THE AFRICAN CANADIAN LEGAL ODYSSEY

Historical Essays

THE AFRICAN CANADIAN LEGAL ODYSSEY

Historical Essays

Edited by
BARRINGTON WALKER

Published for The Osgoode Society for Canadian Legal History by
University of Toronto Press
Toronto Buffalo London

ISBN 978-1-4426-4689-6

Printed on acid-free, 100% post-consumer recycled paper
with vegetable-based inks.

Library and Archives Canada Cataloguing in Publication

The African Canadian legal odyssey : historical essays /
edited by Barrington Walker.

(Osgoode Society for Canadian legal history)
Includes bibliographical references.
ISBN 978-1-4426-4689-6

1. Black Canadians – Legal status, laws, etc. – History.
2. Race discrimination – Law and legislation – Canada – History.
3. Black Canadians – Social conditions.   4. Black Canadians – History.
I. Walker, Barrington, 1970–   II. Series: Osgoode Society for Canadian
Legal History series

KE4395.A47 2012   342.7108'73   C2012-906369-X
KF4483.C59B53 2012

University of Toronto Press acknowledges the financial assistance to its
publishing program of the Canada Council for the Arts and the
Ontario Arts Council.

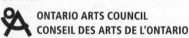

Canada Council   Conseil des Arts   ONTARIO ARTS COUNCIL
for the Arts   du Canada   CONSEIL DES ARTS DE L'ONTARIO

University of Toronto Press acknowledges the financial support of the
Government of Canada through the Canada Book Fund for its
publishing activities.

For David

Contents

Foreword

THE OSGOODE SOCIETY
FOR CANADIAN LEGAL HISTORY

One of the central themes of the new legal history of the past two decades has been exploration of the law's role in shaping the lives and experiences of historically marginalized groups in our society. The Osgoode Society has made a number of contributions to that enterprise, and we are pleased to do so again with this collection. *The African Canadian Legal Odyssey: Historical Essays*, compiled by Professor Barrington Walker, consists of both new essays and a few "classic" articles and is anchored by a sweeping introduction summarizing the state of the field and suggesting new lines of research for the future. The various essays examine both civil and criminal cases, as well as looking at Black legal pioneers and Canadian slave law. A theme that comes through consistently is the contrast between formal legal equality and the ways in which the law, particularly private law, failed to ensure substantive social and economic equality.

The purpose of the Osgoode Society for Canadian Legal History is to encourage research and writing in the history of Canadian law. The Society, which was incorporated in 1979 and is registered as a charity, was founded at the initiative of the Honourable R. Roy McMurtry, formerly attorney general for Ontario and chief justice of the province, and officials of the Law Society of Upper Canada. The Society seeks to stimulate the study of legal history in Canada by supporting researchers, collecting oral histories, and publishing volumes that contribute to legal-historical scholarship in Canada. It has published eighty-eight

books on the courts, the judiciary, and the legal profession, as well
as on the history of crime and punishment, women and law, law and
economy, the legal treatment of ethnic minorities, and famous cases
and significant trials in all areas of the law.

   Current directors of the Osgoode Society for Canadian Legal History
are Robert Armstrong, Kenneth Binks, Susan Binnie, David Chernos,
Thomas G. Conway, J. Douglas Ewart, Violet French, Martin Fried-
land, John Gerretsen, Philip Girard, William Kaplan, Horace Krever, C.
Ian Kyer, Virginia MacLean, Patricia McMahon, Roy McMurtry, Dana
Peebles, Paul Perell, Jim Phillips, Paul Reinhardt, Joel Richler, William
Ross, Paul Schabas, Robert Sharpe, Mary Stokes, and Michael Tulloch.

   The annual report and information about membership may be obtained by writing to the Osgoode Society for Canadian Legal History,
Osgoode Hall, 130 Queen Street West, Toronto, Ontario, M5H 2N6.
Telephone: 416-947-3321. E-mail: mmacfarl@lsuc.on.ca. Website: www
.osgoodesociety.ca.

R. Roy McMurtry
President

Jim Phillips
Editor-in-Chief

Acknowledgments

Many years ago Jim Phillips of the Osgoode Society for Canadian Legal History proposed this collection and I am deeply grateful for his sustained enthusiasm and support for this project. Along with him, Philip Girard, also of the Osgoode Society, and University of Toronto Press editors Len Husband, Wayne Herrington, and Ian MacKenzie all worked very hard to bring it to completion. I would also like to thank all the authors for contributing their new and previously published work. Thanks to Georgina, Ellis, and Miles for supporting me during the long process of finishing this book. It is dedicated in memory of Dr David Sealy.

THE AFRICAN CANADIAN LEGAL ODYSSEY

Historical Essays

1

Introduction:
From a Property Right to Citizenship Rights – The African Canadian Legal Odyssey

BARRINGTON WALKER

This introduction, in the first Osgoode Society collection and reader on the history of Blacks and the law in Canada, makes two main arguments. First, the social history of Blacks in Canada is inextricably bound to the question of law – more so than any other historically disenfranchised group in Canada, save for its First Nations peoples. Second, the profoundly legal dimension of Black Canadian social history is a consequence of the era of European empire and slavery where questions of Blacks' legal and citizenship status, the nature and quality of their freedom, and even their very humanity often hinged upon questions of law. The law had a central role in defining Black Canadian life in the slavery and the post-slavery eras, but this role was often ambiguous and changed over time. Slavery was legally supported in one of two ways: through positive law, and more passively through the recognition of the customary use of slaves (including the recognition of the property right that slave-owners held in their slaves). In the post-emancipation period (after 1833) Blacks enjoyed legal freedom; and yet, during this period the law's role in their lives was ambiguous and the quality of the freedoms they enjoyed was limited. While anti-Black discrimination was not supported by positive law in Canada, throughout Canadian history the law tended to passively support white supremacy by accepting the conditions that allowed it to thrive. Ambiguity thus lies at the heart of the Black Canadian legal odyssey, and this introduction explores the elements and the implications of this ambiguity.

* * *

Legal scholars often note that the essence of the law is storytelling.[1] Two stories illuminate the centrality of questions of law in the histories of Black Canadians. In 1790 the British Parliament, looking to encourage settlement in British North America (as well as Bermuda and the Bahamas) in the aftermath of its defeat at the hands of the new American republic, passed an imperial Act that allowed for the importation of "Negroes, household furniture, utensils of husbandry or cloathing."[2] There is a story here in this simple declaration – one that centres on the list of goods itemized in the Act. What does the juxtaposition of household effects with human beings mean? This is a pattern that was mirrored in the numerous probate court records of white slave-owners in eighteenth- and early nineteenth-century British North America. It is clear that the story being told here is one that we have conveniently forgotten in our selective rendering of the Black past in Canada's self-congratulatory – and only partially true – national narratives as Canada as a "haven" from slavery and racism. This is a claim that is subject to increased scrutiny, but there is far from a clear consensus on the matter. These eight simple words tell a powerful story – a tale about Black people, their bodies, and how they were imagined in the British imperial system and the laws of its empire. Blacks were neither subjects nor citizens; rather, they were commodities, goods, machines for producing wealth, sexual pleasure, and social status.

Here is another story that both encapsulates and complicates our understanding of the position of Blacks in the law. A Nova Scotia case that came before the Annapolis circuit court in 1800, *DeLancey v. Woodin*, was one of the most important historical non–habeas corpus cases in the history of slavery in pre-Confederation Canada.[3] When the courts granted slaves the right of habeas corpus – effectively setting them free – in a series of cases slave-owners turned to the action of trover to maintain their hold on their unruly property. The two parties at the centre of the case were James DeLancey – who as part of the Loyalist elite was an esteemed councillor and slave-owner – and his slave Jack who had run away from him. Jack had fled to join the Royal Nova Scotia Regiment and began to work for wages in the employ of a man named William Woodin. Woodin's lawyer, Richard John Uniake, the attorney general of Nova Scotia, argued that Jack "as well as all the other Negroes in the province were Freemen; there were not any laws to make them other-wise."[4] DeLancey thus brought an action of trover – an action brought to recover the value of personal property, wrongfully converted, by another for his own use – against Jack's employer. At the centre of this case were two diametrically opposed conceptions of rights. Was it the right of the slave-owner to recoup the loss of his property – hence in-herently affirming the validity of his property right in Jack – or Jack's right to earn a living as he saw fit, as a free man (rather than a freed-man) and a subject?

The case was decided in favour of the plaintiff DeLancey; as Barry Cahill argues, there was little that could "turn a sceptical Annapolis jury against an Annapolis plaintiff (who happened to be not only a former member of both the Council and the House of Assembly, but also the most prominent Loyalist in the County), in favour of a Hali-fax merchant defendant, against whom judgment was given for 70 [pounds]."[5] The verdict in this case, like so much in the history of Black Canadians' encounter with the law and legal institutions, does not lend itself to easy conclusions or analyses. The decision seems to have flown in the face of English case law that "trover lay not for a negro, for the owner had not an absolute property in him."[6] More importantly, Cahill argues, the substantive questions of law that this case should have de-cided were whether there was a basis for action in the tort of conversion in the person of a Black man who claimed he was free, or whether or not wages paid to such a person could form the basis of an estimate of the value of property alleged to have been wrongfully converted.[7] The defence moved to arrest the judgment; the arrest of judgment likely led to a new trial, but there is no evidence of another having occurred.

The 1790 imperial Act is an example of how Blacks were assigned a legal position at the nexus of objectification and commodification, but the case of *DeLancey v. Woodin* also demonstrates that while there was considerable legal support for slavery, under British rule the law's role was to support the institution rather than sanction it through positive law. This was in contradistinction to the institution under French rule. Indeed, throughout Canada's history under the British, with only one exception (Prince Edward Island) the law supported slavery only in-directly, and its support for the institution was contestable precisely because of the absence of positive law and the ambiguous legal status of Blacks. Blacks rarely meekly submitted to their enslavement. Run-ning away was common, as evidenced by the myriad ads placed by slave-owners seeking their return published in the newspapers of Hali-

fax, York, and Saint John. The legal questions over the status of Black
peoples in colonial Canada were, I suggest, both a reflection of the social resistance of Blacks and the catalyst of changes that amounted to
what some historians have depicted as a judicial war of attrition against
slavery. Whether the judiciary in Canada waged a war against the institution is debatable, for the anti-slavery positions of many jurists were
ameliorative, rather than abolitionist.

The ambivalent status of Black Canadians before the law during slavery also profoundly framed the post-emancipation period. After 1834,
the question of slavery in Canada was legally settled. Blacks were no
longer to be considered property but citizens under the law. At least
Black men were. Black women, like their white counterparts, would be
denied the franchise until the interwar era. But abolition did not abolish white supremacy in Canada, or the law's central role in maintaining
differential power relations along racial lines, or the hierarchies of race
and racial thought. While the ambiguities that marked the slavery qua
slavery question were resolved with the abolition of slavery across the
British Empire, questions about how the law would substantiate the de
jure freedom of the post-1834 era persisted across space and time. This
was the ambivalent legacy for Black peoples under Canadian law, the
tensions created from within and without of racial liberalism's socio-
legal order. The racism that flowered in the post-emancipation period
was profoundly shaped in both substance and form by the emerging
force of scientific racism and the hardening of social attitudes as the
nineteenth and twentieth centuries unfolded.

This introduction will provide an overview of Black Canadians' relationship with the law in the eras of slavery and post-slavery. This
introduction covers some three hundred years and is organized into
six thematic periods. These themes have been shaped significantly by
both legal history scholarship and the field of critical race studies – the
schema developed and refined by David Theo Goldberg in particular
– on the role and historicity of "race" and racism as social, intellectual,
and "scientific" phenomena. Section 1, "A Right of Property? Slavery
and the Law under French and English Colonialism," explores the legal history of slavery and emancipation. Section 2, "Race and the Law
in the Age of Emancipation and Loyalty, 1783–1833," probes the role
of the law and the colonial state in dispensing with slavery and how
Blacks exercised agency in this process, actively appealing to British
law rather than merely quiescently and passively being the recipients
of largesse. Section 3, "Law and the Underground Railroad, 1833–1865:

A Legal Haven?," discusses the rise of legal liberal racialism in British North America in the context of the dramatic and iconic era of the Underground Railroad. Section 4, "Finding Jim Crow: The Law and Anti-Black Racisms, 1850–1950," discusses the naturalist challenge to legal liberalism racialism in Canada and the law's role in passively – and in the case of immigration policy actively – supporting it. Section 5, "Race, 'Rights,' and the Law, 1918–1967," discusses the legal challenge to racial naturalism in the era between the Great Depression and the liberalization of Canadian immigration policy. Section 6, "The Law in a 'Post-Racial' Order, 1967–Present," discusses the enduring significance of structural and institutional racism in a country that is both legally and (presumptively) societally colour-blind. Following this broad survey, I introduce the individual contributions to this volume.

A Right of Property?
Slavery and the Law under French and English Colonialism

Slave Law under French Rule

Legal institutions and the institution of slavery were closely tied to the histories of various regions and different epochs of colonial Canada. It is true that slavery did not shape Canada as profoundly as it did the slave societies in other parts of the Americas and the Caribbean – a point that has been frequently made elsewhere. This is so well recognized, in fact, that many scholars argue that this renders the institution quite insignificant in the broader context of Canadian history.[8] This is not the case. Slavery was a significant institution in New France, Île Royale, and later British North America because the very existence of the institution laid bare the racialized nature of these settler colonial societies. And for people of African descent in Canada, their relationship with these colonial states and their legal institutions during slavery greatly affected their social status in the post-emancipation period.

In order to understand the law's role in shaping the institution in Canada under French and British rule, one must first understand that events that unfolded in "Canada" were local manifestations of developments in French and English empires. These developments shaped life throughout the African diaspora. Slavery was practised throughout the French Empire, and the law played a pivotal and unequivocal role in the institution throughout it. While the legality of slavery within

France itself was subject to several legal challenges because of France's version of the freedom principle (wherein slaves became free by virtue of entering free territory), slavery in France's late Bourbon era was legally sanctioned through a series laws and edicts emanating from the metropole, crafted to govern slavery in and through the various conduits of its vast empire.

During the reign of Louis XV and XVI the empire depended heavily upon slave labour in its colonies. Forced Black labour in Guadeloupe, Louisiana, Saint Dominique, and Saint Christophe provided a steady stream of revenues for the Crown, underwriting the colonial enterprise and enriching the metropole. Three key edicts legally sanctioned slavery in the empire: the Code Noir, the Edict of 1716, and the 1738 Declaration.

The original version of the Code Noir, written in 1685 and some 485 pages in length, regulated slavery in the West Indies. In 1724 the code was revised to include Louisiana. These codes were essentially a series of rules designed to govern the relationship between masters and slaves. The code protected masters from violence at the hands of their slaves as well as outlawing slave theft, escapes, and revolts. But the code also outlined masters' responsibilities to their slaves. The 1685 code mandated that all slaves be baptized and "instructed in the Catholic religion." And baptized slaves were to be buried on consecrated ground. Those who were not baptized were to be buried at night in a location near to their place of death. The code also stipulated that those who purchased slaves were obligated to inform the governor and intendant who would give their slaves religious instruction. Masters were also required to provide their slaves over ten years old with basic weekly sustenance, specifically "two and a half pots of *Mangoe* flour or the equivalent, with two pounds of salt beef, or three of fish or the equivalent. Children under ten [were] to receive half the amount."[9] Slave-owners also had to legally recognize Sundays and Saints Days, during which no slave would be made to work from "midnight to midnight." Nor could slaves be sold on either of these days. Masters were also "forbidden to shackle their slaves or have them beaten, tortured or mutilated, on pain of forfeiture and criminal prosecution."[10] In the 1724 Act, a provision was added that forbade interracial marriage.[11]

In 1716, another edict was introduced from the metropole that supplemented the Code Noir. This edict emerged after the death of King Louis XIV and in the midst of a constitutional crisis that followed it, leaving the king's regent, the Duke of Orleans, beholden to the Parlement for his power.[12] This edict addressed the "problem" created when masters brought their slaves into France. What was their legal status? Would they retain "the privilege of the soil" ensconced in the freedom principle? As the number of slaves being brought into France by their owners began to increase during the late seventeenth and early eighteenth century, so too did instances where slaves turned to the courts to demand their freedom – many successfully. The Edict of 1716 set the conditions through which slave-owners could bring their slaves into France – conditions that, as mentioned above, dovetailed with the Code Noir. Masters could retain ownership of their slaves if they abided by certain principles. Slaves could be brought to France only for the purposes of religious instruction or to learn a trade for the benefit of the slave colonies. But slave-owners needed written permission to do so (from the colonial governor) – a detailed permit describing the slave – and were required to register the slave with court clerks in both their colony of origin and in France once they landed. Masters who failed to comply with these provisions risked losing their slaves. "For the first time," argues Sue Peabody, "the Edict of 1716 gave slaves a statutory, in addition to a customary, basis for claiming their freedom in France" and an "intermediate" slave status "that restricted the master's rights over a slave more than in the colonies, yet was not so lenient as to equate a French slave's status with that of a free person in the kingdom." There was another complication with the edict, again linked to the constitutional crisis, and which further added to the uncertainties surrounding slavery in France. It was not registered by the Parlement of Paris in retaliation for disagreements over religious and fiscal matters, "creating a limbo for slaves who came to Paris or other cities within the Parlement's jurisdiction."[13]

Roughly two decades after the 1716 edict a third major decree legally regulated slavery: the 1738 Declaration. It stipulated that masters who failed to legally register their slaves risked having them seized by the clerk of Admiralty of the Admiralty court of France and returned to the colonies *"au profit du roi."*[14]

Just as in France, slavery was a legally sanctioned institution in New France. In slavery's formative stages, the French Crown deemed slave labour necessary for the colony. The law was used to provide both form and legitimacy to an institution that was central to the life of the colony. Louis XIV gave his royal assent to the use of Black and panis slaves in New France in 1689 and again in 1701.[15] This royal assent was further entrenched by ordinances and proclamations by colonial officials (intendants and governors) until 1738. On 13 April 1709, for example, Intendant Jacques Raudot issued an ordinance that affirmed the need for masters to acquire "certainty of ownership" of their slaves who "leave their masters almost daily under the pretext that there are no slaves in France," which, he added, was "not wholly true since in the islands of the Continent all Negroes bought as such are regarded as slaves."[16] Raudot felt strongly that it was necessary for the colonial state to assure the property rights of both present and future slave-owners in the colony.[17] In 1736, as the number of slaves grew, Intendant Gilles Hocquart issued another ordinance in an attempt to formalize the ad hoc means by which masters had been freeing their slaves. Heretofore, masters who decided to free their slaves required the sanction of the state through a notary.[18]

Slavery also received legal support of sorts through the customary use of the Code Noir in New France (particularly those portions along the St Lawrence), Île Royale, and Île St Jean. Slaves in these colonies did not have as many opportunities to contest their enslavement directly or indirectly – or benefit from legal developments such as the 1716 Edict or the 1738 Declaration – as did those who were enslaved in France. If the possibilities for freedom were limited in the French colonies, there was evidence, nonetheless, of tacit recognition of their humanity under the laws that governed slavery in French North America. The earliest historians of slavery in Canada, Riddell and Winks, made this (now rather contentious) point; they argue that slavery in New France was relatively humane because of the ameliorating effects of the provisions in the code (mentioned above) that outlined a master's duty to his slaves. More recent scholarship parts company with Winks.[19] Nonetheless, it is clear that, through key provisions in the Code Noir and their customary application by slaveholders in New France (as well as Île Royale), slaves occupied a status that was property with some of the characteristics of legal personhood.[20] Slavery endured under French rule until the Conquest, though in reality the institution was in decline by the early eighteenth century. Most slaves in New France were First Nations people, commonly called "panis," from the Pawnee or related tribes. Of the 4,000 slaves recorded in New France, 2,472 were panis.[21] But with the fall of New France, the complexion of slavery began to change. The institution would become renewed – its population decidedly more Black – under British rule. And once again the law would play a pivotal role in shaping the institution.

Slave Law under British Rule

Slavery was practised widely in the British colonies in the Caribbean and North America. What distinguished slave law in the British Empire from its French counterpart is that while slave law under the French was centrally moulded by edicts from the metropole, slave law under the British did not emanate from the colonial centre.[22] Kenneth Morgan argues that, because by the seventeenth century slavery had not existed for centuries, the body of English common law was silent on the issue of the treatment of slaves, regarding slaves as property rather than human beings. Individual colonies were permitted to craft their own slave laws and codes. One can see the pivotal role of slave law in both shaping colonial British slave societies and reflecting the socio-economic anxieties of white settlers most markedly in the period around the mid-seventeenth century. In colonial Virginia, for example, a 1640 law forbade Blacks from carrying arms; by 1662 miscegenation was outlawed in the colony. A Virginian slave code was created in 1680 and revised in 1705.[23]

In 1669 the white British settlers to the Carolinas were accompanied by an embryonic constitutional document named the "The Constitutions." This document both formally recognized the existence of slavery and decreed the extension of religious tolerance towards slaves, "but it was made explicit that any slave converting to a Christian denomination remained, during his worldly life, in ye same State and Condition he was in before." And further that "every Freeman of Carolina, shall have absolute power and authority over Negro Slaves, of what opinion or Religion soever."[24] In the 1690s more laws were enacted that required masters to search their slaves' quarters for weapons and prevented masters from giving slaves Saturdays off, as was the custom. Over the course of the Carolinas' eighteenth century, yet more laws were passed that cemented Blacks' inferior legal status. After the Stono Rebellion of 1740, a Negro Act was passed that greatly restricted slaves' travel between plantations. A subordinate and separate legal system for slaves and free Blacks alike was created and presided over by slaveholders and JPs, who were empowered to deal with cases in a summary fashion. Blacks were not allowed to testify in these courts. Blacks were also barred from owning guns, boats, or domestic livestock. Other provisions discouraged interracial sex between Black men (slave and free) and white women (free and indentured servants). Overall, says

Morgan, "a statutory law of race and slavery existed in all thirteen British North American colonies by the middle of the eighteenth century." These laws were "draconian and created the condition of slavery characterized by the master's almost total control over his slaves, permitting an array of brutalizing physical punishments for those slaves who transgressed the law." It was much the same pattern in the British Caribbean. Slaves' lives in Barbados were regulated by a slave code enacted in 1688; Jamaica's code of 1696 was closely modelled upon it.[25]

Slave-owners in those regions that would become British North America in the post-revolutionary era did not craft a social and economic order through similar slave codes. Local conditions did not warrant it, for these were economies and societies with slaves rather than slave societies. Nonetheless, once again the law played an important role in shaping the experience of slavery through the recognition of slaveholders' property and the common law's support of customary slavery throughout the empire. The British conquest of Acadia between 1710 and 1713 was finalized by the Treaty of Utrecht. Under its terms, the French lost Acadie (peninsular Nova Scotia and New Brunswick) and Newfoundland to the British, managing to hold on to only Île Royale (Cape Breton Island) and Île St Jean. And these possessions fell to the British in 1758, Île Royale having been captured in 1745 by New Englanders with British assistance, then returned to France in 1748 at the end of the War of Austrian Succession. Over the four decades between the treaty and the expulsion, the Acadians – even after they were compelled to pledge allegiance to the British Crown – found themselves under the constant suspicion of their new colonial masters. In 1745 the inhabitants of Île Royale were deported to France en masse. In 1755 the Brits deported the Acadians from the mainland (peninsular Nova Scotia).[26]

These seismic events ushered in an era of British settlement upon the "vacated" lands of Acadie. In 1758 and 1759, at the behest of Nova Scotia's Lieutenant-Governor Charles Lawrence, New Englanders "from Massachusetts, Connecticut, and Rhode Island began to move to the Nova Scotian frontier." This diverse group came to be known as the New England Planters and were the primary beneficiaries of the appropriated lands of the Acadians and of the Mi'kmaq before them. Slave-owning Planters were given the largest land allotments.[27] Probate court records show slavery was firmly entrenched as a property right – an important marker of wealth and status.[28] In 1762 customary slavery in

Nova Scotia received tacit legal recognition from the colonial assembly by way of an Act that prohibited the sale of liquor in the colony to "any soldier, sailor, servant, apprentice, bound servant or negro slave." In 1767, the Nova Scotia census counted 104 slaves out of a total population of 3,022.[29] This number would grow dramatically in the aftermath of the American Revolution.

If Britain's conquest of Acadie had implications for the maintenance and influx of slavery into this historic Mi'kmaq and later French territory, its conquest of New France had similar implications for slavery in that region. After the Conquest, between 1760 and 1763 slavery – an institution that was in decline during the last days of French rule – was reinvigorated. Slavery continued to enjoy the support of the state. The French negotiated the right to keep their slaves, sell them, and instruct them in the Catholic faith.[30] James Murray, the first governor of Quebec, in an oft-cited missive reflecting the future importance of slavery in Quebec under British rule, is worth citing at length:

I must earnestly entreat your assistance, without servants nothing can be done. Had I the inclination to employ soldiers, which is not the case, they would disappoint me, and Canadians will work for nobody but themselves. Black slaves are certainly the only people to be depended upon, but it is necessary, I imagine they should be born in one of our Northern Colonies, the winters here will not agree with a Native of the torrid zone pray therefore if possible procure for me two Stout Young Fellows, who have been accustomed to County Business, and I shall wish to see them happy, I am of the opinion there is little felicity with the Ladys, you may buy for each a clean young wife, who can wash and do the female offices about a farm. I shall begrudge no price, so we hope we may, by your goodness succeed.[31]

Slavery would become part of the social and legal fabric of Quebec, supported by the British colonial state (though not through positive law) and well established in its social and economic customs. In 1763 the British introduced English civil and criminal law to Quebec, restoring French civil law in 1774 under the provisions of the Quebec Act. But these changes did not affect slavery: "The English civil and criminal law that was introduced into Quebec in 1763 contained no effective strictures against slavery; indeed the entire weight of law and custom in the British colonies tended to support the legality of the institution overseas."[32]

Recent scholarship has ably demonstrated that post-Conquest Quebec was one place among many in the empire in which slavery enjoyed legal support. But as we shall see below, this legal support was never absolute; it was always contested and became increasingly tenuous over time. In Montreal in particular, slaves constituted a visible and yet absented presence. If this sounds inherently contradictory, it is meant to, for Blacks in colonial Montreal occupied a contradictory space in the history and culture of the city. There were not many slaves in a numerical sense, but they were highly visible in an overwhelmingly white city.[33] Their presence, in other words, was not overwhelming but nor was it atypical. Frank Mackey has unearthed several examples of what he calls the "Black fact" in Montreal. Though slaves were few in numbers, it was nonetheless true that slavery was "accepted by the many as part of the fixed order of a hierarchical society."[34] Slaves in British colonial Montreal were the chattels of priests and nuns, parliamentarians, "missionaries, military officers [and] fur traders."[35]

Slaves in British North America, then, were no aberration; while they did not toil on vast sugar-cane or indigo plantations, they were not anomalous. The arrival of the Loyalists in the aftermath of the American Revolution brought renewed vigour to the institution. In Nova Scotia, "an estimated 1,232 slaves, often designated as 'servants' or 'servants for life,' were brought by Loyalists from the former American colonies."[36] Quebec witnessed an influx of Loyalist-owned slaves, though the exact numbers are unknown. Loyalist settlements in the Eastern Townships of Quebec and Eastern Ontario – along the shores of the Bay of Quinte and the Cataraqui River – were also dotted with Loyalist slaveholding families.[37] The further importation of slaves was supported and encouraged by the colonial state when in 1790, as we have seen, Britain passed the Act allowing slave-owners from other parts of the empire to immigrate to British North America with their property, including slaves.[38]

The Loyalist age of slavery was nonetheless contradictory, for while clearly slaves were an important part of the Loyalist social, political, and, to a very limited extent, economic order in British North America, the influx of slaves into British North America after 1783 also signalled the beginning of its slow death – much of it via legal instruments and institutions – and its eventual demise across the empire and in British North America. The courts of British North America played a pivotal role in slavery's demise.

Race and the Law in the Age of Emancipation and Loyalty, 1783–1833

Emancipation Debates and the Law

For Blacks in British North America, the period between 1783 and 1833 was a complex one that belies easy analysis. Black freedom was very much at the centre of events that unfolded between the end of the American Revolution and the abolition of slavery in the British Empire. The question of slavery and Black freedom was broad and complex, marked by debates on slavery's economic viability and desirability, its religious morality, and its legal bearings. This conversation took place amidst the reverberations of one of the world's most important slave revolts in French colonial Saint Dominigue (present-day Haiti). The economic, social, and moral justification for the slave trade and slavery was being debated among elite whites (and a handful of elite Blacks) while the enslaved chipped away at the institution through the agency represented by both the idea and the practice of Black Loyalism in British North America, for example, and acts of resistance ranging from marronage to rebellion.[39] In the grand scheme of things – in the context of the Atlantic World – British North America was a minor catalyst for and a reflection of a broader, imperial conversation and historical processes on slavery, the slave trade, and abolitionism.[40] The debates surrounding the legality of slavery during the age of Loyalty will be our focus here.

While the recognition of the slave-owner's right to own, alienate, and bequeath slaves to heirs gave slavery its legal force in British North America, legal institutions were nonetheless key to slavery's demise in Canada. In the courts of British North America, slavery was challenged by white legal activists and Blacks who fought the institution in fairly well-known cases. Recall the eighteenth-century Nova Scotia case of *DeLancey v. Woodin* cited above: the case of a slave who withstood his master's trover action against his employer, a ploy to recoup the property of "lost wages" and ultimately return him to servitude. Trover cases were most often, of course, brought by putative masters; habeas corpus cases were brought when slaves invoked one of the most fundamental pillars of the common law in a bid to secure their freedom. This proved to be a very important strategy of slaves and their allies who benefited from the court rulings that did not recognize slavery's legal basis.[41]

British North American colonial legislatures were also important arenas for the crucial legal questions that confronted slavery in Canada during the turn of the nineteenth century. In Nova Scotia and New Brunswick, slaveholders attempted to garner legal recognition for the institution in the face of mounting losses suffered before judges who, they deemed, were far too sympathetic to their slaves and scornful of their property rights. Slave-owners in Nova Scotia attempted to pass bills that would legally formalize slavery – "Negro bills" – in 1789 and 1808. In New Brunswick, a similar bill was tabled in 1801.[42] In Upper and Lower Canada, by contrast, legislative bills regarding the slavery question were tabled not to preserve the institution but to dispense with it. In Upper Canada, under the lead of a lieutenant-governor who was hostile to slavery but mindful of the support that the institution enjoyed among many slaveholding members of the legislature, the government successfully shepherded a gradual emancipation act through the legislature in 1793. No new slaves were to be imported into the colony, and children born into slavery were to be freed by the age of twenty-five. It was not an abolitionist measure by any means – it did not free a single slave – but it was unparalleled in British North America and it served as a catalyst for the withering away of the institution elsewhere.[43]

"Mighty Experiments": The Colonial State and Free Black Populations of Loyalists, Maroons, and Refugees

As we have seen, the legal questions surrounding slavery, its basis in law in particular, were prominent in both the courts and in colonial legislatures. The period before 1833 was a complex era. The numbers of slaves increased after 1783 as Loyalist slave-owners brought their slaves to British North America, but so too did the numbers of free Blacks, the largest free Black population in North America, thus creating a situation never before seen in the British Empire. While the slavery question would be definitively answered by 1833–4, the law played a significant role in overtly and tacitly regulating Black life well before then. In many ways it was a precursor to the law's role in shaping Black life in the era of the Underground Railroad, its complexities and contradictions.

The end of the American Revolution ushered in what Seymour Drescher calls the age of the mighty experiment of 1833 in the British Empire. Between 1791 and 1833, says Drescher, "alternative visions to slavery" were proposed. Sierra Leone and Haiti were lauded by abolitionists, who, in pitched ideological battles with their pro-slavery opponents, sought examples of the success of post-emancipation Black societies. Referring specifically to the "return" of London's Black poor to Sierra Leone, Drescher argues that such schemes were seen as "a socioeconomic experiment in the liberation of all Africa. Faith in man's potential to reconstitute the social order in Africa along rational and scientific principles probably reached new heights following the conclusion of the Revolutionary War in 1783."[44]

Drescher has little to say about how this conversation took shape in colonial Nova Scotia, and that is an unfortunate oversight, because the Sierra Leone chapter of the story of Black freedom in the age of Revolution was the second act of a larger story.[45] But others have. Jeffrey McNairn in particular has studied British travellers' observations of Nova Scotia's free Black communities in the period before 1833 and how these conversations formed part of the larger debate on the merits of the experiment in Black freedom. These travellers, argues McNairn, increasingly influenced by the ascendancy of the social and human science of political economy, deemed the "mighty experiment" of Black freedom before 1833 a mighty failure, particularly in the period after 1827.[46]

Such conversations tell us that Black freedom in the age of Revolution was forged in the context of fierce debates about Blacks' suitability for freedom and whether the abolitionists' arguments were governed by the "ill-informed sentiment sustaining abolitionism."[47] What role did the law have in all of this? Tacitly (though far from equivocally, as we have seen above), the law supported the enslavement of some while formally granting the rights of British citizenship to others. But among those in the latter category there were tensions between their formal legal equality, their rights as British subjects, and the willingness of colonial and legal elites to recognize Blacks' full humanity and substantiate Black citizenship. In a pattern that was to shape Black life in British North America and Canada over the course of the post-emancipation period, the law's role in securing Black freedom was dubious at best. As I have argued elsewhere but in a slightly earlier context, Black freedom – and more specifically, Black citizenship – was forged in the precarious space between legal equality and social inequality, with the latter profoundly affecting the quality and scope of the former.[48]

The experiences of Black Loyalists, Maroons, and Refugees, and in particular the fraught nature of their relationship with the colonial state – their second-class citizenship – exemplifies this crucial point. Black

Loyalists expected their loyalty to the Crown during the Revolution to be rewarded with the fruits of full citizenship, and land in particular. They sought a life of independent yeoman farming, the antithesis of slave labour on the large plantations, small farms, or in artisanal settings as hired labour. In reality, the Black Loyalists found they suffered myriad indignities at the hands of the colonial government, what James W. St.G. Walker has aptly called the "bondage of dependence."[49] In a scenario to be repeated in the early to mid-nineteenth century, they found legal freedom but soon came to the embittering realization that "in a society conditioned to thinking of [B]lacks as slaves, their claims for equality were not always to be taken seriously by white individuals or even by white officialdom."[50]

The citizenship afforded to Nova Scotia's (and New Brunswick's) free Black population in the period after 1783 and prior to 1833 was circumscribed by multiple forces: the continued (though waning, especially after the early 1800s) existence of slavery itself, the quasi slavery of exploitative wage labour, debt-peonage, indentured servitude, unequal justice in the courts, white mob violence, and paternalism. The land allotments that the Black Loyalists had so greatly coveted were late in coming. White Loyalists received their land first. When Blacks did finally begin to receive land from the colonial government, their allotments tended to be markedly smaller than those of whites.[51] It does bear mentioning – as recent scholarship on Black–Mi'kmaq relations in Nova Scotia does – that Blacks did enjoy a sort of privilege vis-à-vis the colonial state because they too were the beneficiaries of Aboriginal land that was essentially stolen by the British.[52] By 1793 many of the Black Loyalists were so disappointed by the broken promises of the British – their unfulfilled yearning for full freedom – that many decamped for Sierra Leone to begin their search for freedom anew.

The Maroons and the Refugees were the two groups that followed the Black Loyalist migration. The Maroons arrived in the aftermath of their ignoble defeat at the hands of the British at the end of the Maroon Rebellion. Those recalcitrant runaway slaves, who had taken to Jamaica's mountains under Spanish rule, co-mingled with the island's aboriginal peoples and waged war against colonial masters, until finally subdued in 1795. The Maroons, bereft of options, offered a truce to the British. In spite of the truce, by an act of the Jamaican legislature, some 556 Maroons were herded onto ships pointed in the direction of Nova Scotia.[53] Once they arrived in Halifax they had a persistent champion in Lieutenant-Governor Wentworth, a sympathetic and somewhat paternalistic figure who claimed to understand "the Negro mentality." Nonetheless, the Maroons' time there was brief and difficult. They were subject to the scorn and distrust of many white Haligonians, chaffed against any suggestion that they should co-mingle with the former slaves of the British and their descendants, and found Halifax's winters difficult to manage. Like many of the Loyalists before them, they soon arrived in the fledgling colony of Sierra Leone, just in time to help the British put down a rebellion fomented in large part by former Black Loyalists.[54]

The Refugees' arrival in Nova Scotia, like that of the Maroons and the Black Loyalists before them, was the consequence of war – the War of 1812 in this instance. The British, drawing inspiration from a strategy they employed to weaken American colonists during the Revolution, once again offered those Blacks who absconded and crossed British lines the promise of freedom. And once again, Nova Scotia (and New Brunswick) was to be the destination of these former slaves. The Refugees' experiences have been documented in the secondary literature. Historians' views of the Refugees' story has shifted over time, from an emphasis on their cultural inadequacies and their inability to adapt to the rigours of the life of free Blacks in a market economy, to a celebration of the Refugees' ability to survive the difficult days after slavery, an affirmation of their agency.[55]

The colonial state regarded the Refugees with wary suspicion at best. Government officials were only lukewarm supporters of the noble experiment that the imperial government had foisted upon them. Could these people (who, unlike the Black Loyalists, were all ex-slaves and bereft of the military distinctions of those who had served in the Black Pioneers corps during the Revolution) make the transition to freedom? Similar to the attitudes of the travelogue writers mentioned above, the colonial government held a dim view of the Refugees. Its policy was shaped by duty to the empire and a genuine desire to help a group many deemed unfortunate and inferior. But these altruistic sentiments were restrained by sceptics who, by both their words and deeds, wondered whether these people could – or should, for that matter – live as free, independent citizens.

Upon their arrival, colonial officials housed many Refugees in the colony's poorhouse and upon Melville Island, the infamous site of the British prison for American POWs during the War of 1812; Black Refugees received the same provisions as did U.S. prisoners before them. Placed under the responsibility of the collector of customs by Colonial Secretary Lord Bathurst, the Refugees, under the watchful eye of the colonial assembly, were given the means to (barely) sustain themselves while they were strongly encouraged to move on to Trinidad – a prospect that held far less lustre than did that of the Black Loyalist migration to Sierra Leone because many of the Refugees believed that they would be resold into slavery.

A handful did leave for Trinidad, but most stayed in British North America, occupying small plots of land via "tickets of occupation" rather than the land grants enjoyed by white settlers. The struggle to have their tickets of occupation converted to grants was a central theme in the Refugees' struggle for equality. Invariably these plots were too small to fully sustain a life of independent farming. The Refugees sold the produce they managed to raise on their small farms, as well as berries and trout and household items such as charcoal and brooms. Others ventured into the cities of Halifax or Dartmouth to work for wages as unskilled labourers, although a handful did enter the ranks of skilled labour, while still others took to seafaring.[56] Seafaring, traversing the ocean over the same routes by which many Black men and their recent ancestors had come to North America, South America, and the Caribbean as slaves, was to continue to be one of the most important occupations for Black men in the Atlantic World who sought to make a living in both the slavery and post-slavery eras.[57]

The Refugees attained a liminal form of citizenship in Nova Scotia and New Brunswick: they were not slaves but nor were they free from economic servitude or social inequality. The law offered no protection from the indignities of white supremacy. In 1833, the Nova Scotian assembly, feeling besieged by the influx of Loyalists, Maroons, and Refugees between 1783 and 1815, looked upon Britain's decision to abolish slavery not in terms of its historic significance for people of African descent but as the impetus for another wave of a potential "problem" population of Blacks fleeing slavery. While Britain's act to abolish slavery opened up a vast legal frontier of freedom in British North America, Nova Scotia's assembly moved to extricate the province from any further "experiments" in Black freedom. In 1834 it passed an Act prohibiting the "Clandestine Landing of Liberated Slaves … From Vessels Arriving in the Province." The assembly installed a constable at the harbour to search for such ships, their captains being subject to fines. When the assembly attempted to renew the Act two years later, it was disallowed by the British government, which rightly surmised that it contravened the spirit of the 1834 imperial Act to abolish slavery in the empire.[58]

The British abolition of slavery – preceded only by their abolition of the slave trade in 1807 – represented the most important legal expression of the ascendancy of liberalizing attitudes towards racial slavery. Rather than an indication that the slave system was in economic decline, the imperial Act of 1834 was to a large degree a triumph of humanitarianism over the rigid intractability of the biological racism that provided the ideological ammunition for the pro-slavery position. But this victory was only a partial one. The humanitarian spirit that manifested itself in the success of the anti-slavery position was the legal recognition of the force of arguments against the inhumanity of chattel slavery, but this alone did not constitute a recognition of the full humanity of people of African descent, nor some notion of racial equality between those descended from Africa and those descended from Europe. What it did signal was the increasing currency of the idea that slavery was an abhorrent practice that could no longer be sustained under the weight of the moral arguments marshalled against it by abolitionists, both Black and white.

The consequence of centuries of chattel slavery – the perception that Blacks were inherently racially inferior to whites – could not be abolished along with the institution. Blacks in Nova Scotia and New Brunswick, the beneficiaries of some of the earliest experiments in Black freedom, already knew that the joys of legal freedom were sharply curtailed by the bitter reality of white supremacy. Rarely did even the staunchest white anti-slavery activists support the radical idea of racial equality. While slavery was no longer a recognized institution in the empire, anti-Black racism persisted. And the law played an ambiguous role in its persistence. An instrument of social justice, the law was also (albeit tacitly and often passively) precisely the instrument that allowed the white supremacist order to thrive. Blacks in British North America faced an intellectual, cultural, and legal landscape that was rife with contradictions and ambiguities. This landscape was contoured by broadly liberal intellectual currents in the empire that mounted a challenge to a biologically rooted idea of Black inferiority in the form of Blacks' formal legal freedom and civic equality, and the countervailing forces of slavery's persistent legacy of biological racism, which took the form of pervasive and myriad social forms of anti-Black racism. The legal dimensions of the Underground Railroad era witnessed patterns congruent to those forged during the Age of Emancipation and Loyalty.

Law and the Underground Railroad, 1833–1865:
A Legal Haven?

The Underground Train,
Strange as it seems,
Carried many passengers
And never was seen

It wasn't made of wood,
It wasn't made of steel;
A man-made train that
Ran without wheels.

The train was known
By many a name.
But the greatest of all
Was "The Freedom Train"

The Quakers, the Indians,
Gentiles and Jews,
Were some of the people
Who made up the crews.

Free Blacks and Christians
And Atheists, too,
Were the rest of the people
Who made up the crews.

Conductors and agents
Led the way at night,
Guiding the train
By the North Star Light.

The passengers were
The fugitive slaves
Running from slavery
And its evil ways.

Running from the whip
And the overseer,

> From the slave block
> And the Auctioneer.
>
> They didn't want their masters
> To catch them again,
> So men dressed as women
> And the women dressed as men.[59]

These lyrics, invoking the powerful imagery and iconography of the Underground Railroad era, are from a Negro spiritual called "The Ballad of the Underground Railroad" by Charles Blockson. The era of the Underground Railroad is, without a doubt, the most widely known and widely studied aspect of the Black experience in Canada. The period is revered by many as the genesis of a great Canadian human rights tradition that would calcify in the twentieth century, particularly in the post-war era, marked by a Pearsonian internationalist ethos, liberalizing immigration policies that would turn increasingly to the non-white areas of the world for immigrants, and the policy of multiculturalism. In a country like Canada where Blackness is considered peripheral – if not entirely irrelevant – to its founding narratives, the Underground Railroad era is an anomaly of sorts, albeit a powerful one. Canadians have a deep psychic and emotional attachment to the idea of Canada as a refuge and a haven from U.S. slavery and racial injustice.

In 1918, Fred Landon, a scholar of Black Canadian history in the age of the Underground Railroad, argued that British North Americans' treatment of Blacks, particularly its "coloured refugee settlements" in western Ontario, was "a chapter of our provincial history that does us credit. To the Black men in bondage," wrote Landon, "Canada was always the haven of refuge. With the Fugitive Slave Law," he continued,

and other repressive measures in force, they were not safe, even in Boston. In some states supposedly free, the were subject to fierce persecution, but in Canada they always found protection and fullest freedom. They were given a welcome and an opportunity to show themselves worthy of citizenship. Hundreds who made their escape from slave plantations in the South never halted until they had crossed the boundary and, to use their very own expressive phrase, "had shaken hands with the lion." Out of the free states of the North there came, too, a steady stream of coloured folk who had found their dreams of security and peace rudely disturbed by pro-slavery sentiment.[60]

Blacks' "dreams of security and peace," and whether they found it under the British flag, are at the heart of understanding the Black experience in Canada during this era. While one must be careful of succumbing to the temptation to set Landon up as a straw man, it is important, nonetheless, to interrogate his portrayal of Canada precisely because it has had such a powerful influence over time. Landon viewed Canada as a place where fugitive slaves and free Blacks alike from the United States experienced the "fullest freedom" juxtaposed to the bondage of the South and the "supposed freedom" of the antebellum North. Landon's assumptions about Black life in Canada (as well as the tone and tenor of his text) are examples of the a priori assumptions that have shaped the writing of Black Canadian history in the era of the Underground Railroad, and Black Canadian history more generally. Questions of law have always been an integral part of Black life – more specifically Blacks' struggle for full humanity – in nineteenth-century British North America.

Landon, who wrote at a time when little value was placed in Canadian history, not to mention the history of Blacks in Canada, is still regarded as one of the most important scholars of Black Canada; his work is still widely read, cited, and reproduced. But his vision of Black life at the end of Underground Railroad on the British side, while accurate in many of its particulars, was certainly overdrawn. While Landon had little to say about the eras that pre- and post-dated the age of the Underground Railroad, his body of work greatly influenced scholars' perceptions of Black Canadian life until the publication of Robin Winks's *The Blacks in Canada* in 1971 with Yale University Press, one of most prestigious university presses in North America. Contrary to Landon, Winks argued that Blacks faced severe cultural and socioeconomic barriers, but they were nonetheless equal before the law: "If social and economic realities did not conform to legislative forms, these forms at least limited the ways in which prejudice might make itself felt."[61]

The nature and the significance of Blacks' legal freedoms – both formerly enslaved and freeborn – were rather obvious: the right of British citizenship/subjecthood and property rights (a key register of how Blacks imagined themselves as free subjects under the British Empire), the right to serve on juries, sell, and, in rarer instances, hire labour and alienate property. The legal and psychic benefits of life under the "lion's paw" cannot be overstated. Freeborn Blacks from states such as California found respite in Canada from the spread of "Black codes" in states that sought to curtail their freedom, making them second-class citizens.[62] Fugitive slaves enjoyed these very same rights, and most crucially they were protected from the threat of U.S. slavery. Between 1833 and 1842, the overwhelmingly favourable outcomes of a number of cases involving fugitive slaves from the United States affirmed Canada's status as a formal legal haven for Blacks when the Upper Canadian government refused to extradite fugitive slaves to the United States and certain re-enslavement.[63] In the vast majority of such cases, the legislature and the courts held firm the frontier of legal freedom that had opened up in front of those so hungry for it. While it is not true that the British refused to extradite all fugitives,[64] the general principle through which the courts adjudicated these cases was simple, yet powerful and profound: no slave could face extradition to the United States for a crime that did not exist under British law (i.e., theft of a slave). Slaves who committed the act of theft were similarly protected as long as that theft (e.g., theft of a horse) was done in a necessary bid to win freedom. And in one case where a slave committed theft that clearly contravened this principle, the British government looked the other way and, hewing to the greater and more noble principle of anti-slavery, decided to offer protection. The fugitive-slave cases were instructive instances of the nature of a key element of the legal freedoms Blacks enjoyed in Canada.[65]

And yet as powerful as they are as examples of Blacks' legal freedoms in the age of the Underground Railroad – legal freedoms that had clearly evolved from the more tenuous freedoms Blacks had enjoyed in the age of Loyalty – in neither era did Blacks enjoy the full freedom invoked in Landon's work. Winks correctly identified the ways in which the law could, and did, check overt expressions of racial animus towards Blacks. But it would be left to works subsequent to Winks to point out how the law also passively supported anti-Black prejudice. Its passive support of the dominant culture's pervasive belief in Blacks' racial inferiority compelled Black Canadians to negotiate the space between the veneer of their formal legal equality and pervasive societal inequality. The legal order tacitly supported white supremacy and the constellation of attitudes that consigned Blacks to second-class citizenship where they were unable to access the exalted citizenship – to invoke Sunara Thobani's analytical lens – reserved for whites.[66]

How did this tension between legal freedom and legally sanctioned inequality play out? The schools question of 1840s and 1850s Upper Canada / Canada West and nineteenth-century Nova Scotia are poignant examples. In each province, the law was taken up in different ways – ambiguously in the first instance and more positively and concretely in the latter – to deny Blacks access to education, a key register of their desire for full civic equality. In Upper Canada, segregated schools were prohibited by the 1843 School Act. By 1850, the Act had been amended, allowing "any group of five Negro families to ask a local public school official to establish such a school for them." This occurred in the context of the virulent "Negro-phobia" that was gripping Upper Canada at the time. This racial animus was largely a product of the demographic pressure of fugitive slaves entering the province at an unprecedented rate and the cusp of the ascendance of racial naturalism – the belief that Blacks were inherently biologically inferior to their white counterparts. Racial naturalists also believed that this was an inevitable and incontrovertible consequence of nature. They lacked the optimism of their liberal racialist counterparts who believed that with time and tutelage, Blacks could rise above their inferior status. It was a line of reasoning that had much in common with official and unofficial policy towards the governance of Aboriginal peoples in Canada. The mid-nineteenth century was the beginning of a wave of scientific racist thought that would reach its height by the turn of the century. Racists seized upon the amendment to the Schools Act to deny Blacks access to the common schools. Affronted by these efforts to keep their children out, Blacks fought back in Canada West's civil courts. This strategy produced mixed results but it was, on balance, unsuccessful. The Act remained in force in Ontario until 1964.[67]

The law also had a prominent role in determining equal access to Nova Scotia's schools. Unlike Canada West, where the law had only an indirect role in maintaining separate schools, Nova Scotia's schools were also segregated via social custom and express legal statute. Most Black children in Nova Scotia attended Black schools because they lived in a highly segregated society. These deeply entrenched social customs of segregation were augmented by an act of the Nova Scotian legislature that allowed "the school commissioners of any municipality ... [to] establish separate institutions if necessary and if the government approved." Black families actively fought segregated schools in Nova Scotia over the course of the late nineteenth century and over much of the twentieth. Explicit racial language was dropped from the Act in 1918; nonetheless, these schools remained a fact of life in Nova Scotia until the post-war era.[68]

Finding Jim Crow: The Law and Anti-Black Racisms, 1850–1950

The schools question shows that during the Underground Railroad era and beyond, Canada was no refuge from social prejudice. Canada's status as a legal haven for Blacks was limited. Indeed, the law was an imperfect instrument in offering protections from social prejudice and, contrarily, often enabled it. The era between 1850 and 1950 was one of ascendant naturalist and scientific racism in Canada. The law's role – tacit in the instance of criminal law, civil law, and civil society, and uniquely overt in the instance of immigration policy – will be explored in this section.

I have argued elsewhere that one key to understanding the Black experience in Canada lies in grappling with its legacy of "Jim Crow."[69] C. Vann Woodward, in his foundational work, *The Strange Career of Jim Crow*, demonstrates that Jim Crowism was the quintessence of a white supremacist order that emerged in the aftermath of slavery. During slavery, legal statutes or "Black codes" regulated Black life in many southern states, but as Woodward explains in a passage worth citing at length, for a Black in the days after U.S. slavery,

the public symbols and constant reminders of his inferior position were the segregation statutes, or "Jim Crow" laws. They constituted the most elaborate and formal expression of sovereign white opinion upon the subject. In bulk and in detail as well as in effectiveness of enforcement the segregation codes were comparable with the black codes of the old regime, though the laxity that mitigated the harshness of the black codes was replaced by a rigidity that was more typical of the segregation code. That code lent the sanction of law to a racial ostracism that extended to churches and schools, to eating and drinking. Whether by law or by custom, that ostracism extended to virtually all forms of public transportation, to sports and recreations, to hospitals, to orphanages, prisons, and asylums, and ultimately to funeral homes, morgues, and cemeteries.[70]

Here Woodward clearly delineates both the legal and the customary aspects of Jim Crow in the antebellum South, but what of Canada? The concept of Jim Crow in Canada is contentious. Among students of Canadian history there is a consensus that the concept is an American import that has little to do with Canada's history. Nonetheless, a handful of scholars have written at length about a "Canadian version" of Jim Crow that emerged in the late nineteenth and early twentieth centuries. While the racist culture of the south was a creation of social customs and legal support, the balance was towards the latter. The opposite was true in Canada: the balance tipped towards Jim Crow as a function of social custom, while the law passively supported it, in the main. Nonetheless, the key similarity between the two countries is that Jim Crowism was neither exclusively customary nor exclusively legally sanctioned. In many parts of Canada, just as in the antebellum South, Blacks tended to live in segregated neighbourhoods that were supported by restrictive covenants, could be barred from private establishments such as pubs and theatres, or could find themselves subject to segregation in these publicly accessed private establishments.[71] Blacks also had to contend with a gendered labour market segmented and stratified along racial lines.[72] As Walter Tarnopolsky has shown, when Blacks turned to the courts to address these issues, the judicial record was mixed but tended to support the right to segregate. It is true that in some cases judges supported plaintiffs after being denied service in a restaurant or seats in a theatre. The law generally recognized two sets of competing rights: the customer's right to service and, just as importantly, the proprietor's freedom of commerce and association.[73] But the balance of decisions tilted towards the proprietors. The few Black lawyers who attempted to fight this racial order found that they had only a tenuous foothold in the profession. The difficulties of these exceptional figures who struggled to gain access in a racially exclusive legal profession is being unearthed by some of the most important research in the history of Blacks and the law in Canada (see below).

The law's tendency to support anti-Black racism and social segregation in Canada served as pillars of Canada's version of "Jim Crow"; it also played this role in its unequal treatment of Blacks in the criminal justice system. While criminal law was formally neutral in procedures and rules, its practice was a social creation and thus both reflected and reinforced Blacks' marginal social status. The criminal courts were a key institution among many that positioned Black Canadians as outsiders – people who were "in" the country but not "of" it, a social problem, quintessential "others." While there has not yet been a comprehensive national study of the treatment of Blacks in the criminal justice system, some work has been done in the province of Ontario in the nineteenth and twentieth centuries. Clayton Mosher's exhaustive study of the treatment of Blacks and "Asians" in Ontario's criminal justice system between 1892 and 1961 concluded that there was compelling historical evidence of systemic and institutionalized racism against Blacks and Asians in the criminal justice system and that such continued to be the case well into the 1990s.[74] In my own work, *Race on Trial: Black Defendants in Ontario's Criminal Courts, 1858–1958,* I found, as Mosher did, convincing evidence of systemic biases against Black defendants. I argued that Blacks lived in the spaces carved out by liberal racism, between legal equality and pervasive forms of societal discrimination. In the criminal courts this meant that though the law was formally neutral, the practice of law was a product of long-standing social forces and attitudes that held that Blacks were inferior to whites and not fully human.

These societal attitudes took on a range of legal expressions. Some cases were characterized by harsh prison sentences for Black defendants. Others featured the commutations of death sentences based on racially produced ideas about the diminished criminal responsibility (and mental capacities) of Black defendants, and the courts' (or the government's) desire to paper over convictions that were potentially racially biased (and hence legally suspect), and they were an opportunity, through the extension of mercy, to showcase the superiority of Canadian nationhood and British justice over the lynch law and mob rule of the United States.[75]

If discussions of lynch law and British justice were symbolically important aspects of nation-building, immigration law and practice in Canada have been their literal counterparts. The histories of racism and immigration have been inextricably bound together in Canadian history.[76] The first immigration Act of 1869 was designed primarily to promote the safe passage of potential immigrants to Canada. The ascendancy of racial naturalism in the form of scientific racism, eugenics, and educational psychology began to shape public policy profoundly. Through subsequent amendments to the original Act (1892, 1906, 1910), immigration policy gradually shifted in emphasis from an "open posture" designed primarily to attract newcomers to newly "empty lands" (a product of the territorial dispossession of First Nations peoples) to one that was increasingly oriented towards keeping undesirables out of Canada. In 1885, with the completion of the railroad nearing and the need for Chinese labour no longer pressing, the federal government moved to implement the Chinese Immigration Act, which restricted Chinese immigration and imposed a fifty-dollar head tax on all but a select few of them. By 1923, the Chinese Immigration Act was revised to effectively exclude the Chinese from entry to Canada. That same year both naturalized and non-naturalized Chinese were barred from the franchise. The 1906 and 1910 policy changes allowed for more scrutiny of prospective immigrants with an eye to excluding "undesirables" from entry. The federal Cabinet was now imbued with the power to prevent the entry of anyone it deemed to be at odds with the best interests of the country.[77]

Blacks were also affected by the climate of racial exclusion that permeated Canada's immigration policy during this era. Indeed, immigration policy was a major vector of state power through which Jim Crowism was institutionalized in Canada. Prospective Black immigrants were profoundly affected by the 1906 and 1910 amendments to the Immigration Act, which bequeathed vast discretionary powers upon the Cabinet. Black Oklahomans' attempt to migrate to the Canadian prairies in the early twentieth century is one of the best-known examples of how hardening racial attitudes closed the border to Black migrants. The Canadian government, determined to open up the "last best west" to agricultural settlement, was dismayed at the interest that their campaign generated among Black Oklahomans who, disappointed by the failed promise of a life of equality in a new state, looked towards the Canadian plains as a possible respite from myriad Jim Crow laws that consigned them to second-class citizenship. What they were confronted with, however, was a Canadian state that employed various measures to keep them out of the country. The implementation of invasive medical examinations upon Black migrants at the border was a favourite tactic. Canadian immigration officials also dispatched an African American doctor to Black communities south of the border with the mission to embark upon a disinformation campaign to dissuade Black Oklahomans from making the trek north. But even these efforts to stem the tide of Black migrants were not enough for the Laurier government. On 12 August 1911, the federal government approved – though never acted upon – an Order in Council barring Black immigration to Canada.[78] This sad tale was the cause of a broader trend: from the late nineteenth century to the end of the Second World War, most Blacks in Canada were native born.[79]

Race, "Rights," and the Law, 1918–1967

This era witnessed a broad shift from the church as the primary site of Black community mobilization and resistance to a turn to secular institutions and instruments – including the law – for the fight for full social and civic equality. The turn to secular provincial and national organizations was in full swing after 1945, and the world wars were pivotal periods in this transformation. The immediate post–First World War period was the catalyst for this change, while the aftermath of the Second World War – a landmark era in Canada's rights revolution – reanimated and furthered developments of the interwar period.

The outbreak of the First World War signalled a shift in Black Canadians' relationship to the Canadian state. Many Black men relished the opportunity to serve in the conflict; similar to many other groups of historically racially marginalized "visible minorities," they saw the opportunity to serve in the larger goal of making claims for full inclusion in Canadian society. Their desires were met with considerable resistance from a government that, although it had no formal policy that banned Blacks from military service, employed an informal policy of strongly discouraging it. It was only during the latter stages of the war when the casualties among white soldiers began to mount that the government allowed Blacks to serve (at this point many, ironically, had to be conscripted), albeit in units such as the No. 2 Construction Battalion.[80]

The wartime experience of agitation for full inclusion into the military carried over after the war. In Halifax, for example, church-led community initiatives such as the United Baptist Association and the Baptist Young Peoples Union represented Black Nova Scotians in both the secular and spiritual realms, until the founding of the Nova Scotia Association for the Advancement of Coloured People after the Second World War.[81] In Ontario, the era after the Great War saw the rise of the Canadian League for the Advancement of Coloured People, which had among its founding members white jurist William Renwick Riddell.[82] Transnational and Pan-Canadian organizations also began to flourish during this era. Marcus Garvey's United Negro Improvement Association, the first important Pan-African and Black nationalist movement, which began in Jamaica and spread to Harlem, began to make inroads into Toronto, Montreal, and Sydney between 1920 and 1940.[83] Labour mobilization of Black workers, among whom Black sleeping-car porters took a crucial and leading role, began in earnest after the First World War and continued throughout the interwar period.[84]

As it had been during the First World War, the government was reluctant to allow Blacks to serve in the Second World, and once again Blacks had to fight for the right to fight. Many more served in the Second World War than did during the First. Emboldened by their wartime experiences and bitterly disappointed by the unfulfilled promises after having served the empire during wartime, Black Canadians directed their efforts at political mobilization, which grew in sophistication and the determination with which it was carried out.

And what of the law in Canada as a site of Black struggle for racial equality? In much of the story of Blacks and the law, the picture is decidedly mixed. Canada's courts played a peripheral role in this story. In the United States, landmark civil rights cases in the 1930s and 1940s such as *Missouri ex rel. Gaines v. Canada* (1938), *Sipuel v. Board of Regents of the University of Oklahoma* (1948), and *Sweatt v. Painter* (1950) dramatically shaped African Americans' civil rights story, culminating in *Brown v. Board of Education at Topeka, Kansas* (1954). The *Brown* decision declared segregated schools unconstitutional, striking down vestiges of the "separate but equal" doctrine in *Plessy v. Ferguson* (1898) that was given renewed legal sanction at the highest levels of government despite the 14th and 15th Amendments to the U.S. Constitution.[85]

Beginning at the turn of the century, few civil cases appeared before Canadian courts concerning Black Canadians who were denied access to private establishments. In 1899 the *Johnson v. Sparrow et al.* ruling stipulated that it was unlawful to exclude Blacks from public entertainments, but the ruling was overturned in 1921 in *Lowe's Montreal Theatre Ltd. v. Reynolds* when it was ruled that such policies were lawful. *Lowe's* was overturned on appeal, not on grounds of racial inequality but breach of contract. The defendant in the case argued that he never seated Blacks in his theatre, and this was disproven by several witnesses. In Kitchener in the 1920s, *Franklin v. Evans* involved a Black watchmaker from Kitchener who was denied service in a local London Ontario restaurant. The court dismissed the case, ruling that "because the restaurant had no monopoly on service ... the plaintiff was free to seek a meal elsewhere." In 1924 in the case of *Rogers v. Evans*, Evans – a regular at Vancouver's Clarence Hotel – was denied service when the ownership of the bar changed hands. Rogers won his initial case but lost on appeal. There were strong dissenting voices in the appellate court, but ultimately the proprietor's right to deny service trumped Evans's right to service.

A similar pattern emerged in two cases that appear in this volume: the 1940 case of Fred Christie who, like Evans, was denied service in the York Tavern, his favourite bar, and the case of Viola Desmond, a beautician who was denied a seat in a New Glasgow, Nova Scotia, movie theatre. In the *Christie* case, when the bar's ownership changed hands, Christie found he too, like other "coloured" patrons, was denied service. He sued the bar. The case, which made it to the Supreme Court of

Canada, was ultimately decided against him.[86] In 1940, Viola Desmond was forcibly removed from a theatre because she refused to sit in the section of the theatre reserved for Blacks. Her decision to sit in the section reserved for whites meant that she was in violation of provincial sales tax in the amount of one cent, for which she was promptly arrested, taken to jail, and fined twenty dollars. Viola Desmond brought a suit against the theatre, which was eventually dismissed because her lawyer had failed to file an appeal within ten days, instead issuing a writ of *certiorari*.[87]

What was the significance of these cases? Like so much of the history of Blacks and the law in Canada, their legacy is complicated, but ultimately these cases signalled a failure of legal imagination and moral purpose in the Canadian judiciary. Save for a few dissenting voices of those judges who handed down minority opinions, unlike their counterparts in the United States, Canadian jurists were reluctant to use their courts as instruments of public policy and racial justice and instead cleaved to narrow conservative rulings that carefully sidestepped the racial questions at the heart of these cases, focusing on principles such as the freedom of association, commerce, and the nature of the contract between business owners and customers.[88] These principles, more often than not, reaffirmed the legal right to discriminate. It is also true that without an American-style bill of rights, the few judges who might have been inclined to use their rulings to shape public policy had little to work with. The outcome of these cases was a central irony of how race was articulated in a racial liberal order: racial exclusion was much harder to fight. In much of the United States, particularly in the Midwest and the South, the baldness of Jim Crow expressed through legally sanctioned ideas of racial naturalism made for a formidable yet tangible target. If U.S. law made Jim Crow – and with it, the denial of Black citizenship – through rulings such as *Dred Scott* and *Plessy v. Ferguson*, it followed that the law could be used reasonably as an instrument to undo it (at least partially).

In Canada, by contrast, Blacks had been full citizens on paper since 1833, and there was no body of case law that had threatened their legal status. As we have seen, however, in the post-slavery era Blacks were denied full social equality in myriad areas. The difficulty that faced Black Canadians then was how to use civil cases to fight racism in a social order where Blacks already had formal legal equality, but throughout their history had suffered inequalities that were a product of social customs supported through legal rulings that granted the right to discriminate. This central paradox of Black life in a racial liberal order – the spaces between formal legal equality and social inequality – proved to be difficult terrain to navigate through the civil courts alone.

This paradox meant that Black litigants who sued for equal access to private establishments met very limited success in Canada, and Blacks soon realized they needed to take collective action across differences of class, national origin, and faith within the Black community. They also joined forces with other "ethnic"/racialized communities by assuming a prominent role in multi-ethnic, multiracial, and multi-faith campaigns for human rights in Canada. Black Canadians thus turned their gaze outside the courts to engage the state and civil society in a bid to achieve substantive equality.[89]

Whereas Canadian courts lagged behind their U.S. counterpart in substantive civil rights cases, governments in Canada were well ahead of the United States in legislative process and the growing significance of administrative law and human rights legislation. In Ontario, for example, these efforts led to key anti-discriminatory legislative acts: the Racial Discrimination Act (1944), the Fair Employment Practices Act (1953), and the Fair Accommodation Practices Act (1954). Other provinces enacted similar legislative acts during the same era, following the path blazed by Ontario.[90]

On the immigration front, human rights activists, among whom Blacks were prominent, also fought to lift immigration restrictions to non-whites. The Negro Citizenship Council, formed in 1951 (later renamed the Negro Citizenship Association), was at the forefront in efforts to open Canadian immigration to groups the government had deemed "non-preferred" in its early- and mid-twentieth-century immigration Acts. The human rights activism of the post-war era had little initial effect on the federal government, which introduced a new immigration Act in 1952 that bore fundamental similarities to the 1906 and 1910 Acts in that the racially exclusionary orientation of the Act remained intact. The NCA sent a delegation to meet with the immigration minister in 1954 to lobby for changes to the government's treatment of West Indian immigrants.

At the same time that human rights activists were lobbying the Canadian government, West Indian government officials began to press for immigration agreements with the Canadian government to allow small numbers of nurses and domestics into Canada. By 1955, under both internal and external pressure, the government agreed to allow a small number of domestics into the country (similar to a scheme in the interwar era that brought Black domestics from Guadeloupe to Quebec, and nurses to the country as a whole). The Caribbean nursing and domestic schemes by definition were only a crack in the artifice of Canada's exclusionary immigration policy (at least where Blacks were concerned). But it is also clear that Canada's need to address shortages in its labour market was as big a factor as diplomatic pressure and the poor optics of overt racial exclusion in the post-war (and more specifically, post-Holocaust) era in the government's decision to allow some West Indian Blacks in. By 1962, largely – but certainly not exclusively – due to the efforts of Black Canadian activists, Ellen Fairclough, minister of immigration, moved to eliminate racial preferences from Canadian immigration policy. By 1967, under a Liberal government, the "points system" was introduced, legally formalizing and operationalizing the process of (ostensible) colour blindness that informs much of Canada's immigration policy.

The Law in a "Post-Racial" Order, 1967–Present

The liberalization of Canadian immigration and the dawn of official multiculturalism policy signalled an important shift in Canadian public policy and the Canadian polity. Both are often heralded as the beginnings of a multicultural and even "post-racial" country where ideas about "race" and the practice of racism no longer characterize the public conduct of individuals or expressions of the law as they once did in Canada.[91] The Bill of Rights, human rights codes, and the protections for minority groups under the Charter of Rights and Freedoms are the legal and legislative expressions of a Canada that sought to move away from the legal support for acts of social discrimination, to a more substantive citizenship for those who had been deemed unsuitable in an earlier era. The question that confronts us here is whether this is an accurate picture of the post-1967 period.

The answer is yes, but it is a qualified yes. Blacks have achieved more substantive access to the rights of full citizenship than at any time in their history in Canada. Yet, similar to so much of the history of Blacks and the law and the Canadian state, their access to full citizenship still remains partial. Thus we must be wary of a teleological understanding of Blacks' rights in Canada that inevitably regards the period after the Second World War as the fount of unprecedented racial equality for Blacks in Canada. While it is true that since the post-war era Blacks have had an expanding array of tools to redress social wrongs, the rights revolution remained unfinished for them. Black inequalities stubbornly persist in Canadian society. Even the more substantive legal freedoms and citizenship rights that Blacks enjoy now exist alongside pervasive systemic barriers to full citizenship and equality. Blacks continue to live in the shadow of slavery. They confront profound inequalities in myriad areas, for theirs was a socio-economic and civic existence in the margin of society. They continue to live, in the words of one Black Canadian sociologist, in the "economic apartheid" of "racialized poverty" characterized by high rates of unemployment (even among university graduates) and precarious and insecure work (contract, temporary, and part-time).[92] And Blacks continue to face differential outcomes in the criminal justice system, with longer sentences than their white counterparts and markedly higher rates of incarceration. In fact, many scholars now locate the genesis of Blacks' differential treatment in the criminal justice system with the vexing issue of racial profiling in policing, broadly defined to encompass state and non-state actors (e.g., private security firms).[93] The question that confronts us in Canada is whether, as proponents of critical race theory argue, the very foundation of law itself is inherently designed to maintain white supremacy in its myriad material and ideological manifestations. Are the ideas of legal impartiality and neutrality social fictions designed to mask the law's role in maintaining unequal power relations? Or is there still hope for African Canadians that they can work through the law, as they have in the past, in their quest to achieve full citizenship? While there is much room for optimism that Canadian law can help African Canadians to realize the dream of full equality they have been searching for since 1833, the jury is still out.

Conclusion and Chapters in This Volume

There are eleven chapters in this volume. Six are original pieces (including this introduction) and five are well-known (or relatively well-known) reprints or a reworking of significant published work in the field. Each contribution explores a major theme in the history of Black Canadians and the law, covering the historical period from slavery until the late twentieth century.

Part One, "Legal Pioneers," is a study of influential Black Canadian jurists who left an indelible mark on the history of the legal profession, Black Canadian communities, and Canada itself. In chapter 2, Susan Lewthwaite provides a legal and extra-legal biography of Ethelbert Lionel Cross, Toronto's first Black lawyer, who, she argues, lived life as an "outsider" and sought to "uphold the principles of British justice as he saw them in interwar Toronto." Chapter 3 reflects upon the little-known peripatetic life and career of Trinidadian-born Henry Sylvester Williams. J. Barry Cahill traces his life from an educator in Port of Spain to a stint as a railway porter in the United States. From there Williams went to Dalhousie Law School, where he studied from 1893 to 1895, and then on to London, where he was once again a student at King's College (University of London). Once there, he worked in the temperance movement, founded the Black British imperialist African Association, and was called to the London Bar in 1902. Cahill's study, the result of careful research of fragmentary sources, asks us to consider the importance of Williams's Halifax sojourn and his encounters with Halifax's Black community and its leaders and the importance of this period in framing the consciousness of the race leader who would emerge in early twentieth-century London.

Part Two "Formal Legal Equality and Anti-Black Discrimination: Case Studies" fleshes out the tensions between legal formalism and discriminatory attitudes in criminal and civil cases during the early twentieth century. Chapter 4 is Constance Backhouse's widely read account of Viola Desmond's challenge to racial discrimination in a New Glasgow, Nova Scotia, movie theatre. Chapter 5, by Susan McKelvey, explores the myth of "racelessness" in the law – a term coined in Backhouse's pioneering work – in the case of *R. v. Richardson* in Sandwich, Ontario, in 1903. Chapter 6, by David Steeves, is a meticulously researched account of the Dany Sampson murder trial in Depression-era Halifax. Steeves's analysis of Sampson's trial for the murder of two young white boys provides us with a window upon a racially divided (and charged) city and the contours of a trial marked by societal racism, the rule of law, and the ways in which the former affected the quality of the latter through historic practices of racially biased jurymandering. Chapter 7 is James W. St.G. Walker's previously published work on the Supreme Court case of Fred Christie, a Black man who was denied service in a Montreal tavern in 1936. Chapter 8, Eric M. Adams's reconsideration of the Fred Christie trial, complicates our understanding of the trial itself and its legal legacy by asking us to consider the role that basic errors of fact and law have had in limiting our previous understanding of the case.

Part Three, "Slavery, Race, and the Burden of History," bookends (chronologically speaking) the long fraught relationships between slavery, race, and the law. The first contribution, chapter 9, by D.G. Bell, J. Barry Cahill, and Harvey Amani Whitfield, is a study of slavery and slave law in the Maritimes. The next piece in the collection, chapter 10, by the late sociologist, criminologist, and philosopher David Sealy, explores questions of race, law, and culture in the late-twentieth-century case of *R. v. Hamilton*. Lastly, chapter 11 is James W. St.G. Walker's study of the 1997 case of *R. v. R.D.S.* This case, which is well known and has been thoroughly discussed and debated, began as a trial of a Black youth, "RDS," for assault and obstruction of a police officer. When the case was found in favour of the defendant, the Crown launched an appeal, contending that the (Black) presiding judge was racially biased against the arresting police officers. Walker engages with this case through the lens of critical race theory and its call for analyses of the law framed by awareness of racism and power differences, and challenges to the "objectivity" of conditions that oppress racialized people. *R.D.S.*, Walker tells us, was the first case where the Supreme Court of Canada "openly discussed racism in our society." For this reason, it can be considered a pioneering case.

NOTES

1 My favourite newer book that makes the argument for the law as a form of storytelling, and storytelling as law, is John Borrows's *Drawing Out Law: A Spirit's Guide* (Toronto: University of Toronto Press, 2010). Of course law as storytelling is a key tenet of the critical race theory movement – a point that James W. St.G. Walker makes in chapter 11 of this collection. See also, for example, Carol Aywlward, *Canadian Critical Race Theory: Racism and the Law* (Halifax: Fernwood Publishing, 1999); and Derrick Bell, *And We Were Not Saved: The Elusive Quest for Racial Justice* (New York: Basic Books, 1979).

2 Robin Winks, *The Blacks in Canada: A History* (Montreal and Kingston: McGill-Queen's University Press, 1997), 26.

3 This case is explored in chapter 9 in this volume.

4 Barry Cahill, "Slavery and the Judges of Loyalist Nova Scotia," *University of New Brunswick Law Journal* 43 (1994): 98.

5 Ibid., 101.

6 Ibid., 102.

7 Ibid.

8 Frank Mackey, *Done with Slavery: The Black Fact in Montreal* (Montreal and Kingston: McGill-Queen's Press, 2010); and Winks, *Blacks in Canada*.

9 William R. Riddell, "Le Code Noir," *Journal of Negro History / Association for the Study of African American Life and History* (1925): 322, 324.

10 Ibid., 322.

11 Sue Peabody, *There Are No Slaves in France: The Political Culture of Race and Slavery in the Ancien Regime* (New York: Oxford University Press, 1996), 7; Riddell, "Le Code Noir," 321–9; Winks, *Blacks in Canada*, 7.

12 The death of King Louis XIV sparked a constitutional crisis in France around the question of his successor. According to Sue Peabody, in the days prior to his death, Louis XIV lacked a suitable heir, as two years prior to his passing they all died, leaving only his great grandson, a boy of five. The king's illegitimate sons –the Duke of Maine and the Count of Toulouse – were to be given some influence as part of a council that would rule until his great-grandson came of age. The king's nephew, the Duke of Orleans, was also part of the council, which was to rule until his great-grandson was of age. Instead, the Duke of Orleans colluded with the parliament to annul Louis XIV's will to make him "the boy king's sole regent." This made Orleans the sole ruler of France but a ruler beholden to parliament for his power. Peabody, *There Are No Slaves in France*, 16.

13 Ibid., 14–22.

14 This phrase means "in favour of the king." Ibid., 41, 49.

15 Winks, *Blacks in Canada*, 7–8.

16 William Renwick Riddell, "The Slave in Canada," *Journal of Negro History / Association for the Study of African American Life and History* 5 (1920): 265.

17 Ibid.

18 Ibid., 267.

19 Two notable examples of works that consider graphic bodily violence to be at the centre of the slave experience in colonial New France are Afua Cooper's *The Hanging of Angelique: The Untold Story and the Burning of Montreal* (Toronto: Harper Collins, 2005); and Maureen Elgersman's *Unyielding Spirits: Black Women and Slavery in Early Canada and Jamaica* (New York: Garland Publishing, 1999), 1–16.

20 David Gilles, "La norme esclavagiste, entre pratique coutumière et norme étatique: les esclaves panis et leur statut juridique au Canada (XVIIe–XVIIIes)," *Ottawa Law Review* 1 (2008–9): 90.

21 Winks, *Blacks in Canada*, 9.

22 Kenneth Morgan, *Slavery and the British Empire: From Africa to America* (Oxford: Oxford University Press, 2007), 112–14.

23 Ibid.

24 Peter H. Wood, *Black Majority: Negroes in Colonial South Carolina from 1670 through the Stone Rebellion* (New York: W.W. Norton, 1975), 19.

25 Ibid., 99, 103; Morgan, *Slavery and the British Empire*, 112–13.

26 Roughly two thousand managed to escape to Île St Jean, helping the overall population grow four-fold from the decade earlier from one thousand to four thousand. Their respite there was short lived. The British rounded up the Acadians of Île St Jean and deported them to France shortly thereafter in 1758. Some managed to hide on the island. And of those who eventually made it to France, many decided to leave. "A few actually made it back to Acadie, but the largest number found their way to Louisiana." Quoted in James Laxer, *The Acadians: In Search of a Homeland* (Toronto: Doubleday Canada, 2006), 96–7.

27 Harvey Amani Whitfield, *Blacks on the Border: The Black Refugees in British North America, 1815–1800* (Burlington: University of Vermont Press, 2006), 15.

28 Gary Hartlen, "Bound for Nova Scotia; Slaves in the Planter Migration, 1759–1800," in *Making Adjustments: Change and Continuity in Planter Nova Scotia, 1759–1800*, ed. Margaret Conrad, 123–8 (Fredericton, NB: Acadiensis, 1991). The literature on the planter migration to Nova Scotia is a long-neglected area of scholarship that has a dedicated following among both a core group and an ever-increasing group of scholars who study the migration from various perspectives and through various analytical, empirical perspectives. Also see Margaret Conrad, ed., *Intimate Relations: Family and Community in Nova Scotia* (Fredericton, NB: Acadiensis, 1995); Margaret Conrad, ed., *They Planted Well: New England Planters in Maritime Canada* (Fredericton, NB: Acadiensis, 1988); Margaret Conrad and Barry Moody, eds., *Planter Links Community and Culture in Colonial Nova Scotia* (Fredericton, NB: Acadiensis, 2001). However, a perusal of this scholarship reveals that very little of it deals with slavery. See also Winks, *Blacks in Canada*, 27.

29 James W. St.G. Walker, *The Black Loyalists: The Search for a Promised Land in Nova Scotia and Sierra Leone, 1783–1870* (Toronto: University of Toronto Press, 1992), 40; Winks, *Blacks in Canada*, 24.

30 According to Afua Cooper, these terms were negotiated by the Marquis de Vaudreuil under the 47th article of the treaty of capitulation. Cooper, *Hanging of Angelique*, 81.

31 Cited in Elgersman, *Unyielding Spirits*, 23; and Daniel G. Hill, *The Freedom*

Seekers: Blacks in Early Canada (Agincourt, ON: Book Society of Canada, 1981), 7.

32 Winks, *Blacks in Canada*, 25.

33 Cooper, *Hanging of Angelique*, 288.

34 Mackey, *Done with Slavery*, 108.

35 Ibid., 112–35.

36 St.G. Walker, *Black Loyalists*, 40.

37 Winks, *Blacks in Canada*, 33.

38 Cooper, *Hanging of Angelique*, 91.

39 See Elgersman, *Unyielding Spirits*, 101–7; and St.G. Walker, *Black Loyalists*, 1–12.

40 While, again, I can't do justice to the complexity of this story in this intro-duction, interested readers should turn to Seymour Drescher's work for a fine analysis of the key debates on this issue. Unfortunately, Drescher does not have much to say about these issues in the "Canadian" context, but his work was and is an answer to two predominant schools of thought on what is often vaguely and somewhat over-simplistically referred to as the abolitionist impulse of the turn of the nineteenth century. The first is a Whiggish celebratory notion of the emergence of a human rights golden age (a posture that is now evident on much of the newer post-revisionist work on the Underground Railroad era in Canada). The second is the Marxian thesis of the decline of slavery in the wake of capitalism's intrac-table ascendance à la Eric Williams's *Capitalism and Slavery*. See Seymour Drescher, *Econocide: British Slavery in the Era of Abolition* (Pittsburgh, PA: University of Pittsburgh Press, 1977); and his more recent work, *The Mighty Experiment: Free Labour versus Slavery in British Emancipation* (New York: Oxford University Press, 2002).

41 In his foundational work, Cahill discusses the habeas corpus case that, in his words, "verged most closely on the judicial abolition of slavery": *R v. Ross*. This case featured a slave named Catherine who brought an ac-tion against a "Shelburne Loyalist," presenting him with a writ of habeas corpus that her putative master "daringly ignored." He was subsequently prosecuted for contempt of court. Cahill, "Slavery and the Judges of Loyal-ist Nova Scotia," 117–18. See also the case of a slave named Robin (alias Robert) in Montreal in 1800 in Mackey, *Done with Slavery*, 29.

42 Cahill, "Slavery and the Judges of Loyalist Nova Scotia," 128, 132.

43 Winks, *Blacks in Canada*, 97–8.

44 Drescher, *Mighty Experiment*, 91.

45 The seminal work on the story of Black Nova Scotians in the age of Revo-lution is St.G. Walker's *Black Loyalists* (see chaps 1 through 4).

46 Jeffrey L. McNairn, "British Travellers, Nova Scotia's Black Communities
    and the Problem of Freedom to 1860," *Journal of the Canadian Historical
    Association / Revue de la Société historique du Canada* 19, no. 1 (2008): 27–56.
    McNairn's arguments are based primarily upon his analysis of the trav-
    elogues of "failed colonial merchant and office-holder turned political
    economist and ardent free trader" John MacGregor and Captain William
    Scarth Moorsom, a military engineer.

47 Ibid., 38.

48 I have made these arguments in my first book. See Barrington Walker, *Race
    on Trial: Black Defendants in Ontario's Criminal Courts, 1858-1958* (Toronto:
    Osgoode Society for Canadian Legal History and University of Toronto
    Press, 2010), 3–4.

49 St.G. Walker, *Black Loyalists*, 41.

50 Ibid. Walker goes on to say argue that in the United States, slavery was
    synonymous with the exploitation of Black labour, and Nova Scotians of
    European descent had a similar attitude towards Blacks, as primarily a
    source of labour. "It was this economic attitude," says Walker, "taken by
    white people, rather than any identifiable belief in racial inferiority, that
    was to cause most discriminatory situations experienced by Black Loyal-
    ists during the 1780s." I disagree with this point, for while there was an
    economic dimension to anti-Black racism in Nova Scotia, the elements of
    white supremacist culture were a more complex phenomenon than this
    economically reductionist formulation. In fairness I would also add that
    Walker's more recent work has evolved from his analysis of anti-Black
    discrimination in *Black Loyalists*, 42.

51 Ibid., 45–6.

52 Given the limitations of space, I cannot do justice to this important emerg-
    ing conversation on the sometimes fruitful and fraught relationship be-
    tween Blacks and First Nations peoples from the colonial era to the present
    in Canada, but suffice it to say that from the standpoint of students of
    Black studies and history, this work asks difficult and even painful ques-
    tions of Black Canadians' historic and ongoing relationship to the Cana-
    dian state project of white settler colonialism. While its proponents often
    overstate what can be called (somewhat over-simplistically, I admit) the
    Blacks-as-settler-colonists thesis, their work has posed a serious challenge
    to those of us who have ignored Blacks' (marginal but nonetheless real)
    privilege as settlers in favour of a more comfortable narrative of anti-Black
    oppression and Blacks' triumphant acts of agency and resistance in the
    face of it – a criticism that may well be levelled at much of my own writ-
    ing, including this piece. The seminal work in this field is Zainab Ama-

dahy and Bonita Lawrence, "Indigenous People and Black People: Settlers or Allies?," in *Breaching the Colonial Contract: Anti-Colonialism in the US and Canada*, ed. A. Kempf, 105–36 (New York: Springer Science + Business Media B.V., 2009); and Paula C. Madden's *African Nova Scotian–Mi'kmaq Relations* (Halifax: Fernwood Publishing, 2008).

53 Winks, *Blacks in Canada*, 81.

54 Ibid., 94; St.G. Walker, *Black Loyalists*, 234.

55 W.A. Spray, *The Blacks in New Brunswick* (New Brunswick: Brunswick Press, 1972); and Winks, *Blacks in Canada*, chap. 5. A much more recent interpretation that focuses on Black agency is again Harvey Amani Whitfield's excellent study, *Blacks on the Border* (Lebanon, NH: University Press of New England, 2006).

56 Whitfield, *Blacks on the Border*, chaps 3 and 4; Winks, *Blacks in Canada*, 128–34.

57 In his seminal work on the Black Atlantic, Paul Gilroy argues, "The involvement of Marcus Garvey, George Padmore, Claude MacKay and Langston Hughes with ships and sailors lends … support to … [the] prescient suggestion that 'the ship remained perhaps the most important conduit of Pan-African communication before the appearance of the long-playing record.'" Paul Gilroy, *The Black Atlantic: Modernity and Double Consciousness* (Cambridge, MA: Harvard University Press, 1993), 13.

58 Winks, *Blacks in Canada*, 129.

59 Charles L. Blockson, "The Ballad of the Underground Railroad," Owen Sound's Black History, http://www.osblackhistory.com/ballad.php.

60 Fred Landon, "The History of the Wilberforce Refugee Colony in Middlesex County," in *Ontario's African-Canadian Heritage*, ed. Frost Smardz et al. (Toronto: Natural Heritage Press / Dundurn, 2009), 75.

61 Winks, *Blacks in Canada*, 248–52.

62 For the history of free-born U.S. Blacks who left California in the 1850s to begin life anew in Victoria, BC, see Crawford Kilian, *Go Do Some Great Thing: The Black Pioneers of British Columbia* (Vancouver: Douglas and McIntyre, 1978). See also Winks, *Blacks in Canada*, 155–6, for the story of the free Black settlers who in 1829 left Ohio and its restrictive Black Codes to found the Wilberforce settlement in Upper Canada.

63 Karolyn Smardz Frost, *I've Got a Home in Gloryland: A Lost Tale of the Underground Railroad* (Toronto: Thomas Allen Publishers, 2007); Sharon Hepburn, *Crossing the Border: A Free Black Community in Canada* (Urbana: University of Illinois Press, 2007).

64 In 1841 Nelson Hackett stole a "racing mare," a gold watch, and an overcoat from his master during his escape to Canada West. For the theft of

these items the governor general ordered his extradition to the United States. Winks, *Blacks in Canada*, 172.

65 See C. Peter Ripley, *Canada, 1830–1865*, vol. 2 of *The Black Abolitionist Papers* (Chapel Hill: University of North Carolina Press, 1986), 4–6.

66 Sunera Thubani, *Exalted Subjects: Studies in the Making of Race and Nation in Canada* (Toronto: University of Toronto Press, 2007).

67 See Winks, *Blacks in Canada*, 368–76. Winks cites the cases of *Washington v. Trustees of Charlotteville, Hill v. Camden, Simmons v. Chatham, Hutchinson v. St Catharines, Dunn v. Windsor*, and *Stuart and Sandwich East*. In *Washington* the plaintiff won his fight to get his children into the common school rather than the gerrymandered separate school district the trustees had devised. But the plaintiff had to pay his own court costs (the defendants had not the means to do so) and thus had to sell his own farm to cover the costs. As I have written elsewhere, this constituted a pyrrhic victory of sorts. While the strategy of gerrymandering school districts was no longer available to racists, the plaintiff had to endure near financial ruin. In *Hill, Hutchinson,* and *Dunn*, in all three instances the courts denied Black families access to common schools. In the *Simmons* case another attempt to gerrymander school districts was quashed, and in the *Stewart* case, which was legally ambiguous, it was ruled that if a Black separate school had fallen into disuse, Blacks had the right to the common schools. It ensured, said Winks, that "segregationists would have to be active rather than passive if they wished to maintain separate school systems" (see above). It was not, of course, a repudiation of the idea of separate schools themselves.

68 Ibid., 376–80.

69 Barrington Walker, "Finding Jim Crow in Canada, 1789–1967," in *A History of Human Rights in Canada: Essential Issues*, ed. Janet Miron, 81–98 (Toronto: Canadian Scholars' Press, 2009).

70 C. Vann Woodward, *The Strange Career of Jim Crow*, 3rd rev. ed. (New York: Oxford University Press, 1974), 7.

71 Constance Backhouse, *Colour-Coded: A Legal History of Racism in Canada, 1900–1950* (Toronto: University of Toronto Press and the Osgoode Society for Canadian Legal History, 1999), 175–6; Sarah-Jane Mathieu, *North of the Color Line: Migration and Black Resistance in Canada, 1870–1955* (Chapel Hill: University of North Carolina Press, 2010), chap. 2, "Jim Crow Rides This Train: Segregation in the Canadian Workforce"; James W. St.G. Walker, *"Race," Rights and the Law in the Supreme Court of Canada* (Waterloo, ON: Wilfrid Laurier University Press and the Osgoode Society for Canadian Legal History, 1997), 124–37.

72 Some of the very best work in this area is Agnes Calliste on railway por-

ters and Caribbean domestics. See Agnes Calliste, "Race, Gender and Immigration Policy: Blacks from the Caribbean, 1900–1932," *Journal of Canadian Studies / Revue d'études canadiennes* 28 (1993/4): 131–48; and "Sleeping Car Porters in Canada: An Ethnically Submerged Split Labour Market," *Canadian Ethnic Studies* 19 (1987): 1–20.

73 Walter S. Tarnopolsky, *Discrimination and the Law in Canada* (Toronto: Richard De Boo, 1982), 21.

74 Clayton Mosher, *Discrimination and Denial: Systemic Racism in Ontario's Legal and Criminal Justice Systems, 1892–1961* (Toronto: University of Toronto Press, 1998), 197–9.

75 Barrington Walker, *Race on Trial.*

76 See Barrington Walker, ed., *The History of Immigration and Racism in Canada: Essential Readings* (Toronto: Canadian Scholars' Press, 2008).

77 Ninette Kelley and Michael Trebilcock, *The Making of the Mosaic: A History of Canadian Immigration Policy* (Toronto: University of Toronto Press, 2000), 15, 97, 133, 203.

78 For a detailed discussion, see R. Bruce Shepard, *Deemed Unsuitable: Blacks from Oklahoma Move to the Canadian Prairies in Search of Equality in the Early 20th Century Only to Find Racism in Their New Home* (Toronto: Umbrella, 1997), chap. 6. The Order in Council read, "His Excellency in Council, in virtue of the provisions of Sub-Section (c) of Section 38 of the Immigration Act, is pleased to Order and it is Hereby Ordered as follows:- For a period of one year from and after the date hereof the landing in Canada Shall be and the same is prohibited of any immigrants belonging to the Negro race, which is deemed unsuitable to the climate and requirements of Canada."

79 James W. St.G. Walker, *Racial Discrimination in Canada: The Black Experience* (Ottawa: Canadian Historical Association, 1985).

80 James W. St.G. Walker, "Race and Recruitment in World War I: Enlistment of Visible Minorities in the Canadian Expeditionary Force," *Canadian Historical Review* 70 (Mar. 1989): 1. See also Bridglal Pachai, *The Nova Scotia Black Experience through the Centuries* (Halifax: Nimbus Publishing, 2007), 165–74.

81 Pachai, *Nova Scotia Black Experience*, 180–1, 189.

82 Melissa Shaw, "Blackness and British 'Fair Play': Responses to Anti-Black Racism, 1919–1939" (unpublished, 2011), 1, 69; Frost Smardz et al., *Ontario's African-Canadian Heritage*, 22–3.

83 Carla Marano, "'Rising Strongly and Rapidly': The Universal Negro Improvement Association," *Canadian Historical Review* 91 (June 2010): 237.

84 Mathieu, *North of the Color-Line*, 184, 185–212.

85 Darlene Clarke Hine, William C. Hine, and Stanley Harrold, eds., *The Af-*

rican-American Odyssey, combined vol. 4th ed. (New Jersey: Prentice Hall, 2010), 359–60, 574–5.

86 St.G. Walker, *"Race," Rights and the Law*, chap. 3.

87 Backhouse, *Colour-Coded*, 263; Winks, *Blacks in Canada*, 433.

88 This point is made in Backhouse, *Colour-Coded*, 256.

89 Mathieu, *North of the Color-Line*, 208.

90 Fair Employment Acts were passed in Manitoba (1953), Nova Scotia (1955), New Brunswick, Saskatchewan, and British Columbia (1956). Fair Accommodation Acts were passed in Nova Scotia and New Brunswick in 1959 and British Columbia in 1961. Alberta and Nova Scotia passed human rights codes in 1963 and 1965 respectively. Winks, *Blacks in Canada*, 428; Bromley L. Armstrong and Sheldon Taylor, *Bromley: Tireless Champion for Just Causes* (Pickering, ON: Vitabu Publications, 2000), 76–7. For a newer piece that explores the importance of the Ontario Human Rights Commission and administrative law in Ontario, see Frank Luce and Karen Schuler, "The Right to Discriminate: Kenneth Bell versus Karl McKay and the Ontario Human Rights Commission," in *Property on Trial: Canadian Cases in Context*, ed. Eric Tucker, James Muir, and Bruce Ziff (Toronto: Osgoode Society and Irwin Law, 2012).

91 An example of this sort of interpretive orientation can be found in Cecil Foster, *Where Race Does Not Matter: The New Spirit of Modernity* (Toronto: Penguin Canada, 2005). This book's normative and celebratory enunciation of multiculturalism was widely celebrated in the mainstream media when it was published.

92 Grace-Edward Galabuzi, *Canada's Economic Apartheid: The Social Exclusion of Racialized Groups in the New Century* (Toronto: Canadian Scholars' Press, 2006), 126–7. See also Joseph Mensah, *Black Canadians: History, Experiences, Social Conditions*, 2nd ed. (Black Point, NS: Fernwood, 2010), 139.

93 See, for example, David M. Tanavich, *The Colour of Justice: Policing and Race in Canada* (Toronto: Irwin Law, 2006); and Carol Tator and Frances Henry, *Racial Profiling in Canada: Challenging the Myth of "A Few Bad Apples"* (Toronto: University of Toronto Press, 2006).

PART ONE

Legal Pioneers

2

Ethelbert Lionel Cross: Toronto's First Black Lawyer

SUSAN LEWTHWAITE

Ethelbert Lionel Cross was the fourth known Black lawyer called to the bar in Ontario and the first to establish a law practice in Toronto.[1] Until recently, nothing was written about him, and he appears to have been forgotten. However, in a pioneering article on Black lawyers in Ontario, Lance Talbot notes Cross's call to the bar and states that his "career was short-lived when, in 1937, after encountering professional difficulties, he left the practice of law."[2] Still more recently, Constance Backhouse has presented a far richer portrait of Cross as a spokesman for the Black, Jewish, and trade union communities in events that took place following Ku Klux Klan (KKK) activities in Oakville, Ontario, in 1930.[3] In this instance, Cross successfully pressured the attorney general of Ontario to prosecute the local KKK leaders, one of whom was convicted and sentenced to a term in jail, to considerable public outcry in some circles.

This study seeks, through newspaper and other contemporary accounts, to flesh out the life and career of Lionel Cross and demonstrates that Cross was an "outsider" in the Toronto legal profession not only because of his race, but also because of his immigrant status and his views on religion and other issues. Cross neither kept a low profile nor

Previously published in Constance Backhouse and W. Wesley Pue, eds., *The Promise and Perils of Law: Lawyers in Canadian History*, 193–223 (Toronto: Irwin Law, 2009).

attempted to join the city's elite. He remained an "outsider" and from that position consistently held virtually all of the entrenched local authorities – the police, the judiciary, the criminal law, and the church – to account. His is a fascinating story that shows an outsider's attempts to uphold the principles of British justice as he saw them in interwar Toronto.

Ethelbert Lionel Cross was born on 29 October 1890 in San Fernando, Trinidad, the son of Eloise and François Cross.[4] His only sibling was a sister nine years his junior. He attended Naparima College in Trinidad, a secondary school founded by Presbyterian missionaries from Nova Scotia in 1900, modelled loosely on the Pictou Academy.[5] Judging from the writing skills and wide-ranging interests evident in Cross's later life, it appears that the education Naparima College provided him was of high quality and that Cross must have been an eager pupil. At the school, Cross learned to play cricket and later said that "his enthusiasm for the game is as much a manifestation of the ardent love he has for it as a tribute to the institution of his student days."[6]

In 1910, at the age of twenty, Cross left the West Indies and moved to New York, where he began a journalistic career principally with the *New York News*. While he was in New York in 1912, his father died, leaving Cross the sole supporter of his mother and sister back in Trinidad. After his father's death, he sent his mother thirty dollars a month. Cross relocated to Halifax in 1915, where he got a job as editor of the *Atlantic Advocate*, a newspaper that served Nova Scotia's Black community.[7]

Cross was in Halifax when the First World War erupted, and he enlisted for military service on 2 January 1917, at the age of twenty-six, joining the Second Construction Battalion, which consisted primarily of "Negroes."[8] On his attestation papers, Cross reported that he was unmarried and had no children. He listed his religion as Roman Catholic and his occupation as "journalist." Cross and the other members of his battalion sailed out of Halifax on 28 March 1917 on the SS *Southland*, "crossing the Atlantic during one of the worst weeks of unrestricted submarine warfare."[9] They landed at Liverpool, England, on 7 April and proceeded to France on 17 May. Shortly after arriving in England, Cross was promoted to sergeant. The Second Construction Battalion was attached to the Canadian Forestry Corps, and the military service of most of its members consisted of logging and milling near the Franco-Swiss border to provide desperately needed lumber for the war effort.[10] Cross served nineteen months in France and then six months in England before his discharge in June 1919. He sailed back to Halifax on the SS *Aquitania*. Upon discharge, Cross was reported in good health, 5'8½" tall, and weighing 172 pounds – having gained 5 pounds since his enlistment. His discharge certificate refers to him as "colored," the only indication of his race that appears in his military service file: his enlistment papers describe his complexion as "dark." One of the addresses Cross listed on his discharge papers was that of C.C. Ligoure, a medical doctor originally from the same hometown in Trinidad as Cross, with whom Cross might have lived for a short time after his enlistment or from whose Halifax home Cross's mail was forwarded.[11]

Lionel Cross was almost twenty-nine years old when he returned to Halifax after the war. Why he did not resume his journalistic career we do not know,[12] but he enrolled in the law program at Dalhousie University, then articled with John Eaglen Griffith, a Black lawyer in Halifax,[13] and, having passed all his final year examinations, was called to the bar of Nova Scotia on 12 December 1923.[14] Cross was one of seven West Indians who graduated from Dalhousie Law School between 1900 and 1931, most of whom articled with Griffith, and all of whom subsequently left the province.[15]

After Cross's call to the Nova Scotia bar he appears to have returned to Trinidad briefly[16] but then moved to Toronto, where he enrolled at Osgoode Hall Law School. He articled with Ephraim Frederick Singer, a Toronto-based Jewish lawyer,[17] and was called to the bar in Ontario on 20 March 1924, the fourth known Black lawyer to have been called in the province and the first since 1900.[18] He set up a law office at 131½ Queen Street West, which must have been roughly across Queen Street from Osgoode Hall, establishing the first Black law practice in the city.[19] Shortly afterwards, he made his first appearance at the Toronto Police Court, an event covered by the *Toronto Daily Star*. In a brief column in the Police Court news, the *Star* reported, "There was something of a mild sensation in court to-day, when E. Lionel Cross, LL.B., Toronto's solitary colored advocate, appeared." According to the reporter, Cross "exhibited all the assurance of a seasoned habitue [*sic*] of court precincts."[20] In many instances when newspaper articles mentioned or quoted Cross, they included a reference to his race. In early years the uniqueness of his position was noted as above,[21] and in some later instances he was referred to in more complimentary terms such as "a cultured colored barrister," "a colored gentleman," and "noted negro lawyer."[22]

As Toronto's sole "colored advocate" for five years,[23] and one of two for the remainder of his career, Cross was something of a local personality. He built up his law practice, which the Toronto Daily Star described as "wide." Reportedly the majority of his clients were "white folk rather than the people of his own color."[24] What is possible to reconstruct about his legal career from newspaper reports is far from complete. However, we do know that Cross appeared at every level of court from the Toronto Police Court to the Court of Appeal at Osgoode Hall. Of the six known trials in which he represented people accused of criminal offences, we know the outcome of five, and Cross did not win any of them. His apparent lack of success in the courtroom does not necessarily reflect poorly on his abilities as a lawyer, however. Cross attracted the kinds of clients not likely to appear sympathetic to juries or police magistrates and whose situations may have made successful defence cases difficult. Most of them were probably immigrants, if their names are any indication, and on the margins of contemporary Toronto society. In April 1924, his first appearance in a Toronto courtroom, Cross appeared as defence counsel for a man named Petrio Bolsu on an unspecified charge. He later represented John Kogonock on a charge of reckless driving, and Martti Laine, a Finn, on a charge of wounding. Only one of his clients that we know about was "colored": Charles Winn, convicted of assault at the Toronto Police Court in late December 1932.[25]

In the last three cases, evidence suggested guilt and despite his best efforts on behalf of his clients, Cross was unable to save them from conviction. John Kogonock had been sitting dazed at the wheel of his car at a railway crossing at King and John Streets at 4:20 in the morning, "Micawber-like, waiting for something to turn up," when a policeman happened upon him and arrested him. At the Police Court trial, Cross tried to argue that the conduct of the accused had not endangered anyone: "It was a quiet hour of the morning" and only the milkmen on their rounds were on the streets. The police officer had reported that the man had been drinking. "What do these drinking motorists care about people on the streets?" asked Magistrate Browne and sentenced Kogonock to pay twenty-five dollars and costs and to serve seven days in jail.[26] At the criminal Assizes trial of Martti Laine, accused of stabbing fellow Finn William Keskinen in the face with a knife, scarring him for life, according to newspaper headlines, Cross repeatedly tried to get the victim to admit that he could not positively identify his attacker. However, Keskinen stalwartly insisted, through an interpreter, that Laine, whom he knew, was the man who had stabbed him, and the jury convicted Laine.[27] The complainant who had charged Charles Winn with assault testified at the Police Court trial, "He sprawled into my car and there was liquor on his breath." Cross, apparently trying to cajole the complainant into dropping the charge, declared, "It was the spirit of the occasion," and asked the complainant, "Aren't you willing to forgive?" But appealing to the good nature of the complainant did not work; "he didn't feel in the forgiving mood." The magistrate asked, "What was the spirit of the occasion? Gin?" "No, jackass whiskey," replied Cross, and the magistrate fined Winn five dollars or five days;[28] so much for the success of humour in the courtroom.

Cross's law practice included civil matters as well as criminal. He represented the members of the First Baptist Church in seeking an injunction to restrain the trustees and clerk of the church "from interfering with the pastor of the church in his duties."[29] Most of this kind of work has not left much trace in published sources such as the newspapers from which most of this research into Cross's practice was drawn.

Much of what we are able to find out about Cross's legal career in such sources arises from his involvement with an organization called the Rationalist Society, a "free-thought" group of secularists, atheists, and agnostics formed in 1925 and active until about the mid-1930s.[30] The officers of the Rationalist Society were white, working-class Torontonians, yet they retained Cross as legal counsel for their organization, a relationship that was maintained for the thirteen years during which Cross practised law in the city.[31] Cross's representation of the rationalists led him to act as defence counsel at two criminal trials that took place in 1927, one for theft and the other for blasphemous libel. Such clients as the rationalists, who challenged the moral authority of religion and the legitimacy of police authority, were not likely to be heard sympathetically by devout and conformist judges or jury members, and the prosecution won both cases – verdicts that were upheld upon appeal. Cross also represented the Rationalist Society in 1932 when it sought an injunction against the Toronto police to restrain them from interfering in rationalist public meetings.[32]

Cross appears to have supported the rationalist cause philosophically, in addition to acting as the society's legal counsel. On at least two occasions, Cross was the featured speaker at Rationalist Society Sunday night meetings, once speaking on capital punishment and on another occasion, intriguingly, on "The Female of the Species and Satan."[33] When one of the rationalists put together a newsletter called the

Christian Inquirer,[34] Cross, whose law office was in the same building from which the *Inquirer* was published, was one of the few advertisers.[35] Cross had identified his religion as Roman Catholic on his attestation papers when he enlisted for military service in the First World War – an affiliation he appears to have shed by the mid-1920s. Perhaps his experience overseas during the war had turned him against religion.[36]

The publication of the first edition of the *Christian Inquirer* in January 1927 led to its editor's arrest by Toronto Morality Police on a charge of blasphemous libel, possibly the only occasion upon which such a charge was levied in English-Canadian legal history.[37] The editor, Ernest Victor Sterry, and his Rationalist Society supporters immediately retained Cross to defend Sterry on this charge. Cross remained Sterry's lawyer throughout the ensuing trial and appeal. Ironically, it was left to those outside the local elite to articulate the principles of freedom of speech that ought to be, they argued, the basis of civic life.

When Sterry appeared in court to find out whether he would have to face trial for blasphemous libel, both he and Cross appeared stunned when Crown officials brought forward an additional charge against him – one of theft.[38] That complaint, which had apparently been made more than two years before,[39] had been brought forward by Joseph Ying, who accused Sterry of having stolen two hundred dollars from him. Ying alleged that he had given Sterry a deposit of that amount to arrange for a laundry licence. That licence had never materialized, and Sterry never paid Ying the money back. Sterry's trial on the theft charge took place at the Toronto Police Court on 1 February 1927 before Magistrate Browne. The main argument of Cross's defence was that Sterry had merely acted as the middleman in the transaction and that he had been an employee of a man named John Pearson, who had taken the money and disappeared.[40] The fact that Sterry had signed a paper that documented the arrangement with Ying showed that his intention had not been theft, argued Cross. The defence also questioned the motives of the police who had not acted on Ying's complaint for some time; as Cross said, "Sterry has been around town for three years and not until the charge of blasphemous libel [was] brought against him does the theft charge appear against him." Sterry himself testified that he was "well-known" in the city: "I spoke on the streets and at Queen's Park," he was reported in the *Star* as having said on the stand.[41] In other words, if the police had wished to arrest him they had plenty of opportunities to do so before, and they had not, until the blasphemous libel charge had been laid against him.

Police Magistrate Browne dismissed the defence arguments and said he did not believe Sterry's account of the transaction. His judgment may have been based on the insistence of Joseph Ying and his friend John Sing, who appeared as a witness, that they had never met or seen this Mr Pearson and knew nothing of him, whereas Sterry testified that the four of them[42] were together on the occasion when Sterry had signed the agreement.[43] Pearson was described in both the *Star* and the *Telegram* as a man so big as to have been unforgettable. Sterry was convicted and sentenced to four months determinate and for an indeterminate period not to exceed six months. According to the *Telegram*, "The sentence appeared to come as a big surprise to the accused and also to his counsel, Lionel Cross, colored barrister, who fought the charge every inch of the way."[44]

Sterry appealed the theft conviction, and the appeal represents one of two known occasions when Lionel Cross appeared at the superior courts at Osgoode Hall, in this case at the Supreme Court of Ontario.[45] In both instances, Cross's demeanour before the superior court judges was not as deferential as the judges expected. Cross tried to link his arguments to larger philosophical issues, for which the judges had no patience. Cross based the appeal of Sterry's conviction for theft in part on the admissibility of the evidence of Joseph Ying: "I objected at the trial," said Mr Cross, "to the Chinaman swearing on the bible, believing that his conscience was not bound as he was not a Christian."[46] Justice Orde said there was no appeal on that ground, and the lawyer representing the Crown at the appeal, Francis Patrick Brennan, objected: "My honorable friend should not say they are not Christians without proof." Chief Justice Latchford urged Cross to "pass up that point" or "pass from that."[47]

Cross moved along to his next point, arguing that there had been no offence of theft. There was some discussion with the judges over the issue of colour of right[48] and about the agreement Sterry had signed with Ying. Chief Justice Latchford admonished Cross for touching on questions of fact: "There is no appeal to this court on questions of fact," he said, and urged Sterry to "come to the point." Cross contended that Sterry might be the object of a civil suit but not a criminal action, because there had been no intention of theft. "But how will you get around the fact that the criminal code says it is a crime?" asked Judge Latchford. Cross replied, "I argue that this case does not come within the province of the section of the Code." Mr Justice Middleton "remarked that Mr Cross seemed to be arguing on the law as it existed 100 years ago," and

Chief Justice Latchford said that the wording of the law had changed "to meet conditions in which men steal money now," the old wording of *steal, take*, and *carry away* having been removed. "Your lordships seem to be en bloc against me," said Cross.[49] "The law is against you," replied the Chief Justice. "The facts established by the evidence in this case show that a crime has been committed under the law." Cross's final argument was that the sentence appeared rather severe. "But you have not leave to appeal the sentence," replied Mr Justice Orde. Mr Justice Middleton said that the sentence did not seem severe to him, "four months definite only." With that, the appeal was dismissed.

It was the Sterry blasphemy trial, however, that made Lionel Cross a local celebrity.[50] Toronto Morality Police officers arrested Ernest Victor Sterry in the late afternoon of 10 January, after Inspector David McKinney had read and taken exception to the contents of the first issue of the *Christian Inquirer*, "a new effort in Toronto's literary field" that purported to be "different from anything obtainable in Canada today."[51] "It was so different," wrote the *Globe*, "that it has landed Sterry in the police net."[52] In the *Inquirer*, Sterry wrote, in part, "It is blasphemy of the worst description to call any pretended history a Divine Revelation, which sets forth God as a being who delights in the murder of those creatures he has brought into existence. Read your Bible, if you have not done it before, and you will find in it hundreds of passages relating to the Divine Being, which any moral and honest man would be ashamed to have appended to his character."[53]

The police charged Sterry with blasphemous libel under section 198 of the Criminal Code.[54] "Whether any particular published matter is a blasphemous libel or not is not a question of law," the Code said, "providing that no one is guilty of blasphemous libel for expressing in good faith and in decent language, or attempting to establish by arguments used in good faith and conveyed in decent language any opinion whatever upon any religious subject."[55] The case was very unusual, "practically unique in British legal annals," according to the *Globe*. Assistant Crown Attorney Edward J. Murphy, who represented the Crown at the trial, said, "This is almost the only one in a century."[56] "It is the most unusual charge ever tried in a Canadian court," said the *Telegram*, "and has but one precedent in the past 100 years in the British Empire."[57] Cross recognized the unique nature of this case: "There have been two cases under this charge in England, and so far as I am aware there have been only two," he told a reporter for the *Telegram*. "Mr Sterry is an atheist, and the case is one to decide whether he has contravened the *criminal code* by expressing his opinion on the Christian religion."[58]

Cross was the principal defence counsel in this case from the time of Sterry's arrest[59] through the appeal of his Sessions Court conviction. One other lawyer was also involved: Nathan Waldo assisted Cross at the trial.[60] The case rapidly became a cause célèbre not only in Toronto, but even outside Canada, and it got a lot of attention in the press.[61] The American Rationalist Association, the Chicago and Detroit chapters of which were particularly strong, sent moral support and funds to help with the defence.[62] For a time, a rumour circulated that the great American lawyer Clarence Darrow would come to Toronto to help defend Sterry.[63] Cross may even have corresponded with Darrow about it.[64] Some members of the executive of the Toronto Rationalist Association told newspaper reporters that if Darrow were to come, he would have to act as junior to Lionel Cross,[65] that suggestion showing the extent to which local Rationalists desired to stir things up. To insist that one of the most famous lawyers on the continent, a white American, should defer to the local lawyer, a "colored" Torontonian, represented a reversal of the usual order of things that contemporaries must have noted and that some must have found shockingly presumptuous. After such rumours had circulated for a couple of months, Cross let it be known that "Darrow would be unable to attend the proceedings on account of illness."[66]

There was never any doubt that Sterry was responsible for the contents of the *Christian Inquirer*, as he freely admitted that he had published the paper and delivered about five hundred copies of it himself at various locations around the city, including City Hall and Queen's Park.[67] So the legal issue involved in the trial focused on whether or not the language could be regarded as "decent." The *Star* summarized the issue: "What is blasphemous libel? How far can anyone go in criticism of the Christian religion before he or she has committed a blasphemous libel and is therefore liable to prosecution under Section 198 of the *Criminal Code*?"[68] "It is the choice of language that is involved in Mr Sterry's case," wrote the *Telegram*, "it is not whether his education is inferior to that of other apostles who couch their arguments in decent language. There is the more important fact that vulgar or profane language can transform a legitimate philosophical argument into a blasphemous libel. Vulgar or profane language can make a statement which in itself is not vulgar or profane, a vulgar or profane statement."[69]

From early on, it became clear that Cross would face an uphill battle defending Sterry. Police Magistrate Browne, committing Sterry for trial, declared that the Crown had to establish "that the statements contained in the publication are blasphemous and I believe that they are blasphemous, inasmuch as it is a most indecent and offensive attack on Christianity and the scriptures, couched in the most scurrilous and opprobrious language. I find it was the defendant's intention to asperse and vilify Almighty God in composing and publishing these scandalous, impious, blasphemous and profane libels of God."[70]

This statement pretty much sums up the view of the police and the Crown, a view with which the judges involved in the appeal did not disagree. Sterry was committed for trial, Cross entered a plea of not guilty, the Crown asked for a remand for one week, and Sterry was released on one thousand dollars bail.[71] The trial was postponed twice, and it finally began on 14 March 1927, with Sterry appearing before Judge Coatsworth and a sessions jury. The courtroom was filled long before the proceedings began, demonstrating the fever pitch of public interest in the case.[72]

From the outset, Cross expressed the view that this was an important case, stating that a "tremendous issue was at stake."[73] He consistently explained to newspaper reporters that he had chosen to take on Sterry's blasphemy case because of his "appreciation of the freedom of thought." On the day following Sterry's arrest, Cross told a *Star* reporter that the case at issue was one that dealt with the fundamentals of liberty, itself. "I am a colored man," he said, "but I can truthfully say that I prefer the slavery of the body to the slavery of the mind and, if I had to make a choice, I would go back to the slavery of the body."[74]

Cross's belief in freedom of thought and speech was one of the main tenets throughout his defence of Sterry: "Any one was free today to criticize the Bible or any other book."[75] That argument remained one of the main principles in the defence case throughout the trial and the appeal.

Cross and the other rationalists deeply resented insinuations that they were foreign agitators. During the days following Sterry's arrest, some newspapers, particularly the *Evening Telegram*, emphasized the link between the Canadian rationalists and the American body of the same name in a series of articles.[76] Cross reacted with some hostility to insinuations that he was American and "denied with considerable warmth that he came originally from the United States. 'I was born in the British West Indies, saw war service overseas, and am now pleased to call myself a Canadian,'" he asserted.[77] Others branded the rational-

ists and Sterry as Communists, an allegation Sterry "wished to correct."
He denied being Communist himself and explained, "The Rationalist
Society is not interested in political affairs as a body ... There may be
one or two who have some leaning in that direction, but the larger element are either Conservative or Liberal in their politics ... So far as
Communism is concerned we have always held that rationalist thought
should take up all our efforts."[78]

When the trial opened on 14 March, Cross objected to the reading
of the indictment before the jury, arguing that "the wording would
prejudice the case of his client."[79] Cross objected to the indictment on
a number of points.[80] Crown Attorney Murphy said that the wording
of the indictment conformed to section 852 of the Criminal Code and
so "no credence" should be given to Cross's objections. When Cross
tried to insist that the jury be sent from the courtroom when the indictment was read, Judge Coatsworth said, "But the indictment must be
read. You can't swear the jury unless they hear the indictment."[81] The
indictment was duly read, and Cross entered the plea of not guilty.
The jurors were then selected; according to the *Star*, thirteen were
"stood aside" by the Crown and four challenged by the defence.[82] The
jury was then sent away while Cross presented his objections to the
indictment, which the judge dismissed, and ordered the jury called
back in.

The trial lasted less than two days, beginning 14 March and ending before noon the following day. Unsurprisingly, the trial focused
on the language of the *Christian Inquirer*. The arresting officer, David
McKinney, was the principal witness during the first day of proceedings. At one point Nathan Waldo, assisting Cross in the defence, asked
permission to distribute copies of the *Christian Inquirer* to the jury so
they could look at them while Inspector McKinney was being cross-
examined. "We don't want to spoil the jury's appetite for dinner by pe-
rusing these," said the Crown, to which Cross objected.[83] The defence
counsel argued that "the charge involved alleged blasphemy against
the Christian religion," and if it was an attack on the Jewish God, there
was no crime.[84] This line of thought caused the pious Inspector McKinney to remark that he did not know that there was more than one God.
Nathan Waldo asked if he had heard of Jupiter and Zeus, and whether
he believed in the Trinity.[85] Mr Murphy objected. The defence asked
Inspector McKinney if he would be prepared to lay charges with regard
to other books "being circulated in Toronto by well known authors"
that contained similar statements. Mr Murphy again objected: "That

has nothing to do with this case. Surely the inspector does not have to crawl all over the bookshelves."[86]

The other principal witness at the trial was Sterry himself, who took the stand in his own defence. Sterry claimed his objective was "to liberalize the public opinion." The churches in Toronto were always doing that, he said, and "he thought that he was sufficiently learned to voice his thoughts." Sterry claimed to be a "hylo idealist," the term coming from the Greek word for *matter*. He expounded at length on the subjects he had studied that made him qualified to voice an opinion on religious issues. Sterry said that he "was doing this in good faith ... and firmly believed everything that he had printed." Cross said, "This man says that he does not believe in God. If so he did not commit blasphemy. What Sterry has written is no different than recognized ministers have said." Murphy countered, "My learned friend is trying to prove that two wrongs make a right ... he thinks because a half dozen people think like Sterry that it is the proper thing." Cross tried to read excerpts from Sir George Fraser and other prominent experts on the question of blasphemy, but was cut off. "I will go to others higher than this court. Perhaps your honor will be a little more charitable to me then," Cross stated, which was "vehemently objected to by the crown." Sterry, not doing his case any favour, launched into an "excited harangue" about his beliefs, and the judge ordered him not to make a speech. Sterry said he wanted to disillusion the jurors in regard to certain biblical passages, "trying to show the crudity, absurdity and blasphemy of this Bible." Sterry made a remark about "'hard-shelled Baptists,' who still believed all that was in the Bible," and Cross interrupted, warning him, "Don't mention any particular creed, please."[87]

The defence and prosecution cases wrapped up the following day, on 15 March. "Cross emphasized 'freedom of speech' in his remarks to the jury and pleaded that Sterry had published *The Christian Inquirer* for the purpose of giving to the world the result of long and careful study. Any man had the right to express a personal opinion." The defence wondered, "Why did the police have to defend the Christian religion?"[88] In his address to the jury, Crown Attorney Edward J. Murphy said, "Were the crown to tolerate and permit such a wicked and profane libel of God to go unnoticed it would deal a death blow to the state as a Christian state ... [A] man who in a place of public resort applies opprobrious epithets to names held in reverence by all Christians, ought in my opinion to be severely punished not for differing from us in opinion, but for permitting a nuisance which gives us pain and disgust."[89] Murphy concluded, "He is no more entitled to outrage our feelings by obtruding his impiety on us and to say he is exercising his right of discussion than [he is] to ... run up and down the street naked and to say he is exercising his right of locomotion. He has a right of discussion, no doubt ... but he must use all his rights so as not to infringe the rights of others."[90]

Judge Coatsworth made a charge to the jury in which he emphasized the importance of the Christian religion and the Bible to Canadian law and society, leaving no doubt about the "official" view of the link between the Christian religion and the state.[91] It took the jury less than half an hour to convict Sterry.[92] Sterry appeared for sentencing on 16 March. Cross asked for a suspended sentence: "In view of the fact that a conviction has been found ... I think the law has been sufficiently vindicated ... I think the ends of justice might be fairly met by suspended sentence and an undertaking not to publish any more such statements. I recommend that to your honor," said Cross. According to the *Star*, Cross spoke "in tones slightly nervous and strained," the only time his courtroom demeanour was described in such terms. Judge Coatsworth thought "the offence is too serious to pass by without some punishment." He sentenced Sterry to sixty days, to run consecutively to the sentence he was currently serving for theft. He also recommended an order for Sterry's deportation.[93]

Cross filed notice of appeal in the middle of April. The appeal was based on several criticisms of the police and the Sessions Court judge: that the conviction was contrary to law and evidence and against the weight of evidence; that the evidence did not disclose any criminal offence; that the indictment was defective; that the trial judge wrongfully excluded certain defence evidence; and that the trial judge wrongfully misdirected the jury on the law and the evidence "and included in his address material that prejudiced the minds of the jury against the accused."[94] The appeal was thus based on several arguments that had been presented at Sterry's original trial, along with a few new points. Cross argued that the Crown's view that Sterry's publication was offensive to devout Torontonians was never substantiated at the trial because no witnesses had been called to testify to that effect other than the arresting police officer. Cross also argued that the judge's charge to the jury was prejudicial to his client.

As had been the case at the appeal of Sterry's theft conviction, at this appeal Cross was less deferential towards the judges than they were accustomed to, and he tried to raise philosophical issues, to which the judges responded with impatience. The appeal was heard on 4 May 1927 and, despite the lengthy list of grounds upon which the appeal was based, it was dismissed in less than an hour. Cross "was told in no uncertain terms that the language used by Sterry was an offence against the Christian religion. Chief Justice Latchford said he could not understand how any jury could have found otherwise," a sentiment to which his four colleagues concurred.

Cross tried to argue that "blasphemy laws are a heritage of the past, born of intolerance."[95] Chief Justice Latchford retorted, "A history of blasphemy may be of interest to you. It is not of interest to the court. Let us get down to the facts."[96] There was some discussion about the meaning of the word *decent* as applied to language, and Cross said, "Language used should not indict any man," and referred to George Bernard Shaw and H.G. Wells. "You don't happen to have looked up the definition of the word 'decent' in the English dictionary?" asked Mr Justice Riddell. "'Decent' means 'seemly.' You seem to have the wrong conception of the meaning of the word." The judges expressed impatience at Cross's attempt to bring authors other than Sterry into the discussion. When Cross "pointed out that learned authors had used terms similar to those for which Sterry had been found guilty," Chief Justice Latchford replied, "What if they did? ... We are not concerned with that. We are concerned with Sterry." Mr Justice Riddell "said he was firmly convinced that Sterry's language was indecent in the eyes of Christians." Cross "contended that such a law should not exist in the present age." Mr Justice Orde "stressed that Canada was 'a country which had been based on religion.'" Chief Justice Latchford lost patience when Cross tried to argue that point, and said, "I must ask you to come to the point," adding that unless counsel did so, his lordship would refuse to listen. Cross said that Sterry had not been given a chance, to which Justice Riddell replied, "What chance does he want? Does he want us to say that that language was decent?" The appeal court judges considered Judge Coatsworth's charge to the jury quite proper, and the appeal was dismissed.[97]

The Sterry trials had taken up four months of Lionel Cross's time. One wonders how much he was paid for his efforts. Sterry himself would not have had the money and neither would the executive of the Rationalist Association of Canada, all of whom were working-class men and women. Funds for the Sterry defence were solicited at Rationalist Society public meetings, but we have no way of knowing how much money those efforts raised.[98] Some newspaper articles suggested

that American and British Rationalist Associations had sent money towards a defence fund but, again, whether they did and how much that
might have amounted to, and how much Cross might actually have
pocketed for his services, is unknown. Cross continued working on the
case, trying to win Sterry early release from prison. Cross visited Sterry
at the Ontario Reformatory at Guelph one weekend in September and
told the *Star*, "It looks now as though he will probably have to serve the
full term. I do not anticipate that he will be out until probably early in
November. So far the parole board has taken no action about his release
though I have made representations in his behalf."[99] Sterry was eventually released from the reformatory and remained in the city, despite the
efforts of the Toronto police to have him deported. Sterry set himself up
as an art dealer,[100] and although he remained involved in the rationalist
cause, he kept a relatively low profile after his release from jail.[101]

Apart from his legal career, Cross is also of interest as an eloquent
writer who expressed views on several subjects that might be regarded
as ahead of their time. Between 1926 and 1930, he wrote at least ten letters to the editor that were published in the *Toronto Daily Star*. The con-
tent of some of these letters is worth examining in some detail because
they appear to be the only surviving documents that Cross wrote himself.[102] Three themes run through these letters. Foremost is Cross's commitment to freedom of thought, speech, and assembly, and his criticism
of the Toronto police for perceived violations of those deeply held principles. Second is scepticism about organized religion. Frequently these
two threads are related, as much of what Cross says about freedom and
about the police arose from his view that the Toronto police targeted
groups of Torontonians unfairly, such as the rationalists, whose beliefs
did not coincide with those of the majority of the city's population. A
third subject on which Cross wrote and spoke was race relations.

Cross's views on religion might be inferred from his support of the
rationalists and some of his own writings. He appears to have thought
of religion as a backward way of thinking that ill-prepared people for
life in the modern world. In response to an article that appeared in the
Toronto Daily Star in late January 1926, in which the writer quoted U.S.
President Calvin Coolidge and a "well-known psychologist" who recommended religion as a cure for crime, Lionel Cross wrote a lengthy
letter to the editor. "Too often is the baseless assertion made as to the
relationship between crime and religion," he wrote. "I shall let Have-
lock Ellis, the great English criminologist, answer that question. He
says: 'It seems extremely rare to find intelligently irreligious men in

prison.'" Cross continued, "Is it not time that we got away from that barbaric idea about the depravity of man and his fallen nature? Man is not naturally depraved, nor is his nature fallen. He is gradually but steadfastly progressing upwards in the arts and civilization and these are accomplishments to his honor and not to his shame ... I feel sure ... that if half the effort devoted to religion were given to the promulgation and teaching of the social sciences and the real things concerning man's nature most of the ills which now afflict us would vanish."[103]

Similarly, Cross argued for the relaxation of laws that restricted various activities on the Sabbath: "The times do change, and we with them," he wrote. "Some day Toronto (and, for that matter, all Canada) will fall in line with other countries ... which have realized that Sunday is a creation of man, and not man a creation of Sunday; thus disproving, as countries having the open Sunday have done, that a nation that does not make a fetish of the Sabbath still prospers, and is no worse off thereby, despite the jeremiads of its puritans."[104]

Police suppression of Rationalist Society meetings brought scathing criticism from Cross. "I have been trying to reconcile our ideas of British liberty with the attitude of the police in breaking up the meetings on the street of those with unconventional ideas, while religious gatherings are undisturbed," he wrote in a letter to the editor of the *Star*.[105]

What can be the reason for this form of persecution? I got it straight from the lips of a police inspector in charge of the division where these speakers hold forth. This officer did not deny the right of speech to these persons, but informed me that their views were objectionable to many people and to the police, and that was sufficient reason for dispersing them; furthermore, the police were under no obligation to protect any speakers on the street but religious ones.

The meetings of the Rationalist Society, whose counsel I am, are well conducted; the crowds are model, and the attendants do everything to cooperate with the police in seeing that the sidewalks are kept clear. These people try to obey the law.

I have appealed to the police commissioners and the chief of police to remedy this condition of things as doing an injustice to a body of citizens whose only fault is that their views are unorthodox. But this appeal has been to no purpose. Is it not possible to arouse an enlightened public sentiment to correct this?[106]

Cross consistently opposed attempts by the police to extend their powers in the interwar years. In response to anti-communist hysteria, the "Red Scare" of the 1920s, the municipal government contemplated the introduction of a bylaw that would require all persons wishing to speak on the streets to secure a permit from the chief of police. An editorial in the *Toronto Daily Star* opposed this measure, which would in effect make the police chief the "censor of opinions for the city." Cross wrote a letter of support to the *Star*, declaring the editorial "a gem" that "should reflect the considered opinion of every reader. A reactionary spirit is now stalking," said Cross, "and what cannot be done directly it is being endeavored to do indirectly."[107]

In addition to criticizing the police, Cross took on some members of the clergy who were well-ensconced among the ranks of the city elite. Cross attended St Alban's Cathedral to hear the Rev. F.C. Ward-Whate respond to the "atheists of Toronto" and reported back to a rationalist gathering that the reverend had said if he were the attorney general, he would have put the rationalists in jail and then had them all deported, and would "have a disinfecting squad visit the office of *The Christian Inquirer*." A copy of Cross's letter to Ward-Whate was published in the *Star*, in which Cross said, "On behalf of the Rationalist Society, and *The Christian Inquirer*, whose counsel I am, I take up the gauntlet thrown down by you, and I am authorized by these two organizations to invite you to leave the security of your coward's castle – the pulpit – and engage with me in public debate on the merits of this question." When he received no response to this challenge, Cross threatened, on behalf of the Rationalist Society and the *Christian Inquirer*, to sue for slander.[108]

Despite his tough words, Cross abhorred brutality, including that practised by the judicial and educational systems. "Can we ever 'reach men's hearts through their skins'?," he pondered. "Retributive measures on the subject of crime is a good theme for magistrates, crown attorneys and the clergy to expatiate upon; but retribution is an evil." He urged fuller scientific investigation into the causes of the evils that led men to commit crimes.[109] Similarly, he supported "the new state of things which humanize the attitude of the school towards the child," writing a scathing response to a critic of the new system: "Such views are antiquated and pernicious, and need to be repudiated ... If your correspondent could appreciate the mischief that has been done to the child mind out of sheer ignorance to sympathize with its workings, rather than tanning the youngers' hides, he would be inclined to feel that in most cases the process should be reversed."[110]

Lionel Cross was not afraid to take on the white establishment for its racist views, as Constance Backhouse has shown.[111] Cross's comments on race issues show his courage, fearlessness, and deeply held views on principles of justice, as well as an eloquent turn of phrase. In early June 1926, representatives of the Ku Klux Klan visited Toronto as part of a campaign to boost membership north of the border, "to bring about the biggest Protestant revival the world has known."[112] On 2 June, one of them, "an emissary of this world-saving body," went to Lionel Cross's Queen Street office and tried to convince him to "enlist the members of my race to lend a helping hand in the redemption of this sorely stressed world," in return for which Cross would be given half the membership fee per "each Kleagle cub I had taken into the fold," at the time the considerable sum of five dollars.[113] "One marvels at the superb and unabashed nerve of some of the genus *homo*," wrote Cross in a letter to the *Toronto Daily Star*. Describing the views of his interviewer as "iridescent tosh," Cross said that once his visitor had finished presenting his case, Cross "flayed this movement most unmercifully ... I am convinced," he went on,

that this scheme stands unmasked as having the same motives as those self-appointed saviors in the United States whose activities have left a train of bloodshed and crime in their wake; Under the cloak of patriotic sentiment they have been able to enfold their dupes in their meshes, gulling them by appealing to their baser passions and arousing all the ignoble fires of prejudice both religious and racial.

And all this in the name of Christianity! Verily, the Christian has been dubbed the most intolerant of all religionists.

My answer is that if Canada needs the Ku Klux Klan or any other organization of its ilk, then I, for one, am sorry for Canada.[114]

Constance Backhouse has written in depth about an incident that occurred in Oakville in early 1930, in which local representatives of the KKK interfered in a relationship between a white woman and an allegedly Black man.[115] Backhouse describes how Cross mobilized the Black, Jewish, and trade union communities to pressure the attorney general to lay charges against one of the main perpetrators, which he did, and the man, a chiropractor named Phillips, was convicted – a conviction that stood on appeal. It is worth quoting here some of what Cross said, in this case at a public meeting "largely composed of white people." As Cross had argued in the Sterry case, he related the specific issue in this instance to a more general one of rights: "This is not a question of intermarriage, but of constitutional rights. It is a question of whether we are to allow this secret order to exist, whether the law is to be obeyed."[116] Cross continued, "It is absurd, and is treason to the state that a body of men, perhaps 2,000 should say to 8,000,000 Canadians: 'We shall enforce the laws; you can't.'" He went on,

Most of you as white people, may have peculiar ideas of the negro. You are not to blame. Must he be considered a man or should he be considered an indefinable, something ranging between a man and a beast?

There were great negro civilizations in Africa decades ago, explorers have discovered ... The present dominance of the white race did not always exist. One Roman has said that the ugliest and stupidest of the early slaves were the Anglo-Saxons.

So long as we have these hooded bands we have a form of slavery ... We are not entirely free here. Certain theatres and hotels exclude colored people. I look to labor as being the institution above all others – certainly not the church – as the solution of this terrible situation wherein the minority must suffer.[117]

At another public meeting at which a number of people spoke out against the activities of the KKK, Cross said, "Once we were brutes and chattels, but we are gradually winning respect and a place in the world ... I am not concerned with the supremacy of any one race. If it were possible for the negro race to become so, I would do anything to defeat that end. I am interested in the welfare of all races. I plead for equal opportunity and tolerance that would make us 'brothers all for a' that.'"[118]

Cross claimed that the Klan issued threats against him when he would not stop making comments about them – an accusation Klan members hotly denied. Despite the potential dangers to his safety, Cross consistently argued that the Klan's behaviour was outside the law and ought not to be tolerated, a view that many Torontonians of all races and religions shared.

About a year and a half after the Oakville KKK incident, Cross was called upon to comment on a policy that the University of Western Ontario enacted that would ban "colored" students not born in Canada from enrolment. This measure was intended to limit the number of Black students entering the university's medical school, purportedly "for clinical reasons." As the university's executive secretary, Walter James Brown, explained, "White patients in hospitals repeatedly objected to their being examined by negro students, so that we found this step necessary to maintain our standards of learning."[119] When the To-

ronto Daily Star reporter asked Cross for his views on the university's policy, Cross clarified that the real objection was to the examination of white women by Black medical students, and went on, "It is regrettable that such narrow prejudice should be shown and that a colored man should be asked to qualify himself in order to command the respect of his white brothers. And when he attempts to do so that every difficulty should be placed in his path so as to keep him down."[120] Throughout his career in Toronto, then, Cross spoke out on race relations and stood up to white authorities who expressed racist views or attempted to implement or enforce racist policies.

In addition to being known for his legal career and his social activism in interwar Toronto, Cross was a celebrated sports figure in the city, a noted cricketer who played for several Toronto clubs. Before emigrating, he had played "big cricket" in the West Indies, "the youngest player representing the southern part of the island on an eleven that opposed a formidable array of international cricketers." He remained involved in the sport after leaving the West Indies, first in New York, then in Halifax and Montreal before moving to Toronto, and he had been chosen to represent Ontario in interprovincial games "on more than one occasion." E.S. Jackson, author of the regular *Toronto Daily Star* column at the time "With the Cricketers," acknowledged Cross's abilities as a player – "the man of many centuries" would be the nickname Jackson would call him – and his authority on the sometimes arcane rules of that sport: "Perhaps there are few men in Toronto more thoroughly conversant with the rules of cricket than Mr Cross." Jackson considered Cross an ambassador for cricket: "It is men like E. Lionel Cross who are helping to make cricket more popular in Canada."[121]

Lionel Cross's legal career and his life in Toronto came to an end when he was disbarred in January 1937, having practised law in Toronto for almost thirteen years. According to the notice published in the *Globe*'s "Osgoode Hall News," he was disbarred for "conduct unbecoming a barrister and solicitor in that he appropriated to his own use funds belonging to a client."[122] Constance Backhouse, noting that several subsequent Black members of the Ontario bar shared the same fate as Cross, has speculated that members of the legal community used the concept of professionalism to exclude outsiders.[123] As was mentioned early in this chapter, Cross tended to have clients on the margins of society, principally immigrants. He spent a lot of time and energy working on behalf of the Rationalist Society, and one wonders how they could have paid him for a fraction of the time he devoted to their cause. He must have struggled even harder than usual to maintain his law practice during the Depression.[124] Cross appears to have been such a strongly and consistently principled man that it is hard to accept that he would have intentionally deceived and stolen from clients. He would have been painfully aware that as one of only two Black lawyers in the city at the time, his behaviour would set an example. During his legal career, Cross had been deferential to no authority except to the concepts of liberty and justice. Cross had been a thorn in the side of Toronto authorities for years, lecturing the police and the public about the concept of British liberty, arguing that the laws were antiquated and should be changed, questioning the legitimacy of the authority of the Christian religion as the basis for civic society, skewering institutions for racist views and policies, and challenging the views of Ontario judges and the law in the Sterry trials and appeals. With Cross's disbarment, that thorn was extracted.[125] The fact of Cross's disbarment should not be ignored, but neither should his career be forgotten because it ended badly.[126] On the contrary, it should be celebrated. Cross's courage at representing unorthodox and unpopular views so doggedly throughout his thirteen-year practice in Toronto is remarkable, and the fact that he was Toronto's first Black lawyer makes his achievements even more noteworthy.

NOTES

I am grateful to Mike Sulek for research assistance and to the Law Foundation of Ontario for providing funding for the larger project of which the research in this chapter represents one small part. Several people provided comments on an earlier draft, and I thank each of them: Elise Brunet, Katherine Corrick, Jim Phillips, and Sophia Sperdakos. I also thank Barry Cahill of Nova Scotia Archives, and Kathryn Harvey of Dalhousie University Archives for providing information and copies of documents from the time Cross spent in Nova Scotia. I am particularly grateful to Kathryn Harvey for providing a copy of Cross's graduation photograph from Dalhousie Law School, the only photograph of good quality of Cross that I have been able to locate.

1 The first Black lawyer in Ontario is now believed to be Robert Sutherland, who was called to the bar in 1855. On Sutherland, see Ian Malcolm, "Robert Sutherland: The First Black Lawyer in Canada?," *Law Society of Upper Canada Gazette* 26 (June 1992): 183–6; Christopher Moore, "Walkerton: Not

about the Water!," *Law Times*, 19 June 2000, 9. For years it was thought that Delos Rogest Davis, who was called in 1886, was the first Black lawyer in Ontario; see *Dictionary of Canadian Biography Online*; Julias Isaac, "Delos Rogest Davis, K.C.," *Law Society of Upper Canada Gazette* 24 (Dec. 1990): 293–301; Lance C. Talbot, "History of Blacks in the Law Society of Upper Canada," *Law Society of Upper Canada Gazette* 24 (Mar. 1990): 65–70. For a summary of what was known about early Black Ontario lawyers in the late twentieth century, see Constance Backhouse, *Colour-Coded: A Legal History of Racism in Canada, 1900–1950* (Toronto: University of Toronto Press and the Osgoode Society, 1999), 177n18, 177n20; Christopher Moore, *The Law Society of Upper Canada and Ontario's Lawyers, 1797–1997* (Toronto: University of Toronto Press, 1997), 177–9; and Talbot, "History of Blacks." Robert Sutherland practised principally in Walkerton, while Delos Davis and his son, Frederick Homer Alphonso Davis, the third Black lawyer called in Ontario (in 1900), practised in Amherstburg. The uncertainty about the race of early members of the bar is not unique to Ontario or indeed to Canada. As Walter J. Leonard wrote, "No one … is exactly certain who the first black lawyer in America was, or the exact number and nature of those who followed him until the 1940s." Leonard, "The Development of the Black Bar," *Annals of the American Academy of Political and Social Science* 407 (1973): 135.

2 Talbot, "History of Blacks," 66. The official record of Cross's legal career as represented by information of a public nature in the Law Society of Upper Canada's records is very sparse. Those records show that Cross was called to the bar in Nova Scotia on 12 December 1923, after which he moved to Ontario, where he enrolled with the Law Society, articled with E.F. Singer, and was called to the bar on 20 March 1924. He practised in Toronto until 1937, when he was disbarred.

3 Backhouse, *Colour-Coded*, chap. 6; "History Will Judge," speech at the London, Ontario, call to the bar, 30 Sept. 2002. I will not repeat here all the details of this interesting case, which Backhouse covers thoroughly in her book.

4 The biographical sketch of Cross's life before he became a lawyer in the first few paragraphs is, unless otherwise noted, derived from an interview that formed part of the newspaper coverage of the arrest of Ernest Victor Sterry, an event discussed more fully below, in "Learned to Be Atheist at His Mother's Knee," *Toronto Daily Star* (hereafter *Daily Star*), 12 Jan. 1927, and documents in Cross's First World War military service file in: Cross, Ethelbert Lionel Regimental No. 931405, box 2165-11, accession 1992–1993/166, RG ISO, Library and Archives Canada, Ottawa. I am grate-

ful to Library and Archives Canada staff for providing photocopies of the contents of this file. Some newspaper reports from 1930 report Cross's birthplace as England, which appears to be incorrect; in, for example, "Klansmen's Names Demanded of Price by Negro Barrister," Toronto *Globe* (hereafter *Globe*), 17 Mar. 1930. Cross is described as "a negro barrister of British birth." Perhaps these reports intended to identify Cross as a British citizen.

5 "With the Cricketers," *Daily Star*, 20 Feb. 1929. Naparima College, or "Naps," as it is referred to by those intimately acquainted with it, continues to educate young Indo-Trinidadians and counts among its graduates past prime ministers of Trinidad and Tobago. Information on the college was found online: www.naparimacollege.edu.tt and www .naparima.org in August 2007.

6 Ibid.

7 Cross was editor of this publication by June 1916 and until January 1917, but I have been unable to pinpoint the exact date when he took on this position. Few issues of the *Atlantic Advocate* appear to have survived, and none outside of Nova Scotia. On the publication, see Barry Cahill, "The 'Colored Barrister': The Short Life and Tragic Death of James Robinson Johnston, 1876–1915," *Dalhousie Law Journal* 15 (1992): 371–2; Philip L. Hartling, "'Devoted to the Interests of Colored People': The Atlantic Advocate, Nova Scotia's First Black Magazine," Halifax, Nova Scotia Archives and Records Management pamphlet, Jan. 1992, V/F v. 371 #25. I am grateful to Barry Cahill of NSARM for sending me a copy of the Hartling piece.

8 Military officials did not permit Blacks to enlist in the war's early days. For restrictions on Black enlistment and the formation of the Second Construction Battalion, see Calvin W. Ruck, *The Black Battalion 1916–1920: Canada's Best-Kept Military Secret* (Halifax: Nimbus, 1987), 6–13; Robin Winks, *The Blacks in Canada: A History*, 2nd ed. (Montreal and Kingston: McGill-Queen's University Press, 1997), 313–18.

9 Winks, *Blacks in Canada*, 318; see also Ruck, *Black Battalion*, 20. According to Ruck, before leaving for overseas duty, the battalion held a street parade in Dartmouth led by its own brass band; ibid., 19.

10 C.W. Bird and J.B. Davies, *The Canadian Forestry Corps: Its Inception, Development and Achievements* (London: HM Stationery Office, 1919); Ruck, *Black Battalion*, 20; Winks, *Blacks in Canada*. Some battalion members were eventually assigned to line units and participated in trench combat.

11 Discharge papers from military service file; information on Dr Ligoure from Hartling, "Devoted to the Interests of Colored People," 4.

12 Journalistic opportunities must have been hard to come by in a city still reeling from the devastation wrought by the 1917 Halifax Explosion. The newspaper of which Cross had been editor before he went overseas, the *Atlantic Advocate*, appears to have ceased publication in 1917, probably a casualty of the explosion; in any case, it did not long survive Cross's departure. Another possibility is that Cross had lost faith in journalism. As P. Fussell notes, "A lifelong suspicion of the press was the one lasting result of the ordinary man's experience of the war." Fussell, *The Great War and Modern Memory* (London: Oxford University Press, 1975), 316.

13 Griffith followed a similar path, as Cross did after him. Having been born in Nevis in the British West Indies, he emigrated to the United States and later to Canada. Griffith was educated at New York University, where he obtained an LLB degree, and at McGill University, from which he graduated with a BCL. Griffith arrived in Halifax in late 1916 and was admitted to the bar of Nova Scotia four months later. He practised in Halifax until his death in 1944. Cahill, "Colored Barrister," 372–4.

14 In his final-year examinations, Cross got a Class I in Domestic Relations, Class II in Equity, Conflicts, and Practical Statutes, and Pass in Evidence, Constitutional Law, Mortgages, and Procedure. I thank Kathryn Harvey of Dalhousie University Archives for providing Cross's examination results.

15 Barry Cahill identifies seven West Indian graduates of Dalhousie Law School in this period and assumes they were all Black: Cahill, "Colored Barrister," 374. According to Philip Girard, new research identifies one of them, Lionel Ryan, born in St Kitts, as white and of Irish Catholic descent; Philip Girard to the author, 9 Nov. 2007.

16 The Dalhousie student newspaper printed the following notice in November 1923: "Lionel Cross of the '23 Class has returned to his home in the British West Indies where he will practice." *Dalhousie Gazette*, 7 Nov. 1923, 3. I am grateful to Kathryn Harvey of the Dalhousie University Archives for taking the trouble to find and send me this useful reference.

17 It was not unusual for Black law students to article with Jewish lawyers. For the difficulties early Black students faced in finding articling principals, see Constance Backhouse, "Gender and Race in the Construction of 'Legal Professionalism': Historical Perspectives," paper presented to the chief justice of Ontario's Advisory Committee on Professionalism, First Colloquium, October 2003, 6–7; Backhouse, *Colour-Coded*, 177n20; and for a general discussion of the difficulties Black lawyers faced, see Talbot, "History of Blacks," 66–8.

18 Talbot notes, "Between 1900 and 1923 no Blacks were called to the Bar in Ontario." "History of Blacks," 66.

19 The street address of Osgoode Hall is 130 Queen Street West. Cross re-
    mained at that Queen Street address until 1930, when he moved to the
    Yonge Street Arcade, where his office was located from 1930 to 1934, and
    then to 33 Adelaide Street West, where he remained until his disbarment
    in 1937. *Canada Law Lists, 1925–36* (Toronto: Canada Law List, 1937). Cross
    is not listed in the 1937 Law List.

20 "Like Seasoned Habitue [*sic*]," *Daily Star*, 3 Apr. 1924.

21 Similarly, he was referred to as "Toronto's sole colored legal practitioner"
    in "Fraud Charge Delayed," *Daily Star*, 15 Oct. 1925.

22 "Arrest Atheist Editor / Charge of Publishing a Blasphemous Libel," *Daily
    Star*, 11 Jan. 1927; "Blasphemy Charged against Editor of 'Christian Inquir-
    er,'" *Daily Star*, 11 Jan. 1927; "Blasphemous Libel Is Charged against Editor
    of Pamphlet," *Globe*, 11 Jan. 1927; "Colored Citizens Are Represented in
    Many Professions and Trades," *Daily Star*, 15 Mar. 1930.

23 Cross was joined by Bertrand Joseph Spencer Pitt, who appears to have
    been the only Ontario lawyer to have articled with Lionel Cross, in 1928.
    Pitt was originally from Grenada. On Spencer Pitt, see Talbot, "History of
    Blacks," 67–8; Backhouse, above note at 177n20; S. Taylor, "B.J. Spencer
    Pitt: A Forgotten Icon," *Share*, 21 Feb. 2002, 9. Talbot notes that the bulk of
    Pitt's clients were Canadians of Polish origin: ibid., 67.

24 "Learned to Be Atheist at His Mother's Knee," *Daily Star*, 12 Jan. 1927.

25 Newspaper coverage of these trials is from *Daily Star*: On Petrio Bolsu, see
    "Like Seasoned Habitue [*sic*]"; on John Kogonock, under the subheading
    "Hour before the Dawn," see "Men's Police Court: Question by Accused
    Delays Proceedings," 26 Dec. 1930; on Martti Laine, under the subheading
    "Slashed Cheek," see "Men's Police Court: Youth Admits Theft / Goes to
    Reformatory," 17 Apr. 1931; "Stabbed in Cheek / Has Scar for Life," 29
    Apr. 1931; and on Charles Winn, see "Men's Police Court: Some 50 Cele-
    brants Sorry and Penitent," 27 Dec. 1932, 2.

26 "Men's Police Court: Question by Accused Delays Proceedings," *Daily
    Star*, 27 Dec. 1932.

27 "Men's Police Court: Youth Admits Theft / Goes to Reformatory," under
    subheading "Slashed Cheek" and "Stabbed in Cheek / Has Scar for Life,"
    Daily Star, 17 and 29 Apr. 1931.

28 "Men's Police Court: Some 50 Celebrants Sorry and Penitent." The offence
    may have taken place on Christmas Day, the "occasion" to which Cross
    referred.

29 "Ask No Interference with Church Pastor," *Daily Star*, 3 Sept. 1932.

30 There had been predecessor free-thought organizations in the city from
    about the time of Confederation, but the older organizations appear to

have disappeared before the First World War. The publication of *Secular Thought*, founded in the 1880s as the principal organ of free-thought news and discussion in Canada, ceased publication around 1911. See R. Cook, *The Regenerators: Social Criticism in Late Victorian English Canada* (Toronto: University of Toronto Press, 1985), chap. 4, for a discussion of the earlier organizations. After a hiatus of close to fifteen years, the Rationalist Society of Canada formed in 1925 and incorporated the following year. I have not been able to trace any relationship between the Rationalist Society and its predecessors, but as Cook notes, "The threads of free thought activities are difficult to pull together, for much of the documentation has disappeared" (52).

31 The two leading figures in the Rationalist Society of Canada were William Henry Styles and Bertram Elijah Leavens. We know they were white because their photographs appeared in the newspaper: "Rationalist Society Officers," *Daily Star*, 20 Jan. 1927. The incorporation papers for the society list Styles's occupation as rigger and Leavens's as cabinet maker. Rationalist Society letterhead named Cross as the organization's counsel from 1926 to 1938. The organization's documents are in the file "Rationalist Society of Canada," C. 26135, Companies and Personal Property Security Branch, Toronto, Ministry of Government Services.

32 "Asks Court to Enjoin Police Interference," *Daily Star*, 29 Aug. 1932; "Halt Street Meet Case," *Daily Star*, 24 Oct. 1932.

33 Notices of Rationalist Society Sunday-night meetings appeared regularly in the Saturday *Daily Star*. The notices of the meetings at which Cross was to speak appeared 7 Jan. 1928 and 9 Feb. 1929. The meetings took place on the day following the appearance of the notices: on 8 Jan. 1928 (females and Satan) and 10 Feb. 1929 (capital punishment). Unfortunately, the newspapers did not cover those meetings, so exactly what Cross said is not known.

34 "A Pithy, Popular Presentation of Profound Problems Perplexing the Public," Toronto *Evening Telegram* (hereafter *Evening Telegram*), 11 Jan. 1927, reprinted parts of the first issue under the heading "Paper on Which Charge Is Based."

35 "Blasphemous Libel Is Charged against Editor of Pamphlet." When the police broke up a rationalist street meeting in August 1929, an eyewitness reported that "a colored man" had been speaking critically about Chief of Police Draper just before the police moved in. It could have been Lionel Cross, who was an outspoken critic of the city's police. "Police Disperse Two Street Meetings," *Daily Star*, 19 Aug. 1929.

36 As one historian of the British rationalist movement has noted, "Many

men either became unbelievers or met unbelievers during their military service." B. Cooke, *The Blasphemy Depot: A Hundred Years of the Rationalist Press Association* (Oldham: Rationalist Press, 2003), 77. Perhaps Cross, like Wilfred Owen, the First World War poet, became disillusioned at the "inability of the civilian world – especially the church – to understand what was going on." Fussell, *Great War*, 289.

37   The exact nature of the case is explored in detail below. Although the Sterry case appears to be the only blasphemous libel case in English-Canadian history, there were several instances of such cases in Quebec; Marika Tamm, "Blasphemy Trials in Quebec, 1900–1935," May 1992 (unpublished). I thank the author for permission to use the information contained in her paper and Jim Phillips for bringing the paper to my attention.

38   The headline in the *Evening Telegram*, 11 Jan. 1927, reads, "Remand on Blasphemy Charge / Sterry Also Accused of Theft," and the subheading "Chinaman's Allegation Comes as Surprise to Editor of 'Christian Inquirer.'" According to this account, "the latter charge [of theft] appeared to have come as a surprise to the accused editor and kept his colored counsel, E.L. Cross, and himself wagging their heads for a long time."

39   The charge had been laid originally in August 1924: "Arrest Atheist Editor / Charge of Publishing a Blasphemous Libel."

40   This trial was reported in the local newspapers as part of their regular coverage of Police Court news: "Sterry Is Sentenced to Four Months' Term," *Daily Star*, 1 Feb. 1927; "Editor Sterry Is Jailed," *Evening Telegram*, 1 Feb. 1927.

41   "Sterry Is Sentenced to Four Months' Term."

42   Sterry, Ying, Sing, and Pearson.

43   Cross stated in court, "The Chinaman must have met Pearson," in "Sterry Is Sentenced to Four Months' Term."

44   "Editor Sterry Is Jailed."

45   Although Cross appeared on behalf of Sterry at the appeal, he did not file the appeal documents himself. Isadore Levinter did so: "Sterry Appeal Likely to Be Heard To-morrow," *Evening Telegram*, 3 Feb. 1927; "Sterry Theft Appeal Entered at Osgoode," *Daily Star*, 9 Feb. 1927.

46   "Sterry Loses Appeal from Theft Verdict," *Daily Star*, 11 Feb. 1927. This is an interesting argument, given that Sterry "affirmed" but would not swear on a Bible before giving evidence at his blasphemous libel trial. According to the *Daily Star*, when Sterry took the stand, "he affirmed, not taking the oath, saying that he belonged to no religious denomination." "Why He Doesn't Believe in 'The God of the Jews,'" *Daily Star*, 15 Mar. 1927.

47 "Sterry Appeal Is Dismissed"; "Sterry Loses Appeal from Theft Verdict," *Evening Telegram*, 11 Feb. 1927. This account of the appeal is based on these two newspaper reports.

48 Colour of right "generally, although not exclusively, refers to a situation where there is an assertion of a proprietary or possessory right to the thing which is the subject-matter of the alleged theft ... The term ... is also used to denote an honest belief in a state of facts which, if it actually existed would at law justify or excuse the action done." *The Dictionary of Canadian Law*, 2nd ed. (Toronto: Carswell, 1995), 203.

49 That remark of Cross's appears in identical wording in both the *Daily Star* and the *Globe*.

50 The discussion of the Sterry trial in this paper focuses on Cross's role as defence counsel. Much more could be said about the case, about which I am writing another paper.

51 "Blasphemous Libel Is Charged against Editor of Pamphlet."

52 Ibid.

53 The *Inquirer* went on:

> The God of the Bible is depicted as one who walked in the Garden of Eden, talked with a woman, cursed a snake, sewed skins together for clothes, preferred the savoury smell of roast cutlets to the odors of boiled cabbage, who sat in a burning bush or popped out from behind the rocks, this irate Old Party who thunders imprecations from the mountain or mutters and grouches in the tabernacle, and whom Moses finds, so hard to tame, who in his paroxysms of rage has massacred hundreds of thousands of his own Chosen People, and would often have slaughtered the whole lot if cunning old Moses hadn't kept reminding him of "What will the Egyptians say about it?" This touchy Jehovah whom the deluded superstitionists claim to be the Creator of the whole universe, makes one feel utter contempt for the preachers and unfeigned pity for the mental state of those who can retain a serious countenance as they peruse the stories of His peculiar whims, freaks and fancies, and His frenzied megalomaniac boastings.

I have been unable to track down a surviving copy of the *Christian Inquirer* in any library or archives. There is no copy in the indictment file at the Archives of Ontario.

Excerpts were published verbatim in the newspapers and copied into the indictment.

This transcription is from "Paper on Which Charge Is Based," *Evening Telegram*, 11 Jan. 1927.

54 R.S.C. 1906, c. 146.

55 J. Crankshaw, J.E. Crankshaw, and A. Chevalier, *Crankshaw's Criminal Code of Canada*, 5th ed. (Toronto: Carswell, 1924) s. 198.

56 "Blasphemous Libel Is Charged against Editor of Pamphlet."

57 "Will Prosecute the Second Blasphemy Case in over 100 Years," *Evening Telegram*, 11 Jan. 1927.

58 "Remand on Blasphemy Charge / Sterry also Accused of Theft," *Evening Telegram*, 11 Jan. 1927. The cases referred to involved publications by free-thought organizations in England, whose example Sterry may have intentionally followed. The literature on blasphemy prosecutions in England is vast; recent surveys include Joss Marsh, *Word Crimes: Blasphemy, Culture, and Literature in Nineteenth-Century England* (Chicago: University of Chicago Press, 1998); David Nash, *Blasphemy in Modern Britain, 1789 to the Present* (Aldershot: Ashgate, 1999).

59 Cross accompanied Sterry to the police station when he was arrested. "Blasphemous Libel Is Charged against Editor of Pamphlet."

60 Waldo was Jewish and the son of a rabbi. In 1928, Toronto police issued a warrant for Waldo's arrest on a charge of attempting to influence a juror in the trial of Waldo's brother-in-law, Dr Benjamin Cohen, for performing an illegal operation, most likely an abortion. After he learned that Toronto police were looking for him, Waldo fled the city, possibly crossing the border into the United States. When Cohen took the stand on the charge of conspiracy arising from the alleged attempt to influence the juror, the Crown attorney asked him, "Where's Waldo?" to which Cohen responded that he did not know. It was this charge of conspiracy that led to Waldo's disbarment: "No Further Arrests in the Jury Scandal," *Daily Star*, 1 June 1928; "Decision Is Reserved on Appeal for Bail," *Daily Star*, 30 June 1928; "Dr Cohen Committed on Conspiracy Count," *Daily Star*, 14 Sept. 1928; "Struck Off Roll," *Daily Star*, 21 Feb. 1929.

61 According to an editorial, "The Sterry Case," *Daily Star*, 30 Mar. 1927, "All over the world, it seems, literary persons are discussing [it]." The Sterry trial was mentioned in *Time* on three occasions: "Atheist," 24 Jan. 1927; "Blasphemy," 7 Feb. 1927; and "Jehovah, Jupiter, Baal," 28 Mar. 1927. An article in the *Daily Star*, "Handling of Sterry Case Is Criticized in U.S. Press / Too Much Dignity Given It," 2 Apr. 1927, quoting the following American newspapers, provides an indication of the extensive coverage the case was given outside Canada: *Brooklyn Daily Eagle*, *Fort Worth Record-Telegram*, *Indianapolis News*, *Louisville Times*, *New Orleans Item*, *Omaha World-Herald*, *Peoria Transcript*, and *Rock Island Argus*.

62 "Defence Fund for Sterry Being Launched in U.S.A.," *Evening Telegram*, 13 Jan. 1927.

63 "Would Send Darrow to Aid Blasphemy Case," *Evening Telegram*, 12 Jan. 1927; "Says Darrow's Help Promised to Sterry," *Daily Star*, 14 Jan. 1927; "Sterry Will Be Defended by Darrow," *Evening Telegram*, 14 Jan. 1927. The Sterry case took place only two years after the famous Scopes "monkey trial," in which Clarence Darrow had unsuccessfully represented Tennessee schoolteacher John Scopes. Scopes had been fired for teaching evolution to students in his science class. This case pitted evolutionists against creationists, and although the latter won, Darrow had made the creationists appear sufficiently inconsistent and irrational that many awarded Darrow the moral if not the actual victory in the trial. Darrow himself was a lifelong agnostic.

64 Newspaper reports show that Cross was in contact with other representatives of the American rationalist movement. For example, in "Sterry Will Be Defended by Darrow," Cross told a reporter, "I have had word from our friends in New York," who had told him that Darrow would come.

65 "May Ask for Darrow But Only a Junior," *Daily Star*, 24 Jan. 1927; "Sterry Will Be Defended by Darrow."

66 "Darrow Not Coming," *Daily Star*, 12 Mar. 1927.

67 "Why He Doesn't Believe in 'The God of the Jews.'"

68 "Arrest Atheist Editor / Charge of Publishing a Blasphemous Libel."

69 "Blasphemy Charged against Editor of 'Christian Inquirer.'"

70 "References to Deity Called Blasphemous / Sterry Is Committed," *Daily Star*, 25 Jan. 1927.

71 Aaron Newton, a Yorkshireman, "who says he has been an atheist since he was a boy," provided bail. Newton said that reading Fox's *Book of Martyrs* had "set him 'against religion,' though his grandfather was a clergyman." "Remand on Blasphemy Charge / Sterry Also Accused of Theft," *Evening Telegram*, 11 Jan. 1927. Newton was not an office holder in the Rationalist Society of Canada at this time.

72 "Sterry Puts Up Fight Disputing Allegation of Blasphemous Libel," *Daily Star*, 14 Mar. 1927. By the time this trial began, Sterry was in jail, having been convicted of theft.

73 "Sterry Committed with Renewed Bail," *Globe*, 26 Jan. 1927. The same comment is reported in "References to Deity Called Blasphemous/Sterry is Committed." The *Star* quotation continued, "If the Godhead has a sense of humor, He might laugh at the things we say about religion."

74 "Learned to Be Atheist at His Mother's Knee."

75 "Expect Sterry Case to Go to Jury Today," *Globe*, 15 Mar. 1927.

76 "Would Send Darrow to Aid Blasphemy Case," *Evening Telegram*, 12 Jan. 1927; "Defence Fund for Sterry Being Launched in U.S.A.," *Evening Tele-*

gram, 13 Jan. 1927, 1; "U.S. Is Controlling Centre of Toronto's Rationalism," *Evening Telegram*, 13 Jan. 1927.

77 "Says Aid Offer Meant Betrayal of Client," *Daily Star*, 15 Jan. 1927.

78 "Says Darrow's Help Promised to Sterry," *Daily Star*, 14 Jan. 1927.

79 "Sterry Puts Up Fight Disputing Allegation of Blasphemous Libel," *Daily Star*, 14 Mar. 1927.

80 "First, the language … of the indictment is archaic and obsolete; second, the accusation and description is very much to the prejudice of the accused; third, we must be limited to the four corners of the section of the code, under which we are charged, there is no similar description of the offence in the code; fourth, we are not being tried under English decisions; fifth, the indictment should be amended striking out objectionable matter; sixth, the code does not define what is blasphemous libel and the Crown has no right in the indictment positively to describe it. It is a question of fact for the jury." "Didn't Intend Libel of God, Says Cross"; and "Sterry Puts Up Fight Disputing Allegation of Blasphemous Libel," *Evening Telegram*, 14 Mar. 1927. These two accounts are almost identical.

81 "Didn't Intend Libel of God, Says Cross."

82 "Sterry Puts Up Fight Disputing Allegation of Blasphemous Libel."

83 "Didn't Intend Libel of God, Says Cross."

84 "Sterry Puts Up Fight Disputing Allegation of Blasphemous Libel."

85 "Didn't Intend Libel of God, Says Cross."

86 "Sterry Puts Up Fight Disputing Allegations of Blasphemous Libel."

87 The quotations from this paragraph are all from "Why He Doesn't Believe in 'The God of the Jews.'"

88 Ibid.

89 "Find Sterry Guilty of Blasphemous Libel," *Daily Star*, 15 Mar. 1927.

90 Ibid.

91 Ibid. One sub-headline of this story reads, "An Impressive Charge to the Jury Was Delivered by Judge Coatsworth."

92 All the newspapers consistently report that the jury deliberated for twenty-five minutes. "Find Sterry Guilty of Blasphemous Libel." "Verdict of Guilty Returned by Jury in Blasphemy Case," *Globe*, 16 Mar. 1927.

93 "Sixty Days to Editor / Deportation to Follow / Sentence upon Sterry," *Daily Star*, 16 Mar. 1927. This newspaper account noted that such an outcome was unusual; under Canadian law, a person was not liable to deportation if he or she had resided in the country for more than five years, and Sterry had lived here for sixteen. Other newspaper reports mentioning the possibility that Sterry might be deported are "May Deport Sterry," *Daily Star*, 16 Mar. 1927; "To Deport Sterry," *Daily Star*, 16

Mar. 1927; "Deportation of Sterry Being Sought by Police," *Globe*, 16 Mar. 1927; "To Do 60 Days in Jail and to Be Deported, Sentence on Sterry," *Globe*, 17 Mar. 1927. For the use of deportation as a tool to rid the country of "undesirable" immigrants in the early twentieth century, see Barbara Roberts, *Whence They Came: Deportation from Canada, 1900–1935* (Ottawa: University of Ottawa Press, 1988).

94 Grounds for the appeal are listed in "Ask Leave to Appeal Sentence on Sterry," *Daily Star*, 13 Apr. 1927.

95 "Blasphemous Libel Appeal Is Dismissed," *Evening Telegram*, 4 May 1927.

96 The appeal was reported in "Sterry Conviction Upheld / Court Considers Language an Insult to Christianity" and "Blasphemous Libel Appeal Is Dismissed," *Daily Star*, 4 May 1927; "Appeal by E.V. Sterry Is Dismissed by Court," *Globe*, 5 May 1927.

97 Unless otherwise noted, the quotations in this paragraph are from "Sterry Conviction Upheld / Court Considers Language an Insult to Christianity."

98 For example, a notice, "The Sterry Blasphemy Appeal," appeared in the *Daily Star*, 21 and 23 Mar. 1927. The subheading read, "Freedom of Speech and the Liberty of the Press Are in Peril!"

99 "Cross Sees Sterry in the Reformatory," *Daily Star*, 28 Sept. 1927.

100 Toronto City Directories for 1929 and 1933–8 list Sterry's occupation as fine art and stamp dealer. Advertisements for Sterry's shop appeared in the *Daily Star*, 24 Nov. 1933 and 19 Feb. 1938.

101 Sterry chaired a Rationalist Society meeting in October 1928, which broke out in an uproar. On that occasion, Joseph McCabe, "England's leading exponent of evolution," spoke at Margaret Eaton Hall: "McCabe Meeting Ends in Disorder," *Globe*, 15 Oct. 1928. McCabe had been a Catholic priest known as Father Anthony before his "conversion" to free-thought and was a leading free-thought speaker in Britain, North America, and the Antipodes. A brief account of McCabe's career can be found in F.J. Gould, *The Pioneers of Johnson's Court: A History of the Rationalist Press Association from 1899 Onwards*, rev. ed. (London: Watts, 1935), 18–20. For a full biography, see Bill Cooke, *A Rebel to the Last Breath: Joseph McCabe and Rationalism* (Amherst, NY: Prometheus, 2001). Sterry also spoke at a Rationalist Society meeting in October 1932, on "My Objections to the Christian Scheme of Salvation," notice in *Toronto Daily Star*, 8 Oct. 1932.

102 I have been unable to locate papers of Cross or records relating to his legal practice in any archival repository. Nor have I been able to locate records of the Rationalist Society apart from the organization's incorporation file, "Rationalist Society of Canada," C. 26135, Companies and Per-

sonal Property Security Branch, Toronto, Ministry of Government Services.

103 "Crime and Its Causes," *Daily Star*, 2 Feb. 1926. In the letter, Cross disputed the contention that the crime rate, particularly among young people, was increasing, quoting statistics from a *New York Times* editorial of 28 Dec. 1925.

104 "Toronto's Sabbath," *Daily Star*, 15 Sept. 1928.

105 "Rationalists' Meetings," *Daily Star*, 3 Aug. 1929. This letter is quoted here in full because it represents an important theme in Cross's writings, that of freedom of speech, which Cross consistently articulated throughout his entire legal career.

106 Ibid.

107 "No Civic Censor Wanted," *Daily Star*, 19 Sept. 1929; "Reactionism Abroad," *Daily Star*, 27 Sept. 1929.

108 "Bible Is Ridiculed by Rationalists," *Daily Star*, 17 Jan. 1927; "Calls Upon Pastor for Public Debate," *Daily Star*, 19 Jan. 1927; "He Threatens to Sue on St Alban's Sermon," *Daily Star*, 21 Jan. 1927.

109 "Crime and Its Causes." It is not difficult to see why one of Cross's lectures to a Rationalist Society meeting was on the subject of capital punishment, to which Cross was most likely opposed.

110 "Punishing Children," *Daily Star*, 10 July 1929. Cross went on to say that the "best opinion on pedagogies" on the issue of gender of teachers was that "there should be an equal number of teachers of both sexes in the schools. The adult hand of both is equally necessary to mould the adolescent mind and give it true balance and perspective."

111 Backhouse, *Colour-Coded*, chap. 6.

112 "Canada Doesn't Need It," *Daily Star*, 2 June 1926.

113 The membership fee was ten dollars, of which Cross was to be given five, according to the arrangement his visitor proposed. By this time the KKK had broadened its targets to include Jews, Roman Catholics, and immigrants, as well as Blacks, to become a nativist organization anxious to preserve "American values." Although the KKK had broad support in parts of the United States, such support was on the wane by 1926 and dwindled rapidly after that. The KKK made inroads into some Canadian communities, particularly in Saskatchewan, but it did not gain a lot of popular support in most of Ontario; in fact, many Ontarians viewed Klan activities with concern. For summaries of KKK activities in Canada, see Backhouse, *Colour-Coded*, 181–93; Winks, *Blacks in Canada*, 320–5. For more detail, see William Peter Baergen, *The Ku Klux Klan in Central Alberta* (Red Deer, AB: Central Alberta Historical Society, 2000); Allan Bartley,

"A Public Nuisance: The Ku Klux Klan in Ontario, 1923–1927," *Journal of Canadian Studies* 30, no. 3 (1995): 156; Martin Robin, *Shades of Right: Nativist and Fascist Politics in Canada, 1920–1940* (Toronto: University of Toronto Press, 1992); Julian Sher, *White Hoods: Canada's Ku Klux Klan* (Vancouver: New Star Books, 1983). Bartley argues that the robust culture of the Orange Order prevented the KKK's infiltration into Ontario.

114 "Canada Doesn't Need It."

115 Backhouse, *Colour-Coded*, chap. 6. The man later claimed to be not Black, but part Aboriginal.

116 "Says Law Not Vindicated in Oakville Klan Episode," *Daily Star*, 17 Mar. 1930.

117 Ibid.

118 "Has No Negro Blood, Klan Victim Declares," *Daily Star*, 5 Mar. 1930. The reference to "brothers all for a' that" is to a poem by the Scottish poet Robert Burns, "For A' That."

119 This account is from "Western Draws Color Line Except for Canadian-Born," *Daily Star*, 13 Aug. 1931. The *Star* took care to solicit the views of representatives of the Black community, including "colored Toronto barrister" Lionel Cross, as well as university officials.

120 Ibid.

121 "With the Cricketers," *Daily Star*, 23 Oct. 1928, and 20 Feb. 1929.

122 "At Osgoode Hall," *Globe*, 25 Jan. 1937. Law Society member files and records of disciplinary proceedings before February 1986 are closed to researchers, so the precise nature of the charge against him is never likely to be known.

123 Backhouse, "Gender and Race Legal Professionalism."

124 Lance Talbot speculates that the Depression must have lain behind the difficulties that led to Cross's disbarment. Talbot also points out that the most lucrative types of legal practice, such as corporate litigation and real estate, would have been largely closed to Black lawyers in Cross's time. The types of law that would have been open to him would have been criminal and small-scale civil causes, neither of which would have generated much income for lawyers. The evidence found in researching this paper bears out Talbot's view, "History of Blacks."

125 I have tried without success to find out what happened to Lionel Cross after his disbarment. He appears to have left Toronto and never to have returned, for which one could hardly blame him. City directories show him listed for the last time in 1936, after which he disappears permanently. I wondered whether he might have returned to Trinidad and tried contacting the Law Society, Bar Association, National Archives and Li-

brary but got no response to my queries. Perhaps Cross went elsewhere, to make a fresh start in a new place where no one knew his history.

126 Writing about the first Black lawyer in Halifax, James Robinson Johnston, Barry Cahill speculates that the manner of Robinson's death – he had been murdered by his brother-in-law – had come to overshadow his life and career and he had largely been forgotten until recently. Cahill, "The Colored Barrister." Cross's case is similar. The cloud of his disbarment seems to have hung over his reputation, so that although he had been a well-known figure in Toronto for about a decade from the mid-1920s to the mid-1930s, he too had been largely forgotten.

3

Constructing an "Imperial Pan-Africanist": Henry Sylvester Williams as a University Law Student in Canada

J. BARRY CAHILL

In 2004 George and Darrill Fosty published *Black Ice*, "the lost history of the colored hockey league of the Maritimes, 1895–1925." They included a timeline of "Notable dates in black Canadian history," among which was the enrolment at Dalhousie Law School of Henry Sylvester Williams (1867–1911), an ex-schoolmaster from Trinidad who became the father of modern organizational pan-Africanism.[1] Most of two chapters of the Fosty brothers' book is devoted to an imaginative reconstruction of Williams's involvement with Black people in Halifax during two years spent in the city in the early 1890s.[2] For them, Williams was a political refugee par excellence, the "last passenger" on the fabled Underground Railroad, ultimately driven out of Halifax by a cabal of white supremacists who disapproved of his advocacy of Black empowerment. What role did Canada, Nova Scotia, Halifax, and Dalhousie University *really* play in launching the career of this short-lived Caribbean W.E.B. Du Bois?

In September 1893 Williams became the first Black student in Dalhousie University's Faculty of Law. Though poor examination results compelled him to abandon the LLB course in 1895 without graduating, Williams was a pioneer in Black Canadian legal history. He blazed a trail not only for James Robinson Johnston (LLB 1898) – Dalhousie University's first Black graduate[3] – but also for a generation of Black West Indians who afterwards came to Nova Scotia to study law and be called to the bar.[4] This paper examines why Williams came to Dalhousie, considers his experience there, and shows how a false start in the colonial hinterland led to a renewed, successful effort in the metropolis of the imperium.

In or about 1891 Henry Sylvester Williams was teaching school in suburban Port of Spain when he decided to go abroad seeking higher education. There was no university in the British West Indies, nor had Williams been privileged to attend grammar school or college. He may not have made up his mind to become a lawyer before leaving Trinidad; yet his very leaving implies a desire to become a barrister. As historian Carl Campbell points out, Trinidadians "could not become barristers without expensive study abroad."[5] Though locals had been qualifying as solicitors since 1875, Williams presumably had no interest in becoming a mere solicitor without status inside the legal profession or influence outside and beyond.[6] According to historian Bridget Brereton, "school teaching, and the company of a few young 'radical' black and coloured teachers and lawyers in the city, were not enough for Williams and he left Trinidad in 1891."[7] He intended to go to the United States and England for higher education, but a fortuitous encounter with an eminent Québécois lawyer would ensure that the path from one to the other lay through Canada and Nova Scotia. Williams's brief sojourn in Canada irrevocably set his face towards public service and politics.

Immediately after leaving Trinidad, Williams is supposed to have spent a year or two in the United States, where Black lawyers were well established and relatively numerous.[8] In Halifax newspapers, he could have read about the committee appointed by the recent national convention of Black lawyers in Chattanooga (Tennessee) arriving in Washington, DC, in autumn 1893 to lobby Congress on the convention's recommendation that if the federal government would not or could not protect Black people, then $1 billion should be appropriated to relocate America's Black population somewhere outside North America.[9]

Williams was working as a Pullman porter[10] – it is not known where – when he met Henri-Gustave Joly de Lotbinière, QC (1829–1908), an *avocat* who practised law in Quebec City.[11] In a political career spanning twenty-five years Joly had been a Liberal MP, premier of Quebec, leader of the provincial opposition, and chair of the National Liberal Federation; he had refused a seat in the Senate twice and one in the federal Cabinet once. In 1885 Joly withdrew completely from politics to protest the Quebec Liberal/nationalist response to the Riel affair, and for ten years afterwards practised law with his eldest son, Edmond.

Joly was what would today be called a social democrat. A supporter of progressive causes such as feminism and the metric system, he was also a pioneering environmentalist. Known all over the continent as a speaker and writer on silviculture, in 1885 Joly served as vice-president of the American Forestry Congress. In 1893 he prepared Quebec's forestry exhibits for the Chicago World's Fair, and in 1900 he would be among the founders and serve as first president of the Canadian Forestry Association. Joly travelled extensively in the United States and Canada, so it is hardly surprising that he and Williams met on a passenger train.

Williams found in Joly, who was nearly forty years his senior, an enlightened and disinterested mentor. For Williams, Joly was the very model of the sophisticated cosmopolite and internationalist. It was likely his tutelage that converted Williams to an imperial federationist and "new imperialist" à la Joseph Chamberlain, then leader of the breakaway liberal unionist parliamentary party and later Conservative colonial secretary during Williams's years in England. Joly inculcated in Williams, in the words of James R. Hooker, "an excessive anglophilia, an extreme belief in the theory ... of British imperialism."[12] This ideology would influence Williams's outlook and action at the outset of his career as a pan-Africanist. In effect Joly helped turn Williams into an "Afro-Saxon" – a Black British imperialist dedicated to the proposition that the blessings of empire should flow equally to its Black subjects. Before the end of his career, however, Williams would begin to evolve towards a Black nationalist who believed in self-determination for colonized Black people around the world. He thus foreshadowed both a younger generation of pan-Africanists and developments within the pan-Africanism of his own generation.

In other respects too, Joly represented Williams's deepest aspiration: to be a successful lawyer-politician playing on the international stage. Though it is impossible to determine whether Williams decided to become a lawyer because of Joly's influence and example, it is clear that for him lawyering was the means to an end. It is not an overstatement that Williams modelled himself on Joly. A coming man in search of a role, he needed an appropriate mentor to inspire and assist him.

But if law was the ticket to public service and politics, Williams had first to strike a path to the legal profession in a country not his own where there were but two Black lawyers – New Brunswick's Abraham Beverly Walker and Ontario's Delos Rogest Davis. Vocational law schools were few. The Law Society of Upper Canada had a law school, and McGill University and Université Laval had law faculties. Victoria University's thirty-year-old law faculty was suspended in 1892 when the institution merged with the University of Toronto. Also in 1892 Nova Scotia's University of King's College opened a law school in Saint John, New Brunswick.[13]

In 1893 "Dalhousie's little law school" was ten years old and something of a via media between academic faculty and vocational school. The Nova Scotia Barristers Society had not been involved in its establishment, except to the incidental extent that one of the school's promoters and founders, Attorney General John S.D. Thompson (afterwards prime minister of Canada) was president of the society at time. In 1894 the society's generally indifferent attitude prompted a complaint from law undergraduates that the Council of the society (benchers) did not take university legal education seriously.[14] Most lawyers then did not possess, nor did they need, the LLB, which neither substituted for articled clerkship nor was required for a call to the bar. The most the LLB could effect was the reduction of articled clerkship from four years to three. The minimum requirement for admission to the three-year law degree program was junior matriculation (Grade 11).[15]

Yet Dalhousie's faculty of law also reflected what P.B. Waite has described as the university's "maturing confidence": "in the 1890s [Dalhousie Law School] set about its task of imbuing its students with the idea of duty to the public and the state with becoming modesty."[16] The Weldon tradition, as the school's ethos came to be eponymously known, in honour of its first dean, Richard Chapman Weldon, a sometime MP, held politics to be the epitome of public service.[17] In that sense, if in no other, the law school and Henry Sylvester Williams were exceedingly well met.

In March 1893 Joly wrote Dean Weldon (a fellow MP) about Williams.[18] Weldon replied within the week, expressing pleasure that Williams had "enlisted the sympathy of such influential friends." Understandably assuming that Williams intended to become a barrister in Trinidad, Weldon assured Joly that he would do everything possible to assist, and urged that Williams appear in time for registration.[19] Williams did so, easily meeting the "recognized equivalent" of junior matriculation in order to waive the matriculation examination.

The university's year when Williams arrived in 1893 began on 21 September, registration day. Williams was not an undergraduate (degree candidate) but a "general student" who registered and matriculated while pursuing a make-up or probationary year in order to ease the transition to undergraduate status. In effect, "General" was the first year of a four-year law degree program for those without a first degree or any university education at all, those who were in-course BA candidates considering or decided on law as a profession, or those undergraduates who wished to save time and money by commencing law studies before completing their arts or letters degree.[20] Academic legal study did not suit everyone's taste or capacity; six of the ten General students in Williams's year did not proceed to the LLB. The high rate of attrition was perhaps due in part to the low admission requirements.[21] Williams was by no means alone in failing to make the undergraduate cut.

His appearance in law school must have caused a sensation, the more so for his exoticism. Unlike James R. Johnston, scion of a prominent Halifax Black family, Williams was not local. Having no roots among Halifax's Blacks – an alien among the disadvantaged – inevitably complicated his experience as a Black intellectual "from away." Xenophobia and culture shock were both factors, and the learning curve must have been steep indeed. The heart, centre, and soul of Black Halifax was the old North Suburbs,[22] home to Black people continuously since the late eighteenth century. Lying in the foothills of the Citadel, the North Suburbs were also home to the city's two principal Black churches – Zion African Methodist Episcopal and African Baptist (now Cornwallis Street Baptist Church) – and to a flourishing petite-bourgeoisie among whom was James R. Johnston's influential extended family. It would have been in the North Suburbs that Williams lodged with the otherwise unidentified Black family about whom Dean Weldon made discreet enquiries and "learned nothing unfavourable."[23]

Though a member of the Church of England, Williams worshipped at Zion AME, established by and for African-American refugees from slavery ca. 1846 but by the 1890s stoutly British West Indian.[24] He had little choice, for Black people were not welcome in Halifax's mainstream churches. Black Christians worshipped in a Black church. To that extent a victim of customary racial segregation, Williams nevertheless exploited the opportunity to make the second of his two important Canadian contacts: the Reverend Henry B. Brown, pastor of Zion Church, who arrived in Halifax the same year as Williams. Brown, a West Indian formerly of Kingston, Jamaica, seems to have been a person of some consequence, as is clear from the later testimonial of Black lawyer A.B. Walker.[25]

Henry Sylvester Williams came from an ethnically diverse but racially integrated society where lawyers of colour were routine and where an uneasy peace more òr less obtained among African descendants like himself, East Indians, Creoles, and the Anglo-British white ruling class. He came to an ethnically homogeneous society where the racially visible were an oppressed minority, segregation and discrimination were the rule, and racial tensions were deepening.[26] In 1876 the Halifax school board had exercised its discretion to segregate the city's hitherto integrated public schools.[27] Efforts by "respectable" Black people to improve themselves along the lines of white urban society were tolerated but resisted.[28]

Williams had no reason to come to Halifax except to study law at an institution where he was at full personal liberty to do so. Dalhousie, which had begun to admit women in 1892, erected no barriers to the admission of Black people, and James R. Johnston became an arts undergraduate in 1892. Unfortunately, there is little documentary evidence and no oral tradition on Williams's time in the city. Apparently it was neither a successful venture nor a pleasant memory. What is known is that he threw himself into his studies with zeal and zest. His participation in the Model Parliament[29] in autumn 1893 suggests how much he had learned from his mentor, Joly. On one occasion, according to Dalhousie's student newspaper, Williams "was brought to task by the hon. member for Pictou East for not having introduced a resolution of which he had given notice a few nights previous. A constitutional question then arose as to the relations between Trinidad and Nova Scotia which was ably handled by our constitutional lawyers."[30]

A week later, "the great event of the evening" was the introduction by Williams of a private member's bill to change Trinidad's constitution from that of a Crown colony ruled by governor and council to representative government – a reform not completely achieved until 1956.[31] On that occasion Williams, the would-be imperial parliamentarian, spoke at such length and with such impassioned eloquence that debate on the bill had to be adjourned.[32] He was already looking ahead to a time where he might play such a role in public and political life. Williams's star turns in the Model Parliament were well remembered in Dalhousie law school. Two years after his departure the student newspaper featured an article entitled "An Historic Session of Mock Parliament":

At the beginning of the college year [1893] a new candidate with a longing to becoming a disciple of Coke and Blackstone, presented himself at the Dean's office. That respected personage looked the new-comer over, and, after the usual questioning, admitted him to the bosom of the freshman class. The stranger gave us fellows to understand that he was a product of the West Indies, and we at once decided that his jet complexion was owing to climatic conditions. However, he was genial, and even went so far as to invite some of the "grave and reverend Seniors" up to his room, where they feasted on oyster stews and chewing tobacco. When Mock Parliament began its sittings, our friend from the Southern climes evinced much interest, and it was a rare occasion when a Saturday evening passed without seeing his smiling countenance among the embryo politicians who haunted the big room in the north wing. Shortly before the Xmas holidays it was rumoured in the library that the member from the Antilles was to address the house at its next sitting, when a bill affecting the West India trade was to have its second reading.[33]

The next academic year, 1894–5, saw Williams a candidate for the LLB, studying the mainstream curriculum: real property, crimes, contracts, torts, and constitutional history. He could not have fared well, for there is no record of his examination results. Moreover, failing in more than two subjects meant that the academic year was lost. Perhaps understandably, Williams did not inform Joly, who learned of the situation only after writing Dean Weldon in January 1896. Weldon replied, "With reference to young Williams, the colored student from Trinidad, I regret to say that he made an extremely poor record at the sessional examinations in February last [1895]. He had the gift of fluent speech, but had no power of thinking and no exact knowledge. I saw a good deal of him during the time of his stay in our University, and was won by his manners, but was much disappointed at his complete failure in his studies ... I know that you will be much disappointed, with this unpromising turn in a career from which you hoped for better results."[34]

Nothing more is heard of Williams until February 1896, when he registered at the Canadian high commissioner's office in London.[35] In September he entered King's College (University of London) to study Latin. In those days Latin was as important technically for lawyers as English was practically. It was also required both for graduation from Dalhousie Law School and for a call to the Nova Scotia bar.

Williams, a strict teetotaller, next became a lecturer on the Church of England temperance circuit throughout the British Isles. In September 1897 he founded the African Association, the mandate of which was "to encourage a feeling of unity and to facilitate friendly intercourse among Africans in general: to promote and protect the interests of all [British] subjects claiming African descent, wholly or in part, in British colonies and other places, especially in Africa, by circulating accurate information on all subjects affecting their rights and privileges as subjects of the British Empire, by direct appeals to the Imperial and local Governments."[36]

Three months later Williams was admitted to Gray's Inn, the smallest of the four Inns of Court with the exclusive right of summoning to the English bar. Why Gray's? Other Trinidadians had preceded him there, and there was in Port of Spain a Gray's Inn Literary Association, which suggests a significant presence of old members in the capital of Trinidad and Tobago. Williams remained an intending barrister for some five years. During this time, however, he was thoroughly distracted both by family matters – he married a white Englishwoman in 1898 – and by the necessity of establishing himself in London and attending to Pan-African Association business.

In July 1900 the African Association sponsored the world's first Pan-African Conference, organized and convened by Williams as honorary secretary. The conference gave rise to a new, though short-lived Pan-African Association of which Williams was again general secretary and chief publicist.[37] The only Canadian delegate to the conference was his former Halifax pastor, the Reverend Henry B. Brown,[38] who became executive vice-president of the new organization. Williams never saw Canada again. The closest he got was when he addressed the annual meeting of the National Afro-American Council (predecessor of the NAACP) in Philadelphia in August 1901.[39]

Called to the English bar in June 1902, Williams was probably the first Black barrister actively to practise law in England, though he was not the first Black person to be called. Most Black members of the English bar practised law outside England, in their homeland or in British colonial Africa, as Williams himself was soon to do briefly. To mark his accession to the bar Williams sent Joly a fine studio portrait of himself in barrister's gown and wig.[40] In August 1902 he published his only monograph, *The British Negro: A Factor in the Empire ... Two Lectures*, describing himself on the title page as "Member of Dalhousie University Law School (Canada)."[41]

An English barrister's certificate was a credential giving the holder automatic standing, *ad eundem gradum*, at the bar of any colony or country in the British Empire. In October 1903 Williams was called as the first and only Black member of the bar in Cape Colony (1910 Union of South Africa). While living and working in Cape Town, he was involved in founding the African People's Organization, predecessor to the African National Congress. Rather than summon his wife and family to join him and settle permanently in South Africa, however, Williams returned to London early in 1905, determined to work for and speak to the interests of the Black people of South Africa in the Mother of Parliaments. As it happened, a general election had to be called before the end of that year. Perhaps Williams hoped to emulate the example of M.M. Bhownaggree (the Anglo-Indian barrister who was only the second visible minority MP) and stand for an east London constituency, such as Bhownaggree had represented since 1895. Williams was unsuccessful in securing a Liberal nomination; Liberals in Romford, for example, whom Williams is known to have addressed, selected instead a banker and municipal politician who was successful in taking the constituency away from the Conservatives. East Indians like Bhownaggree were perhaps more familiar to constituency selection committees than African-West Indians, and therefore more acceptable as prospective parliamentary candidates. The general election of January 1906 saw Sir Henry Campbell-Bannerman's new Liberal ministry returned by a landslide, and the Conservative Bhownaggree defeated. There would not be a West Indian immigrant MP of African descent until 1987.[42]

Williams had to settle finally for municipal rather than national politics. Later in 1906 he became the first Black person elected to local government in England. That achievement occasioned a renewal of correspondence with Joly, who learned about Williams's election from one of his correspondents in the Caribbean and wrote to congratulate him and re-establish contact.[43] Early in 1908 Williams visited Liberia, the African-American republic in West Africa, and in February he addressed the second annual meeting of the Liberian National Bar Association on "The Object of a Bar Association." Later that year, unable to support his wife and children otherwise, Williams returned permanently to Trinidad, where he was called to the bar and practised law with moderate success for the balance of his short life. He died of chronic nephritis in March 1911, in his forty-fourth year.

Meeting Rev. Brown in Halifax in 1893 had put Williams indirectly in touch with advanced African-American thinking on civil rights, personified by Black Methodist bishops such as Henry McNeal Turner and Alexander Walters, who became the first and only president of the Pan-African Association. In any case, his time at Dalhousie University thrust Williams into the midst of a long- and well-established urban Black quartier (really a town within a city), where he confronted challenges quite different from what he had ever experienced in either Trinidad or the United States. Black Halifax was metaphorically halfway between Port of Spain and New York City.

Williams's Canadian sojourn focused more sharply his desire and determination to become a race leader along the lines of Booker T. Washington (with whom he corresponded). Though Canada had a significant Black population – centred in Nova Scotia, southern New Brunswick, and southwestern Ontario – it nevertheless lay well outside and beyond the horizons of the Pan-African movement. Blacks in Canada, lacking critical mass and coherent race leadership, were not on the agenda of international pan-Africanism. The Pan-African Association, born of the 1900 London conference, had no Canadian among its national vice-presidents, while its executive vice-president, Rev. Brown,[44] the only Canadian delegate to the conference, seems to have remained where he already was – in England.

Williams's two years as a law school student in Halifax played a significant role in his professional, political, and intellectual development. While at Dalhousie Law School in the early 1890s, the twenty-six-year-old Williams was an inspired race leader in the making, devoted to equal rights and equality of opportunity for Black people and legal and political action to attain them. He also had the opportunity to live among and observe a vibrant and self-consciously "respectable" urban Black population, which in a short time would give rise to Canada's third Black lawyer – James Robinson Johnston.[45]

NOTES

The author is grateful to Dr Marika Sherwood (senior research fellow, Institute of Commonwealth Studies, University of London) for sharing her then unpublished chapter on Williams's years in the United States and Canada; to Theresa Thom, librarian, Gray's Inn, for sharing research on Williams and responding to many queries; to Ronald Noel for permitting his MPhil thesis at University of the West Indies, St Augustine, Trinidad and Tobago, to be photocopied; and to Heather Long CG(C), Diana Fancher, and Lesley Stevens for professional research assistance.

1 See generally Marika Sherwood, "Williams, Henry Sylvester (1869–1911)," *Oxford Dictionary of National Biography* (hereafter *ODNB*), accessed 25 May 2008, http://www.oxforddnb.com/view/article59529; now, definitively, Sherwood's *Origins of Pan-Africanism: Henry Sylvester Williams, Africa and*

the African Diaspora (London: Routledge, 2010). See also Ronald Court-
ney Noel, "Henry Sylvestre-Williams: A New Inquiry into an Old Hero"
(MPhil thesis, University of the West Indies at St Augustine, 2006); Noel
has for the first time established Williams's correct year of birth as 1867.
For historical context, see Philip D. Morgan and Sean Hawkins, eds., *Black
Experience and the Empire* (Oxford: Oxford University Press, 2004); and
Marilyn Lake and Henry Reynolds, *Drawing the Global Colour Line: White
Men's Countries and the International Challenge of Racial Equality* (Cambridge:
Cambridge University Press, 2008). Proceedings of the academic confer-
ence, "Henry Sylvester Williams and Pan-Africanism: A Retrospection and
Projection," University of the West Indies at St Augustine, Trinidad and
Tobago, 7–11 Jan. 2001, held to memorialize the centenary of the July 1900
London conference of the African Association, which Williams organized,
are as yet unpublished and inaccessible.

2 George Fosty and Darril Fosty, *Black Ice* (New York: Stryke-Indigo Publishing, 2004), chaps 6 and 7, 51–75. The evidence for Williams's alleged
involvement is not clear. There are no notes, and only a single printed
primary source appears in the bibliography: the Halifax newspaper *Acadian Recorder*. For a scholarly treatment, see the third chapter of Sheldon
Gillis, "Putting It on Ice: A Social History of Hockey in the Maritimes,
1880–1914" (MA thesis, Saint Mary's University, 1996), 72–96; Williams is
nowhere mentioned.

3 On this subject generally, see Judith Fingard, "Johnston, James Robinson,"
Dictionary of Canadian Biography (hereafter *DCB*) (Toronto: University of
Toronto Press, 1998), 14:543–4.

4 Most did not remain in Nova Scotia. An exception was Frederick Allan
Hamilton of Scarborough, Tobago (LLB 1923), who settled in Sydney
and in 1950 became Nova Scotia's first Black king's counsel. Another was
H.A.J. (Gus) Wedderburn (LLB 1973), who spent his entire distinguished
career in Nova Scotia. See the chapter 2 on Ethelbert Lionel Cross (LLB
1923) in this volume, and especially Philip Girard and Jeffrey Haylock,
"Stratification, Economic Adversity and Diversity in an Urban Bar: Halifax, Nova Scotia, 1900–1950," in *The Promise and Perils of Law: Canadian
Lawyers in History*, ed. Constance Backhouse and W. Wesley Pue, 75–102
(Toronto: Irwin Law, 2009), which looks at the experiences of this group of
transplanted West Indians.

5 Carl C. Campbell, *The Young Colonials: A Social History of Education in Trinidad and Tobago, 1834–1939* (Kingston: University of the West Indies Press,
1996), 73.

6 In the British West Indies, as in the United Kingdom, the legal profession

was divided between *barristers*, who argued cases in court, and *solicitors*, who briefed barristers, advised clients, and performed other legal or notarial services.

7 Bridget Brereton, *Race Relations in Colonial Trinidad, 1870–1900* (Cambridge: Cambridge University Press, 1979), 92; she does not mention that Williams eventually became a lawyer.

8 On this subject generally, see J. Clay Smith Jr, *Emancipation: The Making of the Black Lawyer, 1844–1944* (Philadelphia: University of Pennsylvania Press, 1993).

9 "The Color Question," *Halifax Daily Echo*, 30 Oct. 1893.

10 The chief and almost the only employment opportunity available at the time to upwardly mobile young Black men in Canada. See generally Agnes Calliste, "Blacks on Canadian Railways," *Journal of Ethnic Studies* 20 (1988): 36–52; Calliste, "Sleeping Car Porters in Canada: An Ethnically Submerged Split Labour Market," *Canadian Ethnic Studies* 19 (1987): 1–20; Calliste, "The Struggle for Employment Equity by Blacks on American and Canadian Railroads," *Journal of Black Studies* 25 (1995): 297–317; and Sarah-Jane Mathieu, "North of the Colour Line: Sleeping Car Porters and the Battle against Jim Crow on Canadian Rails, 1880–1920," *Labour / Le Travail* 47 (Spring 2001): 9–42.

11 Joly was Quebec's leading Protestant Liberal politician. See Marcel Hamelin, "Joly de Lotbinière, Sir Henri-Gustave," in *DCB*, 13:518–24, and also the article, as revised by Hamelin, in *ODNB*.

12 James R. Hooker, *Henry Sylvester Williams: Imperial Pan-Africanist* (London: Rex Collings, 1975), 20. Further evidence of his neo-imperialism is to be found in Williams's only known published work, *The British Negro: A Factor in the Empire, and the Ethiopian Eunuch; Two Lectures* (Brighton, 1902). The same view is taken by Pennybacker in her study of the Universal Races Congress, which took place in London four months after Williams's death: "But Williams ... was an empire reformer, not an anti-imperialist." Susan D. Pennybacker, "The Universal Races Congress, London Political Culture, and Imperial Dissent, 1900–1939," *Radical History Review* 52 (Spring 2005): 107. If Williams was, in Pennybacker's words, a "radical cosmopolitan," it would have been the result in no small measure to the influence and example of Joly.

13 See generally John P.S. McLaren, "The History of Legal Education in Common-Law Canada," in *Legal Education in Canada*, ed. Roy J. Matas and Deborah J. McCawley, 111–45 (Montreal: Federation of Law Societies of Canada, 1987).

14 "Law Department," *Dalhousie Gazette*, 7 May 1894.

15 On the law school in Williams's time, see John Willis, *A History of Dalhousie Law School* (Toronto: University of Toronto Press, 1979), 52–66. It is worth noting that the law faculty's former librarian, lawyer John Thomas Bulmer, was a known friend and outstanding supporter of Black people in Halifax; see Philip Girard, "Bulmer, John Thomas," *DCB*, 13:132–4.

16 P.B. Waite, *Lives of Dalhousie University, vol. 1, 1818–1925, Lord Dalhousie's College* (Montreal and Kingston: McGill-Queen's University Press, 1994), 169.

17 Concerning Dean Weldon, see Philip Girard, "Weldon, Richard Chapman," *DCB*, 15:1064–7, and sources cited.

18 The letter has not survived.

19 Weldon to Joly de Lotbinière, [20?] Mar. 1893, Fonds de famille Joly de Lotbinière, Bibliothèque et Archives du Québec, Centre d'archives de la capitale (BANQ-Q) P 351. Joly's side of the correspondence does not survive.

20 Among them was Robert Harper Murray, son of a prominent Presbyterian minister, latterly judge of the County Court for Halifax and a constant and conspicuous friend of Black people.

21 See generally Willis, *Dalhousie Law School*, 60.

22 Not to be confused with the North End; informally, the northern boundary of the North Suburbs is North Street. See generally Paul A. Erickson, *Historic North End Halifax* (Halifax: Nimbus, 2004), 9–20.

23 Weldon to Joly de Lotbinière, 6 Feb. [1896], p. 6306, BANQ-Q P 351.

24 See generally "The African Methodist Episcopal Church: Its Work among the African Race and the Problems Which Press on Its Pastors," *Halifax Evening Mail*, 4 Nov. 1929.

25 A Black lawyer in Saint John, New Brunswick, Walker was president of the Afro-British League of which Brown was senior vice-president. See generally [anon., comp.], *Missionary Enterprise among the Coloured People of the Maritime Provinces of Canada* [London, 1899?]; Canadian Institute for Historical Microreproductions microfiche no. 05672.

26 On this subject generally, see Bridglal Pachai, *Beneath the Clouds of the Promised Land: The Survival of Nova Scotia's Blacks, vol. 2, 1900–1989* (Halifax: BEA, 1990), 69–134.

27 On the community response to this outrage, see Sheridan J. Hay, "Black Protest Tradition in Nova Scotia, 1783–1964" (MA thesis, Saint Mary's University, 1997).

28 On this subject generally, see Judith Fingard, "Race and Respectability in Victorian Halifax," *Journal of Imperial and Commonwealth History* 20 (1991–2): 169–95; and Suzanne Morton, "Separate Spheres in a Separate World:

African Nova Scotian Women in late 19th-Century Halifax County," *Acadiensis* 22, no. 2 (Spring 1993): 61–83.

29 Willis, *Dalhousie Law School*, 52–3.

30 "Mock Parliament," *Dalhousie Gazette*, 25 Nov 1893.

31 On this subject generally, see H.B.D. Johnson, "Crown Colony Government in Trinidad and Tobago, 1870–1897" (DPhil thesis, University of London, 1969).

32 "Mock Parliament," *Dalhousie Gazette*, 22 Jan. 1894. He would also have participated in the unanimous resolution expressing sympathy for John Valentine Ellis, editor of Saint John's *Globe*, who had been arbitrarily imprisoned by the Supreme Court of New Brunswick ("the most contemptible judicial institution in Canada") for criticizing a judge of the Court: "Sympathy for Mr Ellis," *Halifax Daily Echo*, 7 Nov. 1893.

33 [C.L.M.], "An Historic Session of Mock Parliament," *Dalhousie Gazette*, 26 Mar. 1897.

34 Weldon to Joly, 6 Feb. 189[6], p. 6306, fonds de famille Joly de Lotbinière.

35 *Halifax Morning Chronicle*, 17 Feb. 1896.

36 Qtd in Mathurin, *Henry Sylvester Williams*, 41. See generally Peter Fryer, *Staying Power: The History of Black People in Britain* (London: Pluto, 1984), 279–81; see also Mathurin, *Henry Sylvester Williams*, chap. 4.

37 Williams can lay claim to both the word and idea of common action by persons of African descent around the world in order to achieve not "back-to-Africa" (Garveyism) but "Africa for Africans" – an emancipation from colonial oppression just as Africans of the Diaspora had been emancipated from slavery. Williams saw pan-Africanism as a worldwide system of race uplift initiated by African descendants for the benefit of indigenous Africans. It was Black Power *avant la lettre*.

38 Brown left Halifax for New Brunswick in September 1896 to become pastor of the AME church in Saint John; in autumn 1898 went to England.

39 Sir Henri-Gustave Joly de Lotbinière was then in distant British Columbia serving as lieutenant-governor; Williams seems to have made no effort to contact Joly or to establish a Canadian branch of the Pan-African Association.

40 It is item 9467 in the Joly de Lotbinière papers.

41 This had no bearing on his credentials as regards reading for the bar in England. Williams's academic path to the law was rocky; the surviving records have been analysed exhaustively by Noel, "Henry Sylvestre-Williams."

42 On this subject generally, see Sumita Mukherjee, "'Narrow-Majority' and 'Bow-and-Agree': Public Attitudes towards the Elections of the First Asian

MPs in Britain, Dadabhai Naoroji and Mancherjee Merwanjee Bhownag-gree, 1885–1906," *Journal of the Oxford University History Society* 2 (Michael-mas 2004).

43 Mathurin, *Henry Sylvester Williams*, 139. Williams's letters in reply either were not received or have not been preserved in the extensive Joly de Lot-binière family archive; but Joly's letters were carefully preserved among Williams's papers.

44 He is definitely *not* to be identified with Henry "Box" Brown, the slavery escapee born in 1816; see Mathurin, *Henry Sylvester Williams*, 165. This er-ror is made by nearly everyone who has written on the 1900 Pan-African Conference.

45 Johnston was called to the bar of Nova Scotia the very month – July 1900 – Williams was organizing in London the first pan-African conference. See generally Barry Cahill, "Paths to the Law in Late-Victorian Africadia: The Odyssey of James Robinson Johnston" (paper delivered to Department of Justice Canada, Atlantic Regional Office, 28 Feb. 2012), http://nsbs.org/james-robinson-johnston.

PART TWO

Formal Legal Equality and Anti-Black Discrimination: Case Studies

4

"Bitterly Disappointed" at the Spread of "Colour-Bar Tactics": Viola Desmond's Challenge to Racial Segregation, Nova Scotia, 1946

CONSTANCE BACKHOUSE

The contentious racial incident began on Friday, 8 November 1946, when Viola Irene Desmond's 1940 Dodge four-door sedan broke down in New Glasgow, Nova Scotia.[1] The thirty-two-year-old, Halifax-born Black woman was en route to Sydney on a business trip. Forced to wait overnight for repairs, she decided to take in the seven o'clock movie at the Roseland Theatre. Erected on the northeast corner of Forbes and Provost Streets in 1913, the theatre was designed in the manner of grand old theatrical halls and graced with colourful wall murals featuring paintings of "the land of roses." In its early days, the Roseland introduced New Glasgow audiences to silent pictures, with enthusiastic local musicians providing background sound with piano, cymbals, sirens, and bass drums. One of the most popular proved to be the American blockbuster *Birth of a Nation*. Outfitted with the latest modern equipment for sound in 1929, the theatre premiered Al Jolson's celebrated blackface performance in *The Jazz Singer* in the first month of "talkies." In time, the Roseland came to be New Glasgow's premier movie theatre.[2]

Handing the Roseland cashier a dollar bill, Viola Desmond requested "one down please." Peggy Melanson, the white ticket-seller on duty

Previously published in Constance Backhouse, *Colour-Coded: A Legal History of Racism in Canada, 1900–1950* (Toronto: University of Toronto Press, 1999).

that evening, passed her a balcony ticket and seventy cents in change. Entirely unaware of what would ensue from her actions, Viola Desmond proceeded into the theatre and headed towards the main-floor seating area. Then Prima Davis, the white ticket-taker inside the theatre, called out after her: "This is an upstairs ticket, you will have to go upstairs."

Thinking there must have been some mistake, Viola Desmond returned to the wicket and asked the cashier to exchange the ticket for a downstairs one. The ticket-seller refused, and when Viola Desmond asked why, Peggy Melanson replied, "I'm sorry but I'm not permitted to sell downstairs tickets to you people."

Peggy Melanson never mentioned the word *Black*, or the other terms, *Negro* or *coloured*, which were more commonly used in the 1940s. But Viola Desmond recognized instantly that she was being denied seating on the basis of her race. She made a spontaneous decision to challenge this racial segregation, walked back inside, and took a seat in the partially filled downstairs portion of the theatre. As Prima Davis would later testify, "[When] she came back and passed into the theatre, I called to her. She never let on she heard me. She seated herself below."[3]

Prima Davis followed Viola Desmond to her main-floor row. Confronting the Black woman, who was now sitting quietly in her seat, she insisted, "I told you to go upstairs." When Viola Desmond refused to budge, Prima Davis left to report the matter to the white manager, Harry MacNeil. MacNeil was New Glasgow's most prominent "showman," his family having constructed MacNeil's Hall in the late 1870s to serve as the town's first theatre. The MacNeils brought in a series of concert artists, ventriloquists, astrologists, musicians, bell-ringers, jugglers, and tumblers to entertain theatre-goers. Town historians recall innumerable performances in MacNeil's Hall of *Uncle Tom's Cabin*, with "boozy has-beans of the classic theatre emoting lines of black face roles with Shakespearean declamations." When moving pictures killed off live theatre, Harry MacNeil built a series of movie houses in New Glasgow, ultimately settling on the Roseland Theatre as the best location in town.[4]

Harry MacNeil came down immediately and "demanded" that Viola Desmond remove herself to the balcony. She had already "been told to go upstairs," MacNeil pointed out, and a notice on the back of the ticket stipulated that the theatre had "the right to refuse admission to any objectionable person." Viola Desmond replied that she had not been refused admission. The only problem was that her efforts to purchase a downstairs ticket had been unsuccessful. Politely but firmly, she requested the manager to obtain one for her. "I told him that I never sit upstairs because I can't see very well from that distance," she later told the press. "He became angry and said that he could have me thrown out of the theatre. As I was behaving very quietly, I didn't think he could." The agitated Harry MacNeil turned heel and marched off in pursuit of a police officer.

The Arrest at the Roseland Theatre

In short order, Harry MacNeil returned with a white policeman, who advised Viola Desmond that he "had orders" to throw her out of the theatre. "I told him that I was not doing anything and that I did not think he would do that," advised Viola Desmond. "He then took me by the shoulders and dragged me as far as the lobby. I had lost my purse and my shoe became disarranged in the scuffle." The police officer paused momentarily to allow Viola Desmond to adjust her shoe, while a bystander retrieved her purse. Then the forcible ejection resumed. As Viola Desmond recounted, "The policeman grasped my shoulders and the manager grabbed my legs, injuring my knee and hip. They carried me bodily from the theatre out into the street. The policeman put me into a waiting taxi and I was driven to the police station. Within a few minutes the manager appeared and the Chief of Police [Elmo C. Langille]. They left together and returned in an hour with a warrant for my arrest."

She was taken to the town lock-up, where she was held overnight. Adding further insult, she was jailed in a cell alongside male prisoners. Mustering every ounce of dignity, Viola Desmond deliberately put on her white gloves and steeled herself to sit bolt upright all night long. She later described her experience in the lock-up as follows: "I was put in a cell which had a bunk and blankets. There were a number of men in the same block and they kept bringing in more during the night. The matron was very nice and she seemed to realize that I shouldn't have been there. I was jailed for twelve hours."[5]

The Trial

The next morning, 9 November 1946, Viola Desmond was brought before New Glasgow magistrate Roderick Geddes MacKay. Born and bred in nearby St Mary's in Pictou County, MacKay had graduated in law from Dalhousie University in 1904. He was appointed town solicitor for New Glasgow in 1930, where he managed his law practice while simultaneously holding down a part-time position as stipendiary magistrate. The sixty-nine-year-old white magistrate was the sole legal official in court that day. Viola Desmond had no lawyer; she had not been told of her right to seek bail or to request an adjournment, or of her right to counsel. Indeed, there was no Crown attorney present either. Harry MacNeil, "the informant," was listed as the prosecutor.[6]

Viola Desmond was arraigned on a charge of violating the provincial Theatres, Cinematographs and Amusements Act. First enacted in 1915, the statute contained no explicit provisions relating to racial segregation. A licensing statute to regulate the operations of theatres and movie houses, the act encompassed such matters as safety inspections and the censorship of public performances. It also stipulated that patrons were to pay an amusement tax on any tickets purchased in provincial theatres. Persons who entered a theatre without paying such tax were subject to summary conviction and a fine of "not less than twenty nor more than two hundred dollars." The statute authorized police officers to arrest violators without warrant, and to use "reasonable diligence" in taking them before a stipendiary magistrate or justice of the peace "to be dealt with according to law."[7]

The statute based the rate of the amusement tax upon the price of the ticket. The Roseland Theatre's ticket prices were forty cents for downstairs seats, and thirty cents for upstairs seats. These prices included a tax of three cents on the downstairs tickets, and two cents on the upstairs. The ticket issued to Viola Desmond cost thirty cents, of which two cents would be forwarded to the public coffers. Since she had insisted on sitting downstairs, she was one cent short on tax.[8]

This was the argument put forth by Harry MacNeil, Peggy Melanson, and Prima Davis, all of whom gave sworn evidence against Viola Desmond that morning. The trial was short. The three white witnesses briefly testified that the accused woman had purchased an upstairs ticket, paying two cents in tax, and then insisted on seating herself downstairs. After each witness concluded, Magistrate MacKay asked the prisoner if she wanted to ask any questions. "I did not gather until almost the end of the case that he meant questions to be asked of the witnesses," Viola Desmond would later explain. "It was never explained to me of whom I was to ask the questions." So there was no cross-examination of the prosecution witnesses whatsoever.[9]

At the close of the Crown's case, Viola Desmond took the stand herself. The minutes of evidence from the trial record contain a succinct report of her testimony: "I am the accused. I offered to pay the difference in the price between the tickets. They would not accept it." Magistrate MacKay convicted the defendant and assessed the minimum fine of twenty dollars, with costs of six dollars payable to the prosecuting informant, Harry MacNeil. The total amount of twenty-six dollars was due forthwith, in default of which the accused was ordered to spend one month in jail.[10]

Viola Desmond was quite properly angry that she was offered no opportunity to speak about the real issues underlying the taxation charges. "The Magistrate immediately convicted and sentenced me without asking me if I had any submissions to make to the Court on the evidence adduced and without informing me that I had the right to make such submissions," she later explained. Even a casual observer can see that many arguments might have been raised to preclude a conviction. It was far from clear that Viola Desmond had actually transgressed the statute. According to her testimony, she tendered the difference in the ticket prices (including the extra cent in tax), but the manager and ticket-seller refused to accept her money. It is difficult to find the legally required *actus reus* (criminal act) in Viola Desmond's behaviour here. Indeed, if anyone had violated the statute, it was the theatre owner, who was in dereliction of his statutory duty to collect the tendered taxes and forward them to the designated government board.[11]

Furthermore, the price differential between upstairs and downstairs seats was not prescribed by statute. It was simply a discretionary business policy devised by the management of the theatre. The manager could have decided to collapse the two admission prices and ask one single fee at whim. In this instance, Harry MacNeil chose to charge Viola Desmond a mere thirty cents for her ticket, and on this amount she had paid the full tax owing. She was not charged forty cents, so she did not owe the extra cent in tax. The court might have construed the rules regarding alternate seating arrangements as internal business regulations having nothing whatsoever to do with the revenue provisions in the legislation.

Even more problematic was the prosecution's questionable attempt to utilize provincial legislation to buttress community practices of racial discrimination. The propriety of calling upon a licensing and revenue statute to enforce racial segregation in public theatres was never addressed. Did the legislators who enacted the statute design the taxing sections for this purpose? Were racially disparate ticket-selling practices contemplated when the statutory tax rates were set? Were the penalty sections intended to attach alike to theatre-goers deliberately evading admission charges and Blacks protesting racial segregation? As the press would later attest, Viola Desmond "was being tried for being a negress and not for any felony."[12]

Observers of the trial would have been struck by the absence of any overt discussion of racial issues. In the best tradition of Canadian "racelessness," the prosecution witnesses never explained that Viola Desmond had been denied the more expensive downstairs ticket on the basis of her race. No one admitted that the theatre patrons were assigned seats on the basis of race. In an interview with the Toronto *Daily Star* several weeks later, Harry MacNeil would insist that neither he nor the Odeon Theatres management had ever issued instructions that main-floor tickets were not to be sold to Blacks. It was simply a matter of seating preferences: "It is customary for [colored persons] to sit together in the balcony," MacNeil would assert.[13] At the trial, no one even hinted that Viola Desmond was Black, that her accusers and her judge were white. On its face, the proceeding appears to be simply a prosecution for failure to pay provincial tax. In fact, if Viola Desmond had not taken any further action in this matter, the surviving trial records would have left no clue to the real significance of the case.[14]

Viola Desmond: The Woman Accused

The day of her conviction, Viola Desmond paid the full fine, secured her release, and returned to her home on 4 Prince William Street in Halifax. She was deeply affronted by her treatment at the hands of the New Glasgow officials. Her decision to protest the racially segregated seating practices at the Roseland Theatre had initially been a spontaneous gesture, but now she was resolved to embark upon a more premeditated course of action. She was also "well known" throughout the Black community in Nova Scotia and consequently in a good position to do something about it.[15]

Viola Desmond, whose birth name was Viola Irene Davis, was born in Halifax, on 6 July 1914, into a prominent, middle-class, self-identified "coloured" family. Her paternal grandfather, a Black self-employed barber, had established the Davis Barber Shop in Halifax's North End. Barbering was an occupation within which a number of Canadian Blacks managed to carve out a successful living in the nineteenth and early twentieth centuries. Hair-cutting and -styling were rigorously segregated by race in many portions of the country, with white barbers and beauticians reluctant to accept Black customers. Black barbers were quick to seize the business opportunities rejected by racist whites and set up shop servicing both Black and white clientele.[16]

James Albert Davis, Viola's father, worked in the Davis Barber Shop for a time and then took up employment as a shipwright in the Halifax Shipyards. Eventually, he established a career for himself as a business-man, managing real estate and operating a car dealership. Although it was extremely difficult for Blacks to obtain positions within the civil service, two of Viola's male relatives worked for the federal postal ser-vice.[17]

Viola's mother, Gwendolin Irene Davis, was the daughter of a Bap-tist minister who had come to Halifax from New Haven, Connecticut. Gwendolin Davis's mother, Susan Smith, was born in Connecticut and identified herself as white. Gwendolin's father, Henry Walter Johnson, was "seven-eighths white," and although he is described as being "of mixed race," Gwendolin Davis seems to have been generally regarded as white.[18]

The question of racial designation, inherently a complex matter, be-comes even more problematic when individuals with different racial designations form blended families. Some have suggested that a funda-mental premise of racial ideology, rooted in the history of slavery, stip-ulates that if individuals have even "one Black ancestor," regardless of their skin colour they qualify for classification as "Black." However, it is equally clear that some light-skinned individuals are able to "pass" for white if they choose, or can be mistaken for "white," regardless of their own self-identification.[19]

Viola's parents married in 1908, creating what was perceived to be a mixed-race family within a culture that rarely welcomed interracial marriage. It was not the actual fact of racial mixing that provoked such concern, for there was undeniable evidence that interracial reproduc-tion had occurred extensively throughout North American history. It was the formalized recognition of such unions that created such unease within a culture based on white supremacy. The tensions posed within a racist society by an apparently mixed-race family often came home to roost on the children born to James and Gwendolin Davis. Viola's younger sister recalls children taunting them in the schoolyard, jeering: "They may think you're white because they saw your mother at Par-ents' Day, but they haven't seen your father." Viola self-identified both as "mixed-race" and as "coloured," the latter being a term of preference during the 1930s and 1940s.[20]

Viola Davis was an extremely capable student, whose initial schooling was obtained within a racially mixed student body at Sir Joseph
Howe Elementary School and Bloomfield High School. Upon her graduation from high school, Viola took up teaching for a brief period at
Preston and Hammonds Plains, racially segregated schools for Black
students. She saved all of her teaching wages, since she knew from the
outset that she wanted to set up a hairdressing business of her own.
Modern fashion trends for women, first heralded by the introduction
of the "bobbed" haircut in the 1920s, created an explosion of adventur-
ous career opportunities for "beauticians," who earned their livelihood
by advising women on hair care and cosmetics. Beauticians provided
much-sought-after services within the all-female world of the new
"beauty parlours," which came to serve important functions as neighbourhood social centres. Beauty parlours offered steady and socially
respectable opportunities to many entrepreneurial women across Canada and the United States.[21]

Despite severely limited employment opportunities in most fields,
some Black women were able to create their own niche in this new
market, as beauticians catering to a multiracial clientele with particular
expertise in hair design and skin care for Black women. This was Viola
Desmond's entrepreneurial goal, but the first barrier she faced was in
her training. All of the facilities available to train beauticians in Halifax restricted Black women from admission. Viola was forced to travel
to Montreal, where she was able to enrol in the Field Beauty Culture
School in 1936. Her aspirations took her from Montreal to New York,
where she enrolled in courses to learn more about wigs and other styl-
ing touches. In 1940, she received a diploma from the acclaimed Apex
College of Beauty Culture and Hairdressing in Atlantic City, founded
by the renowned Black entrepreneur Sarah Spencer Washington.[22]

Shortly before she left for her first training in Montreal, Viola met
John Gordon (Jack) Desmond, a man ten years her senior. Their court-
ship would ultimately lead to her marriage at the age of twenty-two.
Jack Desmond was a descendant of generations of Black Loyalists who
had settled in Guysborough County in 1783, when several thousand
free Blacks took up land grants from the Crown. He was born into a
family of eight children in Tracadie, Nova Scotia, on 22 February 1905,
and lived for some years in New Glasgow. He moved to Halifax in 1928
and took employment with a construction company, but the loss of his
eye to a metal splinter in a work accident in October 1930 cost Jack
Desmond his job.[23]

Shifting careers by necessity, in 1932 Jack Desmond opened his own business, Jack's Barber Shop, on Gottingen Street, a central thoroughfare in the "Uptown Business District" in a racially mixed neighbourhood in the old north end of Halifax. The business attracted a racially mixed clientele, drawn in part from the men who came in on the ships at the naval dockyard. The first Black barber to be formally registered in Nova Scotia, Jack Desmond was popular, with an easy-going personality that would earn him the title "The King of Gottingen Street." Jack became romantically interested in the young Viola Davis, took the train up to Montreal to see her while she was in training, and ultimately proposed marriage there. In 1936, the couple was married before a Baptist minister in Montreal.[24] When Viola returned to Halifax in 1937, she set up Vi's Studio of Beauty Culture alongside her husband's barbershop on Gottingen Street. She offered her customers a range of services, including shampoos, press and curl, hair-straightening, chignons, and hairpieces and wigs. Former customers recall the weekly Saturday trip to "Vi's" as the social highlight of the week. Viola Desmond amassed a devoted clientele, many of whom still recollect with great fondness her sense of humour, her sympathetic nature, and her cheerful, positive outlook on life. The younger women thought of her as inspirational, someone who "took all of us kids from this area under her wing, and was like a mother to us all."[25]

Ambitious and hard-working, Viola Desmond soon developed plans to expand her business. She branched out into chemistry and learned how to manufacture many specialized Black beauty powders and creams, which she marketed under the label "Vi's Beauty Products." She added facials and ultraviolet-ray hair treatments to her line of services. Viola Desmond's clientele encompassed legendary figures such as the Black classical singer Portia White, who came for private appointments on Sundays because her hectic schedule did not permit regular appointments during the week. Gwen Jenkins, the first Black nurse in Nova Scotia, began weekly visits to "Vi's Children's Club" for washing and braiding at the age of ten. Despite the hectic pace of business, Viola continued to take courses in the latest hairstyles and make-up, travelling to New York every other year to update her expertise. In 1945, she was awarded a silver trophy for hairstyling by the Montreal Orchid School of Beauty Culture. Recognizing that there were additional opportunities outside of Halifax, Viola began to travel around the province, setting up temporary facilities to deliver products and services to other members of the Black communities.[26]

Although Jack was initially supportive of his wife's choice of career, her ambitious business plans began to cause him some distress. He became concerned that all of the travel required was inappropriate for a married woman. Both spouses in Black families frequently held down jobs in the paid labour force, contrary to the pattern in white middle-class households. But middle-class Black women who sought work outside the home often faced bitter tensions within their marriages. Their careers tended to clash with society's prevailing ideals of gender, which required that men be masters in their own homes, ruling over dependent women and children. Even women who remained childless, such as Viola Desmond, found themselves subject to pressure to retire from the paid workforce.[27]

At odds with her husband on this point, Viola Desmond held firm convictions that Black women ought to have greater access to employment opportunities outside their traditionally segregated sphere of domestic service. A few years after she set up her own studio, she opened the Desmond School of Beauty Culture, which drew Black female students from across Nova Scotia, New Brunswick, and Quebec. Viola Desmond's long-range plans were to work with the women who graduated from her school to establish a franchise operation, setting up beauty parlours for people of colour across Canada. Her former students recall that she kept the shop immaculately; that all the beauticians, including Viola, wore uniforms and regulation stockings; and that their appearance was rigorously inspected each day. Viola Desmond personified respectability to her students, who always called her "Mrs Desmond" and were struck by the "way that she carried herself" and her "strength of character."[28]

The evidence suggests that most legal challenges to racial segregation in Canada seem to have come from middle-class individuals. This appears not to be a coincidental factor, for class issues are intricately related to such matters. A certain level of economic security furnished a base that enabled such individuals to consider taking legal action against discriminatory treatment. Furthermore, given contemporary class biases, middle-class status appears to have underscored the indignity of racist treatment. Viola Desmond's elite position within the province's Black community was well established. She and her husband, Jack, were often held up as examples of prosperous Black entrepreneurs, whose small-business ventures had triumphed over the considerable economic barriers that stood in the way of Black business initiatives. Yet regardless of her visible financial standing in the community, Viola Desmond remained barred from entry into the more expensive seating area of the New Glasgow theatre. For those who believed that economic striving would eventually "uplift" the Black race, the response of the manager of the Roseland Theatre crushed all hope of eventually achieving an egalitarian society.[29]

The matter of gender is also important in understanding the significance of Viola Desmond's ejection from the Roseland Theatre. In making her decision to challenge racial segregation in the courts, Viola Desmond became one of the first Black women in Canada to do so. As the controversy spread, Viola Desmond also came to symbolize the essence of middle-class Black femininity. She was a celebrated Halifax beautician, described as both "elegantly coiffed and fashionably dressed," a "fine-featured woman with an eye for style." Her contemporaries recall that she was always beautifully attired, her nails, make-up, and hair done with great care. Described as a "petite, quiet-living, demure" woman, who stood four foot eleven inches and weighed less than 100 pounds, Viola Desmond was a well-mannered, refined, demonstrably feminine woman, manhandled by rude and forcibly violent white men. The spectacle would undoubtedly have provoked considerable outcry had the principal actors all been middle-class whites. Customary white gender relations dictated that, at least in public, physically taller and stronger men should exercise caution and delicacy in their physical contact with women. Roughing up a lady violated the very core of the ideology of chivalry.[30]

The extension of traditional white gender assumptions to Black women provoked more pause. Racist practices condoned and nurtured throughout North America during times of slavery denied Black women both the substance and the trappings of white femininity. Slave masters compelled their male and female slaves alike to labour alongside each other, irrespective of gender. Black women found their reproductive capacity commodified for material gain and frequently experienced rape at the hands of their white owners and overseers. Denied the most fundamental rights to their own bodies and sexuality, Black women were barred by racist whites from any benefits that the idealized cult of "motherhood" and "femininity" might have offered white women. The signs on the segregated washrooms of the Deep South, "White Ladies" and "Black Women," neatly encapsulated the racialized gender assumptions. As Evelyn Brooks Higginbotham has described it, "No black woman, regardless of income, education, refinement, or character, enjoyed the status of lady."[31]

Whites who ascribed to attitudes such as these were somewhat unsettled by women such as Viola Desmond. Throughout her frightening
and humiliating ordeal, she had remained the embodiment of female
respectability. Her challenge to the racially segregated seating policies
was carried out politely and decorously. Her dignified response in the
face of the volatile theatre manager's threat to throw her out was that
she "was behaving very quietly," and so "didn't think he could." Even
the white matron from the New Glasgow lock-up recognized the incon-
gruity of exposing a refined woman to the rough-and-tumble assort-
ment of men collected in the cell that night: "She seemed to realize that
I shouldn't have been there," emphasized Viola Desmond. By the standards of the dominant culture, Viola Desmond was undeniably feminine in character and deportment. The question remained whether the
ideology of chivalry would be extended to encompass a Black woman
who was insulted and mauled by white men.

The Community Responds to the Conviction

The first to hear about the incident was Viola Desmond's husband, Jack,
who was upset but not surprised. Jack was quite familiar with New
Glasgow's Roseland Theatre. In fact, he had watched the Roseland Theatre being built while he worked as a child in the drugstore next door.
"There were no coloreds allowed downstairs," he recalled later. "She
didn't know that – I knew it because I grew up there." A deeply religious man, Jack Desmond held philosophical views that were rooted in
tolerance: "You've got to know how to handle it," he would counsel.
"Take it to the Lord with a prayer."[32]

Viola Desmond was considerably less willing to let temporal matters
lie, as the interview she gave to the Halifax *Chronicle* shortly afterward
indicates: "I can't understand why such measures should have been
taken. I have travelled a great deal throughout Canada and parts of the
United States and nothing like this ever happened to me before. I was
born in Halifax and have lived here most of my life and I've found relations between negroes and whites very pleasant. I didn't realize a thing
like this could happen in Nova Scotia – or in any other part of Canada."[33]

The shock that underlies this statement clearly communicates the
magnitude of the insult that Viola Desmond experienced in the Roseland arrest. She must have been no stranger to racial segregation. She
taught in segregated schools, was denied occupational training on the
basis of race, and was keenly aware of segregated facilities in her own

business. But unexpectedly to encounter segregated seating in a Nova Scotian theatre seems to have struck Viola Desmond as a startling injustice. The unforeseen discrimination was magnified by the heinous actions of the theatre manager and various officials of the state, who responded to her measured resistance with violence and criminal prosecution. To see the forces of law so unanimously and spontaneously arrayed against her quiet protest must have struck Viola Desmond as outrageous. Couching her complaint in the most careful of terms, with polite reference to the "very pleasant" relations that normally ensued between the races, she challenged Canadians to respond to this unconscionable treatment, to side with her against the legal authorities who pursued her conviction.

A considerable portion of the Black community in Halifax seems to have shared Viola Desmond's anger and concern over the incident. Pearleen Oliver was one of the first to take up the case. One of the most prominent Black women in Nova Scotia, Pearleen Oliver was born into a family of ten children in Cook's Cove, Guysborough County, in 1917. She "put herself through high school by doing housework," the first Black graduate of New Glasgow High School in 1936. After graduation, she married the young Reverend William Pearly Oliver. The Olivers presided over an almost exclusively Black congregation at Cornwallis Street Baptist Church, where the Rev. Oliver was posted as minister. Viola and Jack Desmond belonged to the Cornwallis Church, and the morning after her arrest Viola Desmond came over to seek advice from the Olivers. Only Pearleen was home, but she recalls vividly that Viola Desmond was shaken and tearful as she related her experience. "I said, 'Oh Dear God, Viola, what did they do to you, what did they do to you?'" Pearleen Oliver was appalled by what had happened and told Viola that she should seek legal advice. "I figured it was now or never," explained Mrs Oliver. "Hitler was dead and the Second World War was over. I wanted to take it to court."[34]

Pearleen Oliver had an enviable record as a confirmed proponent of racial equality. In 1944, she spearheaded a campaign of the Halifax Coloured Citizens Improvement League to force the Department of Education to remove racially objectionable material from its public school texts. The insulting depiction of "Black Sambo" in the Grade 11 text should be stricken from the books, she insisted, and replaced by the "authentic history of the colored people" and accounts of "their contribution to Canadian culture." The leader of the Ladies Auxiliary of the African United Baptist Association, who campaigned extensively to eliminate racial barriers from the nursing profession, Pearleen Oliver also took matters affecting Black women extremely seriously.[35]

When he learned of Viola's treatment later that weekend, the Rev. William Oliver was equally concerned. An influential member of the African United Baptist Association of Nova Scotia, the Rev. Oliver had achieved public acclaim as the only Black chaplain in the Canadian army during the Second World War. A confirmed proponent of racial equality in education and employment, William Oliver was no stranger to humiliating practices of racial segregation himself. He had been refused service in restaurants, barred from social activities organized by whites, and challenged when he attempted to participate in white athletic events. William Oliver was on record as opposing racial segregation in hotels, restaurants, and other public facilities, stressing that businesses should "cater to the public on the basis of individual behavior, regardless of race."[36]

The Olivers were shocked by the visible bruises on Viola Desmond's body, and they advised her to get immediate medical attention. The Black physician whom Viola consulted on 12 November treated her for injuries to her knee and hip and also advised his patient to retain a lawyer to appeal the conviction.[37]

Recognizing that they needed to gather assistance from the wider community, Pearleen Oliver sought public support for Viola's case from the Nova Scotia Association for the Advancement of Colored People (NSAACP). The NSAACP, dedicated to eradicating race discrimination in housing, education, and employment, was founded in 1945. Pearleen Oliver found about half of the NSAACP members supportive of Viola Desmond's court challenge, while half expressed initial reluctance. Divisions of opinion about strategies for change seem to be inherent in all social reform movements, and the NSAACP was no exception. Fears of fostering racist backlash, concerns about using the law to confront racial segregation, and questions about whether equal admission to theatres was a pressing issue seem to have motivated the more cautious.[38]

Pearleen Oliver made a convincing case for supporting a legal claim, however, and all of the members of the NSAACP ultimately backed the case. They pledged to call public meetings about Viola Desmond's treatment and to raise funds to defray any legal costs. As Pearleen Oliver would explain to the Halifax *Chronicle*, the NSAACP intended to fight Viola Desmond's case to prevent "a spread of color-bar tactics" across the province.[39]

Some dissent continued to linger within the Black community. One individual wrote to the *Clarion*, a bi-weekly Black newspaper founded in New Glasgow in July 1946, "About all we have to say about our Country is 'Thank God' for it. With all its shortcomings it is still the best place on earth. I would like to start complaining about segregation in theatres and restaurants, but as I look around me and see the food stores filled to overflowing while countless millions are starving I just can't get het up over not eating in certain places. I am EATING and REGULARLY. Later on, maybe, but not now. Canada is still all right with me."[40]

The argument made here seems partially rooted in economic or class-based concerns. The letter focused on issues of basic sustenance, intimating indirectly that those who could afford to eat in restaurants or attend the theatre were not fully representative of the Black community. In contrast, Carrie M. Best, the forty-three-year-old Black editor of the *Clarion*, believed that the question of racial segregation in public facilities was extremely important to the entire Black population. She wrote back defending those who would challenge such discrimination:

It is sometimes said that those who seek to serve are "looking for trouble." There are some who think it better to follow the line of least resistance, no matter how great the injury. Looking for trouble? How much better off the world would be if men of good will would look for trouble, find it, and while it is merely a cub, drag it out into the open, before it becomes the ferocious lion. Racial and Religious hatred is trouble of the gravest kind. It is a vicious, smouldering and insidious kind of trouble, born of fear and ignorance. It often lays dormant for years until some would be Hitler, Bilbo or Rankin emerges to fan the flame into an uncontrollable catastrophe.

It is heartening to know how many trouble shooters have come to the aid of *The Clarion* since the disgraceful Roseland incident. They are convinced, as are we, that it is infinitely wiser to look for trouble than to have trouble looking for them.[41]

Carrie Best would profile Viola Desmond's treatment on the front pages of the *Clarion*, denouncing it as a "disgraceful incident," and claiming that "New Glasgow stands for Jim-crowism, at its basest, over the entire globe." She also gave prominent placement to a notice from Bernice A. Williams, NSAACP secretary, announcing a public meeting to solicit contributions for the Viola Desmond Court Fund. The *Clarion* urged everyone to attend and give donations: "The NSAACP is the Ladder to Advancement. Step on it! Join today!" Money began to trickle in from across the province, with donations by whites and Blacks alike.[42]

Carrie Best, who was born and educated in New Glasgow, was well acquainted with the egregious forms of white racism practised there. A woman who defined herself as an "activist" against racism, she did not mince words when she claimed there were "just as many racists in New Glasgow as in Alabama."[43] She was thrown out of the Roseland Theatre herself in 1942, for refusing to sit in the balcony, and tried unsuccessfully to sue the theatre management for damages then.[44]

Nor was she a stranger to the heroism of Black resisters. One of her most vivid childhood memories involved a race riot that erupted in New Glasgow at the close of the First World War. An interracial altercation between two youths inspired "bands of roving white men armed with clubs" to station themselves at different intersections in the town, barring Blacks from crossing. At dusk that evening, Carrie Best's mother was delivered home from work by the chauffeur of the family who employed her. There she found that her husband, her younger son, and Carrie had made it home safely. Missing was Carrie's elder brother, who had not yet returned from his job at the Norfolk House hotel. Carrie described what ensued in her autobiography, *That Lonesome Road*:

In all the years she lived and until she passed away at the age of eighty-one my mother was never known to utter an unkind, blasphemous or obscene word, nor did I ever see her get angry. This evening was no exception. She told us to get our meal, stating that she was going into town to get my brother. It was a fifteen minute walk.

At the corner of East River Road and Marsh Street the crowd was waiting and as my mother drew near they hurled insults at her and threateningly ordered her to turn back. She continued to walk toward the hotel about a block away when one of the young men recognized her and asked her where she was going. "I am going to the Norfolk House for my son," she answered calmly. (My mother was six feet tall and as straight as a ramrod.) The young man ordered the crowd back and my mother continued on her way to the hotel. At that time there was a livery stable at the rear entrance to the hotel and it was there my mother found my frightened older brother and brought him safely home.[45]

This was but one incident in an increasingly widespread pattern of white racism, which exploded with particular virulence across Canada during and immediately following the First World War. White mobs terrorized the Blacks living near New Glasgow, destroying their property. White soldiers also attacked the Black settlement in Truro, Nova Scotia, stoning houses and shouting obscenities. Throughout the 1920s, Blacks in Ontario and Saskatchewan withstood increasingly concerted intimidation from the hateful Ku Klux Klan. But race discrimination had a much longer history in Canada.[46]

The History of Black Segregation in Canada

From the middle of the nineteenth century, Blacks and whites in two provinces could be relegated to separate schools by law.[47] Ontario amended its School Act in 1849 to permit municipal councils "to authorize the establishing of any number of schools for the education of the children of colored people that they may judge expedient." The preamble to the statute was quite specific. The legislation was necessary, it admitted, because "the prejudices and ignorance" of certain Ontario residents had "prevented" certain Black children from attending the common schools in their district. The statute was amended in 1850, to direct local public school trustees to establish separate schools upon the application of twelve or more "resident heads of families" in the area. In 1886, the legislature clarified that schools for "coloured people" were to be set up only after an application had been made by at least five Black families in the community.[48]

Although it was drafted in permissive language, white officials frequently used coercive tactics to force Blacks into applying for segregated schools.[49] Once separate schools were set up, the courts refused Black children admission to any other schools, despite evidence that this forced many to travel long distances to attend schools they would not have chosen otherwise.[50] Separate schools for Blacks continued until 1891 in Chatham, 1893 in Sandwich, 1907 in Harrow, 1917 in Amherstburg, and 1965 in North Colchester and Essex Counties.[51] The Ontario statute authorizing racially segregated education would not be repealed until 1964.[52] As white historian Robin Winks has noted, "The Negro schools lacked competent teachers, and attendance was highly irregular and unenforced. Many schools met for only three months in the year or closed entirely. Most had no library of any kind. In some districts, school taxes were collected from Negro residents to support the [white] common school from which their children were barred ... The education received ... could hardly have been regarded as equal."[53]

Similar legislation dating from 1865 existed in Nova Scotia, where education authorities were authorized to establish "separate apartments or buildings" for pupils of "different colors."[54] A campaign for racial integration in the schools, organized by leaders of the Black community in 1884, prompted an amendment to the law, stipulating that Black pupils could not be excluded from instruction in the areas in which they lived.[55] The original provisions for segregation within the public school system remained intact until 1950.[56] In 1940, school officials in Lower Sackville, in Halifax County, barred Black children from attending the only public school in the area, and until 1959 school buses would stop only in the white sections of Hammonds Plains. In 1960, there would still be seven formal Black school districts and three additional exclusively Black schools in Nova Scotia.[57]

Beyond the schools, racial segregation riddled the country. The colour bar was less rigidified than in the United States, varying between regions and shifting over time.[58] But Canadian employers commonly selected their workforce by race rather than by merit.[59] Access to land grants and residential housing was frequently restricted by race.[60] Attempts were made to bar Blacks from jury service.[61] The military was rigorously segregated.[62] Blacks were denied equal access to some forms of public transportation.[63] Blacks and whites tended to worship in separate churches, sometimes by choice, other times because white congregations refused membership to Blacks.[64] Orphanages and poorhouses could be segregated by race.[65] Some hospitals refused access to facilities to non-white physicians and service to non-white patients.[66] Blacks were even denied burial rights in segregated cemeteries.[67] While no consistent pattern ever emerged, various hotels, restaurants, theatres, athletic facilities, parks, swimming pools, beaches, dance pavilions, skating rinks, pubs, and bars were closed to Blacks across the country.[68]

There were as yet no Canadian statutes expressly prohibiting such behaviour. The first statute to prohibit segregation on the basis of race did not appear until more than a year after Viola Desmond launched her civil suit, when Saskatchewan banned race discrimination in "hotels, victualling houses, theatres or other places to which the public is customarily admitted." The 1947 Saskatchewan Bill of Rights Act, which also barred discrimination in employment, business ventures, housing, and education, constituted Canada's first comprehensive human rights legislation. The act offered victims of race discrimination the opportunity to prosecute offenders upon summary conviction for fines of up to $200. The Court of King's Bench was also empowered to issue injunctions to restrain the offensive behaviour.[69] But none of this would assist Viola Desmond in November 1946.

Preparing for Legal Battle

Had Viola Desmond wished to retain a Black lawyer to advise her on legal options, this would have presented difficulties. Nine Black men appear to have been admitted to the bar of Nova Scotia prior to 1946, but few were available for hire.[70] The only Black lawyer practising in Halifax in 1946 was Rowland Parkinson Goffe. A native of Jamaica, Goffe practised initially in England, taking his call to the Nova Scotia bar in 1920. Goffe travelled abroad frequently, operating his legal practice in Halifax only intermittently. For reasons that are unclear, Viola Desmond did not retain Goffe. He may have been away from Halifax at the time.[71]

Four days after her arrest, on 12 November Viola Desmond retained the services of a white lawyer named Frederick William Bissett. Rev. William Oliver knew Bissett, and it was he who made the initial arrangements for Viola to see the lawyer. A forty-four-year-old native of St John's, Newfoundland, Bissett graduated in 1926 from Dalhousie Law School with a reputation as a "sharp debater." Called to the bar in Nova Scotia that year, he opened his own law office in Halifax, where he practised alone until his elevation to the Supreme Court of Nova Scotia in 1961. A noted trial lawyer, Bissett was acclaimed for his "persistence and resourcefulness," his "keen wit and an infectious sense of humour." Those who knew him emphasized that, above all, Bissett was "gracious and charming," a true "gentleman." This last feature of his character would potentially have been very helpful to Viola Desmond and her supporters. Their case would be considerably aided if the courts could be induced to visualize Viola Desmond as a "lady" wronged by rough and racist men. The affront to customary gender assumptions might have been just the thing to tip the balance in the minds of judges who would otherwise have been reluctant to oppose racial segregation. A "gentleman" such as Bissett would have been the perfect choice to advocate extending the mantle of white chivalry across race lines to cover Black women.[72]

Bissett's first task was to decide how to frame Viola Desmond's claim within the doctrines of law. One option might have been to mount a direct attack on the racially restrictive admissions policy of the theatre. There was an excellent precedent for such a claim in an earlier

Quebec Superior Court decision, *Johnson v. Sparrow*. In 1899, the court awarded fifty dollars in damages to a Black couple barred from sitting in the orchestra section of the Montreal Academy of Music. Holding that a "breach of contract" had occurred, a white judge, John Sprott Archibald, reasoned that "any regulation which deprived negroes as a class of privileges which all other members of the community had a right to demand, was not only unreasonable but entirely incompatible with our free democratic institutions." The Quebec Court of Queen's Bench affirmed the ruling on appeal, although it focused exclusively on the breach of contract and held that the issue of racial equality did not need to be directly addressed at the time.[73]

A similar position was taken in British Columbia in 1914, in the case of *Barnswell v. National Amusement Company, Limited*. The Empress Theatre in Victoria promulgated a "rule of the house that coloured people should not be admitted." When the white theatre manager turned away James Barnswell, a Black man who was a long-time resident of Victoria, he sued for breach of contract and assault. The white trial judge, Peter Secord Lampman, found the defendant company liable for breach of contract and awarded Barnswell fifty dollars in damages for humiliation. The British Columbia Court of Appeal affirmed the result.[74]

A string of other cases had done much to erode these principles. In 1911, a Regina newspaper announced that a local restaurant was planning to charge Black customers double what whites paid for meals, in an effort to exclude them from the local lunch-counter. When William Hawes, a Black man, was billed $1.40 instead of the usual $0.70 for a plate of ham and eggs, he took the white restaurant-keeper, W.H. Waddell, to court one week later. His claim was that Waddell had obtained money "by false pretences." The case was dismissed in Regina's Police Court, with the local white magistrates concluding that Hawes had known of the double fare when he entered the restaurant, and that this barred a charge of false pretences.[75]

Another example of judicial support for racial segregation occurred during the upsurge of racial violence at the close of the First World War. In 1919, the majority of the white judges on the Quebec Court of King's Bench held in *Loew's Montreal Theatres Ltd v. Reynolds* that the theatre management had "the right to assign particular seats to different races and classes of men and women as it sees fit." White theatre proprietors from Quebec east to the Maritimes greeted this ruling with enthusiasm, using it to contrive new and expanded policies of racially segregated seating.[76] In 1924, in *Franklin v. Evans*, a white judge from the Ontario

High Court dismissed a claim for damages "for insult and injury" from W.V. Franklin, a Black watchmaker from Kitchener, who was refused lunch service in "The Cave," a London restaurant.[77] In 1940, in *Rogers v. Clarence Hotel*, the majority of the white judges on the British Columbia Court of Appeal held that the white female proprietor of a beer parlour, Rose Elizabeth Low, could refuse to serve a Black Vancouver businessman, Edward Tisdale Rogers, because of his race. The doctrine of "complete freedom of commerce" justified the owner's right to deal "as [she] may choose with any individual member of the public."[78]

Fred Christie v. The York Corporation, ultimately reaching a similar result, wound its way through the Quebec court system right up to the Supreme Court of Canada in 1939. The litigation began when the white manager of a tavern in the Montreal Forum declined to serve a Black customer in July 1936. Fred Christie, a resident of Verdun, Quebec, who was employed as a private chauffeur in Montreal, sued the proprietors for damages. Judge Louis Philippe Demers, a white judge on the Quebec Superior Court, initially awarded Christie twenty-five dollars in compensation for humiliation, holding that hotels and restaurants providing "public services" had "no right to discriminate between their guests." The majority of the white judges of the Quebec Court of King's Bench reversed this ruling, preferring to champion the principle that "chaque propriétaire est maître chez lui." This philosophy was endorsed by the majority of the white judges on the Supreme Court of Canada, who agreed that it was "not a question of motives or reasons for deciding to deal or not to deal; [any merchant] is free to do either." Conceding that the "freedom of commerce" principle might be restricted where a merchant adopted "a rule contrary to good morals or public order," Judge Thibaudeau Rinfret concluded that the colour bar was neither.[79]

In contrast, a series of judges dissented vigorously throughout these cases. In *Loew's Montreal Theatres Ltd v. Reynolds*, white judge Henry-George Carroll took pains to disparage the situation in the United States, where law was regularly used to enforce racial segregation. Stressing that social conditions differed in Canada, he insisted, "Tous les citoyens de ce pays, blancs et noirs, sont soumis à la même loi et tenus aux mêmes obligations." Carroll spoke pointedly of the ideology of equality that had suffused French law since the revolution of 1789 and reasoned that Mr Reynolds, "un homme de bonne éducation," deserved compensation for the humiliation that had occurred.[80]

In *Rogers v. Clarence Hotel*, Judge Cornelius Hawkins O'Halloran wrote a lengthy and detailed rebuttal to the majority decision. Noting that the plaintiff was a British subject who had resided in Vancouver for more than two decades, with an established business in shoe repair, O'Halloran insisted that he should be entitled to obtain damages from any beer parlour that barred Blacks from admission. "Refusal to serve the respondent solely because of his colour and race is contrary to the common law," claimed the white judge. "All British subjects have the same rights and privileges under the common law – it makes no difference whether white or coloured; or of what class, race or religion."[81]

In *Christie v. The York Corporation*, the first dissent came from Antonin Galipeault, a white judge of the Quebec Court of King's Bench. Pointing out that the sale of liquor in Quebec taverns was already extensively regulated by law, he concluded that the business was a "monopoly or quasi-monopoly" that ought to be required to service all members of the public. Galipeault noted that if tavern-keepers could bar Blacks, they could also deny entry to Jews, Syrians, the Chinese, and the Japanese. Bringing the matter even closer to home for the majority of Quebecers, he reasoned that "religion" and "language" might constitute the next grounds for exclusion. Galipeault insisted that the colour bar be struck down.[82]

At the level of the Supreme Court of Canada, Henry Hague Davis expressly sided with Galipeault, concluding that racial segregation was "contrary to good morals and the public order." "In the changed and changing social and economic conditions," wrote the white Supreme Court justice, "different principles must necessarily be applied to new conditions." Noting that the legislature had developed an extensive regulatory regime surrounding the sale of beer, Davis concluded that such vendors were not entitled "to pick and choose" their customers.[83]

What is obvious from these various decisions is that the law was unsettled, as Judge Davis frankly admitted: "The question is one of difficulty, as the divergence of judicial opinion in the courts below indicates."[84] Where the judges expressly offered reasons for arriving at such different results, their analysis appears to be strained and the distinctions they drew arbitrary. Some tried to differentiate between a plaintiff who had prior knowledge of the colour bar and one who did not. Some considered the essential point to be whether the plaintiff crossed the threshold of the premises before being ejected. Ad nauseam the judges compared the status of theatres, restaurants, taverns, and hotels. They argued over whether public advertisements issued by commercial establishments constituted a legal "offer" or merely "an invitation to buy." They debated whether a stein of beer had sufficient "nutritive qualities" to be regarded as food.

Despite the endless technical arguments, the real issues dividing the judges appear to be relatively straightforward. There were two fundamental principles competing against each other: the doctrine of freedom of commerce and the doctrine of equality within a democratic society. Although the judges seem to have believed that they were merely applying traditional judicial precedents to the case at hand, this was something of a smokescreen. Some judges were choosing to select precedents extolling freedom of commerce, while others chose to affirm egalitarian principles. Nothing irretrievably compelled them to opt for one result over the other except their own predilections. A white law professor, Bora Laskin, made this explicit in a legal comment on the *Christie* case, written in 1940: "The principle of freedom of commerce enforced by the Court majority is itself merely the reading of social and economic doctrine into law, and doctrine no longer possessing its nineteenth century validity."[85]

Furthermore, no court had yet ruled on the validity of racial segregation in hotels, theatres, or restaurants in the province of Nova Scotia. A cautious lawyer, one easily cowed by the doctrinal dictates of *stare decisis*, might have concluded that the "freedom of commerce" principle enunciated by the majority of judges in the Supreme Court of Canada would govern. A more adventuresome advocate might have surveyed the range of judicial disagreement and decided to put the legal system to the challenge once more.

The reform-minded lawyer could have gone back to the original decisions in *Johnson v. Sparrow* and *Barnswell v. National Amusement Co.*, which most of the judges in the later cases had curiously ignored.[86] Quebec Judge John Sprott Archibald, in particular, laid a firm foundation in *Johnson v. Sparrow*, eloquently proclaiming the right of Canadians of all races to have equal access to places of public entertainment. Roundly criticizing the policy of racially segregated seating, he explained,

This position cannot be maintained. It would perhaps be trite to speak of slavery in this connection, and yet the regulation in question is undoubtedly a survival of prejudices created by the system of negro slavery. Slavery never had any wide influence in this country. The practice was gradually extinguished in Upper Canada by an act of the legislature passed on July 9th, 1793, which forbade the further importation of slaves, and ordered that all slave children born after that date should be free on attaining the age of twenty-one years.

Although it was only in 1834 that an act of the imperial parliament finally abolishing slavery throughout the British colonies was passed, yet long before that, in 1803, Chief Justice Osgoode had declared slavery illegal in the province of Quebec. Our constitution is and always has been essentially democratic, and does not admit of distinctions of races or classes. All men are equal before the law and each has equal rights as a member of the community.[87]

Judge Archibald's recollection of the legal history of slavery in Canada is something of an understatement. The first Black slave arrived in Quebec in 1628, with slavery officially introduced by the French into New France on 1 May 1689.[88] After the British Conquest in 1763, the white general Jeffery Amherst confirmed that all slaves would remain in the possession of their masters.[89] In 1790, the English Parliament expressly authorized individuals wishing to settle in the provinces of Quebec and Nova Scotia to import "negroes" along with other "household furniture, utensils of husbandry or cloathing" free of duty.[90] In 1762, the Nova Scotia General Assembly gave indirect statutory recognition to slavery when it explicitly adverted to "Negro slaves" in the context of an act intended to control the sale of liquor on credit.[91] In 1781, the legislature of Prince Edward Island (then Île St Jean) passed an act declaring that the baptism of slaves would not exempt them from bondage.[92]

The 1793 Upper Canada statute, of which Judge Archibald was so proud, countenanced a painfully slow process of manumission. The preamble, noting that it was "highly expedient to abolish slavery in this province, so far as the same may gradually be done without violating private property," said it all. The act freed not a single slave. Although the statute did ensure that no additional "negro" slaves could be brought into the province, it confirmed the existing property rights of all current slave-owners. Furthermore, children born of "negro mother[s]" were to remain in the service of their mothers' owners until the age of twenty-five years (not twenty-one years, as Judge Archibald had noted). The act may actually have discouraged voluntary manumission, by requiring slave-owners to post security bonds for slaves released from service, to cover the cost of any future public financial assistance required.[93] Confronted with litigants who contested the legal endorsement of slavery, white judges in Lower Canada, Nova Scotia, and New Brunswick dispatched inconsistent judgments.[94] Portions of the area that was to become Canada remained slave territory under law until 1833, when a statute passed in England emancipated all slaves in the British Empire.[95] Slavery persisted in British North America well after it was abolished in most of the northern states.[96] Even after abolition, Canadian government officials approved the extradition of fugitive African Americans who escaped from slavery in the United States and sought freedom in Canada.[97]

However, Judge Archibald's ringing declaration that the constitution prohibited racial discrimination was an outstanding affirmation of equality that could potentially have been employed to attack many of the racist practices currently in vogue. Long before the enactment of the Canadian Bill of Rights or the Canadian Charter of Rights and Freedoms, here was a judge who took hold of the largely unwritten, amorphous body of constitutional thought and proclaimed that the essence of a democracy was the legal eradication of "distinctions of races or classes." A thoughtful attorney could have created an opening for argument here, reasoning that the "freedom of commerce" principle should be superseded by equality rights as a matter of constitutional interpretation. These arguments had apparently not been fully made to the Supreme Court of Canada when the *Christie v. York Corporation* case was litigated. There should have been room for another try.

In addition, the Supreme Court had expressly admitted that "freedom of commerce" would have to give way where a business rule ran "contrary to good morals or public order." No detailed analysis of the ramifications of racial discrimination was ever presented in these cases. A concerted attempt to lay out the social and economic repercussions of racial segregation might have altered the facile assumptions of some of the judges who could find no fault with colour bars. So much could have been argued. There was the humiliation and assault on dignity experienced by Black men, women, and children whose humanity was denied by racist whites. Counsel could have described the severe curtailment of Black educational and occupational opportunities that placed impenetrable restrictions upon full participation in Canadian society. The distrust bred of racial segregation had triggered many of the instances of interracial mob violence that marred Canadian history. A creative lawyer might have contended that rules that enforced racial divisions undeniably fomented immorality and the disruption of public peace.

Similar arguments had been made before the Ontario Supreme Court in 1945, in the landmark case of *Re Drummond Wren*. The issue there was the legality of a restrictive covenant registered against a parcel of land, enjoining the owner from selling to "Jews or persons of objectionable nationality." Noting that there were no precedents on point, Judge John Keiller Mackay, a white Gentile, quoted a legal rule from *Halsbury*: "Any agreement which tends to be injurious to the public or against the public good is void as being contrary to public policy." Holding that the covenant was unlawful because it was "offensive to the public policy of this jurisdiction," Mackay stated,

In my opinion, nothing could be more calculated to create or deepen divisions between existing religious and ethnic groups in this Province, or in this country, than the sanction of a method of land transfer which would permit the segregation and confinement of particular groups to particular business or residential areas ... It appears to me to be a moral duty, at least, to lend aid to all forces of cohesion, and similarly to repel all fissiparous tendencies which would imperil national unity. The common law courts have, by their actions over the years, obviated the need for rigid constitutional guarantees in our polity by their wise use of the doctrine of public policy as an active agent in the promotion of the public weal. While Courts and eminent Judges have, in view of the powers of our Legislatures, warned against inventing new heads of public policy, I do not conceive that I would be breaking new ground were I to hold the restrictive covenant impugned in this proceeding to be void as against public policy. Rather would I be applying well-recognized principles of public policy to a set of facts requiring their invocation in the interest of the public good.

The common law was not carved in stone. Nor was the judicial understanding of "public policy," which as Judge Mackay stressed, "varies from time to time."[98]

In assessing his strategy in the *Desmond* case, Bissett had to consider many factors: the wishes of his client, the resources available to prepare and argue the case, the social and political climate within which the case would be heard, and the potential receptivity of the bench. Viola Desmond would have been soundly behind a direct attack on racial segregation. She had come seeking public vindication for the racial discrimination she had suffered. The community support and funding from the NSAACP would have strengthened her claim. The Halifax beautician would have been viewed as a conventionally "good" client, a successful business entrepreneur, a respectable married woman who had proved to be well mannered throughout her travails. The traditional assumptions about race relations were also under some scrutiny. Although white Nova Scotians continued to sponsor racial segregation in their schools, housing, and workforce, the unveiling of the Nazi death camps towards the end of the Second World War riveted public attention upon the appalling excesses of racial and religious discrimination. In October 1945, the Canadian Parliament entertained a motion to enact a formal Bill of Rights, guaranteeing equal treatment before the law, irrespective of race, nationality, or religious or political beliefs. Public sentiment might have been sufficiently malleable to muster support for more racial integration. Viola Desmond's case potentially offered an excellent vehicle with which to test the capacity of Canadian law to further racial equality.[99]

But Frederick William Bissett decided not to attack the racial segregation directly. Perhaps he simply accepted the Supreme Court of Canada ruling in *Christie v. York Corporation* as determinative. Perhaps he could not imagine how to push the boundaries of law in new, more socially progressive directions. Perhaps he was intimately acquainted with the white judges who manned the Nova Scotia courts and knew their predilections well. Whatever the reason, Bissett settled upon a more conventional litigation strategy. That he would fail, even in this more limited effort, may suggest that a more dramatic challenge would have fallen far short of the goal. I prefer to think that the stilted narrowness of the vision dictated an equally narrow response.

Rex v. Desmond

Bissett issued a writ on Wednesday, 14 November 1946, naming Viola Desmond as plaintiff in a civil suit against two defendants, Harry L. MacNeil and the Roseland Theatre Co. Ltd. Bissett alleged that Harry MacNeil acted unlawfully in forcibly ejecting his client from the theatre. He based his claim in intentional tort, a legal doctrine that contained little scope for discussion of race discrimination. The writ stipulated that Viola Desmond was entitled to compensatory damages on the following grounds: (1) assault, (2) malicious prosecution, and (3) false arrest and imprisonment. Bissett did not add a fourth and lesser-known tort, "abusing the process of the law," which might have offered more scope for raising the racial issues that concerned his client. The three grounds he did enunciate were all advanced in racially neutral terms.[100]

Whether there would have been an opportunity to address the issue of race discrimination indirectly within the common-law tort actions will never be known. The civil claim apparently never came to trial, and the archival records contain no further details on the file. Why Bissett decided not to pursue the civil actions is unclear. Perhaps he felt that the tort claim would be difficult to win. The common-law principle of "defence of property" might have been invoked to justify the use of force by property owners against trespassers. The defendants would also have been entitled to raise the defence of "legal authority," asserting that they were within their rights in removing someone who had breached the tax provisions of the Theatres Act. The conviction registered against Viola Desmond bolstered this line of argument, confirming that at least one court had upheld the defendants' actions. It also served as a complete defence to the claim for "malicious prosecution." Upon reflection, Bissett may have decided that he needed to overturn the initial conviction before taking any further action upon the civil claim.[101]

On 27 December 1946, Bissett announced that he would make an application for a writ of certiorari to ask the Supreme Court of Nova Scotia to quash Viola Desmond's criminal conviction. There was "no evidence to support" the conviction, he contended, and the magistrate lacked the "jurisdiction" to convict her. Bissett filed an affidavit sworn by Viola Desmond, outlining how she had asked for a downstairs ticket and been refused, describing in detail her manhandling by the theatre manager and police officer, and documenting the failings in the actual trial process itself. Nothing in the papers filed alluded directly or indirectly to race. Viola Desmond, Reverend W.P. Oliver, and William Allison (a Halifax packer) jointly committed themselves to pay up to two hundred dollars in costs should the action fail.[102]

A writ of certiorari allowed a party to transfer a case from an inferior tribunal to a court of superior jurisdiction by way of motion before a judge. In this manner, the records of proceedings before stipendiary magistrates could be taken up to the Supreme Court for reconsideration. The availability of this sort of judicial review was restricted, however. Parties dissatisfied with their conviction could not simply ask the higher court judges to overrule it because the magistrate's decision was wrong. Instead, they had to allege that there had been a more fundamental denial of justice or that there was some excess or lack of jurisdiction.[103]

There is no written record of what Bissett argued when he appeared before Nova Scotia Supreme Court Justice Maynard Brown Archibald on 10 January 1947.[104] But the white judge was clearly unimpressed. A native of Colchester County, Nova Scotia, Judge Archibald had studied law at Dalhousie University and was called to the Nova Scotia bar in 1919. He practised law in Halifax continuously from 1920 until his appointment to the bench in 1937. Although he was an erudite lecturer in Dalhousie's law school, Archibald did not choose to elaborate upon legal intricacies in his decision in the *Desmond* case. Viola Desmond had no right to use the process of certiorari, he announced, and he curtly dismissed her application on 20 January. The cursory ruling of less than two pages contained a mere recitation of conclusion without any apparent rationale. "It is clear from the affidavits and documents presented to me that the Magistrate had jurisdiction to enter upon his inquiry," Archibald noted. "This court will therefore not review on certiorari the decision of the Magistrate as to whether or not there was evidence to support the conviction."[105]

The best clue to deciphering the decision is found in the judge's final paragraph: "It was apparent at the argument that the purpose of this application was to seek by means of certiorari proceedings a review of the evidence taken before the convicting Magistrate. It is obvious that the proper procedure to have had such evidence reviewed was by way of an appeal. Now, long after the time for appeal has passed, it is sought to review the Magistrate's decision by means of *certiorari* proceedings. For the reasons that I have already given, this procedure is not available to the applicant."[106]

A part-time stipendiary magistrate for a brief period during his days of law practice, Judge Archibald was concerned that lower court officials be free from unnecessary, burdensome scrutiny by superior court judges. Earlier Nova Scotia decisions had reflected similar fears, suggesting that access to judicial review be restricted to prevent "a sea of uncertainty" in which the decisions of inferior tribunals were subjected to limitless second-guessing. The proper course of action, according to Archibald, would have been to appeal Magistrate MacKay's conviction to County Court under the Nova Scotia Summary Convictions Act.[107]

Why Bissett originally chose to bring a writ of certiorari rather than an appeal is not clear. The Summary Convictions Act required litigants to choose one route or the other, not both. An appeal permitted a full inquiry into all of the facts and law surrounding the case, with the right to call witnesses and adduce evidence, and the appeal court entitled to make a completely fresh ruling on the merits. Although an appeal would seem to have offered greater scope to the defence, Bissett may have preferred to make his arguments before the more elevated Nova Scotia Supreme Court, which heard applications for certiorari, rather than the County Court, which heard appeals from summary convictions. Or he may simply have missed the time limit for filing an appeal, which was set as ten days from the date of conviction. He issued the civil writ a mere five days after the initial conviction, but the writ of certiorari was not filed until almost a full month afterwards. Possibly by the time Bissett turned away from the civil process to canvas his options with respect to the criminal law, it was already too late for an appeal.[108]

Since the limitation period for appeals had already run, Bissett had no other option but to seek to overturn Archibald's ruling before the full bench of the Nova Scotia Supreme Court.[109] The case was set down for argument on 13 March. Jack Desmond refused to accompany his wife to court, since he continued to oppose Viola's actions and blamed her for stirring up trouble. The tensions within the marriage were increasing by the day and would ultimately result in the couple's permanent marital separation.[110] Carrie Best, who did accompany Viola Desmond to court, acknowledged in the *Clarion* that it was an emotionally tense experience to sit through the hearing, "hoping against hope that justice will not be blind in this case." Carrie Best admitted that she "watched breathlessly as the calm, unhurried soft spoken Bissett argued his appeal." Bissett conceded that the time to lodge the original appeal had "inadvertently slipped by," but that this should not bar the court from reviewing on certiorari. "The appellant is entitled to the writ," claimed Bissett, "whether she appealed or not, if there has been a denial of natural justice."[111]

The affidavit Viola Desmond filed to support her case set out in detail the many ways she felt the trial had been procedurally unfair. She had not been told of her right to counsel or her right to seek an adjournment. She did not understand that she was entitled to cross-examine the prosecution witnesses. She was sentenced without any opportunity to make submissions to the court. These several omissions would have more than sufficed to constitute a denial of natural justice, as lawyers understand the meaning of that term in the latter half of the twentieth century. But at the time of the *Desmond* appeal the concept of due process was much less clear. Judge John Doull, who issued his decision on this case on 17 May 1947, even disputed the use of the term *natural justice*. A former attorney general of Nova Scotia, Doull wrote, "A denial of justice apparently means that before the tribunal, the applicant was not given an opportunity of setting up and proving his case. (The words 'natural justice' were used in some of the opinions of the judges but I doubt whether that is a good term.) At any rate a denial of the right to be heard is a denial of a right which is so fundamental in our legal practice that a denial of it vitiates a proceeding in which such denial occurs."[112] The white judge conceded that if a "denial of justice" was established in Viola Desmond's affidavit, the failure to appeal would no longer suffice to bar her claim. But then Judge Doull, a former mayor of New Glasgow, concluded that there had been no such procedural omissions in the present case. None of the other white Supreme Court judges differed from this view.[113]

Bissett's other argument, on the lack of jurisdiction, was vigorously disputed by respondent's counsel, Edward Mortimer Macdonald, Jr, KC. Harry MacNeil's lawyer was a forty-seven-year-old white New Glasgow resident who had received degrees from Dalhousie University, Bishop's College, and McGill. He practised law in Montreal from 1924 to 1930, then returned to practice in his birth province of Nova Scotia, where he served as the town solicitor for New Glasgow. "The magistrate [had] jurisdiction, [and] tried the case on the evidence before him," asserted Macdonald. "The sole objection remaining to the appellant is that the evidence does not support a conviction. The proper remedy therefore is by way of appeal."[114]

Bissett did not argue that it was beyond the jurisdiction of a magistrate to apply the Nova Scotia Theatres, Cinematographs and Amusements Act to enforce racial segregation. He should have. Courts had long held that it was an abuse of process to bring criminal charges as a lever to enforce debt collection. Here the theatre manager was not trying to help the province collect tax, but to bring down the force of law upon protestors of racial segregation. That Bissett might have drawn an analogy to the abuse of process decisions was suggested months later in a *Canadian Bar Review* article written by J.B. Milner, a white professor at Dalhousie Law School. Calling the *Desmond* case "one of the most interesting decisions to come from a Nova Scotia court in many years," Milner asserted that Harry MacNeill was prosecuting Viola Desmond "for improper reasons." MacNeill's "desire to discriminate between negro and white patrons of his theatre" transformed the criminal proceeding into "a vexatious action," Milner argued.[115]

None of this was addressed before the court. Instead, Bissett confined his jurisdictional point to the insufficiency of evidence at trial, leaving himself wide open to procedural critique. Judge Robert Henry Graham emphasized that the evidentiary matters in this case did not relate to jurisdiction: "A justice who convicts without evidence is doing something that he ought not to do, but he is doing it as a Judge and if his jurisdiction to entertain the charge is not open to impeachment, his subsequent error, however grave, is a wrong exercise of a jurisdiction which he has, and not a usurpation of a jurisdiction which he has not." There could be no question "raised as to the jurisdiction of the stipendiary magistrate" in this case, concluded Judge Graham, himself another former white mayor and stipendiary magistrate from New Glasgow. Furthermore, Judge Graham added, "no reason except inadvertence was given to explain why the open remedy of appeal was not taken." William Francis Carroll and William Lorimer Hall, the other two white judges who delivered concurring opinions in the case, agreed that certiorari was not procedurally available to overturn the conviction.[116]

Three of the judges, however, felt inclined to make some comment about the sufficiency of evidence at trial. Graham's view was that the charge had been substantiated: "[Viola Desmond] knew that the ticket she purchased was not for downstairs and so that she had not paid the full tax." Carroll disagreed: "The accused did actually pay the tax required by one purchasing such a ticket as she was sold." Hall, the only judge to make even passing reference to the racial issues, was most explicit:

Had the matter reached the Court by some method other than *certiorari*, there might have been opportunity to right the wrong done this unfortunate woman.

One wonders if the manager of the theatre who laid the complaint was so zealous because of a *bona fide* belief there had been an attempt to defraud the Province of Nova Scotia of the sum of one cent, or was it a surreptitious endeavour to enforce a Jim Crow rule by misuse of a public statute.[117]

Despite their differing opinions, all four judges took the position that Viola Desmond's efforts to overturn Magistrate MacKay's original ruling should be denied. Her conviction would stand.

The decision to apply for certiorari rather than to appeal had cost Viola Desmond dearly. Respondent's counsel, E.M. Macdonald, laid the blame squarely at Bissett's feet. "The appellant had full benefit of legal advice before the expiry of the delays for appeal," he insisted at the Supreme Court hearing. More than five days before the expiration of the time for appeal, Bissett was actively on the case, having already launched the civil action for assault, malicious prosecution, and false arrest and imprisonment. His decision to opt for judicial review rather than an appeal of the original conviction proved disastrous. He chose to argue the case in a conservative and traditional manner, relegating the race issues to the sidelines of the legal proceeding. Even within this narrow venue, Bissett failed to deliver.

The Aftermath

What must Viola Desmond have thought of the ruling? Although she left no letters or diaries reflecting her views, her sisters recall something of her feelings at the time. Wanda Robson, Viola's younger sister, explains: "The day she came back from the court, knowing she had lost the case, she was very disappointed. A person like my sister never liked to lose. A person like my sister, who was such a hard worker, had always been told if you do hard work, you're going to win. If you're Black or Negro or whatever, you're going to work hard, get that scholarship and win. We forgot about our colour and educated ourselves. She felt that she should have won the case, and she was bitterly disappointed."[118]

Viola Desmond must have been appalled, not only by the ruling, but by the way her attempt to seek legal protection from racial discrimination was turned into a purely technical debate over the intricacies of criminal procedure. None of the judges even noted on the record that she was Black. The intersection of "white male chivalry" with "Black womanhood" lay completely unexamined. Nor was there any direct reference to the Roseland Theatre's policy of racially segregated seating. Judge Hall was the only one to advert to the "Jim Crow rule," a reference to the practices of racial segregation spawned in the United States after the abolition of slavery. Even Judge Hall's professed concern did not dissuade him from reaching the same conclusion as his brothers on the bench: that the court was powerless to intervene.

Professor Milner took up this very point in his review of the case: "Discrimination against colour," he noted, took place "outside the sphere of legal rules." The theatre manager "apparently violated no law of human rights and fundamental freedoms in this free county in refusing admission to part of his theatre to persons of negro extraction." What struck Milner as particularly unfair was that the manager not only removed Viola Desmond, "as our democratic law says he may," but also successfully prosecuted her for violating a quasi-criminal provision in a provincial statute.[119]

The *Clarion*'s coverage of the "disappointing" decision, on 15 April 1947, was muted. Politely expressing appreciation for "the objective manner in which the judges handled the case," the editor noted, "It would appear that the decision was the only one possible under the law. While in the moral sense we feel disappointed, we must realize that the law must be interpreted as it is. The Clarion feels that the reason for the decision lies in the manner in which the case was presented to the Court. This was very strongly implied by the Supreme Court. This is a regrettable fact."[120]

Bissett, who is not mentioned by name, is clearly taking the fall here. It was his choice of an application for certiorari, rather than appeal, which was singled out as the reason for the legal loss. His conservative strategy of camouflaging race discrimination underneath traditional common-law doctrines, his decision not to attack the legality of racial segregation with a frontal assault, was not discussed.

The *Clarion* did, however, take some solace from Judge Hall's "Jim Crow" remarks, which it quoted in full, adding, "The Court did not hesitate to place the blame for the whole sordid affair where it belonged ... It is gratifying to know that such a shoddy attempt to hide behind the law has been recognized as such by the highest Court in our Province. We feel that owners and managers of places of amusement will now realize that such practices are recognized by those in authority for what they are, – cowardly devices to persecute innocent people because of their outmoded racial biases."[121]

Some Blacks believed the whole incident better left alone. There were accusations that Viola Desmond had caused all the trouble by trying to "pass" for white, that her mother's white heritage caused her to put on airs and sit where she ought never to have sat. Walter A. Johnston, a Black Haligonian employed as a chef with the immigration department, made a point of criticizing Viola Desmond at an Ottawa national convention of the Liberal party in October 1948. Viola Desmond had been "censured by the Halifax colored group" for her activism, he advised. "We told her she was not helping the New Glasgow colored people by motoring over there to cause trouble." Johnston complained of racial "agitators" who would "increase the racial problem and set back the progress towards good feeling." The policy he counselled: to "shrug ... off the trouble we met" with a "soft-answer-that-turneth-away-wrath."[122]

James Calbert Best, Carrie Best's son and the associate editor of the *Clarion*, had an entirely different perspective. Calling for legislation that would put the right to racial equality above the privileges of those in business, he claimed, "People have come to realize that the merchant, the restaurant operator, the theatre manager all have a duty, and the mere fact that such enterprises are privately owned is no longer an excuse for discrimination on purely racial grounds ... Here in Nova Scotia, we see the need of such legislation every day."[123]

Comparing the situation of Blacks in Nova Scotia with those in the American South, Best castigated Canadians for their complacency:

We do have many of the privileges which are denied our southern brothers, but we often wonder if the kind of segregation we receive here is not more cruel in the very subtlety of its nature ...

True, we are not forced into separate parts of public conveyances, nor are we forced to drink from separate faucets or use separate washrooms, but we are often refused meals in restaurants and beds in hotels, with no good reason.

Nowhere do we encounter signs that read "No Colored" or the more diplomatic little paste boards which say "Select Clientele," but at times it might be better. At least much consequent embarrassment might be saved for all concerned.[124]

Bolstered by the apparent inability of the courts to stop racial discrimination, Canadian businesses continued to enforce their colour bars at whim. The famous African-American sculptress Selma Burke was denied service in a Halifax restaurant in September 1947. "We had expected to find conditions in Canada so much better than in the States," explained her white companion, "but I'm sorry to say we were mistaken."[125] Grantley Adams, the Black prime minister of Barbados, was refused a room in a Montreal hotel in 1954 because the hotel had "regulations."[126] The racial intolerance in New Glasgow intensified and spread to other groups. In September 1948, a gang of hooded marauders burned a seven-foot cross on the front lawn of the home of Joe Mong, the Chinese proprietor of a New Glasgow restaurant. Police investigated but pronounced themselves sceptical that the incident had "anything to do with K.K.K. activities." It was simply "a private matter," they concluded.[127] Akin to "freedom of commerce."

After her loss in court, Viola Desmond seems to have withdrawn from public gaze and taken steps to consolidate her business. Her younger sister recalls that Viola sought advice from her father: "She was wondering what she should do, and my father said: 'Viola, I think you've gone as far as you should go. It's time to get on and put this behind you. I won't say that nothing's been gained. Something has, but at what cost? Your business is sliding.' So she set her lips, and got back to her business."[128] But even the business seems to have lost some of its lustre. Angry at the failure of the legal system to erase her conviction, Viola Desmond set aside her plans to establish franchise operations throughout Canada. She began to invest her money in real estate, believing that this represented greater security in a racially torn society. She bought up homes, renovated them, and rented them out to Black families. Eventually she closed up her shop and moved to Montreal, where she enrolled in business classes, hoping to become a consultant in the entertainment industry. She moved down to New York City, where she had just begun to establish her business when she fell ill. On 7 February 1965, at the age of fifty, Viola Desmond died in New York of a gastro-intestinal haemorrhage.[129]

As a matter of legal precedent, the *Viola Desmond* case was an absolute failure. The lawsuit was framed in such a manner that the real issues of white racism were shrouded in procedural technicalities. The judges turned their backs on Black claims for racial equality, in certain respects openly condoning racial segregation. But the toll that her battle with racial segregation took on Viola Desmond was not entirely for naught. According to Pearleen Oliver, the legal challenge touched a nerve within the Black community, creating a dramatic upsurge in race consciousness. The funds raised for legal fees were diverted to serve as seed money for the fledgling NSAACP, after Frederick William Bissett declined to bill his client, substantially strengthening the ability of the Black organization to lobby against other forms of race discrimination.[130]

While there were undeniably those who thought the struggle better left unwaged, the leaders of Nova Scotia's Black community felt differently. Asked to reflect on Viola Desmond's actions fifteen years later, Dr William Pearly Oliver tried to explain the enormous symbolic significance of the case. His appreciation for her effort transcends the failures of the legal system, and puts Viola Desmond's contribution in clearer perspective: "This meant something to our people. Neither before or since has there been such an aggressive effort to obtain rights. The people arose as one and with one voice. This positive stand enhanced the prestige of the Negro community throughout the Province. It is my conviction that much of the positive action that has since taken place stemmed from this."[131]

NOTES

Extensive notes with complete details, indicated by an asterisk, can be found under Endnotes to Chapter Seven at www.utppublishing.com/pdf/Colour_Coded.pdf.

1 Details surrounding the arrest are taken from "Affidavit of Viola Irene Desmond," 29 January 1947, *His Majesty the King v. Viola Irene Desmond,* Supreme Court of Nova Scotia no. 13347, vol. 937, RG39 "C" Halifax, Public Archives of Nova Scotia (hereinafter cited as PANS); "Negress Alleges She Was Ejected from Theatre," Halifax *Chronicle,* 30 Nov. 1946, 2; "Ban All Jim Crow Rules Is Comment on N.S. Charge," Toronto *Daily Star,* 30 Nov. 1946, 3. Material from this chapter was presented as the Seventh Annual Gibson-Armstrong Lecture in Law and History at Osgoode Hall Law School in February 1994, and an earlier version was published as "Racial Segregation in Canadian Legal History: Viola Desmond's Challenge, Nova Scotia 1946," *Dalhousie Law Journal* 17, no. 2 (Fall 1994): 299–362.

2 On the history of the Roseland Theatre and the racist nature of *The Birth of a Nation* (film) and blackface minstrelsy, see *.

3 For details concerning a number of Canadian cases that set historical precedents for Viola Desmond's direct-action approach, see *.

4 On MacNeil and his theatre, see *.

5 "Negress Alleges She Was Ejected from Theatre," Halifax *Chronicle;* "Affidavit of Viola Irene Desmond," PANS. For the reference to the gloves and posture, see the notes of the researcher who assisted with the compilation of material for this chapter: Tanya Hudson, "Interview with Dr Pearleen Oliver," Halifax, 28 Aug. 1995.

6 For biographical details on MacKay, see "Former Magistrate Dies at 84," Halifax *Chronicle-Herald,* 29 Sept. 1961, 2.

7 See R.S.N.S. 1923, c. 162, s. 8(8), 9, 10, 14. The initial enactment is *Theatres and Cinematographs Act,* S.N.S. 1915, c. 9, as amended.

8 For details of the statutory provision and the pricing arrangement at the Roseland, see *.

9 "Record," Rod G. MacKay, stipendiary magistrate for the Town of New Glasgow, County of Pictou, 9 Nov. 1946, *R.- (Inf. Henry MacNeil). Viola Desmond,* PANS; "Affidavit of Viola Desmond," PANS.

10 "Record," Rod G. MacKay. The ultimate disposition of the costs is unclear. One handwritten document signed by Magistrate MacNeil indicates that the accused was to pay Harry MacNeil, "the Informant herein, the sum of six dollars for his costs in this behalf." Another handwritten document signed by the magistrate indicates that the costs were broken down: $2.50 to be paid to himself as magistrate, and $3.50 to Police Chief Elmo C. Langille.

11 "Affidavit of Viola Desmond," PANS; R.S.N.S. 1923, c. 162, s. 8(3), 8(10). *Saturday Night* raises this point in its coverage of the trial, 7 Dec. 1946, 5: "The action of the magistrate in fining the lady in question for defrauding the province, when she had most expressly tendered to the box office the

proper price, including tax, of the seat in which she later insisted on sitting, is a travesty of justice."

12 "Negress Alleges She Was Ejected from Theatre," Halifax *Chronicle*. On the historical use of the terms *Negro* and *Negress* and the preference of the Black community for the word *coloured*, see *.

13 "Ban All Jim Crow Rules Is Comment on N.S. Charge," Toronto *Daily Star*, 30 Nov. 1946, 3. MacNeil continued: "We have a large colored patronage at our theatre and we don't permit color discrimination to be a determining factor. It would be poor policy for us to set up a color bar ... There was no discrimination."

14 This raises the important question of how many other trials lie buried, lost to historical scrutiny, because the real issues relating to racial divisions were (consciously?) unspoken or camouflaged with unrelated legal matters. On the tendency to delete references to race in evidence filed on racial-discrimination matters, see Robin W. Winks, *The Blacks in Canada: A History*, 2nd ed. (Montreal and Kingston: McGill-Queen's University Press, 1997), 424, discussing the 1920 hearing under the Industrial Disputes Investigation Act into the racially motivated discharges of thirty-six Black porters from the Canadian Pacific Railway. On a comparative note, see the discussion of the appeal of the conviction of Rosa Parks in the Montgomery bus boycott in Alabama in 1955, which never mentioned the Alabama bus segregation statute or racial segregation. "One reads the opinion in vain trying to understand the issue that her appeal raised," notes Robert Jerome Glennon in "The Role of Law in the Civil Rights Movement: The Montgomery Bus Boycott, 1955–1957," *Law and History Review* 9 (1991): 88.

15 Viola Desmond's elder sister recalls her sister's actions as unpremeditated: "I think it was a spontaneous action. She was aware of prejudice, but she had not been exposed to that kind of prejudice. In Halifax, you could sit where you liked in the theatre. So I think it came as a shock to her. She was well-known in Halifax, she felt herself to be an entrepreneur, she paid taxes, and she was part of the city. She knew people at different levels, so it was more of a shock for her. She acted spontaneously and I truly believe she never thought she would be physically mishandled. I think she was more shocked than surprised." See Constance Backhouse, "Interview with Mrs S.A. (Emily) Clyke, Viola Desmond's older sister," Montreal, 28 Apr. 1995. For reference to Viola Desmond as "well known throughout the province," see the *Clarion* 1, no. 1 (Dec. 1946), reel 4340, PANS.

16 Constance Backhouse, "Interview with Wanda Robson, Viola's younger sister," North Sydney, 22 Mar. 1995; Backhouse, "Interview with Mrs S.A. (Emily) Clyke." Judith Fingard, "Race and Respectability in Victorian Hali-

fax," *Journal of Imperial and Commonwealth History* 20, no. 2 (May 1992): 169, nn180–2, 185, that the Davises were well-established members of the Black elite in Halifax. For information on the racial segregation of barbershops and the niche that Black barbers established in Canada, see *.

17 James Albert Davis managed the sizeable family real estate holdings of his own family and that of his wife until the Depression knocked the bottom out of the market. At that point, James Davis became the service manager of the Argyle Street Garage. He continued to cut hair for family and friends in his home throughout his life; Backhouse, "Interview with Wanda Robson"; Backhouse, "Interview with Mrs S.A. (Emily) Clyke." Viola Desmond's grandfather secured a position as a letter carrier when he retired from barbering. Viola's uncle (and godfather) John Davis also obtained employment in the Post Office Division in Halifax. On the rarity of Blacks achieving the status of civil service or Post Office employees, see correspondence from Beresford Augustus Husbands, president of the Colored Men's Conservative Social and Athletic Club, to the mayor of Halifax, 17 May 1937, protesting that "there is no representative of the colored race in any of the local civic departments," no. 42, vol. 7, RG35-102 (3B), PANS; W.P. Oliver, "Cultural Progress of the Negro in Nova Scotia," *Dalhousie Review* 29, no. 3 (1949): 297–8, reprinted in George Elliott Clarke, ed., *Fire on the Water: An Anthology of Black Nova Scotian Writing* (Lawrencetown Beach, NS: Pottersfield, 1991), 1:129–33.

18 Henry Johnson was born in Richmond, VA. Full information concerning his parents is not available, although Wanda Robson was able to provide the following details: "His father was a white plantation owner ... I can't tell you about his mother – I don't know. This is where the mixed race comes in. Henry Walter Johnson was maybe seven-eighths white – who is white, who is Black, I don't know. Henry was a Baptist minister in New Haven, Connecticut, and he also was at Cornwallis Street Baptist Church in Halifax for one year. While in New Haven, he worked as a businessman. He was a real estate entrepreneur who also sold antiques. He married Gwendolin's mother, Susan Smith, who was a white woman born in Connecticut. Henry bought property when living in Halifax. Gwendolin inherited those properties." See Backhouse, "Interview with Wanda Robson." For biographical details on Viola Desmond's parents, who married on 9 Mar. 1908, see Churches: Halifax: Trinity Anglican: Baptisms no. 735, 736, 844, PANS Micro.; Marriages: Halifax County: 1908: no. 92, 249, RG32; notes of the researcher who assisted with the compilation of material for this chapter, Allen B. Robertson, "Interview with Pearleen Oliver," Halifax, July 1993.

19 Canadians appear to have accepted that any known Black ancestry resulted in a racial classification as "Black." For one example, see *Gordon
v. Adamson* (1920), 18 O.W.N., 191 at 192 (Ont. High Ct.), in which Judge
Middleton describes the child of a "white" mother and a "negro" father as
"coloured." Judith Fingard notes in "Race and Respectability," 170, that
"regardless of skin colour," members of "the Afro-Nova Scotia community
were universally identified as 'coloured.'" W. Burton Hurd, "Racial Origins and Nativity of the Canadian People," *Census of Canada 1931* (Ottawa:
Supply and Services, 1942), 13:vii, notes that the instructions given to
Canadian enumerators for the 1931 census were as follows: "The children
begotten of marriages between white and black or yellow races will be
recorded as Negro, Chinese, Japanese, Indians, etc., as the case may be."
James W. St.G. Walker, *"Race," Rights and the Law in the Supreme Court of
Canada* (Waterloo: Osgoode Society and Wilfrid Laurier University Press,
1997), 18, notes that these instructions contradicted the provisions of the
Indian Act at the time: see discussion of *Re Eskimos* in chapter 2. On the
extensiveness of racial intermixing (some voluntary and some coercive)
and the accepted rules of racial designation in the United States, see *.

20 At the turn of the century, interracial marriages appear to have been on
the decline: Fingard, "Race and Respectability," 179. Ruth I. McKenzie,
"Race Prejudice and the Negro," *Dalhousie Review* 20 (1940): 201 notes that
"intermarriage [of Blacks] with whites is not approved." Wanda Robson
discusses Viola Desmond's racial identification in the following terms:
"Would Viola have defined herself as 'mixed race'? Of course. Would you
be wrong in describing her as Black? Not as far as I am concerned. I am of
the generation that was raised to be proud of being Black. Viola is clearly
Black. I know what I am, she is my sister." See Backhouse, "Interview
with Wanda Robson." On the experience of claiming mixed-race heritage
in Canada, see Carol Camper, ed., *Miscegenation Blues: Voices of Mixed
Race Women* (Toronto: Sister Vision, 1994). James and Gwendolin Davis
produced twelve children. See Churches: Halifax: Trinity Anglican: Baptisms no. 735, 736, 844, PANS Micro.; Robertson, "Interview with Pearleen
Oliver." Viola's obituary in the Halifax *Chronicle-Herald*, 10 Feb. 1965, 26,
lists nine surviving siblings. There were five sisters and one brother in
Montreal: Gordon Davis, Emily (Mrs S.A. Clyke), Eugenie (Mrs F.L. Par-
ris), Helen (Mrs B.W. Fline), Constance (Mrs W. Scott), and Olive (Mrs A.
Scott). There were two brothers and one sister in Halifax: John Davis, Alan
Davis, and Wanda (Mrs W. Neal). See also the obituary in Halifax *Mail
Star*, 10 Feb. 1965, 8.

21 During the Depression, Viola worked after school as a mother's helper in

order to make ends meet; notes of the researcher who assisted with the compilation of material for this chapter, Allen B. Robertson, "Interview with Jack Desmond," Halifax, 16 June 1993 and 23 June 1993; Backhouse, "Interview with Wanda Robson"; Backhouse, "Interview with Mrs S.A. (Emily) Clyke." For details on the large number of Black women who chose teaching, and the expansion of occupational opportunities in hair-dressing, see *.

22 Viola's sister, Wanda Robson, recalls that Viola Desmond lived at the "Y" and worked part-time as a cigarette girl at Small's Paradise nightclub in Harlem to make ends meet. Viola Desmond took great pains to conceal her Harlem employment from her mother, because she knew her parents would not have approved. While in New York, she also worked as an agent for musicians and obtained copyright for some lyrics for her clients. See notes of David Woods, who assisted with the compilation of material for this chapter, "Interview with Wanda Robson," North Sydney, Oct. 1995; Backhouse, "Interview with Mrs S.A. (Emily) Clyke"; Robertson, "Interview with Jack Desmond"; Brigdlal Pachai, *Beneath the Clouds of the Promised Land: The Survival of Nova Scotia's Blacks* (Halifax: Lancelot Press for Black Educators Association of Nova Scotia, 1991), 152–3, 297; Back-house, "Interview with Wanda Robson." For details on the specific servic-es that Black women sought from hairdressers and the spectacular career of Madame C.J. Walker, see *.

23 Jack's father, Norman Mansfield Desmond, was a hack driver for John Church's Livery Stable and a founding deacon of the New Glasgow Black Baptist Church. Jack Desmond's mother, Annie Williams, worked as a domestic servant. Both Jack's parents were born into farming families in Tracadie in Antigonish County: Robertson, "Interview with Jack Des-mond"; Pachai, *Beneath the Clouds*, 152–4, 297; New Glasgow *Clarion* 1, no. 1 (December 1946); *Halifax-Dartmouth City Directories* (Halifax: Might Directories Atlantic, 1938–46). On the emigration of Blacks to Nova Scotia, see *.

24 Jack Desmond's sister, Amelia, married a Black barber, Sydney Jones, who initially offered Jack the opportunity to take up barbering. Wanda Robson recalls that Jack Desmond's customers were approximately 80 per cent Black and 20 per cent other races. She also notes that he was "easy-going" and not nearly as hard-working as Viola. Jack Desmond worked from his shop on Gottingen Street continuously until his retirement. When he closed his barbershop, he sold the site to Frank Sobey, who ultimately sold the store to Foodland groceries. Jack Desmond continued to work for both of the new owners and to cut hair in people's homes for many years

after: "Jack's Got All the Answers: King of Gottingen," Halifax *Mail-Star*, Saturday insert in the *Leader*, 31 May 1986, 13; Backhouse, "Interview with Wanda Robson"; Pachai, *Beneath the Clouds*, 152–4; Robertson, "Interview with Jack Desmond." On the residence patterns of Black Haligonians and the importance of Gottingen Street to the Black community, see *.

25 The precise opening date for Vi's Studio of Beauty Culture is unclear, with various sources suggesting 1937, 1940, and 1941. See Backhouse, "Interview with Wanda Robson"; Backhouse, "Interview with Mrs S.A. (Emily) Clyke"; Tanya Hudson, "Interview with Clara Adams," Halifax, 24 July 1995; Tanya Hudson, "Interview with Barbara Bowen," Halifax, 26 July 1995; Woods, "Interview with Pearleen Oliver."

26 Robertson, "Interview with Pearleen Oliver"; Constance Backhouse, "Interview with Gwen Jenkins," London, March 1995; Hudson, "Interview with Clara Adams"; "Takes Action," New Glasgow *Clarion* 1, no. 1 (Dec. 1946); advertisements for her business in New Glasgow *Clarion* 2, no. 4 (28 Feb. 1947), and 11, no. 5 (15 Mar. 1947); "Beauty School Graduation," Truro *Clarion* 2, no. 9 (2 July 1947); Pachai, *Beneath the Clouds*, 153; Robertson, "Interview with Jack Desmond"; *Halifax-Dartmouth City Directories*, 1938–46; Elaine McCluskey, "Long-Established Minority Still Excluded from Power," Halifax *Chronicle-Herald*, 16 Mar. 1989, 41.

27 Backhouse, "Interview with Wanda Robson"; Robertson, "Interview with Pearleen Oliver." On the employment patterns of middle-class Black women and the resulting gender tensions, see *.

28 Graduates of the school included: Nora Dill, Rose Gannon, Rachel Kane, Verna Skinner, Joyce Lucas, Helen Davis, Bernadine Bishop, Bernadine Hampden, Evelyn Paris, Vivian Jackson, Ruth Jackson, Maddie Grosse, Gene States, Patricia Knight, Mildred Jackson, and Barbara Bowen. Students were required to pay tuition of forty dollars a month and to sign on for a minimum of six months' training. They were taught shampoo, press and curl, manicures, and hygiene: Backhouse, "Interview with Mrs S.A. (Emily) Clyke"; Hudson, "Interview with Barbara Bowen"; Hudson, "Interview with Clara Adams"; David Woods, "Interview with Rose Gannon-Dixon," Halifax, Aug. 1995.

29 For details regarding Viola Desmond's reputation in Nova Scotia, see "Takes Action," New Glasgow *Clarion* 1, no. 1 (Dec. 1946). On the restricted business opportunities available to Black Nova Scotians, and the predominantly middle-class status of Blacks who contested racial segregation in Canadian courts, see *. The issue of class designation is complex, especially when overlaid by race. Within the Black community, Viola Desmond would probably have been viewed as upper class. From the vantage point

of whites, a married woman who worked outside the home as a beautician would probably have been classified as working class. Class definitions, when examined through distinct racial perspectives, can become as slippery as race definitions themselves. On the complex racial dynamics associated with the promulgation of and resistance to white middle-class culture within the African-American community, see Evelyn Brooks Higginbotham, *Righteous Discontent: The Women's Movement in the Black Baptist Church, 1880–1920* (Cambridge, MA: Harvard University Press, 1993).

30 See, for example, "Takes Action," New Glasgow *Clarion* 1, no. 1 (Dec. 1946); Pachai, *Beneath the Clouds*, 152–5; McCluskey, "Long-Established Minority"; Robertson, "Interview with Pearleen Oliver"; Hudson, "Interview with Barbara Bowen"; Hudson, "Interview with Clara Adams"; Backhouse, "Interview with Wanda Robson." Although there were a number of cases brought by Black men earlier, and a few brought by Black couples (see further discussion in this chapter), Viola Desmond appears to have been the first Black woman in Canada to take legal action against racially segregated seating practices independently in her own right. This claim is based upon an appraisal of reported cases only. There may have been others whose cases were unreported, or whose cases do not reveal on the face of the documents that race was the issue. For details of similar challenges brought by Black women in the United States, see *.

31 Evelyn Brooks Higginbotham, "African-American Women's History and the Metalanguage of Race," *Signs* 17, no. 2 (Winter 1992): 254, 257, 261. For further analysis and references on the racialized configuration of gender, see *.

32 McCluskey, "Long-Established Minority"; Pachai, *Beneath the Clouds*, 154.

33 "Negress Alleges She Was Ejected from Theatre," Halifax *Chronicle*, 30 Nov. 1946, 2.

34 Hudson, "Interview with Pearleen Oliver"; Ken Alexander and Avis Glaze, *Towards Freedom: The African-Canadian Experience* (Toronto: Umbrella, 1996), 155. Prior to her marriage to Jack Desmond, Viola belonged to the racially mixed congregation of the Trinity Anglican Church. She switched affiliations to her husband's church upon marriage.

35 For biographical details on Pearleen (Borden) Oliver, whose own attempts to enter the nursing profession were barred because of race, see Doris McCubbin, "The Women of Halifax," *Chatelaine*, June 1954, 16; Colin A. Thomson, *Born with a Call: A Biography of Dr William Pearly Oliver, C.M.* (Dartmouth, NS: Black Cultural Centre, 1986); George Elliott Clarke, ed., *Fire on the Water* (Lawrencetown Beach, NS: Pottersfield, 1991), 1:171; reference by Frances Early in her review of "Rethinking Canada: The Promise

of Women's History," *Resources for Feminist Research* 21 (Spring 1992): 25,
to oral interviews of Pearleen Oliver, held by Saint Mary's University Library, Halifax; Alexander and Glaze, *Towards Freedom*, 155. For reference
to Pearleen Oliver's public-speaking campaign in the 1940s to publicize
cases of Black women refused admission to nursing schools, see Agnes
Calliste, "Women of 'Exceptional Merit': Immigration of Caribbean Nurses
to Canada," *Canadian Journal of Women and the Law* 6 (1993): 92. For reference to Pearleen Oliver's interest in discrimination against Black women,
see Clarke, *Fire on the Water*, 146, where he notes that Pearleen Oliver's *One
of His Heralds* (Halifax: Pearleen Oliver, n.d.) discusses the situation of Agnes Gertrude Waring (1884–1951), whose attempt to receive ordination to
preach at the Second Baptist Church in New Glasgow was refused by the
Maritime Baptist Convention because she was female. For reference to the
"Little Black Sambo" campaign, see correspondence from Beresford Augustus Husbands to the Mayor of Halifax, following Pearleen Oliver's address on 26 Jan. 1944, in PANS. Helen Campbell Bennerman's *Story of Little
Black Sambo*, first published in 1899, became a Canadian classic, according
to Robin Winks, "still selling well in its sixteenth printing in 1969": Winks,
Blacks in Canada, 295.

36 Born in 1912, Rev. Oliver grew up in a predominantly white community in
Wolfville, NS, and graduated from Acadia University with a BA in 1934,
and a Master's of Divinity in 1936. For biographical details on Rev. Oliver
(who would later become the chair of the Black United Front), see Thomson, *Born with a Call*; "Halifax Cleric Elected," Halifax *Chronicle-Herald*, 3
Sept. 1960, 13; Clarke, *Fire on the Water*, 1:171; Marjorie Major, "The Negroes in Nova Scotia," no. 42K, vol. 1767, Mg1, PANS; Oliver, "Cultural
Progress of the Negro," 134; W.P. Oliver, "Urban and Rural Life Committee of the African United Baptist Association of Nova Scotia," no. 42L, vol.
1767, Mg1, PANS; Winks, *Blacks in Canada*, 350–2; Robin Winks, "Negroes
in the Maritimes: An Introductory Survey," *Dalhousie Review* 48, no. 4
(1969): 469; Nancy Lubka, "Ferment in Nova Scotia," *Queen's Quarterly* 76,
no. 2 (1969): 213–28.

37 Viola Desmond sought medical treatment from a physician from the West
Indies who resided in the same building as her parents and maintained
an office on the corner of Gottingen and Gerrish Streets. Being Black, this
physician had no access to city hospitals and had to perform all procedures in his office: Robertson, "Interview with Pearleen Oliver." Wanda
Robson believes the doctor's name may have been F.B. Holder, a British
Guiana–born Black physician practising in Halifax at this time; Backhouse,
"Interview with Wanda Robson."

38 Pearleen Oliver sought support from a number of other Black organizations: the Halifax Coloured Citizens Improvement League, the president
of the Ladies' Auxiliary of the Cornwallis Street Baptist Church, and the
president of the Missionaries' Society. She was disappointed how few
people came to the meeting and discouraged by the reluctance many expressed to "make trouble": Hudson, "Interview with Pearleen Oliver";
Robertson, "Interview with Pearleen Oliver." For the mission statement of
the NSAACP, a list of its charter members, and information about predecessor organizations, see *.

39 "Negress Alleges She Was Ejected from Theatre," Halifax *Chronicle*, 30
Nov. 1946, 2. This position was supported by Mrs M.H. Spaulding, chair
of the emergency committee for civil rights of the Civil Liberties League,
whose views are quoted in "Ban All Jim Crow Rules Is Comment on N.S.
Charge," Toronto *Daily Star*, 30 Nov. 1946, 3: "'Jim Crow practices, such as
segregating Negroes or any other group in certain sections of theatres, or
in keeping them out of hotels, have no place in Canada and should be forbidden by law. There is no place for second-class citizenship in this country,' said Mrs Spaulding. She added there had been instances of the same
sort of racial discrimination in other parts of Canada. When Negroes tried
to buy a ticket at a theatre, they are told the only seats available were in
the balcony, she asserted. 'When Paul Robeson was in Toronto in *Othello*
at the Royal Alexandra he said he would not appear if there was any discrimination against colored people, and they were seated in all parts of the
house.'"

40 New Glasgow *Clarion* 1, no. 1 (Dec. 1946). For information on the *Clarion*
and other Black newspapers in Canada, see *.

41 "Editorial, Taking Inventory," New Glasgow *Clarion* 2, no. 4 (28 Feb. 1947):
2.

42 "Takes Action" and "Viola Desmond's Appeal," New Glasgow *Clarion*
1, no. 1 (Dec. 1946): 1; "Editorial: A New Year's Message," *Clarion* 2, no.
1 (Jan. 1947). The latter article notes that "one of New Glasgow's leading
business men" (race unspecified) donated ten dollars to the case, leading
the editor to applaud him for his "courage and generosity." Pearleen Oliver recalls that money came in from all over the province, in amounts both
large and small, with more white donors than Black: Robertson, "Interview with Pearleen Oliver." On the origins and meaning of the American
phrase *Jim Crow*, see *.

43 Carrie Best Interview, Collection Ar2265–2268 and 2279, CBC Radio, SMI
Division, PANS. Dr Carrie M. Best, whose birth name was Carrie Prevoe,
was born in New Glasgow in 1903 and completed high school in New

Glasgow. She married Albert Theophilus Best, a Barbadian-born Black porter for the Canadian National Railway, and had one son, J. Calbert Best. Carrie Best was an editor and publisher of several Black newspapers, founding the *Clarion* in 1946 and publishing the nationally circulated *Negro Citizen* in 1949. In 1956, she began to write columns in the Pictou *Advocate* on matters of human rights and produced and narrated radio shows for five stations for twelve years. In 1970, she was awarded the Lloyd McInnes Memorial Award for her contribution to social betterment. She received the Order of Canada in 1974 and an honorary degree from St Francis Xavier University in 1975. Her son, Calbert Best, became national president of the Civil Service Association of Canada in Ottawa in 1960 and an assistant deputy minister for Manpower and Immigration in 1970. See Dr Carrie M. Best, *That Lonesome Road: The Autobiography of Carrie M. Best* (New Glasgow, NS: Clarion Publishing, 1977); Clarke, *Fire on the Water*, 1:171; Winks, *Blacks in Canada*, 405, 408; "Albert Best Dies Sunday," New Glasgow *Evening News*, 5 Aug. 1971; "The Gracious Activist," *Novascotian*, 10 Apr. 1982, cover story and 3–4; "Nova Scotia's Best, Buckler Honored," Halifax *Chronicle-Herald*, 21 Dec. 1974; "St FX Confers Honorary Degrees on Two N.S. Women, N.B. Lawyer," New Glasgow *Evening News*, 12 May 1975; "Three Honorary Doctorates to Be Awarded at Convocation," New Glasgow *Evening News*, 24 Apr. 1975, 9; "Two to Receive Decorations in Order of Canada Tonight," New Glasgow *Evening News*, 16 Apr. 1980; "J.C. Best Accepts New Post," Halifax *Chronicle-Herald*, 19 Jan. 1966; "Cal Best Reelected Civil Servants' Chief," Halifax *Chronicle-Herald*, 1 Oct. 1960.

44 On 18 Feb. 1942, Carrie Best issued a writ of summons against Norman W. Mason and the Roseland Theatre Co. Ltd for ejecting her and her son, Calbert, from the theatre on 29 Dec. 1941. The event was a deliberate, planned attack on the policy of racial segregation that the theatre began to impose in the 1940s, apparently at the request of some white patrons. Carrie Best wrote to Mason, the white owner of the theatre, challenging him on the policy and advising that she and her son intended to sit on the main floor on 29 Dec. 1941. When she tried to do so that afternoon, she was asked to leave by the white assistant manager, Erskine Cumming, white police officer George S. Wright, and white police chief Elmo Langille. When she refused to leave, Officer Wright placed his hands under Mrs Best's arms and raised her from her seat. She apparently announced, "That's all I wanted you to do, put your hands on me. I will fix you for this." Then she and her son left the theatre. Carrie Best retained James Hinnigar Power, a white New Glasgow lawyer, and commenced litigation, claiming assault and battery and breach of contract. She sought $4 in repairs to her coat, $5,000

in general damages for the assault and battery, and $500 general damages for the wrongful revocation of the licence given to her to witness the performance. Trial was held on 12 May 1942, in the Pictou Court House, before Robert Henry Graham of the Supreme Court of Nova Scotia, the same judge who would later hear Viola Desmond's case. The white judge charged the all-white jury to answer the following questions, to which they responded:

1. Did the Defendant Company's ticket seller sell any tickets to the Plaintiff? No.
2. Did the Defendant ticket seller sell her a downstairs ticket? No.
3. Did the Plaintiff know the Defendant Company would not sell her a downstairs ticket? Yes.
4. Had the Plaintiff any reasonable grounds for thinking the ticket seller sold her a downstairs ticket? No.
5. Did the Plaintiff do as she did because she knew Defendant Company's ticket seller would not sell her a downstairs ticket? Yes.
6. Was any more force used to remove the plaintiff than was necessary? No.
7. What damage, if any, did the Plaintiff sustain? None.

Upon the return of these findings, Judge Graham dismissed Carrie Best's action and charged her with the defendant's bill of costs, which amounted to $156.07. See *Best v. Mason and Roseland Theatre*, file A4013 (1942), RG39 "C" (PI) 1986550/099, PANS; "Case Dismissed against Mason and Roseland Theatre," New Glasgow *Evening News*, 15 May 1942; "Case Dismissed," New Glasgow *Eastern Chronicle*, 19 May 1942; "Two Sentences Are Imposed in Supreme Court," Pictou *Advocate*, 21 May 1942; "Jury Dismisses Suit for Damages," Halifax *Herald*, 15 May 1942; "Colored Woman's Action Dismissed," Halifax *Chronicle*, 15 May 1942. For a fuller account, see Constance Backhouse, "'I Was Unable to Identify with Topsy': Carrie M. Best's Struggle against Racial Segregation in Nova Scotia, 1942," *Atlantis* 22, no. 2 (Spring 1998): 16–26. I am indebted to Barry Cahill for bringing the archival file to my attention.

45 Best, *That Lonesome Road*, 43–4. The Norfolk House, where Carrie's brother worked, had a history of refusing to support the practices of racial discrimination so common in the area. The Halifax *Eastern Chronicle*, 28 May 1885, noted that Mr H. Murray, a white man, refused to close his Norfolk hotel to the Fisk Jubilee Singers, a Black choir group. Members of the choir had earlier been refused admission to hotels in Pictou and Halifax.

46 Truro, which would earn itself the designation "the Alabama of Canada"
and "Little Mississippi," also maintained a "Whites Only" waiting room in
the railway station: Lubka, "Ferment in Nova Scotia," 215; Winks, *Blacks in
Canada*, 319–25, 420; Winks, "Negroes in the Maritimes," 466–7; Thomson,
Born with a Call, 467. On the activities of the KKK, see discussion of *R. v.
Phillips* in chapter 6 of Constance Backhouse, *Colour-Coded: A Legal History of Racism in Canada, 1900–1950* (Toronto: University of Toronto Press,
1999).

47 Although similar legislation was not passed in provinces other than Ontario and Nova Scotia, New Brunswick's legislature enacted two statutes
giving explicit recognition to the existence of Black schools. For details
of the 1842 and 1843 New Brunswick provisions, and information about
more informal segregation methods used in other provinces, see *. For a
comparison with the segregated schooling offered First Nations children,
see discussion of *R. v. Wanduta* in chapter 3.

48 For legislative details of the 1849, 1850, 1859, and 1886 provisions, see *.

49 Winks, *Blacks in Canada*, 365–76; Robin W. Winks, "Negro School Segregation in Ontario and Nova Scotia," *Canadian Historical Review* 50, no. 2
(1969): 174, 176; Jason H. Silverman and Donna J. Gillie, "The Pursuit of
Knowledge under Difficulties: Education and the Fugitive Slave in Canada," *Ontario History* 74 (1982): 95; Claudette Knight, "Black Parents Speak:
Education in Mid-Nineteenth-Century Canada West," *Ontario History* 89
(1997): 269. For some discussion of the resistance offered by Blacks to these
practices, see Peggy Bristow, "'Whatever you raise in the ground you can
sell it in Chatham': Black Women in Buxton and Chatham, 1850–65," in
*"We're Rooted Here and They Can't Pull Us Up": Essays in African-Canadian
Women's History*, ed. Peggy Bristow Dionne Brand, Linda Carty, Afua P.
Cooper, Sylvia Hamilton, and Adrienne Shadd (Toronto: University of
Toronto Press, 1994), 114–16; Afua P. Cooper, "Black Women and Work in
Nineteenth-Century Canada West: Black Woman Teacher Mary Bibb," in
Bristow et al., *We're Rooted Here*, 148–68.

50 *Washington v. The Trustees of Charlotteville* (1854), 11 U.C.Q.B. 569 (Ont.
Q.B.), held that school authorities could not exclude Black children unless
alternative facilities for "colored pupils" had been established, but *In re
Dennis Hill v. Schools Trustees of Camden and Zone* (1854), 11 U.C.Q.B. 573
(Ont. Q.B.), ruled that Black children could be forced to attend separate
schools located miles away from their homes and outside of their school
sections. *An Act to Amend the Act respecting Common Schools in Upper Canada*, S.O. 1868-69, c. 44, s. 9, provides "that no person shall be deemed a supporter of any separate school for coloured people, unless he resides within

three miles in a direct line of the site of the school house for such separate school; and any coloured child residing farther than three miles in a direct line from the said school house shall be allowed to attend the common school of the section within the limits of which the said child shall reside." These provisions are continued by *An Act respecting Separate Schools*, R.S.O. 1877, c. 206, s. 2–5; *The Separate Schools Act*, R.S.O. 1897, c. 294. After the amendment, several cases acknowledged that race should not be the sole ground for exclusion from common schools, but then accepted the testimony of school authorities regarding overcrowding and "insufficient accommodation," using this to defeat the claims of Black parents to register their children in non-segregated schools: see *In re Hutchison and School Trustees of St Catharines* (1871), 31 U.C.Q.B. 274 (Ont. Q.B.); *Dunn v. Board of Education of Windsor* (1884), 6 O.R. 125 (Ontario Chancery Division). For two examples of cases where the efforts of education officials to bar Black children from common public schools were challenged successfully, see *Simmons and the Corporation of Chatham* (1861), 21 U.C.Q.B. 75 (Ont. Q.B.), quashing for uncertainty a by-law that purported to enlarge substantially the geographic catchment area of a separate school, and *Stewart and Schools Trustees of Sandwich* (1864), 23 U.C.Q.B. 634 (Ont. Q.B.), which accepted evidence that the separate school operated only intermittently as a reason to overrule the common school's refusal to register a Black female student. See also Winks, *Blacks in Canada*; Winks, "Negro School Segregation," 175–82; Knight, "Black Parents Speak."

51 Winks, *Blacks in Canada*; Winks, "Negro School Segregation,"182, 190.

52 For legislative details of the specific provisions relating to "coloured people" between 1887 and 1964, see *.

53 Winks, "Negro School Segregation," 177.

54 For legislative details of the 1865 and 1873 provisions, see *.

55 For legislative details of the 1884 provision, see *.

56 For legislative details of the provisions in force between 1900 and 1950, see *.

57 In Lower Sackville, Mrs Pleasah Lavinia Caldwell, a Black Nova Scotian, responded by opening a "kitchen school" in her home, which educated Blacks in the area until her death in 1950: Helen Champion, "School in a Kitchen," unlabelled clipping dated 9 Nov. 1949, no. 42a, vol. 1767, Mg1, PANS. In 1964, four such districts continued: Beechville, Hammond Plains, Lucasville, and Cherry Brook, all in Halifax County: Winks, *Blacks in Canada*, 376–80. For details of the lack of funding and difficulties recruiting teachers and obtaining equipment, premises, and transportation in Nova Scotia, see Winks, "Negro School Segregation," 186–91.

58 Winks, *Blacks in Canada*, comments on the "formlessness of the racial barrier" (325), noting, "In the United States the Negro was somewhat more
sure – sure of where he could and could not go, of when to be meek and
when to be strong. In Canada he was uncertain" (326).

59 Oliver, "Cultural Progress of the Negro," 129–35, notes that most Black
males could not find work except in the heaviest and most poorly paid
jobs: agriculture, mining, lumbering, steel, railway, and shipping industries. In most cases, they were also barred from membership in unions.
Business ventures were limited to barbershops, beauty parlours, taxi
businesses, trucking, shoemaking, a newspaper, and one co-operative
store. See also James W. St.G. Walker, *Racial Discrimination in Canada:
The Black Experience* (Ottawa: Canadian Historical Association, 1985), 15,
where he notes that, during the interwar years, Black men were concentrated in the following jobs: waiters, janitors, barbers, and labourers. The
elite among the men worked as railway waiters and porters: see Stanley
G. Grizzle, *My Name's Not George: The Story of the Brotherhood of Sleeping
Car Porters in Canada* (Toronto: Umbrella, 1998); Judith Fingard, "From
Sea to Rail: Black Transportation Workers and Their Families in Halifax,
c. 1870–1916," *Acadiensis* 24, no. 2 (Spring 1995): 49–64; Agnes Calliste,
"The Struggle for Employment Equity by Blacks on American and Canadian Railroads," *Journal of Black Studies* 25, no. 3 (Jan. 1995): 297–317;
Calliste, "Blacks on Canadian Railways," *Canadian Ethnic Studies* 20, no.
2 (1988): 36–52; Calliste, "Sleeping Car Porters in Canada: An Ethnically Submerged Split Labour Market," *Canadian Ethnic Studies* 19, no. 1
(1987): 1–20. Prior to the Second World War, Black females were limited
to teaching school or domestic work. On the pervasive restriction to domestic work, Suzanne Morton, "Separate Spheres in a Separate World:
African–Nova Scotian Women in late-19th Century Halifax County," *Acadiensis* 22, no. 2 (Spring 1993): 67,notes, "African–Nova Scotian women
had virtually no legal wage-earning opportunities outside domestic
service, taking in laundry, or sewing. Regardless of the status in the community, property holdings or occupation of the husband, married women
and widows charred, and young women were servants." Dorothy W.
Williams, *Blacks in Montreal, 1628–1986: An Urban Demography* (Cowansville, QC: Yvon Blais, 1989), 45, notes that the superintendent of nurses
of the Montreal General Hospital admitted in the 1930s that Black nurses
could not find employment in Montreal, "since there were not enough
Black patients to care for in the hospitals (and White patients would not
allow Black nurses to touch them)." See also "Girl Barred by Color from
Nurses Training Course," New Glasgow *Clarion* 2, no. 15 (6 Oct. 1947):

1, recounting race barriers against Black women throughout Ontario. The nursing field opened to women in Nova Scotia in 1949, when two Blacks graduated as registered nurses. See also Dionne Brand, *No Burden to Carry: Narratives of Black Working Women in Ontario, 1920s to 1950s* (Toronto: Women's Press, 1991), 155, 184, 207. Williams notes (45) that Blacks were barred from doing medical internships in Montreal between 1930 and 1947. The Faculty of Medicine at McGill University arranged instead for Blacks to serve their internships with Howard University in Washington, DC. Donald H. Clairmont and Dennis W. Magill, "Nova Scotia Blacks: Marginality in a Depressed Region," in *Canada: A Sociological Profile*, ed. W.E. Mann (Toronto: Copp Clark, 1971), 179, 183, quote P.E. MacKerrow, *A Brief History of the Colored Baptists of Nova Scotia* (Halifax, 1895): "The United Sates with her faults, which are many, has done much for the elevation of the coloured race. Sad and sorry are we to say that is more than we can boast of here in Nova Scotia. Our young men as soon as they receive a common school education must flee away to the United States and seek employment. Very few ever receive a trade from the large employers, even in the factories, on account of race prejudices." Rev. Adam S. Green, MS, "The Future of the Canadian Negro" (1904), no. 11, vol. 144, V/F, PANS, at 17, notes, "How many negroes do you find as clerks, book-keepers, or stenographers within the provinces? I know of but *one* ... Our people are excluded from such lucrative positions, not so much from disqualification, as from race-prejudice."

60 On the history of residential segregation by race across Canada, see *.

61 Although there was no legislation explicitly barring Blacks from jury service, some legal officials took steps to eliminate their names in the empanelling of jury lists. Winks, *Blacks in Canada*, 251, 284–6, notes that a challenge to Black jurors and jury foremen in Toronto in 1851 was unsuccessful, but that Blacks were excluded from jury service in Victoria between 1864 and 1872. James W. St.G. Walker, *The Black Identity in Nova Scotia: Community and Institutions in Historical Perspective* (Halifax: Black Cultural Centre for Nova Scotia, 1985), 8, notes that Blacks "could not serve on juries or claim a jury trial." See also James M. Pilton, "Negro Settlement in British Columbia" (MA thesis, University of Victoria, 1951); "Colored Men as Jurors," Victoria *Colonist*, 7 May 1872, 3; "Colored Jurors," Victoria *Colonist*, 21 Mar. 1872, 3; 27 Nov. 1872, 3; "Have Them Right," New Westminster *Times*, 18 Feb. 1860.

62 On the history of military segregation, see *.

63 For a case documenting the resistance of a Black man to racial segregation on a Chatham steamer in the 1850s, see *.

64 Winks, "Negroes in the Maritimes," 466; Winks, *Blacks in Canada*, 286, 325;
    Daniel G. Hill, *The Freedom-Seekers: Blacks in Early Canada* (Agincourt, ON:
    Book Society of Canada, 1981), 104.
65 On the racial segregation of orphans and paupers in Nova Scotia, see *.
66 On the denial of hospital services to Blacks in Halifax and Edmonton,
    see *.
67 On segregated cemeteries, see *.
68 Winks, *Blacks in Canada*, 248, 283–4, 286, 325, notes that hotels in Hamil-
    ton, Windsor, Chatham, and London refused admission to Blacks in the
    mid-nineteenth century. In the 1860s in Victoria, the chief theatre refused
    Blacks access to the dress circle or to orchestra seats, the Bank Exchange
    Saloon refused service to Blacks, and they were also excluded from Queen
    Victoria's birthday ball and from the farewell banquet for Governor James
    Douglas. The colour line remained visible in British Columbia in restau-
    rants and places of entertainment prior to the First World War. Blacks
    were not admitted to the boy scout troops or the YMCA in Windsor, and
    Black musicians had to establish their own orchestra in Owen Sound.
    Winks, *Blacks in Canada*, 325–6, 388, 420, 457 notes, "In 1924 the Edmonton
    City Commissioner barred Negroes from all public parks and swimming
    pools – and was overruled by the city council; in Colchester, Ontario, in
    1930, police patrolled the parks and beaches to keep blacks from using
    them. In Saint John all restaurants and theatres closed their doors to Ne-
    groes in 1915; two years later the chief theatres of Hamilton also did so …
    In 1929, when the World Baptist Conference was held in Toronto, Negro
    delegates were denied hotel rooms … Only one hotel in Montreal could be
    depended upon not to turn Negroes away in 1941 … Many dance pavil-
    ions, skating rinks and restaurants made it clear that they did not welcome
    blacks; and several pubs in Saskatchewan and British Columbia insisted
    that Negroes sit in corners reserved for them." Even into the 1960s, Black
    residents were virtually barred from community restaurants, and Windsor
    barkeepers designated separate "jungle rooms" for Blacks until 1951. See
    also "Hotels Refuse to Take Negroes," Vancouver *Province*, 13 Aug. 1945,
    2, recounting how Black members of the cast of *Carmen Jones* were denied
    hotel accommodation in Vancouver; and "Color Bar Said Drawn in Local
    Pub," Vancouver *Sun*, 30 July 1948, 1. Howard Lawrence, New Glasgow
    Clarion 2, no. 2 (Dec. 1946), urged the Black community to establish a com-
    munity centre because "every place is closed to us." Anna-Maria Galante,
    "Ex-Mayor Lewis Broke New Ground," *Afro-Nova Scotian Portraits* (Hali-
    fax: Chronicle-Herald and Mail-Star, 19 Feb. 1993), 7, quotes Daurene
    Lewis stating that the dances in Annapolis Royal were always segregated

(ca. 1940s and 1950s) and attempts were made to segregate the movie house as well. McKenzie, "Race Prejudice and the Negro," 201, notes that "[Negroes] are not always served in the best restaurants, nor admitted to high-class hotels. They are restricted, in cities, to the poorer residential districts, and are not accepted socially." See also Daniel G. Hill, "Black History in Early Ontario," *Canadian Human Rights Yearbook* (Ottawa: Human Rights Research and Education Centre, University of Ottawa, 1984–5), 265; Grizzle, *My Name's Not George*, 54–5; Winks, "Negroes in the Maritimes," 467; Winks, "Negro School Segregation," 189; Allen P. Stouffer, *The Light of Nature and the Law of God: Antislavery in Ontario, 1833–1877* (Montreal and Kingston: McGill-Queen's University Press, 1992), 200–1; Brand, *No Burden to Carry*, 134, 149–50, 153, 210–11, 278. For reference to comparable treatment of First Nations peoples, see George Manuel and Michael Poslums, *The Fourth World: An Indian Reality* (Don Mills, ON: Collier-Macmillan Canada, 1974), 101.

69 For legislative details regarding the 1947 and 1949 Saskatchewan provisions, and similar legislation enacted in Ontario in 1951 and 1954 on the heels of a concerted lobby campaign, see *.

70 On the admission of Black lawyers (including James Robinson Johnston, Joseph Eaglan Griffith, Frederick Allan Hamilton, and George W.R. Davis) to the bar of Nova Scotia, to the bar of British Columbia (Joshua Howard), and to the bar of New Brunswick (Abraham Beverly Walker), see *. For details concerning Ontario, see chapter 6, Backhouse, *Colour-Coded*.

71 Barry Cahill, "The 'Colored Barrister': The Short Life and Tragic Death of James Robinson Johnston, 1876–1915," *Dalhousie Law Journal* 15 (1992): 373, notes that Goffe was admitted to Gray's Inn in 1905 and called to the bar by Gray's Inn in 1908. He practised at the English bar for six years and "was employed in various government departments" during and after the First World War. He died in 1962 in his ninetieth year.

72 For biographical details on F.W. Bissett, the son of Frederick W. Bissett and Ethel Gray (Smith) Bissett, see "Bissett, Frederick William, B.A., LL.B.," *Maritime Reference Book: Biographical and Pictorial Record of Prominent Men and Women of the Maritime Provinces* (Halifax: Royal Print, 1931), 34; "Bench Vacancy Filled," Halifax *Chronicle-Herald*, 11 Mar. 1961; "Mr Justice F.W. Bissett," Halifax *Mail-Star*, 11 Nov. 1978, 6; "Mr Justice Bissett, 76, Dies in Halifax," Halifax *Mail-Star*, 10 Nov. 1978, 1–2; "Tributes Paid to Mr Justice F.W. Bissett," Halifax *Mail-Star*, 11 Nov. 1978, 1–2. Apart from Rev. Oliver's recommendation, it remains unclear why Viola Desmond selected F.W. Bissett. She seems to have been familiar with at least some other white members of the legal profession. Earlier, in November 1946, she

retained Samuel B. Goodman, a white lawyer from Halifax, to issue a writ against Philip Kane, the white car dealer who sold her the 1940 Dodge, for overcharging her in violation of the Wartime Prices and Trade Board Order. See *Viola Desmond v. Philip Kane*, no. S.C. 13304, vol. 936, RG39 "C" Halifax, PANS.

73 *Johnson v. Sparrow* (1899), 15 Que. S.C. 104 (Quebec Superior Court), at 108. For details of Judge Archibald's decision, see *. When the case went on appeal to the Quebec Court of Queen's Bench, Judge Bossé refused to equate a hotel and a theatre under the common-law rule, but upheld the $50 damage award based on the breach of contract. The court did not overturn Judge Archibald's explicit racial analysis but stated that it was unnecessary to decide the question of whether Blacks were entitled to the same rights of admission as whites in this case; *Johnson v. Sparrow* (1899), 8 Que. Q.B. 379. Walker, *"Race," Rights and the Law*, 146, suggests that "in dismissing Justice Archibald's reasoning the appeal decision undermined any general application of the non-discriminatory principle." With respect, this is arguably an over-reading of the appeal decision. Judge Bossé adverts to the legislation in the United States endorsing racial segregation, explicitly questions whether these enactments might be unconstitutional as violating the principle of equality, notes that similar legislation has not been enacted in Canada, and then concludes that the present dispute, which can be resolved on a purely contractual basis, does not require any further rulings on racial discrimination. This does not appear to be an overt rejection of Judge Archibald's analysis on racial equality, but a reluctance to rule on the matter in the present case. For further discussion of the common-law duty to serve, and another Ontario case that followed *Johnson v. Sparrow*, see *. Several earlier cases premised on an innkeeper's duty to serve the public were brought by Jacob Francis, an English-born Black saloon-keeper in Victoria. In the spring of 1860, Francis was refused service of two bottles of champagne in a billiard saloon at Yates and Government Streets. On 20 Apr. 1860, a civil jury heard his claim for forty shillings in damages in *Francis v. Miletich*, Rule and Order Book, 1859–61, 63, 69, Supreme Court of Civil Justice, Vancouver Island, C/AA/30.3D/2, Archives of British Columbia (ABC); Supreme Court of Civil Justice, 118–19, 123, Vancouver Island, C/AA/30.3P/5; Charge Books, Vancouver Island, GR848; "Refusing a Drink to a Coloured Man," Victoria *Gazette*, 21 Apr. 1860, 3. The jury held that Miletich was an innkeeper, that Francis was refused liquor but not received as a guest, and that Francis sustained no injury and was not entitled to damages. In 1862, Jacob Francis was refused service at the Bank Exchange Saloon in Victoria and again sought legal relief. According to

newspaper accounts, a white Victoria police magistrate, Augustus F. Pemberton, ruled that saloons that refused service to Black men would either not get a licence or would be fined and their licence not renewed when it expired. According to the charge book, the case was dismissed by Magistrate Pemberton on 4 July 1862. See *Jacob Francis v. Joseph Lovett*, vol. 3, Charge Books, GR848, ABC; "Wouldn't Let Him Drink," Victoria *Colonist*, 26 June 1862, 3; "Shall a Black Man Drink at a White Man's Bar?," Victoria *Colonist*, 28 June 1862, 3; "The Vexed Question Settled," Victoria *Colonist*, 5 July 1862, 3; "Shall a Colored Man Drink at a White Man's Bar?" Victoria *British Colonist*, 5 July 1862, 3. For more details on Francis, who was earlier denied the right to take up an elected seat in the colonial Legislative Assembly because of his race, see Pilton, "Negro Settlement in British Columbia"; S. Stott, "Blacks in B.C.," NW/016.325711/B631, ABC. For a similar case in 1913, see *Moses Rowden v. J.B. Stevens, Prop., Stratford Hotel*, British Columbia County Court (Vancouver) Plaint and Procedure Books, 1886–1946 [B7314–B7376], GR1651, ABC; Indexes to Plaint and Procedure Books, 1886–1946 [B7897–B7901], British Columbia County Court (Vancouver), GR1651; Judgments 1893–1940 [B2611–B2643], British Columbia County Court (Vancouver), GR1418; "Negro Sues Because Color Line Is Drawn," Vancouver *Province*, 4 Oct. 1913, 15; "Hotel Bar Refused to Serve Negro," Vancouver *Province*, 10 July 1913, 17; "Enters Suit for Damages for Being Refused Drink," Vancouver *Sun*, 1 Oct. 1913, 1. Rowden sought relief before the city's licence commissioners, who refused to intervene. He then claimed $500 damages on the basis that Stevens failed to meet his common-law obligation as an innkeeper to serve travellers. The outcome of the case is unclear from the surviving documentation.

74 *Barnswell v. National Amusement Company, Limited* (1914), 21 B.C.R. 435, [1915] 31 W.L.R. 542 (B.C.C.A.). See also "Suit against Theatre," Victoria *Times*, 30 May 1914, 18; "Damages Are Awarded," Victoria *Times*, 10 Dec. 1914, 16; "Legal Intelligence," Victoria *Daily Colonist*, 10 Dec. 1914, 3. For further details, see *.

75 "Colored Patrons Must Pay Double," Regina *Leader*, 9 Oct. 1911, 7, announces, "One of the city's restaurants has decided to draw the colored line and in future all colored patrons will pay just double what their white brothers are charged. This, of course, is not a money-making venture, but is a polite hint to these people that their patronage is not wanted. It is understood that the change is made at the urgent request of some of the most influential patrons, and not on the initiative of the management. It is an innovation in the running of hotels, cafes and restaurants of the city and the experiment will be watched with interest." The exact basis for the

ruling, which is not reported in the published legal reports, is somewhat difficult to reconstruct from the press account in "May Charge Double Price," Regina *Leader*, 16 Oct. 1911, 7. The newspaper specifies that the case was "a charge of obtaining money under false pretences" laid against W.B. Waddell by William Hawes. There was some factual dispute over whether Hawes had been notified of the double charge prior to ordering, with Hawes claiming he had not, and Waddell claiming he had. White magistrates Lawson and Long concluded that Hawes had and held that therefore there was no case of false pretences. The press seems to have been less convinced, claiming that the case stood for the proposition that "a restaurant keeper has the right to exclude colored patrons by charging double prices without, however, taking proper steps to make the charge known to those whom he proposes to exclude." The press report also hints that the claim may have been rooted in breach of contract, recounting that the plaintiff tried to show that Hawes "had no knowledge of [the double price] arrangement when he gave his order, and that the bill of fare from which he ordered constituted a contract." The contract issues appear to have been ignored by the court. Counsel for Hawes, Mr Barr, sought leave to appeal, but this was denied. For another example of a case where Blacks were charged extra, see *R. v. J.D. Carroll*, file 21/1860, box 1, B.C. Attorney General Documents, GR419, ABC; and "Police Court," Victoria *Colonist*, 14 Jan. 1860, 3, where William Bastion, a Black man, charged J.D. Carroll, a white innkeeper, with extortion after he charged him $1.50 for three drinks he had already consumed on 10 Jan. 1860. Charles Jackson and Arthur Wiggins, white men who were with Bastion at the time, testified that they had never been charged more than 12 1/2 cents per drink. Carroll was committed for trial by Magistrate Augustus Pemberton in Victoria Police Court on 12–13 Jan. 1860, but the outcome of the case is not clear from the surviving records. The Victoria *Colonist*, 19 Jan. 1860, suggests that the case was dismissed because Carroll was a spirit dealer and not an innkeeper; see Diba B. Majzub, "'A God Sent Land for the Colored People'? The Legal Treatment of Blacks in Victoria, 1858–1865," unpublished manuscript, 23.

76 *Loew's Montreal Theatres Ltd. v. Reynolds* (1919), 30 Que. K.B. 459 (Quebec King's Bench) per John-Edward Martin, J., at 466; Winks, "Negroes in the Maritimes," 467; "Court Says Color Line Is Illegal; All Equal in Law," Montreal *Gazette*, 5 Mar. 1919, 4. For details of the case, and a 1912 case in Edmonton that reached a more informal but similar resolution, see *.

77 *Franklin v. Evans* (1924), 55 O.L.R. 349, 26 O.W.N. 65 (Ont. High Court). See also "Dismisses Suit of Colored Man," London *Evening Free Press*, 15 Mar. 1924, which gives the name as W.K. Franklin. Strangely, neither *Johnson v.*

Sparrow nor *Barnswell* was cited in the legal decision, and Judge Haughton Lennox concluded that there were no authorities or decided cases in support of the plaintiff's contention. Most of the decision centred on common-law rules requiring hotel-keepers to supply "accommodation of a certain character, within certain limits, and subject to recognized qualifications, to all who apply." Contrasting restaurants with innkeepers, Lennox held that the common-law obligations did not apply to the defendant. The white judge did, however, seem to have been ambivalent about the result he reached in this case. Disparaging the conduct of the white restaurant owner and his wife, whose attitude towards the plaintiff Lennox described as "unnecessarily harsh, humiliating, and offensive," Lennox contrasted their situation with that of the plaintiff: "The plaintiff is undoubtedly a thoroughly respectable man, of good address, and, I have no doubt, a good citizen, and I could not but be touched by the pathetic eloquence of his appeal for recognition as a human being, of common origin with ourselves." Lennox then expressly ducked the issue: "The theoretical consideration of this matter is a difficult and decidedly two-sided problem, extremely controversial, and entirely outside my sphere in the administration of law – law as it is." Lennox dismissed the action without costs. Curiously, the account in the local Black newspaper, *Dawn of Tomorrow*, suggests that the plaintiff won: "W.V. Franklin Given Damages," London *Dawn of Tomorrow*, 2 Feb. 1924, 1; "Mr W.V. Franklin's Victory," London *Dawn of Tomorrow*, 16 Feb. 1924, 2. This coverage appears erroneous in asserting that "the jury took only 20 minutes to decide that Mr Franklin should be awarded damages," since the law report notes that there was no jury and that the claim was dismissed. However, the Black press, unlike the white press, did recount the plaintiff's testimony in valuable detail: "When Mr Franklin was called to the witness box for the defence counsel [and asked], 'Have you any ground for damages?' Mr Franklin's eloquent and polished reply was: 'Not in dollars and cents, but in humiliation and inhuman treatment at the hands of this fellow man, yes. Because I am a dark man, a condition over which I have no control, I did not receive the treatment I was entitled to as a human being. God chose to bring me into the world a colored man, and on this account, defendant placed me on a lower level than he is'" (London *Dawn of Tomorrow*, 2 Feb. 1924, 1). Reference was also made in the Black press, on 16 Feb. 1924, to the views of the Black community on the necessity of bringing the case: "In a recent article in our paper we stated that the colored people of London stood solidly behind Mr Franklin. On the whole we did stand behind him but a few there were who doubted the wisdom of his procedure, believing, as they expressed it, that his case

would cause ill feeling between the races ... [N]othing in respect is ever
gained by cringing or by showing that we believe ourselves to be less than
men. Nothing will ever be gained by submitting to treatment which is less
than that due to any British subject" (London *Dawn of Tomorrow*, 16 Feb.
1924, 2). The financial cost of bringing such an action was acknowledged
by the *Dawn of Tomorrow*, which made an express appeal to readers to contribute money to assist Mr Franklin in defraying the costs of the case, since
"the monetary damages awarded him by the courts is far below the actual
cost to him."

78 *Rogers v. Clarence Hotel et al.,* [1940] 2 W.W.R. 545, (1940), 55 B.C.R. 214
    (B.C.C.A.).
79 *Christie and Another v. York Corporation* (1937), 75 Que. C.S. 136 (Que. Supe-
    rior Court); rev'd *York Corporation v. Christie* (1938), 65 Que. B.R. 104 (Que.
    K.B.); leave to appeal granted *Fred. Christie v. The York Corporation,* [1939]
    80 S.C.R. 50 (S.C.C.); upheld *Fred Christie v. The York Corporation,* [1940] 81
    S.C.R. 139 (S.C.C.). For a more detailed account of this case, see *.
80 *Loew's Montreal Theatres Ltd. v. Reynolds* (1919), 30 Que. K.B. 459 (Quebec
    King's Bench), at 462–3.
81 *Rogers v. Clarence Hotel et al.,* [1940] 2 W.W.R. 545, (1940), 55 B.C.R. 214
    (B.C.C.A.); 257, vol. 39, Judgments, 1893–1947 [B6321], British Columbia
    Supreme Court (Vancouver), GR1570, ABC; 319–25, vol. 368, British Co-
    lumbia Bench Books, GR1727; "Court Rules Beer Parlor Must Serve Col-
    ored Patron," Vancouver *Province,* 23 Feb. 1940, 11; "Owner's Right: May
    Refuse to Serve Beer," Vancouver *Province,* 22 Feb. 1940, 2; "Negro Suing
    Proprietor of Beer Parlor," Vancouver *Sun,* 22 Feb. 1940, 1; "Negro Wins
    Right to Use Beer Parlor," Vancouver *Sun,* 23 Feb. 1940, 17. For a more de-
    tailed account of the case, see *.
82 *York Corporation v. Christie* (1938), 65 Que. B.R. 104 (Que. K.B.), at 125–39.
83 *Fred Christie v. The York Corporation,* [1940] S.C.R. 139 (S.C.C.), at 147, 152.
84 *Fred Christie v. The York Corporation,* [1940] S.C.R. 139 (S.C.C.), at 152. On
    the significance of the many dissenting judges, see Frank R. Scott, *Essays on
    the Constitution* (Toronto: University of Toronto Press, 1977), 333.
85 Bora Laskin, "Tavern Refusing to Serve Negro – Discrimination," *Canadian
    Bar Review* 18 (1940): 316. See also Frank R. Scott, *The Canadian Constitution
    and Human Rights* (Toronto: Canadian Broadcasting Company, 1959), 37.
86 None of the later cases mentioned *Barnswell v. National Amusement Co.* The
    reluctance of Canadian judges to discuss matters of race explicitly may
    have had something to do with this. County Court Judge Lampman's trial
    decision in *Barnswell* was the only portion of the judgment that mentioned
    the plaintiff's race. In the report of the decision in the *Western Law Reporter,*

Lampman's trial decision is not included, even in summary form. Since the appeal rulings make no express mention of race, a legal researcher would have been hard-pressed to conclude that the case was an anti-discrimination precedent. The report in the *British Columbia Reports*, however, does make the issue of race explicit. *Johnson v. Sparrow* was mentioned briefly, in *Loew's Montreal Theatres Ltd. v. Reynolds*, which distinguished it on two rather peculiar grounds: that the plaintiff in *Johnson* had already purchased a ticket prior to the refusal of entry while the plaintiff in *Reynolds* had not, and that the plaintiff in *Johnson* had been unaware of the colour bar, whereas the plaintiff in *Reynolds* was deliberately challenging the policy. Although the Quebec Court of King's Bench in *Christie v. York Corporation* also cited *Johnson v. Sparrow*, the Supreme Court ruling made no mention of the decision, nor did the other cases discussed above. The curious erasure of the earlier anti-discrimination rulings is underscored by the comments of Judge Lennox in *Franklin v. Evans*, who noted that counsel for the Black plaintiff, Mr Buchner, "could find no decided case in support of his contention." A scholarly article written years later, Ian A. Hunter, "Civil Actions for Discrimination," *Canadian Bar Review* 55 (1977): 106, also fails to mention the *Johnson v. Sparrow* case or the *Barnswell v. National Amusement Co.* case, although the author discusses the others in detail. See also D.A. Schmeiser, *Civil Liberties in Canada* (London: Oxford University Press, 1964), 262–74, who erroneously refers to *Loew's Montreal Theatres* as "the earliest reported Canadian case in this area," ignores *Johnson v. Sparrow* and *Barnswell v. National Amusement Co.*, and then concludes, "The foregoing cases clearly indicate that the common law is particularly barren of remedies guaranteeing equality of treatment in public places or enterprises."

87 *Johnson v. Sparrow* (1899), 15 Que. S.C. 104 (Superior Court), at 107.

88 On the history of slavery under the French regime, see *.

89 For reference to the clause in the 1763 Treaty of Paris, see *.

90 For the 1790 English provision, see *.

91 For details of the 1762 legislative provision, see *.

92 For details of the 1781 legislative provision, which was repealed in 1825, see *.

93 For details of the 1793 provisions and their re-enactment through 1897, see *.

94 For details of the judicial cases, see *.

95 For details of the 1833 English provision, see *.

96 On the tenacity of slavery in Canada, see *.

97 For details of the 1842 decision to permit the extradition of Nelson Hackett and the 1860–1 extradition of John Anderson, see*.

98 *Re Drummond Wren*, [1945] O.R. 778 (Ont. Supreme Court), at 780–3, and
quoting 7 Halsbury, 2d ed. 1932, at 153–4. See also *Essex Real Estate v.
Holmes* (1930), 37 O.W.N. 392 (Ont. High Court), in which the court took a
narrow interpretation of the following restrictive covenant: "that the lands
shall not be sold to or occupied by persons not of the Caucasian race nor
to Europeans except such as are of English-speaking countries and the
French and the people of French descent," holding that a Syrian was not
excluded by such a clause. See also *Re Bryers & Morris* (1931), 40 O.W.N.
572 (Ont. High Court). One year after the *Desmond* litigation, another set
of white, Gentile judges would disagree with Judge Mackay's ruling. In
Re Noble and Wolf, [1948] 4 D.L.R. 123, O.W.N. 546 (Ont. High Court), affirmed [1949] O.R. 503, O.W.N. 484, 4 D.L.R. 375 (Ont. C.A.), they explicitly upheld a restrictive covenant prohibiting the sale or lease of a summer
resort property to "any person of the Jewish, Hebrew, Semitic, Negro or
coloured race or blood." Fearful of "inventing new heads of public policy"
that would impede "freedom of association," the judges espoused racial
exclusivity as an obvious social right. Ontario Court of Appeal Chief
Justice Robert Spelman Robertson wrote, "It is common knowledge that,
in the life usually led at such places, there is much intermingling, in an
informal and social way, of the residents and their guests, especially at the
beach. That the summer colony should be congenial is of the essence of
a pleasant holiday in such circumstances. The purpose of [the restrictive
covenant] here in question is obviously to assure, in some degree, that the
residents are of a class who will get along well together. To magnify this
innocent and modest effort to establish and maintain a place suitable for
a pleasant summer residence into an enterprise that offends against some
public policy, requires a stronger imagination than I possess … There is
nothing criminal or immoral involved; the public interest is in no way
concerned. These people have simply agreed among themselves upon a
matter of their own personal concern that affects property of their own in
which no one else has an interest." This ruling was later overturned, *Annie Maud Noble and Bernard Wolf v. W.A. Alley et al.*, [1951] 92 S.C.R. 64, 1
D.L.R. 321 (S.C.C.). The Supreme Court justices made no explicit comment
on the public policy reasoning of the earlier decisions. Instead they held
the covenant void for uncertainty: "It is impossible to set such limits to the
lines of race or blood as would enable a court to say in all cases whether a
proposed purchaser is or is not within the ban." See also *Re McDougall and
Waddell*, [1945] O.W.N. 272 (Ont. High Court), where the court considered
a restrictive covenant that prohibited the sale or occupation of lands "by
any person or persons other than Gentiles (non-semetic [*sic*]) of European

or British or Irish or Scottish racial origin." The court held that such provisions did not violate the newly enacted Ontario Racial Discrimination
Act, and that there were no legal restrictions to affect their implementation. For the first legislation to ban racially restrictive covenants on land,
see *An Act to amend The Conveyancing and Law of Property Act*, S.O. 1950, c.
11; *An Act to amend The Law of Property Act*, S.M. 1950, c. 33. These statutes
are discussed in more detail in chapter 6, Backhouse, *Colour-Coded.*

99 The debate on the motion, which failed to lead to the incorporation of
a Bill of Rights in the British North America Act is recorded in *House of
Commons Debates* (10 Oct. 1945), p. 900.

100 See *Viola Irene Desmond v. Henry L. McNeil and Roseland Theatre Co. Ltd.,*
filed 14 Nov. 1946, no. 13299, Supreme Court of Nova Scotia, vols 936–7,
RG39 "C" Halifax, PANS. On 12 Dec. 1946, Bissett filed a notice of discon-
tinuance against the Roseland Theatre Company Ltd, along with a writ
alleging the same claim against the parent corporation: *Viola Irene Desmond v. Odeon Theatres of Canada Ltd. and Garson Theatres Ltd.*, no. 13334,
Supreme Court of Nova Scotia, vols 936–7, RG39 "C" Halifax, PANS. For
details concerning the law of "assault," "battery," "false imprisonment,"
"malicious prosecution," and the tort of "abuse of process," see *. Under
the latter cause of action, Bissett could have argued that MacNeil invoked
summary criminal prosecution under the Theatres Act, a process not unlawful in itself, for the collateral and improper motive of enforcing racial
segregation. The conviction would have become irrelevant, with the sole
focus being whether racial segregation constituted an "unjustifiable" ulte-
rior motive for the theatre manager's acts, which necessitated harm to
others.

101 For details of the common-law defence, see *.

102 "Recognizance for Certiorari," 24 Dec. 1946; "Notice of Motion," 27 Dec.
1946; and "Affidavit of Viola Irene Desmond," PANS. The notice was
served upon Rod G. MacKay and Harry MacNeil on 30 Dec. 1946. Litigants were required to put up financial sureties before filing actions for
judicial review.

103 For information on the availability of certiorari applications, see *.

104 There is no published report of the case brought before Judge Archibald,
and the press coverage contains no further details: see "Supreme Court
Ruling Sought," Halifax *Herald*, 10 Jan. 1947, 18. The "Notice of Motion"
lists three grounds, although the vagueness of the claims permits little
analysis: 1. That there is no evidence to support the aforesaid conviction.
2. That there is evidence to show that the aforesaid Viola Irene Desmond
did not commit the offence hereinbefore recited. 3. That the information

or evidence did not disclose any offence to have been committed within the jurisdiction of the convicting magistrate. The report of the appeal of Judge Archibald's ruling, *The King v. Desmond* (1947), 20 M.P.R. 297, at 298 and 300 (N.S.S.C.), suggests that Bissett also tried at first instance to make a technical argument that the prosecution failed to allege the location where the offence took place. Apparently he abandoned this claim when the original information, stipulating that the acts occurred "in the Town of New Glasgow," was located.

105 "Decision of Archibald, J.," 20 Jan. 1947, PANS; *The King v. Desmond* (1947), 20 M.P.R. 297 (N.S.S.C.), at 298–9. Judge Archibald was born in Manganese Mines, Colchester County, to John H. Archibald and Mary Alice (Clifford) Archibald. He was educated at public schools in Truro and received his LLB from Dalhousie in 1915. A Liberal in politics and United Church by religion, Judge Archibald lectured in Criminal and Statute Law at Dalhousie in the mid-1920s. He was appointed to the Supreme Court in 1937, and in 1948 he was appointed to the Exchequer Court of Canada, a post he held until his death in 1953. See "Archibald, The Hon. Maynard Brown," *Who's Who in Canada, 1945–46* (Toronto: International Press, 1946), 1042; *Who's Who in Canada, 1951–52*, 612; *Maritime Reference Book*, 23–4; *Annals – North British Society: 1950–1968* (Kentville, NS: Kentville Publishing, 1969), 58–9; and "Prominent Jurist Held Many Important Posts," Halifax *Chronicle-Herald*, 10 July 1953, 1, 6.

106 "Decision of Archibald, J.," 2, PANS; *The King v. Desmond*, at 299.

107 For earlier Nova Scotia decisions see, for example, *The Queen v. Walsh* (1897), 29 N.S.R. 521 (N.S.S.C.), at 527. See also *The Nova Scotia Summary Convictions Act*, S.N.S. 1940, c. 3, s. 58.

108 S.N.S. 1940, c. 3, ss. 59, 60, 62, 66, as amended S.N.S. 1945, c. 65.

109 "Notice of Appeal," 20 Jan. 1947, and "Entry of Appeal," 21 Feb. 1947, PANS. See also "Reserve Appeal Decision in Desmond Case," Halifax *Herald*, 14 Mar. 1947, 18. For details of the appellant's and respondent's arguments, see *The King v. Desmond* (1947), 20 M.P.R. 297 (N.S.S.C.), at 299–301.

110 Some cite the couple's disagreement over the case as the main source of the marital breakdown: Hudson, "Interview with Pearleen Oliver." Others suggest that there were long-standing, additional strains within the marriage caused by Jack Desmond's drinking and his distrust of Viola's ambitious business prospects: Woods, "Interview with Gannon-Dixon"; Backhouse, "Interview with Wanda Robson."

111 "Clarion Went A-Visiting!" New Glasgow *Clarion* 2, no. 5 (15 Mar. 1947): 2.

112 *The King v. Desmond* (1947), 20 M.P.R. 297 (N.S.S.C.), at 307. Other reports of the case appear as (1947), 89 C.C.C. 278, 4 C.R. 200, [1947] 4 D.L.R. 81. For biographical details on Doull, who was born in New Glasgow on 1 Nov. 1878, see Halifax *Chronicle-Herald*, 1 Oct. 1960, 32; *Who's Who in Canada, 1945–46*, 474.

113 Doull's comment is found at 309. Doull served as mayor of New Glasgow in 1925. Judge Robert Henry Graham noted at 304 that Bissett had argued a denial of natural justice, relying on *R. v. Wandsworth*, [1942] 1 All E.R. 56, in which the court overturned the conviction of a defendant who had been denied the opportunity to defend himself. Judge Graham, however, made no reference to Viola Desmond's detailed affidavit alleging similar treatment and refused to find a denial of natural justice in the present case.

114 The son of a New Glasgow lawyer and politician Hon. Col. Edward Mortimer Macdonald, PC, Macdonald, Jr, was born in Pictou, called to the bar of Quebec in 1924, and the Nova Scotia bar in 1929. He practised with the law firm of Macdonald & MacQuarrie, with offices in Pictou and New Glasgow. He was a Liberal and a Presbyterian. See *Maritime Reference Book*, 11; "Macdonald, E.M.: Death: Town Solicitor for New Glasgow Dies," no. 20, vol. 2022, MG1, PANS; Charles G.D. Roberts and Arthur J. Tunnell, *The Canadian Who's Who* (1936–7) (Toronto: Murray Printing, 1936), 2:660.

115 J.B. Milner, "Case and Comment," *Canadian Bar Review* 25 (1947): 915–22. Interestingly, Milner did not believe that the trial decision to convict Viola Desmond was incorrect, describing it at 919 as "technically perfect." For biographical details about Milner and further details concerning his article, see *.

116 For Judge Graham's ruling, see *The King v. Desmond* (1947), 20 M.P.R. 297 (N.S.S.C.), at 305, quoting in part Viscount Caldicott in *Rex v. Nat Bell Liquors Limited*, [1922] 2 A.C. 128 (H.L.), at 151. For biographical details on Judge Graham, who was born in New Glasgow on 30 Nov. 1871, the son of John George Graham and Jane (Marshall) Graham, see "Mr Justice Graham Dies at Age 85," Halifax *Mail-Star*, 28 May 1956, 1, 6; *Who's Who in Canada, 1945–46*, 466; *The Canadian Who's Who* (Toronto: Trans-Canada, 1948), 4:380; *Catalogue of Portraits of the Judges of the Supreme Court of Nova Scotia and other Portraits* (Halifax: Law Courts, n.d.), 110, F93C28, PANS. Graham received a BA and LLB from Dalhousie, was called to the Nova Scotia bar in 1894, and named a KC in 1913. He served as town councillor in New Glasgow in 1898, mayor from 1899 to 1900, and represented Pictou County as a Liberal in the House of Assembly between 1916 and

1925. He served as stipendiary magistrate from 1906 to 1910 and was appointed puisne judge of the Supreme Court in 1925.

117 *The King v. Desmond* (1947), 20 M.P.R. 297 (N.S.S.C.), at 305–7. Unlike Doull and Graham, Judge Carroll was not born in New Glasgow, but in Margaret Forks, NS, on 11 June 1877. Educated at St Francis Xavier College in Antigonish and at Dalhousie University, he was called to the bar of Nova Scotia in 1905, serving several terms as a Liberal MP. For biographical details, see obituary, Halifax *Chronicle-Herald*, 26 Aug. 1964, 16; *Who's Who in Canada, 1945–46*, 666. The decision on file at the archives, "Decision of Hall, J.," PANS, shows that the original typed version reads, "Had the matter reached the Court by some method other than certiorari, there might have been opportunity to right the wrong done this unfortunate woman, *convicted on insufficient evidence*" (emphasis added). The latter phrase was crossed out by pen, initialled by Judge Hall, and did not appear in the reported version of the decision. Judge Hall was born in Melvern Square, Annapolis County, in 1876, to Rev. William E. and Margaret (Barss) Hall. He was educated at Acadia and Dalhousie University and admitted to the bar in 1900. He practised law in Liverpool, NS, from 1902 to 1918, and then became Halifax Crown prosecutor. Active in the Conservative party, he was elected to the provincial legislature and served as attorney general in 1926. He was also an active worker for welfare organizations in Halifax. Judge Hall was appointed to the Nova Scotia Supreme Court in 1931. For biographical details see *Prominent People of the Maritime Provinces* (St John: McMillan, 1922), 77–8; o "Veteran Jurist Dies at 81," Halifax *Mail-Star*, 27 May 1958, 3; 262, vol. 41, MG9, Biographical Card File, PANS; *Who's Who in Canada, 1945–46*, 1494–5.

118 Backhouse, "Interview with Wanda Robson." Similar reactions were expressed by Ida B. Wells, the famous African-American campaigner against lynching, after she lost a lawsuit in Memphis, Tennessee, in the late nineteenth century, when she was denied accommodation in the "Ladies Only" (white) railway carriage. Ida B. Wells's diary entry reads, "I felt so disappointed because I had hoped such great things for my people generally. I have firmly believed all along that the law was on our side and would, when we appealed to it, give us justice. I feel shorn of that belief and utterly discouraged, and just now, if it were possible, would gather my race in my arms and fly away with them": Alfreda M. Duster, ed., *Crusade for Justice: An Autobiography of Ida B. Wells* (Chicago: University of Chicago Press, 1970), xvii.

119 Milner, "Case and Comment," 915–16, 922.

120 "The Desmond Case," Truro *Clarion* 2, no. 15 (Apr. 1947), 2; and "Dismisses Desmond Application," Truro *Clarion* 2, no. 15 (Apr. 1947), 4.

121 "The Desmond Case," Truro *Clarion*, 2. The *Clarion* would later reprint a 15 July 1947 editorial from *Maclean's* magazine, in which the *Desmond* case is described and critiqued: "In a free country one man is as good as another – any well-behaved person may enter any public place. In Nova Scotia a Negro woman tried to sit in the downstairs section of a theatre instead of the Jim Crow gallery. Not only was she ejected by force, but thereafter she, not the theatre owner, was charged and convicted of a misdemeanour. Most Canadians have been doing a fair amount of grumbling lately about the state of our fundamental freedoms. Maybe it's time we did more than grumble." See "Is This a Free Country?," Truro *Clarion* 2, no. 12 (15 Aug. 1947): 2.

122 On the allegations that Viola Desmond might have been trying to "pass," see Backhouse, "Interview with Wanda Robson." For Johnston's comments, see "N.S. Negroes Libelled by Attack," Truro *Clarion* 3, no. 8 (13 Oct. 1948): 1.

123 "Toronto Leads the Way," Truro *Clarion* 2, no. 12 (15 Aug. 1947): 2. The same paper reports that the City of Toronto Board of Police Commissioners passed a regulation (inserted in a city by-law governing the licensing of public places) providing a penalty of licence cancellation for any hall, rink, theatre, or other place of amusement in the city that refused to admit anyone because of race, colour, or creed. See "Toronto Law against Discrimination" and "Toronto Leads the Way," Truro *Clarion* 2, no. 12 (15 Aug. 1947): 1–2.

124 "No Discrimination," Truro *Clarion* 2, no. 12 (15 Aug. 1947): 2. *Saturday Night* also draws a comparison with the United States, on 7 Dec. 1946, 5: "Racial segregation is so deeply entrenched in what the American people are accustomed to call their way of life that the problems which it raises in a democracy (it raises none in a totalitarian state) will not be solved in the United States without a good deal of conflict. Canada is in a position to avoid most of that conflict if she avoids getting tied into the American way of life in that respect, and now is the time to take action to avoid it."

125 "American Artists Score Racial Discrimination," Halifax *Chronicle*, 15 Sept. 1947, no. 18, vol. 16, Mg15, PANS; "More Discrimination," Truro *Clarion* 2, no. 14 (1 Nov. 1947): 2. Selma Burke's female companion was A.F. Wilson, a noted American author of several books on race discrimination. The *Clarion* reports in 2, no. 11 (1 Aug. 1947): 1–2, that a New Glasgow restaurant refused service to a young West Indian student working with the provincial highways department. The same article

notes that a Black couple, Mr and Mrs A.T. Best, was also refused seating in a small fruit store and fountain in New Glasgow.

126 Esmerelda Thornhill, "So Often against Us: So Seldom for Us, Being Black and Living with the Canadian Justice System," plenary presentation to the Ninth Biennial Conference of the Congress of Black Women of Canada, Halifax, 1989, 3 (copy on file with the author).

127 "New Glasgow," Truro *Clarion* 3, no. 6 (8 Sept. 1948): 3. For further discussion of the KKK, see chapter 6.

128 Backhouse, "Interview with Wanda Robson."

129 Ibid.; Backhouse, "Interview with Mrs S.A. (Emily) Clyke"; obituaries in the Halifax *Chronicle-Herald*, 10 Feb. 1965, 26, and Halifax *Mail Star*, 10 Feb. 1965, 8.

130 Robertson, "Interview with Pearleen Oliver." Paula Denice McClain, *Alienation and Resistance: The Political Behavior of Afro-Canadians* (Palo Alto: R. & E. Research Associates, 1979), 59, notes that the NSAACP was responsible for integrating barbershops in Halifax and Dartmouth, sponsoring the first Blacks for employment in Halifax and Dartmouth stores, integrating the nurses' training and placement programs, persuading insurance companies to sell Blacks policies other than industrial insurance, and initiating a controversy that resulted in the Dartmouth school board hiring Blacks.

131 Thomson, *Born with a Call*, 84.

5

Creating the Myth of "Raceless" Justice in the Murder Trial of *R. v. Richardson*, Sandwich, 1903

SUSAN McKELVEY

On 25 September 1903, a jury of twelve men returned a verdict of manslaughter in the case of *R. v. Richardson* in Sandwich, Ontario. Oliver Richardson had been charged with murder for killing his neighbour Edmund Matthews. The men, who were both farmers, had been engaged in an ongoing land dispute, which was described by local newspapers as "one the longest and fiercest family quarrels in the history of the County."[1] The murder and subsequent trial garnered a great deal of attention, but it was not just because a murder had occurred in a small farming community. Rather, what was significant about the murder and subsequent trial was that the victim was Black, while his killer was white. According to *Globe* coverage of the trial, this was the first time in Ontario that a white man was tried for murdering a Black man.[2]

This trial provides an opportunity for analysis of the racialization of the criminal justice system at the beginning of the twentieth century. There are two drastically different narratives of race in Canada. On the one hand, Canadians perceive themselves as demonstrating exemplary racial neutrality and equality; on the other, racism and racial discrimination is said to be pernicious and pervasive. So how can we reconcile these contrasting perspectives? Carolyn Strange's analysis of the trials of Clara Ford and Carrie Davies can help to provide a framework within which to examine the Richardson case.[3] Both of these lower-class women were acquitted of murdering wealthy men. While many criminologists have argued that their acquittals reflected the leniency of the criminal justice system towards women, Strange argues that the selective mercy they received actually reflected a type of chivalric justice that merely obfuscated the sexism, classism, and racism inherent in the system as a whole. Acquitting the women perpetuated patriarchal ideologies by reinforcing dominant stereotypes of female frailty and masculine heroism. The notion of "British justice" in the case of *R. v. Richardson* served a similar function. By prosecuting Oliver Richardson, society was able to claim that all men are equal before the law, regardless of race. But similar to the trials of Clara Ford and Carrie Davies, solitary acts of leniency or impartiality by criminal courts did not eliminate inequality and systemic racism within the society as a whole; rather they obscured it. This chapter will explore the case of *R. v. Richardson* in order to understand how the prosecution of a white man for the murder of his Black neighbour contributed to the Canadian myth of "raceless" justice.

For much of Canadian history, an ideal of neutral "British justice" has been put forward as one way to distinguish Canadians from their overtly racist American counterparts. Embedded within the idea of British justice is the belief that British institutions, such as the law, act as protection against injustice. Liberty and equality before the law form the central tenets of this popular ideology.[4] In the nineteenth century, British North America featured numerous examples of British justice, many of them in contrast with the American institution of slavery. During the American Revolution and the War of 1812, the British offered emancipation to all slaves who volunteered to fight against the Americans, while the Abolition Act of 1833 formally abolished slavery in the British Empire, almost thirty years before the United States engaged in a lengthy and bloody civil war.[5] Blacks therefore gained the same formal legal status as other Canadians, including full legal equality and rights of citizenship. As a result, Canada became the destination of choice for many Black individuals from the United States, some of whom had escaped slavery by travelling through the Underground Railroad. Stories about Blacks reaching Canada and attaining freedom became part of the national myth. A story in which it is epitomized appeared in R.M. Fuller's history of Windsor, Ontario.[6] In 1830, an escaped slave from Kentucky managed to cross the border into Ontario and was given work by members of the Baby family, a prominent white family in Windsor. His master came after him and tried to kidnap him, but the escaped slave was saved by his new employers, who let him choose whether or not he wanted to return with his old master. In recounting the history of a city that has had a Black population since the eighteenth century, this is the only mention Fuller makes of the Black community. Their existence is reduced to an archetypal narrative that glorifies white British notions of justice and equality.

Even after the end of the American Civil War and the abolition of slavery, Canadians still felt moral superiority over their American counterparts with regards to race and justice. In the early twentieth century the *Toronto Globe* carried numerous reports of lynchings in the United States.[7] These featured stories of legal officials pleading with mobs to allow the law to take its course and refrain from lynching those accused of crimes.[8] Many of the transgressions for which Black men were lynched were minor, including stealing a bottle of pop, firing a shot at a white man who was uninjured, and claiming ignorance about the whereabouts of an alleged murderer.[9] Given these stories, it is not surprising that the perception in Canada was that Black men could be killed by whites with relative impunity in the United States. An editorial written in response to an article in an American newspaper that suggested Canada unite with the United States to improve the growth of the population stated the matter quite plainly: "Our ideals in some respects are very different from those of our neighbours. In the very copy of the [New York] Sun in which the editorial appears there is a paragraph headed 'Negro Burned to Death – Texas Mob Catches him in Indian Territory and Soon Puts Him to Death.' ... This is not an unusual or sporadic event, for similar occurrences are of almost daily record. The Sun may fail to understand our point of view, but we would not consider it an honor to be included within the bounds of a nation so helpless to enforce the first requisite of civilized society."[10]

This editorial demonstrates how many Canadians perceived the quality of justice in the United States. In contrast to this deplorable state of affairs south of the border, Canadians could feel proud that their legal institutions dealt with all crimes equally and justly and were even willing to prosecute a white man for killing his Black neighbour. While vigilante justice dominated and the nefarious Jim Crow laws were implemented throughout the United States to enforce racial segregation, Canadians were proud of the "racelessness" of their legal system, a pride that helped to define Canadian identity.

Although the Canadian justice system was constructed – and may superficially have appeared – to be "raceless," racism was nevertheless pervasive because it was inherent in the underlying systems and structures of the legal system. Statutes and laws might have bestowed all individuals with formal legal equality, but they were applied in a racist society, which ultimately led to differential treatment on the basis of race. Stereotypes deeply entrenched within society depicted Black people as innately inferior to whites. In 1911, the federal Cabinet passed an order to prevent Black immigration, based on the assumption that Black people were unsuited to the cold Canadian climate.[11] Although the order never became formal legislation because of the potential diplomatic repercussions from the United States, an informal policy of exclusion nevertheless remained. Racism also existed in housing, employment, and services. There were restrictive racial covenants in many parts of Canada and Ontario that were enforced by the courts, while Blacks were regularly refused entry to theatres, restaurants, and taverns.[12] Discrimination in hotel accommodation, which did receive some acknowledgment, was blamed on the racist attitudes of Americans.[13] It was claimed that racist American hotel patrons would not be willing to stay at hotels where Blacks were guests. This example demonstrates how, even when confronted with racial discrimination within their own borders, Canadians were able to avoid accepting culpability by pointing across the border to the south. The most serious source of racial anxiety for the white community, however, was the possibility of miscegenation. In particular they feared hypersexual and aggressive Black men mixing with white women.[14]

Discrimination and inequality were also revealed within the criminal justice system. Blacks were over-represented relative to the percentage of the total number of people executed in Canada, and they tended to receive longer terms of imprisonment when convicted of property crime.[15] Clayton James Mosher noted that one reason Blacks had a higher rate of imprisonment for both property and violent crimes was that sentencing judges tended view the testimony of Black offenders as unreliable.[16] Also noted by both Mosher and Barrington Walker was that Blacks were treated particularly harshly when the victim of a crime was white, but less so when the victim was another Black or Asian.

Oliver Richardson and Edmund Matthews lived between the third and fourth concessions of Colchester South, near the Town of Harrow in Essex County. As a result of its close proximity to Detroit, Essex County had been the main terminus of the Underground Railroad and many Blacks chose to settle there. Colchester in particular had a significant Black population, with seven known settlements of Black people.[17] By 1821 there were enough Black people to establish the first Black Baptist Church in Ontario, and by the 1850s it was estimated that

close to one-third of the township was Black. There has been substantial debate about the size of the Black population in Canada, and the
degree of decline caused by the return of Black settlers to the United
States after the abolition of slavery there, but according to one study by
Michael Wayne, in 1861 Colchester had the third-largest Black population in Canada West.[18] He also argues that what is frequently depicted
as a mass exodus of former slaves returning to the United States after
the Civil War was more likely a decline of about 20 per cent between
1861 and 1871.[19] Although this does not provide a precise number for
the Black population in 1903, it suggests that the Black population in
Colchester was significant.

In the mid-1850s, white settlers occupied most of the land from the
lake to the fourth concession, but north of the fourth concession was
largely Black settlers.[20] Matthews's and Richardson's farms were therefore at the boundary between the two groups. Although many of the
Black settlers were materially successful and owned their own farms,
there was tension between white and Black residents. In 1830 white
inhabitants of Colchester and Gosfield petitioned the legislature to prevent the planned immigration of a group of Blacks from Cincinnati,
Ohio, while in 1852 Black members of the community tried to insist on
their right to vote in a township meeting, but were prevented by the
white men present.[21] The Black community filed a grievance with the
county magistrate, who insisted that they be allowed to vote.[22]

The subject that was the most contentious, however, was schools. In
1846 the superintendent in the area requested government legislation
for separate Black schools in his report,[23] and in 1850 the provincial
legislature passed the *Separate School Act*.[24] Although this act was allegedly created to allow Black families to request a separate school, it was
frequently used by white families to enforce segregation – a use that
was strengthened by subsequent legislation throughout the 1850s.[25]
Although the schools were reintegrated throughout the 1860s, a report
by the superintendent in 1871 provides some insight into the attitudes
of the white community who protested school integration: "Though
there is no animosity against the colored people in the ordinary outdoor business of life there is a deeply rooted prejudice against admitting them to a footing of equality in matters of a more strictly social
nature. A white man who should admit a colored person to his table,
or allow his children to sit beside a colored child in school would by so
doing exclude himself and his family from the society of white persons.
A feeling so universal, so inveterate, cannot be ignored, however much

we may deplore its existence."[26] This statement demonstrates the type of policy that was pervasive in Canada, which bestowed legal equality by allowing Blacks to have access to funds for schools, but prevented them from exercising that equality in a meaningful way because of social prejudice.

In spite of this prejudice, Colchester was the home of notable Black Canadians. Josiah Henson, the model for Harriet Beecher Stowe's character Uncle Tom, lived there for seven years, while Elijah McCoy, the famous inventor, was born there in 1844.[27] Delos R. Davis, who was one of the first Black lawyers in Canada, also grew up there in the Black settlement of New Canaan.[28] The special act passed by the Ontario legislature in 1884 to allow him to take the bar admission exams was introduced by his local South Essex MPP, William Balfour, who also co-founded the *Amherstburg Echo*, a local liberal newspaper that served both the Black and white communities.[29] Although Balfour died in 1896 and was therefore not in office when the trial took place in 1903, he was succeeded as MPP by the co-founder of the *Echo*, John Auld. Auld also appears to have been on good terms with members of the Black community, as his funeral was described as "one of the most representative funerals ever held in the county" with "people of all classes, creeds and colors."[30] In the debate on Black immigration in 1911, the MP from South Essex objected to the proposed actions of the government and stated, "Coloured people in my experience have been amongst the most loyal citizens of this country."[31] Clearly at least some of the politicians in the area were supportive of the Black community. This is not surprising, given that politicians needed the Black vote, but it does add another dimension to the racial atmosphere of Essex County. While full social equality was lacking and some topics generated tension between the Black and white communities, positive signs suggest that there was also a degree of shared respect and amicable relations. It was in this mixed-race farming community that a white man, Oliver Richardson, shot and killed his Black neighbour, Edmund Matthews, on 10 July 1903.

On that day, a mare and a colt, both belonging to Matthews, escaped from their enclosure. While the mare went out onto the highway, the colt went over a line fence into Richardson's field. The men had been engaged in an ongoing land dispute for a few years, so as Matthews went to retrieve the mare from the highway, Richardson came out and told him to get the colt out of his field. An altercation followed, culminating in Richardson drawing a revolver and shooting Matthews four times. Sons of both men were present and witnessed the events leading up to and including the shooting; Richardson's wife also came out at some point in the fray. After being shot, Matthews fell into a ditch, while the Richardson family retreated to their home.

No one in the community was surprised by what happened. The men had been engaged in a quarrel for years over the location of a line fence that divided their properties. Matthews had purchased two pieces of property decades earlier that were divided by a strip of approximately forty acres. He surveyed the boundary lines with the white seller, who retained the property in between. For the next thirty years, these boundary lines were respected, and there were no disputes. The original seller eventually died, and two or three years prior to 1903, his son sold the land to Richardson. The deed of sale stated it was for "40 acres, more or less," and although the seller claimed in court to have told Richardson that the property was only thirty-seven acres, as soon as he purchased it Richardson began to dispute the boundary, claiming that he was entitled to a full forty acres.[32] He also argued that since his property was short of what he was entitled to, the two men should share the difference, and pulled out the fence between the properties. This act began a feud that saw both men in court multiple times for accusations of trespassing and making threats, as well as half a dozen replevin suits. In June both men had agreed to allow the dispute to be settled by the arbitration of a local judge, a process that was underway when the shooting occurred.[33] A reporter from the *Detroit Free Press* spoke to Oliver Richardson's brother, Eligh, a day after the shooting occurred.[34] Eligh had not gone to Oliver's house after the shooting and refused to have anything to do with his brother. He stated, "Oliver is of a headstrong nature ... and it was impossible for his relatives to reason with him over the matter of the line fence which was the cause of the feud between the two men. He insisted that he had been robbed and that he would yet have his own. It was pointed out that he was only losing about two acres of land at the most and that he allowed twice as much to go to waste every year. But it was no use talking, so I refused to have anything more to do with him. He has brought this trouble on himself and will have to get out of it without any assistance or sympathy from me."[35] The statement demonstrates the extent to which the sympathy of the whole community, both Black and white, lay with Matthews. Although Matthews had also made threats, the consensus within the community was that Richardson had been the primary instigator and that Matthews had merely been responding in kind.[36]

Both men had been born in Colchester, and both were said to be from respectable families. Both were married with children; Matthews had two sons and a daughter, while Richardson had five sons ranging in age from five to nineteen. But while Matthews was described by newspapers as industrious, peaceable, law-abiding, and a good citizen, whose only quarrel had been with Richardson, Richardson was described as being "the black sheep of the family."[37] The *Amherstburg Echo* also reported, "He possesses a fine rich farm and but for the numerous lawsuits in which he has been engaged the past 10 years ought to be one of the most prosperous farmers in the township."[38] Richardson certainly seemed to demonstrate a tendency towards litigiousness. Ten to twelve years earlier he had been involved in another legal dispute with Edmund Matthews's father, Matthew Matthews Sr, when Richardson tried to claim a portion of the older Matthews's land.[39] The verdict of the High Court was against Richardson, and he was also ordered to pay the whole costs. Rather than comply with the order he deeded his property to his wife and left the country.[40] What was certainly notable about Richardson's landholding over the decades was that he appeared on the tax assessment rolls only sporadically.[41] In contrast, Edmund Matthews, Matthew Matthews Sr, and Richardson's father all appear consistently as landowners in each assessment roll examined. This is not surprising, since as farmers their livelihood would be dependent on their land.

Richardson's questionable character was not limited to civil law suits and unusual land ownership history; it also included previous criminal charges. On New Year's Day in 1897, Richardson had allegedly attacked a white man named Sylvester McLean.[42] Richardson had been in possession of sheep that had been stolen from McLean, which a third white man, William Stewart, had pleaded guilty to stealing. Richardson had been arrested and charged with having stolen goods in his possession, leading him to assault McLean when he encountered him on the road on New Year's Day. McLean was apparently so badly injured that he was unable to see out of either eye and was under the care of a doctor for three weeks. Despite testimony by Sylvester McLean, the doctor who treated him, and William Stewart, who had witnessed the assault from a distance, Richardson was acquitted. When testifying on his own behalf, Richardson claimed that this was the first fight he had been in for fifteen years, but that he had previously been in a fight with his brother-in-law, in which he had bitten off a piece of his ear. In charging the jury, the judge had strongly favoured the prosecution;

when the jury returned with a verdict of not guilty, he stated that he did not know how they could have arrived at such a verdict.

In contrast, all of the altercations that Edmund Matthews had had with the law appeared to centre on his dispute with Richardson. He had previously been convicted of assaulting Richardson and damaging a line fence.[43] There was also an incident where Matthews had pointed a gun at Mrs Richardson. Maxime Laporte, the Amherstburg chief of police, had arrested Matthews on a number of occasions based on the complaints of Richardson.[44] In testifying in the coroner's inquest he stated that sometimes Matthews had been difficult to deal with. He had never resisted arrest but had hidden from Laporte several times when he had come to arrest him. Laporte also recounted a conversation that he had with one of the men he had brought on one occasion to help arrest Matthews. They had been downstairs in the courthouse with three others discussing their opinions of the case when one of the men stated, "Richardson was the biggest nigger of the two," the man having known Richardson for twenty-five years.[45] It is interesting how this racial slur was appropriated and redefined. By applying it to Richardson this man was reversing their racial stereotypes; although Matthews was Black, Richardson was unworthy of being categorized as white, because he was a bully.

Apart from these encounters with Richardson and the brief descriptions included in the newspapers, not much is known about Matthews. He was a farmer and fifty-five years old when he died.[46] He had lived in Colchester South his whole life, and as of 1897, he had owned just over 85 acres of land. He had eight brothers and sisters, all of whom lived in Colchester, and the whole family was described as "among the most highly respected colored people in the township."[47] Matthews's father, Matthew Matthews Sr, in particular was very well known and respected. He had been born in Virginia in 1822, and immigrated to Canada with his father in 1833, the same year that the act to abolish slavery in the British Empire was passed.[48] Once in Canada, Matthew Matthews Sr and his father settled between the second and third concessions of Colchester, in what became known as the Matthews Settlement.[49] By 1881 he owned 345 acres, for several years he was a school trustee, and in the historical atlas published that year he not only paid to be included in the biographical directory, but his farm was one of the few that was labelled on the map of Colchester.[50] He was a local Baptist preacher, and in 1889 he was nominated in a contest that was held to honour the most influential Black man in Colchester South.[51]

Michael Radelet has explored the relationship between race and the death penalty in the United States, examining cases where a white defendant was executed for crimes against Blacks.[52] He looked at both the frequency of these cases and whether or not status characteristics other than race could explain why the executions occurred. Of the over fifteen thousand executions reviewed for the study, only thirty fit the criteria outlined.[53] In each case Radelet found that other status considerations, such as class, occupation, economic value, marginality, and prior criminality played a role in condemning the white man. This is an American study, but Barrington Walker has also noted a similar pattern in Canada with respect to social factors determining whether or not a "Black-on-Black" murder would result in an execution.[54] One execution occurred in Essex County in 1900 only a few years before Edmund Matthews was killed. Levi Steward, a Black man, was executed for murdering Jim Ross, another Black man who was affectionately known as "Old Jim." While Steward had been lower-class, Ross had been a man of considerable wealth who was also well respected and established. Walker argues that the racist discourse that accompanied the case was more typical of a crime that had occurred across the colour line. Steward was described by a local doctor testifying against him to be "a stupid ignorant mulatto of a very low mental type."[55] In the case of Edmund Matthews there was no evidence of this type of racist discourse, and the crime appeared to have been taken seriously from the outset. It is likely that his family's long-term standing within the township, along with Matthews's own reputation as a law-abiding citizen and member of the community, contributed to the general response to the shooting, rather than any abstract notion of British justice or equality.

After the shooting, people passing by and neighbours who had witnessed the scene from afar went over to Matthews, and a local doctor was called. Matthews was unable to get up, so the doctor had a stretcher constructed, and Matthews was carried to his father's house nearby. Dr Campeau found four wounds, three of which were superficial, but the fourth had penetrated the body. When Campeau found blood in the urine he knew that the bullet had injured the kidney, and he advised Matthews to make a will. Fred H.A. Davis, a Black barrister from Amherstburg,[56] was called to draw up the will, along with R.M. Dennis, a justice of the peace. Both witnessed a deposition by Matthews about the shooting. The local constables had also been called, and Dr Campeau told them to arrest Oliver Richardson, who was then taken, along with his eldest two sons who had witnessed the shooting, to the local lockup. At this point, prior to the establishment of a local police force in Colchester South Township and the Town of Harrow, county constables were responsible for patrolling the area, and then reported incidents to the Windsor Police Department.[57] Detective Campeau[58] of Windsor thus received a telephone message to inform him of the incident, and he set off that evening, along with Detective Mahoney and Constable Laporte of Amherstburg for the home of the victim's father, where Matthews lay dying.

The next day, Oliver Richardson was brought, along with his wife and his sons who had been arrested, to the Police Court in Windsor. While his wife and sons were discharged, Oliver Richardson was arraigned on a charge of "shooting and wounding with intent to kill."[59] Meanwhile, in Colchester, a local constable returned to the scene of the shooting to investigate. He found a stone that he described in later testimony as being "a little larger than an ordinary tumbler," a hat, and a piece of suspender near the fence where the shooting took place.[60] He collected the clothes Matthews had been wearing, and then proceeded to the Richardson home, where he found a pitchfork, an axe with blood on the handle, and a crowbar, which were leaning against the house.[61]

Around this time, a dying Edmund Matthews was interviewed by a journalist from the *Detroit Free Press*, I.M. Cady. Describing Matthews's demeanour, Cady wrote, "There was no hate in his voice and he spoke of Richardson more in sorrow than in anger. He bitterly regretted that he had not run away from Richardson instead of remaining to have it out with him."[62] Matthews also claimed that when he went to retrieve his mare from the road, Richardson came out and told him to get the colt out of his field. Matthews said that he told him that he would do so as soon as he got the mare. Richardson told him again to retrieve the colt, or he would do it himself. This led to an argument between the two men, and Matthews claimed that he climbed the fence into his own field. When Richardson followed him, Matthews claimed that he forbade him to do so, but that he crossed the fence anyway. At this point, as Richardson pulled a revolver out of his pocket he yelled, "You black —, I intend to shoot you now and put an end to this trouble."[63] Because Richardson had made similar threats before, Matthews told him to go ahead and shoot. Richardson fired three shots in rapid succession, at which point Matthews realized that Richardson really was going to kill him, and he began to fight back. Richardson fired one more shot as Matthews began to wrestle with him and Matthews managed to get the revolver away from Richardson, which he threw to his son Joe. At this point Mrs Richardson came out carrying an axe, and along with her younger son, who had a pitchfork, began to hit him from behind. He finally let Richardson go, and the entire Richardson family retreated to their house. The article also described how Matthews had been in extreme pain throughout the interview, but that he had persevered to the end of his story. Later that evening around 5 p.m., however, Matthews finally succumbed to his injuries and died.

Three hours later, Dr McKenzie of Harrow performed an autopsy on the body at the behest of the coroner. His findings were laid out in a five-page report and were consistent with Dr Campeau's earlier examination, which found three superficial wounds and one that had punctured the body.[64] The bullet had entered the body between the tenth and eleventh ribs, cutting through the body before passing through the kidney and lodging in one of the back muscles where it was found. Other than some small tubercles in the lungs, Edmund Matthews had been a healthy man. In concluding his report Dr McKenzie wrote, "The cause of death was hemorrhage and shock due to the penetrating wound of the left side."[65]

Three days later, on Tuesday, 14 July, Oliver Richardson was brought back by train to Harrow from Sandwich for the coroner's inquest, which was held in the town hall. Richardson was escorted by Detectives Campeau and Mahoney and met at the train station by members of his family, as well as a crowd of Black people. There were no hostile demonstrations, however, and the group followed Richardson and the detectives to the hall, which was packed full of spectators. Coroner Hassard of Harrow presided over the inquest, which began soon after 10 am with testimony from the son of the victim, Joseph Matthews. According to the *Windsor Weekly Record* he "gave his evidence very intelligently."[66] He had been with his father when the shooting took place and told a story similar to the statement his father made before he died. He had heard Richardson's sons shout to their father to "Shoot the black son of a b—h" before the defendant fired.[67] He said that Richardson shot his father twice before his father threw a stone at him, and that after two more shots his father had managed to tackle Richardson to the ground and take the gun away. Richardson's sons, who were holding a pitchfork and an axe, had been holding Joseph back, while Mrs Richardson attacked his father with an axe and the younger son hit him with a pitchfork. Joseph Matthews's testimony was followed by Dr McKenzie who gave his written report of the ante-mortem examination. Fred H.A. Davis and R.M. Dennis then presented the statement Matthews had made to them before he died, over the objections of the defence counsel.

Next were the defendant's sons, Frank and George Richardson.[68] The story that they told was very different from what Edmund and Joseph Matthews had claimed. They said that when their father had told Matthews about the colt being in their field, he had told him to go to hell and refused to get the colt. When they went to retrieve the colt themselves, Matthews started to throw stones at their father. They claimed that while they had not been carrying anything, both Matthews and his son were carrying clubs. While backing away from Matthews, their father tripped and they heard Edmund Matthews calling to his son Joseph, telling him to come help him kill the "white sons of b—h's."[69] Their father then drew his revolver and shot three or four times, after which he retreated to the fence and Matthews fell on top of him. After George rolled Matthews off his father, Matthews picked up a stone and threw it at their mother, knocking her down. Under cross-examination by Mr Bartlet the boys claimed that their father had owned the revolver for five or six years, but that he had started to carry it only since the trial at Harrow.

This testimony was followed by Andrew Thompson, a white neighbour who lived north of the fourth concession. He had been on his farm and had witnessed the scene from a distance. Although he could not identify the men from where he had been, he had seen only a stone thrown after the first two shots, and before the second two shots, and the man who threw the stone did not appear to be holding a club. He had not gone over to intervene because his sons had urged him not to get involved, and he went over only after Richardson and his family had left the scene. The last witness of the day was Della Heaton, a white girl about twenty-four years old, who arrived on the scene after the shooting and found Edmund Matthews lying in the ditch.[70] She testified that Matthews said that he was dying, and when his wife came out he told her that he would not have gone for the horse if he had known what was going to happen. One detail in her testimony that was mentioned only in the *Amherstburg Echo* was that Matthews asked her to fan him.[71] Given the social fears about the relationship between Black men and white women that were dominant at the time, it seems notable that a Black man could ask a young white woman to fan him: it suggests that the racial barriers within this community were not so stringent that they could not be put aside in extreme circumstances.

The coroner's inquest resumed on Friday, 17 July, and included the testimony of three neighbours.[72] One had heard Matthews shout "keep off my place" along with four shots on the day of the shooting, while the other two claimed that they had heard Oliver Richardson threaten the life of Edmund Matthews on two separate occasions.[73] They were followed by Dr Campeau who had treated Matthews, and had also attended to Mrs Richardson. Despite her claims that she had been injured in the melee by the victim, the doctor stated that when he had examined her he had not seen any bruises, only a minor abrasion on her lip. Since the fight, however, she had been acting as though she had been severely injured. While the local newspapers and Dr Campeau shared the opinion she was exaggerating her injuries, the *Toronto Star* showed her much more sympathy by stating, "The woman's head and neck show evidence of severe injury."[74] The final witnesses were two white fence-viewers who had been called in to resolve the land dispute and had heard Richardson threaten to shoot Matthews, and Constables Laporte and Swegles, who had dealt with the men's ongoing dispute and investigated the shooting. The verdict of the jury was unanimous and expected.[75] They found that Edmund Matthews had died because of a bullet wound that had been shot by Oliver Richardson with intent to kill. Oliver Richardson was then returned to the Sandwich jail, where he was held without bail until the fall assizes in September.[76]

The Crown attorney for the Sandwich fall assizes had already been set before the shooting took place. At the end of June 1903, Col. J.C. Hegler of Ingersoll asked Col. John Morison Gibson, the attorney general, for the position.[77] This was early for a request for an assize, but Hegler felt that he had special knowledge related to one of the cases, *King v. Holman*, in which it was alleged that Ben Holman, a representative of the Dominion Express Co., had appropriated over eight hundred dollars of the company's money.[78] Thus Hegler received much more than he bargained for when he volunteered to prosecute a matter of theft from an employer; he ended up being responsible for prosecuting an interracial murder. The case appears to have been a priority. As an MLA, Attorney General Gibson was known for his "progressive" tendencies, which included the introduction of the Gibson Act in 1893 that was intended to protect children and prevent cruelty against them.[79] Although there is no evidence that Gibson was directly involved in working to protect the rights of Black people, he did have political connections to George Brown, who founded the *Toronto Globe* and was a staunch supporter of the abolitionist movement.[80] According to Donald Simpson, "When one turns to the commercial press, one paper, the *Globe*, stands out in its defence of the rights of the black immigrant and in its attack on the institution of slavery."[81] To what extent Gibson may have been influenced by Brown it is hard to say, but in another letter to Gibson in early August, Hegler stated, "I fully recognize the responsibility resting on me in the murder case and as I said to Mr Cartwright [the deputy attorney general] I want to make the most I can of it properly for my own sake and will leave nothing undone that I can do."[82] This included the possibility of Hegler personally going with Detective Campeau to see the location of the shooting. Regardless of whether he was able to go or not, Hegler maintained contact with Detective Campeau and worked hard to prepare for the case.[83]

The Sandwich fall assizes opened on Monday, 21 September 1903 in the Essex County Courthouse. Chancellor John A. Boyd, president of the High Court of Justice, presided, and his opening address to the grand jury focused on the case of *R. v. Richardson* and the notion of British justice. He began by commending the county for the fact that although they shared a border with the United States there were only two criminal cases to be tried, but regretted that one of those cases involved the most serious offence. He continued,

It is a deplorable state of affairs when one man raises his hand to crimson it with the heart's blood of a fellow being – to bring to an untimely end a mortal being before the time allotted him to die by God, the Giver of Life. Were we in some of the states of the sister nation whose fair shores lie in such close proximity to our borders, it might be necessary to inform you that he whose blood was spilt belongs to the despised and down trodden race of former slaves, the Negro. There it might be in keeping to stretch the law a little in favor of the more fortunate white man. But, I am proud to say we are on Canadian soil where the life of the colored man is as much revered, and where the blood of the Negro is as precious to justice and mercy as that of any other of our subjects. Where the British flag, the loved union jack, floats, there must justice reign. I charge you not to let the race question alter your unbiased opinions or convictions.[84]

This flowery prose and nationalistic symbolism demonstrate that, from the very beginning, one purpose of this trial was to demonstrate the superiority of British justice. While Americans will manipulate the law to achieve a desired outcome, in Canada "the despised and down trodden race of former slaves, the Negro" will receive equal justice. What is slightly ironic about the statement is the fundamental contradiction Boyd invokes. He claims that were the shooting to have happened in the United States it would be necessary to inform them that the victim was Black. But his entire statement is built around the race of the victim, regardless of the claims of British justice, thereby providing the grand jury with the information he claimed to be irrelevant within a Canadian context. He therefore rejects race as an important factor, while simultaneously bringing it to the fore. This address was followed by a short examination of ten key witnesses before the grand jury, who returned a true bill against Richardson.

Hegler was aided in the prosecution by white county Crown Attorney A.H. Clarke and Black Attorney Delos R. Davis. Davis's specialty was in drainage litigation, but he acted as counsel in six murder cases.[85] He did not play an active role within the courtroom, as Hegler was responsible for the addresses to the jury and the examination of the witnesses.[86] Although he may have known the victim's family, as his son was the lawyer called to make Matthews's will before he died, Davis's inclusion as counsel appears largely symbolic as a demonstration of the "racelessness" of the legal system. Not only was a white man being charged with murder for killing a Black man, but one of the men representing the Crown in the case was himself Black, thereby making it clear that race in the Canadian justice system was not a topic of concern.[87]

Defending Richardson was another local white attorney John H. Rodd and eminent white defence attorney E.F.B. Johnston from Toronto. Johnston's most famous case was his defence of Clara Ford in 1895, a mulatto seamstress who had confessed to killing a wealthy young white man.[88] Johnston managed to save his client by taking advantage of racial stereotypes and claiming that she had been tricked by unchivalrous detectives intent on advancing their careers by solving a notorious murder. In the case of *R. v. Richardson*, Johnston had a very different task: convince an Essex County jury that a white man had been acting in self-defence when he had shot his Black neighbour with whom he had an ongoing dispute.

The trial began on Wednesday, 23 September. About an hour was needed for jury selection, with most of the challenges coming from Richardson's counsel. The final jury was made up of men from all over the county. All were farmers and had been born in Ontario, although there was some diversity reflected in other respects.[89] In terms of "racial or tribal origin" the men were English, Scottish, and French. Some were married with children, others were married with no children, and some were single. Two spoke French as their first language, and, notably, one, a French-Canadian farmer from Rochester named John Walker, was Black.[90]

Hegler's opening statement echoed many of the same sentiments expressed by Chancellor Boyd in his opening address. He called on the jury to do their duty and to render a verdict based on the evidence. He asked them not to let racial prejudice influence or interfere with their decision-making: "Let not prejudice or ill will toward the colored race alter your decision, gentlemen … Our law and justice should protect alike all citizens, whether red, white or black. Our colored citizens must get justice, and I am pleased to say that there are no burnings at the stake in our Dominion as in countries not far away."[91] In a supposedly "raceless" system, there was nevertheless much emphasis placed on the race of the victim. Hegler's statement makes it appear as though it were an accepted fact that Canadian society was divided into red, white, and Black, but the most important point was that this socially accepted racial hierarchy did not interfere with the administration of justice. In spite of this contradiction between the simultaneous acceptance and denial of race as an important social category, it is clear that this address reinforced the theme of British justice to the jury. Similar to the ideology of chivalric justice invoked by Johnston in the case of Clara Ford, Hegler reminded the jury of British justice, which was a concept deeply embedded in Canadian popular culture.[92] Hegler appealed to the ideologies they held as citizens of Canada and Britain, and called on them to uphold the institutions that defined them as a nation distinct from the United States.

The first witness was James Laird, a civil engineer who provided the court with a plan of the properties and the scene of the murder. He was followed by Andrew Thompson, Dr Campeau, and Dr Mackenzie. Many of the witnesses had testified at the coroner's inquest, and their testimony remained largely consistent with what they had stated then. In the afternoon the trial resumed and the courtroom was even more crowded than it had been in the morning, with every seat taken and even standing room at a premium. A significant number of Black people had come on the morning train from the towns nearest Colchester, and many brought lunch baskets so they could stay for the entire day.[93] Within the courtroom there was a "color line" drawn next to the railing, where "a row of damsels stood patiently listening to the evidence."[94] Regardless of whether or not this racial segregation was a social convention or a legal rule, it demonstrates the pervasiveness of racism within the legal system. Even in a murder trial where the victim was Black and was intended to exemplify the "racelessness" of the Canadian justice system, there was still a visible reminder that the racial hierarchy of Canadian society extended into the courtroom.

Joseph Matthews then testified, followed by the neighbour who had heard the shots. At this point the prosecution attempted to introduce statements given by Edmund Matthews before his death. Mrs Matthews, the victim's wife, was called, but the defence objected to her testimony; the defence then called I.M. Cady, the representative from the *Detroit Free Press* who had interviewed Matthews a couple of hours before he died. Matthews appears to have made two statements about the shooting before he died: one was a deposition given in the middle of the night to Barrister Fred Davis and Justice of the Peace R.M. Dennis, which was introduced over the objections of the defence at the coroner's inquest; the other was given to the press representative from the *Detroit Free Press*. In Hegler's correspondence with Gibson in August, he acknowledged a fear that the dying declaration would be rejected on the grounds that it was not based on "a settled and hopeless expectation of death."[95] Hegler was not explicit in the letter as to which statement he was referring to, but it seems likely that he chose to introduce the second statement at the trial, since it was taken later and was therefore more likely to satisfy the condition that it be a dying declaration.[96] When it was discovered through cross-examination by Johnston that the testimony Cady had given was not a verbatim report of the interview, however, Chancellor Boyd deemed it inadmissible according to the rules of evidence. Although the court offered to dismiss the jury and postpone the trial until the spring assizes, after a conference with his wife and Johnston, Richardson chose to continue.[97]

The rest of the afternoon consisted of the testimony of Constable Swegles, who had investigated the scene, and those who had witnessed Richardson threaten to shoot Matthews. Of those who were called to give evidence of the threats were two Black labourers, a white deputy sheriff, and one of the white fence-viewers whose brother was the sheriff. Also called during this series of witnesses, but not examined, was Constable Nathan Powell, a Black man who was listed as a labourer in the 1901 Canadian census.[98] Although there is no information as to why Powell did not testify, Chancellor Boyd's benchbook includes the note: "knew Matthews; he was a *very* dark *colour*."[99] It is instructive that this was considered a relevant piece of information for Chancellor Boyd to record; apparently the "racelessness" of British justice did not extend to the judge's personal benchbook.

The court adjourned at 7 p.m. and began again the next morning at 9 o'clock. Another series of witnesses were called to prove that Richardson had threatened to kill Matthews on numerous occasions. These witnesses included the reeve of Colchester, both white and Black labourers, and a Black barber.[100] Coroner Hassard was then called to testify about the proceedings at the inquest, Joseph Matthews was recalled to identify the clothes of his father, and County Crown Attorney A.H. Clarke produced a list of convictions against both men beginning in June 1902.

It was then time for the defence to present their case. Richardson's sons, Frank and George, were the first to testify, and although their testimony under direct examination was largely consistent with what they had said at the inquest, they were "badly rattled" under cross-examination by Hegler.[101] They contradicted themselves and were forced to admit that they had told at least one person that Edmund Matthews's son Joseph had done the shooting.[102] Despite this error, they claimed that their father had shot Matthews only *after* he had started to throw stones. The boys were followed by their mother, who testified that Matthews had threatened to kill her husband on two occasions. She told a story of the shooting similar to her sons', but claimed that Joseph Matthews had thrown a stone at her, which hit her in the head, loosening some of her teeth.[103] Under cross-examination a letter was entered into evidence, which the prosecution alleged that she had sent. The letter had been mailed from Michigan and was dated 17 July 1903. It claimed that Oliver Richardson had not committed the murder he was charged with, but that it had been a double or a lookalike. The letter went on to say, "I do not think that you will be able to catch the right party that done it [sic] as said party is able to disguise himself completely and look different altogether."[104] Mrs Richardson denied writing the letter and claimed ignorance when confronted with the fact that she had admitted to giving false testimony under oath in a civil suit a few years before.[105] Hegler could do nothing to get her to change her story, and when challenged by anything that contradicted it she claimed she could not remember.

Mrs Richardson was followed by Dr Samson, who had examined both Oliver and Mrs Richardson the day after the shooting. He had noted an abrasion on Richardson's face, some skin knocked off his hand, and a small bruise on his back, which the doctor stated could not have been done with a club. Mrs Richardson had a minor injury to her mouth, but her teeth were naturally bad. The final witnesses for the defence were a series of white men, all around the same age as Richardson, who testified that Matthews had threatened Richardson.[106] Last, there was a Crown rebuttal witness; the official stenographer from Mrs Richardson's civil case was called to definitively prove that she had previously admitted to lying under oath.[107]

Oliver Richardson was never called to testify in his own defence. This is not surprising, as it was a typical strategy of Johnston's, who felt that there was little to gain and much to lose by allowing a prisoner to testify, especially if the prisoner was a man.[108] Whatever he said would be perceived as necessary for self-preservation and not persuasive with a jury. Another important consideration, especially in this case, was the fact that putting the prisoner on the stand would have opened the door to questions about character. Only two references were made to Richardson's previous charge of assault against Sylvester McLean,[109] but had Richardson been put on the stand, it is possible that all of the details would have been drawn out.

All of the evidence was complete by 3 o'clock, at which point counsel made their closing arguments. Johnston began his two-hour oration with the exclamation, "Murder or nothing!"[110] He argued that since the prosecution alleged that the defendant had committed murder with malice, the jury had to choose between murder and acquittal. In framing the jury's choice in such a manner, Johnston must have felt extremely confident that the jury would not convict his client for the murder, even though it was an undisputed fact that Richardson had pulled the trigger multiple times. He then moved on to discuss the question of race. He claimed that it would be an insult to the jury to plead for justice for any man based on his race; colour did not matter. He believed that the *real* danger lay in whether or not a white man would receive the same justice as a Black man, since too much sympathy for the Black man would lead to discrimination against the white man. He therefore asked the jury to ignore the question of race so justice could be done. In reviewing the evidence, however, Johnston again returned to the question of race. He pointed out that Matthews had been a strong, healthy man in the prime of life, and that they "must not forget the race to which he belonged."[111] Rather than ignoring race, Johnston attempted to appeal to racial stereotypes regarding the comparative strength between Black and white men. The implication was that Richardson had to defend himself with a revolver because Matthews's natural strength as a Black man would overpower him otherwise. According to this theory, the fact that Richardson was fifteen years younger than Matthews and was described as "a big, burly fellow" did not seem to overwhelm the natural advantage Matthews possessed.[112] Johnston also referred to the extreme provocation Richardson endured over the years with their constant quarrelling. In doing so he reinforced Richardson's claim of self-defence by incorporating a claim of provocation, which would have reduced the offence only from murder to manslaughter. Johnston pointed out that the time and place of the shooting were clearly not ideal for a premeditated attack. Richardson carried his revolver with him at all times, and the shooting had not been part of a premeditated plan. If the jury was going to convict Richardson of murder, then it would be based "on the unsupported evidence of the negro boy, Joe Mathews, son of the deceased," which Johnston did not believe the jury would do.[113] Johnston's closing address therefore closely followed the convention already established by Boyd and Hegler; despite claiming that race was not an issue, Johnston spent a great deal of his closing speech invoking racial stereotypes and prejudices, such as Matthews's supposed strength and the unreliability of Joseph Matthews's testimony. While racial stereotypes had helped Johnston to acquit Clara Ford, he would repurpose them to defend Oliver Richardson.

Johnston's forceful address was followed by a quieter but earnest speech by Col. Hegler. Hegler called on the jury to provide a fair and impartial verdict based on the evidence. He then reviewed the facts in the case and pointed out that none of the most important elements were in dispute. Matthews had died because of a gunshot wound that had been inflicted by Richardson. Richardson had been trespassing on Matthews's land when he had pulled out his revolver, a deadly weapon that he had been carrying around. By carrying the revolver around, there could be no doubt that he was courting a quarrel. Hegler briefly pointed out contradictions in Richardson's sons' testimonies and was scathing in his condemnation of Mrs Richardson. He also reminded the jury that they could convict Richardson of either murder or manslaughter. If they did not believe that Richardson's actions were premeditated with malice, they could also find him guilty of manslaughter if they believed that the shooting had been done by accident. He concluded by asking the jury to do justice for both the people and the prisoner.

The next morning Chancellor Boyd provided his charge to the jury. He advised them to avoid the extreme statements that had been given by both families, and to place the most weight on the impartial evidence in between, in particular the eyewitness account of Andrew Thompson. Boyd reviewed the most important pieces of evidence, focusing on the conflicting assertions by the different parties about whether or not Matthews had had a club, and when he had used it against Richardson. If Matthews had not attacked Richardson until after he was shot, it had nothing to do with a claim of self-defence. Boyd emphasized that Thompson did not see any sign of a club until after the last shot, and Dr Samson found no marks on Richardson that could have been made by a club. After he asked them not to let any sympathy for either Matthews or Richardson prevent them from rendering a just verdict, he also questioned what right a farmer had in carrying around a loaded pistol daily. Boyd then moved on to outline the three courses available to the jury: murder, manslaughter, or acquittal. If they believed that Richardson was in fear for his life or of grievous bodily harm, and that Matthews was the aggressor, it was their duty to acquit the prisoner. If they felt that the shooting had been intentional, but not premeditated, their verdict should be manslaughter. If it was "the result of a deliberate determination to take the life of another," however, they should return with a verdict of murder.[114] Johnston raised several objections to the charge, including the fact that they could convict on manslaughter, but was ultimately overruled on all of them.

It took one hour for the jury to reach their verdict.[115] When they had returned to the courtroom and the foreman was asked if the jury had come to a unanimous decision, he responded "Guilty," and sat down. According to the *Amherstburg Echo*, this "startling reply" almost created a panic.[116] The prisoner, who had been stoic throughout the trial, grew pale, and his wife buried her face in her hands. The clerk then asked the foreman what Richardson was guilty of, to which the foreman replied "manslaughter." This was followed by a feeling of relief in the prisoner and his family, but the *Echo*'s description of the scene makes it appear that a verdict of murder was unexpected. While the white community was satisfied with the verdict of manslaughter, many in the Black community were openly disappointed with the result and felt that if Matthews had been white the verdict would have been murder.[117] Although it is impossible to know for certain, it seems likely that the jury was split along the same racial lines. The jury apparently took as long as they did to reach their verdict because one juror believed the verdict should be murder. Whether that lone juror was the single Black man is impossible to know, but it seems likely. In deciding on a sentence, Chancellor Boyd took into consideration the fact that Richardson had a family, but also noted that the victim had also left a wife and children. Although he could have received a penalty of life imprisonment, Oliver

Richardson was ultimately sentenced to fifteen years in the Kingston Penitentiary.

In one sense it seems fairly evident that a genuine effort was made to achieve justice for Edmund Matthews. But while those who were prosecuting Oliver Richardson believed that they were demonstrating the "racelessness" of the Canadian justice system, a more careful contextual analysis reveals that the trial merely hid the more deeply entrenched racism and prejudices within society. Edmund Matthews was a well-respected and integrated member of the community from a prominent local family, while Oliver Richardson was a bully with a shady past, whose own family wanted nothing to do with him. The fact that the community was willing to prosecute Richardson does not demonstrate the existence of a "raceless" society; it merely demonstrates that many other social factors come into play in the administration of justice.

Moreover, racialized discourse was present throughout the trial, from the opening remarks of Chancellor Boyd to the grand jury, to the closing address of the defence. These legal actors would simultaneously disavow and contribute to racial stereotypes and hierarchies. No attention was paid to the fact that Matthews, an otherwise law-abiding citizen, would feel the need to hide from the local constable when he came to arrest him. Perhaps Matthews recognized that he would not receive a fair hearing when his word was pitted against a white man's, even when that white man had Richardson's notorious reputation. Richardson had certainly been able to threaten Matthews's life with impunity in front of countless legal officials, and it was only when Matthews was shot multiple times at point-blank range with numerous witnesses that the law intervened on his behalf. Some newspapers even claimed that Richardson had never expected any penalty for what he had done.[118] While it would be dishonest to claim that Matthews had been an innocent victim, he had been forced to navigate a system that was stacked against him. He was drawn into the dispute by a confrontational neighbour who showed little respect for the property of others, and the only thing Matthews could do was try his best to stand his ground. As noted by Barrington Walker in his study of the experiences of Black defendants in criminal cases, Matthews may have been entitled to formal legal equality, but this equality was constantly undermined by the informal racism inherent within society.[119]

The verdict and sentence also leave much to be desired. A contemporary legal perspective may believe that a verdict of manslaughter was justified under the circumstances, but the case of *R. v. Slaughter*, which was tried in Sandwich the following year, reveals the disparities of justice based on race.[120] The Slaughter case represented an almost mirror image of *R. v. Richardson*, and it even featured many of the same legal actors; County Crown Attorney A.H. Clarke acted for the prosecution, while Delos R. Davis was the defence counsel. In that case a Black American man killed an intoxicated white man who called him a "nigger" by hitting him over the head with a pool cue. Although these men were strangers with no previous contact or relationship, and the weapon had been merely what was on hand, the Black defendant was convicted of murder. These facts precisely fit Boyd's definition of manslaughter, and yet the verdict was murder. It is therefore hard to argue against the fact that there appeared to be different standards for manslaughter and for murder, depending on the race of the victim and the defendant. Regardless of the purported "racelessness" of British justice, it was ultimately up to the jury to decide what was just, and although these men may have striven to uphold the lofty ideals of British justice, their decisions nevertheless reflected the informal racism inherent within society.

The inequality in justice between the two verdicts was so obvious that as soon as the verdict was given in the Slaughter case, the judge expressed doubt in meting out the mandatory penalty of death. In a letter to the minister of justice arguing for commutation of the sentence, County Crown Attorney Clarke argued, "It was generally expected in the community that the verdict would be manslaughter and I think that under the circumstances justice would be done by commuting the punishment to life imprisonment. It is not long since a white man in this County was tried on the charge of murdering a colored man there being a great deal of ill-will between them. In that case the verdict of the Jury was manslaughter and not murder, and in view of the unequal position of the colored man in society I think it would be in the interests of justice that the Government should intervene."[121]

While it was commendable that this miscarriage in justice was recognized so quickly, and the Black man's death sentence was commuted to life imprisonment, it nevertheless highlights one of the many gaps between the rhetoric and reality of British justice. While solitary acts of apparent impartiality like *R. v. Richardson* could help to temporarily hide some of these gaps, it did nothing to resolve the underlying racial inequality pervasive within Canadian society. While British justice may have been "raceless," entitling everyone to formal legal equality, it was implemented by men who implicitly and uncritically accepted racial hierarchies, ultimately leading to different justice for those who were white and those who were not. In the end, notions of British justice may have led the jury in Richardson's case to feel that Richardson should be punished for killing a Black man, but they did not feel that Richardson should be hanged for killing a Black man. The fact that he was tried and punished by the law would be enough to distinguish themselves from their uncivilized American counterparts. *R. v. Richardson* therefore does not demonstrate that the Canadian justice system was "raceless," but that Canadians built a sense of identity based on idealized ideological notions of justice and equality that could be contrasted against American vigilantism.

What are truly needed to understand the relationships between race, nationalism, and the law, however, are more studies that explore race from this neglected perspective. While numerous studies focus on discriminatory government practices and the over-prosecution of minority populations for crimes, research into the extent to which the justice system prosecuted white Canadians for crimes against minorities seems to be lacking. Was this really the first time a white man was charged with murdering a Black man in Ontario? How representative is this case? These are questions that are yet to be answered, but they provide an opportunity to add another necessary dimension to the discussion of race within Canada.

NOTES

This paper was the result of a fourth-year undergraduate legal history seminar at York University. I would like to thank Professor Paul Craven for his guidance throughout the research process, as well as his instrumental role in getting this paper published. Further, I would like to thank editor-in-chief Jim Phillips; my parents for funding the project; and Ashwin Fernandes for his ongoing support and patience. I would also like to acknowledge the Marsh Historical Collection for their remarkably complete collection of the *Amherstburg Echo*, as well as the wonderful volunteers at the Harrow Early Immigrant Research Society.

1 *Amherstburg Echo*, 17 July 1903. The newspapers of the period along with the criminal assize clerk indictment file were the principal primary sources for this study.

2 *Toronto Globe*, 24 Sept. 1903.

3 Carolyn Strange, "Wounded Womanhood and Dead Men: Chivalry and the Trials of Clara Ford and Carrie Davies," in *Gender Conflicts: New Essays in Women's History*, ed. Franca Iacovetta and Mariana Valverde, 149–88 (Toronto: University of Toronto Press, 1992).

4 While there is considerable debate about the nature of "liberty" in Canadian history, most historians would accept that in some form it can be seen as a dominant ethos in Canada after ca. 1840. Equality before the law is a less contentious notion; while at times not observed, it was always a crucial tenet of Canadian political and legal ideology. For an introduction to recent debates on the nature of liberty and equality in Canadian political thought, see Jean-Francois Constant and Michel Ducharme, eds., *Liberalism and Hegemony: Debating the Canadian Liberal Revolution* (Toronto: University of Toronto Press, 2009); and Philip Girard, "Liberty, Order and Pluralism: The Canadian Experience," in *Exclusionary Empire: English Liberty Overseas, 1600–1900*, ed. Jack P. Greene, 160–90 (New York: Cambridge University Press, 2010).

5 Although the Act received royal assent in 1833 it took effect only on 1 August 1834.

6 R.M. Fuller, *Windsor Heritage* (Windsor: Herald, 1972), 127–8.

7 A search of the *Toronto Globe* database for the term *lynching* revealed reporting of over fifty incidents of lynching and attempted lynching of Black men in the United States from July 1900 to September 1903. Of these only about four focus on the crime that was allegedly committed. There were also reports about the number of men who had been lynched in the United States and commendations for charges that were brought against lynchers.

8 *Globe*, 12 Feb. 1901; 26 Aug. 1901; 18 Feb. 1902; 4 May 1903; 27 July 1903; 22 Sept. 1903.

9 *Globe*, 11 May 1901; 17 July 1901; 18 July 1903.

10 *Globe*, 23 Aug. 1901.

11 Clayton James Mosher, *Discrimination and Denial: Systemic Racism in Ontario's Legal and Criminal Justice, 1892–1961* (Toronto: University of Toronto Press, 1998), 93.

12 Mosher, *Discrimination and Denial*, 103; James W. St.G. Walker, *"Race," Rights and the Law in the Supreme Court of Canada: Historical Case Studies* ([Toronto]: Osgoode Society for Canadian Legal History and Wilfrid Laurier University Press, 1997), 190.

13 Mosher, *Discrimination and Denial*, 89.

14 The most well-known case of racial violence in Canada before the 1950s was an event that occurred in Oakville in 1930, when a young interracial

couple who were living together planned to marry against the wishes of the white girl's mother. The Ku Klux Klan intervened, returning the girl to her mother and warning the Black fiancé to stay away from the girl in the future. Although the group claimed that they were acting within the laws because they never used force, they had acted at night while wearing Klan uniforms (including masks), and burned a cross on the lawn of the young man. Although criminal charges were laid against some of the Klansmen who had participated, they were for minor offences, and only one was actually convicted, and initially he was not even sentenced to any jail time. Constance Backhouse, *Colour-Coded: A Legal History of Racism in Canada, 1900–1950* (Toronto: Osgoode Society for Canadian Legal History, 1999), 173–225. The incident was also mentioned by Walker, *"Race," Rights and the Law*, 135–7.

15 Mosher, *Discrimination and Denial*, 176; Barrington Walker, *Race on Trial: Black Defendants in Ontario's Criminal Courts, 1858–1958* (Toronto: University of Toronto Press, 2010), 19.

16 Mosher, *Discrimination and Denial*, 179, 187.

17 Donald G. Simpson, *Under the North Star: Black Communities in Upper Canada*, ed. Paul E. Lovejoy (Trenton, NJ: Africa World, 2005), 281. Those settlements were the town of Colchester, New Canaan, Kingsville, Gilgal, Pleasant Valley, the Matthews Settlement, and Cannonsburg. Although there is not much information about the Matthews Settlement, it was named after the victim's father and grandfather who settled there in the 1830s, and included a school.

18 Michael Wayne, "The Black Population of Canada West on the Eve of the American Civil War: A Reassessment Based on the Manuscript Census of 1861," *Histoire sociale / Social History* 28, no. 56 (1995): 482–5. Colchester was third after Chatham and Raleigh, both in Kent County.

19 Ibid., 471.

20 Simpson, *Under the North Star*, 281.

21 Ibid., 161.

22 Mosher, *Discrimination and Denial*, 85.

23 Simpson, *Under the North Star*, 283.

24 Robin W. Winks, *The Blacks in Canada: A History*, 2nd ed. (Montreal and Kingston: McGill-Queen's University Press, 1997), 368.

25 Colchester itself had four Black school sections, including one on the Third Concession in the Matthews Settlement. While most schools became integrated again in the 1860s, the school in the Matthews Settlement remained predominantly Black until the 1960s.

26 As quoted in Simpson, *Under the North Star*, 284.

27 Daniel G. Hill, *The Freedom Seekers: Blacks in Early Canada* (Agincourt, ON: Book Society of Canada, 1971), 196; Harrow Early Immigrant Research Society (HEIRS), *Harrow and Colchester South, 1792–1992* (Harrow, ON: Harrow History Book Committee, 1993), 148.

28 Owen Thomas, "Davis, Delos Rogest," *Dictionary of Canadian Biography On-line*, 2000, http://www.biographi.ca/009004-119.01-e.php?&id_nbr=7322.

29 Thomas, "Davis, Delos Rogest"; Ronald G. Hoskins, "Balfour, William Douglas," *Dictionary of Canadian Biography Online*, 2000, http://www .biographi.ca/009004-119.01-e.php?&id_nbr=5944. The newspaper at the time of the trial regularly included notices for events at the local Black churches, suggesting that it was a medium of communication for the Black community.

30 *Echo*, 15 Aug. 1924.

31 Canada, *House of Commons Debates* (1910–11), p. 5911, qtd by Mosher, *Discrimination and Denial*, 92.

32 *Echo*, 17 July 1903.

33 Ibid.

34 Eligh was described in the article as a highly respected farmer.

35 As quoted in *Detroit Free Press*, 12 July 1903.

36 *Windsor Weekly Record*, 17 July 1903.

37 Ibid. Although a common turn of phrase, this is certainly an ironic statement, given the racial issues inherent in the dispute.

38 *Echo*, 17 July 1903.

39 While it is possible that this portion of land was the same property that was in dispute in 1903, since Matthew Matthews Sr was the original purchaser of one of the pieces of land, a topographical plan of the area published in the *Echo* shows that Richardson's home was on a piece of land immediately adjacent to a large plot of land still owned by Matthew Matthews Sr at the time of the murder. These properties were separated by a side road bordering the properties in dispute at the time of shooting. Since Richardson bought the property between Edmund Matthews's two properties only a few years before the shooting, it seems more likely that this was a separate dispute involving other properties. *Echo*, 17 July 1903.

40 Ibid.

41 Assessment Rolls for Oliver Richardson, Edmund Matthews, Matthew Matthews Sr, and Francis Richardson, 1880, 1885, 1887, 1893, 1895, 1897, Township of South Colchester diffusion material, D 301, microfilm GS 870(a), Archives of Ontario. Richardson first appears on the assessment rolls in 1887 with one property of fifty acres; in 1893 he appears again, but

without any property listed. He is not listed at all on the assessment rolls
in 1895, while in 1897 his wife is listed as the owner of the property.

42 Defendant: Richardson, Oliver; Charged with Assault occasioning Bodily
Harm; Receiving Stolen Good, Essex County, 1897, Criminal Assize Clerk
criminal indictment file, RG 22-392-0-1477, Archives of Ontario. A detailed
account of the assault and trial is also given in *Echo*, 8 Jan. 1897, and 26
Mar. 1897.

43 *Weekly Record*, 25 Sept. 1903.

44 *Echo*, 24 July 1903.

45 Ibid.

46 Edmond Matthews household, family 62, p. 6, Colchester South division 3,
Essex South (district 60), Ontario, 1901 census of Canada.

47 *Echo*, 17 July 1903.

48 Although Virginia was a slave state, there is no mention that Matthew
Matthews Sr was ever a slave. There were significant populations of free
Blacks in some of the slave states, including Maryland, Virginia, and Kentucky, but as conditions in the United States became more oppressive as
the country neared the Civil War, many emigrated. Wayne, "Black Population of Canada West," 472.

49 *Echo*, 16 Nov. 1906.

50 *Historical Atlas of Essex and Kent Counties* (repr., Toronto: H. Belden, 1973),
35.

51 HEIRS, *Harrow and Colchester South*, 148.

52 Michael L. Radelet, "Executions of Whites for Crimes against Blacks: Exceptions to the Rule?," *Sociological Quarterly* 30, no. 4 (1989): 529–44.

53 Radelet's source of information for the executions is what he contends to
be the most extensive archive of American executions, which is located
in Headland, AL, and has been developed and maintained by Watt Espy.
Espy has accumulated information on 15,978 executions that have occurred in American jurisdictions since 1608. The range of dates for the
cases studied by Radelet is from 1739 to 1944.

54 Walker, *Race on Trial*, 51–3.

55 Ibid., 52. The other piece of information that we can take from the execution of Levi Steward is that there was no community disinclination away
from execution. A community history of Sandwich, ON, that was published in 1909 includes an account of all executions that had occurred there
in the preceding hundred years. It begins by stating, "During the early
part of this town's existence as a District or County seat punishment was
dealt out with a liberal hand." Apart from Steward, who was the most
recent execution listed, there were fourteen other executions in Sandwich,

all but one for murder (another man was also convicted of murder in 1904, although his sentence was commuted). This can be contrasted to the experience of Prince Edward County, which was discussed by Robert Sharpe in *The Lazier Murder*. In 1884 two men were hanged for murder, but a subsequent sense of guilt within the community based on the feeling that at least one of the men had been innocent meant that no future Prince Edward County jury convicted an accused charged with a capital offence; Robert J. Sharpe, *The Lazier Murder: Prince Edward County, 1884* (Toronto: University of Toronto Press, 2011).

56 His father and legal partner was Delos R. Davis.

57 HEIRS, *Harrow and Colchester South*, 30.

58 The doctor who treated Matthews and the detective who was called in Windsor shared the same last name. The Campeau family was one of the oldest French families of the locality, the French having been the first Europeans to settle in the area (Detective Campeau himself was fifth generation). While it is certainly possible that the two men were related, there is no information on how closely. *Commemorative Biographical Record of the County of Essex, Ontario: Containing Biographical Sketches of Prominent and Representative Citizens* (Toronto: J.H. Beers, 1905), 508; John Clarke, *The Ordinary People of Essex: Environment, Culture, and Economy on the Frontier of Upper Canada* (Montreal and Kingston: McGill-Queen's University Press, 2010), 77.

59 *Weekly Record*, 14 July 1903.

60 *Echo*, 24 July 1903.

61 Ibid.

62 *Detroit Free Press*, 12 July 1903.

63 Ibid.

64 Defendant: Richardson, Oliver; Charged with Murder, Essex County, 1903, Criminal Assize Clerk criminal indictment file, RG 22-392-0-1500, Archives of Ontario (henceforward Richardson Murder criminal indictment file).

65 Ibid.

66 *Weekly Record*, 17 July 1903.

67 Ibid.

68 Constrained by space considerations, I have combined the two testimonies of Richardson's sons. They were largely consistent with one another, although there were some conflicting reports between the coverage of the *Weekly Record* and the *Echo*. I have tried to include the most salient details.

69 *Weekly Record*, 17 July 1903. This statement is attributed to both Edmund and Joseph Matthews, depending on which newspaper account is read.

I have chosen to attribute it to Edmund Matthews, as I believe it would most strengthen Richardson's claim of self-defence.

70 David P. Heaton household, family 96, p. 9, Colchester South division 3, Essex South (district 60), Ontario, 1901 census of Canada.

71 *Echo*, 17 July 1903.

72 Note that George Johnson and Frank Powell, the men who claimed that they heard the threats, were both Black, but there is conflicting information about the race of the third witness, Frank Harris. The *Weekly Record*, 21 July 1903, states that all three witnesses were "colored," but the 1901 Canadian census lists Harris as white; Frank Harris household, family 73, p. 7, Colchester South division 3, Essex South (district 60), Ontario, 1901 census of Canada.

73 *Echo*, 24 July 1903.

74 *Toronto Star*, 13 July 1903.

75 *Weekly Record*, 14 July 1903.

76 There was also a preliminary hearing in Sandwich on 22 July 1903 before the police magistrate. The only witnesses were Joseph Matthews and Dr Mackenzie; *Weekly Record*, 24 July 1903.

77 J.C. Hegler to Col. Gibson, 30 June 1903, in A.G.O. [Attorney General's Department]; Correspondence re Fall Assizes, 1903, Attorney General Central Registry Criminal and Civil Files, RG 4-32, microfilm MS 7593, Archives of Ontario (henceforward AGO Correspondence).

78 *Echo*, 25 Sept. 1903; Holman was ultimately acquitted.

79 Carolyn E. Gray, "Gibson, Sir John Morison," *Dictionary of Canadian Biography Online*, 2000, http://www.biographi.ca/009004-119.01-e.php?&id_nbr=8157.

80 Simpson, *Under the North Star*, 73. Although Brown died in 1880, the reporting of the *Globe* at the turn of the century still appeared very supportive of the rights of the Black community. As already discussed, it gave a notable amount of coverage to reports of lynching in the United States. While the *Toronto Star* gave coverage to the initial shooting and Coroner's inquest, it tended to favour Richardson's account of the events, and the subsequent reports of the trial were very short, with no mention of the final verdict. In contrast, the *Globe* followed the entire sequence of events, which included front page coverage of the shooting and the closing addresses of the trial.

81 Ibid.

82 12 Aug. 1903, AGO Correspondence.

83 Detectives Campeau and Mahoney appear to have gone on their own to Harrow to collect evidence and get witnesses for the prosecution on Fri-

day, 4 Sept. 1903; J.H. Rodd went to Harrow for the defence the next day; *Echo*, 11 Sept. 1903.

84 As quoted in *Echo*, 25 Sept. 1903.

85 Thomas, "Davis, Delos Rogest."

86 Clarke played a small role in the courtroom as he introduced a list of some of the convictions against the two men.

87 The amount of difficulty Davis had in obtaining an articling position and the fact that he ultimately had to rely on a special act of Parliament to be admitted to the bar completely undermines any claim that his presence on a case reflects the "racelessness" of the legal system.

88 Strange, "Wounded Womanhood and Dead Men."

89 Information about the jurors was taken from the 1901 Canadian census. Elgin Corbett is listed as a fruit grower. Two of the jurors (Harvey/Harry Wilson of Walkerville and William Murray of Malden) could not be located on the census and therefore information about their language, race, profession, etc. is unknown.

90 On the Canadian census of 1901, Walker is listed as Catholic, single, living with his mother, able to read and write, and his mother tongue is French; John Walker household, family 41, p. 5, Rochester division 6, North Essex (district 59), Ontario, 1901 census of Canada.

91 *Echo*, 25 Sept. 1903.

92 Greg Marquis, "Doing Justice to 'British Justice': Law Ideology, and Canadian Historiography," in *Canadian Perspectives on Law and Society: Issues in Legal History*, ed. W. Wesley Pue and Barry Wright (Ottawa: Carleton University Press, 1988), 70.

93 *Weekly Record*, 25 Sept. 1903.

94 Ibid.

95 12 Aug. 1903, AGO Correspondence.

96 The first statement was made at around the same time that Matthews made his will, which his doctor had suggested he do. The statement was taken under oath and began, "I feel in a critical condition at the present time and I don't feel that I am going to get well again. I feel that unless there is a change I am not going to get well." As quoted by *Echo*, 17 July 1903. In contrast, the article in the *Detroit Free Press* describes Matthews as "suffering agonies from his wounds," and ends with the statement: "This is the true version of the story, and as I realize that I will not get better, I am telling you God's truth about the whole affair." As quoted by *Detroit Free Press*, 12 July 1903.

97 *Detroit Free Press*, 24 Sept. 1903.

98 The only mention of Nathan Powell's testimony in the newspapers was

in the *Weekly Record*, which stated "Constable Powell was called but not examined." *Weekly Record*, 25 Sept. 1903; Nathan S. Powell household, family 55, p. 6, Colchester South division 1, Essex South (district 60), Ontario, 1901 census of Canada.

99 Since Powell must have said something to be noted in Boyd's benchbook, it is frustrating that there is no information regarding his testimony in the newspaper accounts of the trial, apart from what is mentioned above. Emphasis in original; Benchbooks of Justice John A. Boyd, 15 June–20 November 1903, p. 63, box 3, RG 22-439-1-34, Archives of Ontario.

100 The definition of *reeve* that applies in this context is the council president in some Canadian municipalities. Definition retrieved from *Webster's New College Dictionary* (Toronto: Thomas Allen & Sons, 1973).

101 *London Free Press*, 26 Sept. 1903.

102 *Weekly Record*, 25 Sept. 1903. I found contradictory reports on which brother made this statement, but it does not seem particularly important to definitively attribute it to either one. It is interesting to note, however, that when the *Detroit Free Press* agent went to the Richardson house the day after the shooting, the three youngest boys also claimed that Joseph Matthews had done the shooting; *Free Press*, 12 July 1903.

103 *Weekly Record*, 25 Sept. 1903; this is the story the boys appear to have told in the trial, but it contradicts the evidence they gave at the coroner's hearing.

104 Unsigned letter from Albion, Michigan, to Coroner Geo. A. Hassard, 17 July 1903, part of Richardson Murder criminal indictment file.

105 See extract from cross-examination of Alenna Richardson in *Richardson v. Thompson* tried at a sitting of the County Court, town of Sandwich, December 1899, part of Richardson Murder criminal indictment file.

106 Ages and race of the witnesses obtained from the 1901 Canadian census and local newspaper reports.

107 *Free Press*, 25 Sept. 1903.

108 E.F.B. Johnston, "The Prisoner as a Witness," *Canada Law Journal* 33, no. 18 (1897): 666–73.

109 The first was by one of the fence-viewers in the coroner's inquest who said that he heard Edmund Matthews say, "Richardson, you cannot whip me like you did Sylvester McLean by jumping on his back like a dirty dog" (*Echo*, 24 July 1903). It was also briefly mentioned after the list of previous convictions (*Weekly Record*, 25 Sept. 1903).

110 He began his speech the same way in the case of Clara Ford; see Strange, "Wounded Womanhood and Dead Men," 168.

111 *Weekly Record*, 29 Sept. 1903.

112 *Globe*, 13 July 1903. Kingston Penitentiary intake records state that Richardson was 5'11" and 204 lbs; Inmate: D767 Oliver Richardson, Kingston Penitentiary inmate history description ledger 1886–1912, vol. 558, RG73-C-6, Library and Archives Canada.
113 *Weekly Record*, 29 Sept. 1903.
114 *Echo*, 2 Oct. 1903.
115 The *Weekly Record* stated that it took two hours, but the *Echo*, the *Globe*, and the *Free Press* all agree that it was one hour.
116 *Echo*, 2 Oct. 1903.
117 *Globe*, 26 Sept. 1903. The satisfaction of the white community was evident in a letter from County Crown Attorney A.H. Clarke to Deputy Attorney General J.R. Cartwright. In reporting on the outcome of the trial Clarke states, "I think that the result of the trial will be quite satisfactory to the body of the people." Apparently the "body of the people" to whom he is referring is not the Black community; 25 Sept. 1903, AGO Correspondence.
118 *Weekly Record*, 25 Sept. 1903.
119 Walker, *Race on Trial*.
120 Ibid., 61–4.
121 A.H. Clarke to Charles Fitzpatrick, minister of justice, qtd in Walker, *Race on Trial*, 63–4.

6

Maniacal Murderer or Death Dealing Car: The Case of Daniel Perry Sampson, 1933–1935

DAVID STEEVES

On the evening of 19 July 1933, the bodies of young brothers Edward and Bramwell Heffernan were found a short distance from each other along the railway tracks that ran near their home on the outskirts of Halifax, Nova Scotia. With their clothes torn to shreds and their bodies bloodied, it was believed by many that their deaths had been caused by a tragic misadventure with a passing train, while others speculated that a deranged killer was in their midst. Following an inconclusive coroner's inquest and months of fruitless investigation by local police and the RCMP, Daniel Perry Sampson, an African Nova Scotian veteran of the Great War, was arrested for the brutal murder of both boys. Sampson's passage through the courts included two sets of trials and appeals before Nova Scotian jurists as well as an appearance before the Supreme Court of Canada. Throughout, graphic details of the boys' deaths as well as Sampson's plea of insanity and his counsel's allegations of bias, procedural unfairness, and judicial error were fodder for the front pages of Halifax's four daily newspapers, making this one of the city's most notorious cases of the 1930s. Although there has been some limited attention paid to Sampson since, a closer examination of this case not only clarifies important aspects of Halifax's social history but also exposes a previously unknown piece of Canadian legal history.

The tragic deaths of these two young boys were met with a significant response by authorities and the media representative of the general approach to crime in Halifax during the 1930s. Although Haligonians had long perceived their city to be one of law and order, Halifax was challenged by the exceptional social and economic changes it faced throughout the interwar period (1918–39). Many within the city took a dim view on these transformations and saw them as the precursors to such social ills as the loosening of public morals, drug addiction, prostitution, vagrancy, gambling, and even murder, caused by an identifiable "criminal class" of outsiders in their midst.[1] With little evidence and few leads emerging in the weeks following the horrific discovery, investigative attention focused on connecting the few items found near the scene with an eyewitness account noting the presence of a "coloured" man in the area where the boys were last observed. At the same time, Halifax's daily newspapers had concluded that only a criminally deranged individual could have committed such an act. With the arrest of Daniel Sampson, authorities had finally found a suspect who matched their public portrayal. However, Sampson's passage before Nova Scotian courts presented two significant hurdles over which the Crown would have to pass. First, amid a racially divided city, a panel of twelve unbiased jurors had to be found. Second, characterized by the local media as a cold-blooded, maniacal killer, Sampson would have to be adjudged sufficiently sane if a trial was to occur and a sentence rendered. The related procedural steps taken by the Crown, defence, and the Court provide significant context in this case as well as for other offenders under similar circumstances who faced a Nova Scotian court.

While this case may have captured the attention of Halifax's media and citizenry over the course of almost two years, little is known about Sampson today. Admittedly, my attention was first piqued not by a case law or archival reference but by a mention in the work of noted African-Canadian writer and academic George Elliott Clarke. However exhaustive the contemporary coverage of this case may have been, a closer examination of its legislative, procedural, and cultural underpinnings reveals a previously unknown aspect of racial discrimination that affected most, if not all, jury trials of African Nova Scotians in Halifax from 1890 until 1943. Much has been written about the historically troubling legacy of discrimination faced by African Nova Scotians, with specific focus on its legal dimensions emerging in the wake of the Royal Commission on the Donald Marshall Jr Prosecution. Additionally, recent scholarship has demonstrated how discriminatory policies were made manifest on the Halifax landscape with the ghettoization and subsequent demolition of Africville. Employing an interdisciplinary framework that bridges literature, legal history, doctrinal legal scholarship, and geography, this chapter excavates from case files further examples of discrimination towards the city's minority communities.

The Deaths of Inseparable Brothers

The sudden deaths of Bramwell and Edward Heffernan shocked the city of Halifax – in 1933 a community in the midst of its second decade of economic depression and corresponding social instability. In spite of the significant reconstruction efforts that followed the city's tragic 1917 explosion, Halifax did not share in the same economic prosperity found in central and western Canada during the 1920s. Instead, the significant reduction of Canada's peacetime navy and naval infrastructure, coupled with losses in the manufacturing and resource sectors, among other factors, plunged the city into severe unemployment and resulting poverty from which it would emerge only after Canada's return to conflict in 1939. Unwilling or unable to accept such harsh conditions, many Haligonians, particularly skilled tradesmen, left their families and the city during the 1920s in search of work in the United States and other parts of Canada. This escape route, however, was largely cut off after an American prohibition against further immigration in the early 1930s.[2]

For those who remained, government as well as other groups attempted to confront the social ills afflicting Halifax with varying degrees of success and coverage. Halifax's labour movement, still reeling from its failure in the 1920 Halifax Shipyard strike, saw its numbers diminish and dissention enter its ranks. Attempts to assure job security, such as the Halifax Building Trades Council's issuance of membership cards, proved helpful during the brief construction boom of the late 1920s, but by the 1930s skilled tradesmen were being undercut by others willing to work for lower wages. The provincial government addressed this issue of un- and underemployment with legislation restricting out-of-province workers, but it was the eventual passage of the *Industrial Standards Act* in 1936 and its imposition of binding arbitration on the building trades that would most affect the working class. Charity, both personal and institutional, proved to be only a stopgap measure against the widespread poverty experienced within Halifax. Ultimately, the responsibility for the poor fell on the municipality, which, despite a provision in its charter, provided modest amounts of income support to those who continued to live in their own homes (known as "outdoor relief") as well as sanctioned "indoor relief" to the worst cases through incarceration at the City Home.[3]

Whether by choice or circumstance, Janet and Edward Heffernan were among those who remained in Halifax during the interwar period. It would appear that Edward had enjoyed work as a carpenter during the brief construction boom of the late 1920s, but by the early 1930s had found himself unemployed. In spite of these financial challenges, both parents tried to maintain a closely knit family environment grounded in their faith as Salvationists. This strong sense of family might explain why the Heffernans' two eldest daughters chose not to start their own households but rather, like many of their peers, remain at home, where they could contribute to the family income through their employment at a downtown department store. Unlike other families, however, the two Heffernan boys were not forced to leave school in search of low-paying jobs. Instead, by the summer of 1933 both boys had completed their years at Alexandra School and would be enrolling in grades five and six at Armdale School in the fall.[4]

This change in schools reflects a move by the Heffernans off peninsular Halifax and suggests a further worsening of their financial situation. During this period, many families left the higher rents and close confines of the downtown core for the city's outskirts, where they could supplement their pantries and possibly their modest incomes through small gardens and the keeping of hens, pigs, and even cows.[5] With Edward's lengthening unemployment, the Heffernans appeared to follow this trend with a move from their downtown residence at 944 Barrington Street to the Chain Lake District of Halifax. There, they occupied a small house on the Pipe Line Road that was located a short distance from the meter house of the city's water supply at Chain Lake.[6]

During the afternoon of 19 July 1933, Edward Heffernan and a friend, Richard Matthews, set out from the family home to pick berries in the surrounding woods. Unknown to their father, his two young sons had similar plans and ventured out shortly thereafter with berry pails in hand for their own search. Later, both boys were seen happily picking away amid the bushes that lined the railway tracks a short walk from their home. On their return home at 9:30 that evening, Heffernan and Matthews made the horrific discovery of Bramwell's body lying face-down across the railway tracks less than a half mile from the family home. Distraught, Heffernan picked up his son and attempted to carry him home, but he was soon overcome with grief and was unable to bear his son's body further: Matthews would carry Bramwell's body the rest of the way home. After leaving Bramwell's body with his mother and sisters, both men sought additional assistance from their neighbours and continued to look for the youngest boy. At approximately 10:00 p.m., the body of Heffernan's namesake, Edward, was found a short distance from his brother, lying in a wooded area down a short incline from the railway tracks, clutching leaves in his hands.

The family's physician, H.C.S. Elliott, was summoned to the Heffernan residence at 10:25 p.m. that evening, but there was nothing he could do. Both boys were pronounced dead following what appeared to be a tragic encounter with a train. The circumstance of their sons' deaths hit both parents particularly hard as they had previously warned their boys about the dangers of playing around the nearby railway tracks. Mrs Heffernan was so affected that she had to be removed from the family home and spent the evening with a family friend, Mrs Crozier, in Halifax.[7]

An Inconclusive Verdict

Although front page headlines in each of Halifax's four daily newspapers reported that Bramwell and Edward had been struck and killed by a train, rumour and conjecture in the days following their deaths led many to speculate that a more sinister motive had been at play.[8] Given the sudden nature of their deaths, and quite possibly a desire to quell any public uncertainty, an inquest was convened on 20 July 1933 before Stipendiary Magistrate Ian Ross. The inquest opened at the Heffernan home, at which time jury members, Ross, the Crown, and witnesses examined the locations where both bodies were discovered, as well as an approximately 500-foot-long trail of blood along the nearby railway tracks. Later, the proceedings reconvened in Ross's office at the Halifax courthouse where the bulk of the inquest's testimony and evidence was tendered on its first day.

Any hope by authorities for a swift and decisive determination of what or who had caused the deaths of Bramwell and young Edward Heffernan was quickly dispatched. Testimony in the inquest began with the statements of the elder Edward Heffernan and the men who assisted him in the search for both boys: Matthews, Lewis Nicholson, and Stephen Dwyer. Each testified to the events of the previous evening, but the men were unable to provide any evidence that pointed towards a cause of death.[9]

It was, however, in the initial comments of Dr H.C.S. Elliott that doubt surrounding the cause of death first arose. Elliott testified to his findings from a preliminary examination of both bodies the night before, at which time he concluded that the boys had been deceased for a period of between one and three hours, placing the time of death between 7:30 and 9:30 p.m. Of the two boys, Elliott noted that Edward was the most gravely injured and had succumbed within minutes of his injuries to massive internal and external bleeding from three deep, penetrating chest wounds. Bramwell, on the other hand, had received only one chest wound and may have lived for up to thirty minutes before he bled to death on the railway tracks, thus explaining the trail of blood as his failed attempt to return home in search of help. What troubled Elliott was his belief that the injuries did not point towards a violent collision with a train. Indeed, neither boy presented with any signs of head or bone trauma, nor did their clothing bear marks of grease or grime suggesting contact with heavy equipment. Furthermore, a striking similarity in the mechanism of injury led Elliott to the opinion that a common instrument had been used to wound both boys. Accordingly, Elliott was unwilling to assign the cause of death to a train at that time.[10]

The remaining witnesses that day proved to be equally inconclusive and unenlightening for the jury. After examining both bodies, RCMP Corporal Joseph Walsh testified that he continued his investigation at the Halifax rail terminals where he was told that the last train to pass the area in question was Engine 2645 of the Halifax and South Western Railway that arrived at the terminals at approximately 7:00 p.m. The train, unfortunately, offered little evidence as its cars had been broken up and its engine had been recently cleaned. Assuring the inquest that these actions were not part of a larger cover-up but simply normal practice, the CNR's chief of police was adamant in his testimony that the railway was cooperating fully with authorities in securing evidence and would, if requested, make the men who cleaned the engine available for questioning. Paul Langille, the train's engineer, testified that he did not believe his train had hit both boys. At 6:35 p.m., he recalled passing the Pipe Line Road where he observed a boy and a nearby object which easily could have been another boy standing fifteen and forty feet away from the tracks on an embankment. Given the train's speed (20–25 mph) and the boys' distance from the tracks, he thought it would be unlikely that either boy could have reached the train before it passed. Further, having attended the inquest's proceedings earlier that day, he noted that the location where both bodies were found did not appear to be the same as where he had seen the two boys the evening before. This information was corroborated by the train's fireman, Harry Dalton, who also recalled seeing a woman and two children picking berries farther up the track from where he had observed the two boys. Unfortunately, the train's engineer and brakeman did not see the boys and were unable to offer any relevant testimony.[11]

As the inquest drew to its originally intended conclusion there was little to indicate an exact cause of death. A majority of the witnesses had given testimony that led away from the Crown's theory of tragic misadventure, and the only evidence entered (two "battered berry cans with blueberries remaining" and a nondescript kit bag similar to those carried by sailors containing a heavy stone) did not speak to the events of the night before. Echoing their uncertainty, Jury Foreman William Brennan advised Stipendiary Magistrate Ross that he and his members were unanimous in their inability to release a finding without the assistance of a post-mortem and further evidence on the condition of the train upon its arrival. Accordingly, so as not to interfere with the family's funeral plans set for the next day, Ross ordered that a post-mortem take place following the close of proceedings that day at Snow's Undertaking Parlours under the supervision of Dr Elliott and Provincial Pathologist R.P. Smith. Lastly, before adjourning until 25 July, Ross made a public appeal for assistance in the case. Carried on the front pages of the *Halifax Chronicle* and the *Halifax Star*, the message indicated that "authorities [were] anxious to locate any one [sic] who may have information which will bear on the tragedy." Specifically, Ross and the RCMP were interested in speaking with the woman who had been seen picking berries in the area with two children as they believed she "may have some information which will be helpful."[12]

Given the significant media coverage the case had engendered, response to Ross's request was almost immediate. On 22 July, George and Elizabeth Parsons of 2½ Clifton Street came forward insisting that they were the individuals who had been seen picking berries a short distance from the Heffernans. Both recalled meeting two boys matching Edward and Bramwell's description by a spring near Chain Lake where they gave the boys a cup to get a drink of water. They also remembered encountering a "coloured" man at the spring, whom they would later observe walking down the nearby railway tracks in the direction opposite from where the boys were found. Both spouses, however, differed in their account of whether they had seen anyone else in the area that day. Quoted in the *Halifax Chronicle*, Elizabeth initially asserted that the "coloured" man was the only person she and her husband had come across. Later, under oath at the preliminary hearing in this case, her memory would improve as she recalled seeing a young girl together with a man earlier in the day but stressed that the "coloured" man was the last person she saw near the boys.[13] George, on the other hand, never mentioned a young girl but did recall seeing three men around the spring that afternoon: the previously mentioned "coloured" man, a workman in blue overalls, and a third he failed to describe. Given these significant discrepancies, it is possible that the Parsons had fabricated their stories and were engaging in a practice of racial stereotyping that was particularly inflammatory for African Nova Scotians around cases involving violence at the time.[14] Regardless, both George and Elizabeth Parsons would later testify for the Crown, with Elizabeth acting as the primary witness for the purpose of identification.[15]

Even with the Parsons' information and extensive efforts by the Halifax police and RCMP, there were indications that the investigation had stalled. With no new evidence or reports of individuals being taken into custody for questioning, the *Halifax Chronicle* reported that investigators had suggested that "little would be done" prior to the inquest's resumption, and that even those proceedings might be adjourned. This did not occur, as three men came forward with information that caused authorities to seriously consider the possibility of foul play in the deaths of Bramwell and Edward.[16]

On the evening of 18 July, Patrick Kelly and brothers James and Ernest Riley were camping in the woods near Chain Lake when a man stopped by their campfire for the night. Known to Kelly as Pius McLean, the man appeared to be quite intoxicated and proceeded to act rather abusively towards the three campers. Kelly testified at the inquest that he observed McLean in the woods the following day drinking rubbing alcohol and "acting like a man under a delusion." In addition to McLean's questionable behaviour at camp, what concerned the men and caused them to question whether McLean might have been involved in the deaths of Bramwell and Edward were comments he made about an altercation he had with two boys who were carrying a knife. For his part, McLean admitted to being drunk when he arrived at the camp but stated that he spent next day sleeping, not drinking, in the woods. Furthermore, he stated that the altercation had, in fact, occurred two weeks prior and involved two older youths carrying fishing gear as opposed to two young boys with a knife.[17]

Any suspicion surrounding McLean, however, was quickly dismissed by Halifax County Medical Officer W.D. Forrest. Forrest told the inquest that he had known McLean for over thirty years and had occasion to come into frequent contact with him through McLean's work as a waterfront employee. Over that time, Forrest had come to know McLean as "harmless and a well-behaved man" who possessed an education that was "above average for a man of his class." Most significantly, he expressed his medical opinion that McLean had "an above average mental condition" and was, therefore, incapable of committing such a horrific crime. The injuries sustained by both boys, he asserted, could have been inflicted only by a criminally deranged individual. As a direct result of this testimony, McLean was released from custody as a material witness and received no further investigative attention as a suspect. The question of mental capacity in the deaths of Edward and Bramwell would continue to be a significant, if conspicuously avoided, aspect of the subsequent investigation and prosecution in this case.[18]

With the exclusion of Pius McLean as a suspect and no progress resulting from the Parsons' information, the jury was left with the findings of their requested post-mortem and the testimony of two CNR employees to resolve this mystery. While both physicians agreed that the boys had suffered wounds caused by a long, slender object, they were at odds over what, or who, had administered the fatal blows. Dr Elliott was unshaken from his earlier findings and asserted that the lack of grease or grime on the boys' clothing and a similarity in their injuries pointed towards homicide. Dr Smith, on the other hand, was unwilling to believe that a person could have administered the fatal blows in such a similar fashion. In his words, "Its [sic] possible, of course, but it would take terrible force." With that said, he did not believe that either boy had been struck by the train's engine. CNR employees Charles Greenough and Edward Pelham then testified to their observations after inspecting the train's engine and cars on the evening of 19 July. Both men stated that they had not observed anything unusual such as blood or other damage to the engine or cars of Engine 2645 that evening. The only damage they found was to a piece of equipment called a spring hammer on the underside of one of the cars that had moved inwards from its normal upright position. After deliberating for thirty minutes, the jury returned a rather inconclusive verdict: "We can in no way connect the deaths of Edward and Bramwell Heffernan with a Railway train and our report is that the above named met their deaths from other causes which we are unable to determine." Ultimately, they recommended that the attorney general continue his investigation into the deaths.[19]

Death Dealing Car or Maniacal Murderer

There is little, if anything, to indicate that the jury's recommendation for further investigation actually led to an arrest in this case. Authorities were quick to assure the public through the media that they were "delving deeper and deeper into the case" by "scour[ing] the vicinity [of the alleged crime] and minutely search[ing] the district for the slightest trace of persons who might have been there." The results of these redoubled efforts proved empty, as Halifax police and the RCMP failed to identify either a new suspect or even a motive in the deaths of the two boys in the days following the inquest's conclusion. As before, this inability to move forward was blamed on "an apparent lack of tangible clues" or leads provided by the public. In the hope of bringing forth new evidence in the investigation, the *Halifax Herald* and the *Halifax Mail* offered a $250 reward for "information leading to the arrest and conviction of any person or persons responsible for the deaths of these two boys." Unfortunately, the reward failed to elicit either new information or suspects. If anything, it provoked more speculation on the cause of death in this case.[20]

The lack of progress in the investigation caused many to question the conclusions made thus far by authorities, while others provided their own theories on what, or who, had killed the boys. These individuals generally fell into two camps: those who believed the boys had died by human hands and those who rejected the jury's findings and believed that a train was at fault; or, as the *Halifax Herald* pithily inquired, those who wondered whether a "death dealing car" or "maniacal murderer" was at large. Several police officers, unwilling to view the death as homicide and allow the already troubled investigation to drag on further, maintained that a train had hit the boys. Citing experience gleaned from past cases, they attempted to reconcile their explanation with the jury's verdict by suggesting that the boys might not have been hit by the engine itself but by another part of the rolling stock. Those who viewed the deaths as homicide tended to be more macabre in their depiction of a suspect. One such example appeared in the *Halifax Mail*, which reported the recent discovery of a stained military knife as well as a toad "which had been cut in two and otherwise frightfully mutilated" found approximately two hundred yards from where one of the boys had been located. Certainly, the writer speculated, this was "definite evidence that some frenzied or insane person was operating near the spot where the bodies of Bramwell and Edward Heffernan were discovered."[21]

Quite possibly the most speculative (albeit plausible) explanation for the deaths of Bramwell and Edward appeared in the pages of the *Halifax Chronicle*. Acknowledging that its theory was "unsupported by anything else but circumstantial evidence," the *Chronicle* cited the expertise of veteran woodsman, hunter, and fisherman Thomas Kennedy, who believed that the deaths "were caused by a steel headed arrow sped by the hand of an archer." Although hunting season had closed, Kennedy suggested that the recent rise of interest in archery might lead a hunter to the woods for practice where "[a] small boy half hidden by the dense brushes might easily be mistaken for one of the varieties of small game and the excited archer would discover, too late ... that he might have sped an arrow which ended a life." Desperate to conceal his mistake, the hunter might then remove the only witness to his crime and conceal both bodies by removing his arrows and weighing the bodies down to be sunk in the nearby lake, thus explaining the wounds found by Drs Smith and Elliott as well as the kit bag and stone. The hunter's inability to carry out his terrible act, Kennedy suggested, was most likely due to his being startled by someone or something near the tracks. When told of this new theory, RCMP officers responded predictably that they were still "actively interested in the case and [were] checking up every possible angle." No arrests were forthcoming.[22]

As the weeks passed into months and the case fell from the headlines, there was little indication that the deaths of Bramwell and Edward Heffernan would be solved. What, then, explains the rather "sudden and unexpected" arrest of Daniel Perry Sampson almost five months after the investigation had begun? Unlike other theories or suspects in this case, no mention of Sampson was ever made by the media or police prior to his arrest. This is not to say that Sampson was unknown to police. The forty-nine-year-old African Nova Scotian veteran of the Canadian Construction Battalion from the Great War had been a familiar face to Corporal Walsh during the latter's time as a municipal police officer in Halifax. Indeed, it was a series of visits Walsh paid to the home Sampson shared with his mother on the edge of the city's North End at 76 Market Street that gave rise to suspicion about the labourer and eventually led to his arrest. What exactly prompted these visits was never made clear by Walsh; however, his interest in Sampson as a suspect was raised by some "discrepancies" he noted in their conversations over the course of these visits. Certainly the fact that Sampson, an African Nova Scotian, matched the vague description of one of the men last seen near the Heffernan boys was not lost on Walsh in his investigation.

The visits between Walsh and Sampson took place over a period of almost three months between 20 October and 13 December 1933. According to his testimony at Sampson's preliminary hearing, Walsh recalled six specific visits but added that he would often stop by the house if he happened to be in the neighbourhood. Walsh's visits with Sampson at his home tended to be short: often lasting only ten to twenty minutes, with only one visit lasting an hour. On two occasions, however, Sampson accompanied Walsh to the RCMP Headquarters on Doyle Street, where his questioning continued.[23] During one such visit in late October, Sampson took part in a line-up for Elizabeth Parsons. Surrounded by uniformed and plainclothes officers, Parsons identified Sampson as the "coloured" man she saw near the Heffernan boys.[24] Despite this positive identification, Sampson was not arrested but, instead, released and returned home, where Walsh's visits would continue.

On the morning of 14 December, Sampson reported to RCMP Headquarters at the request of Detective Constables Thomas W. McKay and William M. Beazley, who had visited his home the previous day while he was out. Even after Walsh's numerous visits with Sampson, no written statement had ever been taken, and this meeting was intended to record the details discussed thus far. Without the benefit of counsel, Sampson found himself in Inspector J.P. Blakeney's office with the three officers. According to Blakeney, Sampson was asked if he could recount the details of his trip to Chain Lake on the day in question. Although not under arrest at the time, he was given the standard evidentiary warning by McKay before being questioned further. Sampson was then said to have described his meeting with the two boys and the events that led to their deaths. He was also shown the previously discovered knife and asked if it was the one he had used to stab both boys, to which he retorted that the knife was so dull that its only usefulness would be to "double as a hoe" and that "[he] would be a fool to bring it in for [his mother] to cut bread with." He did, however, reportedly state that his knife was most likely still at Chain Lake "if no one had picked it up" and indicated to the officers that he could find it if asked. As with his previous encounters, and contrary to the stated purpose of this meeting, no record was taken of Sampson's comments by the officers present.[25]

After a brief break for lunch, Sampson accompanied a group of officers on a drive to Chain Lake. Upon arrival, Sampson directed the officers to proceed further down the path to a spot between the middle dam at Chain Lake and the highway where he stated he had initially found and hidden his knife. He then exited the car and, according to the officers present, led the group around the area identifying the locations where he had found the mysterious kit bag, met a man and woman (presumably the Parsons), and first encountered the Heffernan boys. Following a short walk along the tracks, Sampson reportedly indicated to the officers where he had stabbed both boys, as well as where he had disposed of his knife by tossing a stick in its assumed direction. A quick search returned a knife from a rocky patch of ground just steps from the tracks in an area that had been "minutely" searched previously by police without any success. With Sampson's comments as well as the discovery of a knife, the officers believed they had finally found their suspect in one of the most notorious murders Halifax had seen. Sampson was placed in the back of the police car for a quiet ride back to the detachment where no words were reportedly exchanged between the officers and their prisoner.[26]

On returning to the detachment, Sampson was again placed in Inspector Blakeney's office. This time, however, Blakeney was not present, as he would later state that he had other business to tend to in the detachment. Over the course of approximately the next thirty minutes, without either threat or inducement according to both McKay and Beazley, Sampson was said to have recounted once again the story of his initial meeting with the Heffernan boys and what had led to their deaths in a manner similar to his comments earlier that day. These comments would form the basis of a handwritten statement that was transcribed and read back by McKay to Sampson, who was himself unable to either read or write. The document describes two altercations between Sampson and the boys. The first occurred after Sampson had met the Parsons at the spring. Contradicting the Parsons' earlier statements that had him walking in the direction opposite from the two boys, Sampson's statement indicates that he first met up with the boys on the tracks where they "[made] fun of me and called me names and began firing rocks at me." Sampson then located the "large knife" he had previously found and hidden a month prior and put it in his pocket. At their second meeting, both boys continued to call Sampson names such as "coon, nigger, and baboon face" and hurl rocks in his direction as the three walked towards Halifax. As Sampson walked away, the epithets and rocks continued, and he lost his temper. In his statement Sampson indicates that, after walking back towards the boys, he took out his knife, stabbing Bramwell in the back and then stabbing Edward twice. With the document bearing his mark, Sampson was arrested and placed in the Halifax jail to await his trial.[27]

The Trial: Part 1

Dressed in the same blue double-breasted suit that he was arrested in almost four months prior, Daniel Sampson stood quietly in the prisoner's dock as his murder trial began. African Nova Scotians have experienced a long-standing pattern of racialized bias and abuse within an unrepresentative justice system that has, only recently, started down the path of redress through contemporary reform. During the early 1930s, this bias manifested itself in a grossly under-representative bar,[28] an all-white judiciary,[29] and rather tenuous relations with the police.[30] Certainly, as a mirror on the community, the local media were keenly aware of Sampson's race when they acknowledged his "ebony features" amid a courtroom filled with white lawyers, a white pool of potential jury members, and a white judge. Neither Sampson nor his lawyer, however, was aware of the circumstances that assured this representation and were thus unprepared for the unique form of Nova Scotian justice that would be meted out for Sampson as well as all other African Nova Scotians facing jury trials in Halifax during this period.[31]

The trial was presided over by Justice John Doull with R.M. Fielding acting on behalf of the Crown and Ormond Robert Regan, KC, representing Sampson. A former corporate solicitor and provincial attorney general, Doull rose to the bench during the previous session, making this not only one of his first capital trials but also his first full session of criminal trials.[32] Both lawyers were well-respected members of the bar. Fielding was an experienced practitioner who would later teach criminal law as a lecturer at Dalhousie Law School.[33] A former civic politician who left Halifax for Moose Jaw and later for service in the Great War, Regan returned to Nova Scotia in 1930, at which time he established a sole practice. Albeit a senior criminal practitioner in his own right, Regan's experience with murder trials was decidedly less than his colleague's, with his last having taken place slightly more than twenty years prior.[34]

From the outset of the trial it was clear that what Regan lacked in experience he intended to make up for in the enthusiasm with which he defended his client. Interrupting the court as the charge against Sampson was being read, Regan rose and objected to the trial proceeding any further until a jury had been empanelled to assess whether his client "was of sufficient mentality to understand the nature of the charge" against him. In support of this objection, Regan put forward a written statement from the superintendent of the Nova Scotia Hospital, Dr

Murray MacKay, who had been one of the two physicians to examine Sampson shortly following his arrest. According to MacKay, Sampson was a "high moron" who possessed the mental abilities of a twelve- to thirteen-year-old child. In spite of this submission, Doull chose to overrule the objection on two grounds. On a purely evidentiary point, Doull noted that because MacKay's statement was not in affidavit form it was inadmissible as evidence. In addition, he noted that the statement did little to raise doubt about Sampson's ability to understand the proceedings, given MacKay's comment that the accused understood what effect stabbing a person with a knife would have, thus demonstrating an awareness of the nature and consequences of his alleged acts and satisfying the test for capacity, as it stood at the time.[35] Accordingly, Doull ruled that the trial should proceed. Undeterred, Regan was on his feet again with a request that the charges against Sampson be tried separately. It was his submission that, given the horrific nature of the boys' deaths, trying both murder charges simultaneously might bias the jury against his client. Unlike his previous objection, Regan succeeded, and the murder charge pertaining to Edward was put over to the fall term. With these preliminary matters taken care of, Doull asked Sampson what he intended to plead regarding the murder of Bramwell Heffernan. Speaking for his client, Regan responded that Sampson would plead not guilty by reason of insanity.[36]

As the trial opened, the Crown's case appeared to be relatively straightforward, given its widely reported possession of Sampson's alleged confession. This, however, was not to be, as Fielding advised the court that the document had recently gone missing. The jury was immediately excused, and a heated discussion ensued as to how the evidence at issue should be handled. Fielding argued that the information contained in Sampson's statement was still available to the court through the oral testimony of the officers present. The document, he suggested, was merely a recounting of Sampson's original confession that had occurred earlier in the day and had been witnessed by the officers. For his part, Regan challenged the officers' memory and asserted that the application of the "best evidence rule" called for the document itself to be produced instead of evidentiary bootstrapping though oral testimony. In his ruling, Doull disagreed with Regan's submissions and found the oral testimony to be admissible evidence of Sampson's confession. He concluded that because the Crown was not putting forth the document itself, arguments concerning its admissibility were moot.[37]

After his vigorous cross-examination of the Crown's evidence, Regan's defence of Sampson could only be described as slight. Choosing not to outline his case to the jury, Regan launched into the examination of his four witnesses, which he concluded just fifteen minutes later. It would seem that each witness was intended to support Regan's defence of insanity or, in the case of Sampson's mother, provide an alibi. However, their initial testimony was quickly undermined during the Crown's cross-examination. Dr Murray MacKay's medical evidence was, once again, shown not to support a valid defence of insanity. Additional testimony was heard from Dr George Bateman, superintendent of the School for the Deaf and Blind, as well as Major Wilfred Smith of the Salvation Army, who knew Sampson in their capacity of employer and pastor respectively. Both noted that Sampson "was a man of simple, low intellect." However, neither was able to state that he would be unaware of his actions or their consequences and thus insane. Probably the most emotional testimony occurred during the testimony of Sampson's mother, Elizabeth Lambert, who was adamant that her son had not killed both boys as he had been at home with her that day "fixing a window." During Fielding's cross-examination, her story fell apart as she revealed that her son had not been at home all day but had, in fact, left at 3:00 p.m. to see a ball game, only to return at 7:30 p.m., potentially allowing him sufficient time to be in the Chain Lake area at the estimated time of death.[38] With these witnesses excused, Regan concluded his case.

While the jury addresses by both counsel were relatively succinct, Justice Doull occupied almost an hour with his instructions. After deliberating briefly, the jury returned a verdict of guilty with a recommendation for mercy. As Doull read out the verdict, Sampson displayed his first reaction to the proceedings by gulping visibly as he stood in the prisoner's box. His mother, present throughout the trial, was also noticeably moved and watched the verdict with a persistent swaying motion and her eyes tear-stained. Regan responded to the verdict by echoing his previous objection of mental capacity. He asked the court for a stay of judgment as "the verdict of the jury can mean one thing only and that is that they believed the accused to be mentally afflicted. Otherwise how could mercy be extended to a man convicted of the horrible offence charged in the indictment?" As before, Doull ruled against the motion. He did, however, convey to the jury and Regan that although he was bound to pass sentence he would communicate the jury's request for mercy to the proper authorities.[39] Although Sampson was scheduled to face his second charge of murder in the death of Edward during the fall session, a date of execution was set for 26 June. As he waited for his sentence to be carried out, Sampson was remanded to the provincial jail and placed in solitary confinement on death row.[40]

Appeal: Part 1

Sampson's guilty verdict was touted on the front pages of Halifax's four daily newspapers. Many viewed the trial's outcome as the obvious and just conclusion to a horrific chapter in the city's recent history. Regan, however, had an alternate opinion and took significant issue with how the trial had unfolded. In a notice of appeal filed on 25 April 1934 he alleged that errors in law had led to an unjust verdict for his client: the improper admission of Sampson's alleged confession to the RCMP, a failure to direct the jury as to the appropriate weight of Elizabeth Parson's positive identification of Sampson from the RCMP line-up, the improper admission of a rebuttal witness by the Crown without prior notice to the defence,[41] and the highly prejudicial comments by the Crown noting that the accused had failed to testify in his own defence.[42] As a result, Regan contended, Sampson deserved a new trial.

Sampson's appeal took place on 9 June 1934 and was dispensed with quickly with written reasons filed just one week later. In allowing the appeal and ordering a new trial, the majority of the Supreme Court of Nova Scotia chose to address only two of Regan's four points of appeal. Speaking for the majority, Mr Justice Humphrey Mellish first expressed significant concern towards the manner in which Doull had dealt with Sampson's alleged confession. In his jury address, Doull stated that his reliance on witness testimony instead of the confession itself was not because of "any doubt as to the document being correct – I don't think any doubt was raised about that," but because Sampson's illiteracy generated concerns "about taking the signature by his mark at full value." Mellish questioned the logic of such an approach, given that "the prisoner's sanity was in issue." In his opinion, "the character of a document which [Sampson] was willing to sign might be quite relevant on that point." Moreover, Mellish was of the view that the very mention of the document as a "confession" was "comprehensive and cogent evidence of its contents" that demanded its admission as evidence. Certainly, as Mellish asserted, "there is enough of the 'best evidence' rule left to maintain this principle of law both in civil and criminal cases."[43]

In commenting on Sampson's alleged confession, Mellish revealed a troubling aspect of the trial that suggested either sloppiness by the police and Crown, or worse, a serious ethical lapse and misdirection towards the court. At trial, the unexpected loss of Sampson's alleged confession was attributed by Doull to a filing error: "As it turned out the document is locked up and cannot be found." This, however, was not the case. Mellish was suspect of such claims, given that "there was no evidence that the document was locked up or could not be found." In fact, he remarked that not only had copies been made of the alleged confession but the document itself "which had been before the committing Magistrate is and was where it ought to be, on file in the Supreme Court."[44] That it was not admitted into evidence at Sampson's first trial was, Mellish asserted, an error, and any subsequent proceeding would necessarily have the opportunity of considering this document.

Mellish reserved the Court's most pointed criticism for the comments made by the Crown at trial that indicated Sampson's failure to testify in his own defence. In his decision he noted that Mrs Parsons had identified Sampson on two separate occasions while under direct examination: first, at the RCMP detachment, and then again at trial. By calling the jury's attention to Sampson's lack of comment upon first being identified, Mellish concluded that the Crown's motivations could only have been "calculated to mislead the jury." There was no justification for such an inference by the Crown, Mellish asserted, as "there was no evidence that the prisoner even knew that he was being identified." What was even more egregious for Mellish was that, in the face of Regan's strenuous objections, "nothing was apparently done [by Doull] to prevent the jury from giving effect to the remarks of the Counsel for the Crown in this regard."[45] With these two stated reasons, the Court set aside Sampson's conviction and ordered a new trial. As he waited, Sampson was removed from solitary confinement on death row and returned to the general population at the provincial jail.

A Fatal Error

On its face, there was little that distinguished Daniel Sampson's second trial from that of his first as the same cast of characters appeared before the Court proffering evidence that eventually resulted in another finding of guilt and a corresponding death sentence from the jury.[46] What makes these proceedings significant emerges on a closer examination of Regan's jury challenges specifically, and the jury selection process in Nova Scotia generally. Such an analysis not only places the trial and its outcome in an entirely new light but also provides a valuable context for an aspect of Canadian legal history that has, thus far, received "scant attention."[47]

During the nineteenth century, the use of jury challenges within Nova Scotia had been an infrequent occurrence. This was perhaps due to a perception that "challenging was a procedural safeguard of the guilty."[48] The *Halifax Chronicle* did little to alter such public opinion during Sampson's second trial when it decried the procedural steps taken by Regan as a "bitter attempt to reverse the verdict of the first trial."[49] Although the record indicates numerous jury challenges at Sampson's first trial, the manner with which Regan employed them (specifically the challenge for cause) at Sampson's second trial was decidedly different and suggests a more progressive, almost activist, approach to jury selection. After a further application to have Sampson found unfit to stand trial was quashed by Doull, Regan indicated his intent to challenge all forty-eight potential jurors. Uncertain about the exact nature of his challenge, Doull inquired whether Regan was proceeding with a challenge to the entire panel (challenge to the array) or a series of challenges to potential jurors on an individual basis (challenge to the poll). Regan's response did little to clarify the situation as he indicated that he would challenge all jurors on the ground that their impartiality had been affected by the extensive publicity that had emerged from the first trial.

For some, this approach might suggest a degree of confusion on Regan's part about the procedural and technical requirements of jury challenges as they stood at the time.[50] A review of the trial record proves otherwise and reveals Regan's statement, whether he was conscious of it or not, to be a rather deft use of rhetoric and strategy that not only highlighted the exercise of widespread community biases but also exposed their presence within the trial. By characterizing the pool's bias as being common among all members, prior to having examined even one member thereof, Regan was making a logical, yet highly political, assertion that each member was emblematic of the community from which they were drawn and wherein his client could not receive a fair trial – a point that would become clearer upon his subsequent questioning. Furthermore, while pretrial publicity was the stated reason for Regan's challenges, it was not the only source of bias he would explore. Amid inquiries about potential jurors' exposure to local newspapers and other discussion of the previous trial, Regan broached the question of whether jurors might be "prejudiced in respect of colour" with four members of the pool. With no mention of race at any point in the earlier proceedings, the manner in which Regan raised the issue was almost as telling as the question itself.[51]

While lacking in experience surrounding murder trials, Regan nonetheless evidenced a unique degree of insight towards the practical implications that questions concerning racial intolerance within Halifax might have for his client. By choosing not to base the stated reason for his challenge on racial bias but rather introduce it tangentially within a widely accepted ground of challenge, Regan raised a rather controversial issue in a trial and city already seized with racial tension. What was equally noteworthy was that there were no later objections made by the Crown on any of Regan's three subsequent inquiries about the role that race might play in a potential juror's opinion of Sampson. As an experienced criminal practitioner, Fielding would have been keenly aware that the city's widespread intolerance towards African Nova Scotians might potentially bias a juror against Sampson and yet remained silent. What might this say about the jury selection process in Nova Scotia at that time?

The challenges for cause within Sampson's second trial signal a continued adherence to English jurisprudence during a period for which there has been no scholarship on the jury selection process in Canada generally. During the latter nineteenth century, Canadian courts indicated that they would continue to follow English jurisprudence on challenges for cause. This approach allowed potential jurors to form and express opinions on the outcome of a trial, provided that their views were not motivated by "ill will" against the defendant. The English approach was further complicated by a prohibition against any questions by the defence that might expose a juror's ill will or whether he or she had expressed a related opinion: any proof thereof had to be supplied by extrinsic evidence. In contrast, the American approach had no such "ill will" provision to save potential jurors from exclusion.[52]

The examination of C.A.B. Bullock and Andrew Merkel illustrate the contemporary approach to jury challenges by both counsel. Examined first by Regan, Bullock's responses demonstrate the continued adherence to the principles of English jurisprudence with questions of a juror's preconceived opinions quickly followed by an inquiry of whether such opinions were motivated by ill will:

Q. Did you form an opinion?
A. Yes, I thought he was guilty.

Q. Are you of the same opinion still?
A. Naturally; there has been nothing to change it since.
Q. It would take a lot to switch you?
A. No, not necessarily; I should base my opinion on the evidence.
Q. And if the evidence was the same as appeared at the last trial you would be of the same opinion still?
A. I would.

Fielding's subsequent cross-examination of Bullock further highlights the continued requirement for ill will to be demonstrated prior to a potential juror's disqualification:

Q. The evidence you would hear would be the evidence on which you would try the case.
A. Absolutely.
Q. And solely on that?
A. Absolutely.
Q. Could you give a fair and impartial verdict?
A. Certainly.[53]

Andrew Merkel, a prominent figure within the Halifax community and the Halifax bureau chief for the Canadian Press, faced a similar examination. When asked by Regan if he had previously expressed an opinion on the case, Merkel could not recall ever doing so. He was, however, quite forthright in disclosing that he had formed an opinion that Sampson was, indeed, guilty of the crime alleged. Once again, Fielding's cross-examination probed the question of ill will by asking whether Merkel could give a "fair and impartial" verdict based solely upon the evidence presented. As with Bullock, Merkel responded that he would. Ultimately, both men were deemed competent to serve as jurors and, because of an acknowledged familiarity with Doull, were appointed to act as triers responsible for the further selection of all other jurors who would serve throughout the trial.[54]

Bullock and Merkel were not the only two potential jurors within the pool to express an opinion on what they believed to be the proper outcome of the trial. In fact, of the forty-eight men assembled, several expressed a similar opinion. This noticeably disturbed Regan and prompted an objection by the defence to the entire selection process: At least half of the jurymen called to the stand to give evidence respecting their own competency admitted frankly that they were prejudiced against the prisoner and hence incapable of rendering a true and fair verdict. Most of them said they had already arrived at the conclusion that the prisoner was guilty since they had read the evidence given at the first trial and some added that it would take a lot to shake them in their belief.[55] Of the twelve jurors ultimately selected to preside over the second trial, four members of the panel expressed a preconceived belief that Sampson was guilty.[56]

A rather telling comment that foreshadowed Sampson's eventual fate came in the challenge for cause of Halifax telegraph operator J.H. Trapnell. Although familiar with the case from prior newspaper accounts, Trapnell stated that he had yet to form an opinion at the time of his examination. When questioned further by Regan on the effect of entering the jury room "with an opinion fixed in [his] mind," Trapnell replied candidly that such a mindset "would be fatal." Trapnell was eventually found to be competent by the triers but did not serve as a juror.[57]

Nova Scotian Jurymandering

For Sampson, the related issues of race and bias were obvious impediments to the exercise of justice within a Halifax courtroom and, accordingly, were the subject of Regan's numerous challenges. There were, however, other less conspicuous factors that had a far greater impact on the jury selection process in this case as well as those for all other African Nova Scotians and members of the working class who would face trial by jury in Halifax. Historians and social scientists have documented numerous instances of social, economic, and educational segregation that restricted African Nova Scotians' access to justice. However, until now, there has never been an examination of the legislative provisions that effectively jurymandered[58] all trials in Halifax from 1796 until 1943.

A survey of the jury legislation in the Maritime Provinces at the time of Sampson's trial demonstrates how subtle legislative differences can speak to the larger practice of social control and, thereby, patterns of systemic discrimination. Among the provinces, the respective legislation was generally quite similar, with a common framework that set out who could or could not serve as a juror. The basic requirements in all three provinces were that a juror had to be a male, between the ages of twenty-one and sixty-five years, who was a resident of the province.[59] Jurors who otherwise met these criteria could still be excluded for a variety of prescribed reasons.[60] Furthermore, it was common in all three provinces to exclude certain individuals because of their office or employment. While the range of these positions varied from province to province, they were generally restricted to senior civil servants, members of the legislature or local government, judges, lawyers, and others whose employment was deemed to be essential, such as officers, clerks, and labourers in the military, medical practitioners, police officers, teachers and professors, members of the clergy, and lighthouse keepers, among others.[61] Of the provinces, Nova Scotia had the most instances of legislative control over who could or could not serve as a juror as prescribed by its *Juries Act*.

In spite of their relative similarities, there were three unique sections of Nova Scotia's *Juries Act* in force at the time of Sampson's trials that set it apart from legislation in the other two Maritime Provinces and suggest a conscious manipulation of the demographic permitted to serve on juries within Halifax. On its face, the first of these might be viewed as a residency requirement that was common during the period.[62] This provision, however, was unique in the singular legislative attention paid to Halifax County and the requirement that jurors for the entire county be drawn from an enumerated list of ten polling districts within the municipality.[63] The second section of the Act in question appears, at first glance, to be equally benign, with a requirement that potential jurors be assessed with a certain amount of real or personal property.[64] New Brunswick also had a similar provision that required potential jurors to own an estate of real or personal property with a value of at least three hundred dollars.[65] What distinguished the legislation in both provinces was that, while New Brunswick's threshold applied equally across the province, Nova Scotia established separate thresholds for grand and petit juries with amounts that differed dramatically between Halifax and the other counties.[66] Lastly, on a somewhat related point, the Act seemingly relaxed the property requirement with a provision that permitted individuals who were members of a firm with assets that, if divided equally, would qualify all members of the firm for service on either a grand or petit jury, as the case may be, to be deemed qualified, regardless of their own financial wherewithal.[67] The effect of each section will be discussed in turn.

The geographic delimitation of eligible jurors within Halifax County echoed the racialized settlement patterns of African Nova Scotians. Black settlement in Nova Scotia generally took place on the fringes of white townships or in more secluded areas of the province, with what little land new African Nova Scotians received tending to be small in size and barren, with little prospect of self-sustaining development. Halifax was no exception, with the majority of its African Nova Scotian population originally settling a short distance from the urban core in communities such as Preston, Beechville, and Hammonds Plains. With the War of 1812, a further wave of Black settlement would increase the population of these communities. Shortly thereafter, legislators directed their attention to what they stated was the troubling frequency with which insufficient panels of potential jurors were being returned and a "perceived inequality" towards the frequency with which Halifax citizens were chosen for jury duty.[68] Prior legislation had specified that jurors were "to be returned and summoned from the Town and Peninsula of Halifax."[69] As such, the catchment for jury eligibility was extended to a distance of fifteen miles from the town, with the stated intent that "all inhabitants within the vicinity of [Halifax] should attend as Grand and Petit Jurors."[70] While this may have increased the numbers of potential jurors, it also created a situation where citizens from the more rural parts of Halifax County could face trial before a jury on which they were ineligible to sit. Although some members of Halifax County's African Nova Scotian population may have been excluded, this is not to say that all African Nova Scotians were geographically excluded at this time, as the large communities of Beechville, East and North Preston were still within the catchment.

As the face of Halifax changed, so, too, was the province's *Juries Act* with amendments that further excluded most, if not all, African Nova Scotians from jury service within the county. Throughout the nineteenth century, many within Halifax's African Nova Scotian community left their homes on the outskirts of town and moved into the urban core. Most would settle in the old North End of the peninsula, with a significant community emerging in the area bounded by Brunswick, Cogswell, Robie, and North Streets, while others would settle on land in an area overlooking the Bedford Basin that would come to be known as Africville.[71] This shift towards a larger African Nova Scotian community within peninsular Halifax was not welcomed by all, and instances of overt and more covert segregation as well as racial discrimination have been well documented with examples such as the presence of segregated schools and questionable hiring practices amid a wider community animus against its newest neighbours. It was during this period that the province chose to amend its *Juries Act* in 1890.[72] By requiring that all potential jurors reside in ten specific polling districts on the peninsula, the amendment appeared to move the Act back to its pre-1827 formula for the summoning of jurors. On closer examination, the amendment was actually far more restrictive as the drafters had selected only polling districts that were situated in the most affluent and predominantly white areas of the downtown core and residential South End, with no overlap into areas with significant numbers of African Nova Scotian population.[73] Whether conscious or not, the adverse effect of this amendment was clearly one that precluded African Nova Scotians in Halifax, like Sampson, from appearing before a jury of their peers.

But if the Nova Scotian government wished to shape the demographic of eligible jurors, it would not be restricted solely by the criteria of geography. Although faced with economic depression, Halifax in 1933 was still the province's seat of both political and, equally important, economic power. Both factors perpetuated a disparity in the concentration of wealth in Halifax as compared to the province's other counties. The *Juries Act* reflected this financial reality with an 1864 amendment that established different property requirements to sit on a jury in Halifax County as compared with other counties in the province.[74] When placed in context, this amendment, and future ones like it, were less an exercise in equity than a means to ensure economic dominance by the middle and upper classes within the jury system. In 1864, the requirement for service on a grand jury in Halifax was raised to two thousand dollars, with eight hundred dollars needed for admission to a petit jury panel. By the time of Sampson's trial, the amount required for grand jury service had grown to four thousand dollars, while the petit jury requirement remained eight hundred dollars. These amounts were well beyond the average property assessments for members of the working class living on peninsular Halifax.[75] Thus, only Halifax's most affluent could determine what charges would go to trial, while significant assets were also required to sit in judgment of one's fellow citizens at trial.[76] It is important to note that, although few in number, there were members of Sampson's North End community who would have qualified financially for jury service had they not been excluded geographically.[77] In effect, this provision not only excluded the large numbers of Halifax's African Nova Scotian population but also a significant portion of the working class who simply could not demonstrate such levels of wealth.[78]

Even with the above-mentioned provisions, Halifax's establishment was not guaranteed a place on all juries within the county. The *Juries*

Act's legislative restrictions had created a rather limited pool of potential jurors who were permitted to serve on only one jury panel every three years. How, then, were the establishment's views to be reflected on juries if they were not always present? By relaxing the property requirement for those men employed as partners to a firm who might otherwise not qualify, the *Juries Act* appeared to expand its reach outside of Halifax's most affluent citizens.[79] What it actually accomplished was to place individuals on juries who could be assumed to be sympathetic to the viewpoints of their more affluent partners or employers and to whom they would have to report following the trial. It should be noted, however, that while the geographic and personal financial requirements of the *Juries Act* influenced jury selection in each of Sampson's trials, there is no indication that any relaxation of the property requirement was made in this case. Ultimately, all of these provisions represent the first example of jurymandering documented in Canada.

While there is no evidence on the record to indicate that Regan was aware of the impact such provisions had on the selection of a jury in Sampson's case, it is clear that even after his extensive use of challenges the panel selected was not acceptable to the defence. Rising immediately upon the addition of the final juror to the panel, Regan put forth a motion requesting that the trial take place outside of Halifax. Although overstating his case, Regan was adamant that the bias he exposed within his challenges would adversely affect Sampson's chances for a fair trial: "Out of 50 men questioned yesterday ... all of them had apparently formed an opinion. I think it is a difficult proposition for the jurors to disabuse themselves of their preconscious ideas respecting this case." In refusing to grant the motion, Doull confined his reasoning to the stated objection of pretrial publicity. Addressing Regan's objection, Doull stated that "the same conditions you complain of would apply anywhere in Nova Scotia" because "the two Halifax papers go into every community."[80] While this case undoubtedly captured the attention of many Nova Scotians, it is clear that the same conditions were not equally applicable across the province.

Mental Illness

Regan's procedural objections were not limited solely to his suspicions of the jury selection process. As mentioned, each of Sampson's trials was prefaced by a motion asserting his mental incompetence. Quashed on both occasions, Regan may have been concerned that Doull refused to place more weight on the assessment of Dr Murray MacKay that Sampson was a "high moron" rather than Halifax County Jail Physician W.D. Forrest's conflicting determination that the accused was "normal," as he possessed a "mental condition average for one of his class." The real basis for his objections, however, emerged in comments he made to Doull at the outset of Sampson's second trial. Characterizing the proceedings as "a disgrace to the county," Regan lamented that his client had been denied "the ordinary common decencies of assistance." Specifically, this referenced what Regan believed to be the "negligence" of the attorney general in not "grant[ing] the accused a more thorough mental examination" based on purely financial reasons.[81] As such, Regan took issue with both Doull's judicial assessment of Sampson's capacity and the means by which it was determined.

Although Doull was unwavering in his findings of Sampson's sanity, the basis for his conclusions was not without qualification. On 18 December 1933, four days following his arrest, Sampson was examined in the Halifax County Jail by Drs MacKay and Forrest. This would be his only mental evaluation prior to trial. An explanation emerged in Regan's comments to Doull prior to sentencing at the first trial when he stated that his client had received "no government assistance financially to obtain medical assistance at his trial." In stark contrast to the current practice of court-ordered mental health assessments as set out in the *Criminal Code*, expenses related to evaluation under Nova Scotia's then-Lunacy Act were assessed against an individual's available personal property or, for those with insufficient funds, billed to the municipality in which the individual was resident.[82] While it is clear that Sampson was initially assessed pursuant to the *Lunacy Act*, Dr MacKay's testimony raised an obvious concern about the thoroughness of the assessment and the weight it should have received. Given that Sampson was admittedly "without funds," Doull's refusal to revisit what appeared to be a deficient basis for his initial opinion not only assured that a verdict would be rendered in this highly publicized case but also denied Sampson the opportunity and only means available to challenge his competency ruling.

Whether perpetuating the belief that Halifax's crime problem was the product of "alien" outsiders, a blatant attempt at increased sales through front page sensationalism, or both, the construction of Sampson's mental capacity by the Halifax media was markedly different from what emerged inside Justice Doull's courtroom. With the inconclusive findings of the coroner's inquest, each of Halifax's four newspapers focused its attention on the search for a "criminally deranged" individual, and Sampson's eventual arrest only confirmed their suspicions. Downplaying Doull's judicial findings, Halifax's newspapers ascribed a detached, cold-blooded persona to Sampson and interpreted his actions within this frame. A photo of Sampson carried throughout his time before the courts illustrates this portrayal. Captured "at leisure ... in the County Jail court yard [sic]," Sampson is shown posing expressionless and staring off into the camera.[83] Within the courtroom, Sampson's actions were portrayed as emotionless and detached from the reality that surrounded him. Described "calmly stuffing his pipe" or "resting his head against the prisoner's box," Sampson appeared disinterested in his own trials and "unaware" of his ultimate fate.[84] The media even attempted to portray Sampson's mental deviance as a familial trait. In the Halifax Mail, the writer provides an account of Sampson's time in jail and notes he spends his day sitting "idly and moody" alone in his cell, "allowed to see nobody but his mother who visits daily." In spite of the serious charges against her son, the reporter remarks with some surprise that these visits between mother and son were significantly subdued: "Neither showed signs of emotion but sat quietly chatting in the jail office."[85]

A Question of Race

With no mention on record until Sampson's second trial and appeal, the issue of race had been conspicuously avoided by both the Crown and defence. Regan's extensive challenges and the jury selection process itself were merely indicative of a long-standing animus against African Nova Scotians and others within Halifax's ethnic minority community. The catalyst for the emergence of this racist undercurrent was the interwar period's economic depression that led some whites to feel threatened, both socially and economically, by the "alien" communities in their midst. Events such as the 1919 attacks on Chinese restaurant owners as well as ongoing assaults against African Nova Scotians not only demonstrated individual bigotry but also pointed towards an institutionally systemic racial bias.[86] Indeed, just one year prior to Sampson's arrest, the Herald reported that a five-foot cross had been burned on land beside St John the Baptist Roman Catholic Church situated on Halifax's North-West Arm. Although the paper reported that the "melodramatic spectacle served only to amuse a group of youths who gathered," notes found at the scene suggest otherwise. The first, placed beside the cross, stated, "The Knights of the Ku Klux Klan Is [sic] In Halifax. Their Court is now Opened for the good of the People. Watch." The second, written on cards found scattered in the field, read, "K.K.K. Remember – Every criminal, gambler, thug, libertine, home wrecker, wife beater, dope peddler, moonshiner, every crooked politician, white slaver, shyster, lawyer ... and black spider – is fighting the Klan. Think it over. Which side are you on?"[87]

Local police acknowledged they were aware of the individuals involved; however, no arrests occurred. During an unstable period in Halifax's recent history, this event represented not only a significant voicing of hatred against those within Halifax's ethnic community but also an attempt by some to associate the city's criminal element with a question of race.[88]

The extent to which racial bias had affected Halifax was further evidenced in a letter submitted to the court by Regan on 17 October 1934. Unwilling to have the letter read in the presence of the jury, Doull excused the panel prior to the letter being read to the open court. Purportedly written by Angus Harnish of 52 Argyle Street, the letter outlined a plan by its author to organize a mob and attack the jail so that Sampson might be lynched unless he "were [sic] hanged by November 21." Doull turned the letter over to Inspector Blakeney and ordered that Harnish, if found, was to be brought before the court. The *Chronicle*, the only one of the city's four daily newspapers to report this lynch plot, indicated that the city directory contained no entry for Angus Harnish, and the address provided was rather that of Weeks Printing Company. When queried, a representative of the company denied any knowledge of such a person or the letter itself. Ultimately, no arrest was ever made, and the trial proceeded as scheduled.[89]

Apart from the brief revelation of the lynch plot against Sampson, and Regan's jury challenges, the question of race did not factor heavily throughout Sampson's second trial. Shortly after the second death sentence was pronounced by Doull, this time without a recommendation for mercy from the jury, Regan filed a Notice of Appeal on grounds virtually identical to those he had put forth in Sampson's first appeal. Unlike those proceedings, Regan raised two points of contention surrounding the selection of jurors: the jury panel had included a significant number of members who were adversely predisposed to Sampson, and the selection of triers had been in error, as Doull should have chosen individuals from outside the panel of jurors returned by the sheriff. In his dissenting opinion, Justice Mellish addressed Regan's points

briefly but felt compelled to raise a further ground not found in Sampson's Notice of Appeal nor argued at the hearing. According to Mellish,
Doull's instructions to the jury on the question of manslaughter had
been lacking because the learned trial judge had either disregarded important evidence or failed to consider mitigating factors that spoke to
Sampson's status as an "ordinary person" under the law. Proper jury
instructions, Mellish asserted, should have noted "that there was evidence that [Sampson] was a man of low mentality, and that his conduct
should have been judged having that in view." It was Mellish's belief
that Sampson "was perhaps peculiarly susceptible for this reason and
by reason of his race to the insults offered him and perhaps might not
unreasonably be presumed to have lost control of himself so as to justify a finding of manslaughter." In Mellish's opinion, this "was the *real*
question before the jury."[90]

Mellish's suggestion that a trial judge direct a jury to consider such
factors as mental capacity and race in their determination of whether
the provocation at issue was "sufficient to deprive an ordinary person
of the power of self-control" was not simply an insightful and forward-
thinking approach for the time but one that has yet to gain complete
acceptance in Canada more than seventy years later.[91] With that said,
Mellish's assertion that "all evidence relevant" to the determination of
provocation be directed to a jury was an incorrect interpretation of the
law as it stood at the time of Sampson's appeal. At that time, courts
viewed provocation through a purely objective lens that examined
whether the provocation was "sufficient to deprive an ordinary person of the power of self control."[92] It would be almost thirty-five years
before a British court accepted that a trial judge should raise factors
such as age, gender, and race with a jury prior to their deliberations.[93]
Eventually, the Supreme Court of Canada adopted the substance of the
British jurisprudence in a 1985 ruling, thereby establishing a modified
objective approach for cases pleading provocation. In the Court's decision, the majority opinion written by Chief Justice Dickson expressed
reservations that, although such information might be helpful, requiring a trial judge to direct a jury accordingly in each case was not "wise
or necessary," as "sufficient guidance" was to be found in the *Criminal Code* itself.[94] A review of the majority decision demonstrates that
the application of a purely objective standard by Nova Scotian courts
resulted in decisions that were, for Sampson and other African Nova
Scotians, inherently colour blind.[95]

Writing for the majority of the Nova Scotia Supreme Court, Justice Hugh Ross asserted that there were "no grounds set out in the notice of appeal on which a new trial should be granted," nor was there any exception that could be taken to Doull's jury charge. Mellish's belief that a jury be instructed on an accused's mentality was dismissed by Ross, as he correctly cited that "the weight of authority [was] against" such a position. Although Ross identified Sampson as a "coloured man" and listed the racial epithets levelled against the accused by the Heffernan boys, it is worth noting that he chose not to consider race as a factor in determining provocation. This is clearly evident in Ross's assessment of Doull's comment to the jury that "[words alone have] been very seldom if ever held to be that kind of provocation" was nothing more than "an expression of [Doull's] own opinions as to the sufficiency of the proof of provocation," as opposed to a direction on the law. Ultimately, Ross concluded that, "even if exception [could] be taken to the parts of the learned Judge's charge …, no substantial wrong or miscarriage of justice has occurred."[96]

A Final Verdict

The Nova Scotia Supreme Court's affirmation of Doull's second guilty verdict and corresponding death sentence was presented by the Halifax media as not only a just conclusion for the only plausible suspect of this horrific crime but also as a restoration of order to the city as a whole. Within days of the decision, Sampson's case had fallen from the headlines, with what little mention it did receive tending to criticize any further attempts to clear Sampson's name as the acts of a man trying to cheat the gallows. Public sentiment, however, did not deter Regan, as he indicated on 20 December 1934 Sampson's intent to seek leave to appeal to the Supreme Court of Canada. A stay of execution was sought the following day and granted until 7 March 1935.

Although Regan continued to act as Sampson's barrister of record in correspondence with the Supreme Court of Canada, it is interesting to note that he did not appear before the Court in what would be his client's final appeal. Instead, that task fell to D.K. MacTavish of the Ottawa firm of Herridge, Gowling, MacTavish, and Watt. In a letter addressed to the minister of justice, Regan indicated that this was due to Sampson's continued financial difficulties.[97] The appeal took place before a panel of five justices, with MacTavish as appellant's counsel and J.H.

MacQuarrie as well as Fielding acting on behalf of the Crown. The appeal focused on a single point of law stemming from Mellish's dissenting opinion on the sufficiency of Doull's instructions on the question of provocation. Shortly following the hearing, the Court issued a two-line decision dismissing the appeal.[98] In slightly lengthier supplementary reasons for judgment filed the following month, Chief Justice Lyman Poor Duff expressed deference towards Mellish as a jurist "from whose opinions I never dissent without real hesitation." However, citing the law as it stood in the *Criminal Code*, he stated that he was unable to find any error in Doull's directions to the jury. In fact, Duff lauded Doull's judicial clarity in his comments to the jury by stating, "I do not think [the question of provocation] could have been put more fairly and more clearly and I, therefore, think the appeal should be dismissed."[99] With this decision, Sampson's death sentence was again restored and scheduled to be carried out on 7 March 1935.

After a lengthy investigation and a series of contested Court proceedings, what little doubt remained for many Haligonians about Sampson's guilt was lessened by the events that preceded his execution. On the afternoon of 6 March 1935, Sampson was visited by his mother, Regan, and his spiritual advisor, Rev. W.A. White. Later that evening, Regan returned, at which time Sampson gave what would be his last statement: a final admission of guilt. As with his first statement, the following comments were again transcribed and read back to Sampson prior to his signature of the document using his mark:

I, Daniel P. Sampson, on the even of my execution admit that I killed the two Heffernan boys, but because I was tormented by them.

I have been in the County Jail for over a year and I wish to thank Jailor Mitchell, Assistant Jailor Mr Hood, and all the other officials in the Jail for their generous and kind treatment and I have only praise to make of the treatment I received during the time I have been in Jail.

I am sorry for what I did and I wish to apologize and extend sympathy to the parents of the children.[100]

The account of Sampson's final moments was framed with the same imagery used by the media since his arrest. Carried in the *Chronicle* on 7 March 1935, the writer portrayed Sampson as an unrepentant and cold-blooded killer in the moments before his execution at 1:05 that morning: "With the same stolidness with which he twice heard himself declared guilty of the crime and condemned to death, Sampson walked to the gallows and a few seconds after he had stepped on the platform the trap was sprung by Hangman Samuel Edwards. Seconds later, the man was pronounced dead by the County jail physician."[101]

Shortly following the execution, a coroner's jury was convened by Sheriff R.A. Brenton before Stipendiary Magistrate Ross. After viewing the body, the jury released its finding that Sampson had died because of a fracture and dislocation of the cervical vertebrae by Court-ordered execution. Following a service at Snow's Mortuary, Sampson was buried in Fairview Cemetery on 8 March 1935.

Conclusion

That the case against Daniel Perry Sampson received significant contemporary attention, yet remains relatively unknown today, is not entirely surprising, as this case was, and is, characterized as an example of African-Canadian criminality.[102] The sudden deaths of Bramwell and Edward Heffernan shocked a city that quickly went looking for answers. With an inconclusive verdict from a hastily convened coroner's jury, many Haligonians (particularly those in the media) concluded that this unfortunate incident indicated the threat posed by a "criminal class" of outsiders within their city. After months of investigation, with no new evidence and only speculative explanations, the rather sudden arrest of a mentally challenged African Nova Scotian confirmed the city's worst fears and, in concert with the prevalent racialization and marginalization of violent crime, rendered Sampson guilty in the minds of many, even before his trial had begun. With examples of questionable investigative and prosecutorial practices as well as two threatened lynchings, among other incidents, this case demonstrates further overt examples of a racially biased response to crime in Halifax during the interwar period. However, it also illustrates the pervasive impact of systemic discrimination towards those within Halifax's marginalized communities who often found themselves before the city's courts.

The significant pursuit of law and order in Halifax throughout the interwar period has been characterized as a response to the "storms of modernity" that was fuelled by socio-economic inequalities.[103] While Sampson's case certainly confirms this, it also reveals that the city's response to crime was, in part, legally constructed and, thereby, self-perpetuating. By effectively excluding all African Nova Scotians and members of the working class from jury service within Halifax County based on discriminatory geographic and economic criteria, legislators ensured that the only time these individuals were seen in court would be as alleged outlaws from inside the prisoner's box. Similar socio-economic factors confronted those accused of a crime and suffering both mental illness and a lack of funds. The resultant media coverage inevitably led many to associate these individuals and the areas of Halifax where they resided as being inherently criminal and helped perpetuate a criminal stigma that attached even before they arrived in court.

Sampson's case may have grabbed headlines during its time before the Canadian courts. However, the reasons for this are not limited to the tragic circumstances of the evening of 19 July 1933, nor are they readily apparent from the various trial and appellate decisions. A closer examination of newspaper accounts, court transcripts, case files, legislation, and tax assessment rolls reveals a more accurate narrative of racial and socio-economic bias. Daniel Perry Sampson's case illustrates that the question of crime and the response thereto in the city of Halifax during this period not only express social relationships but also react back upon them.[104] Given the recent findings of cases such as *R. v. R.D.S.*[105] and *R. v. Parks*[106] that recognize the presence of anti-Black racism in Nova Scotia specifically and Canada generally, it is clear that further examples do exist; the challenge is in excavating these previously erased narratives from the archives.

They put Sampson in what he called the *penatenrinary* –
the petty tyranny.
Gallant, pallid guards played at shooting him.
One morning he was sitting with the Bible
and his head popped open;
his black scalp puffed up fatally scarlet.[107]

NOTES

The case of Daniel Perry Sampson was first brought to my attention by George Elliott Clarke in February 2005. Subsequently, Dr Clarke has been an invaluable sounding board for my research. I also wish to thank Professors R. Blake Brown and Philip Girard for their insight and helpful comments in the composition of this chapter. Elements of this chapter were initially presented at the University of Toronto Criminology Graduate Students Association Conference on 19 October 2007 and later to the Toronto Legal History Group on 24 February 2010. Thanks are extended to those present for their helpful feedback. With that said, all errors or omissions are entirely mine.

1 Michael S. Boudreau, *Crime and Society in a City of Order: Halifax, 1918–1935* (PhD thesis, Queen's University, 1996), 255–62 and 423. Boudreau notes that this "criminal class," albeit a somewhat problematic descriptor, was constituted by the "deviant alien" and those who often lived on the socio-economic margins of society. Boudreau also notes a significant "public fear" associated with acts of crime committed by members of Halifax's ethnic minority communities. Specifically, this racialization of crime led to a belief that African Nova Scotians demonstrated a criminal disposition towards acts of violence.

2 Judith Fingard, Janet Guildford, and David Sutherland, *Halifax: The First 250 Years* (Halifax: Formac, 1999), 140.

3 Additionally, the Department of National Defence established a work camp at the Halifax Citadel for unemployed single men. This camp, however, was often not at capacity, most likely the result of a humiliating admissions process and substandard living conditions. Ibid., 141–4.

4 "2 Dead, 3 Injured in Series of Accidents: Father Finds Sons Dead on Rail Tracks," *Halifax Mail*, 20 July 1933.

5 Fingard et al., *Halifax*, 144.

6 "2 Dead, 3 Injured in Series of Accidents: Father Finds Sons Dead on Rail Tracks," *Halifax Mail*, 20 July 1933.

7 Ibid.

8 "Violent Death of Two Boys Remains Mystery," *Halifax Chronicle*, 21 July 1933.

9 The only remarkable detail in their testimony came from Heffernan, who recalled being passed by a train the night before, approximately two miles from where his sons were found but not hearing the train's whistle: a point that contradicted testimony given later by a member of the train's crew. Ibid.

10 "Violent Death of Two Boys Remains Mystery," *Halifax Chronicle*, 21 July 1933.

11 "Inquest Jury Puzzled by Brothers: Identity of Woman and Children Sought by Court and Police," *Halifax Star*, 21 July 1933.

12 Ibid.; "Violent Death of Two Boys Remains Mystery."

13 Preliminary hearing examination of Elizabeth Parsons, 28 Dec. 1933, no. 1033, Halifax County Supreme Court, vol. 722 (1933–34), series C, RG 39, Public Archives of Nova Scotia, Halifax.

14 Boudreau, *Crime and Society*, 423–47. Boudreau cites the stabbing of young William Walsh by an unknown "colored slasher." After word of the alleged attack got out, Walsh's neighbours "wanted to lynch his assailant and might well have attacked the first black man they encountered had the police not intervened."

15 "Police, Medical Men, Investigate Dual Fatality: Mounties Find Witnesses in Boys' Deaths," *Halifax Herald*, 22 July 1933.

16 "Police Seeking to Solve Mystery of Boys' Deaths: Continue Probe into Fatality Near Halifax; Secrecy Surrounds Efforts," *Halifax Herald*, 25 July 1933.

17 "Boys Not Killed by Train Is Jury's Belief," *Halifax Daily Star*, 26 July 1933. See also "Jury Declares Youth Were Not Killed by Train," *Halifax Herald*, 26 July 1933.

18 "Boys Not Killed by Train Is Jury's Belief," *Halifax Herald*, 26 July 1933.

19 "Boys Killed by Long Rod, Doctors Say," *Halifax Mail*, 21 July 1933. See also "Boys' Death Mystery Unsolved," *Halifax Herald*, 26 July 1933; "Police Probe Mysterious Deaths: Mystery Deepens as Jury Says Boys Were Not Killed by Train," *Halifax Mail*, 26 July 1933.

20 "Fear Maniacal Slayer in Chain Lake Tragedies: Interest Is Heightened by Reward," *Halifax Mail*, 27 July 1933; "Offer Reward for Solving Boys' Death Mystery: Slayer Eludes Police," *Halifax Herald*, 27 July 1933.

21 "Hunt Boys' Murderer or Death-Dealing Car," *Halifax Herald*, 28 July 1933; "Police Hunt Boys' Murderer or Death-Dealing Car: Developments Lacking in Wide Search," *Halifax Mail*, 28 July 1933; "Find Stained Knife Near Death Scene: Added Weight to Theory of Human Slayer," *Halifax Mail*, 2 Aug. 1933.

22 "Police Still Probe Death of Children: Experienced Woodsman Advances Theory in Killing of Heffernan Brothers," *Halifax Chronicle*, 28 July 1933.

23 Preliminary hearing examination of Corporal Joseph Walsh, 28 Dec. 1933, no. 1033, Halifax County Supreme Court, vol. 722 (1933–4), series C, RG 39, Public Archives of Nova Scotia, Halifax.

24 It was later revealed under cross-examination that Sampson was the only African Nova Scotian man in the array. Preliminary hearing examination of Elizabeth Parsons, 28 Dec. 1933.

25 Preliminary hearing transcripts of T.W. MacKay, W.M. Beazley, and J.P. Blakeney, 28 Dec. 1933, no. 1033, Halifax County Supreme Court, vol. 722 (1933–4), series C, RG 39, Public Archives of Nova Scotia, Halifax.

26 "Offer Reward for Solving Boys' Death Mystery: Slayer Eludes Police," *Halifax Herald*, 27 July 1933; "Fear Maniacal Slayer in Chain Lake Tragedies: Interest Is Heightened by Reward," *Halifax Mail*, 27 July 1933.

27 Statement of Daniel Perry Sampson, 14 Dec. 1933, no. 1033, Halifax County Supreme Court, vol. 722 (1933–4), series C, RG 39, Public Archives of Nova Scotia, Halifax.

28 While Dalhousie Law School had educated a lawyer of colour previously, Henry Sylvester Williams (1893–4), James Robinson Johnson was the first

African Nova Scotian to be admitted to the provincial bar upon his call in 1900. The numbers of African Nova Scotian lawyers in the province have begun to rise to significant levels only following the institution of the Indigenous Black and Mi'kmaq Program in 1989 that encouraged more African Nova Scotian lawyers to be educated at Dalhousie Law School. See Justin Marcus Johnston, *James Robinson Johnston: The Life, Death and Legacy of Nova Scotia's First Black Lawyer* (Halifax: Nimbus, 2005), 19–23.

29 Judge Corrine Sparks became the province's first African Nova Scotian judge upon her appointment in 1987.
30 The troubling relations between African Nova Scotians and the police received judicial notice in *R. v. R.(D.S.)*, [1997] 3 S.C.R. 484. See also Nova Scotia, *Report of the Royal Commission on the Donald Marshall, Jr, Prosecution* (Halifax: Province of Nova Scotia, 1989), 4:25.
31 "Insanity Is Sampson's Defence: Colored Man Shows No Trace of Emotion as Murder Trial Opens," *Halifax Daily Star*, 10 Apr. 1934.
32 Nova Scotia Barristers' Society, "Justice John Doull," in *The Supreme Court of Nova Scotia and Its Judges, 1754–1978* (Halifax: Nova Scotia Barristers' Society, 1978), 84.
33 *The Canadian Law List* (Toronto: Carswell, 1941), 360.
34 "Obituary: Ormond Robert Regan," *Halifax Chronicle-Herald*, 10 July 1951.
35 Don Stuart, *Canadian Criminal Law: A Treatise* (Toronto: Carswell, 2001), 382–3. See also *Criminal Code*, S.C. 1927, c. 36.
36 Minutes of Evidence, *R. v. Sampson*, 10 Apr. 1934, 1, vol. 1587 (1933–4), RG 13, Library and Archives Canada, Ottawa; "Insanity Is Sampson's Defence: Colored Man Shows No Trace of Emotion as Murder Trial Opens," *Halifax Daily Star*, 10 Apr. 1934.
37 Minutes of Evidence, *R. v. Sampson*, 10 Apr. 1934, 36, vol. 1587 (1933–4), RG 13, Library and Archives Canada, Ottawa; "Mounties Tell of Accused Murderer's 'Confession,'" *Halifax Herald*, 11 Apr. 1934.
38 Minutes of Evidence, *R. v. Sampson*, 10 Apr. 1934, 11, vol. 1587 (1933–4), RG 13, Library and Archives Canada, Ottawa; "Mentality Low, Says Dr McKay," *Halifax Mail*, 11 Apr. 1934; "Sampson Guilty of Boy's Murder; Will Learn His Sentence Today," *Halifax Chronicle*, 12 Apr. 1934.
39 In his reporting letter for the governor general, Justice Doull did convey the jury's recommendation for mercy. However, he did say that such indulgence could refer only to provocation or mental incapacity. In spite of finding Sampson sufficiently sane to stand trial, Justice Doull wrote, "Some further examination might be made of the man's mental condition. If he is sane, I do not think that under the Law, the provocation which he alleges in his confession is sufficient to reduce Murder to Manslaughter."

John Doull to Secretary of State of Canada, 14 Apr. 1934, vol. 1587 [1933–4), RG 13, Library and Archives Canada, Ottawa.

40 "Death Sentence Is Pronounced: Prisoner's Counsel Appeals in Vain for Probe by Alienists," *Halifax Mail*, 12 Apr. 1934.

41 The rebuttal witness, George Renner, testified that he had observed Sampson approximately one mile from the alleged crime scene on the road from Chain Lake to Halifax at approximately 5:00 or 5:30 p.m. Renner's name was not placed on Sampson's indictment, nor was any notice given prior to his appearance.

42 Notice of Appeal, 25 Apr. 1934, no. 1033, Halifax County Supreme Court, vol. 722 (1933–4), series C, RG 39, Public Archives of Nova Scotia, Halifax. At the hearing, Regan was given leave to argue a further ground: that there had been insufficient direction as to what constituted reasonable doubt.

43 *R. v. Sampson*, [1934] 8 M.P.R. 237 (N.S.S.C. [A.D.]) 241.

44 Ibid., 241–2.

45 Ibid., 242–3.

46 Elizabeth Parsons was not present at Sampson's second trial because of illness. Her testimony was permitted to be read into evidence over Regan's objection.

47 The most recent survey of juries in Canadian legal history occurs in R. Blake Brown, *A Trying Question: The Jury in Nineteenth-Century Canada* (Toronto: University of Toronto Press, 2009). An earlier work by the author is also illustrative: R. Blake Brown, "Challenges for Cause, Stand-Asides, and Peremptory Challenges in the Nineteenth Century," *Osgoode Law Journal* 38, no. 3 (2000): 454.

48 Brown, "Challenges for Cause," 482.

49 "Sampson Again in Fight for His Life: Defence Counsel Challenges Entire Panel of Jurors as Second Murder Trial Begins," *Halifax Chronicle*, 16 Oct. 1934.

50 Written notice was required for challenges to the array, see *Criminal* Code, S.C. 1927, s. 925(2). Additionally, while bias by the sheriff responsible for the compilation of a jury pool was a valid ground for a challenge to the array, individual juror bias was subject to a challenge to the poll. See Brown, "Challenges for Cause," 456–7.

51 Challenges for cause of Herbert Hemming, John G. Gregg, Thomas Wambolt, and C.A.B. Bullock, 15 Oct. 1934, no. 1033, Halifax County Supreme Court, vol. 722 (1933–4), series C, RG 39, Public Archives of Nova Scotia, Halifax.

52 Brown, "Challenges for Cause," 466, 472–5.

53 Challenge for cause of C.A.B. Bullock, 15 Oct. 1934, no. 1033, Halifax

County Supreme Court, vol. 722 (1933–4), series C, RG 39, Public Archives of Nova Scotia, Halifax.

54 Challenge for cause of Andrew Merkel, 15 Oct. 1934, no. 1033, Halifax County Supreme Court, vol. 722 (1933–4), series C, RG 39, Public Archives of Nova Scotia, Halifax; Report of the Trial Judge to the Attorney General, 12 Nov. 1934, no. 1033, Halifax County Supreme Court, vol. 722 (1933–4), series C, RG 39, Public Archives of Nova Scotia, Halifax.

55 Challenges for cause of the poll, 15 Oct. 1934, no. 1033, Halifax County Supreme Court, vol. 722 (1933–4), series C, RG 39, Public Archives of Nova Scotia, Halifax.

56 Ibid.

57 Challenge for cause of J.H. Trapnell, 15 Oct. 1934, no. 1033, Halifax County Supreme Court, vol. 722 (1933–4), series C, RG 39, Public Archives of Nova Scotia, Halifax.

58 *Jurymandering* is a hybrid term that references the more commonly known gerrymandering and describes the manipulation of jury composition through the delimitation of a jury pool and the subsequent challenges put to potential jurors. See Susanne H. Vikoren, "Justice of Jurymander? Confronting the Underrepresentation of Racial Groups in the Jury Pool of New York's Eastern District," *Columbia Human Rights Law Review* 27 (1995–6): 605.

59 Note that Nova Scotia used the term *person* in its jury legislation. Accordingly, such language might have presented an opportunity for women to be considered for jury service following the *Persons' Reference* of 1929. Records from both of Sampson's trials, however, suggest that the practice in Nova Scotia was still to select only men for jury panels through the mid-1930s. *The Juries Act*, R.S.N.S. 1923 c. 223, ss. 3, 5(ee); *The Jury Act*, S.N.B. 1927, c. 130, s. 2; *The Jury Act*, S.P.E.I. 1924, c. 8, s. 4.

60 All provinces excluded men who had been convicted of a serious criminal offence, with Nova Scotia and Prince Edward Island permitting service by those who had been granted a pardon. Also, to ensure the capacity of their jurors, both Nova Scotia and Prince Edward Island excluded any individual found to be blind, deaf, or suffering any "other mental or physical infirmity incompatible with the discharge of the duties of a juror." See *The Juries Act*, R.S.N.S. 1923 c. 223, ss. 5(1)(dd) & 7; *The Jury Act*, S.P.E.I. 1924, c. 8, ss. 5(a) & 5(b).

61 *The Juries Act*, R.S.N.S. 1923 c. 223, s. 5; *The Jury Act*, S.N.B. 1927, c. 130, s. 3; *The Jury Act*, S.P.E.I. 1924, c. 8, s. 6.

62 Prince Edward Island required that jurors serve on trials only within the county where they resided. *The Jury Act*, S.P.E.I. 1924, c. 8, s. 4.

63 *The Juries Act*, R.S.N.S. 1923 c. 223, s. 5(ff).

64 Ibid., ss. 3 and 4.
65 *The Jury Act*, S.N.B. 1927, c. 130, s. 2. R. Blake Brown notes the historical
    presence of property qualifications in England from the fifteenth until
    the nineteenth century. See "'A Delusion, a Mockery, and a Snare': Array
    Challenges and Jury Selection in England and Ireland, 1800–1850," *Cana-
    dian Journal of History* 39 (2004): 4.
66 In 1933, men qualified to serve on a grand jury within Halifax County
    were required to own real or personal property with a value assessed for
    the purposes of taxation of at least four thousand dollars. Potential mem-
    bers of grand juries within Guysborough and Richmond Counties were
    required to be assessed with at least four hundred dollars of personal or
    real property, whereas all other counties within the province required an
    assessment of at least five hundred dollars of real property or a combined
    estate of real and personal property assessed at six hundred dollars. In the
    case of petit juries, these amounts decreased significantly but still varied
    across the province. In Halifax County, men wishing to serve on a petit
    jury were required to be assessed for taxes with real or personal property
    valued at eight hundred dollars. In Guysborough and Richmond Counties
    this amount was three hundred dollars, whereas the requirement for all
    other counties was five hundred dollars of real or personal property. *The
    Juries Act*, R.S.N.S. 1923 c. 223, ss. 3–4.
67 *The Juries Act*, R.S.N.S. 1923 c. 223, s. 4(2)(b).
68 Brown, *Trying Question*, 17–42.
69 *An Act to Regulate Juries*, S.N.S. 1796, c. XI.
70 *An Act to Regulate Juries*, S.N.S. 1827, c. XXXII.
71 Donald H. Clairmont and Dennis William Magill, *Africville: The Life and
    Death of a Canadian Black Community*, 3rd ed. (Toronto: Canadian Scholars'
    Press, 1999).
72 *The Juries Act*, S.N.S. 1890, c. 7.
73 See Appendix 1.
74 *The Juries Act*, S.N.S. 1864, c. 7.
75 The majority of households in Halifax's North End fell under the $800
    threshold for service on a petit jury. General Assessment Rolls 1934–5,
    Halifax, HRM Municipal Archives (RG 35-102, series 19, A. 116–118).
76 The impact of property requirements on the class composition of juries
    is explored in Douglas Hay, "The Class Composition of the Palladium
    of Liberty: Trial Jurors in the Eighteenth Century," and in J.S. Cockburn
    and Thomas A. Green, eds., *Twelve Good Men and True: The Criminal Trial
    Jury in England, 1200–1800* (Princeton: Princeton University Press, 1988),
    309–16.

77 General Assessment Rolls 1934–5, A. 116–18, series 19, RG 35-102, HRM Municipal Archives, Halifax.

78 The Nova Scotia Law Reform Commission noted that the requirement to own property had disproportionately disadvantaged women, the working class, and people of colour until as late as 1985, when that provision was removed from the Act. See Law Reform Commission of Nova Scotia, *Juries in Nova Scotia* (Halifax: Law Reform Commission of Nova Scotia, 1994), 21.

79 By expanding the property requirement to include partners of Halifax's most affluent citizens, those senior merchants could avoid what had become acknowledged as "so oppressive a duty." Brown, *Trying Question*, 23.

80 "Lawyer Asks That Trial Be Staged Outside Halifax," *Halifax Star*, 16 Oct. 1934.

81 "Says Trial Was Disgrace to Country," *Halifax Mail*, 17 Oct. 1934.

82 *The Lunacy Act*, R.S.N.S. 1923, c. 171, ss. 17 and 21.

83 "Labourer Accused of Slaying Heffernan Lads Is Remanded," *Halifax Mail*, 15 Dec. 1933.

84 "Remand Alleged Slayer: Adjournment Is Asked by Prosecutor," *Halifax Mail*, 21 Dec. 1933.

85 "To Examine Accused Man Next Week," *Halifax Mail*, 16 Dec. 1933.

86 Fingard et al., *Halifax*, 105. See also Clairmont and Magill, *Africville*; and Donald H. Clairmont and Dennis William Magill, *Nova Scotian Blacks: An Historical and Structural Overview*, 4th ed. (Halifax: Institute of Public Affairs, Dalhousie University, 1973).

87 Boudreau, *Crime and Society*, 415.

88 Ibid., 415–17.

89 "Letter Threatens Lynch Plot," *Halifax Chronicle*, 17 Oct. 1934. A second letter with the threat of a lynch plot was sent to Doull by Harris Coleman of Halifax. It is worth noting that the writing in both letters is strikingly similar. Harris Coleman to John Doull, n.d., vol. 722 (1933–4), series C, RG 39, Library and Archives Canada, Ottawa.

90 *R. v. Sampson*, [1935] 2 D.L.R. 197 (N.S.S.C. [A.D.]) (emphasis in original).

91 *R. v. Hill* 1986 CanLII 58 (S.C.C.) (CanLII). Prof. Don Stuart suggests that the procedural approach adopted by the Supreme Court of Canada in *Hill* is "troubling." Rather, he suggests, "The Supreme Court should have made it mandatory for a trial judge to direct the jury as to the individual factors that can be taken into account on the reasonable person test. It should have adopted the full approach of the House of Lords in *Camplin*." Stuart, *Canadian Criminal Law*, 382–3.

92 Stuart, *Canadian Criminal Law*, 537.

242 The African Canadian Legal Odyssey

93 *R. v. Camplin* [1978] A.C. 705, [1978] 2 All E.R. 168 (H.L.).

94 *R. v.* Hill 1986 CanLII 58 (S.C.C.) (CanLII) at para. 40.

95 Stuart, *Canadian Criminal Law*, 533–43.

96 *R. v. Sampson*, [1935] 2 D.L.R. 197 (N.S.S.C. [A.D.]) at para. 97.

97 O.R. Regan, to Hugh Guthrie, 16 Dec. 1934, vol. 722 (1933–4), series C, RG 39, Library and Archives Canada, Ottawa.

98 *R. v. Sampson*, [1935] S.C.R. 634 (S.C.C.) (QL).

99 *R. v. Sampson*, [1935] 3 D.L.R. 128 at para. 1 (S.C.C.) (QL).

100 "Condemned Man Confesses to Murder of Two Boys: Statement Is Given to Counsel," *Halifax Chronicle*, 7 Mar. 1935.

101 "Condemned Man Confesses to Murder of Two Boys: Statement Is Given to Counsel," *Halifax Chronicle*, 7 Mar. 1935.

102 George Elliott Clarke notes that Canada has expressed a significantly different, and far less copious, legacy of African Canadian criminality than that found in America, in spite of conditions that provide numerous examples. George Elliott Clarke, "Raising Raced and Erased Executions in African-Canadian Literature: Or, Unearthing Angélique," in *Racism, Eh?: A Critical Inter-Disciplinary Anthology of Race and Racism in Canada*, ed. Camille A. Nelson and Charmaine A. Nelson (Concord, ON: Captus, 2004), 66.

103 Boudreau, *Crime and Society*.

104 I have paraphrased the concept initially expressed by Henri Lefebvre in "The Production of Space." This concept was subsequently used by Jennifer J. Nelson to illustrate how the ghettoization of Africville through neglect and the denial of essential services "produced the community, in the 'outside' public mind, as a place of dirt, odour, disease, and waste. These associations, which came to be manifested as the conflation of Africville with degeneracy, filth and 'the slum,' justified the further denial of essential services on the basis of how Africville had come to be known." Certainly this socially generated viewpoint could be applied to the practice of jurymandering in Halifax. Jennifer J. Nelson, "The Space of Africville: Creating, Regulating and Remembering the Urban 'Slum,'" in *Race, Space, and the Law: Unmapping a White Settler Society*, ed. Sherene H. Razack (Toronto: Between the Lines, 2002), 217.

105 *R. v. R.(D.S.)*, [1997] 3 S.C.R. 484.

106 (1993), 84 C.C.C. (3d) 353 (Ont. C.A.) (leave to appeal refused [1994] 1 S.C.R. x).

107 George Elliott Clarke, "1933," *Execution Poems* (Wolfville, NS: Gaspereau, 2000), 24.

7

The Law's Confirmation of Racial Inferiority: *Christie v. York*

JAMES W. ST.G. WALKER

The Incident

By the mid-twentieth century, people of African descent had been in Canada for generations, lived in family units, attended Christian churches, spoke English and/or French, fought on behalf of king and empire in every war since the American Revolution, and publicly comported themselves according to the norms established by the majority society. The only significant distinguishing characteristic was colour. And yet African Canadians were subjected to restrictions in employment, housing, education, services, and recreation. Chiefly they were set apart and kept down, marginalized as neighbours, as employees, and as citizens. With only a few exceptions the law did not impose segregation and inequality on African Canadians; rather, the law upheld the right of Canadian individuals, organizations, and institutions to discriminate on grounds of "race." The most significant statement in support of this situation came from the Supreme Court of Canada in the case of *Christie v. York*.[1]

Previously published as chapter 3 of Walker, *"Race," Rights and the Law in the Supreme Court of Canada: Historical Case Studies* (Toronto and Waterloo: Osgoode Society for Canadian Legal History and Wilfrid Laurier University Press, 1997), 122–80.

Fred Christie was a Black man, a chauffeur by occupation, a member of the Union (United) Church, a resident of Montreal for over twenty years when the incident in question occurred. A tall man with a fit and healthy demeanour, impeccably clean and well dressed, Mr Christie is described as having the deportment of a gentleman and an impressive manner in his carriage and speech. In complexion he was pale brown.[2] Born in Jamaica in 1902, he migrated to Montreal as a teenager at the end of the First World War. His Jamaican accent had long since been modified, but its legacy was a precise way of speaking, which added to his courtly and dignified air. Among his Canadian acquisitions was a passion for the sport of ice hockey. He had a season ticket to a box seat at the Montreal Forum, and he rarely missed a game.[3]

In the spring of 1936 the York Tavern moved from its previous location into the ground floor of the Montreal Forum. To announce its move, the tavern took out newspaper advertisements and displayed a large sign inviting the public to visit its new premises and taste its wares. Fred Christie and his friends had often enjoyed a glass of beer in the old York Tavern, which had been located just to the north of the largest concentration of Black population in Montreal. The new location, however, brought with it a new policy: management instructed the staff that under no circumstances were "Negroes" to be served.[4]

On the evening of Saturday, 11 July 1936, Mr Christie and two friends, Emile King and Steven St Jean, entered the Forum to attend a hockey game. Mr King was a Texas-born African American who had lived in Montreal for nineteen years and was employed as a butler. Mr St Jean was a French-Canadian salesman. They often attended athletic events together. At Christie's invitation the three friends decided to stop for a beer before the game. He had no reason to suspect that they might be unwelcome. A waiter approached, and Fred Christie placed a 50-cent piece on the table, politely ordering "three steins of beer." The waiter responded, "Gentleman, I am very sorry. I cannot serve colored people." Mr Christie asked, "Why? Since when?" "It is an order from the manager," he was told. Incredulous, Christie demanded an interview with the manager. First to arrive was bartender George Gressie, who confirmed that ever since the tavern opened in the Forum, its policy had been to refuse service to Black people. Christie insisted on seeing someone more senior, and eventually assistant manager Roméo Lajoie was brought to the table. Quietly and politely, so that neighbouring tables could not overhear, Mr Lajoie explained to the party that even had he wanted to, he was not permitted by the York Corporation's regulations to accommodate "colored" men in the tavern. "Is that the only reason?" Christie asked. "Yes," said Lajoie. His demeanour slipping, Christie stalked to a pay telephone just outside the tavern and called the police. Apparently anticipating some disorder, the two constables who responded were less than tactful, alerting the crowd of seventy patrons to the dispute at the Christie table. In the presence of the police witnesses Mr Christie again insisted on being served. Mr Lajoie repeated his polite refusal one last time. The policemen, whose impatience was directed more at Christie than Lajoie, said there was absolutely nothing they could do. They left, followed by Fred Christie and his two friends.[5]

Fred Christie and Emile King were no strangers to racial discrimination, but they were outraged by this incident. Like most other African Canadians in Montreal, they had learned which shops and theatres to avoid, which jobs were unavailable, which residential districts would exclude them. But when they expected service, in an establishment so publicly located, they felt betrayed and humiliated. The "colour line" had advanced toward them, or so it seemed, and they decided it was time to fight back.[6] Confident that they had an absolute right to equality and insulted at the inferiority implied by their rejection, Christie and King decided to sue the York Tavern for the humiliation they had suffered.[7]

"Jim Crow" in Canada

An 1891 magazine article predicted that "to the end of time Africa will bless Canada for the refuge and home given to her children in that period of their trouble and trial."[8] New World slavery was undoubtedly a period of trouble for the children of Africa, but Canada's innocence was less obvious than the quotation might suggest. Between 1628 and the first decade of the nineteenth century, approximately three thousand people of African origin were held as slaves in what is now Canada, their status duly noted in the legal documents of the times.[9] As late as 1808 the Nova Scotia Assembly debated a "Bill for regulating Negro Servitude," prompted by a petition from slave-owners seeking to confirm the legality of slavery.[10] Nor did the extinction of slavery bring equality to Canada's Black population. In his classic description of American racial segregation, *The Strange Career of Jim Crow*, C. Vann Woodward identified the areas of life where legalized segregation tended to apply, following the end of slavery in the United States. He listed "churches and schools," "housing and jobs," "eating and drinking," "public transportation," "sports and recreations," "hospitals, orphanages, prisons and asylums," and, in death, "funeral homes, morgues and cemeteries."[11] In virtually every one of these areas of life and death, African Canadians, too, experienced exclusion and separation from mainstream institutions, amounting to a Canadian version of "Jim Crow."

Canada's free Black community dates from the American Revolution, when British officials promised freedom and equality to rebel-owned slaves who joined the Loyalist cause. Over 3,500 Black Loyalists were transported to the Maritimes during the British evacuation from the new republic in 1783. They were settled on the fringes of larger white towns, close enough to offer their daily labour, yet far enough to maintain social distinctions. The legacy of slavery consigned them to a labouring and service role, and they would never receive the recognition and rewards as Loyalists that their service during the war had earned them.[12] They were joined during the War of 1812 by more than two thousand other former American slaves, known as the Black Refugees, who similarly had fled to the British upon a wartime promise of land and freedom.[13] In their segregated settlements the free African Canadians continued to experience a barrier defined by their colour, doomed to menial employment, denied access to public institutions, and locked in poverty. Discrimination and disadvantage were mutually reinforcing, as the consequences of restricted opportunity were attributed to racial inferiority.

Elsewhere in Canada the patterns of Black settlement were less abrupt than in the Maritimes, but the "refuge and home" eulogized in 1891 were never untarnished. Tens of thousands of fugitive American slaves migrated to Ontario in the decades leading up to the American Civil War; almost a thousand others moved from California to Vancouver Island. Social separation and economic deprivation destroyed the dreams of the American runaways who crossed the border expecting a sanctuary, not just from slavery but from the inequalities imposed by racism. Approximately three-quarters of them returned to the American South after Emancipation.[14] It was not until the new century that Black migration to Canada was resumed. Between 1900 and 1912 about 1,300 Blacks from Oklahoma settled in Alberta and Saskatchewan, but rejection and harassment ensured that the renewed movement was brief.[15]

Throughout the period when white Canadians prided themselves for offering a haven to African Americans, negative stereotypes rendered a positive reception virtually impossible. In 1815 the Nova Scotian Assembly observed the arrival of the Black Refugees "with concern, and alarm" and passed a resolution "to prohibit the bringing any more of these people, into this Colony." Their reason, the resolution explained, was

that the proportion of Africans already in this country is productive of many inconveniences; and that the introduction of more must tend to the discouragement of white labourers and servants, as well as the establishment of a separate and marked class of people, unsuited by nature to this climate, or to an association with the rest of his Majesty's Colonists.[16]

Apart from the implication that African people must be labourers and servants, a direct product of Black slavery, the resolution reveals an acceptance of the notion that Blacks and whites were separate classes who could not suitably associate with one another. Such ideas prevailed throughout British North America. The Upper Canadian Assembly received petitions as early as 1830, when the "Underground Railroad" was just beginning, calling for restrictions on Black settlement in the province because of the African Americans' alleged degradation and defects of character.[17] During American Reconstruction, between 1865 and 1877, Canadian newspapers regarded the Southern experiment in racial equality with an interest, and often a horror, that directly reflected the conventional wisdom. Reconstruction was doomed to failure because of the former slaves' inherent laziness. "If they work at all, they will do just enough to secure themselves from starvation," proclaimed a typical editorial. As natural servants, Black people could not operate without white direction. Careful supervision was required as well, to curb the "animal passions" of African sexuality, which could burst forth in "demoniacal rage and lust." Above all, the "instinctive feelings of repugnance" that whites naturally held toward Blacks made "mixing and even association" of whites and Blacks unthinkable.[18]

What was true in the United States must be true in Canada. Writing in the popular *Canada and Its Provinces* series, Superintendent of Immigration W.D. Scott maintained, "The negro problem, which faces the United States and which Abraham Lincoln said could be settled only by shipping one and all back to a tract of land in Africa, is one in which Canadians have no desire to share."[19] Or as the *Toronto Mail and Empire* bluntly asserted, "If negroes and white people cannot live in accord in the South, they cannot live in accord in the North."[20] These and similar attitudes existed quite independently of personal experience. When sixteen Black men arrived in Virden, Manitoba, in the summer of 1908 they found "the farmers in the neighbourhood have a strong objection to the employment of coloured labour."[21] Despite the fact that no Black people had ever been through Virden before, the mayor explained that "farmers' wives are afraid of them."[22] The most dramatic expression of similar sentiments came from the Edmonton chapter of the Imperial Order of the Daughters of the Empire. In March 1911 the chapter met in emergency session to consider "the influx of Negroes" from Oklahoma then in progress. They sent a petition to Immigration Minister Frank Oliver:

We view with alarm the continuous and rapid influx of Negro settlers into Northern Alberta and believe that their coming will bring about serious social and political conditions.

This immigration will have the immediate effect of discouraging white settlement in the vicinity of the Negro farms and will depreciate the value of all holdings in such areas.

We fear that the welcome extended to those now coming will induce a very large black population to follow them.

The problems likely to arise with the establishment of these people in our thinly populated province must be plain to all, and the experience of the United States should warn us to take action before the situation becomes complicated and before the inevitable racial antipathies shall have sprung up.

We do not wish that the fair fame of Western Canada would be sullied with the shadow of Lynch Law but we have no guarantee that our women will be safer in their scattered homesteads than white women in other countries with a Negro population.

We would therefore urge upon the Government the need for immediate action and the taking of all possible steps to stop Negro immigration into Alberta.[23]

In line with the same sexual mythology, Mrs Isobel Graham, described as a "Manitoba suffragist," wrote in the *Grain Growers' Guide* of 3 May 1911 that atrocities would inevitably be committed by African-American immigrants against white Canadian women, and warned that lynching and even burning at the stake would become necessary.[24] Dr Ella Synge, speaking on behalf of prairie women, pointed to "the enormous increase in outrages on white women that has occurred" in South Africa as a result of liberal British policies, and predicted that "the finger of fate is pointing to lynch law which will be the ultimate result, as sure as we allow such people to settle among US."[25]

When members of Parliament raised the concerns of their African-Canadian constituents that Black immigrants were being excluded on grounds of colour, the federal government denied that any policy existed to refuse entrance on grounds of "race, colour, or previous condition of servitude," but Minister Frank Oliver admitted that

there are many cases where the admission or exclusion of an immigrant depends on a strict or a lax interpretation of the law, so that if the immigrant is of what we would call the desirable class it may be that they are administered laxly, and if he is of the presumably less desirable class then they are administered more restrictedly.[26]

When the minister rejected the suggestion being proposed in the popular press that a restrictive head tax be imposed to discourage Black immigration, MP William Thoburn from the Ontario riding of Lanark cried out in the House of Commons, "I would like to ask the government if they think it in the interests of Canada that we should have negro colonization in our Canadian Northwest? Would it not be preferable to preserve for the sons of Canada the lands they propose to give to niggers?"[27]

Sentiments such as these readily explain the substantial extent of racial segregation in Canada. The most significant area of separation, at least in legislative terms, was in education.[28] In Nova Scotia the *Education Act* of 1836 permitted local commissioners to establish separate schools for "Blacks or People of Colour."[29] Since the Black schools were irregularly funded by special legislative grants and charitable donations, teachers and equipment were inevitably inferior, and educational quality suffered. Black parents organized protests against the limitations placed upon their children, culminating in an 1883 petition campaign demanding the full integration of provincial schools. This precipitated a debate in the legislature, resulting in amendments to the *School Act* in 1884 and a partial but significant victory for African Canadians. The revised Act continued to permit school commissioners to establish segregated facilities, but added that "colored pupils shall not be excluded from instruction in the public school in the section or ward where they reside."[30] In the city of Halifax this provision gained African-Canadian youths access to secondary education for the first time. A later section of the 1884 Act was less helpful, stipulating that no school receiving special aid could hire a teacher with anything higher than a fourth-class certificate.[31] Since every all-Black school in the province at that time received provincial aid, this ensured that they would be served by the most poorly qualified teachers. Separate must also be inferior, according to Nova Scotia law.

Ontario's *Common School Act* of 1850 allowed twelve or more heads of family to request a separate Black school.[32] The intention of the Act may have been to permit Black families to opt for their own school, but in practice twelve white family heads could request separate schools for Black children. Under this legislation segregated education was imposed in most Ontario districts with a sizeable African-Canadian population. Several court cases refined the administration of the segregated schools. In *Washington v. The Trustees of Charlotteville* Chief Justice John Beverley Robinson ruled that where no separate school existed, Black children must be admitted to the common school with white children.[33] In a second case immediately afterwards, however, Robinson decided that if a Black school had been established in the school district, even if it was as far as four miles away from their homes, Black children could be forced to attend the segregated facility.[34] The trustees in Chatham exploited this ruling to create a separate school district comprising every Black family wherever they lived in the town, but this practice was rendered illegal in *Simmons v. Chatham* in 1861 when the chief justice concluded that such subjective school section boundaries were too uncertain to be administered effectively.[35] In 1864 the courts found that when a separate school fell into disuse the Black children thus displaced should be accepted in the nearest common school.[36] Under this principle, parental actions, including the withholding of school taxes, led gradually to the closing of most separate Black schools and the integration of the children, though the segregation provision remained in the Ontario legislation until repealed in 1964.[37] In New Brunswick, where de facto separate schools served all-Black communities, the law recognized but did not require the separate education of Black children;[38] on the prairies, though the law was silent on the question, African-Canadian children were frequently rejected from public schools because of their colour.[39]

The separation accepted in education was acceptable too in many other areas of life, though not with the support of positive legislation. Early African-Canadian settlers in Ontario were moved to declare "our perfect contentment with our political condition, living, as we do, under the influence of free and equal laws, which recognize no distinction of colour in the protection which they afford and the privileges which they confer."[40] But "legal equality" would not mean freedom from racial restriction and exclusion in Canada. Ida Greaves was not far from the mark when she wrote in 1929, "The Negro has exactly the same rights as anybody else until he tries to use them, then he can be quite legally restrained."[41] Legally acceptable racial segregation had a long and full history in Canada before Fred Christie ever set foot in the York Tavern. The barriers were by no means absolute, but across Canada, from Halifax to Victoria, there were establishments normally open to the public where African Canadians were refused admission. Segregation in housing, employment, restaurants and bars, transportation, recreation, hospitals, orphanages, and cemeteries – every one of Vann Woodward's "Jim Crow" categories – had its Canadian example.[42]

Most Canadian cities had a district where the majority of Black residents lived, with boundaries enforced by racially restrictive covenants or more usually by consent among white homeowners and real estate agents. As the *Windsor Herald* explained to Black citizens in that city:

If a certain locality is prohibited, let them avoid it, as they will experience no difficulty in finding places for settlement; but if they endeavor to force themselves into positions where they are not wanted, under the idea that the British constitution warrants them in so doing, they may discover in the end that the privileges which they now enjoy will become forfeited.[43]

In 1920 four Black families moved into the Victoria Park district of Calgary, where no Black people had lived before. A petition was organized and signed by 472 of the district's 670 households, asking city council to relocate the Black families and to restrain any further purchases. Calgary council had little experience with this kind of issue – there were only seventy African Canadians in the city and none had caused any "trouble" before – and so after a brief debate the city clerk was instructed to write to sixteen other Canadian cities for guidance from those more experienced:

Would you be so kind as to inform me by return mail as to any legislation that might be in effect in your municipality segregating the residences of negroes to any particular district or districts. Further, if there is any legislation preventing negroes from locating in your City at all.

This last request is prompted by a statement which has been made to the effect that such legislation does exist in certain municipalities in Canada.[44]

There were no such by-laws in Canada in 1920,[45] though several respondents (including Windsor's city clerk) volunteered that Black people tended to live in concentrated areas anyway. Nevertheless it is surely significant that Calgarians assumed examples must exist and were ready to implement legal segregation in their city. In fact Calgary solved its problem in the typical Canadian fashion: whites resident in Victoria Park agreed to sell no more homes to Blacks, and the Blacks there agreed to sell their homes only to white purchasers.[46]

Employment discrimination was widespread, encompassing the civil service as well as the private sector.[47] African Canadians complained that public transportation and accommodations were denied to them without legal recourse. When a Black man was physically ejected from the Mansion House hotel in London, Ontario, and sought a warrant against the owner from a local magistrate, it was the Black man who found himself convicted of assault.[48] *Saturday Night* magazine expressed no sympathy when Toronto's Queen's Hotel barred the Rev. C.O. Johnson, declaring, "In Canada there is no active prejudice against the colored race" and Black people were never affronted "except when they forget that no well-bred person will endeavour to force himself into a place where he is not wanted."[49] An Edmonton newspaper reported in 1912,

Irate Negroes were turned down services in two hotels. They ask, "Have Edmonton bartenders the right to draw the colour line?" The attorney general's department said while it gives the hotel keeper the right to sell liquor, "it cannot compel him to sell to anyone if he does not wish to do so."[50]

Only a few days after Fred Christie's ordeal in Montreal, *Saturday Night* took editorial note of a Black singer denied access to the dining room in the Toronto hotel where she was a guest. "[T]he situation in Canada, with regard to discrimination against colored persons in public hostelries, is little if at all better that it is in [the United States]," the magazine admitted, though blame was placed on Americans who "dictate their policies" when they patronized Canadian hotels. While this was acknowledged to be "an intolerable anomaly in a free, liberal and supposedly Christian country," no legal solution was offered.

The only feasible way of dealing with the situation appears to be the establishment of international clubhouses in the larger urban centres in which foreigners of any race, color, religion or political philosophy, provided that they are personally acceptable, will be admitted to the full enjoyment of all privileges.[51]

Canadian theatres frequently had separate seating for Black patrons, and this could be enforced by mob violence on occasion: a riot erupted in the Empress Theatre in Victoria when a group of prominent African-Canadian citizens took seats in the dress circle, contrary to local convention.[52] In Windsor, Ontario, the Palace Theatre maintained a "Crow's nest" for Black customers; Loew's (later the Capital) had its "Monkey cage." These practices were still in existence when the York Tavern incident occurred.[53] Ontario's deputy attorney general explained in a letter to Stephen Leacock in 1929 that

Coloured people have exactly the same rights as others in the matter of public places of entertainment, but as the obligation of a proprietor to sell seats in his theatre or meals in his restaurant does not ordinarily exist, he can refuse to sell to Negroes if he pleases, just as he could refuse to sell to any other person or class of people, as long as the refusal is not accompanied by insult or violence.[54]

Across Canada, hospitals typically would not accept African Canadians as nurses, Black doctors were denied hospital privileges in several cities, and in at least one Edmonton hospital Blacks were not even received as patients in the 1920s and 1930s.[55] A separate orphanage was established in Nova Scotia for African-Canadian children in 1921.[56] Black veterans of the First World War were buried in a segregated section of Camp Hill cemetery in Halifax,[57] and the Nova Scotia municipality of St Croix had a by-law passed in 1907, still enforced as late as 1968, excluding African Canadians from burial in the local cemetery.[58]

White reluctance to associate intimately with African Canadians extended even into the emergency conditions of the First World War. The appeal to save the empire and democracy in the fall of 1914 did not carry any colour implications, but Black volunteers were systematically rejected by recruiting officers. Many protested, convinced that a contribution to the war effort would earn the gratitude and respect of the white majority. From Saint John came a letter to the governor general: "I beg to call your attention to the fact that Colored men of good repute have been denied the chance of enlistment in the Forces for overseas service etc. on the ground of Color."[59] The Hamilton Black community advised the minister of militia that virtually every eligible young man had sought to enlist, but had been

turned down and refused solely on the ground of color or complexional distinction; this being the reason given on the rejection or refusal card issued by the recruiting officer.

As humble, but as loyal subjects of the King, trying to work out their own destiny, they think they should be permitted in common with other peoples to perform their part, and do their share in this great conflict.[60]

Similar letters were received from every part of Canada in 1914, 1915, and 1916. "It is certainly shameful and insulting to the Race," one such letter concluded.[61] Vancouver's chief recruiting officer complained, "Coloured candidates are becoming insistent, and I should like to know what course I am to pursue."[62]

Militia headquarters had an issue on its hands, and several queries were sent to regional and unit commanders to determine their attitudes. In typical replies, the Victoria district commander reported that Black enlistment "would do much harm, as white men here will not serve in the same ranks with negros [sic] or coloured persons,"[63] and from the East Coast that whites would withdraw if Blacks were accepted, as "neither my men nor myself, would care to sleep alongside them, or eat with them, especially in warm weather."[64] The issue became especially insistent after a group of Toronto Blacks formed a platoon of their own and offered it to Militia Minister Sam Hughes. Every commanding officer in the military district administered from Toronto was canvassed to find a battalion willing to accept the African-Canadian platoon in the spring of 1916. Some replies were simple: "I have no desire to have a coloured platoon in my Battalion"; "I would object very strongly to accepting the Platoon mentioned." Some sought to blame their reluctance on the prejudices of the common soldiers: "It would seriously affect our recruiting"; "It would cause great dissatisfaction among the men now enlisted." Some even attempted humour: "Thank goodness, this battalion is over strength and does not need a 'colored' platoon, nor even a colored 'drum-major'!"; the Canadian Highlanders suggested coyly that "these men would not look good in kilts." At a time when Prime Minister Borden had committed Canada to the daunting task of keeping 500,000 men in the battlefields, not a single battalion would take a Black platoon.[65]

The policy set by the militia council was that "coloured men can be enlisted in any Overseas Unit provided that the Commanding Officer is willing to accept them, but it is not thought desirable, either in the interests of such men themselves or of the Canadian Forces, that Commanding Officers should be forced to take them."[66] But when Black

Nova Scotians gained the ear of several prominent Nova Scotia politicians, including Fleming McCurdy, John Stanfield, and Robert Borden, Chief of General Staff Willoughby Gwatkin was ordered to conduct a study and report on the feasibility of African-Canadian enlistment. His reply encapsulates the feelings prevalent in 1916:

Memorandum on the enlistment of negroes in Canadian Expeditionary Force.

1. Nothing is to be gained by blinking facts. The civilized negro is vain and imitative; in Canada he is not being impelled to enlist by a high sense of duty; in the trenches he is not likely to make a good fighter; and the average white man will not associate with him on terms of equality. Not a single commanding officer in Military District No.2 is willing to accept a coloured platoon as part of his battalion; and it would be humiliating to the coloured men themselves to serve in a battalion where they were not wanted.

2. In France, in the firing line, there would be no place for a black battalion, C.E.F. It would be eyed askance; it would crowd out a white battalion; it would be difficult to reinforce.

3. Nor could it be left in England and used as a draft-giving depot; for there would be trouble if negroes were sent to the front line for the purpose of reinforcing white battalions; and, if they are good men at all, they would resent being kept in Canada for the purpose of finding guards, etc.

4. It seems, therefore, that three courses are practicable:

    (a) As at present, to allow negroes to enlist, individually, into white battalions at the discretion of commanding officers.

    (b) To allow them to form one or more labour battalions. Negroes from Nova Scotia, for example, would not be unsuitable for the purpose.

    (c) To ask the British Government if it can make use of a black battalion, C.E.F., on special duty overseas (e.g. in Egypt): but the battalion will not be ready before the fall, and, if only on account of its relatively extravagant rates of pay, it will not mix well with other troops.

5. I recommend courses (a) and (b).[67]

Convinced by Gwatkins's option (b), the militia council voted just three days later to establish a Black labour unit, the Nova Scotia No. 2 Construction Battalion, with authority to recruit Black men from all across Canada.[68] But while African Canadians were at last acceptable into the Canadian Expeditionary Force, if only in the traditional and stereotypical role of labourers, social distance had still to be maintained. Most astonishingly, the Black battalion was transported overseas in 1917 in a separate troop ship to avoid "offending the susceptibility of other troops," and it was actually recommended, though not accepted, that their ship should not join a regular convoy but should cross the submarine-infested Atlantic on its own.[69] Once overseas and engaged in their duties, the men of the No. 2 were segregated in the camp cinema, were provided with their own "coloured chaplain," were treated in a separate hospital wing when ill or wounded, and were incarcerated in a separate punishment compound when they misbehaved.[70] Back in England after the Armistice and awaiting return transport to Canada, a sergeant from the No. 2 arrested a white man and placed him "in charge of a colored escort" en route to the camp jail. White soldiers unwilling to contemplate such an insult attacked the Black party, provoking a riot between white and Black soldiers throughout the camp.[71] Their efforts during the war had not won respect for Black Canadians.

Separation and subordination were to be maintained, by violence and intimidation where necessary. Probably the most dramatic example of community action to enforce "Jim Crow" occurred in Oakville, Ontario, on 28 February 1930. Ira Johnston, described in the press as a "coloured man" or a "Negro" aged thirty, became engaged to marry twenty-year-old Isabella Jones, who bore the description "white girl" ("Johnston," the *Toronto Daily Star* reported, "is a fine-looking man and nearly white"). The pending marriage caused much talk among the neighbours, since it was widely considered improper to mix "race" in this way. Miss Jones's mother tried to prevent the match, applying to the police and an Oakville magistrate for legal intervention and then, when she learned that no law prevented her daughter from marrying a Black man, she wrote to the Ku Klux Klan for assistance. Meanwhile Mr Johnston had difficulty finding a minister who would perform the marriage, though he had received a valid marriage licence, and so late in February Miss Jones moved in with Mr Johnston, still unmarried. The Klan kept watch, and on 27 February, learned that Mr Johnston had arranged with the pastor of the African Methodist Episcopal Church to conduct the marriage on 2 March. This precipitated what the Klan called its first "direct action" in Canada on the night of 28 February. About seventy-five Klansmen, most of them from Hamilton, Ontario, travelled by car to Oakville, where they marched through the streets in their hooded uniforms, burned a large cross at Main and Third Streets in downtown Oakville in the presence of hundreds of spectators, and then went in pursuit of the offending couple. They were found at the home of Ira's aunt, where they were playing cards at about 11 p.m. Isabella was told to get in a Klansman's car, and when Ira "asked what authority they had for taking her away" they made no reply "but closed the door and drove off." Isabella was taken to her mother's home, where before witnesses she swore to have nothing to do with Ira Johnston again. At Mrs Jones's request, the Klan took Isabella to a Salvation Army hostel for safekeeping. Returning to "interview" Ira further on his transgression, the Klansmen surrounded the house and burned another cross on the front lawn. Ira's mother explained that he had gone out in search of his fiancée, whereupon "the spokesman told me that if Ira, my son, was ever seen walking down the street with a white girl again the Klan would attend to him." As they were leaving town, the Klan cavalcade was intercepted by Police Chief David Kerr. He recognized many of them, for they had removed their masks, and he appeared to approve when they told him everything that had happened.[72]

The following day Oakville Mayor A.B. Moat told the press, "Personally I think the Ku Klux Klan acted quite properly in the matter. The feeling in the town is generally against such a marriage. Everything was done in an orderly manner. It will be quite an object lesson." Chief Kerr, explaining why he did not arrest anyone, said, "They used no force nor did they create a disturbance of any kind ... The conduct of the visitors was all that could be desired."

But the Ontario Black community was outraged. An "indignation meeting" was held in Toronto, and Black leaders called upon the attorney general to investigate the incident and prosecute the guilty. Their rights as British subjects were being violated, they claimed; in the recent war they had served their King and empire for the sake of upholding rule of law, and now a disorderly mob was taking the law into its own hands. A Black Baptist minister said, "I hold no brief for the promiscuous intermingling of the races. But I am unalterably opposed to the substitution of the purely authorized law enforcement agencies by such an intolerant organization as the Ku Klux Klan." Rabbi Maurice Eisendrath of Holy Blossom Synagogue joined the protest, claiming that the official apathy served to condone the Klan's illegal act. The attorney general agreed. Charges were laid against four of the Klansmen for having their faces "masked or blackened, or being otherwise disguised, by night, without lawful excuse."

Only one of the four, Hamilton chiropractor William A. Phillips, was found guilty and fined fifty dollars. Phillips appealed his sentence and the Crown cross-appealed. Klan spokesman Dr Harold Orme insisted, "Our only interest in race matters is that we want our country kept pure from contamination by mixed marriages." The "mixture of blood," according to the Klan, created "fiery, subnormal people to whom most of the violent crimes could be traced." Chief Justice Mulock decided, however, "The motive of the accused and his companions is immaterial." They had taken "illegal interference" with the liberty of the young woman. "Their action was unlawful and it is the duty of this Court to pronounce the appropriate punishment." The court upheld Phillips's conviction and increased his penalty to three months in jail. Unrepentant, Phillips declared that he was "happy to serve a term in prison for such a cause as this," and the Klan issued a statement that all its members were ready and willing to sacrifice themselves for Christianity and the flag.

Even Isabella said she felt sorry for Phillips. "He thought he was doing me a kindness. I have a letter that he sent me containing good advice. I don't like to think of him having to go to jail." In an editorial the Toronto *Globe* expressed what may have been majority opinion on the subject. The Klan was denounced for taking the law into its own hands, for intimidation of a fellow-subject, for its un-British conduct committed in secrecy. But the editorial concluded, "The work the nocturnal visitors did at Oakville in separating a white girl from a colored man may be commendable in itself, and prove of benefit, but it is certain that the methods were wrong."[73]

The Montreal Community

The historical pattern in Montreal reflected the national experience for African Canadians. There were Black slaves in Montreal at its foundation in 1641, and from then until the Conquest more than six hundred slaves resided in the city and its environs. Slavery was an acceptable and respectable institution in the ancien régime: Mother Marie-Marguerite d'Youville, founder of the Sisters of Charity, was one of Montreal's more prominent slaveholders, a fact that did not interfere with her canonization in 1990.[74] Undoubtedly the slave who left her mark most emphatically on Montreal history was Marie-Joseph-Angélique, who in April 1734 set fire to her mistress's home to distract attention from an attempt to escape. The fire spread, destroying forty-six houses and the Hôtel-Dieu. Following a highly publicized trial and unsuccessful appeal, the twenty-five-year-old slave was hanged in Montreal's public square, her body burned, and her ashes thrown to the winds.[75]

The legal status of slavery was confirmed by an order signed by Intendant Jacques Raudot on 13 April 1709 clarifying title to panis (native Indian) and African slaves held in the colony. Apparently some habitants were encouraging slaves to leave their masters on the pretext that slavery was illegal. Raudot declared slaves to be the property of the persons who bought them, and announced a fine of fifty livres for anyone assisting a runaway.[76] In 1734 Intendant Gilles Hocquart ordered the militia to arrest runaway slaves and two years later introduced a complicated procedure to register manumissions in an effort to discourage masters from freeing their own slaves. Voluntary manumissions, Hocquart noted, were causing confusion, making it "nécessaire de fixer d'une manière invariable l'état des esclaves."[77] When Montreal fell to the British in 1760, Article 47 of the Capitulation provided that slaves should remain the property of their masters, as before: "[L]es nègres et panis des deux sexes resteront en leur qualité d'esclaves en la possession des français et canadiens à qui ils appartiennent; il leur sera libre de les garder à leur service dans la colonie ou de les vendre; ils pourront aussi continuer à les fair lever dans la réligion catholique."[78]

The day after the capitulation, the governor of Montreal wrote to the commandant at Detroit, explaining that although he had been required to surrender to General Amherst, he had managed to do so "à des conditions très avantageuses pour les colons … En effet ils conservent le libre exercice de leur réligion, et sont maintenus en leur possessions de leurs biens …; ils conservent leurs Nègres et Panis."[79] As a Missouri judge would point out a century later,

the 47th article is not only a clear recognition of the existence of slavery [in Montreal], but of the value of the interests connected with it. Only the most prominent objects seem to have engaged the attention of the retiring governor, for he secures nothing for his master's subjects but their religion and their slaves.[80]

The new British rulers had, in any case, no intention of challenging slavery. General James Murray, the first English governor, wrote to a friend in New York in November 1763,

I must most earnestly entreat your assistance, without servants nothing can be done. Had I the inclination to employ soldiers, which is not the case, they would disappoint me, and Canadians will work for nobody but themselves. Black slaves are certainly the only people to be depended upon.

Murray went on to ask his friend to buy him some slaves in New York, and added, "You may buy for each a clean young wife, who can work and do the female offices about a farm. I shall begrudge no price."[81]

A few free Black Loyalists landed in Lower Canada, but they were far outnumbered by the approximately three hundred slaves brought by white Loyalist masters. In 1783 the Montreal press carried an advertisement announcing

TO BE SOLD

A Negro Wench about 18 years of age, who came lately from New York with the Loyalists. She has had the Small Pox – The Wench has a good character and is exposed to sale only from the owner having no use for her at present. Likewise to be disposed of a handsome Bay Mare.[82]

A bill introduced in the Lower Canada legislature in 1793 "tendant à l'abolition de l'esclavage" was tabled by a decisive vote of twenty-eight to three.[83] Advertisements for the sale of slaves were published in Montreal at least until 1805, at which time there were about 150 slaves in the city.[84]

As slavery died out in Lower Canada in the nineteenth century, former slaves and their descendants either moved away or lost their identity. In the 1871 census there were only seventy-two persons of African descent dispersed throughout Montreal, and there was no identifiable "Black community" when the city again became a destination for Black migrants in the 1880s. The American Pullman Company already used Black porters and waiters on its continental service, and when Montreal was connected with New York and Boston in 1886, and became the eastern Canadian headquarters for both the Canadian Pacific Railway and the Grand Trunk, the practice spread across Canada. Canadian railway agents were sent to the major American urban centres and to campuses of Black colleges in the South to recruit African Americans as porters and waiters. They were housed in Montreal and travelled from coast to coast serving white passengers. Initially comprising a community of temporary male sojourners, by the 1890s many railway workers were beginning to settle in Montreal and to bring their families. Their commitment to Montreal was later enhanced by the establishment of the headquarters there for the Order of Sleeping Car Porters, for employees of the Canadian National Railway, and the Porters' Mutual Benefit Association for those working on the CPR.[85]

To this initial core of American railway workers there was added a small but increasing flow of young Black men from rural Ontario and Nova Scotia seeking work on the Pullman cars. Most were not considered sophisticated enough for this kind of service, but they could become red caps in Windsor Station or shoeshiners or elevator operators. Those who found jobs brought their families and settled permanently in Montreal. West Indians, too, were attracted to the opportunities of Montreal. Though white passengers might regard their porters and waiters as menial servants, for African Canadians in the early twentieth century, railway work was stable, reasonably well paid, and generally the most satisfactory kind of employment available. The Montreal Black community grew from 293 persons in the 1911 census to 928 in 1921 and 1,202 in 1931, with men and women gradually coming into balance.[86] Because of rampant housing discrimination in most districts of Montreal,[87] the Blacks inhabited a fairly defined area close to the Canadian National and Canadian Pacific railway yards. Although African Canadians were not a majority in this area, and some resided outside it (including Fred Christie, who participated in a small Black movement to Verdun in the mid-1920s), this neighbourhood constituted the physical community of Black Montreal, with St Antoine Street as its main thoroughfare. The area was characterized by poor-quality housing and low rents, but physical proximity fostered the development of Black community institutions and a sense of identity. The African Canadians of Montreal tended to stay in their own neighbourhood for shopping and recreation as well. In most other parts of the city, hotels, restaurants, and stores regularly refused service to Black customers, and even some churches rejected Black members.[88]

The most significant discrimination experienced by Black people in Montreal was in employment. Even those Americans and West Indians who arrived with skills discovered that they could not find appropriate jobs, either because employers preferred to hire whites or because the American-affiliated unions would not admit them to membership.[89] Apart from the railroads, their chief employer, African-Canadian men could get work as dishwashers, janitors, and occasionally as unskilled or semiskilled factory and construction hands.[90] Because wages were low, both adult partners were required to work in order to support a family, with almost all the women working as domestic servants in white homes.[91] Montreal hospitals would not train or employ Black nurses for, as one priest explained, "les malades ne voudront certainement pas recevoir les soins d'une noire."[92] Even the railways were no safe place for Black men. In the 1920s Black waiters in the dining cars were replaced by whites, first on the CPR and then on the CN.[93] The sleeping-car porter's position remained Black, but regardless of qualifications or length of service, a Black porter could not be promoted to sleeping-car conductor, a post reserved for whites.[94]

The situation in Montreal was perceived by many African Canadians to be worsening in the years following the First World War.[95] Quebec society was experiencing disruption from an economic recession beginning in 1920, and social dislocation caused by rapid industrialization and urbanization. The sense that the French-Canadian equilibrium was being upset by alien forces, coming from outside the francophone community, provoked a resurgence of nationalism and an articulated resentment against "foreigners."[96] In this respect Quebec was not unique: nativist movements swept across Canada in the 1920s, and south of the border the Americans shared the experience of "the tribal twenties."[97] Still the nativist phenomenon in Quebec had its own special features. One was the intimate link, indeed the identification, between the Roman Catholic Church and Quebec nationalism, which rendered any non-Catholic virtually ineligible for inclusion. Another was the appeal to history, the glorification of the struggle against a hostile nature and overwhelming enemies that had produced a singular people, specially adapted to conditions in Quebec. Combined, these features created a sense of divine mission, a "social priesthood," to which the French-Canadian nation had to be faithful.[98]

This nationalist spirit was epitomized in the teachings of the priest and historian Lionel Groulx. The first professor of Canadian history at the University of Montreal, Groulx presented Canadian history as a contest between "races": on the one side "a stock that is more princely than any on earth. We are of a divine race, we are the sons of God"; on the other "barbarians," aliens, the forces of cosmopolitanism and "hermaphroditism."[99] Above all, Groulx exhorted the French-Canadian people, "rester d'abord nous-mêmes." As editor of the nationalist journal *L'Action française*, he wrote in 1921,

it is this rigorously characterized French type, dependent upon history and geography, having ethnical and psychological hereditary traits, which we wish to continue, on which we base the hope of our future; because a people, like all growing things, can develop only what is in itself, only the forces whose living germ it contains.[100]

To protect the French-Canadian nation, Groulx warned against foreign corruptions, from intermarriage to American movies and magazines.[101]

An economic element was present in French-Canadian nationalism throughout the 1920s, but it was accentuated in the 1930s as a result of the Great Depression, when the ethnic conflict became identified in economic terms. *L'Action française*, which had ceased publication in 1928, was succeeded in 1933 by *L'Action nationale* and a program of economic nationalism symbolized by the slogan "Achat Chez Nous." This "campaign of commercial chauvinism"[102] was most obviously directed against Jewish shopkeepers, but a participant explained to the sociologist Everett C. Hughes that it targeted anyone who was not French and Catholic: "He could be a Chinaman or a Negro."[103] The cultural homogeneity demanded by Groulx had produced "un courant de pensée hostile à la présence de non-francophones, et notablement de Juifs, au sein des institutions et services de la majorité."[104] Jews were included within a generalized xenophobia, as revealed in Andre Laurendeau's explanation of 1930s Quebec anti-Semitism as "revulsion directed against *foreigners.*"[105] Black people, mostly migrants from the United States, West Indies, or Nova Scotia, were outsiders by virtue of their origin, their language, and their religion. Some French-Canadian shopkeepers grew reluctant even to serve Black customers, and personal association, always remote, became less likely than ever.[106] It was during the 1930s that Montreal hospitals began refusing Black medical students as interns, leading the McGill University Faculty of Medicine to make an arrangement with Howard University for African Canadians to serve their internships in Washington, DC.[107] In 1936, the year Fred Christie tried to enter the York Tavern, Maurice Duplessis led his Union Nationale party to electoral victory on a platform of nationalism. These developments did not produce a Montreal that was more discriminatory than British Columbia or southwestern Ontario, for example, but they did serve notice to African Canadians that the situation in Montreal was worsening and it was time to take a stand.

This was the context of open suspicion and occasional hostility within which Montreal's African-Canadian population sought to survive as a community. In the early decades of the century, the community produced institutions and societies to serve the needs of its own members. Most important was Union Church, founded in 1907 and affiliated with the Congregational Church until 1925, when it joined

the United Church of Canada. There were other Black churches, introduced by American immigrants, but Union Church on Delisle Street
would become the mother institution for the entire community.[108] The
two porters' organizations provided recreational facilities at their headquarters, and there was a host of smaller social or mutual benefit associations and athletic clubs.[109] The largest secular organization was
the Universal Negro Improvement Association. Marcus Garvey, its Jamaican founder, visited Montreal in 1917, and a formal UNIA branch
was organized in 1919. Openly political and directed at instilling pride
in Black hearts and dignity in Black lives, the UNIA enlisted hundreds
of African Canadians in Montreal in the 1920s. Sunday morning was
devoted to church; Sunday afternoon belonged to the UNIA, with
meetings at Liberty Hall, speeches extolling the virtues of Black independence, debates, dances, and picnics.[110]

Despite poverty and rejection, it was a vital, vibrant community, and
never more so than during the tenure of the Rev. Charles Este as pastor of Union Church. Este arrived in Montreal from Antigua in 1913,
hoping to find work on the railroad, but was forced instead to become
a shoeshiner at a hotel. Night school courses over many years prepared
him to enter the Congregational seminary, and in 1925 he became the
minister at Union Church. Charles Este was the unrivalled spiritual
leader of Black Montreal, and he also had considerable influence in secular affairs. He campaigned vigorously for African-Canadian employment opportunities and admission to training programs. In 1927 Este
founded the Negro Community Centre, located first in the basement
of Union Church, as a focal point for Black social life and community
consciousness. During the Depression, when many other organizations
drifted or declined and even the UNIA went into hibernation, the centre and its parent church provided the energy and the confidence to
enable the community to survive.[111]

It was to this community that Fred Christie turned for support. Many
of its members had grown to believe that nothing could be done about
discrimination; Christie's defiance was regarded as unusual, curious,
and thrilling, and attracted widespread attention among African Canadians.[112] A group of men responded to Christie's challenge by forming
The Fred Christie Defence Committee. The committee was chaired by
Dr Kenneth Melville, professor of biology at McGill, and the vice-chair
was Alfred Potter, a red cap. Treasurer was A.E. Smith, chief red cap for
the CPR, and as publicity director they recruited E.M. Packwood, publisher of Montreal's only Black newspaper, the *Free Lance: Afro-Canadian*

Weekly. They opened a campaign office at 1314 St Antoine Street and organized a mass meeting at the UNIA Hall. Money flowed in, literally in nickels, dimes, and quarters, collected in the Black barbershops and newsstands, at Union Church and the campaign office. African-Canadian women organized a social evening at the Coloured War Veterans' Hall, with the proceeds going to the Christie fund. Through circular letters and "authorized collectors" almost every Black family in Montreal learned of the campaign and made some small contribution. The red caps', CN, and CP porters' associations pledged their formal support. Fred Christie had sparked a mass community crusade to confront the humiliations of racial discrimination. As the *Free Lance* editorialized, "Unless we are prepared to fight for equal treatment under the law of the land, we ought not and will not be regarded or treated as responsible citizens."[113]

Issues and Initiatives

When a group of African Canadians asked the federal government in 1916 whether racially discriminatory practices were legal, the deputy minister of justice replied that legislation was silent on this issue: "The remedy is in the courts."[114] It was therefore to the courts and the common law that the Christie Defence Committee had resort. As far as the committee was concerned, the issue involved was simple: racial discrimination should not be permitted in a democratic society. For the courts, however, there were complications.

Since medieval times the common law of England had required an innkeeper to serve any traveller who applied for lodging and refreshment, subject only to limitations of space or some other reasonable excuse. Over the years certain kinds of behaviour by the customer were deemed a reasonable ground for refusal, primarily drunkenness or other disorderly conduct. The particular tastes and preferences of the innkeeper could not be exercised.[115] The original principle was that a traveller was at the mercy of the innkeeper, perhaps literally for life or death in medieval conditions, and so in exchange for the right to engage in public business the innkeeper accepted the obligation to receive the public without discrimination. This same principle had been extended to other services, in particular to common carriers who could not refuse to carry a customer's goods without a lawful excuse. Both the innkeeper and the carrier were "common" in that they offered their services to anyone, without an explicit contract being required. Similarly, any business granted a state monopoly or position of privilege, by analogy, could not arbitrarily refuse service to a bona fide customer. This was articulated in Lord Hale's doctrine, which set out that enterprises (in this case, a public wharf) that held an exclusive licence to provide a certain service must receive everyone, for they "are affected with a public interest, and they cease to be *juris privati* only."[116] Elaborating this principle, Chief Justice Holt ruled in 1701,

Where-ever any subject takes upon himself a public trust for the benefit of the rest of his fellow-subjects, he is *eo ipso* bound to serve the subject in all the things that are within the reach and comprehension of such an office, under pain of an action against him … [O]ne that has made profession of a public employment, is bound to the utmost extent of that employment to serve the public.[117]

The issue before the court in Christie's case was therefore not the legality of discrimination per se, but the right of the York Tavern, as a licensed business offering to serve the public, to refuse service arbitrarily. Would Lord Hale's doctrine extend to a tavern in the province of Quebec?

The question was not without its Canadian precedents. On 11 March 1898 a Black man named Frederick Johnson, who worked at Montreal's Queen's Hotel as a bellhop, presented a coupon at the box office of the Academy of Music in exchange for two tickets for a theatrical performance the following evening. The clerk, believing Mr Johnson must be on an errand for a white customer, gave over the tickets for seats 1 and 3 in row K of the orchestra. In fact, Johnson had received the coupon as a tip from a Mr Swizzell, the manager of the touring theatrical group, who was staying at the Queen's Hotel. When Mr Johnson and a Black woman attended the theatre the next night, the usher refused to seat them in the orchestra section because of a house regulation restricting Blacks to the dress circle only. Some commotion occurred as Johnson declined the offer of alternate seats in the dress circle, and he and his friend had finally to be ejected forcibly from the theatre. They took a cab to the Théâtre Français, where they were admitted to a performance. Then Mr Johnson sued the Academy of Music for damages.

Justice John Sprott Archibald of the Quebec Superior Court agreed with Johnson and awarded him fifty dollars damages for the humiliation, trouble, and expense to which the academy's action had subjected him.[118] Dismissing the theatre's claim that as a "high class" establishment its exclusive seating arrangement was reasonable, Justice

Archibald articulated two fundamental questions raised by this case. First, could a theatre legally make "invidious regulations" restricting coloured persons to certain sections, and second, having exchanged the patron's pass for tickets to two actual seats, could the theatre refuse to admit him to those seats?[119]

In responding to his first question Justice Archibald gave a ringing denunciation of racial discrimination. The theatre's seating regulation, he maintained,

is undoubtedly a survival of prejudices created by the system of negro slavery ... Our constitution is and always has been essentially democratic, and it does not admit of distinctions of races or classes. All men are equal before the law and each has equal rights as a member of the community ... I should certainly hold any regulation which deprived negroes as a class of privileges which all other members of the community had a right to demand, was not only unreasonable but entirely incompatible with our free democratic institutions.[120]

On the second and more technical question, Justice Archibald held that a theatre is essentially similar to a hotel, and just as a hotel is obliged to receive every traveller, so a theatre must accept every paying guest. The analogy was supported by the fact that both hotels and theatres require public licences and operate under municipal regulations; they are not therefore strictly private enterprises and are not free to discriminate among their customers. Furthermore, the theatre's advertising constituted an offer to the public to attend performances without distinction. Finally, since the theatre issued Mr Johnson with tickets to seats K1 and K3 for 12 March 1898, refusal to grant those seats constituted a breach of contract.[121] The Academy of Music immediately launched an appeal.

The appeal decision was written by Justice Bossé of the Quebec Court of Queen's Bench.[122] The original award of fifty dollars to Mr Johnson was upheld, but the grounds were more limited than those assigned by Justice Archibald. On the point that as a publicly licensed enterprise the theatre could not discriminate in admitting members of the public to performances, Justice Bossé wrote on behalf of his colleagues that theatres did not bear the same obligations as hotels:

Nous n'adoptons pas ces raisons, non pas l'assimilation, pour la décision de la question, d'un théâtre à une auberge ou un hôtel.

L'hôtelier ou aubergiste est, par nos lois, soumis à des obligations spéciales nécessaires pour la sécurité et la santé des voyageurs.

Un théâtre est placé dans des conditions essentiellement différentes. Il n'y a plus la nécessité, mais simple question d'amusement. C'est une entreprise de commerce dans un but d'intérêt privé.[123]

On the other hand, Mr Johnson did have tickets for specific seats and therefore a contract existed between him and the Academy of Music. By refusing him admission to those seats, the theatre had broken the contract and was liable for the damages.[124] The broader question – "si les noirs ont, en cette province, le même droit d'admission que les blancs" – was irrelevant to the case,[125] the court decided, but in dismissing Justice Archibald's reasoning the appeal decision undermined any general application of the non-discriminatory principle. That principle was sustainable only when an explicit contract existed.

"A few years later," Ida Greaves reports, a similar case occurred in Toronto. An African-Canadian mother "who looked white under the electric light," purchased a ticket for her darker-skinned son at a roller-skating rink. The management refused to admit the son when he presented his ticket, so the mother sued for damages. In Divisional Court "the Judge held that the woman was damaged the price of the ticket," and the company owning the rink had to refund her twenty-five cents. No other damages were sustained "since they had a perfect right to refuse to sell the ticket."[126]

A decision closer in principle to Johnson came in a British Columbia case in 1914, *Barnswell v. National Amusement Company*. Mr Barnswell, a long-time resident of Victoria, purchased a ticket to the Empress Theatre in that city. He entered the lobby but was refused admission at the door of the auditorium because "there was a rule of the house that coloured people should not be admitted." Mr Barnswell called the police, and a constable witnessed the theatre's insistence not to admit a Black patron. When Mr Barnswell continued to protest, the manager asked the policeman to remove him from the premises. Barnswell sued the theatre for damages for breach of contract and for assault.[127]

In County Court the theatre admitted to damages only for the amount paid for the ticket, ten cents, but Justice Peter S. Lampman decided that "the defendant broke its contract, and I have no doubt the plaintiff was humiliated."[128] Damages were fixed at fifty dollars, the same as in *Johnson*, though the Montreal case was not raised in argument.

The Empress Theatre's appeal was heard in Vancouver in April 1915.

Justice A.E. McPhillips declared in favour of the theatre, on the grounds that "it is in the public interest and in the interest of society that there should be law which will admit of the management of places of public entertainment having complete control over those who are permitted to attend all such entertainments."[129] His four colleagues on the appeal bench, however, dismissed the appeal because Mr Barnswell's money had been accepted and he was already on the premises before being ejected. No reference was made in *Barnswell* to the issue of racial discrimination: the damages arose exclusively from breach of an established contract.

The limitations of the "contract" principle were made apparent in another Montreal theatre case in 1919. Loew's Theatre was known for its practice of seating Black people only in the balcony. In 1917 Montreal, Blacks had formed the Coloured Political and Protective Association, intended to promote "racial advancement" through coordinated action, particularly at election times.[130] On 26 January 1919 the association sent Messrs Sol Reynolds and Norris Augustus Dobson and their wives to test Loew's Theatre's seating policy. Mr Reynolds purchased four general admission tickets at the box office and proceeded with his companions to sit in the main orchestra section, where there were many empty seats. When theatre staff insisted that they move to the balcony, Mr Dobson protested loudly. All four African Canadians were then ejected from the theatre. Reynolds and Dobson entered suits for damages on the strength of *Johnson*.[131]

In Mr Reynold's case, Justice Thomas Fortin of the Superior Court awarded the plaintiff ten dollars damages, declaring,

In this country the colored people and the white people are governed by the same laws, and enjoy the same rights without any distinction whatever, and the fact that Sol Reynolds was a colored man offers no justification for Loew's Montreal Theatre Limited, refusing him admission to the orchestra chairs in its theatre after issuing to him a ticket for such seat and after acceptance of the same by its collector.[132]

The theatre argued that an admission ticket did not entitle Mr Reynolds to a reserved seat but only to a seat on *either* the ground floor or mezzanine "as the management might desire and as the comfort and convenience of other patrons might demand." Furthermore there appeared on each ticket a printed condition: "The management reserves the right to refund the amount paid for this ticket and to revoke all privileges originally granted purchaser." But Justice Fortin ruled that the purchaser "had the option of choosing his own seat" and that the printed condition "can only justify such revocation before the contract is executed or in the course of execution. It cannot justify the revocation after the acceptance by the theatre's ticket collector." However, in the companion suit brought by Mr Dobson, Justice Fortin found rather ingenuously that Mr and Mrs Dobson were removed from the theatre not on grounds of colour but because they raised their protest "in such a tone of voice that attracted quite a large number of people and blocked the entrance way." This behaviour, according to the judge, was "unjustified," and overlooking the house rule on segregated seating that he had castigated in *Reynolds* he found the theatre had not violated the Dobsons' contract when it ejected them.[133]

Loew's Theatre appealed the *Reynolds* decision to the Court of King's Bench. In a dissenting judgment Justice Henry-George Carroll held that a contract did exist between Reynolds and Loew's, giving the customer the right to sit where he chose. There was nothing distinctive about his ticket to indicate a limitation on the usual right to any seat in the house. He could be denied a seat only for a reasonable cause, such as drunkenness or disturbing behaviour; colour was not a valid reason for cancelling the contract. Reiterating Justice Archibald's 1899 denunciation of racial discrimination, Justice Carroll insisted, "Tous les citoyens de ce pays, blancs et noirs, sont soumis à la même loi et tenus aux mêmes obligations."[134] American cases brought by Loew's as precedents could not be applied, since American social conditions and consequent legislation authorizing discrimination did not exist in Canada. French legal precedents restricting access of certain classes of people had been obviated by the French Revolution. Reynolds, Carroll concluded, "a été gravement blessé" and must be awarded damages.[135]

The other four members of the appeal court decided in favour of the theatre, reversing Justice Fortin's decision. Reynolds's ticket was not for a specific seat; the theatre's discriminatory regulations were legal; it was Reynolds who rejected the seat offered him in the balcony and insisted on sitting in the orchestra section where he knew he was not allowed. Conditions were therefore quite different from the *Johnson* case, and Reynolds had no claim for damages.[136] Chief Justice Lamothe was most eloquent on behalf of the majority: since no explicit law stated otherwise, managers were authorized to set any rules for their own establishments, however arbitrary or discriminatory, provided they did not contravene good morals and public order.

En achetant un billet, Reynolds savait que ce billet lui donnait droit de prendre un siège aux endroits désignés et non ailleurs. C'est donc délibérément qu'il s'est exposé au refus dont il se plaint dans son action. Il a voulu, malgré la règle, prendre place dans les fauteuils d'orchestre, endroit prohibé.

Aucune loi, dans notre province, n'interdit aux propriétaires de théâtres de faire une règle semblable. Aucun règlement municipal ne porte sur ce sujet. Alors, chaque propriétaire est maître chez lui; il peut, a son gré, établir toutes règles non contraires aux bonnes moeurs et à l'ordre public. Ainsi, un gérant de théâtre pourrait ne recevoir que les personnes revêtues d'un habit de soirée. La règle pourrait paraître arbitraire, mais elle ne serait ni illégal ni prohibée. Il faudrait s'y soumettre, ou ne pas aller à ce théâtre. Tenter de violer cette règle à l'aide d'un billet, serait s'exposer à l'expulsion, ce serait s'y exposer volontairement.[137]

In 1916 the Ministry of Justice had advised African Canadians to seek redress in the courts, in the absence of positive law relating to discrimination. The Court of King's Bench was now declaring that in the absence of positive law, discrimination was legal. It was up to the proprietor to decide, on any basis he chose. As Justice Pelletier elaborated, the theatre could lose white patrons if Blacks were admitted: "Il est prouvé que la présence des noirs dans les sièges d'orchestre empêche d'autres citoyens d'aller au théâtre et l'appelante n'est pas obligée de subir une perte de revenus qui résulte de ce fait."[138] Discrimination justified discrimination.

Another case to test the issue occurred in Ontario, where the distance from a proprietor's "duty to serve" was broadened by another significant step. On 20 July 1923 Mr W.V. Franklin, a watchmaker and diamond specialist from the city of Kitchener, was visiting London, Ontario, and stopped at The Cave restaurant for lunch. When the waitress told him that "they did not serve coloured people," Mr Franklin complained to the police and then returned to speak to the restaurant owner, Alfred Evans. Mr Evans and his wife both repeated, in terms the court would later call "unnecessarily offensive," their absolute refusal to serve a Black person on their premises. With the support of London's African-Canadian community and "some of London's foremost [white] citizens," and a fundraising campaign organized by the Black newspaper *The Dawn of Tomorrow*, Mr Franklin sued the Evanses "for the establishment of what he believes to be a right as a Canadian citizen." "I am not fighting," he insisted, "to soothe my own injured feelings. I am taking this stand for the benefit of all peoples of color, for generations of colored children yet unborn. Again, I want to prove to Mr Evans and to all the world that the majesty of the British law will b[r]ook no prejudice."[139]

In 1899 Justice Archibald had found that a theatre, or any publicly licensed and regulated enterprise, had the same obligation to serve the public as a common innkeeper. The appeal court had narrowed this obligation to those occasions when a contract existed, at least in a theatre that offered amusement rather than an essential of life. In 1919 the definition of contract was made more specific, as was the right of a proprietor to set conditions upon the terms of the service offered. Franklin's case seemed clearly distinct from *Reynolds*: a restaurant does provide an essential and is far more analogous to the innkeeper's situation than is a theatre. Restaurants and inns are subject to similar licences and regulations. Mr Franklin was indisputably a traveller and had been previously unaware of the restaurant's regulations. The Evanses had not simply set conditions but had refused to serve him any refreshment at all.

Justice Haughton Lennox sympathized with Mr Franklin, whom he regarded as "a thoroughly respectable man," and he admitted to being "touched by the pathetic eloquence of his appeal for recognition as a human being, of common origin with ourselves."[140] Asked whether he had any ground for damages, Mr Franklin told the court,

Not in dollars and cents, but in humiliation and inhuman treatment at the hands of this fellow man, yes. Because I am a dark man, a condition over which I have no control, I did not receive the treatment I was entitled to as a fellow human being. God chose to bring me into the world a colored man, and on this account, defendant placed me on a lower level than he is.[141]

Yet Justice Lennox found himself required to decide in favour of the restaurant. There was, he explained, an "obvious dividing line" between a restaurant and an inn or hotel. That line, apparently, was the monopolistic nature of the innkeeper's licence:

[The] restaurant-keeper is not at all in the same position as persons who, in consideration of the grant of a monopoly or quasi-monopoly, take upon themselves definite obligations, such as supplying accommodation of a certain character, within certain limits, and subject to recognized qualifications, to all who apply.[142]

The fact that an enterprise was publicly licensed did not in itself carry any "duty to serve." Municipalities grant licences "partly for the purpose of regulating trade, but mainly for the purpose of producing a revenue ... [N]o limit is placed upon the number of licences issued." Butcher shops and department stores in London were also licensed, Justice Lennox reasoned, yet no one could deny the department store proprietor's right to refuse to sell his goods to any particular customer. The Canadian theatre cases – *Johnson*, *Barnswell*, and *Reynolds* – might have suggested another analogy, but they were not considered by the court. Citing a series of British precedents, the judge concluded that a common innkeeper's duty could not be applied to other commercial enterprises.[143] Franklin's only consolation was that because of "the unnecessarily harsh, humiliating, and offensive attitude of the defendant and his wife toward the plaintiff," the action was dismissed without costs.[144] Had the refusal been expressed more politely, presumably, the costs would have been assigned against Mr Franklin. Racial discrimination per se was legally acceptable.

La question de la liberté

In September 1936 the Christie Defence Committee engaged Lowell C. Carroll, an independent attorney and a scholar with publications in landlord and tenant law.[145] The York Tavern hired Brown, Montgomery, and McMichael, a firm of twenty-two members including twelve KCs, with experience representing Loew's Theatre in its successful appeal against Reynolds.[146] They met before Mr Justice Philippe Demers in the Quebec Superior Court in February 1937. Carroll argued that the tavern had a public licence and should therefore serve the public, and besides, by its general publicity advertising the sale of beer, it had offered an implicit contract that was broken when Christie's order was refused. Fred Christie was asked,

Q. Did you notice a large sign outside bearing the words York Tavern?
A. Yes.
Q. Was there anybody at the door to refuse your entrance?
A. No ...

Mr Carroll pursued the same line when examining assistant manager Roméo Lajoie:

Q. Did you put any notice up that negroes were not to be sold beer?
A. No.
Q. Did you ever put a notice in the papers?
A. No.
Q. Did you ever advertise that in the newspapers generally or in the publicity for the tavern?
A. No.
Q. When the tavern was opened, was there any publicity in the newspapers?
A. Yes.
By the Court: Publicity to the effect that negroes were not admitted?
By Plaintiff's Counsel: No.
Q. That publicity, did it say negroes were not to be allowed to get beer?
A. No.
Q. It was unconditional.
By the Court: Do you hold a license by the Government to sell beer?
A. Yes.

Carroll argued further that Fred Christie and Emile King had been insulted and humiliated by the tavern's refusal to serve them, and asked for two hundred dollars each in damages. Defendant's counsel Hazen Hansard picked at this contention in his cross-examination of Christie:

Q. [Y]ou complain of being exposed to ridicule and contempt, humiliation, pain and suffering, injury to reputation, damage to honour and sensibility and deprival of the pleasure of consuming beer with your friends at the time mentioned, and you say that is a value to you of at least a sum of two hundred dollars. Are you in a position to divide the two hundred dollars into those various allegations, or can we take it the real thing you are complaining about is the refusal to serve you with beer, and you want to find out what your rights are?
A. It is a very funny question.
Q. There is no catch in it, Mr Christie ...
By Plaintiff's Counsel: All Mr Hansard wants to know is, are those real damages or not?
A. Yes.

In response Hansard maintained that no humiliation had occurred because the tavern staff had behaved quietly and politely. He asked the waiter, René St Jean,

Q. You heard the evidence given by Mr Christie and Mr King of your refusal
   to serve them was on the grounds that they were colored people, is that
   correct?
A. Yes.
Q. Did any of the people there hear you say that?
A. No …
By the Court: Didn't you think it was humiliating?
A. Well, if it is humiliating to them, then it is humiliating.
By the Court: You did it as quietly as possible?
A. Yes.
By the Court: You had your orders, and gave them politely?
A. Yes.

Hansard insisted that as "a private enterprise operated for gain" the
tavern had the right to make any rules it deemed necessary to protect
its business interests. Since it was not a restaurant or an inn, it was
under no obligation to serve any member of the public. He asked Mr
Lajoie whether the tavern served any meals.

A. Just sandwiches.
Q. Are those sandwiches hot?
A. They are not made at the tavern, they are made at a restaurant, and we call
   for them when needed.

Finally, Hazen Hansard sought to prove that the discrimination practised by the York Tavern was commonplace among similar establishments. Since waiter René St Jean had worked "in taverns and similar
places" since 1907, with experience at the Russell House in Ottawa, the
Senate restaurant, and the Chateau Laurier, and at the CPR's Royal Alexandra Hotel in Winnipeg, Hansard claimed that he could properly be
considered "an expert in tavern practice." St Jean was asked,

Q. Are you able to say from your experience whether or not there is a preju-
   dice amongst white people to be thrown amongst colored people?
A. In the places where I have worked, they did not care to receive colored
   people.
By the Court: They did not care?
A. No, they had a special place for them.
By the Court: Was it a bar?

A. Yes.

By the Court: Did you not admit them at the bar in any of those places?

A. No, Sir, we never saw one or served one either.

By Defendant's Counsel: Did you have any rule about admitting them?

A. If I remember rightly, at the Chateau Laurier we were told not to serve colored people. They had a special place for them, where the porters would go over to them and go right to that service bar.

By Plaintiff's Counsel: Was that rule well known to the porters?

A. Yes, because they all went there ...

By the Court: Did you refuse them at the Chateau Laurier?

A. I never had a chance to refuse them because they never came in there.

By Defendant's Counsel: Would the serving of negroes, in any numbers, in the York Tavern, have any effect on the business of the tavern, are you able to say? ...

By the Court: He never served them and cannot say what effect it would have ...

By Defendant's Counsel: Do you know whether or not there are taverns down on St Antoine St, what might be said to be the negro quarter?

A. Yes, there is a tavern and a restaurant licensed there.

Q. And negroes may be served down there?

A. Yes, that is what I was told.

By the Court: That is not the question. It is a question of rights, that is if you have the right to refuse a man on account of his color. It is a question of law, not of evidence.

By Defendant's Counsel: The circumstances vary for different places.

By the Court: No, no circumstances, it is a question of law whether you have the right or not.

By Defendant's Counsel: I have another witness.

By the Court: I do not require to hear him.

By Defendant's Counsel: Your Lordship rules I cannot examine any more witnesses.

By the Court: It is not necessary.[147]

Philippe Demers's frequent interventions indicated that he was not impressed by the waiter's testimony, nor was he convinced by the legal precedents brought by the tavern, including *Loew's v. Reynolds* and *Franklin v. Evans*. Unfortunately for the tavern, Justice Demers stated, the previous cases occurred in circumstances where there was no law restraining the proprietor's liberty, but the Quebec *Licence Act* had a specific provision protecting the customer. According to Section 33 of that Act, "No licensee for a restaurant may refuse, without reasonable cause, to give food to travellers." Section 19 defined a "restaurant" as "an establishment, provided with special space and accommodation, where, in consideration of payment, food (without lodging) is habitually furnished to travellers"; and a "traveller" was "a person who, in consideration of a given price ... is furnished by another person with food or lodging or both."[148] In the view of Justice Demers, beer is nourishment and should fall within the definition of food. "Quand je prends une verre de lait, une tasse de café, une verre de bière, je mange tout autant que lorsque je mâche du pain." Furthermore, sandwiches were available for purchase in the tavern. On both counts, then, the York Tavern must be considered a "restaurant." As persons seeking "food," Christie and King were definable as "travellers" under the *Licence Act*. This meant that the tavern's regulation was illegal, and the humiliation caused by the refusal of service must be compensated. Since Emile King had not actually placed an order or offered money, only Fred Christie was awarded damages: twenty-five dollars plus costs.[149]

The *Montreal Gazette* announced on its front page, "Court Bars Color Line": "Hotels and restaurants in the Province of Quebec have no right to discriminate between their guests and must serve anyone who pays ... The case established jurisprudence in the province."[150] But the *Gazette*'s excitement was premature, for the York Tavern appealed the Demers decision to the Court of King's Bench.

In presenting Christie's case this second time, Lowell C. Carroll reiterated his contention that when the patron accepted the tavern's offer to sell beer, a contract was completed and could be broken only for reasonable cause. He added that a tavern, like a restaurant or inn, was obliged to serve the public, and that discrimination was contrary to the Criminal Code. Four of the five King's Bench judges disagreed.[151] In the first place, the majority concluded, there was no contract. Justice Bond found that because Christie was immediately and politely informed that he could not be served, there was "no contract ever completed – no bargain struck."[152] Justice Barclay decided that the tavern's general advertisement announcing the sale of beer "does not constitute an offer to sell but is merely an invitation to buy."[153] There was therefore "no foundation for an action *ex contractu*."[154]

Turning more specifically to Justice Demers's Superior Court decision, the majority decided that a tavern was not governed by the same law as a restaurant. The Quebec statutes themselves made a distinction: in the *Alcoholic Liquor Act*,[155] under which taverns were licensed, "tavern," "restaurant," and "hotel" were all defined differently; the requirement in the *Licence Act* that restaurants and hotels must serve all travellers was significantly silent on taverns.[156] In any case, according to Justice St Germain, no evidence had ever been offered to suggest that Christie was a genuine traveller and thereby entitled to service.[157] Just because food was available in the York Tavern did not in itself make it a restaurant; sandwiches were sent from a neighbouring establishment when a York customer placed an order, and even if beer had nutritive value Christie sought it only as a beverage.[158]

British and French cases were cited to indicate that no obligation required taverns to serve the public without discrimination. In British courts an "inn" had been defined concisely, excluding taverns from the duty to serve.[159] *Franklin v. Evans* was added to illustrate that British common law did not impose the innkeeper's responsibility on restaurants either.[160] In France the principle was that a proprietor's choice was limited only if public order required it or if the business enjoyed a monopoly or privilege, and neither of these conditions could be applied to the situation before the court.[161] Article 13 of the Quebec *Civil Code* invalidated any action that might contravene "the laws of public order and good morals," but the terms were left undefined.[162] In the opinion of the King's Bench majority, the York Tavern's action did not fall into this category. Nor did the Court find that licensing restrictions constituted any infringement on the status of a tavern as a private enterprise: licences had as their object the raising of revenue; they did not create a condition of monopoly or privilege.[163] The public interest was not involved. "The fact that a tavern-keeper decides in his own business interests that it would harm his establishment if he catered to people of colour cannot be said to be an action which is against good morals or public order."[164]

For these various reasons, the Court concluded, there were no restraints on the right of the York Tavern to choose its own customers. Since there was no fault, there could be no liability for damages.[165] The fundamental issue in this case was "la question de la liberté": the freedom of a proprietor, in the absence of positive law, "d'entrer ou de ne pas entrer en relations d'affaires avec les personnes qu'il lui plaît."[166] The Court was "not called upon to express any opinion upon the abstract philosophical concept that all men are born equal," Justice Bond insisted, quoting Sir William Scott that "to vindicate the policy of the law is no necessary part of the office of a Judge."[167] "The function of this Court or of any court is to interpret the law as it is passed by the

Legislature – not to change it or alter it or add to it," Justice Barclay added. "When a situation arises which is of public concern, then it is the Legislature and not the courts which should be called upon to remedy the situation."[168]

One judge saw the issue differently. In a thoroughly dissenting opinion, Justice Antonin Galipeault shifted the question of liberty from the proprietor to the patron. Christie was a British subject, a respectable citizen and personally well behaved; he had a right to purchase a glass of beer in a public establishment such as a tavern.[169] Point by point Justice Galipeault found that the precedents argued in favour of Fred Christie. Contradicting his colleagues, he maintained that a contract did exist. In *Sparrow v. Johnson*, when the Court of King's Bench defined the sale of a theatre ticket as a contract, the judgment had been supported in part by the fact that "no notice of the existence or public announcement" of any racially restrictive policy had ever been made.[170] In *Loew's v. Reynolds*, the judgment had stressed that Reynolds did know of the theatre's restrictions before attempting to occupy a certain seat, and this exempted the theatre from the *Sparrow v. Johnson* precedent.[171] The *Loew's* decision, Justice Galipeault emphasized, had permitted the theatre only to seat Black people in a designated section, not to exclude them entirely.[172] Much less so could a tavern exclude them. The numerous regulations imposed on a tavern made it effectively a monopoly or quasi-monopoly; licences were not for the unique purpose of revenue, but to control the numbers, locations, and operating conditions of liquor outlets.[173] The *Alcoholic Liquor Act* repeatedly used the word "privilege" with reference to the sale of alcohol by licence, thus explicitly defining a tavern as a privileged enterprise.[174] The difference between a tavern and a hotel or restaurant was of degree; all three shared the fundamental purpose and nature and should all be subjected to the same responsibility to serve the public.[175] According to the wording in the *Licencing Act*, Christie qualified as a "traveller" and could legitimately expect to be served.[176] Justice Galipeault even agreed with Justice Demers that beer is a food.[177] If a hotel could not refuse lodging to a Black man, and a restaurant could not refuse food, by what logic could a tavern refuse a glass of beer? "Est-il besoin d'un texte pour le tavernier? Était-il besoin d'un texte pour l'hôtelier et le restaurateur? J'estime que non."[178] As for the tavern's claim that it would lose business if Black customers were served, Justice Galipeault found that "un peu enfantin ou ridicule." A tavern is, after all, only a tavern, not a congregation or a club; clients come and go and are not required to socialize with one another.[179] *Franklin v. Evans* had no relevance to Quebec, for it dealt with a restaurant, and in Quebec a restaurant was required by legislation to be non-discriminatory. Had Justice Lennox heard that same case in Quebec he would certainly have decided that hotels, restaurants, and taverns exercised a quasi-monopoly, rendered a public service, and were obliged not to discriminate.[180] It was necessary to push the proposition to the extreme: if a publicly licensed establishment could exclude African Canadians, why not Jews or Chinese or any other "race"? Why not members of certain religions, or persons who spoke certain languages? To support the York Tavern in its discriminatory policy would be tantamount to deciding "contre les bonnes moeurs, contre l'ordre public, contre le droit et la loi."[181]

Justice Galipeault's detailed arguments notwithstanding, the question of liberty was resolved in favour of the proprietor. The principle was reaffirmed that "in the absence of any specific law, a merchant or trader is free to carry on his business in the manner that he conceived to be best for that business."[182]

In the Supreme Court of Canada

The King's Bench decision was announced on 31 May 1938, and the Christie Defence Committee immediately launched a campaign to raise the thousand-dollar bond needed to carry an appeal to the Supreme Court of Canada. Committee chair Kenneth Melville wrote to the Montreal Black community:

The recent decision rendered against Mr Fred Christie of Montreal, in the case of the York Corporation versus Christie, makes it highly imperative that citizens of the Negro race unite solidly to protect themselves against this glaring support of the principle of racial discrimination in public places in Montreal.

To allow this case to be closed without any attempt to appeal this decision to the Supreme Court of Canada, would only tend to encourage further and more open discrimination against members of the Negro race, to encourage the disregard of public order, and indeed, to foster inter-racial discord.

The Appeal Requires Money. Accordingly, a committee of Negro citizens working at their request in conjunction with Mr Christie, have decided to make an appeal to raise sufficient funds by voluntary contributions for this purpose. This committee feels firmly convinced that the Supreme Court of Canada will not uphold this malicious principle of racial discrimination, which is certainly contrary to British principles and traditions.[183]

The response was gratifying. "In the most enthusiastic demonstration of racial solidarity," the *Free Lance* reported, "local public opinion continues to crystallize in united support of the Christie Defence Committee."[184] By September, the impoverished community had scraped together the required bond money, only to learn that the Quebec Court of King's Bench dismissed Mr Carroll's motion for leave to appeal to the Supreme Court. Carroll thereupon enlisted Section 41 of the *Supreme Court Act*,[185] which permitted direct appeal if the matter in controversy was deemed to be of sufficient general importance and if the future rights of the contesting parties might be affected. Leave to appeal was granted on 7 February 1939.[186]

Attorney Carroll prepared the Appellant's Factum around one central issue: racial discrimination was contrary to public order and good morals. Though the *Code* itself left these terms undefined, Carroll insisted that the tavern's policy was a clear violation of the rule and must not be sanctioned by a court of law.

Quebec law is against any discrimination against a citizen on the ground of religion, language, or colour. Bilingualism exists by law in Canada. All religions are free to practise their faiths, without control. All citizens are subject to taxation, without discrimination as to colour. The common law of Quebec is the free enjoyment by all its citizens of the facilities for education, nourishment, and happiness which are available. It cannot be assumed from the fact that the legislature has, in the case of hotels and restaurants, taken care in dealing with their licences, to lay down a statutory obligation to receive, that this was expressly omitted in the case of a tavern. It was omitted because it was not thought necessary, in view of the monopolistic nature of a Quebec tavern, and its privileges under the law, that there would be any question of refusing its facilities to any citizen.

The York Tavern had put out advertisements in the press and in the streets inviting the general public. Nowhere was it stated or implied that Black patrons were not welcome. Mr Christie had frequently visited the tavern before, in its original location. Suddenly and without notice the policy had changed, excluding certain customers on grounds of colour alone.

If this ridiculous exclusion is sanctioned by law, it could be extended without limitation ... until this country bristled with racial, religious, and colour discriminations, like certain European countries. A right to do so, particularly in the case of a Governmentally controlled monopoly, like a Quebec tavern, would certainly be against public order and good morals. Even in the Southern United States the right to discriminate must be granted by statute.

The tavern's refusal to serve Christie "was a direct insult and slander, implying inferiority." For the suffering caused by this humiliation he deserved to be awarded damages. Although a group could not sue a slanderer for a racial insult, an individual could do so if the insult was directly applied to him. Mr Christie's "gentlemanliness and conduct ha[d] not been impeached"; he was deemed "undesirable" only because of colour. According to *Loew's v. Reynolds* and other precedents, management could exclude the unruly and could make certain rules concerning dress requirements and seating arrangements,

But it could not make rules against public order and good morals, and it is respectfully urged that the respondent's rule, refusing negroes, even if it had been made public, which had not been done, was against public order and good morals, particularly in Canada and Quebec, part of an Empire teeming with various races, religions and colours.[187]

The respondent's factum was prepared by Montgomery, McMichael, Common, and Howard, and argued before the Court by Hazen Hansard. There was no dispute over the facts; the tavern's case was that its action was permissible and reasonable, that

the refusal in question was made for purely business reasons on account of the prejudice generally held by white persons to drinking in company with negroes, and that refusal to serve negroes was common in the better class of establishments such as that operated by the Respondent.

The underlying principle was not racial discrimination but the freedom of a private business to choose its customers. "It is essentially a question of contract, and the merchant or trader, in the absence of special statutory provisions, is not under any duty to enter into a contractual relationship with anyone." In the case of Mr Christie, no contract ever existed. "The Respondent refused to enter into a contract for the sale of the beer with the Appellant and, upon being pressed for a reason, gave as its reason the rule it had against serving negroes. The Appellant therefore was told the rule, and knew of it at all material times." The Respondent was not an innkeeper, obliged to supply the wants of travellers, but a merchant "free to deal or not as he may choose." The

Alcoholic Liquor Act specified, "Any person in charge of a tavern ... *may* sell therein beer by the glass"; the language was not compulsory but "purely permissive." The refusal was made "in the exercise of a right – *damnum absque injuria*." The York did not enjoy a monopoly on the sale of beer, for there were taverns on St Antoine Street where Christie could have been served. Numerous functions and enterprises required licences – the operation of a motor car, for example – and they did not thereby become monopolies. Throughout the incident, tavern employees had behaved politely, quietly, and inoffensively. No embarrassment or humiliation had occurred until the Appellant brought it upon himself by calling the police. "On the evidence of record therefore and apart from any question of right, the Appellant suffered no damages at the hands of the Respondent."[188]

The Supreme Court of Canada considered these arguments on 10 May 1939. It was a strong Court, chaired by Chief Justice Sir Lyman Duff, who has been regarded as "the most influential member in the history of the Supreme Court of Canada"[189] and who was the only person on the bench to have heard the Quong Wing case twenty-five years previously. Also present were Justices Thibaudeau Rinfret and Patrick Kerwin, both of whom would later become chief justice (1944–4 and 1954–63, respectively), Oswald Crocket, and Henry Davis. Their judgment was published on 9 December 1939.[190]

Justice Rinfret, appropriately a native of Montreal, delivered the decision for the majority. He accepted the evidence that York employees had behaved

quietly, politely, and without causing any scene or commotion whatever. If any notice was attracted to the appellant on the occasion in question, it arose out of the fact that the appellant persisted in demanding beer after he had been so refused and went to the length of calling the police, which was entirely unwarranted by the circumstances.[191]

"In considering this case," Justice Rinfret continued,

we ought to start from the proposition that the general principle of the law of Quebec is that of complete freedom of commerce. Any merchant is free to deal as he may choose with any individual member of the public. It is not a question of motives or reasons for deciding to deal or not to deal; he is free to do either. The only restriction to this general principle would be the existence of a specific law, or, in the carrying out of the principle, the adoption of a rule contrary to good morals or public order.[192]

The French principle of "la liberté du commerce" articulated this right explicitly, except in cases of privilege or monopoly, and it had been followed in *Loew's v. Reynolds* "where the facts presented a great deal of similarity with those of the present case." Another case "practically identical with the present one" was *Franklin v. Evans*, where Justice Lennox found that the English cases led to the same conclusion.[193] Reviewing the Demers decision, Justice Rinfret felt that it could be supported only if the Quebec *Licence Act* explicitly made it illegal for a tavern to refuse service without reasonable cause. No conditions existed justifying an exception on principle to "la liberté du commerce," for clearly "it cannot be argued that the rule adopted by the respondent in the conduct of his establishment was contrary to good morals or public order." Having thus summarily annihilated the theme of Carroll's factum, Justice Rinfret added, "Nor could it be said, as the law stood, that the sale of beer in the province of Quebec was either a monopoly or a privileged enterprise."[194] A licence does allow certain government controls, but its main purpose is to raise revenue and it does not prevent the operation of a tavern as a private enterprise. "The only point to be examined," therefore, was whether the *Licence Act* could be applied. Such an examination led to the conclusion that "the appellant was not a traveller asking for food in a restaurant within the meaning of the statute ... According to the definitions, he was only a person asking for a glass of beer in a tavern."[195] The legislature had obliged restaurants and hotels to serve the public, but "no similar provision is made for taverns." The decision, in which Duff, Crockett, and Kerwin concurred, was that "[a]s the case is not governed by any specific law ... it falls under the general principle of freedom of commerce; and it must follow that, when refusing to serve the appellant, the respondent was strictly within its rights."[196] Christie's appeal was dismissed with costs, by a count of four to one.[197]

The single dissenting voice belonged to Justice Henry Davis. He agreed that the Quebec *Licence Act* could not be applied to a tavern. He agreed as well that the primary question needing resolution was, "Has a tavern keeper in the province of Quebec under the special legislation there in force the right to refuse to sell beer to any one of the public?"[198] Thereafter Justice Davis's reasoning diverged from his colleagues. Since its first passage in 1921, the *Alcoholic Liquor Act*[199] had established state control over alcoholic beverages, including beer. The sale of beer by the glass with consumption on the premises was strictly limited to specially adapted and licensed establishments defined as taverns. The furniture and equipment required to qualify for a tavern licence were regulated, and the sale of beer was explicitly referred to as a "privilege" conferred by that licence. The hours and days when beer sales were permitted were set out in the Act. Most significantly, the Act listed specified classes who were not to be served alcoholic drinks, including those under the age of eighteen years, convicted drunks, and persons individually prohibited by a decision of the Quebec Liquor Commission.[200] By a separate statute (the *Alcoholic Liquor Possession and Transportation Act*),[201] even the possession and transportation of alcohol, including beer, was placed under state control. The York Tavern had been granted a licence and was privileged, within this strict environment of control and regulation, to sell beer by the glass for consumption on the premises. But did this "special privilege" include "the right to pick and choose those of the public to whom he would sell?" The statute governing the licence already defined the persons to whom the licensee could not sell. Could the licensee impose a separate code of eligibility?[202]

Justice Davis re-examined the precedents to determine whether "freedom of commerce" was as encompassing as the King's Bench decision allowed. In *Loew's v. Reynolds*, for example, Justice Martin had said for the majority that "while it may be unlawful to exclude persons of colour from the equal enjoyment of all rights and privileges in all places of public amusement, the management has the right to assign particular seats to different races and classes of men and women as it sees fit." In *Franklin v. Evans*, Justice Lennox had concluded that English cases did not require a restaurant to serve without discrimination. One of the cases supporting this conclusion was *Sealey v. Tandy*,[203] in which a licensee (not a common innkeeper) was permitted to exclude a customer whom he did not wish to serve. But, Justice Davis pointed out, in the newest edition of Halsbury this case carried a footnote to the effect that "a victualler will be compelled to sell his victual if the purchaser has tendered him ready payment, otherwise not." A victualler, according to the dictionary, was "one who sells food or drink to be consumed on the premises."[204]

Justice Davis admitted, "The question is one of difficulty, as the divergence of judicial opinion in the courts below indicates," but considering the legislation establishing complete state control over alcohol, he concluded that taverns were not free to pick and choose their customers.

In the changed and changing social and economic conditions, different principles must necessarily be applied to the new conditions. It is not a question of creating a new principle but of applying a different but existing principle of the law. The doctrine that any merchant is free to deal with the public as he chooses had a very definite place in the older economy and still applies to the case of an ordinary merchant, but when the state enters the field and takes exclusive control of the sale to the public of such a commodity as liquor, the old doctrine of the freedom of the merchant to do as he likes has in my view no application to a person to whom the state has given a special privilege to sell to the public.

Since the Act already specified the grounds for exclusion, it was up to the legislature itself, not the licence holder, to enact any additional ground such as colour, "race," or religion.[205]

Professor Melville's prediction was not fulfilled; the Supreme Court had upheld the "malicious principle of racial discrimination" and the Christie Defence Committee had to pay the York Tavern's legal costs.[206] Fred Christie was personally humiliated and disillusioned by this betrayal of what he had regarded as "British justice." A few months after the Supreme Court decision was announced, Mr Christie moved to the United States and took up residence in Vermont.[207] The case attracted very little public attention, despite its implications,[208] but lawyers reading the *Dominion Law Reports* were given an editorial note identifying the significance of the *Christie* judgment:

This would appear to be the first authoritative decision on a highly contentious question and is the law's confirmation of the socially enforced inferiority of the coloured races. The principle upon which the judgment is based, though derived from *Code* sources, will be found equally applicable to the common law. The authorities are considered in *Franklin v. Evans*.[209]

Legal scholars have generally lamented the *Christie* decision, perceiving the same consequences as the editor of the *Dominion Law Reports*. Some commentators have expressly found that the judgment was wrong; others have merely regarded it as unnecessary. Closest to the event, and most critical, was Bora Laskin. Commenting in 1940, Professor Laskin wrote,

As between the majority's support of the doctrine of freedom of commerce and Davis J's enunciation of a principle based on legislative assumption of control of an industry the latter ought to be preferred, especially on grounds of policy and where, as in this case, in the absence of a constitutional guarantee of equality of treatment, the result would be the rejection by the courts of tendencies toward discrimination. The principle of freedom of commerce enforced by the

Court majority is itself merely the reading of social and economic doctrine into law, and doctrine no longer possessing its nineteenth century validity. With governmental intervention in the control of certain industries and services in the public interest, the courts may properly conclude that in the absence of legislative pronouncement there is to be no discrimination by government licensees against customers ... Where the government has established legislative control of products or services it seems more desirable to interpret the legislation as not permitting discrimination unless expressly providing therefore rather than as allowing licensees to discriminate unless expressly forbidden.[210]

Douglas Schmeiser has argued that the innkeeper principle could have been extended to cover this situation, had the Court chosen to do so,[211] and Henry Molot has challenged "the wisdom and validity" of the *Christie* judgment:

That a business can simply arrogate to itself and to its premises the immunity which reputedly shelters the private individual in his home ... is belied by the recognition already given by common law and statute to the businessman's more vulnerable position vis-à-vis potential patrons: they are invitees, not trespassers.[212]

Walter Tarnopolsky, like Laskin, has found the dissenting opinion of Justice Davis to be most compelling.[213] For Ian Hunter, too, the decision could have been different. "The judiciary had not lacked opportunities to advance equality, but had preferred to advance commerce; judgments had adumbrated a code of mercantile privilege rather than a code of human rights."[214]

Frank Scott regretted the majority judgment without implying that it was an error:

The freedom of commerce, it was said, enabled the tavern-keeper to choose his customers as he liked. The freedom of Christie from racial insult was not found to be protected by the law ... [O]ne kind of freedom conflicts with another ... The great principle of equality before the law must prevail at some point over the other value of freedom of commerce ... [T]he law as laid down in the Christie case should be changed.[215]

In a separate comment, Professor Scott added, "In choosing the particular result in this case, the majority of the judges exercised a discretion that could as well have gone the other way."[216] The literature lacks absolutely any applause for Sir Lyman Duff and his Court in *Christie v. York*.

It would seem that, as in the case of *Quong Wing*, a different decision was at least possible in 1939. Two precedents were chiefly considered: *Loew's v. Reynolds* and *Franklin v. Evans*. *Loew's v. Reynolds*, however, contained two principal restrictions that limited its application as a precedent for Christie. One, as noted by Justice Davis, was Justice Martin's caution that total exclusion "may be unlawful." For him, it was only the assignment of *particular seats* that was clearly within the right of the proprietor.[217] Justice Pelletier seemed to accept the same narrower definition when he wrote, "Un propriétaire de théâtre a le droit de placer les spectateurs où il veut *dans des endroits*."[218] The second apparent restriction was the emphasis placed by the majority in the 1919 decision upon the fact that Sol Reynolds was aware of the theatre's discriminatory policy before he purchased his tickets. Chief Justice Lamothe began his statement by writing "En achetant un billet, Reynolds *savait*,' and he concluded with *"Dans les circonstances* révélées par la preuve, Reynolds ne peut réclamer des dommages-intérêts."[219] Justice Pelletier distinguished *Sparrow v. Johnson* from *Loew's v. Reynolds* primarily because Johnson had been unaware of the theatre's regulations, whereas "Dans la présente cause, non seulement le demandeur connaissait ce règlement, mais il s'est rendu pour le défier et faire ce qu'il appelle un test case ... *Il résulte de tout cela* que le précédent de *Sparrow v. Johnson* n'est pas applicable."[220] Justice Martin's opinion was equally influenced by the fact that Reynolds "purchased his ticket with the knowledge of the existence of the rule of the theatre that he would not be seated where he asked to be seated, viz., in an orchestra seat, and this en vertu d'un règlement porte à sa connaissance. He could not successfully urge or contend that there was violation of any contractual right and he is not entitled to any damages."[221] The judgment summary in *Rapports Judiciaires de Québec* specifies both these qualifications: "A theatre may impose restrictions and make rules as to *the place which each person should occupy*," and "when a colored man, bearer of a ticket of general admission, wants to take a seat in a part of the house *which he knows* is by a rule of the manager prohibited to colored persons, he cannot complain if he is refused."[222] The York Tavern was refusing service to Fred Christie, not simply assigning him a certain seat. Fred Christie was totally unaware of the York's rule and had been served by the same management before the tavern moved into its Forum location. The cases could have been distinguished.

Nor is *Franklin v. Evans* entirely convincing. Justice Davis drew attention to the footnote that changed the application of *Sealey v. Tandy*, i.e., that a "victualler" must not discriminate against a customer who "tendered him ready payment." Since Justice Lennox found *Sealey* "decidedly pertinent" in dismissing Franklin's claim, that footnote could have affected his decision, and modified his statement that he could "find no authority directly in support" of Franklin.[223] In rendering the majority judgment at the Supreme Court, Justice Rinfret did not himself review the common law cases, but relied on Justice Lennox. This meant that *Barnswell*, for example, continued to be ignored, though it was a case where the plaintiff's admission to the premises before being refused further service was a decisive point. Most of the reasoning in *Franklin v. Evans* builds upon the distinction – "the obvious dividing line"[224] – between an inn and a restaurant. In developing this distinction, Justice Lennox lent great significance to the fact that a restaurant was not a "monopoly or quasi-monopoly."[225] For this to be a "distinction," it must be assumed that an innkeeper did somehow enjoy a monopoly or quasi-monopoly, and this is what imposed the unique obligation to serve the public without discrimination. Yet nowhere did Justice Lennox or any of the cases he quoted specify that an innkeeper's licence gave monopolistic privileges. All the evidence Justice Lennox offered against regarding a municipally licensed restaurant as a monopoly could equally demonstrate that a municipally licensed inn was not a monopoly either. The innkeeper's "duty to serve" had much more complex origins than Justice Lennox implied, and since this duty had been amenable to application by analogy to common carriers and public wharves, there seems to be no "obvious dividing line" preventing its application to restaurants. At least there were some weaknesses in *Franklin v. Evans* that could have been exploited, had the Supreme Court chosen to do so.

But of course the Supreme Court did not choose to do so. In considering the different principles involved, there was a direct confrontation between two sets of rights as then understood. It is only in retrospect that the rights of Fred Christie take obvious precedence. The right of association, for example, contains the right not to associate; the right of a customer to buy or not to buy was matched, with certain specified exceptions, by a proprietor's right to sell or not to sell. The fact that an alternative decision was possible in 1939, as every subsequent authority has maintained, illustrates how context operates upon the judicial process. Although invited to do so by Lowell C. Carroll, the Court did not find racial discrimination to be contrary to good morals or public order. The very notion was summarily dismissed in a single sentence by Justice Rinfret.[226] Henry Davis, like John Idington in 1914, perceived a change in the context within which the law would be interpreted and applied. Increasing state intervention in public affairs would shift the balance of rights between proprietor and public, but on the eve of the Second World War that was not yet generally apparent.

Aftermath

Undoubtedly the Supreme Court opinion that racial discrimination was not immoral or damaging accurately reflected prevailing views on morality and public order. No one ever challenged the York Tavern's contention that white patrons preferred not to associate with Blacks, and evidence at the trial indicated that this kind of prejudice was generally acceptable.[227] Prime Minister Mackenzie King noted his personal distress, about the same time as the *Christie* decision appeared, that Germans and English were killing each other. "It is appalling to think that in this way, the white stocks are making it possible for yellow men and the brown to inhabit the globe."[228] The prime minister notwithstanding, it was the war itself that initiated a process of change.

That change was by no means immediate: the public order assessed by the Court retained its acceptability well beyond the outbreak of hostilities in Europe. Employment discrimination, for example, was enforced by the National Selective Service, the government agency created to direct workers into appropriate employment for the effective prosecution of the war effort. The NSS used a registration form asking an employer's "requirements as to age, skill and race," and it honoured any employer's preference to exclude African Canadians. In fact NSS officers were not merely responsive to the stated prejudices of others: Black applicants were simply assigned to stereotypical positions as domestic servants and unskilled workers. In many parts of the country Black people were not even considered for employment in war munitions factories.[229] Under pressure from Black groups in Toronto, Montreal, and Windsor, the federal agency finally agreed in November 1942 to withdraw the offending questionnaire and to end any racial distinctions in its own job assignments. In its statement dated 14 November the NSS admitted that "discrimination impairs the war effort by preventing the most effective use of our total labour supply and tends ... to defeat the democratic objectives for which we are fighting."[230]

The anomaly was not recognized by the NSS until the war was already three years old. Even more astonishing, for later generations, was the reluctance of the armed services themselves to accept African-Canadian recruits. Regulations of the Royal Canadian Air Force stated, "The following classes of men will not be eligible for enlistment ... (c) Men who are not both of pure European descent and the sons of natural born or naturalized subjects."[231] In 1943 the "pure European descent" rule was dropped;[232] in certain instances prior to that, some Black volunteers were accepted for ground duties but could not be appointed to commissioned rank or to air crew.[233] The navy's similar rule, that a recruit must be "of the white race," was not changed officially until June 1944, after the D-Day landing.[234] Meanwhile public advertisements urging enlistment in the air force and navy, like those of the York Tavern, made no reference to racial qualifications.[235]

As had happened in the First World War, Black Canadians volunteering to serve their country were told that they were not welcome. The army's official policy, once again, was that individual commanding officers must be free to accept or reject volunteers for any reason. The minister of national defence wrote to a leader of the Halifax Black veterans, "I am sure that you will understand why we do not feel that we should interfere with this prerogative and I am sure you will equally recognize that racial questions have had no part in the establishment of it."[236] In a remarkable echo of the previous war, persistent attempts by Black volunteers to enlist prompted a survey of unit commanders in Nova Scotia. Of fourteen officers queried, all responded that Black soldiers would be unacceptable: "would prejudice recruiting," "objection on part of white troops to coloured," "unit would disintegrate" were among the reasons offered.[237] Serious consideration was given to the establishment of a segregated labour battalion, but Ottawa headquarters rejected the idea.[238] In May 1941, in the midst of an urgent recruiting campaign that attracted numbers of prospective Black volunteers, the Halifax district commander sought Ottawa's advice on "the question of the enlistment of Negroes." Recruitment regulations, he pointed out, suggested that any Canadian citizen who was "physically fit and in possession of the necessary educational qualifications" could join the army. He added reassuringly that "the local Negroes are of a low standard of education, which suggests the number of enlistments would not be large."[239] On 5 June 1941 Nova Scotia recruiters were advised that "provided they are physically fit and not illiterate," Black personnel were eligible for enlistment.[240]

If the rejection and segregation of African Canadians was acceptable in a time of national crisis, as the experience in the early years of the war would attest, the Supreme Court's 1939 refusal to enforce integration in a simple tavern can be recognized as consistent with Canadian morality at that time. Even after the dramatic changes brought about by the war – including not only a new sensitivity to the ideology of racism but the increasing involvement of the state in public affairs, with the consequences foreseen by Justice Davis – racial equality was far from won. The experience of Johnson, Barnswell, Reynolds, Franklin, and Christie continued to be true: Black people themselves had to seize the initiative and claim their rights; sometimes they would be successful, and sometimes they would not.

Striking testimony to the vigour and legality of "Jim Crow" in post-war Canada, and to African Canadians' continuing determination to achieve equal rights, was provided by the case of Viola Desmond. Mrs Desmond was a Halifax beautician who made tours to the smaller Black communities in Nova Scotia to promote her line of beauty products and sometimes to do the hair of African-Canadian women. Her service was necessary because many white-operated beauty salons refused to accept Black customers.[241] On one such trip to New Glasgow in November 1946, Mrs Desmond attended a performance at the Roseland Cinema. She asked the ticket-seller for "one down, please" and proceeded to sit in the downstairs section of the theatre. The person collecting the tickets, however, informed her "this is an upstairs ticket, you will have to go upstairs." Coming from Halifax, Mrs Desmond was not familiar with local practice that African Canadians such as herself were required to sit in the balcony. She attempted to exchange her ticket, but was told, "I'm not permitted to sell downstairs tickets to you people." Aware now of the situation, Viola Desmond quietly but determinedly occupied a seat downstairs. Manager Henry MacNeil insisted that she move, indicating the notice on the back of the ticket reserving the right to refuse admission to anybody. When Mrs Desmond expressed her conviction that the cinema had no right to discriminate against her, Mr MacNeil sought the assistance of a policeman who was standing at the back of the cinema, watching the show on his supper break.

Unable to intimidate Mrs Desmond into moving voluntarily, Mr MacNeil and the policeman resorted to physical force. In her later testimony Mrs Desmond referred to a "scuffle" in which her knee and hip were injured and her purse and one shoe were lost. Mr Jack Desmond, Viola's widower, reports that his wife "put up a fight," though other family members claim that Mrs Desmond's small stature and dignified demeanour did not make physical resistance likely. In any case, Mrs Desmond was forcibly removed from her seat, carried by Mr MacNeil and the policeman to a waiting taxi, and taken to the police station, where she was locked up overnight. The next morning, 9 November 1946, Magistrate Rod MacKay found Mrs Desmond guilty of defrauding the province of Nova Scotia of one cent in sales tax: the upstairs price of thirty cents included two cents in tax, the downstairs price of forty cents included three cents tax. By paying for an upstairs ticket and sitting downstairs, Mrs Desmond had failed to pay enough tax. She was fined twenty dollars plus six dollars in costs. The costs were paid over to Mr MacNeil.[242]

With the moral and financial support of the recently established Nova Scotia Association for the Advancement of Coloured People, Viola Desmond engaged Halifax lawyer F.W. Bissett to challenge the New Glasgow decision. Apparently as a strategy to undercut the legitimacy of the entire proceedings against his client, Mr Bissett did not appeal Magistrate MacKay's specific ruling but instead applied for a writ of *certiorari*, arguing that Viola Desmond "was illegally and improperly convicted" and alleging "want of jurisdiction of the convicting magistrate for the reason that the evidence did not support the conviction." Justice Maynard B. Archibald of the Nova Scotia Supreme Court, however, dismissed this application on 20 January 1947: "It is clear ... that the magistrate had jurisdiction to enter upon his inquiry."

It was apparent at the argument that the purpose of this application was to seek by means of *certiorari* proceedings a review of the evidence taken before the convicting magistrate. It is obvious that the proper procedure to have had such evidence reviewed was by way of an appeal.

But the time for an appeal had passed, and *certiorari* was inappropriate.[243] Mr Bissett appealed this ruling to the full bench of the Nova Scotia Supreme Court on 13 March, where he argued that "natural justice" had been denied to Mrs Desmond. Following the precedents, and according to the fundamental purpose for the existence of *certiorari*, "There is a denial of justice where a person is convicted without evidence and the court will grant the writ [of *certiorari*] where an obvious injustice has been done, even though an appeal could have been taken."[244] But the Court unanimously rejected the argument, ruling, "The defendant was convicted on a conviction good on its face and regular in form before a magistrate having jurisdiction."[245] Justice William Hall couched his decision in terms that showed he fully understood, and sympathized with, Mrs Desmond's challenge to racial segregation, and seemed to regret that Bissett had not chosen a straightforward appeal:

Had the matter reached the Court by some method other than *certiorari*, there might have been opportunity to right the wrong done this unfortunate woman.

One wonders if the manager of the theatre who laid the complaint was so zealous because of a *bona fide* belief there had been an attempt to defraud the Province of Nova Scotia of the sum of one cent, or was it a surreptitious endeavour to enforce a Jim Crow rule by misuse of a public statute.[246]

New Glasgow's Black newspaper, the *Clarion*, took Justice Hall's comment as a moral victory. "It would appear that the decision was the only one possible under the law ... [T]he reason for the decision lies in the manner in which the case was presented to court."[247] At least "Jim Crow" had been recognized and denounced.[248] But stories of discriminatory treatment in New Glasgow stores and restaurants continued to appear in the *Clarion*, increasing Black citizens' frustration at the failure of the judiciary to protect them. In August 1947 editors Carrie Best and James Calvert Best launched a campaign for a municipal by-law authorizing council to suspend the licences of any establishment refusing service on grounds of colour.[249] Their model was a Toronto by-law requiring places of amusement licensed by the city to accept all customers regardless of "race, colour or creed," passed in response to public demonstrations after a skating rink ejected a boy simply because he was Black.[250] No by-laws resulted in Nova Scotia, but the Desmond case and the *Clarion*'s editorials forced the provincial Black population to recognize the weakness of the law as it stood and prompted the NSAACP to adopt a program aimed at legislative change rather than judicial enforcement of "rights" that turned out to be deficient.[251]

The route to desegregation through a municipal by-law, following the Toronto model, was attempted in several other Canadian cities. After widespread publicity was given to a refusal by Calgary hotels to accommodate African Canadians in early 1947, organized labour and the Co-operative Commonwealth Federation joined the city's Black community in demanding municipal action against discrimination. A motion was presented to council, but the city solicitor gave the opinion that since persons refused accommodation at a common inn or hotel had recourse to damages under the common law, no by-law was necessary. Any by-law reaching beyond hotels – for example, to include taverns or other places of amusement – would be outside the authority of the council. Instead, Calgary mounted "an educational campaign to eradicate discrimination."[252] The campaign did not convince the manager of a local swimming pool, who admitted in 1948 that Blacks were not permitted to swim there because "if too many Negroes came to swim no one else would want to use the pool and we would go out of business."[253] A Calgary dance hall barred Blacks "because the parents of white girls attending dances there have objected."[254] Oshawa council, on the other hand, passed an anti-discriminatory by-law in December 1949, against the opinion of its city solicitor, who advised, "I don't think the city has the power to legislate in such matters."[255] This same doubt had plagued the town council of Dresden, Ontario, where local African Canadians began pressing for a by-law to eliminate racial discrimination in 1947. Unsure of its authority, the council held a referendum in December 1949, asking Dresden citizens, "Do you approve of the Council passing a by-law licensing restaurants in Dresden and restraining the owner or owners from refusing service regardless of race, color or creed?" The vote was 517 to 108 against the by-law.[256]

Circumstances such as these, and in particular the continuation of blatant discrimination in Dresden, forced Black people and their allies to move into the provincial arena to seek an end to racist practices. Ontario was first to provide a remedy through the *Fair Accommodations Practices Act* in 1954, which forbade racial discrimination in places to which the public was "customarily admitted."[257] Over the next decade most other Canadian provinces passed equivalent laws.[258] Quebec's *Hotels Act* was amended in June 1963 to similar effect.[259] It would no longer be possible for the York Tavern to refuse a Black customer. Fred Christie's campaign, indirectly and eventually, seemed to be vindicated. And yet, late into the 1960s, housing discrimination remained prevalent in Montreal, and most African Canadians still resided in the vicinity of the railroad tracks and St Antoine Street.[260] The situation would finally explode in 1969 when Black and other students at Sir George Williams University occupied the computer centre to protest racial discrimination in their university and in the city generally. In the resulting publicity, far more attention was paid to the destruction of computer equipment than to the problems that had created the student frustration.[261] When, at a Liberal fundraising dinner in Montreal in 1975, Prime Minister Pierre Trudeau warned that racism threatened to appear in Canada, his Montreal audience shared the ignorance of their leader that he was speaking far too late.[262] Fred Christie might never have existed.

Christie as Precedent

But if Fred Christie was unknown to the public, the principles enunciated in his case survived in the courts of Canada. Less than six months after the Supreme Court's *Christie* decision, a case with almost identical circumstances occurred in Vancouver. A Black man named Rogers and a white business colleague entered the Clarence Hotel on Seymour Street, which had recently undergone renovations and had reopened under new management. The new proprietor had taken out newspaper advertisements announcing this fact and inviting "our patrons" to see for themselves. Mr Rogers and his friend, a partner in their shoe-repair business, had often had a beer in the Clarence Hotel under its previous owner and had no reason to think he might be unwelcome now. Yet the new proprietor did refuse to serve Mr Rogers and stated that she did so only because she objected to his "race" and colour. Mr Rogers's suit for damages against the hotel reached the British Columbia Court of Appeal in May 1940.[263]

Chief Justice MacDonald found the refusal of service "contrary to ethics and good morals," but regretfully he felt bound to follow the *Christie* precedent and refuse damages to Mr Rogers. Justice Sloan agreed that *Christie* must be applied, thus giving the hotel a majority of the three-man court. They felt that the "freedom of commerce" principle articulated by the Supreme Court was not confined to Quebec. The Quebec *Licence Act* had substantially the same regulations as the BC *Government Liquor Act*,[264] and neither had any explicit provision inhibiting a proprietor's right to refuse service. The use of the Ontario case of *Franklin v. Evans* in its *Christie* judgment placed it "beyond question" that the Supreme Court intended the principle to apply everywhere in Canada.[265]

Justice Cornelius H. O'Halloran dissented. *Christie* was governed by the civil law of Quebec and could not bind the courts of the common law provinces. According to the legal principles prevailing in British Columbia, Justice O'Halloran found three reasons to decide in favour of Mr Rogers:

First, that it is contrary to common law to refuse service to a person solely because of his colour or race. Furthermore the appellant could not refuse the respondent without showing reasonable cause: in that *secondly*, she "held out" her premises to the public without reservation or limitation, as common and public refreshment rooms where beer might be purchased by the glass; and *thirdly*, the operation of beer parlours in this Province is "affected with a public interest," and is a "public employment" so as to displace any asserted common law right, if such existed in the appellant, to sell only to whom she would.[266]

Justice O'Halloran supported these contentions in a thorough canvas of common law cases. He insisted, "All British subjects have the same rights and privileges under the common law" and regretted that Justice Lennox had overlooked "this elementary principle" in *Franklin v. Evans*.[267] Citing *Rothfield v. North British Ry Co*,[268] in which an Edinburgh hotel was required to pay damages for excluding a Jewish patron, Justice O'Halloran illustrated an explicit denial that "race and nationality" could be a reasonable cause to refuse service. The Clarence Hotel could refuse Mr Rogers for reasonable cause, but obviously not simply because of his "race." The hotel's advertisements constituted "a general invitation" to patronize its beer parlour. Though Rothfield dealt with accommodation in what was legally a common inn, the British court's decision was based on the fact that it "held out" its services to the general public, and not on the innkeeper's duty to serve.[269] Finally, Lord Hale's doctrine of "public interest" must be applied, because the provincial legislature had eliminated "freedom of commerce" in beer and through its *Government Liquor Act* had "affected the sale of beer with a public interest."[270] For these various reasons the Clarence Hotel had no right to refuse Mr Rogers.

We cannot consider the right of the beer parlour operator to refuse the respondent without also considering the right of the respondent to be served. Society is made up of individuals. The common law rights of each individual are necessarily limited by the manner in which their exercise affects the common law rights of other individuals. If the respondent had the right to be served (as he did from the general invitation to the public and the "holding out") it is repugnant to any sense of fair dealing to contend that he could be denied the right except for reasonable cause. It would be unreasonable and unjust, a clear invasion of his common law rights.[271]

The commentator in the *Canadian Bar Review* viewed the O'Halloran dissent as the most interesting part of the *Rogers* decision, but found it mistaken. Common law equality meant only entitlement to equal treatment "under the law or before the Courts or as against the Crown or government"; it had no application between private individuals. The comment also criticized Justice O'Halloran's "holding out" principle: "One might as well say that when a store advertises its wares it makes an offer which can be accepted by anyone who appears in response to the advertisement." On the other hand the *CBR* was impressed with O'Halloran's argument that a licensed beer parlour was "affected with a public interest" and should not therefore discriminate among its customers.[272] Douglas Schmeiser has taken a different line, criticizing Justice O'Halloran's use of the British precedents, since each cited case applied to an innkeeper and not to a liquor establishment. Nor does Professor Schmeiser agree that Lord Hale's doctrine of public interest, as interpreted in subsequent British and American cases, affected a licensed tavern in BC. He concludes, "[I]t must be recognized that no matter how socially desirable the view of O'Halloran J.A. might appear to be, there is little legal authority supporting it." Nevertheless Professor Schmeiser does agree with Justice O'Halloran that "[t]here is nothing in the *Christie* case to indicate that the Supreme Court of Canada intended to lay down a rule binding in other provinces – in fact, the judgment points to the opposite conclusion."[273] The view that *Christie* applied only to Quebec, however, has not been sustained or even argued in other instances.

The federal government, certainly, concluded that *Christie* confirmed the right of taverns and restaurants across Canada to discriminate on grounds of "race." In 1943 Mr Hugh Burnett, a carpenter from Dresden, complained to the minister of justice that he had been refused service in a local restaurant because he was Black. The deputy minister replied:

I beg to inform you that I have been requested to reply to your letter of July 17th complaining that the proprietor of a public refreshment parlour – Mr Morley McKay – refused to permit you to buy refreshment in his establishment. This refusal was apparently based on the fact that you are a member of the negro race. A merchant or restaurant keeper is free to deal as he may choose with such members of the public as he may choose. This rule or principle, in certain circumstances such as you relate, is unfair or discriminatory in its effect; however, to adopt a law requiring a merchant or restaurant keeper to transact business with every member of the public who presented himself, since it would be entirely one-sided, might operate to the serious detriment of business. The principle of freedom of contract which I have mentioned has been recognized and accepted by the Supreme Court of Canada in a decision rendered as recently as 1939. This was on an appeal from the Court of Appeal of the Province of Quebec.[274]

In Calgary in 1947 City Solicitor D.S. Moffat, asked to comment on the legality of an anti-discrimination by-law, cited both *Christie v. York* and *Rogers v. Clarence Hotel* to conclude that, with the sole exception of a common innkeeper, "[t]he right to exclude any person from their premises is a civil right thus established by the Supreme Court of Canada and unless this were changed by a decision of the Privy Council or by Legislation it must stand as the law of this Province."[275] As has been noted previously, the *Dominion Law Reports* editors also assumed that *Christie* would "be found equally applicable to the common law."[276] Justice Rinfret, who wrote the *Christie* decision, would apparently have agreed. He wrote in his 1956 "Reminiscences" that in twenty-nine years on the bench he had never found a single case where the application of common law and civil law would have yielded different results.[277]

Not only was *Christie* used to restrict the "duty to serve" exclusively to common innkeepers. It was also used to limit its application to genuine travellers. On 13 May 1959 Mr Ted King was trying to contact a friend who he believed was staying at Barclay's Motel on Macleod Trail in Calgary. He telephoned the motel to ask if his friend was registered there, describing him as "coloured." Proprietor John Barclay replied that he was not, and added, "We don't allow coloured people here." Mr King was one of the founders, and in 1959 was the president, of the Alberta Association for the Advancement of Coloured People. The purpose of this association was "to promote goodwill and to seek equality in social and civic activities throughout the province"; according to another charter member, this included campaigning "to get rid of some obvious forms of racism."[278] Mr Barclay's statement seemed to offer an opportunity to challenge one obvious form of racism. Mr King and a Black colleague, Mr Harvey Bailey, drove to the motel and asked for accommodation. The "Vacancy" sign was posted outside. Mr Barclay at first said the motel was full, but under questioning from Mr King admitted, "We don't take coloured people." Mr King then sued the motel for five hundred dollars damages, hoping to establish an exemplary precedent.[279]

In Calgary District Court Justice Hugh Farthing accepted the truth of Mr King's charge of racial discrimination, but he decided that the motel was free to do so. Since Alberta had no regulation against discrimination, *Christie* and *Rogers* both indicated that freedom of commerce must allow John Barclay to select his own customers. Only an innkeeper was otherwise obligated, and Justice Farthing noted that an innkeeper was one who provided "lodging and food." No food was available at Barclay's Motel, and so it was not by definition an inn. Even if it had been, it would not be obliged to receive Ted King, because he was not a bona fide traveller. King owned a home in Calgary, drove a car with a Calgary registration, and had taken no luggage to the motel. He admitted in court that he had gone to the motel "for purposes of investigation," to test its discriminatory policies. Judge Farthing dismissed Mr King's action with costs and added "in no uncertain terms" that he did not "appreciate" the way the case had been publicized in the press by Mr King's lawyer, Tony Palmer.[280] The Alberta Supreme Court heard Ted King's appeal on 14 February 1961. No written reasons were offered, but all five justices of the Appellate Division held that King was not a traveller, and four of the five held further that the motel, which did not serve food, was not an "inn." The appeal, accordingly, was dismissed, and Mr King received another lecture from the bench criticizing his attempt to use the courts to effect social change.[281] Shortly thereafter Alberta amended its *Innkeeper's Act* to remove the "food" requirement,[282] so that motels would be required to receive Black travellers. The fundamental purpose of the AAACP action had been achieved, but not through the courts.

An interesting decision in Quebec confronted many of the same issues as *Christie* but did not, ironically, even mention that case. In April 1960 Mrs Joseph, a Black woman, made a deposit on a vacant apartment in Montreal and received the owner's verbal assurance, made by telephone, that she could rent the apartment. When she presented herself to sign the lease, however, the owner refused to confirm the agreement and explained "the reason is because you are coloured." Mrs Joseph's suit for damages came before Justice André Nadeau in October 1965. In granting her damages, including interest from 1960, Justice Nadeau found that an oral contract could be broken only with a valid excuse, and this could not include "race." He concluded that racial discrimination was, in any case, contrary to good morals and public order:

Toute discrimination raciale est illégale parce que contraire à l'ordre public et aux bonnes moeurs; le geste discriminatoire posé par le locateur constitue une violation des règles couramment admises de la morale applicables à la vie en société; il est aussi de la catégorie des actes attentatoires à l'ordre public, étant de nature à troubler la paix dans la société.[283]

Justice Lamothe's denial in *Reynolds* that racial discrimination was contrary "aux bonnes moeurs et à l'ordre public,"[284] echoed by Justice Rinfret in *Christie*,[285] had finally been challenged by a Quebec court. At the time of Justice Nadeau's decision, Quebec did not have legislation covering discrimination in rental accommodation.

Christie's legal career was not yet terminated, though it moved through a phase that was remote from the issue of racial discrimination. A betting agency lost access to Ontario racetracks,[286] but General Electric was required to sell to an electrical contractor because no other suppliers were available in the market.[287] In the latter case, Justice Nadeau explained, "Si répréhensible que fut la conduite du tavernier, il y avait tout de même d'autres alternatives qui s'offraient au client,' and he disavowed the racial element in *Christie*'s value as a precedent: "[L]es standards de conduite de 1940 ont singulièrement évolué depuis, et que ce qui pouvait être acceptable à cette époque ne le serait plus aujourd'hui, la notion d'ordre public évoluant avec le cours des ans."[288] Even in cases where the racial issue per se was not before the courts, it was deemed expedient to distinguish *Christie*'s support for discriminatory behaviour as belonging to a particular time and place. The courts could, therefore, continue to recognize a general right of the freedom of commerce without perpetuating the right to discriminate on grounds of "race." By the 1970s public morality and positive legislation, as Justice Nadeau pointed out, had fundamentally undermined the legality of racial discrimination. One recent case to mention *Christie* does constitute an explicit allegation of racism, and while the different courts reached opposing decisions, the impact at all judicial levels was to confirm that racism should no longer be tolerated in Canadian law.

At issue was the claim of a South Asian woman, an experienced teacher with a PhD in mathematics, that Seneca College of Applied Arts and Technology refused to hire her on grounds of "race" and ethnic origin. Instead of filing a complaint under the *Ontario Human Rights Code*, Dr Pushpa Bhadauria issued a writ for damages for discrimination and for breach of the *Code*. Justice Callaghan dismissed her action, finding that the *Code* itself established a remedy for her complaint and she therefore had no right to a civil action. The Ontario Court of Appeal saw otherwise.[289] The unanimous judgment of the court was delivered by Justice Wilson, who considered the question in two parts: was there a common law duty not to discriminate, which the college had breached, and did a violation of the *Ontario Human Rights Code* give rise to a cause of action? Justice Wilson began her answer with a consideration of *Christie v. York* and *Rogers v. Clarence Hotel*, and was most impressed with Justice O'Halloran's dissenting opinion in the latter that the common law gave a right to equality. If so, she went on, there must be a common law remedy, as the British chief justice had enunciated in *Ashby v. White* in 1703.[290] Furthermore in 1945 Justice Mackay of Ontario had declared a racially restrictive covenant to be void as against public policy.[291] It did not require a positive law: the common law alone grants full protection against discrimination. Acknowledging that the matter was *res integra*, since no authorities directly recognized a tort of discrimination, Justice Wilson argued that the common law was not restricted by the existence of the *Ontario Human Rights Code*, which, after all, had not created but merely recognized the right of every citizen to freedom from discrimination. She therefore concluded that Dr Bhadauria could sue the college, as a common law remedy to the breach of a common law right. The question of whether the *Code* itself gave rise to a civil cause of action was, in the circumstances, irrelevant.[292]

The case came before the Supreme Court of Canada in 1981.[293] Once again the decision was unanimous, but it was this time against Dr Bhadauria's right to a civil claim. Chief Justice Bora Laskin, on behalf of the entire Court, found that "a refusal to enter into contract relations or perhaps, more accurately, a refusal even to consider the prospect of such relations has not been recognized at common law as giving rise to any liability in tort." *Christie* and the other cases brought by Black Canadians had not revealed a common law right against discrimination; Justice O'Halloran's dissent was weakened by its reliance on *Rothfield*, a case involving an innkeeper's obligation, which was not applicable to other situations. The principle in *Ashby v. White* applied only if a right in fact existed. Justice Mackay's 1945 statement that racial discrimination was contrary to public policy, with which Chief Justice Laskin personally agreed, had not been upheld by the Ontario Court of Appeal or the Supreme Court of Canada in a 1950 property covenant case. While he commended Justice Wilson's "bold … attempt to advance the common law," Chief Justice Laskin decided that the common law route was "foreclosed by the legislative initiative which overtook the existing common law of Ontario and established a different regime which does not exclude the Courts but rather makes them part of the enforcement machinery under the *Code*."[294] Dr Bhadauria's proper procedure was to lay a complaint under the *Code*, and seek compensation (i.e., damages) under its explicit provisions. The *Ontario Human Rights Code* contained a declaration that public policy was opposed to racial discrimination, and the *Code* also laid out the necessary procedures to enforce that policy. Justice Wilson's judgment was set aside, and Justice Callaghan's was restored: the remedy established in the *Code* was comprehensive and exclusive; there was no parallel remedy through a civil action.[295]

The Supreme Court did not weaken the prohibition of racial discrimination, it merely channelled the remedy through the provisions of the *Code* rather than through a civil suit for damages. For Dr Bhadauria herself, any vindication of her rights and compensation for the damages she allegedly suffered would be determined if she laid a complaint before the Ontario Human Rights Commission. By 1981 the only dispute was over the means by which a complainant should seek to enforce his or her right to freedom from discrimination. The Supreme Court's *Bhadauria* decision, however, has the effect of lending retroactive approval to *Loew's v. Reynolds, Franklin v. Evans, Christie v. York, Rogers v. Clarence Hotel,* and *R. v. Desmond,* all of which occurred before human rights codes existed in Canada. Although Chief Justice Laskin did not deny the possibility that a common law right existed prior to the enactment of human rights legislation, he confessed that he had "some difficulty in understanding" Justice Wilson's claim that the *Code* "recognized" but did not "create" the right to freedom from discrimination. Indeed he implied that the *Code* had created rather than recognized that right by adding, "There is no gainsaying the right of the Legislature to establish new rights or to create new interests of which the Court may properly take notice and enforce either under the prescriptions of the Legislature or by applying its own techniques if, on its construction of the legislation, enforcement has not been wholly embraced by the terms of the legislation."[296]

In the context this statement was meant to suggest that the legislation did provide for satisfactory enforcement; placed against Justice Wilson's pronouncement, it suggests as well that the right was newly created. This impression is further reinforced by the distinction the chief justice drew between *Rogers v. Clarence Hotel* and *Rothfield*:

The Common Law of innkeepers' liability had, historically, developed along *different lines* from that respecting restaurants and taverns; keepers of common inns were under an obligation to receive travellers or intending guests, irrespective of race or colour or other arbitrary disqualification.[297]

Taverns, such as the York, had therefore not been under any such obligation. *Christie* had survived another test.

NOTES

1 [1940] SCR 139.
2 Interviews: Mr Edward Packwood and Mrs Ann Packwood, Montreal, 13 June 1988; Dr Harold Potter, Montreal, 14 June; Mrs Ann Packwood, 15 June.

    In court Mr Hazen Hansard, counsel for the York Tavern, entered a curious exchange with Mr Christie:

    Q. Of course, I want you to understand, as far as my personal feelings in this matter are concerned, they do not count, but it is the fact that you, Mr Christie, and Mr King, are of the coloured race?
    A. Yes ...
    Q. Are you a full blooded negro?
    A. Yes.
    Q. I notice your complexion is not extraordinarily dark. That is the reason I ask you.
    A. Well, that is a question.
    Q. I just merely want it on the record that you are not extraordinarily black?
    A. As far as I know.
    Q. And similarly I notice Mr King is not extraordinarily black, is he?
    A. No.

    "Evidence on Discovery," case file #6684, Supreme Court.
3 Interview Dr Harold Potter.
4 "Deposition of Rene St Jean," waiter, case file #6684, Supreme Court. Fred Christie insisted that he had been served in the new location, but the waiter claimed that African Canadians had not been admitted since the York opened in the Forum.
5 "Evidence on Discovery," case file #6684, Supreme Court.
6 Interviews: Mrs Martha Griffiths, Montreal, 13 June 1988; Mr and Mrs Packwood.
7 Case file #6684, Supreme Court.
8 J. Cleland Hamilton, "Slavery in Canada," *Magazine of American History* 25 (1891): 238.

9 Older accounts of Canadian slavery include F.W. Harris, "The Black Population of the County of Annapolis," in *The Romance of Old Annapolis*, ed. C.I. Perkins, 60–8 (Annapolis Royal, NS: n.p., 1925); W.R. Riddell, "Notes on the Slave in Nouvelle France," *Journal of Negro History* 8 (1923): 316–30; W.R. Riddell, "Slavery in Canada," *Journal of Negro History* 5 (1920): 261–377; T. Watson Smith, "The Slave in Canada," *Collections of the Nova Scotia Historical Society* 10 (1899), entire issue; M.J. Viger and L.H. Lafontaine, "De l'esclavage en Canada," *Mémoires et documents relatifs a l'histoire du Canada* (Montreal: La Société historique de Montréal, 1859), 1–63. The definitive study of slavery in New France is Marcel Trudel, *L'esclavage au Canada français* (Quebec: Presses universitaires Laval, 1960), to which has been added his *Dictionnaire des esclaves et de leurs propriétaires au Canada français* (Lasalle: Hurtubise, 1990), which contains an entry on almost every slave and slave-owner in French Canada. Other recent discussions are found in David Bell, "Slavery and the Judges of Loyalist New Brunswick," *UNB Law Journal* 31 (1982): 9–42; Barry Cahill, "Habeas Corpus and Slavery in Nova Scotia: R. v. Hecht Ex Parte Rachel, 1798," *UNB Law Journal* 44 (1995): 179–209; and Barry Cahill, "Slavery and the Judges of Loyalist Nova Scotia," *UNB Law Journal* 43 (1994): 73–134; Gary Hartlen, "Bound for Nova Scotia: Slaves in the Planter Migration, 1759–1800," in *Making Adjustments: Change and Continuity in Planter Nova Scotia, 1759–1800*, ed. Margaret Conrad, 123–8 (Fredericton: Acadiensis, 1991); Michael Power and Nancy Butler, "Simcoe and Slavery," in *Slavery and Freedom in Niagara*, 9–39 (Niagara-on-the-Lake, ON: Niagara Historical Society, 1993); James W. St.G. Walker, *A History of Blacks in Canada: A Study Guide for Teachers and Students* (Ottawa: Minister of State, Multiculturalism, 1980), 19–27; Robin Winks, *The Blacks in Canada: A History* (Montreal: McGill-Queen's University Press, 1971), 1–60. A summary of the legal provisions applicable to Canadian slavery is provided by Helen T. Catterall, *Judicial Cases Concerning American Slavery and the Negro*, vol. 5, *Canadian Cases* (New York: Octagon Books, 1968), 340–8.

10 Nova Scotia House of Assembly, *Journals and Proceedings* (hereafter Nova Scotia Assembly Journals), 1808, 155, 156, 159, 272, 281, 295. The Bill was twice examined by a Committee of the Whole and twice deferred.

11 C. Vann Woodward, *The Strange Career of Jim Crow* (New York: Oxford University Press, 1955), 8. According to Woodward, "The origin of the term 'Jim Crow' applied to Negroes is lost in obscurity. Thomas D. Rice wrote a song and dance called 'Jim Crow' in 1832, and the term had become an adjective by 1838" (7). Stuart Berg Flexner dates the term to the 1730s, when African slaves were first called "crows,' and Rice's song to 1828: *I Hear America Talking: An Illustrated Treasury of American Words and*

Phrases (New York: Van Nostrand Reinhold, 1976), 39. Rice, the alleged
originator of blackface minstrelsy in the United States, designed his dance
after seeing a slave with a physical disability jumping and wheeling to
a song with the words "Weel a-bout and turn a-bout / And do just so /
Every time I weel a-bout / I jump Jim Crow": Lerone Bennet Jr, *Before the
Mayflower* (Baltimore: Penguin, 1966), 220. Rice's song-and-dance routine
became a hit and popularized the use of the term *Jim Crow* as a noun to
refer to African Americans and as an adjective to the separate facilities set
apart for Black use, such as those described by Vann Woodward, and the
laws enforcing them. Benjamin Quarles, *The Negro in the Making of America*,
3rd ed. (New York: Collier, 1987), 73, identifies the Jim Crow dance as a
"favorite" among the slaves when celebrating Christmas or 4 July. Since
slave dances at such celebrations were often surreptitious mockeries of
their masters' dancing styles – Lynne F. Emery, "Dance," in *Dictionary
of American Slavery*, ed. R.M. Miller and J.D. Smith, 173–4 (Westport, CT:
Greenwood, 1988) – and since *old Mr Crow* was a term sometimes used by
slaves to mean "slave-owner" (Bennet, *Before the Mayflower*, 221), it is possible that Rice's Jim Crow dance was a satire upon a satire.
12 James W. St.G. Walker, *The Black Loyalists*, 2nd ed. (Toronto: University of
Toronto Press, 1992).
13 John N. Grant, *The Immigration and Settlement of the Black Refugees of the War
of 1812 in Nova Scotia and New Brunswick* (Dartmouth, NS: Black Cultural
Centre for Nova Scotia, 1990); William Spray, "The Settlement of the Black
Refugees in New Brunswick, 1815–1836," *Acadiensis* 6 (1977): 64–79.
14 Crawford Kilian, *Go Do Some Great Thing: The Black Pioneers of British Co-
lumbia* (Vancouver: Douglas and McIntyre, 1978); James Pilton, "Negro
Settlement in British Columbia, 1858–71" (MA thesis, University of British
Columbia, 1951); Jason H. Silverman, *Unwelcome Guests: Canada West's
Response to American Fugitive Slaves, 1800–1865* (Millwood, NY: Associated
Faculty, 1985); Donald G. Simpson, "Negroes in Ontario from Early Times
to 1870" (PhD diss., University of Western Ontario, 1971); James W. St.G.
Walker, "On the Record: The Testimony of Canada's Black Pioneers, 1783–
1865," in *Emerging Perspectives on the Black Diaspora*, ed. A.W. Bonnett and
G.L. Watson, 79–119 (Lanham, MD: University Press of America, 1990).
   Until recently a figure of 30,000 to 40,000 has generally been accepted for
the number of American fugitives who came into Canada. Michael Wayne
suggests a total of only about 20,000 to 23,000, most of whom remained in
Canada following the Civil War: "The Black Population of Canada West
on the Eve of the American Civil War: A Reassessment Based on the Manuscript Census of 1861," *Histoire sociale / Social History* 28 (1995): 465–85.

15 Judith Hill, "Alberta's Black Settlers: A Study of Canadian Immigration Policy and Prejudice" (MA thesis, University of Alberta, 1981); Howard Palmer and Tamara Palmer, *Peoples of Alberta: Portraits of Cultural Diversity* (Saskatoon: Western Producer Prairie Books, 1985), 365–93; R. Bruce Shepard, "Black Migration as a Response to Repression: The Background Factors and Migration of Oklahoma Blacks to Western Canada, 1905–1912" (MA thesis, University of Saskatchewan, 1976); Harold Troper, "The Creek-Negroes of Oklahoma and Canadian Immigration, 1909–11," *Canadian Historical Review* 53 (1972): 272–88.

Bruce Shepard has published a number of articles related to his thesis topic: "Diplomatic Racism: Canadian Government and Black Migration from Oklahoma, 1905–1912," *Great Plains Quarterly* 3 (1983): 5–16; "North to the Promised Land: Black Migration to the Canadian Plains," *Chronicles of Oklahoma* 66 (1988): 306–27; "Origins of the Oklahoma Black Migration to the Canadian Plains," *Canadian Journal of History* 23 (1988): 1–23; "Plain Racism: The Reaction against Oklahoma Black Immigration to the Canadian Plains," *Prairie Forum* 10 (1985): 365–82; and has related the entire episode in *Deemed Unsuitable* (Toronto: Umbrella, 1997).

16 Nova Scotia Assembly Journals.

17 William Pease and Jane Pease, "Opposition to the Founding of the Elgin Settlement," *Canadian Historical Review* 38 (1957): 202–18; Harold Potter, "Negroes in Canada," *Race* 3 (1961): 45; Walker, *History of Blacks in Canada*, 79–83.

18 Allen P. Stouffer, "'A Restless Child of Change and Accident': The Black Image in Nineteenth-Century Ontario," *Ontario History* 76 (1984): 128–50.

19 W.D. Scott, "The Negro," in *Canada and Its Provinces*, ed. Adam Shortt and Arthur Doughty (Toronto: Publishers' Association of Canada, 1914), 7:531.

20 28 Apr. 1911, qtd in Colin Thomson, *Blacks in Deep Snow: Black Pioneers in Canada* (Don Mills, ON: Dent, 1979), 82–3.

21 J. Bruce Walker to W.D. Scott, 21 Aug. 1908, vol. 192, RG 76, Library and Archives Canada (hereafter LAC), Ottawa.

22 George Clingan to J. Bruce Walker, 21 Aug. 1908, vol. 192, RG 76, LAC.

23 Ada Knight, secretary, Edmonton IODE, to Frank Oliver, 31 Mar. 1911, and enclosure, Laurier Papers, MG 26 G1(A), LAC.

24 Carol Lee Bacchi, *Liberation Deferred? The Ideas of the English-Canadian Suffragists, 1877–1918* (Toronto: University of Toronto Press, 1983), 53.

25 *Edmonton Capital*, 27 Mar. 1911, qtd in Thomson, *Blacks in Deep Snow*, 81–2.

26 *Hansard*, 2, 22, and 23 Mar. 1911, 4470–1, 5911–13, 5943–7.

27 *Hansard*, 3 Apr. 1911, 6523–8.

28 Jason Silverman and Donna Gillie, "The Pursuit of Knowledge under Dif-

ficulties: Education and the Fugitive Slave in Canada," *Ontario History* 74 (1982): 95–112; Hildreth H. Spencer, "To Nestle in the Mane of the British Lion: A History of Canadian Black Education, 1820 to 1870" (PhD diss., Northwestern University, 1970); Robin Winks, "Negro School Segregation in Ontario and Nova Scotia," *Canadian Historical Review* 50 (1969): 164–91.

29 Statutes of Nova Scotia (hereafter SNS) 1836, c. 92, s. 5.
30 Revised Statutes of Nova Scotia (hereafter RSNS) 1884, c. 29, ss. 3, 10.
31 Ibid., s. 13.
32 Statutes of Upper Canada (hereafter SUC) 1850, c. 48, s. 19.
33 (1854) 11 Upper Canada Queens Bench Reports (hereafter UCQB) 569.
34 *Hill v. Camden and Zone*, 11 UCQB 573.
35 (1861) 21 UCQB 75.
36 *Re Stewart and School Trustees of Sandwich East*, (1864) 23 UCQB 634.
37 Statutes of Ontario (hereafter SO) 1964, c. 108, s. 1
38 Statutes of new Brunswick (hereafter SNB) 1842, c. 37.
39 V. Carter and W.L. Akili, *The Window of Our Memories* (St Albert, AB: Black Cultural Research Society of Alberta, 1981, 1990), 1:55; R. Bruce Shepard, "The Little 'White' Schoolhouse: Racism in a Saskatchewan Rural School," *Saskatchewan History* 39 (1986): 81–93.
40 "Proceedings of a Meeting of Toronto Blacks," 13 Jan. 1838, in *The Black Abolitionist Papers*, vol. 2, *Canada 1830–1865*, ed. C. Peter Ripley (Chapel Hill: University of North Carolina Press, 1986), 69.
41 Ida Greaves, *The Negro in Canada* (Orillia, ON: Packet-Times, 1930), 63.
42 For an excellent account of the situation in the 1920s, see Greaves, *The Negro in Canada*, chap. 8. A representative list of restrictions during that period is given in Winks, *Blacks in Canada*, 325–6.
43 3 Nov. 1855, qtd in Daniel G. Hill, *The Freedom Seekers* (Agincourt, ON: Book Society of Canada, 1981), 105.
44 J. Miller, Calgary city clerk, letter 13 Apr 1920, Palmer Research Files. I am grateful to the late Howard Palmer and Tamara Palmer Seiler for having allowed me to photocopy the research notes for their chapter on "The Blacks" in *Peoples of Alberta*.
45 In March 1919, Vancouver city council passed a motion asking the city solicitor to design a system of legal segregation confining "Asiatics" to "some well defined given area of the city." After an extensive search undertaken by the city solicitor with the assistance of the Retail Merchants' Association of Canada, council was informed in 1923 that municipalities did not have the power to restrict "Orientals" in this way (Kay Anderson, *Vancouver's Chinatown: Racial Discourse in Canada, 1875–1980* (Montreal and Kingston: McGill-Queen's University Press, 1991), 126–7).

46 *Calgary Herald*, 27 Apr., 29 Apr., 30 Apr., 1 May 1920; *Calgary Albertan*, 27 Apr., 30 Apr., 1 May, 21 May 1920.

47 For example, *Hansard*, 9, 10, and 23 Mar. 1911, 4930, 5040–1, 5941–2, 5946.

48 Peter Gallego to Thomas Rolph, 1 Nov. 1841, *Black Abolitionist Papers*, 2:87–94.

49 *Saturday Night*, 25 Aug. 1888.

50 *Edmonton Capital*, 9 Apr. 1912, qtd in Thomson, *Blacks in Deep Snow*, 82.

51 *Saturday Night*, 1 Aug. 1936.

52 Ralph Weber, "Riot in Victoria, 1860," *Journal of Negro History* 56 (1971): 141–8; Winks, *Blacks in Canada*, 283–4.

53 Lyle E. Talbot, "Black and Canadian: Inside Looking In," unpublished ms., 56.

54 Greaves, *Negro in Canada*, 62.

55 Winks, *Blacks in Canada*, 420.

56 Charles R. Saunders, *Share and Care: The Story of the Nova Scotia Home for Colored Children* (Halifax: Nimbus, 1994).

57 Interview: Calvin Ruck, Dartmouth, NS, 12 Oct. 1993.

58 Don Clairmont and Fred Wien, "Blacks and Whites: The Nova Scotia Race Relations Experience," in *Banked Fires: The Ethnics of Nova Scotia*, ed. Douglas Campbell (Port Credit, ON: Scribbler's, 1978), 157.

59 John T. Richards to the Duke of Connaught, 4 Oct. 1915, file 297-1-21, vol. 1206, RG 24, LAC.

60 George Morton to Gen. Sir Sam Hughes, 7 Sept. 1915, file 297-1-21, vol. 1206, RG 24, LAC.

61 John Richards to military secretary to the governor general, 20 Nov. 1915, file 297-1-21, vol. 1206, RG 24, LAC. See also file 448-14-259, vol. 4739, RG 24, LAC.

62 C.G. Henshaw to brigade major, 23rd Infantry, 7 Dec. 1915, file 297-1-21, vol. 1206, RG 24, LAC.

63 District officer Commanding Military District No. 11, Victoria, to secretary, Militia Council, 9 Dec. 1915, file 297-1-21, vol. 1206, RG 24, LAC.

64 W.H. Allen, Halifax, to 6th Division HQ, 14 Dec. 1915, file 297-1-21, vol. 1206, RG 24, LAC.

65 Various letters in file 34-7-141, vol. 4387, RG 24, LAC.

66 C.S. MacInnes, memo to the secretary, 25 Mar. 1916, file 297-1-21, vol. 1206, RG 24, LAC.

67 Memorandum, 13 Apr. 1916, file 297-1-21, vol. 1206, RG 24, LAC.

68 Militia Council Minutes, 19 Apr. 1916, file 297-1-21, vol. 1206, RG 24, LAC.

69 Mobilization to Gwatkin, 19 Feb. 1917, and reply, n.d., file 600-10-35, vol. 1469, RG 24, LAC; memo to naval secretary, 21 Feb. 1917, and reply, 23 Feb.

70 Vol. 1, OC No. 9 District to director of Timber Operations, 19 Aug. 1918, file E-186-9, box 1698, RG 9 III, LAC; box 4645, assistant to director of Chaplain Services, report, 20 Feb. 1918, RG 9 III; vol. 13, 1918, box 5010, War Diaries, No. 2 Construction Company, RG 9 III.

71 Collier to OC Canadian Troops, Kinmel Park, 10 Jan. 1919, file D-3-13, vol. 1709, RG 24, LAC.

72 *Toronto Daily Star*, 1 Mar. 1930; Toronto *Globe*, 1 and 3 Mar. 1930. The second *Globe* story includes the Klan's own statement on the course of the evening's events.

73 Toronto *Globe*, 3 Mar. 1930; *Toronto Daily Star*, 1 and 24 Mar., 17 Apr. 1930; *Dawn of Tomorrow*, 24 Mar. 1930; *Canadian Forum* (Apr. 1930): 233; *Rex v. Phillips* (1930) 55 Canadian Criminal Cases (hereafter CCC) 49. The young lovers continued to try to find a minister who would marry them. Late on the night of Saturday 22 Mar., they went to the home of Rev. Frank Burgess, the native Indian pastor of the United Church on the New Credit Six Nations reserve. Though his wife "pleaded with her husband not to take the chance of defying the Klan," Mr Burgess finally agreed, and Ira and Isabella were married in the pastor's kitchen with Mrs Burgess as witness. When the Klan learned of the marriage a spokesman said the matter was now closed. "We will not put asunder what God hath joined together" (*Toronto Daily Star*, 24 Mar. 1930).

74 For example, see Toronto *Globe and Mail*, 8 Dec. 1990.

75 The most succinct account of the escape, recapture, and execution of Marie Joseph-Angélique is in Trudel, *Dictionnaire*, 113–14. A very brief reference is in the *Dictionary of Canadian Biography*, online. Another high-profile slave was Mathieu Leveille, purchased in 1733 by the government of New France from his owner in Martinique to serve as public executioner in Quebec. Leveille grew "melancholy" in the pursuit of his profession, so in 1742 Intendant Hocquart purchased a wife for him in the West Indies. Before they could be married Leveille died and his fiancée, baptized as Angélique-Dénise, was sold by the intendant as no longer useful to the government (*Dictionary of Canadian Biography*, online). The position of executioner was considered dishonourable in New France, and government authorities turned to the purchase of a slave because no free white man could be found for the job. Leveille's frequent illness in Quebec suggested the inappropriateness of this solution, and he was replaced after his death by a white man. Apparently Leveille was not involved in the execution of Marie-Joseph-Angélique in 1734. Since the original publication of this chapter, Afua Cooper has brought out a full-length study of this interesting episode. See *The Hanging of Angelique: The Untold Story of Canadian Slavery and the Burning of Old Montreal* (Toronto: HarperCollins, 2006).

76 Viger and LaFontaine, "De l'esclavage en Canada," 4–5.

77 Ibid., 5–6, 17–18.

78 Ibid., 8–9.

79 Ibid., 9, Vaudreuil to Belestre, 9 Sept. 1760.

80 Catterall, *Judicial Cases*, 341–5. The case was *Charlotte v. Chouteau*, heard
    before Judge Richardson in 1857. At issue was the legal existence of slav-
    ery in Montreal, where the plaintiff's mother had been born in 1768. The
    argument was that since slavery did not exist, the mother was born free,
    and consequently the plaintiff was also free. Judge Richardson canvassed
    the French and British laws to conclude that slavery had in fact been legal
    in both French and English Canada.

81 Riddell, "Slavery in Canada," 276.

82 Ibid., 303.

83 Viger and LaFontaine, "De l'esclavage en Canada," 27–8, citing *Lower
    Canada Assembly Journals*, 28 Jan., 26 Feb., 8 Mar., and 19 Apr. 1793.

84 David C. Este, "The Emergence and Development of the Black Church in
    Canada with Special Emphasis on Union Church in Montreal, 1907–1940"
    (unpublished, University of Waterloo, 1979), 50–1.

85 Agnes Calliste, "Sleeping Car Porters in Canada: An Ethnically Submerged
    Split Labour Market," *Canadian Ethnic Studies* 19 (1987): 1–20; Wilfred E.
    Israel, "The Montreal Negro Community' (MA thesis, McGill University,
    1928), 227; Harold H. Potter, Appendix A, "The Sleeping Car Porter," in
    "The Occupational Adjustment of Montreal Negroes, 1941–48" (MA thesis,
    McGill University, 1949), 143–52.

86 Table 14, vol. 2, *Census of Canada*, 1911; table 34, vol. 2, *Census of Canada*,
    1931. In 1931 there were 634 Black men and 568 Black women in Montreal.
    During the Depression the male population declined as African-Canadian
    men sought greater employment opportunities in the United States.

87 In 1917 the Eureka Association introduced a program of communal prop-
    erty purchase for resale or rental to Black Montrealers. It undertook this
    initiative, a pamphlet explained, because "[t]he housing situation among
    Negroes in Montreal gives no hope of improvement in the future. We are
    still forced to live in unsanitary houses, to pay high rentals and suffer hu-
    miliation from landlords whilst endeavoring to procure suitable residenc-
    es." Qtd in Dorothy W. Williams, *Blacks in Montreal, 1628–1986: An Urban
    Geography* (Montreal: Éditions Yvon Blais, 1989), 37.

88 Este, "Union Church in Montreal," 54, 56, 59; Greaves, *Negro in Canada*, 65;
    interviews: Mrs Griffiths, 13 June 1988; Mr and Mrs Packwood, 13 June;
    Mrs Packwood, 15 June; Israel, "Montreal Negro Community," 1–2, 175;
    Potter, "Occupational Adjustment," 6–15.

89 Greaves, *Negro in Canada*, 55–6.

90 Este, "Union Church in Montreal," 55; Israel, "Montreal Negro Commu-
    nity," 77–8; Potter, "Occupational Adjustment," 15–16.
91 Potter, "Occupational Adjustment," 29. A trained and experienced Black
    stenographer, bilingual in English and French, could find work only as a
    domestic (Potter, "Negroes in Canada," 49–50).
92 Potter, "Occupational Adjustment," 118–19.
93 Greaves, *Negro in Canada*, 54–5; Israel, "Montreal Negro Community,"
    230.
94 Calliste, "Sleeping Car Porters"; Potter, "Occupational Adjustment," Ap-
    pendix A, 143.
95 Interview: Mr Eddie Packwood, Montreal, 13 June 1988.
96 Everett C. Hughes, *French Canada in Transition* (Chicago: University of
    Chicago Press, 1943), 219; Susan Mann Trofimenkoff, ed., "Introduction"
    in *Abbé Groulx: Variations on a Nationalist Theme* (Toronto: Copp Clark,
    1973), 15; Michael Oliver, *The Passionate Debate: The Social and Political
    Ideas of Quebec Nationalism, 1920–1945* (Montreal: Véhicule, 1991); Fernand
    Ouellet, "The Historical Background of Separation in Quebec," in *French
    Canadian Nationalism: An Anthology*, ed. Ramsay Cook, (Toronto: Macmil-
    lan, 1969), 15; Mason Wade, *The French Canadians, 1760–1960*, rev. ed. (To-
    ronto: Macmillan, 1968), 2:862.
97 John Higham, *Strangers in the Land* (New York: Atheneum, 1963), 264–99;
    Howard Palmer, *Patterns of Prejudice: A History of Nativism in Alberta* (To-
    ronto: McClelland and Stewart, 1982). Although the first Canadian branch
    of the Ku Klux Klan appeared in Montreal in 1921, the Klan's greatest
    success was in the West, and particularly in Saskatchewan.
98 Jean-c. Bonenfant and Jean-c. Falardeau, "Cultural and Political Impli-
    cations of French Canadian Nationalism," 21–2; Cook, *French Canadian
    Nationalism*, especially Pierre Elliott Trudeau, "Quebec on the Eve of the
    Asbestos Strike," 33–4; Ouellet, "Historical Background of Separatism,"
    61. See also W.D.K. Kernaghan, "Freedom of Religion in the Province
    of Quebec, with Particular Reference to Jews, Jehovah's Witnesses and
    Church–State Relations 1930–1960" (PhD diss., Duke University, 1966),
    58, 146.
99 Lionel Groulx, "French Canadian Nationalism," in *Abbé Groulx*, ed. Trofi-
    menkoff, 87, 94; Susan Mann Trofimenkoff, *Action française: French Canadi-
    an Nationalism in the Twenties* (Toronto: University of Toronto Press, 1975),
    90.
100 Qtd in Wade, *French Canadians*, 2:869.
101 Lionel Groulx, *L'Appel de la race*, 5th ed. (Montreal: Fides, 1962); Trofi-
    menkoff, *Action française*, 77.

102 Kernaghan, "Freedom of Religion," 83.

103 Hughes, *French Canada in Transition*, 135.

104 Pierre Anctil, *Le Rendez-vous Manque : Les Juifs de Montréal face au Québec de l'entre-deux-guerres* (Quebec: Institut Québécois de Recherche sur la culture, 1988), 135.

105 André Laurendeau, *Witness for Quebec*, trans. (Toronto: Macmillan, 1973), 71–2. Emphasis added.

106 Interview: Mr Eddie Packwood, 13 June 1988. "Race relations" in anglophone Montreal are the background for Morley Callaghan's novel *The Loved and the Lost* (Toronto: Macmillan, 1951). Though It occurs after the Second World War, the novel describes a world of restriction and rejection for Black people in Montreal.

107 Williams, *Blacks in Montreal*, 45.

108 Este, "Union Church in Montreal," 60–1; interview: Mrs Packwood, 15 June 1988; Israel, "Montreal Negro Community," 151–64.

109 Greaves, *Negro in Canada*, 55; interview: Mrs Packwood, 15 June 1988; Israel, "Montreal Negro Community," 98, 99, 106, 108–9, 168–88, 227; Potter, "Occupational Adjustment," 143.

110 Leo W. Bertley, "The Universal Negro Improvement Association of Montreal, 1917–1979" (PhD diss., Concordia University, 1979); Este, "Union Church in Montreal," 69–72; interviews: Dr Leo Bertley, Montreal, 14 June; Mrs Packwood, 15 June 1988; Israel, "Montreal Negro Community," 111, 204–7.

111 Este, "Union Church in Montreal"; interviews: Mr Buddy Jones, Montreal, 13 June 1988; Mr and Mrs Packwood, 13 June; Ms Dorothy Williams, Montreal, 13 June; Dr Bertley, 14 June; Mrs Packwood, 15 June; Israel, "Montreal Negro Community," 281; Potter, "Occupational Adjustment," 19; Robert Tremblay, "Les Noirs d'ici," *Parti Pris* 5 (1967–6): 17–23.

112 Interview: Mrs Griffiths, 13 June 1988.

113 Interviews: Mr Packwood, 13 June 1988; Mrs Griffiths, 13 June; Dr Potter, 14 June; Mr Clarence Este, Montreal, 14 June. Mr Packwood has in his possession a list of donors and a file of *Free Lance* issues from the period of the Christie crusade. The quotation is from 9 July 1938.

114 W. Stuart Edwards to E.A. Stanton, 31 Jan. 1916, file 297-1-21, vol. 1206, RG 24, LAC.

115 For a full discussion of the issue, see Henry L. Molot, "The Duty of Business to Serve the Public: Analogy to the Innkeeper's Obligation," *Canadian Bar Review* 46 (1968): 612–42.

116 Cited in Molot, "Duty of Business," 632; and in Douglas A. Schmeiser, *Civil Liberties in Canada* (London: Oxford University Press, 1964), 269.

117 Cited in Molot, "Duty of Business," 637; and Schmeiser, *Civil Liberties in Canada*, 271.
118 (1899) 15 CS 104. In 1994 the Centre de Recherche-Action sur les Relations Raciales announced Le Prix Frederick Johnson, to be awarded annually to a group or individual making an outstanding contribution to the struggle against racial inequality in the Quebec. The two categories under which awards are made, both of which commemorate Mr Johnson's initiative almost a century previously, are *"sensibilisation et pression"* and *"contestation judiciaire."* CRARR news release, 1994.
119 CS, at 106.
120 Ibid., 107–8.
121 Ibid., 108–10.
122 (1899) 8 QKB 379.
123 Ibid., 383.
124 Ibid., 384.
125 Ibid., 379–80.
126 Greaves, *The Negro in Canada*, 62, citing as her source a personal letter from the deputy attorney general of Ontario.
127 (1914) 21 BCR 435; (1915) 31 WLR 542 (BCCA). I am grateful to Mr Paul Winn of Vancouver for sending me the reports on Barnswell.
128 BCR, 436.
129 Ibid., 438.
130 Este, "Union Church in Montreal," 57–8; Israel, "Montreal Negro Community," 108–11.
131 *Montreal Gazette*, 5 Mar 1919; (1921) 30 QKB 459. The newspaper dated the incident as occurring on 26 January 1919; Justice Carroll, hearing the appeal on 29 December 1919, apparently mistakenly said it had occurred on 26 January 1918, QKB at 461.
132 *Montreal Gazette*, 5 Mar. 1919.
133 Ibid. Since it was apparently Mr Reynolds who had purchased all four tickets, Justice Fortin might have decided that the damages were his alone, but this reason was not mentioned in the newspaper account of the trial.
134 (1921) 30 QKB 459, at 462.
135 Ibid., 463.
136 Ibid., 466–7.
137 Ibid., 460–1.
138 Ibid., 464.
139 *Dawn of Tomorrow*, 2 and 9 Feb. 1924; (1924) 55 OLR 349.

140 OLR, at 350.

141 *Dawn of Tomorrow*, 16 Feb. 1924. Misspelling in original.

142 OLR, at 350.

143 Ibid., 350–1.

144 Ibid., 352. *Dawn of Tomorrow* gave a curiously erroneous report on the case, 16 Feb. 1924: "Damages were awarded W.V. Franklin, of Kitchener, in his suit against Alfred Evans at the Middlesex assizes last Saturday before Justice Haughton Lenox. It is alleged that the defendant refused to serve him food on account of his (Franklin's) color. It took the jury only 20 minutes to decide that Mr Franklin should be awarded damages."

145 Lowell C. Carroll, *Landlord and Tenant in the Province of Quebec* (Montreal: Southam, 1934); also Lowell C. Carroll, *Marriage in Quebec: The Conditions of Validity* (Montreal: H.S. Oakes, 1936). He later edited *The Quebec Statute and Case Citator, 1937* (Montreal: Kingsland, 1937); and *Commercial Law of Quebec* (Toronto: I. Pitman and Sons, 1938).

146 Canadian Law List, 1936.

147 Case file #6684, Supreme Court.

148 RSQ 1925, c. 25, s. 33.

149 (1937) 75 SC 136, at 138.

150 *Gazette*, 25 Mar. 1937.

151 (1938) 65 QKB 104. Ad Hoc Justice Pratte joined the majority but on the exclusive ground "that the appellant's refusal herein complained of was made under circumstances such that it could not cause any damage to the respondent" (105).

152 Ibid., at 107.

153 Ibid., at 121.

154 Ibid., at 105.

155 RSQ 1925, c. 37.

156 QKB, at 106–7, 109–10, 113–14, 122–4.

157 Ibid., at 114–15.

158 Ibid., at 110.

159 Ibid., at Ill, 117–19.

160 Ibid., at Ill, 120.

161 Ibid., at 110–11, 116–17.

162 F.R. Scott, "The Bill of Rights and Quebec Law," *Canadian Bar Review* 37 (1959): 145.

163 QKB, at 117, 124.

164 Ibid., at 124–5.

165 Ibid., at 105, 112, 124.

166 Ibid., at 115, 120.
167 Ibid., at 112.
168 Ibid., at 123, 125.
169 Ibid., at 137–8.
170 Ibid., at 128.
171 Ibid., at 128–30.
172 Ibid., at 131.
173 Ibid., at 132.
174 Ibid., at 135.
175 Ibid., at 133.
176 Ibid., at 134.
177 Ibid., at 135–6.
178 Ibid., at 136.
179 Ibid., at 136–7.
180 Ibid., at 137–9.
181 Ibid., at 137, 139.
182 Ibid., at 105.
183 *Free Lance*, 9 July 1938.
184 Ibid.
185 RSC 1927, c. 35.
186 [1939] 4 DLR 723; case file #6684, Supreme Court.
187 Ibid., appellant's factum.
188 Ibid., respondent's factum.
189 Walter S. Tarnopolsky, "The Supreme Court and Civil Liberties," *Alberta Law Review* 14 (1976): 65. See also Gerald Le Dain, "Sir Lyman Duff and the Constitution," *Osgoode Hall Law Journal* 12 (1974): 261.
190 [1940] SCR 139.
191 Ibid., at 141.
192 Ibid., at 142.
193 Ibid., at 142–3.
194 Ibid., at 143–4.
195 Ibid., at 144–5.
196 Ibid., at 145.
197 Ibid., at 146.
198 Ibid., at 147–8.
199 SQ 1921, c. 24, then RSQ 1925, c. 37.
200 SCR, at 148–9.
201 SQ 1921, c. 25, then RSQ 1925, c. 38.
202 SCR, at 150.

203 (1902) 1 KB 296.
204 SCR, at 152.
205 Ibid., at 152–3.
206 Case file #6684, Supreme Court. Respondent's costs were $594.43.
207 Interview: Mrs Griffiths, 13 June 1988.
208 *Montreal Standard*, 9 Dec. 1939, and *Montreal Gazette*, 11 Dec., reported the basic facts of the Supreme Court decision on inside pages without comment. The *Gazette*'s heading was "Negro Loses Suit against Tavern."
209 [1940] 1 DLR 81.
210 Bora Laskin, "Tavern Refusing to Serve Negro – Discrimination," *Canadian Bar Review* 18 (1940): 314–16.
211 Schmeiser, *Civil Liberties in Canada*, 274.
212 Molot, "Duty of Business," 612, 641.
213 Tarnopolsky, "Supreme Court and Civil Liberties," 76.
214 Ian A. Hunter, "The Origin, Development and Interpretation of Human Rights Legislation," in *The Practice of Freedom: Canadian Essays on Human Rights and Fundamental Freedoms*, ed. R. St J. MacDonald and John P. Humphrey (Toronto: Butterworths, 1979), 79.
215 Frank R. Scott, *The Canadian Constitution and Human Rights* (Toronto: Canadian Broadcasting Corporation, 1959), 37.
216 Scott, *Civil Liberties and Canadian Federalism*, 36.
217 (1921) 30 QKB 459, at 465–6.
218 Ibid., at 464. Emphasis added.
219 Ibid., at 460–1. Emphasis added.
220 Ibid., at 463–4. Emphasis added.
221 Ibid., at 466.
222 Ibid., at 459. Emphasis added.
223 (1924) 55 OLR 349, at 350.
224 Ibid.
225 Ibid.
226 SCR, at 144.
227 Justice Galipeault had merely ridiculed the idea that the York would lose business by serving Blacks, since in a tavern the customers were not required to associate intimately ([1938] 65 QKB 104, at 136–37).
228 Mackenzie King Diary, 30 June 1940, MG 26 J13, LAC.
229 Douglas MacLennan, "Racial Discrimination in Canada," *Canadian Forum* (Oct. 1943): 164–5. Potter, "Occupational Adjustment," has extensive evidence of NSS discrimination (see esp. 69–75, 93, 122). "Report of the Audit Committee to the Windsor Interracial Council," mimeo., 1949.

230 NSS Circular 81, 7 Nov. 1942, file 78, reel 1, Canadian Jewish Congress archives; MacLennan, "Racial Discrimination," 165; Potter, "Occupational Adjustment," 70, 93.

231 The King's Regulations and Orders for the Royal Canadian Air Force, 1924, para. 275.

232 King's Regulations for the Royal Canadian Air Force, 1943, art. 171.

233 Interview: Mr James Braithwaite, Toronto, 17 June 1990; Potter, "Negroes in Canada," 47; Potter, "Occupational Adjustment," 106–8, 130–31.

234 Regulations and Instructions for the Royal Canadian Navy, 1942, chap. 7, art. 144(2), amended by PC 4950, 30 June 1944.

235 For example, *Montreal Gazette*, 8 Dec. 1939.

236 Norman Rogers to F. Barrington Holder, 20 Jan. 1940, HQ 61-4-10, Directorate of History (hereafter DHist), Department of National Defence (hereafter DND).

237 "Coloured Troops. Remarks," Halifax, n.d. [Sept. 1939], HQ 61-4-10, DHist, DND.

238 H.E. Boak to secretary, DND, 7 Sept. 1939; Boak to Holder, 22 Sept., HQ 61-4-10, DHist, DND.

239 C.E. Connolly to secretary, DND, 25 May 1941, HQ 61-4-10, DHist, DND.

240 C.W. Clarke, memorandum, "Enlistment – Coloured Personnel," 5 June 1941, HQ 61-4-10, DHist, DND.

241 Segregated hair-care facilities for both men and women were common in Canada, particularly in Nova Scotia and southwestern Ontario (*Clarion*, 15 Dec. 1947; interview: Mr Calvin Ruck, 12 Oct. 1993; Winks, *Blacks in Canada*, 294, 325. The Toronto *Globe and Mail* reported, on 26 Feb. 1947, the predicament of Marguerite Bradley of Toronto, who was accepted by letter as a student at the Marvel Hairdressing School but rejected when she appeared in person. Marvel manager Arthur Ready told the *Globe*, "You realize it would be impossible to have a colored girl here with so many students and business connections. There would be a natural objection by the students." The Marvel attitude was apparently widespread. Viola Desmond was establishing a beauty school in Halifax where Black women could learn hairdressing skills and used her tours around the province to recruit potential students.

242 "Affidavit of Viola Irene Desmond," "Record" and "Conviction," *R. v. Desmond*, file SC 13347, vol. 937, RG 39C, Nova Scotia Archives and Records Management (NSARM); *Halifax Chronicle*, 30 Nov. 1946; *Toronto Star*, 30 Nov. 1946; *Clarion*, 1 Dec. 1946; interviews: Mr Jack Desmond,

Halifax, 19 Feb. 1990; Dr Carrie Best, New Glasgow, 20 Feb. 1990; telephone interview, Mr Henry MacNeil, 14 Oct. 1993; confidential interview with a Desmond relative, 19 June 1995.

Mr MacNeil agreed to continue our discussion in a personal interview on 15 Oct. 1993, but this was prevented by his daughter, who said that the affair "was not a proud moment in Pictou County history and should be left alone." Mr MacNeil himself insisted that the incident was "an unfortunate sequence of coincidences" and he was "glad of an opportunity to set the record straight." He maintained, for example, that Mrs Desmond grew violent and slapped the policeman's face when he politely asked her to move. Mrs Desmond's injuries were treated by a Halifax doctor on Tuesday, 12 Nov., the delay caused by the 11 Nov. public holiday. Her knee soon recovered, but she was still receiving treatment for her hip when interviewed by the *Halifax Chronicle* on 30 Nov. Her husband and another relative confirmed that the hip pain persisted for the rest of her life. Apparently Mrs Desmond was scarcely more than five feet tall, and weighed only about 100 pounds. Reports from those who knew her intimately testify to her sense of absolute shock at what had happened to her in New Glasgow. A detailed account of Mrs Desmond's ordeal in New Glasgow can be found in Constance Backhouse, "Racial Segregation in Canadian Legal History: Viola Desmond's Challenge, Nova Scotia, 1946," *Dalhousie Law Journal* 17 (1994): 299–362.

243 "Notice of Motion," "Judgment of Justice Archibald," file SC 13347, vol. 937, RG 39C, NSARM; 20 MPR 297, at 298–9.

244 MPR at 300. The editors of Criminal Reports added a "practice note" to their report of the Desmond appeal, explaining the application of *certiorari* (4 CR 200): "Ordinarily certiorari is applicable where there is (a) a total want of jurisdiction in the tribunal (e.g., where the subject-matter is not within its jurisdiction); (b) a defect in the jurisdiction of the tribunal (e.g., where an essential step preliminary to its exercise is omitted); (c) an excess of jurisdiction (e.g., where a penalty is imposed beyond that authorised by law); (d) an irregularity of substance appearing on the face of the proceedings; and (e) exceptional circumstances (e.g., fraud or perjury in procuring the conviction of accused)." D.C.M. Yardley later summarized the grounds for *certiorari* as "(i) defect of jurisdiction, (ii) breach of natural justice, and (iii) error of law on the face of the record." Yardley described the features of natural justice to be that the judicial officer must hear both sides of the story, and the accused must be accorded a fair opportunity of replying to a charge; the deciding official must have no inter-

est or any other cause for bias in the outcome; the proceedings must be reasonable; there must be no fraud involved: "The Grounds for Certiorari and Prohibition," *Canadian Bar Review* 37 (1959): 298–99, 310–21.

245 MPR, at 297; 89 CCC 278; 4 CR 200; [1947] 4 DLR 81.

246 MPR, at 307. Justice Hall's contention that Mr Bissett made an error in proceeding by way of *certiorari* rather than an appeal demonstrates the assumptions prevailing on the Nova Scotian court. Since Mr Bissett was challenging the right of the magistrate to make the decision in the first place, an appeal from the decision itself would implicitly have accepted the propriety of the method used in reaching it. He denied not Magistrate MacKay's jurisdiction to hear a case brought under the *Theatres, Cinematographs and Other Amusements Act*, but the validity of using the Act to prosecute Mrs Desmond. Mr Bissett's error was perhaps that he was too subtle in presenting his case as a "denial of natural justice," since a bench schooled in the normalcy of Jim Crow failed to grasp his point that it was more than the fine and the guilty verdict that were being challenged. In the only contemporary published comment on the case, J.B. Milner accepted the "technical" accuracy of the Desmond decision, but he also raised a question that suggests support for Bissett's argument: "The function of the court is to administer justice under the law. If there appears before a magistrate a person who is being prosecuted for improper reasons by misuse of a statute, it is surely the magistrate's duty to explore that misuse. The magistrate has no jurisdiction until an informant lays an information and, if a private informant misuses a statute and improperly lays an information, then is the magistrate acting without jurisdiction?": "Civil Liberties – Theatre Refusing to Admit Negro Person to Orchestra Seat – Violation of Tax Law – Summary Conviction – Certiorari – Abuse of Legal Process," *Canadian Bar Review* 25 (1947): 920. On the other hand, recent analysis of the Desmond case clearly faults Bissett's *certiorari* tactic. Constance Backhouse ("Racial Segregation in Canadian Legal History") appears to accept the judges' interpretation that Bissett used this method in order to have the case reconsidered at the Supreme Court level because he had missed the opportunity to lodge an appeal.

247 15 Apr. 1947.

248 The NSAACP went further and claimed that the Desmond decision had "eliminated Jim Crow" from Nova Scotia theatres. Presumably this was based on an exaggerated interpretation of William Hall's comment. *The Nova Scotia Association for the Advancement of Coloured People: Nova Scotia's No. 1 Human Rights Organization*, n.d. (recruitment and fund-raising pam-

phlet), NSAACP Membership Committee, NSARM. Colin Thomson, *Born with a Call: A Biography of Dr William Pearly Oliver, CM* (Dartmouth: Black Cultural Centre for Nova Scotia, 1986), 83–4, makes a similar error and compounds it by locating final victory for Mrs Desmond in the Supreme Court of Canada.

249 1 and 15 Aug. 1947.
250 170, file 3, vol. 20, Kaplansky Papers, A 53, MG 30, LAC; Harry Gairey, *A Black Man's Toronto, 1914–1980* (Toronto: Multicultural History Society of Ontario, 1981), 26–7; interview: Mr Harry Gairey, Toronto, 22 Feb. 1992. Interestingly this was the solution recommended by Bora Laskin in his 1940 comment on *Christie*, when he wrote, "Administrative oversight by a licensing authority of discriminatory practices by imposing conditions upon the grant of a licence or by exercising a right to refuse renewal is a possible method of dealing with the question raised by the principal case." "Tavern Refusing to Serve Negro – Discrimination," *Canadian Bar Review* 18 (1940): 316.
251 *Nova Scotia Association for the Advancement of Coloured People.*
252 *Calgary Herald*, 22 Feb.; 22 Mar.; 23 Apr. 1947; Alberta Hotel Association to Mayor J.C. Watson, 15 Mar. 1947, Palmer Research Files; city clerk to city solicitor, 18 Mar., to Legislative Committee, 1 Apr.; city solicitor to city clerk, 28 Mar., 8 Apr. 1947; interview: Mr Ted King, Vancouver, 27 Nov. 1993.
253 *Calgary Herald*, 24 Aug. 1948. Mr Ted King reported (interview: 27 Nov. 1993) that until the late 1930s he and other Black children had been allowed to swim in the pool.
254 *Calgary Herald*, 8 May 1951.
255 Canadian Press, 20 Dec. 1949.
256 Council Minutes, 8 Nov. 1949, Dresden Town Hall; *Dresden Times*, 8 Dec. 1949.
257 SO 1954, c. 28.
258 Arnold Bruner, "The Genesis of Ontario's Human Rights Legislation," *University of Toronto Faculty of Law Review* 37 (1979): 236–53; Hunter, "Origin, Development and Interpretation," 77–109; Tarnopolsky, *Discrimination and the Law*, 25–37.
259 SQ 1963, c. 40, s. 8.
260 Tremblay, "Les Noirs d'ici," 17–23; *Montreal Star*, 20 Nov. 1968; "Being Black in Montreal,' *Maclean's*, Dec. 1968, 46–7; Rosemary Brown, *Being Brown: A Very Public Life* (Toronto: Random House, 1989), esp. 23–40.
261 Dennis Forsythe, ed., *Let the Niggers Burn! The Sir George Williams University Affair and Its Caribbean Aftermath* (Montreal: Black Rose Books, 1971);

322 The African Canadian Legal Odyssey

P. Kiven Tungten, "Racism and the Montreal Computer Incident of 1969," *Race* 14 (1973): 229–40.

262 Doug Collins, "Fear and Loathing in the Canadian Mosaic," *Weekend Magazine*, 11 Sept. 1976, 8–10. The new generation of Black Montreal appears to have forgotten Fred Christie as well. Williams, *Blacks in Montreal*, does not even mention the Christie case.

263 [1940] 3 DLR 583.

264 RSBC 1936, c. 160.

265 DLR, at 585–86.

266 Ibid., at 588.

267 Ibid.

268 (1920) SC 805.

269 DLR, at 588–92.

270 Ibid., at 594.

271 Ibid., at 592–93.

272 *Canadian Bar Review* 17 (1940): 730–2.

273 Schmeiser, *Civil Liberties in Canada*, 265–72.

274 F.P. Varcoe, deputy minister of justice, to Hugh Burnett, 3 Aug. 1943, National Unity Association papers, Raleigh Township Centennial Museum.

275 City solicitor to city clerk, 8 Apr. 1947, Palmer Research Files.

276 [1940] 1 DLR 81.

277 Thibaudeau Rinfret, "Reminiscences from the Supreme Court of Canada," *McGill Law Journal* 3 (1956): 2, cited in Peter H. Russell, *The Supreme Court of Canada as a Bilingual and Bicultural Institution* (Ottawa: Royal Commission on Bilingualism and Biculturalism, 1969), 30.

278 Examination for Discovery of Theodore Stanley King, 6 Aug. 1959, file C09863, Calgary District Court; interview: Mrs Hazel Proctor Ostler, 30 May 1979, Palmer Research Files.

279 Examination for Discovery of Theodore Stanley King; (1960) 31 WWR 451; *Calgary Herald*, 26 Oct. 1959; *Calgary Albertan*, 27 Oct., and 28 Oct. 1959; interview: Mr Ted King, 27 Nov. 1993.

280 WWR at 452–59; personal communication from Mr Ted King, 13 Nov. 1993; interview: 27 Nov. Judge Farthing was apparently not alone in resenting the kind of press attention provoked by Mr Palmer. The Toronto *Globe and Mail*, 21 Apr. 1995, described Ontario Chief Justice Charles Dubin as "not enamoured of lawyers who put their case to the reporters before putting it to the judge," and quoted a speech by the chief justice in which he said, "I think one of the most serious threats to professionalism is the increased resort by some members of our profession to argue their cases in the media."

281 (1961) 35 WWR 240; interview, 27 Nov. 1993.

282 SA 1961, c. 40, s. 2.

283 [1966] CS 436.

284 (1921) 30 QKB 459, at 460–1.

285 [1940] SCR 139, at 142.

286 *Adrian Messenger Services v. The Jockey Club Ltd.*, [1972] 2 OR 369.

287 *Philippe Beaubien et Cie v. Canadian General Electric Co*, (1977) 30 CPR (2d) 100.

288 Ibid., at 145.

289 (1979) 27 OR (2d) 142; (1979) 105 DLR (3d) 707. When the plaintiff's husband ran for Parliament in the 1993 federal election, the family name was spelled Bhaduria.

290 (1703) 2 Ld. Raym. 938; 92 ER 126.

291 [1945] OR 778.

292 DLR, at 714–16.

293 (1981) 17 CCLT 106.

294 Ibid., at 120.

295 Ibid., at 119–20.

296 Ibid., at 119.

297 Ibid., at 116. Emphasis added.

8

Errors of Fact and Law: Race, Space, and Hockey in *Christie v. York*

ERIC M. ADAMS

Pre-Game: Introduction

The facts matter. As every lawyer knows, interrogating relevant facts and constructing a sympathetic narrative can win a case.[1] In litigation, facts are always open to question, but by the time those facts take their final form in the written decisions of supreme courts, they usually ossify into something beyond debate. In the confident prose of judges, facts become the incontestable history of the moments they describe. But what if those facts are wrong? This article argues that one famous case, *Christie v. York*,[2] contains errors of fact as illuminating as any of law.

As the story goes, in 1936 Fred Christie and two friends, Emile King and Steven St Jean, were on their way to a hockey game when they entered the Montreal Forum's York Tavern seeking a beer before the game. Turned away by both the waiter and bartender because he was Black,[3] Christie called the police. When the two responding constables failed to intervene, Christie sued the York in contract and in delict under Quebec's *Civil Code of Lower Canada*.[4] Finding the refusal prohibited under Quebec's *Licence Act*,[5] the trial judge concluded that "in this

Previously published in *University of Toronto Law Journal* 62 (2012).

Province, hotels and restaurants have no right to discriminate between their guests, their services being public services," and awarded Christie twenty-five dollars in damages.[6] On appeal, a majority of Quebec's Court of King's Bench held that neither the statutory nor common law of restaurants applied to taverns, and that, in the words of Bond J., "a merchant or trader is free to carry on his business in the manner that he conceives to be best for that business."[7] In his vigorous dissent, Galipeault J., quoting from *Johnson v. Sparrow*, reminded, "Our constitution (Quebec) is and always has been essentially democratic and it does not admit of distinction of races and classes. All men are equal before the law and each has equal rights as a member of the community."[8] At the Supreme Court, Justice Rinfret for the majority found that "complete freedom of commerce" prevailed and held that the York "was strictly within its rights" in refusing service to Christie and his friends.[9] Alone among his colleagues, Justice Henry Hague Davis held that taverns operating under provincial licence were bound by an implied statutory duty to sell libations without discrimination.

Christie raises a number of fascinating issues for the law, perhaps above all the capacity of private and statutory law to enforce human rights norms in the absence of explicit human rights legislation and the language of individual rights.[10] Less abstractly, the case starkly displays a moment of disturbing racism and, equally troubling, its judicial sanction. For these reasons, *Christie* is, or should be, a case of deep interest to legal scholars and historians alike. In its own time, the case generated relatively little public attention.[11] It did, however, draw the criticism of a young Bora Laskin, on the cusp of his career as a law teacher.[12] In his case comment in the *Canadian Bar Review*, Laskin questioned the majority's embrace "of the doctrine of freedom of commerce," urging instead the correctness, on both legal and policy grounds, of Davis J.'s dissent.[13] In the decades that followed, *Christie* served legal scholars such as Frank Scott as evidence for the need for judicial, legislative, or perhaps even constitutional intervention to address racial discrimination in the public and private spheres.[14] In Quebec, legal change finally arrived in 1975 when its *Charter of Human Rights and Freedoms* generally prohibited the discriminatory refusal of goods and services ordinarily available to the public.[15] From that moment, *Christie*, no longer good law in the doctrinal sense, became legal history. In chapter 7 of this volume, historian James W. St.G. Walker provides a useful case study of *Christie*, analysing its doctrinal deficiencies and placing the events in the broader history of racism in Montreal and Canada.[16] Indeed, the current chief justice of the Supreme Court points to *Christie* as emblematic of Canada's unfortunate past of "lawful" discrimination.[17]

Despite the judicial and scholarly attention *Christie* has received, a curious error of fact has never been exposed. What were Christie and his friends doing that night at the Montreal Forum? Of this we can be sure – they were *not* attending a hockey game. This factual error might not be worthy of more than a footnote if it did not also illuminate a number of critical facets of the case. Reconsidered in light of its errors of fact, *Christie* reveals a more complicated terrain than has usually been assumed. Approached as a case not simply about race, but about how race interacted with space and circumstance, this chapter frames *Christie* as a story of legal geography, of how race and racism took shape and found expression in real space – in the neighbourhoods, sports stadiums, and taverns of Montreal.[18] Equally it is a case about how space and circumstance were employed in legal arguments and judicial reasoning either to support or challenge the legality of Christie's exclusion. City space, in these respects, functioned not simply as a back-drop for the factual happenings, but rather as a necessary character in, and jurisprudential feature of, the case itself. More remarkably still, one of these definitional spaces – the hockey game – was itself an error, woven into the facts by Christie's own lawyer. It was, in fact, the boxing ring and not the hockey rink that really mattered.

Whatever one calls the methodological approach employed in this study – legal archaeology, case in context, or simply legal history – this chapter demonstrates the ongoing value of re-examining the cases of our past, not only for deficiencies of law, but for those of fact as well.[19] The results in this instance tell an important historical story not captured in the case reports about how racism in Canada functioned in urban space. Equally germane are the lessons *Christie* contains about the role of space and context more generally in the informal norms that govern city life, in conceptions of citizenship and community, and in the formal resolution of legal disputes. Part 1 begins, as most cases do, with the facts. After introducing Fred Christie, I argue that the divide between Rinfret J.'s majority judgment at the Supreme Court and Davis J.'s dissent can be traced to their divergent approaches to the facts of the case. In particular, I demonstrate that in situating Christie in spatial and contextual terms, Davis J. implicitly argues that Christie's status as a member of the community entitles him to service in quasi-public spaces such as the York. By contrast, Rinfret J.'s denuded approach to the facts supports his abstract turn to freedom of contract in determining the case's outcome. I suggest that *Christie v. York* is really a battle about which facts matter. Part 2 explores the significance of hockey as both a literal and figurative setting to the case. Understanding the history of hockey in Montreal, especially in the 1930s, illustrates why Christie's lawyer, Davis J., and subsequent commentators too, were drawn to its salience as an important framing device for the case. Part 3 reveals that, notwithstanding the hockey game's importance in Davis J.'s dissent, it is, in fact, an error. Hockey, it turns out, matters by its absence: *Christie* occurred because of racial anxieties in and around the boxing ring, the rise and fall of Joe Louis, and the Olympic hopes of a young Canadian boxer named Ray McIntyre.

The First Period: Henry Hague Davis and the Facts

Born in Jamaica in 1902, Fred Christie immigrated to Montreal in 1919, as part of the period's wave of Caribbean (or, as the region was then known, West Indian) migration to Montreal.[20] Christie found work as a chauffeur and settled in Verdun, a southern suburb of Montreal and home to a small Black community. Not far from Verdun, the neighbourhood of St Antoine housed an even larger number of Black residents – Canadian born, together with West Indian and American immigrants.[21] Regardless of their national origin, racism foreclosed most employment fields to Black Montrealers, except domestic labour or as porters (or red caps, as they were known) at the Canadian Pacific Railway (CPR).[22] In the 1920s and 1930s, life in Montreal's Black community revolved around family, the long-distance work schedules of the CPR, church on Sundays, and gatherings of the Universal Negro Improvement Association, while nights pulsed to the new sounds of jazz flowing from the clubs and dance halls.[23] But Verdun would have appealed to Fred Christie for another reason – it was but a short drive to the fabled Montreal Forum.[24]

Christie was a hockey fan – a fact that plays a subtle but important role in the case that would come to bear his name. "The appellant is a British subject residing in Verdun near the city of Montreal in the province of Quebec," Justice Davis's dissent begins, as if placing a finger on a map.

He came from Jamaica and has been permanently resident in the said province for some twenty years. He is a coloured gentleman – his own words are "a negro" though counsel for the respondent, for what reason I do not know, told him during his examination for discovery that he wanted it on record that he is "not extraordinarily black." He appears to have a good position as a private chauffeur in Montreal. He was a season box subscriber to hockey matches held in the Forum in Montreal and in that building the respondent operates a beer tavern ... The appellant had often on prior occasions to the one in question, when attending the hockey matches dropped into the respondent's tavern and bought beer by the glass there. On the particular evening on which the complaint out of which these proceedings arose occurred, the appellant with two friends – he describes one as a white man and the other as coloured – just before the hockey game went into the respondent's premises in the ordinary course. The appellant put down fifty cents on the table and asked the waiter for three steins of light beer. The waiter declined to fill the order, stating that he was instructed not to serve coloured people. The appellant and his two friends then spoke to the bartender and to the manager, both of whom stated that the reason for refusal was that the appellant was a coloured person.[25]

Davis J.'s dissent has usually gathered praise for his conclusion that "in the changed and changing social and economic conditions, different principles must necessarily be applied to the new conditions.'[26] Implicitly, Davis J. suggested that the law should not tolerate discrimination in an expanding definition of the public sphere, including licensed premises like the York Tavern. Unlike Justice Keiller MacKay's bold attack a few years later against a discriminatory covenant in *Re Drummond Wren*,[27] Davis J. never explained what social changes or new conditions mandated a shift in the law. Instead, he left it to the facts to make his argument for him.

Davis J.'s layered construction of Christie's past and present is especially notable when contrasted with Justice Rinfret's terse recitation of the same facts for the majority. "The appellant, who is a negro," Rinfret J. (himself a former Montrealer) writes, "entered a tavern owned and operated by the respondent, in the city of Montreal, and asked to be served a glass of beer; but the waiters refused him for the sole reason that they had been instructed not to serve coloured persons."[28] Here, hockey disappears, and so too does Christie himself (shorn of everything but a declarative racial category) and any sense of history and context. From the sparseness of the facts, Rinfret J. turns to abstract principle. "We ought to start from the proposition that the general law of Quebec is that of complete freedom of commerce," he declares. "Any merchant is free to deal as he may choose with any individual member of the public. It is not a question of motives or reasons for deciding to deal or not to deal; he is free to do either."[29] Having set freedom of commerce as the context, it was easy for the majority to conclude that there was nothing illegal or wrongful in discrimination in the commercial enterprise, whether regulated by the state or not.

History has been kind to Davis J.'s dissent. Beginning with Bora Laskin's case comment,[30] legal scholars have tended to focus their criticism on the majority's legal rationale, particularly the casual racism that so easily championed freedom of contract over individual equality. "The real issues dividing the judges appear to be relatively straightforward," Constance Backhouse argues. "There were two fundamental principles competing against each other: the doctrine of freedom of commerce and the doctrine of equality within a democratic society."[31] Obscured in the focus upon legal principle and the competing precedents on either side of the issue,[32] however, is the critical role of the facts in entitling Christie to equality in the first place. *Christie* was argued and decided just before the ideological rise of new and powerful legal rhetoric about the constitutional status of human rights and freedoms, including the right to equality and non-discrimination.[33] Without recourse to the language of rights, Christie's lawyer and Davis J. relied instead on a much older conception of community as the basis for reciprocal legal obligations.[34] Hence, in the opening lines of his judgment, Davis J. weaved together identity and place to contextualize, humanize, and legalize Christie by constructing him as part of the community.

Davis J. began by identifying Christie as a British subject, by definition a legal member of the political community. But Davis J. gave this legal abstraction deeper texture by localizing Christie further, noting his twenty years in Canada and rooting him in a province, city, and suburb. Thickening the bonds of community still further, Davis J. paused to describe Christie and vividly recreate the scene that gave rise to his legal action. Significantly, Christie is a *gentleman*, employed with working-class respectability and trustworthiness in a *good position* as a chauffeur. He is given the dignity of describing his own race. He has friends, one of whom is white. His demeanour at the York is polite and respectful. Above all, he has adopted that most Canadian of habits, a love of hockey: a passion that Christie indulges not in solitary fashion, but among the jostling masculine crowds of the true fans of the game – in the stands, and in the tavern between periods. Christie and his friends, Davis J. describes, *dropped in* to the York in *the ordinary course*. All of this gave subtle effect to Davis J.'s later pronouncement that the law must keep pace with "changing social ... conditions." What has changed, Davis J.'s facts adumbrate, is that Christie is already part of Montreal life, living, working, and fraternizing among its residents. He deserves equal treatment not because of any free-standing abstract individual right to equality, but because, in a very real and practical sense, he is already a functional and accepted member of the city. Hockey tells us so.

What explains Davis J.'s dissent in *Christie*? Other than the plaudits he has received for his decision in *Christie*, Henry Hague Davis has largely escaped the attention of legal historians, perhaps, in part, because his judicial career was cut cruelly short. He died in 1944 when he was fifty-eight, after serving only nine years at the Supreme Court. Born in Brockville, Ontario, in 1885, Davis was an accomplished student at the University of Toronto, graduating with a bachelor of arts in political science in 1907, a master of arts the following year, and an LLB in 1911.[35] After articling with prominent Brockville lawyer, and later federal Conservative cabinet minister, Hugh Alexander Stewart, Davis was called to the bar. A successful career in corporate-commercial litigation at (what would eventually become) Kilmer, Irving, & Davis in Toronto followed, including several trips to the Supreme Court as counsel. Davis became a King's Counsel in 1928. In 1933, the federal government appointed him to the Court of Appeal of Ontario, where he quickly earned a reputation for "patience and urbanity" on the bench and for producing "lucid and convincing" judgments.[36] Only two years later, the Conservative Minister of Justice Hugh Guthrie elevated Davis to the Supreme Court of Canada – an appointment the *Fortnightly Law Journal* applauded for its injection of legal talent and relative youth (Davis was not yet fifty).[37]

As a testament to Davis J.'s popularity among members of the bar, shortly after his appointment to the Court, the Canadian Bar Association elected him president of the association, an unusual role for a sitting judge. His role on the Court put him in a "somewhat difficult" position, he admitted in addressing the CBA's annual meetings, when it came to delivering "the customary presidential address" typically intended to deal with "concrete questions of law or national problems."[38] Attempting to steer away from anything that might be construed as controversial, Davis J. was prepared to say something about the nature of judging. Citing Lord Bacon's admonition that judges "ought to remember that their office is ... to interpret law and not to make law," Davis J. earnestly explained that the judicial role was a "high calling" demanding "hard work and the greatest of care and the most thought-ful consideration of every case that comes before you."[39] But in closing, Davis J. subverted this more narrow conception of law and judging by celebrating the law's "creative function" in tackling "the changed and changing social and economic conditions which the law exists to regulate and in which it must work"[40] (a phrase he recycled in *Christie*). Davis J. likely saw no contradiction in the two portions of his speech. In private correspondence with Caesar Wright, dean of the University of Toronto, Faculty of Law, Davis advised his friend that policy played no role in his judicial decision-making: the law, and only the law, was what mattered.[41] Yet, for Davis J., the law was clearly protean and flexible, yielding, if not to policy, then certainly to facts.

Davis J.'s blended balance of conservatism, pragmatism, and progressive functionalism earned quick favour, not only with the practising bar, but with Chief Justice Lyman Poole Duff. Despite their twenty-year gap in age, Justices Davis and Duff become close friends on a Court otherwise defined by cordial but cool relations.[42] Their mutual regard often extended into decision-making: Davis J. joined in Duff C.J.'s judgments in the most significant constitutional cases of the period: the New Deal cases,[43] and, perhaps most famously of all, Duff C.J.'s paean to freedom of expression in *Reference re Alberta Statutes*.[44] In both of these instances, Davis J. simply concurred, deferring to Duff C.J.'s reputation as the Court's leading constitutional thinker – which is not to say that the two judges could not disagree – in *Christie*, the chief justice sided with Justice Rinfret, but so did the rest of the panel, Justices Crocket and Kerwin, as well.

Although prepared to join Duff C.J. on occasionally unique constitutional paths, it was largely in business and private law that Davis J. contributed to the Court. The federal government certainly had Davis J.'s business background in mind when they appointed him as a commissioner to investigate a protracted labour dispute among Vancouver's increasingly militant dock workers.[45] Davis approached the issue of communist agitation on Vancouver's waterfront from the perspective one might expect of a former business lawyer: his conclusions, although cautious in tone, placed the blame squarely on the shoulders of the workers for breaking their collective agreement and criticized the union's "unsound and destructive leadership."[46] Again relying on Davis's business acumen, in 1938, the Liberals appointed him to investigate the controversies surrounding the awarding of the Bren machine gun contract to a supposedly Liberal-friendly manufacturing firm.

Finding no wrongdoing, Davis's findings nonetheless recommended that "the making of [munitions or armaments] contracts between Government and private manufacturers ... should be put into the hands of an expert advisory group of competent business men."[47] Davis drafted his report in December of 1938; less than six months later, having returned to his duties at the Court, he heard arguments in *Christie*. Given his background, Davis J. would not have been wholly insensitive, then, to the York Tavern's arguments that the common law protected freedom of contract and the rights of businesses to operate as they saw fit. Yet Davis J. took his dissent in an entirely different direction. He left no specific records that might explain his thinking about *Christie*, but it is not difficult to imagine that, in the summer of 1939, the impending prospects of war had him thinking in broader terms about national unity at home and discrimination abroad; certainly Christie's lawyer pushed the Court to consider the broader international context of discrimination. Moreover, Davis J.'s lively correspondence with Caesar Wright suggests a judge who, in the best sense, puzzled deeply over his cases, earnest and diligent in his efforts to find the just result.[48] Unconvinced by the competing precedents cited by the lawyers in *Christie*, Davis J. looked to the facts. As the opening of his judgment indicates, Davis J. saw in Fred Christie a man constituted by more than race. In Christie, Davis J. saw a dignified working man seeking the pleasures of his friends, hockey, and a drink. He left open, of course, the possibility of continued discrimination in a host of private enterprises (he himself was a member of the exclusive Royal Canadian Yacht Club),[49] but in the publicly regulated spaces where "social conditions" had already changed, social harmony and the common good demanded an equality of service. If Christie could cheer for Montreal's hockey teams, surely he could drink alongside his fellow fans at the Forum's bar before and after the game.

In many ways, Davis J.'s compelling treatment of the facts became the story of *Christie*. More often than not, discussions of the case mention hockey as both the context of the dispute and as a way of describing Christie. "Christie was a Negro who held a season-ticket for the hockey matches in the Montreal Forum," as Frank Scott succinctly put it[50] – all of which is ironic, given that, on the question of hockey, the majority is right and Davis J. is wrong. Christie and his friends walked into the York Tavern at 8:30 on a hot summer night, 11 July 1936.[51] There was no hockey game.

The Second Period: "The Game That Makes a Nation"

Cultural expressions linking hockey and Canadian identity are as pervasive as ice in a Canadian winter. Whether in Al Purdy's poetic celebration of the aesthetics of players in motion (culminating into an end-to-end rush into the northern lights),[52] or in a Tim Hortons commercial peddling the game's unifying appeal,[53] hockey appears across the cultural spectrum as a symbol of Canada and its citizens. To be sure, equating Canadian identity with hockey oversimplifies a complex symbol by skating over the gender, racial, ethnic, and class tensions that mark the sport and cultural practice.[54] Nevertheless, the ties between hockey and Canada have proved remarkably tenacious and enduring. "There has been one expression of nationalism that has remained constant since confederation," Michael Robidoux argues, "ice hockey."[55] While perhaps Richard Gruneau and David Whitson go too far in asserting that hockey "can be understood simply as part of the way Canadians live and make sense of their lives,"[56] it is undoubtedly true that hockey matters a great deal to a great many Canadians.[57] Andrew Holman, in his recent collection on the topic, presses scholars to recognize "the game's ability to tell stories about Canada."[58] Hockey, as it turns out, also has a story to tell about *Christie* and about the practices of inclusion and exclusion in 1930s Montreal.

Although the precise nature of hockey's origins remains contested, there is wide agreement that hockey's history, whatever its actual birth story, is deeply connected to the city of Montreal.[59] It was in Montreal in the 1870s that the modern version of the sport – organized teams, written rules, codes of conduct – began to take shape.[60] The first indoor hockey game took place at Montreal's Victoria Skating Rink in 1875.[61] On 22 March 1894, a team of Montreal amateurs won the first Stanley Cup in a game that seems not so very different from the one played today. "There were fully 5,000 persons at the match," a newspaper reported, "and tin horns, strong lungs and a general rabble predominated. The ice was fairly good. The referee forgot to see many things. The match resulted in favour of Montreal by 3 goals to 1."[62] Montreal amateur hockey continued to flourish in the decades that followed, with teams forming to represent various Anglo-ethnic divisions – the Winged Wheelers for the English, the Shamrocks for the Irish, and the Victorias for the Scottish – before finally converging in one team, the Montreal Wanderers.[63] In 1909, French-speaking Quebecers added a team to call their own when Le Club de Hockey Canadien first took to the ice.[64] It was in Montreal's Windsor Hotel, in a fug of cigar smoke, that the National Hockey League was born in 1917 – complete with two Montreal franchises, the Wanderers and the Canadiens. When a fire destroyed the Wanderers' rink in 1918 the team folded, momentarily leaving only the Canadiens to vie for the affections of Montreal's hockey fans. Montreal's French–English rivalry, however, proved too lucrative an animosity to pass up and, in 1924, the Montreal Maroons joined the NHL to take up the Wanderers' mantle. "Montreal will have two teams," the *Montreal Gazette* trumpeted, "One French-Canadian and one British Canadian!"[65] All the Maroons needed was a place to play.

The Maroons' home became arguably the most famous temple of hockey. Situated at the intersection of Atwater Avenue and Ste Catherine Street, the Montreal Forum opened in 1924 on the former site of an open-air roller-skating rink.[66] Designed by Montreal architect John Alexander Smith and built in an efficient 159 days, the Forum opened to reviews as "the biggest, the most beautiful and the most comfortable rink on the continent."[67] The Canadiens quickly adopted the Forum as their rink too. In the late 1920s and early 1930s, the great rivalry played out between Montreal's two teams in a number of epic battles and Stanley Cup victories – the Canadiens hoisted the Cup in 1924, 1930, and 1931, while the Maroons claimed the championship in 1926 and 1935. From the Forum seats, Canadiens fans fell in love with the goal-scoring prowess of the "Stratford Streak" Howie Morenz, while Maroons fans cheered for the greatest athlete of his generation, Lionel Conacher. The deepening Depression, however, took its toll on paying customers. While matches between the Maroons and Canadiens continued to draw large crowds, by the mid-1930s shrinking attendance led to worries that Montreal could not support two teams.[68]

Despite the sometimes empty brown seats, the Forum had already become something more than just a hockey rink. Ken Dryden's description of the Forum as "hockey's shrine, a glorious melting pot of team, city, and sporting tradition"[69] was true already in the 1930s. Part of its iconic status may have been a function of urban geography: the Forum stood astride both the "affluent and Anglophone residents in the City of Westmount" and the largely French-speaking populace of Montreal.[70] In hockey, if not yet in business or culture, the Forum brought the diversity of Montreal's various communities together. It is no coincidence that the rink often evokes religious imagery too – a fan's relationship to a particular team often extends into quasi-religious devotion.[71] But the Forum became, on occasion, an explicitly religious space as well – hosting, in 1928 and 1931, passion plays for large gatherings of Catholics.[72] Similarly, some ten thousand mourners packed the Forum for Howie Morenz's funeral in the spring of 1937, with fifteen thousand more lining the streets around "that great hushed house."[73] Six weeks after breaking a leg in a game against the Chicago Blackhawks, Morenz suffered a heart attack and died at the age of thirty-six. "They came in the thousands," the *Gazette* reported, "to pay him a last farewell as he lay stilled in death, just as they had come in the thousands to pay him homage when he was lightning loose on skates ... Men, women, and children – judges, doctors, lawyers, industrialists, city and provincial government officials, business executives, milkmen, postmen, house-wives, stenographers, school-children, people of all callings 10,000 strong – thronged the Forum for the Canadian Comet's funeral services."[74]

As Camil DesRoches, another local reporter, observed, "The Forum was absolutely jammed, right up to the rafters ... To me it was the most solemn ceremony I had ever seen no matter what religion you want to name." "I think the best way to explain it," DesRoches claimed, "is that to us, the French people, Morenz was French even though he wasn't. It's as simple as that."[75] After the funeral ended, the Maroons beat the Maple Leafs 3–2.

Community and identity have always taken shape and found expression across a variety of urban settings, perhaps especially so in those "intermediate spaces" situated on the "ragged frontier between public and private" where boundaries of class, gender, and race, among others, are negotiated, reinforced, and sometimes transgressed.[76] The Montreal Forum and the York Tavern within it were just such spaces.[77] There was, of course, a significant private dimension to the Forum's business – access to events was usually restricted to those who could pay for a ticket. But, like other mass spectator sports, commercial imperatives (especially during the Depression) impelled hockey to sell tickets to as many people as possible.[78] The Forum of the 1930s was a place where the wealthy and the working classes gathered together (if still separated by tiered seating) in a united enterprise. In the stands, in the tavern between periods, and over the course of a season, the individual experience of watching and cheering became a shared and collective one.[79] While loyalties to the Canadiens or the Maroons often divided along linguistic lines, when the Maroons folded in 1938, Montreal united behind one team. In the 1930s, whether at Morenz's memorial, or in a hockey season's inevitable triumphs or disappointments, the Forum became a public space for Montrealers to build, express, and share a sense of community.

Undoubtedly, hockey's capacity to construct a sense of national belonging and identity may be over-stretched. In the mid-twentieth century, however, it provided an appealing metaphor for a nation still struggling to find itself.[80] Through much of the 1940s, novelist Morley Callaghan provided a monthly column to the national magazine *New World*, often about sports.[81] Happening upon a snowy game of Toronto street hockey one night, Callaghan observed that the "Anglo Saxon faces and Scandinavian faces and Italian and Slavic faces" became "just a collection of Canadian kids playing shinny." Callaghan spun that romantic observation into "The Game That Makes a Nation" and the assertion that hockey had forged a new national identity.[82] "Hockey does more for the racial unity of this country than all the speeches of all the politicians," Callaghan argued, referring to the French–English divide. "When you saw Canadiens on the ice against the Leafs they became just a lot of Canadian boys joined in something as Canadian as a beaver: they were joined in our great northern ballet, the hockey game. And it belonged to the French just as much as it did to those who speak English."[83] Callaghan returned to the image not ten years later in *The Loved and the Lost*, his novel about divides between rich and poor, Black and white, in post-war Montreal. After "plunging into the [Forum's] cavernous corridors and up the flight of stairs," to take in a game against the Rangers, the novel's protagonist, Jim McAlpine, surveys the crowd. Awash in the "roaring ... like waves rising, falling, breaking, and always in motion," McAlpine notes the diversity of the "sea of faces" (although, to be sure, "the very poor didn't have the money to go to hockey games"): "They came from all the districts of the mountain; they came from wealthy Westmount and solid respectable French Outremount and from the Jewish shops along St. Catherine and of course a few Negroes from St. Antoine would be in the cheap seats. There they were, citizens of the second biggest French-speaking city in the world, their faces rising row on row, French faces, American faces, Canadian faces, Jewish faces, all yelling in a grand chorus; they had found a way of sitting together, yelling together, living together, too."[84]

But as *The Loved and the Lost* and the facts of *Christie* so amply reveal, hockey's bonds could be as brittle as the ice they were fashioned from.

The harmony of hockey's "great chorus" did not always survive beyond the Forum's stands.

As an ideal of citizenry and community emanating from the ice, hockey was as exclusive as it was inclusive. Hockey presented then as it does now a highly gendered image typified by a combination of aggressive masculinity, rugged individualism, and team play. The game could be graceful one moment and violent the next. Like earlier efforts to construct a Canadian identity with the symbolism of sport, hockey "envisioned an idealized image of ... a 'native Canadian' – that is, an overwhelmingly masculine figure of robust health who delighted in rugged, outdoor physical activity and espoused British ideals of order, hierarchy, and fair play."[85] And the tiered hockey stands themselves reinforced a sense of orderly class hierarchy – you sat where you could afford. Hockey was also white.[86] Although Black Maritimers played some of the first organized hockey,[87] the professional game was unofficially foreclosed to Black players until Willie O'Ree broke the National Hockey League's unofficial colour barrier in 1958.[88] Playing semi-pro in Perron, Quebec, in the 1930s and 1940s, Herbert Carnegie, the child of Jamaican immigrants, recalled the racial taunts of the crowd and watching a string of inferior players called ahead of him to NHL training camps. "I will give $10,000 to anyone who can turn Herbert Carnegie white," Conn Smythe, owner of the Toronto Maple Leafs, is reputed to have said.[89] And yet the game beckoned to Fred Christie. He held season's tickets, although whether he cheered for the Montreal Canadiens or the Maroons we do not know. Whether it was the game's athletic lyricism, competitive excitement, the thrill of a streaking Morenz, the acrobatics of a glorious save, or simply the chance to belong to a team, and a city that drew Christie to the Forum, we can only wonder.[90]

It was perhaps with this community-building vision of hockey in mind that Christie's lawyer, Lovell C. Carroll, penned the factum in Christie's appeal to the Supreme Court of Canada in the spring of 1939. "The Appellant was a season box subscriber to hockey contests at the Forum," Carroll mentioned early in setting out the facts. It was at "about 8:30 p.m. on Saturday, July 11th 1936, before a hockey game," Carroll continues, that Christie and his friends entered the York Tavern.[91] That statement cannot be true. The hockey season had ended for both the Canadiens and the Maroons by the end of March.[92] There was no hockey game that night. Christie's factum to the Supreme Court marked the first appearance of this error: neither the Plaintiff's Declaration, filed 10 September 1936, nor the transcripts of the discoveries of the various witnesses, nor the materials filed to respond to the York Tavern's appeal to the Court of King's Bench mentions hockey in relation to the events at issue.[93] What appears likely is that years removed from the actual events, and with limited contact with Fred Christie himself, Carroll drafted his appeal materials endeavouring to place the facts in their best light. In the absence of a discourse of rights, hockey became a powerfully succinct way of emphasizing Christie's belonging – a shorthand way of capturing an argument about community and equality, especially in Montreal. "The common law of Quebec," Carroll asserted, "is the free enjoyment by all its citizens of the facilities for education, nourishment and happiness which are available."[94] Again, this was not so much a question of individual rights as of a society's ability to function in an era of increasing diversity. That need was ever sharper in a place where French and English lived side-by-side, and against the backdrop of impending war. "If this ridiculous exclusion is sanctioned by law," Carroll pointed out, "it would be legal for one tavern to refuse Roman Catholics or Protestants, or to place a sign that 'Only Christians are admitted,' or admit only those speaking English, until this country bristled with racial, religious and colour discrimination like certain European countries."[95] Discrimination, Carroll implied, was impractical in a province of linguistic and religious diversity. Worse still, it was the practice of the enemy.

Carroll was a young and ambitious lawyer when he took on Christie's case. Born in Westmount, Quebec, in 1908, Carroll had been called to the bar of Quebec in 1933 after earning a BA and MA from McGill. He displayed an early aptitude for legal writing, graduating with an LLM in 1933 from the University of Montreal; in short order he produced a number of legal texts dealing with various matters under Quebec law.[96] Politically active, Carroll ran unsuccessfully for the Conservative Party in the 1936 provincial election – his defeat coming just a few weeks before he took on Christie's case.[97] It is not entirely clear how Carroll came to be retained. We do know that the flagrant racism displayed at the York Tavern that night galvanized Montreal's Black community and that the Fred Christie Defence Committee seized responsibility for funding the case. "Money flowed in," Walker writes, "literally in nickels, dimes, and quarters, collected in the black barbershops and newsstands, at Union Church and the campaign office."[98] The committee was chaired by Dr Kenneth I. Melville, a professor in McGill's Department of Pharmacology, and, like Christie, a Black, Jamaican-born immigrant.[99] It seems likely that as the case went from trial, to appeal, and finally, to the Supreme Court of Canada, Carroll's dealings were largely with Melville and the committee rather than Christie. In the context of an ever-diminishing role for Christie in his own case, it is not difficult to see how the error about hockey wove itself into fact, especially when that error offered an implicit and attractive argument bolstering Christie's case.

Third Period: Law and Circumstance

What, then, of the truth? What were Christie and his friends, Emile King and Steven St Jean, doing that hot and humid evening at the York Tavern? It was, as it happened, a busy weekend for sports in the city. The Olympic track and field trials to finalize the Canadian team shortly bound for Berlin were taking place at Molson Stadium, while, across town, the Montreal Royals (nine years before they signed Jackie Robinson) beat the Newark Bears at Delorimier Stadium.[100] At the Forum that Saturday night, the final preparations were being put in place for the upcoming Olympic boxing trials, which were set to commence on Monday evening.[101] Although the boxing tournament had yet to begin, Christie remembered the bar as crowded that night – "some sixty or seventy people" – when the waiter and bartender refused to serve him.[102] The hockey season now a memory, the York was on the cusp of a sporting event of a different sort.

As Christie and his friends discovered that evening, the informal rules that governed racist exclusions – the so-called colour bar – were fluid and contextual.[103] Christie had, as it happened, enjoyed a beer at the York Tavern on a number of previous occasions, including during the hockey season that had ended that spring. That fact seemed to catch the York's lawyer, Hazen Hansard (almost comically) off-guard when he cross-examined Christie before trial:

Q. Have you ever had any beer at the York Tavern and at the Forum?
A. Yes, regularly at the York because I follow athletic sports and I used to go there and drink all the time.
Q. Is that since or before the occasion you refer to in your action?
A. Oh, before the action.
Q. Before the action you had been there?
A. Oh yes, regularly, ever since they have been open.
Q. That is, the York Tavern?
A. Yes.

Q. And when you say since the place has been open, you mean since the tavern has been in the Forum?

A. The York was further down the street; then, they converted this place into a tavern, and they brought the licence ... I have been to both places.

Q. You have been to both places?

A. Yes, repeatedly.

Q. You have been repeatedly to both taverns?

A. Yes.

Q. That is, you have been repeatedly to the York Tavern in the Forum building?

A. Yes.

Q. And you were served with beer?

A. Yes.

Q. Before the occasion in question?

A. Certainly.[104]

This explains, in part, why Christie reacted as he did on the night of 11 July: during the hockey season he and his friends had been to the York many times; in the heat of summer before a boxing tournament, suddenly, the rules changed. The capriciousness of the racism must have been as confounding and frustrating to Christie as it was offensive.

But really there was nothing new in this. In her dated study from the early 1930s, Ida Graves perspicaciously notes that although the Black community possessed "the same rights and status as other races," there existed "scope within the law for the expression of personal prejudice by means that actually impose public disabilities."[105] "The leading hotels," she offers by way of example, "refuse to state whether they have a definite policy with regard to coloured people. Some hotels admit them at times, particularly if other business is not very good, and since the attitude of the management is based, not on a national principle, but on the fear of offending the prejudices of its more profitable clientele, the degree of their colour does much to determine the treatment that Negroes receive."[106]

Hence, it was "the degree ... of colour" that the York's lawyer turned to next. Needing an explanation for why Christie might have been to the York before, Hansard wanted it placed on the record that neither Christie nor King was "extraordinarily black."[107] The notation later confused Justice Davis, but it served a purpose as far as Hansard was concerned: if Christie and King had been served at the York before, it was on account of their having previously passed as white, not because of any inconsistency on the tavern's part. Indeed, their waiter that night was sufficiently uncertain about whether to serve Christie, King, and St Jean that he sought the guidance of his manager before apologizing that he could not take Christie's and King's order.[108] But hockey *had* welcomed Christie and King, and they assumed that extended to the York Tavern when they gathered with fellow fans before and after games, and between periods. If the York maintained a colour barrier during the hockey season – and it claimed that it did – it certainly showed no real interest in enforcing it. But, now summer, the York was keen to reassert its rules of exclusion.

Why? The answer lies in the ring. Among the boxers competing for a coveted spot on Canada's Olympic roster was welterweight hopeful, and "local Negro star," Raymond Clifford McIntyre.[109] Originally from Saint John, New Brunswick, McIntyre now made Montreal home. Still a teenager, McIntyre had earned a reputation as a hard-hitting but elegant fighter.[110] The York surely anticipated McIntyre's presence would draw a large crowd of Black men from St Antoine and Verdun. Indeed, as one press report framed it, McIntyre would be fighting to defend "les couleurs locales."[111] From the York's perspective, a few light-skinned Black fans could slip through the York during the hockey season without much notice or concern, but a larger gathering – exuberant in victory or desultory in defeat – was another matter.

In the 1930s, racial politics still dominated boxing. "Boxing is, and always has been," Jeffrey T. Sammons argues, "a sport of confrontation … fighting between blacks and whites did not indicate comradeship or social acceptance."[112] On the contrary, in the first decades of the twentieth century, sportswriters and promoters alike framed bouts in the ring between Black and white opponents (when they were allowed at all) as contests for racial supremacy.[113] Prejudice still lurked strongly at ringside, in newspaper reporting, and in the sport's backrooms and corridors of power when Detroit's Joe Louis, the "Brown Bomber," emerged as a heavyweight fighter in the 1930s. A symbol of strength and hope to Black Americans, Louis's victories in the ring, like Jack Johnson's earlier in the century, elicited spontaneous celebrations in the streets of Black neighbourhoods.[114] Louis's matches were invariably framed as racial battles as much as individual ones, perhaps never more so than in two historic bouts with German Max Schmeling, a favoured athlete of the Nazi Party.

The first Louis-Schmeling fight took place at Yankee Stadium in New

York City, 19 June 1936, three weeks before Christie's fateful encounter at the York. Like sports fans around the world, Montrealers listened in shock when Clem McCarthy's radio broadcast informed them that Schmeling's powerful right had put Louis down upon the canvas.[115] Schmeling's knockout victory over the previously undefeated Louis unleashed a series of riots across American cities. From the wire service, the *Montreal Gazette* picked up sensational stories reporting "bands of angry Negro hoodlums" attacking whites in Harlem.[116] Separate stories mentioned similarly violent riots in Black neighbourhoods in Chicago and Detroit where "cheering Max Schmeling backers" taunted Louis's dejected fans.[117] Schmeling's defeat of Louis was the biggest sports story in the world, and the extensive newspaper coverage before and after the fight would not have escaped the attention of the York Tavern's owners. Three weeks later, wanting neither Black patrons nor any celebrations or backlash that might accompany a Ray McIntyre win or loss, in the days leading up to the Forum's boxing tournament, the York simply asserted: no Blacks allowed.

Perhaps puzzlingly, the York never attempted to argue the truth – that the context of the boxing tournament and the threat of unrest provided a compelling reason to assert its right to refuse service to Christie and King. We will likely never know why not. It is possible that their lawyer, Hazen Hansard, did not suitably know the facts and missed an opportunity. It is equally possible, however, that he or his clients worried that the York's flexible practices of inclusion and exclusion lacked the static steadiness and consistency of law, or that a history of lax enforcement would implicitly concede that such restrictions were not necessary. Of course, the colour bar's amorphous flexibility was a powerful tool; recall, Graves's observation that Montreal hotels refused to say whether they discriminated by race or not. Such vagueness allowed businesses to tailor the colour bar to the economic climate, or whatever other considerations of time, place, and circumstance suited them. It also allowed owners to evade responsibility for discrimination, to shift the practice from the sunlight to the shadows.[118] But such murkiness might have concerned Hansard. Instead his litigation strategy (ultimately a winning one) seemed premised on drawing sharp and clear lines of acceptable practice across the map of Montreal.

Hansard, like Carroll, was still relatively early in his career, but, as a lawyer with Brown, Montgomery, and McMichael – then the top corporate litigation firm in Montreal, if not Canada – he had acquired considerable experience representing business clients.[119] And it was the practical demands on business and the demarcations of geography that Hansard emphasized when examining his witnesses in defending the York. During questioning of one the York's waiters, Hansard led him to explain that there were other drinking establishments that catered to Black Montrealers: were there not "taverns down on St Antoine St, what might be said to be the negro quarter," where Christie might be served, he asked. There was simply no need for Christie and King to drink where they were not wanted. That line of inquiry brought a strong rebuke from the trial judge, Justice Phillipe Demers. "That is not the question," Demers J. intervened. "It is a question of rights, that is if you have the right to refuse a man on account of his color. It is a question of law, not of evidence." But Hansard persisted. "The circumstances vary for different places," he offered. "No, no circumstances, it is a question of law whether you have the right or not," the judge declared.[120] This minor skirmish between judge and counsel revealed a tension between facts and law that, to greater or lesser degrees, defines all legal cases. Demers J. sought to impose on the messy and uncertain facts the formal logic of law. In refusing to hear from Hansard's other witnesses, the trial judge wanted fewer facts, not more. For Demers J., *Christie* turned on a relatively straightforward question of law: was a state-licensed tavern required to provide service to all? He thought that it was, regardless of the fluidity of the colour bar, the availability of other drinking establishments, or the sport that happened to be featured at the Forum that particular evening.[121]

But for all of Justice Demers's efforts to impose legal clarity and Hansard's attempt to reveal clear rules, the vagaries of context and circumstance tell us more about *Christie* than the relevant precedents and prevailing statutes. The particulars of location, time, and space created the unique features of the facts, just as they anchored Justice Davis's dissent. The importance of space was a point Hansard emphatically conveyed in his opening question to Christie. "You say you reside in Montreal," he challenged, and yet "I notice in the writ you are described as residing at 716 Galt Avenue." "Well," Christie admitted, "at Verdun, I should have said Verdun."[122] Verdun was not Montreal. And neither, for that matter, were the "taverns down on St Antoine" the York Tavern of Ste Catherine. Black was not "extraordinarily black." July was not March. Perhaps most importantly, a summer Saturday night on the eve of a boxing tournament featuring a local Black boxer was not a winter hockey game involving the Canadiens or the Maroons. Such facts mattered intimately to the informal soft law of inclusion and exclusion as practised in the streets, the stadiums, and the taverns of Montreal. Just as Carroll and Davis J. turned to facts – even an erroneous one – to embed Christie in a community and entitle him to equal treatment, Hansard employed the facts to substitute bright lines for blurry ones, to construct an unspoken colour bar that Christie and King insisted on breaking.

The blame for these unfortunate events, Hansard repeatedly and consistently alleged, lay squarely on Christie's and King's shoulders. It was Christie and King, after all, who knew or should have known that they were not welcome at the York, regardless of whether they had slipped past the colour bar on occasions past. "The Plaintiffs well knew," the Defendant's Plea insisted, "when they entered the Defendant's tavern that beer was not sold there to coloured persons, and any notice which was attracted to the Plaintiffs on the occasion in question arose solely out of the fact that the Plaintiffs persisted in demanding beer after they had been so refused and even went to the length of calling the police which was entirely unwarranted in the circumstances."[123]

For the most part, in Montreal as elsewhere in Canada, the colour bar worked because it did not have to work at all. "Did you refuse [Black customers] at the Chateau Laurier?" Justice Demers wanted to know of one of the York's experienced waiters. "I never had the chance to refuse them," he replied, "because they never came in there."[124] "Undoubtedly prejudice and discrimination against the Negro are deep-rooted and widespread in Canada," Ida Graves suggested, "but there has on the whole been little friction or dispute between the white and coloured races. No doubt this is due largely to the fact that they rarely meet in pursuit of ordinary business or recreation."[125] "There weren't many Negros in Montreal," Callaghan wrote in *The Loved and the Lost*, "and those who were there lived between St Antoine and the railroad tracks ... but they couldn't live in the good hotels or go into the select bars and knew it. There was never any trouble."[126]

Fred Christie caused trouble. He did so by refusing to limit his use of urban space, by ignoring the rules of timing and circumstance that suddenly foreclosed the York Tavern to him, by seeking to belong to the community of which he was a part, and by insisting upon legal rights he did not, as it turned out, possess. Sadly, the York tactic worked: Justice Rinfret's majority decision repeats Hansard's accusation of blame almost verbatim.[127] In *Christie*, the soft law of the colour bar proved far stronger than anything Christie could fashion out of the facts, or the hard law precedents and statutes at his disposal. Disappointed and disillusioned by the outcome of his case, Fred Christie left Montreal and moved to Vermont.[128]

Overtime: Conclusion

Today, *Christie* occupies an uncertain place in the legal canon. As a matter of legal history, the case is reasonably well known in broad outline, although it is not widely taught or judicially cited.[129] There are good reasons, however, to keep *Christie* from sinking too deeply into the recesses of legal memory. As A.W.B. Simpson reminds us, cases are in themselves "historical event[s]."[130] Certainly *Christie* has an important historical story to tell about an aspect of Canadian racism that has tended to lurk more quietly in the shadows than its more explicit American counterpart. Canada's colour bar did not need the backing of racist legislation, nor did it require the obviousness of a "Whites Only" sign. The colour bar operated, instead, with invisible lines and quiet whispers. "In refusing to sell beer to [Christie], the [York's] employees did so quietly, politely and without causing any scene or commotion whatever," Justice Rinfret pointed out.[131] Sometimes, as it turns out, the colour bar could be quiet to the point of silence. Christie could drink at the York Tavern in the exuberance of hockey season; in the more racially charged context of a boxing tournament, he could not. A lighter-skinned Black man could sometimes evade the bar, but sometimes not. Flexible and protean, the colour bar was equally adept at disguise, framing itself, as it did in the *Christie* litigation, as a sensitive business practice and clear rule, or, more abstractly still, as a matter of freedom of contract. In practice, however, racial exclusion existed as a pernicious social reality, evasive and slippery even as it mapped urban spaces with racial ideologies and affected the everyday lived experiences of city-dwellers.

But we do a disservice to *Christie* to read the case only as history, and not only because there is a risk of overlooking the ways in which the colour bar's subtle forms may still operate across city space.[132] More than just an illumination of the past, *Christie* is equally a case about the spatial and temporal dimensions of law. "The law both structures our understanding of certain spaces," Desmond Manderson explains, "while at the same time those spaces themselves radically transform the experience, application, and effect of the law."[133] Put another way, "law and space are mutually constitutive."[134] Where and when are key elements of *Christie*, although they lay buried in and beyond the facts.

Rather than simply a case about racism in an abstract sense, *Christie* illustrates how racist practices inscribed themselves in real spaces and in different ways in different moments – in the streets, neighbourhoods, and taverns of Montreal. When Hansard parsed the differences between Verdun and Montreal, drew boundaries between the bars of St Antoine and the York, and castigated Christie for transgressing an invisible colour bar he should have seen, he attempted to transform the case into one of geography. By contrast, Davis J. turned to a different set of spaces to ground his argument about Christie's legal entitlements to service. Rather than a discourse of rights, it was instead a construct of community that Davis J. employed. He did so in explicitly spatial terms, by situating Christie in physical geography – his province, his city, and his neighbourhood – but also in the lived spaces of his community – the streets he drove to earn his living, the seats of the Montreal Forum from where he cheered, and the tavern where he drank among his fellow sports fans. Still another story of space and time is the one that Davis J. and the facts get wrong. If hockey was the game that made the nation, then boxing was the sport that threatened to tear it apart. Set against the backdrop of racial violence in the United States, in the summer of 1936, on the eve of Berlin's racially charged Olympic Games, a boxing tournament infused the York tavern with new rules and meanings about who belonged.

All of this suggests that law unfolds in complex terrains even as the abstract generalities of legal discourse do their part to flatten and homogenize them. And as complicated as are the literal and figurative spaces in which the law operates, so too are the people who give them life. The facts capture something of Fred Christie's quiet dignity and obvious courage in calling out a wrong, but his motivations, personality, and reflections on the case remain obscure. No doubt history will continue to look favourably upon Davis J.'s *Christie* dissent – errors of fact and all. But it is worth remembering that he too could be capable of contradictions. In 1937, Davis J. addressed a gathering of the Minnesota State Bar Association on the topic of judicial appointments in Canada. He never mentioned hockey, but his speech did open with a racist joke. "After hearing the very flattering words of introduction by your distinguished president and by Justice Stone," Davis J. began, "I confess that I feel somewhat as the darkey did when he was asked for the loan of five dollars. He said he was sorry he didn't have it, but he thanked him for the compliment."[135] As for Hazen Hansard, after representing the York in *Christie*, he continued his distinguished litigation career with many return trips to the Supreme Court. In 1964 his peers elected him as president of the Canadian Bar Association, and in that capacity he offered elegant testimony to the ideal of equality that lay at the heart of Canadian law. "Great effort has gone into the building up of this wonderful country by many Canadians without thought of race, creed, colour or national origin," he proclaimed. "Let us not discard that effort and the wisdom of those men."[136]

NOTES

This chapter first appeared in *University of Toronto Law Journal* 62 (2012). This research was aided by an EFF/SAS Grant from the University of Alberta and the assistance of the Osgoode Society for Canadian Legal History. I presented earlier versions at the Canadian Law and Society Annual Conference, the Faculty Seminar at the University of Alberta, Faculty of Law, and the Alberta Legal History Group at the University of Alberta. I thank the participants of those sessions for helpful feedback. I also thank Philip Girard, Sarah Hamill, Robert Leckey, Sarah Krotz, Barry Sullivan, Bruce Ziff, as well as *UTLJ*'s anonymous reviewers for encouragement and criticism. I am grateful to Kelsey Robertson, Matthew Greiner, and Justina Di Fazio for skilled research and editorial assistance. Finally, this chapter owes a particular debt to Jordan Stanger-Ross for many conversations and more than a few hockey games.

1 Indeed, Oliver Wendell Holmes famously worried that facts matter too much by "appeal[ing] to feelings" and "distort[ing] judgment": *Northern Securities Co. v. United States*, 193 US 197, 400 (1904). See also Frederick Schauer, "Do Cases Make Bad Law?," *University of Chicago Law Review* 73 (2006): 883.

2 [1940] SCR 139 [*Christie*].

3 I use the term *Black* in this article – homogenizing and problematic as that description remains – because Christie's racialization as Black mattered deeply to the society that he lived in, and, as it happens, to the facts of his case. It is important to acknowledge, of course, that "races are invented categories – designations coined for the sake of grouping and separating people along lines of presumed difference." Matthew Frye Jacobson, *Whiteness of a Different Color: European Immigrants and the Alchemy of Race* (Cambridge, MA: Harvard University Press, 1999), 4. As Timothy J. Stanley puts it, "It is not human differences per se that make racism but racisms that make 'race.'" *Contesting White Supremacy: School Segregation,*

Anti-Racism, and the Making of Chinese Canadians (Vancouver: UBC Press, 2011), 6.

4 Article 1053 of the Civil Code of Lower Canada provided, "Every person capable of discerning right from wrong is responsible for the damage caused by his fault to another, whether by positive act, imprudence, neglect or want of skill."

5 *Revised Statutes of Quebec* 1925, c. 25. Section 33 provided, "No licensee for a restaurant may refuse, without reasonable cause, to give food to travelers." Section 19 defined a restaurant as "an establishment, provided with special space and accommodation where, in consideration of payment, food (without lodging) is habitually furnished to travelers." A traveller was "a person who, in consideration of a given price ... per meal, à table d'hôte, or à la carte, is furnished by another person with food."

6 *Christie v. York Corporation* (1937), 75 *Recueils de Jurisprudence de Québec* 136, 138 (SC).

7 *York Corporation v. Christie* (1938), 65 *Recueils de Jurisprudence de Québec* 105, 108, 125 (KB). Put another way, Barclay J. added, "The fact that a particular individual has certain preferences is not a matter of public concern."

8 Ibid., 126, quoting *Johnson v. Sparrow* (1899), 15 Quebec Superior Court Reports 104, 108. If taverns could exclude a Black man, Galipeault J. pondered, "pourquoi n'y aurait-il pas des taverniers qui établiraient la même exclusion quant aux Juifs, aux Syriens, aux Chinois, aux Japonais, quant à un certain nombre de races?" ... ou "les gens d'une certaine religion et excluraient les autres?" ou "que seuls les clients parlant une certaine langue seraient admis, quand les autres seraient exclus?" (137).

9 *Christie*, 142, 145.

10 See generally, Daniel Friedmann and Daphne Barak-Erez, eds., *Human Rights in Private Law* (Oxford: Hart Publishing, 2001).

11 The *Montreal Gazette* gave short reports of the decisions at trial and at the Supreme Court of Canada: James W. St.G. Walker, "*Christie v. York*," chap. 7 in this volume.

12 See Philip Girard, *Bora Laskin: Bringing Law to Life* (Toronto: Osgoode Society for Canadian legal History and University of Toronto Press, 2005), 117–18.

13 Bora Laskin, "Tavern Refusing to Serve Negro: Racial Discrimination," *Canadian Bar Review* 18 (1940): 314.

14 Frank R. Scott, *The Canadian Constitution and Human Rights* (Toronto: Canadian Broadcasting Corporation, 1959), 36–7; F.R. Scott, "The Bill of Rights and Quebec Law," *Canadian Bar Review* 37 (1959): 135, 143; F.R. Scott, *Civil Liberties & Canadian Federalism* (Toronto: University of Toronto Press,

1959), 36. See also D.A. Schmeiser, *Civil Liberties in Canada* (Oxford: Oxford University Press, 1964), 263–4.

15 *Statutes of Quebec* [SQ] 1975, c. 6, s. 12. Earlier Quebec statutes had precluded discrimination in hotels, restaurants, and camping grounds (SQ 1963, c. 8) and employment (SQ 1964, c. 46). See Henry L. Molot, "The Duty of Business to Serve the Public: Analogy to the Innkeeper's Obligation," *Canadian Bar Review* 16 (1968): 612. Although the trajectories were similar, different provinces developed their human rights regimes at different times and in slightly different manners. See generally R. Brian Howe and David Johnson, *Restraining Equality: Human Rights Commissions in Canada* (Toronto: University of Toronto Press, 2000), 3–36; Carmela Patrias, "Socialists, Jews, and the 1947 Saskatchewan Bill of Rights," *Canadian Historical Review* 87 (2006): 265; Carmela Patrias and Ruth A. Frager, "'This Is Our Country, These Are Our Rights': Minorities and the Origins of Ontario's Human Rights Campaigns," *Canadian Historical Review* 82 (2001): 1; Walter Suma Tarnopolsky, *Discrimination and the Law in Canada* (Toronto: Richard Boo, 1982), 26–37.

16 Walker, "*Christie v. York.*"

17 Beverley McLachlin, "Racism and the Law: The Canadian Experience," *Journal of Law & Equality* 1 (2002): 23. "Far from being the important step toward equality that many Black Canadians had hoped for," she writes, "the Supreme Court of Canada's decision in *Christie* served only to further entrench and perpetuate racial discrimination in Canada." See also the recent human rights ruling which held that "*Christie* now stands in sharp contrast to the present law in Canada": *Giguere v. Popeye Restaurant*, [2008] *Human Rights Tribunal of Ontario* 2, 74. Of course in relegating *Christie* to the past, there is a danger of overlooking the more subtle but still pernicious forms of racism that operate within the law: see Carol A. Aylward, *Canadian Critical Race Theory: Racism and the Law* (Halifax: Fernwood, 1999), 78–9.

18 See generally Nicholas K. Blomley, *Law, Space, and the Geographies of Power* (New York: Guilford, 1994); David Delaney, *Race, Place, and the Law, 1836–1948* (Austin: University of Texas Press, 1998); Laura Beth Nielsen, "The Power of 'Place': Public Space and Rights Consciousness," in *The New Civil Rights Research: A Constitutive Approach*, ed. Benjamin Fleury-Steiner and Laura Beth Nielsen (Burlington, VT: Ashgate, 2006), 217; Franz Von Benda-Beckmann, Keebet von Benda-Beckmann, and Anne Griffiths, eds., *Spatializing Law: An Anthropological Geography of Law and Society* (Burlington, VT: Ashgate, 2009).

19 On the methodologies of the case-in-context method, see Angela Fernan-

dez, "An Object Lesson in Speculation: Multiple Views of the Cathedral in *Leaf v. International Galleries*," *University of Toronto Law Journal* 58 (2008): 481; Debora L. Threedy, "A Fish Story: *Alaska Packers' Association v. Domenic*," *Utah Law Review* (2000): 185; Debora L. Threedy, "Legal Archaeology: Excavating Cases, Reconstructing Context," *Tulane Law Review* 80 (2006): 1197; Joan Vogel, "Cases in Context: Lake Champlain Wars, Gentrification and *Ploof v. Putnam*," *St Louis University Law Journal* 45 (2001): 791; A.W.B. Simpson, *Leading Cases in the Common Law* (Oxford: Oxford University Press, 1995);. See generally Jim Phillips, "Why Legal History Matters," *Victoria University of Wellington Law Review* 41 (2010): 293.

20 Details from Fred Christie's life are drawn from Walker, "*Christie v. York*," and the discovery and court transcripts located in the original case record, nos 151592-152164, court file 151 809, Bibliothèque et Archives nationales du Québec (hereafter BAQ). See generally, Dorothy W. Williams, *The Road to Now: A History of Blacks in Montreal* (Montreal: Véhicule, 1997), 44. Elsewhere, Williams writes that by the late 1920s, "West Indians made up forty percent of the total Black population in Montreal. Generally they were the most educated, vocal and 'British' of the Black population." Dorothy W. Williams, *Blacks in Montreal 1628–1986: An Urban Demography* (Cowansville, QC: Éditions Yvon Blais, 1989), 33.

21 By 1941, the total population of permanent Black Montrealers was probably somewhere close to four thousand. Williams, *Blacks in Montreal*, 45.

22 As Charles Ashby recalled, the Depression made the limited employment situation even worse: "It was terrible. Half of the men were out of work … everything was in a slump and the Black community suffered like everyone else, except that there was no work at all." See Patti Vipond, "An Interview with Charles Ashby of Montreal," in *A Key to Canada: Part II* (Montreal: The National Black Coalition of Canada, 1976), n.p. On employment prospects generally, see James W. St.G. Walker, *Racial Discrimination in Canada: The Black Experience* (Ottawa: Canadian Historical Association, 1985), 15–16; Williams, *The Road to Now*, 47, 78. On racial discrimination in employment from a slightly later period, see Carmela Patrias, "Race, Employment Discrimination, and State Complicity in Wartime Canada, 1939–1945," *Labour / Le Travail* 59 (2007): 9; for the complicated racializations of life on the railway, see Sarah-Jane Mathieu, *North of the Color Line: Migration and Black Resistance in Canada, 1870–1955* (Chapel Hill: University of North Carolina Press, 2010).

23 On the influence of Marcus Garvey in Montreal, see Carla Marano, "'Rising Strongly and Rapidly': The Universal Negro Improvement Association in Canada, 1919–1940," *Canadian Historical Review* 91 (2010): 233; for image-

ry of Montreal's famed 1930s nightlife, see Wilfred Emmerson Israel, "The Montreal Negro Community" (MA thesis, McGill University, 1928), 189; John Gilmore, *Swinging in Paradise: The Story of Jazz in Montreal* (Montreal: Véhicule, 1988); Nancy Marrelli, *Stepping Out: The Golden Age of Montreal Night Clubs* (Montreal: Véhicule, 2004).

24 Christie lived at 716 Galt Avenue, close to Willibrord Park's many outdoor rinks. Among the working-class kids scoring goals in endless games of wintertime shinny in the 1930s was Scotty Bowman who, after his own promising career was derailed by a serious injury, would go on to attain legendary status as coach of the Montreal Canadiens. Ken Dryden, *The Game: A Thoughtful and Provocative Look at a Life in Hockey* (Toronto: Macmillan, 1983), 35–6.

25 *Christie*, 146.

26 Freedom of contract, Davis J. held, "had a very definite place in the older economy and still applies to the case of an ordinary merchant," but "when the State enters the field and takes exclusive control of the sale to the public of such a commodity as liquor, then the old doctrine of the freedom of the merchant to do as he likes has ... no application." *Christie*, 152.

27 [1945] OR 778.

28 *Christie*, 141.

29 Ibid., 142.

30 Laskin, "Tavern Refusing to Serve."

31 Constance Backhouse, *Colour-Coded: A Legal History of Racism in Canada, 1900–1950* (Toronto: Osgoode Society for Canadian Legal History and University of Toronto Press, 1999), 256.

32 The majority found solace in a series of Canadian cases upholding discriminatory practices in theatres (*Loew's Montreal Theatres v. Reynolds*, [1921] 30 RJ 459 (KB)) and restaurants (*Franklin v. Evans*, [1924], 26 OWN 65 (HC)), while Davis J. distinguished them as not involving "complete government control" of the sale of the commodity. He refused, however, to draw upon the parallel stream of precedent that had served Galipeault J. in dissent in the court below.

33 See Eric M. Adams, "The Idea of Constitutional Rights and the Transformation of Canadian Constitutional Law, 1930–1960" (SJD thesis, University of Toronto, 2009).

34 In the American context, A.K. Sandoval-Strausz convincingly demonstrates that the common law protection of travellers – "a quiet but powerful strand of Anglo-American law" – deeply influenced the development of American civil rights jurisprudence from the late nineteenth century to the 1960s. "The origins of the law of innkeepers and that of common carri-

ers," he writes, "are found not in the natural rights tradition of the Enlightenment, but rather in classical antiquity and with the monarchical state." A.K. Sandoval-Strausz, "Travelers, Strangers, and Jim Crow: Law, Public Accommodations, and Civil Rights in America," *Law and History Review* 23 (2005): 53, 54, 68.

35 "Supreme Court of Canada Judges: The Hon HH Davis," *Fortnightly Law Journal* 4 (1935): 233–4. Unfortunately, Davis's master's thesis, apparently titled, "Unemployment in Canada: A Social and Economic Problem," cannot be located by librarians or archivists at the University of Toronto.

36 Ibid.

37 "Davis Appointed to Supreme Court," Toronto *Globe*, 1 Feb. 1935.

38 "Lawyers and Public Service," *Canadian Bar Review* 15 (1937): 509, 511.

39 Ibid., 513.

40 Ibid., 514. Again, Davis failed to elaborate the changes he had in mind, but he did note Canada's constitutional "evolution" towards legal independence as a sovereign nation.

41 Davis to Wright, 16 Sept. 1938, box 2, B1982-0028, Wright Papers, University of Toronto Archives (hereafter UTA). "That may be a very sound social doctrine," Davis conceded, "but it did not control my consideration or decision in the matter. I attempted to deal with the difficult question as one purely of law."

42 David Ricardo Williams, *Duff: A Life in the Law* (Vancouver: UBC Press, 1984), 83, 182, 247.

43 *Reference Re Section 498A of the Criminal Code*, [1936] SCR 363; *Reference Re Dominion Trade and Industry Commission Act*, [1936] SCR 379; *Reference Re Farmers' Creditors Arrangement Act*, [1936] SCR 384; *Reference Re Natural Products Marketing Act*, [1936] SCR 398; *Reference Re Employment and Social Insurance Act*, [1936] SCR 427; *Reference Re Weekly Rest in Industrial Undertakings Act, Minimum Wages Act, and Limitations of Hours of Work Act*, [1936] SCR 461.

44 *Reference Re Alberta Legislation*, [1938] SCR 100.

45 See generally, R.C. McCandless, "Vancouver's 'Red Menace' of 1935: The Waterfront Situation," *BC Studies* 22 (1974): 56. The strike took place against the backdrop of the settlement march on Ottawa by unemployment workers – hence the anxiety of Vancouver's mayor and federal government alike.

46 "Report of Royal Commission Concerning Industrial Dispute on Vancouver's Waterfront," *Labour Gazette*, Nov. 1935, 982, 995.

47 *Report of the Royal Commission on the Bren Machine Gun Contract* (Ottawa: Government of Canada, 1939), 51.

48 Speaking of an earlier case, Davis J. confided to Wright, "I confess that I have never been without some doubt as to the decision. The case caused me a good deal of worry and I wavered from side to side." Davis to Wright, 6 Nov. 1937, UTA, Wright Papers, B1982-0028, Box 2. "The question is one of difficulty," Davis J. admitted in his dissent in *Christie,* a phrase that appears (with minor variations) in a number of his decisions: see, for example, *Royal Bank of Canada v. Nova Scotia,* [1936] SCR 560; *Toronto Transportation Commission v. Swansea,* [1935] SCR 455.

49 B.M. Greene, ed., "Davis, Hon Henry Hague," in *Who's Who in Canada, 1938–39* (Toronto: International Press, 1939), 132. As well, for a time, Davis served on the General Committee of the Leonard Trust Foundation Association. The trust, established by Colonel Reuben Wells in 1923 to support scholarships, included in its preamble the declaration that "the White Race is, as a whole, best qualified by nature to be entrusted with the development of civilization and the general progress of the world along the best lines." See Bruce Ziff, *Unforeseen Legacies: Reuben Wells Leonard and the Leonard Foundation Trust* (Toronto: Osgoode Society for Canadian Legal History and University of Toronto Press, 2000), 3, 100.

50 Scott, *The Canadian Constitution,* 37. For other references to Christie and hockey see Stephanie Ben-Ishai and David Percy, *Contracts: Cases and Commentaries,* 8th ed. (Toronto: Carswell, 2009), 23; W.S. Tarnopolsky, "The Control of Racial Discrimination," in *The Practice of Freedom,* ed. R. St J. MacDonald and John P. Humphrey (Toronto: Butterworths, 1979), 289, 293; Walker, "*Christie v. York.*" For what it is worth, as of 15 Mar. 2012, even the short Wikipedia entry on *Christie v. York* mentions the hockey game.

51 The temperature that day reached 31.1 degrees Celsius: "Weather Report," *Montreal Gazette,* 13 July 1936.

52 "We sit up there in the blues / bored and sleepy and suddenly three men / break down the ice in roaring feverish speed and / we stand up in our seats with such a rapid pouring / of delight exploding out of self to join them why / theirs and our orgasm is the rocket stipend / for skating thru the smoky end boards out / of sight and climbing up the appalachian highlands / and racing breast to breast across laurentian barrens over hudson's diamond bay and down the treeless / tundra where / auroras are tubercular and awesome and / stopping isn't feasible or possible or lawful." Alfred Purdy, "Hockey Players," in *The Cariboo Horses* (Toronto: McClelland & Stewart, 1965), 60–1.

53 "Hockey? Hockey's our game. But really, it's more than just a game. It's a passion that brings us all together. On frozen ponds. At the community

rink. And in our living rooms ... It's in our dreams ... It's in the streets ...
In every rink across the country. It's in our hearts." Sidney Crosby, Tim
Hortons advertisement (2010).

54 Mary Louise Adams, "The Game of Whose Lives? Gender, Race, and Enti-
tlement in Canada's 'National Game,'" in *Artificial Ice: Hockey, Culture, and
Commerce*, ed. David Whitson and Richard Gruneau (Peterborough, ON:
Broadview, 2006), 71; Jason Blake, *Canadian Hockey Literature: A Thematic
Study* (Toronto: University of Toronto Press, 2010); Andrew C. Holman,
ed., *Canada's Game: Hockey and Identity* (Montreal and Kingston: McGill-
Queen's University Press, 2009); Richard Gruneau and David Whitson,
Hockey Night in Canada: Sport, Identities, and Cultural Politics (Toronto:
Garamond, 1993); Michael A. Robidoux, "Imagining a Canadian Iden-
tity through Sport: A Historical Interpretation of Lacrosse and Hockey,"
Journal of American Folklore 115 (2002): 209; John Chi-Kit Wong, ed., *Coast
to Coast: Hockey in Canada to the Second World War* (Toronto: University of
Toronto Press, 2009).

55 Robidoux, "Imagining a Canadian Identity," 209. Jason Blake adds that
hockey has "been embraced as a symbol of the nation – sometimes lamented, often applauded, but always acknowledged as a ready indicator
of Canadianness." Blake, *Canadian Hockey Literature*, 38.

56 Gruneau and Whitson, *Hockey Night in Canada*, 13. Richard Harrison
waxes similarly that "hockey can be said to be Canada's game not so
much because Canada invented hockey as because hockey invented
Canada." "Between a Puck and a Showpiece," in Holman, *Canada's
Game*, 153. In response to such sentiments, Mary Louise Adams argues,
"If hockey is life in Canada, then life in Canada remains decidedly
masculine and white ... In its roles as national symbol and everyday
pastime, hockey produces a very ordinary but pernicious sense of male
entitlement: to space, to status, to national belonging." Adams, "Game of
Whose Lives," 71.

57 "This identification of hockey with being Canadian seems to be accepted
almost unquestioningly by Canadians and foreigners alike," Chi-Kit Wong
observes in *Coast to Coast*, viii.

58 Holman, "Introduction: Canada's Game? Hockey and the Problem of Identity," in *Canada's Game*, 6.

59 Whether hockey originated in Windsor, NS, or Kingston, ON, or Montreal, QC, or any number of other locales where ice can be found on lakes,
ponds, or rivers continues to be the subject of debate. See Colin D. Howell,
Blood, Sweat, and Cheers: Sport and the Making of Modern Canada (Toronto:
University of Toronto Press, 2001), 43–4.

60 Michel Vigneault, "La Naissance d'un sport organisé au Canada: Le Hockey à Montréal, 1875–1917" (PhD thesis, Laval University, 2001).

61 Gruneau and Whitson, *Hockey Night in Canada*, 37–9.

62 Brian McFarlane, *One Hundred Years of Hockey* (Toronto: Summerhill, 1990), 5.

63 D'Arcy Jenish, *The Montreal Canadiens: 100 Years of Glory* (Toronto: Doubleday Canada, 2008), 7.

64 Ibid., 13.

65 Qtd in William Brown, *The Montreal Maroons: The Forgotten Stanley Cup Champions* (Montreal: Véhicule, 1999), 42.

66 See Robert H. Dennis, "Forever Proud? The Montreal Canadiens' Transition from the Forum to the Molson Centre," in Holman, *Canada's Game*, 161–75.

67 Jenish, *Montreal Canadiens*, 65. See also Wong, *Coast to Coast*, 88–9.

68 Brown, *Montreal Maroons*, 147.

69 Dryden, *Game*, 130.

70 Dennis, "Forever Proud," 163.

71 As Allen Guttmann points out, sports possess "a mythic dimension … which adumbrates a world apart from the rationalized abstractions of modernity." *Sports Spectators* (New York: Columbia University Press, 1986), 178.

72 See Dennis, "Forever Proud," 165.

73 "Last Tribute to Howie Morenz," *Montreal Gazette*, 12 Mar. 1937.

74 Ibid.

75 Qtd in Dick Irvin, *The Habs: An Oral History of the Montreal Canadiens, 1940–1980* (Toronto: McClelland & Stewart, 1991), 19.

76 Bettina Bradbury and Tamara Myers, eds., *Negotiating Identities in 19th- and 20th-Century Montreal* (Vancouver: UBC Press, 2005) 1, 5–6. "Montreal elites and reformers," Bradbury and Myers argue, "shaped the city by founding cultural institutions such as clubs, cemeteries, museums, and urban spaces like parks and neighbourhoods that reflected and perpetuated their class and ethnic identities."

77 On the community aspects of tavern space, albeit from earlier periods, see Julia Roberts, *In Mixed Company: Taverns and Public Life in Upper Canada* (Vancouver: UBC Press, 2009); Peter DeLottinville, "Joe Beef of Montreal: Working-Class Culture and the Tavern, 1869–1889," *Labour / Le Travail* 8 (1981–2): 9.

78 At the same time, NHL team-owners deliberately attempted to "invest commercial hockey with a culture of respectability, enhancing the position of hockey spectatorship within the pantheon of cultural entertainments

as a way of increasing revenue." Conn Smythe described Maple Leaf Gardens (built in 1931) as "a place where people can go in evening clothes … a place that people can be proud to take their wives or girlfriends to." Russell Field, "'There's More People Here Tonight Than at a First Night of the Metropolitan': Professional Hockey Spectatorship in the 1920s and 1930s in New York and Toronto," in Holman, *Canada's Game*, 129.

79 As Janet Laver argues, "Sport is one institution that holds together the people of a metropolis and heightens their attachment to the locale. The pomp and pageantry of sport spectacles creates excitement and arouses fervor, doing for people of the metropolis what religious ceremonies do for people in communal societies." *Soccer Madness* (Chicago: University of Chicago Press, 1983), 14.

80 On the distinctive journey of English Canada, see José E. Igartua, *The Other Quiet Revolution: National Identities in English Canada, 1945–71* (Vancouver: UBC Press, 2006).

81 See Judith Kendle, "Callaghan as Columnist, 1940–48," *Canadian Literature* 82 (1979): 6.

82 Morley Callaghan, "The Game That Makes a Nation," *New World* 3, no. 12 (Feb. 1943). 35. "Hockey is a game that belongs to no one racial group. Hockey is the stuff that is brewed in the melting pot of our nation."

83 Ibid.

84 Morley Callaghan, *The Loved and the Lost* (Toronto: Macmillan, 1951), 176–8.

85 Gillian Poulter, *Becoming Native in a Foreign Land: Sport, Visual Culture, & Identity in Montreal, 1840–85* (Vancouver: UBC Press, 2009), 7.

86 See Robert Pitter, "Racialization and Hockey in Canada: From Personal Troubles in a Canadian Challenge," in *Artificial Ice: Hockey, Culture, and Commerce*, ed. David Whitson and Richard Gruneau (Peterborough, ON: Broadview, 2006), 123.

87 George Fosty and Darril Fosty, *Black Ice: The Lost History of the Coloured Hockey League of the Maritimes, 1895–1925* (Halifax: Nimbus Publishing, 2008).

88 See Cecil Harris, *Breaking the Ice: The Black Experience in Professional Hockey* (Toronto: Insomniac, 2003).

89 Herb Carnegie, *A Fly in a Pail of Milk: The Herb Carnegie Story* (Oakville, ON: Mosaic, 1997), 59, 74, 100. "There was a powerful racial barrier that blocked us from scaling the pinnacle of hockey professionalism. No one wrote about the colour barrier, no one talked about the colour barrier, but it was there."

90 By all accounts, hockey continues to foster a sense of belonging among

immigrants to Canada. Recent research shows that immigrants are more committed to hockey than native-born Canadians. "The results suggest hockey acts as a kind of glue in the Canadian mosaic. Becoming a hockey fan, for the new immigrant, is a very public way of declaring an identification with Canadian culture." Put more simply, as Farah Sleiman, a Lebanese immigrant and Montrealer says, "The city is hockey. You are either a fan, or you or an outcast." Joe Friesen and Les Perreaux, "Study: Canada's Game," *Toronto Globe and Mail*, 21 May 2010. As Steven Brunt puts it, Canadians viewed hockey as "a game that grew out of climate and geography, an organic connection to long, cold winters and vast, open space, to the point that hockey was the single simplest short-form explanation of what made a Canadian a Canadian." *Gretzky's Tears: Hockey, Canada, and the Day Everything Changed* (Toronto: Alfred Knopf, 2009), 76. On the capacity of sports to acculturate in a different context, see Peter Levine, *Ellis Island to Ebbets Field: Sport and the American Jewish Experience* (Oxford: Oxford University Press, 1992).

91 Appellant's factum at paras 5, 7, file 6684, Supreme Court of Canada Archives (hereafter SCCA).

92 The Maroons made it to the semi-final that year, losing to the eventual Stanley Cup winners, the Detroit Red Wings, in late March 1936. The series featured, on 24 March 1936, the longest game in NHL history: 176 minutes and thirty seconds. Brown, *Montreal Maroons*, 179–80. It is possible that Fred Christie was among the 9,000 in attendance.

93 Nos 151592–2164, court file 151 809, BAQ.

94 Appellant's factum, 4, file 6684, SCCA.

95 Ibid., 5.

96 Lowell C. Carroll, *Landlord and Tenant in the Province of Quebec* (Montreal: Southam, 1934); Carroll, *Marriage in Quebec: The Conditions of Validity* (Montreal: H.S. Oakes, 1936); Carroll, *The Quebec Statute and Case Citator, 1937* (Montreal: Kingsland, 1937); Carroll, *Commercial Law of Quebec* (Toronto: I. Pitman & Sons, 1938).

97 Carroll's Westmount riding was taken by William Ross Bulloch for Duplessis's Union Nationale. Carroll managed to garner only 804 votes: "Élections dans Westmount," QuébecPolitique.com, http://www.quebecpolitique.com/elections-et-referendums/circonscriptions/elections-dans-westmount/.

98 Walker, "*Christie v. York.*"

99 Melville went on to great success as the long-time chair of McGill's Pharmacology Department. See "Convocation Speeches 1972," no. 1674, RG 7, McGill Archives.

100 "Track Trials Open Today," *Montreal Gazette*, 10 July 1936. In typical
    racist framing, reporters always distinguished Black athletes, noting,
    in particular, "Sammy Richardson the Negro ace from Toronto" who
    specialized in long jump and the 100 metre dash. Richardson made the
    Olympic squad and competed against the great Jesse Owens in Berlin,
    whom the *Gazette* described as "coffee-coloured" and as "the mercury-
    footed Negro." "U.S. Track Trials Will Start Today," *Montreal Gazette*,
    11 July 1936.
101 "B.C. Boxers Arrive for Olympic Bouts," *Montreal Gazette*, 10 July 1936;
    "Ring Trials Start at Forum Tonight," *Montreal Gazette*, 13 July 1936.
102 Discovery transcript, 11 Feb. 1936, nos 151592–2164, court file 151 809,
    BAQ.
103 "The colour bar was less rigidified than in the United States," Constance
    Backhouse writes, "varying between regions and shifting over time ...
    While no consistent pattern ever emerged, various hotels, restaurants,
    theatres, athletic facilities, parks, swimming pools, beaches, dance pavil-
    ions, skating rinks, pubs and bars were closed to Blacks across the coun-
    try." Backhouse, "'Bitterly Disappointed' at the Spread of 'Colour-Bar
    Tactics,'" in *Colour-Coded*, 251. See also Barrington Walker, "Finding Jim
    Crow in Canada, 1789–1967," in *A History of Human Rights in Canada*, ed.
    Janet Miron (Toronto: Canadian Scholars', 2009), 81.
104 Discovery transcript, 11 Feb. 1936, nos 151592-152164, court file 151 809,
    BAQ.
105 Ida C. Graves, *The Negro in Canada* (Orillia, ON: Packet-Times, 1931), 61.
106 Ibid. "There was a great deal of subtle intimidation," Oscar Peterson re-
    called of Montreal in the 1940s. "They'd refuse you by saying 'I'm sorry
    in front,' but it was still a refusal. The famous Ritz Carlton ... never mind
    getting a room there, they didn't even want me playing there." Qtd in
    Gene Lees, *Oscar Peterson: The Will to Swing* (Toronto: Prospero Books,
    2008), 58.
107 Discovery transcript, 11 Feb. 1936, nos 151592–2164, court file 151 809,
    BAQ.
108 In this respect, both Justices Davis and Rinfret offer truncated versions in
    their summaries of the facts. It was true that the waiter refused to serve
    Christie, but only after he checked with the manager first. "I simply went
    to the bar," he testified, "and asked the manager if I should serve them,
    he said 'No,' so I went to the gentlemen very quietly and said, 'Gentle-
    men, I am very sorry I cannot serve coloured people.'" Transcript, René
    St Jean, 22 Feb. 1936, nos 151592–2164, court file 151 809, BAQ.
109 Harold McNamara, "6 Montrealers Win in Opening Fights of Olympic
    Trials," *Montreal Gazette*, 14 July 1936.

110 The Olympic trials ended in disappointment. McIntyre lost his final bout in a split decision and failed to make the team. The following year, McIntyre became a professional, ultimately capturing the Canadian middleweight title. With the arrival of the Second World War, McIntyre shipped overseas as a member of the 2nd Division Field Ambulance Company. He continued to box in the army, until he suffered a serious shrapnel injury to his right hand during the Dieppe raid. The injury effectively ended his career. McIntyre was inducted into the Canadian Boxing Hall of Fame in 1993, and died, at the age of eighty-nine, in 2006. See Herb Zurkowsky, "McIntyre to Enter Boxing Hall: Former Canadian Champ Was Hero in Ring, at War," *Montreal Gazette*, 2 Oct. 1993; "Ray McIntyre Aiming at Bout with Jock McAvoy," Toronto *Globe and Mail*, 7 Dec. 1940.

111 Paul Parizeau, "Les boxeurs montréalais paraissent en vedette aux essais de boxe olympiques," *Le Canada*, 15 July 1936.

112 Jeffrey T. Sammons, *Beyond the Ring: The Role of Boxing in American Society* (Chicago: University of Illinois Press, 1988), 34.

113 See Thomas R. Hietala, *The Fight of the Century: Jack Johnson, Joe Louis and the Struggle for Racial Equality* (Armonk, NY: M.E. Sharpe, 2002), 34–47.

114 "After he defeated Primo Camera in 1935, for example, Harlem residents poured through the streets 'shouting, clapping, laughing, and even crying.'" Dominic J. Capeci Jr and Martha Wilkerson, "Multifarious Hero: Joe Louis, American Society and Race Relations during World Crisis, 1935–1945," *Journal of Sport History* 10 (1983): 57. See generally Theresa E. Runstedtler, "In Sports the Best Man Wins: How Joe Louis Whupped Jim Crow," in *In the Game: Race, Identity and Sports in the Twentieth Century*, ed. Amy Bass (New York: Palgrave Macmillan, 2005), 47. On Joe Louis's later emergence as a hero across racial divides, see Lauren Rebecca Sklaroff, "Constructing G.I. Joe Louis: Cultural Solutions to the 'Negro Problem' during World War II," *Journal of American History* 89 (2002): 984.

115 Some sixty million Americans listened to the fight, while thirty million Germans tuned in at three a.m. local time to hear the German broadcast. See David Margolick, *Beyond Glory: Joe Louis vs Max Schmeling, and a World on the Brink* (New York: Knopf, 2005), 150–1.

116 "Harlem Hoodlums Attack White Men," *Montreal Gazette*, 20 June 1936.

117 "Celebrants at Detroit Invade Negro Section" and "Chicago Police Called Out," *Montreal Gazette*, 20 June 1936.

118 For an example of the power of inconsistent discrimination in an urban setting, see Thomas J. Sugrue, *The Origins of the Urban Crisis: Race and Inequality in Postwar Detroit* (Princeton: Princeton University Press, 1996).

119 Called to the bar in 1928, Hansard had articled with the noted courtroom lawyer George H. Montgomery, KC. Hansard's career representing large

corporate clients took him to the Supreme Court on several occasions, including just months before he argued *Christie*. On Hansard generally, see his entry in *The Canadian Who's Who* (Toronto: TransCanada, 1967), 168; and his obituary "Veteran Lawyer Hansard," *Montreal Gazette*, 2 May 1985.

120 Transcript, René St Jean, 22 Feb. 1936, nos 151592–2164, court file 151 809, BAQ.

121 *Christie v. York Corporation* (1937), 75 *Recueils de Jurisprudence de Québec* 136 (SC).

122 Discovery transcript, 11 Feb. 1936, nos 151592–2164, court file 151 809, BAQ.

123 Defendant's plea, 28 Sept. 1936, nos 151592–2164, court file 151 809, BAQ.

124 Transcript, René St Jean, 22 Feb. 1936, nos 151592–2164, court file 151 809, BAQ.

125 Graves, *Negro in Canada*, 61.

126 Callaghan, *Loved and the Lost*, 176–8.

127 *Christie*, 141.

128 Walker, *"Christie v. York."*

129 Although *Christie* was among the first cases I read at Dalhousie Law School, a survey of colleagues revealed that the vast majority had not studied the case during their law school careers. *Christie* does not appear in historic or contemporary casebooks on contracts or torts, with the exception of the short note in Ben-Ishai and Percy, *Contracts*, 23.

130 Simpson, *Leading Cases*, 10.

131 *Christie*, 141.

132 Lindsay Jolivet, "Entry Refused Based on Attitude, Not Race, Bartender Says," *Montreal Gazette*, 27 Aug. 2011.

133 Desmond Manderson, "Interstices: New Work on Legal Spaces," *Law Text Culture* 9 (2005): 1.

134 Nielsen, "Power of 'Place,'" 220.

135 Henry Hague Davis, "Judicial Appointments in the Dominion of Canada," *Minnesota Law Review* 22 (1937–8): 128.

136 Hazen Hansard, "Presidential Address," in *1965 Yearbook of the Canadian Bar Association and the Minutes of Proceeding of Its Forty-Seventh Annual Meeting* (Ottawa: National Printers, 1965) 162, 168.

PART THREE

Slavery, Race, and the Burden of History

9

Slavery and Slave Law in the Maritimes

D.G. BELL, J. BARRY CAHILL, AND HARVEY AMANI WHITFIELD

Editor's note: This chapter is an edited version of three previously published articles on slavery and slave law in the Maritime provinces.[1] The text of two of the original articles has generally not been altered, but each has been reduced, repetition between them has been eliminated, and there is some reordering of the material. Professor Bell made more substantial changes to his original piece, incorporating new archival research and refining the focus so that it deals more with the law and less with the judges than his original essay, published in 1982. The articles are presented in the order in which they were published. Taken together, these three works form an important cornerstone of the Canadian scholarship on slavery. The editing is the work of Philip Girard, associate editor of the Osgoode Society, with some assistance from Jim Phillips, editor-in-chief of the Osgoode Society.

Introduction

That slavery existed in the Maritime provinces of Canada is a historical fact. The similarity of the material conditions under which slaves were

Previously published as D.G. Bell, "Slavery and the Judges of Loyalist New Brunswick," *University of New Brunswick Law Journal* 31 (1982): 9–42; J. Barry Cahill, "Slavery and the Judges of Loyalist Nova Scotia," *University of New Brunswick Law Journal* 43 (1994): 73–135; and J. Barry Cahill and H. Armani Whitfield, "Slave Life and Slave Law in Colonial Prince Edward Island, 1769–1825," *Acadiensis* 38 (2009) 29–51.

held there – as domestic rather than plantation slaves – is also well established. Yet the role of the law in upholding or undermining slavery developed in quite different ways in the three jurisdictions. Slavery was upheld by New Brunswick's Supreme Court but undermined by Nova Scotia's, while in Prince Edward Island not only did the Supreme Court permit the recovery of an escaped slave, but the Island legislature also passed, in 1781, the only statute in British North America regulating slavery. These differences, as will be argued below, are largely a function of variations in the legal cultures and attitudes of the relevant elite fragments in each colony. But across the Maritimes, law was the pre-eminent theatre in which slavery was asserted, resisted, justified, subverted, and contested.

This chapter begins with an account of the migration of Black people, slave and free, to the Maritimes, followed by a summary of the English law of slavery. The major sections then analyse the legal controversies over slavery in each of the three provinces.

Black migration to the Maritimes, coerced and by choice, can be divided into two distinct periods: before 1783 and after 1783. The first period was defined by small and scattered numbers of people of African descent who worked within the French and British Empires. The first Africans probably worked as translators and labourers for the French.[2] Ken Donovan points out that, under the French regime on Prince Edward Island, "Jean Pierre Roma owned at least 12 slaves, making him the largest slave owner in the colony."[3] The first substantial contact between Black people and European settlers in the Maritimes occurred in Île Royale (Cape Breton) between 1713 and 1758. As Donovan's work demonstrates, this slave population was multi-ethnic, multicultural, and multilingual. Generally, they worked as domestics but also participated in other forms of work as deemed necessary by their owners.[4] After the Acadian expulsion and the defeat of the French, the British offered land to the New England Planters and, as a result, eight thousand Planters resettled in the Maritimes between 1759 and 1765. It was within this migration that African Americans came as slaves.[5] In the case of Prince Edward Island, separated from Nova Scotia in 1769 in preparation for settlement, Governor Walter Patterson allegedly kept a "mulatto mistress" in 1770. Four years later, however, he noted that there "are no blacks" residing on the Island, which probably meant no Blacks other than slaves.[6] Prior to the American Revolution, Black slaves were a significant presence throughout greater Nova Scotia or old Acadie, but their exact number is unknowable.

The defeat of the British in the American colonies set the stage for the mass migration of free Blacks and Loyalist slaveholders, along with their chattels, to the Maritimes. The total number of Black migrants to the Maritimes in the wake of the Revolutionary War is disputable because documentation is fragmentary, but it may have been as high as 5,000 persons. Of these, approximately 3,500 were ex-slaves who achieved their freedom by escaping to British lines in return for guaranteed mobility and protection against re-enslavement – the "Black Loyalists." The majority settled in Nova Scotia and in what would become New Brunswick.[7] Another aspect of this migration was the importation of slaves to the region by migrant Loyalist slave-owners. Loyalist slaves faced continued bondage, oppression, and possible separation from family and friends. They came from various parts of colonial America and brought diverse cultural and work experiences to the Maritime region. The majority came from New England and the Middle Colonies, with a smaller contingent from the colonies to the south. It is probably safe to say there were not fewer than one thousand Blacks in early New Brunswick and at least half of these were slaves.[8] And within the migration of people of African descent to Nova Scotia and New Brunswick, a trickle of Loyalists with slaves found their way to Prince Edward Island. Two further events had a profound effect on the size and nature of the Black population in the Maritimes. One was the mass exodus of free Blacks to Sierra Leone in 1792, which depopulated the Black communities in Shelburne and Halifax Counties. The other was the large-scale immigration of free Blacks in 1814–16 after the War of 1812. Between these two events, the issue of the legality of slavery was played out in all three colonies.

After 1792 Nova Scotia's residual Black population was largely unfree and was concentrated in Annapolis County. Of course, only the free Blacks emigrated to Sierra Leone; the slave Blacks had no choice but to remain behind. In the first decade of the nineteenth century, that part of greater Annapolis County[9] comprising especially the new Loyalist townships of Digby and Clements, held the largest portion of the Black population of the province; therefore, also the highest percentage of slaves and of frustrated slave-masters determined to maintain and, if possible, reinforce the status quo.[10] That the fear of reduction to slavery had been present continuously among the free Blacks, and gave impetus to the West African colonization scheme, is clear from the second of the two petitions (1791) from Thomas Peters, formerly a sergeant in the Black Pioneers, who effectively laid the groundwork for abolitionist John Clarkson's "mission to America," which resulted in the exodus to Sierra Leone. Peters, who was the chief spokesman of the Annapolis County Blacks, complained of the "public and avowed Toleration of Slavery":[11]

Several of them [free Blacks] thro' this notorious Partiality ... have already been reduced to Slavery without being able to obtain any Redress from the Kings Courts, and ... one ... thus reduced ... did actually lose his Life by the Beating and Ill Treatment of his Master and another who fled from the like Cruelty was inhumanly shot and maimed by a Stranger allured thereto by the public Adver-tisement of a Reward ... who "delivered him up to his Master" in that deplor-able wounded State ... [A]s the poor friendless Slaves have no more Protection by the Laws of the Colony (as they are at present misunderstood) than the mere Cattel or brute Beasts ... and ... the oppressive Cruelty and Brutality of their Bondage is particularly shocking and obnoxious to ... the free People of Colour who cannot conceive that it is really the Intention of the British Government to favour Injustice, or tolerate Slavery in Nova Scotia.

Though the condition of Blacks in Annapolis County, where there had been an unbroken tradition of slavery originating at least as early as the New England Planter period, attracted the most attention, it was pre-exodus Shelburne, the Loyalist metropolis, that had the largest population of Blacks (both slave and free) anywhere in the province. As late as 1806, a refugee slave from Shelburne would precipitate an important Supreme Court case involving the prominent West Indies merchant George Ross, who years before had acted as local agent for Bahamian slave-masters.[12]

Slavery in England and the Empire

The abolition of Negro slavery in 1833 has commonly been hailed as one of the noblest achievements in British history; and, when one re-calls that Britain abolished slavery three decades earlier than many of the American states, there is some basis for such a view. But the enco-mia generally extended to the British record on slavery probably arise not so much from the ending of the slave trade in 1807 and the abolition of the institution itself in the 1830s as from the notion that slavery was never legally tolerated within the borders of the Mother Country her-self, and that Lord Mansfield's celebrated decision in *Somerset v. Stew-art* (1772)[13] put the matter beyond doubt. In a characteristic expression of this still widely accepted misconception Reginald Coupland asserts that after Mansfield's decision "all slaves in England ... were recognized as free men."[14]

Viewed in strictly legal terms, however, *Somerset*'s case is only the most notable of a long series of highly contradictory English decisions that, although they contained many dicta useful to both sides in the broad slavery controversy, did little to weaken the master's legal claim to his Black. All that Lord Mansfield decided, as he himself carefully emphasized, was the narrow point that a slave, once in England, could not be forced to leave. But while he was careful to confine his ratio to the precise question before him, Mansfield did nonetheless cast grave doubt upon the general legality of the institution in obiter dicta that were later an important part of the case against slavery in New Brunswick: "The state of slavery is of such a nature, that it is incapable of being introduced on any reasons, moral or political; but only positive law, which preserves its force long after the reasons, occasion, and time itself from whence it was created is erased from memory: it's so odious, that nothing can be suffered to support it, but positive law."[15]

That *Somerset*'s case did not abolish slavery in England is dramatically illustrated by the fact Lord Mansfield himself died a slave-owner twenty-one years later.[16] Indeed, his decision in *Somerset v. Stewart* only fuelled the controversy, providing support both for those who defended slavery and for those who wished to strike it down. The case itself and the pamphlet literature that immediately sprang up around it did, however, coalesce still further the anti-slavery lobby in Britain. In the 1780s a British Abolition Committee was established, which by the 1790s was causing abolition bills annually to be introduced into Parliament.[17] Finally, in 1807, the anti-slavery forces won legislative abolition of the slave trade in the British Empire, and, three decades later, the progressive phase out of slavery itself. In the meantime, the fact that *Somerset*'s case did not decree slavery abolished in England meant that the question of its legality was very much an open one in the colonies that emerged from the revolutionary war.

Of the North American colonies, the first to take action against slaveholding was Upper Canada. In 1793, the General Assembly enacted, with considerable opposition, that thenceforth no more slaves could be introduced or created in the province. Like some of its neighbouring United States jurisdictions, however, Upper Canada condemned slaves already in the province to serve out their life in bondage. Indeed, the law copied some of the earlier American legislation that actually discouraged manumission by requiring that masters post security, lest freed slaves become a public charge.[18]

In Lower Canada there was also a legislative attempt to phase out slavery in 1793, but the bill died on the order paper. It was, rather, the firm judicial policy of James Monk, chief justice of the King's Bench in Montreal, that effectively doomed the institution in the colony. In cases in 1798, and especially in 1800, Monk denounced slavery and showed that he was determined to free every Black brought before him, if not on a technicality, then on an outright misconstruction of the law. The pro-slavery forces counter-attacked by introducing into the Lower Canadian Assembly a gradualist abolition bill patterned after those in Upper Canada and many of the United States, which would have legalized the status of at least those slaves already held. But passage of these measures failed in 1800, 1801, and 1803. Caught between judicial activism on the one hand and legislative intransigence on the other, slavery in Lower Canada withered away.[19]

Slavery and the Law in New Brunswick

The public records, newspapers, and church registers of Loyalist-era New Brunswick mention Blacks frequently, but references are so scattered and varied that historians have yet to attempt a complete view of the Black experience, free and unfree. The sole aspect to attract more than passing notice is a 1799–1800 test case on the lawfulness of slavery. Historians learned of it through a fascinating correspondence on the legal status of slave-holding that passed between Saint John lawyer Ward Chipman and the chief justice of Nova Scotia. In it Chipman describes his role on behalf of the slave in that test case as one of a "Volunteer for the rights of human nature."[20] The test case failed to end slavery, but Chipman's heroic self-characterization thrilled late-Victorian historians. Eager to interest readers in the New Brunswick past, they seized on slaveholding as a quaintly exotic topic, and most of them depicted Chipman as a chivalrous advocate engaged in a gesture of professional noblesse oblige.[21] More recent historians have echoed this view.[22] This chapter shows that the legal history of New Brunswick slavery amounts to a good deal more than the test case of 1800 and, incidentally, that lawyer Chipman's zeal for the "rights of human nature" did not deter him from arguing the master's side of the question when paid to.

No Act of New Brunswick's General Assembly ever recognized or regulated the existence of slavery.[23] This was greatly to the slaves' advantage. It meant they did not suffer some of the legal disabilities that had prevailed in the older American colonies. They could give evidence in court; they could intermarry with whites; and they were protected by the same criminal law against murder or bodily harm. More importantly, legislative silence meant that the lawfulness of slavery was ambiguous. If the Nova Scotia judiciary were prepared to wear out slavery in face of a 1762 local law explicitly mentioning it – if the Lower Canadian judges were prepared to turn their back on generations of local slave-holding – then surely New Brunswick's judges, faced with neither of these impediments, would do the same.

How often did questions involving the lawfulness of slavery come before the judges of New Brunswick? The various published commentaries discuss only the test proceedings of 1799–1800, to which this chapter adds the cases of Dick and Jim Hopefield in 1805–6. Yet there were others, perhaps many, for in 1800 Ward Chipman noted that the question had been "agitated from the very origin of this Province." Typically such agitation led to an accommodation. Chipman explains, "Some masters have brought Slaves here is true, and that the Slaves have in some instances continued with their masters, without disputing the right of their masters to their service is also true. But it must also be admitted that the Slaves have in many instances controverted this right, and have been manumitted, or indented themselves voluntarily to serve for a term of years upon condition of being discharged at the expiration of it."[24]

But even in a setting where the question of status was blurred and avoided in ways Chipman suggests, the lawfulness of slavery might come before the legal system in many guises: a will purporting to pass slaves might be disputed; sheriffs seizing the property of debtors for sale might be faced with auctioning slaves; a captive might sue the master for false imprisonment; a recaptured escapee might charge the master with kidnapping or sue for battery; or a test of the slave's confinement might be put in motion through a writ of habeas corpus.

Many of the best-known slave cases, including *Somerset* in England, began with a habeas corpus application. In its classic form, a lawyer or other friend on behalf of the captive went before a Supreme Court judge with affidavits alleging that someone was being confined unlawfully. If the judge thought there might be something to it, he would direct the clerk of the Court to issue a habeas corpus (literally "let us have the body") writ to the custodian (slave-master) ordering production of the captive in Court. The custodian was also to write an explanation of the legal basis on which the captive was held. On the appointed day the judge or bench of judges – no jury was used – would hear evidence and argument on whether the custodian's explanation of the captive's confinement was valid. In legal parlance, the process was one of testing the "sufficiency" of the custodian's "return" to the Court's writ. If the return was insufficient, the captive would go free. It was by using writs of habeas corpus in 1799 that a New Brunswick lawyer began what was intended as a "final determination upon principle" of the lawfulness of slavery. "The question," pronounced Ward Chipman, "is now for the first time brought forward, for a legal decision."[25] That test proceeding was the twin case of *R. v. Jones* and *R. v. Agnew.*

The instigator of the 1799–1800 episode was Samuel Street. Born and given his legal training in England, Street had been stationed at Fort Howe on Saint John harbour during the Revolutionary war in one of the colonial military units. From here he led daring covert missions against the rebels in Maine.[26] Street stayed on after the peace and, at the organization of the Supreme Court in the new province, was called to the New Brunswick bar. By the time of the 1799–1800 proceeding he was a prominent member of the opposition faction in the House of Assembly, sitting for Sunbury County. As such, he was a political friend of one of the defendants in the slave litigation, Stair Agnew, and the political enemy of his eventual co-counsel, Solicitor-General Chipman. Within the space of a few years Street would involve himself in five proceedings to free central Saint John Valley slaves, so it fair to say that he became devoted to the abolitionist cause.

Of the background to the proceedings of 1799–1800 little is known. Two distinct cases were involved. The one that came to be argued fully before the Supreme Court was *R. v. Jones*. It concerned the status of "Ann otherwise called Nancy a black woman" whom Caleb Jones had brought from Maryland in 1785 to his new property opposite Fredericton.[27] Now about thirty-seven, Nancy was making her second bid for freedom; thirteen years earlier she had grabbed her toddler and joined in a general escape of Jones's slaves.[28] The other case, *R. v. Agnew*, was over the slave Mary Morton, whom Stair Agnew – a Virginia Loyalist and neighbour of Caleb Jones – had purchased from one William Bailey. Street commenced *R. v. Agnew* three weeks after *R. v. Jones* but apparently did not take it to a hearing once the result of the earlier proceeding became known.[29] Judge Isaac Allen allowed the habeas corpus to issue in *R. v. Jones*, ordering Jones to bring Nancy into court on 18 July 1799. Yet the case did not reach its argument stage until February of the following year. Perhaps when the process opened on 18 July the court took note of Jones's plea that "the said Ann or Nancy was at the time of her birth and ever since hath been a female Negro Slave or Servant for Life, born of African Negro Slaves" and determined that there would be no dispute as to relevant facts. Then it adjourned for seven months to allow the lawyers time to prepare arguments on the great question of principle. It was at this point that Street enlisted Chipman as co-counsel, who then began the exchange with Chief Justice Blowers of Nova Scotia that reveals much of slave law and practice in both colonies. Already Chipman thought he knew the views of the four Supreme Court judges, two favouring abolition and two against, so perhaps all judges had taken part in the July proceedings and expressed tentative opinions or at least gave hints. If the Supreme Court was known to be facing the prospect of impasse, it becomes all the more comprehensible why the case came to engage the talents of a numerical majority of the New Brunswick bar.

R. v. Jones came to argument in the second week of February 1800. Street and Chipman appeared for Nancy, probably with Chipman, the senior lawyer, as leading counsel. Against them were Attorney-General Jonathan Bliss and no fewer than four junior members of the bar. Chipman recalled the case as "very fully argued and lasted two whole days," and the Royal Gazette reported, "The question of Slavery upon general principles was discussed at great length, by the Counsel on both sides."[30] A New Brunswick court argument lasting two whole days would scarcely have had a parallel in either eighteenth or nineteenth centuries. Chipman entered court armed with a massive brief of his anti-slavery argument. Not to be outdone, Jonathan Bliss supported the master's claim from his own lengthy memorandum of legal authorities.[31] The case's immediate result was that Chief Justice George Ludlow and Judge Joshua Upham (a slave-owner himself, and father-in-law of one of the lawyers appearing for the master) supported the contention that slavery was lawful in the province. Judges Isaac Allen (another slave-owner) and John Saunders held that slavery had no legal foundation.[32] The court being evenly divided, Nancy was returned to captivity with Caleb Jones.[33]

R. v. Jones did not strike down slavery but neither did it uphold its lawfulness. Alarmed at the uncertain state of the law, the friends of slavery counter-attacked in the legislature. On 6 February 1801 Stair Agnew, one of the defendants from the year before, rose in the House of Assembly to introduce "a Bill relating to Negroes." Second reading without division came on 12 February and the bill went to committee-of-the-whole. On the following day the committee reported progress; but on 14 February Agnew withdrew the measure altogether.[34] The bill took as its premise a 1790 Act of the British Parliament permitting settlers relocating into British territories from the United States to import their slaves.[35] While it professed to deal with the implications of slaves imported under the 1790 law, Agnew's bill had only slight relationship to it; indeed, it extended to all New Brunswick slaves. It was an ill-disguised attempt to recognize slavery legislatively, thereby undermining one of the most potent anti-slavery arguments urged before the Supreme Court. As such, it anticipated the similarly unsuccessful tactic of Nova Scotia slave-holders in 1808.[36] Agnew was using the 1790 Act merely to give his ploy a guise of legitimacy.

One of the surviving drafts of Agnew's bill would have said much more. It proposed that offspring of slaves would take their status from their mother (as was commonly the case in slave societies) rather than their father (as under the obsolete English law of villeinage), it set a penalty for harbouring escaped slaves, and it provided that, where the sheriff seized the master's property to sell for debt, slaves would be classed as among the chattels. Finally, at the foot of this version was a clause, to be inserted into the provision governing female descent, that would have freed all slaves born in the province after the passing of the bill on their attaining a certain age (which was left blank). It seems that this longer and more radical version of the bill was the one introduced first. When that encountered opposition, Agnew inserted the provision that would have eventually freed slaves born after the bill took effect. Then, when that would not placate opponents, he fell back to the shorter bill. And when that was no more acceptable to fellow legislators, who included the anti-slavery lawyer Samuel Street, he withdrew the whole measure rather than face defeat. By 1801 the tide of opinion in New Brunswick was set so strongly against slavery that Agnew, a member of the faction that usually dominated the lower house, could not persuade Assembly colleagues to recognize that the province's slaves were held lawfully, even in a measure that promised gradual future abolition.

A few months after Agnew withdrew the bill that was based ostensibly on the British Act of 1790, the *Royal Gazette*, acting at the request of "A Constant Customer," reprinted the Act's text. Accompanying it was an analysis by a "worthy and learned Judge." The thrust of the anonymous remarks was that the 1790 law amounted to "Legislative recognition" of the existence of slavery throughout the American empire. In consequence, "the slaves which the Loyalists took with them to their new settlement, were, and are, to this moment, slaves."[37] The printed passage provides no evidence that its author was a local judge, but he may well have been John Saunders. The Saunders Papers at the University of New Brunswick have an undated copy of the opinion in Saunders's own hand but with a slightly longer text. This would suggest that the Saunders version formed the basis of the published account rather than the reverse.[38] That Saunders should harbour pro-slavery sentiments would not be surprising. He came from Virginia and had petitioned the British government for Loyalist compensation for loss of twelve slaves stolen by the rebels. Yet Saunders is not known to have owned slaves in New Brunswick and had been one of the judges who would have freed the slave in *R. v. Jones* just a year earlier. As that case featured full debate on the implications of the 1790 British law, Saunders must have had an alteration in sentiment.

The ultimate stage in New Brunswick's legal debate over the principle of slavery was a complicated cluster of legal proceedings in 1805–6. They reunited several of the established players – Street, Chipman, Ludlow, Agnew – along with a freedom-seeker of notable tenacity, Dick Hopefield. Hopefield's case was years in the making, but direct proceedings began on 6 February 1805 when Chief Justice Ludlow and two associates granted Samuel Street's application for habeas corpus against Stair Agnew to bring Hopefield into court and explain the legal basis for holding him in slavery.[39]

Dick Hopefield's background is known in unusual detail. A woman identified later in court documents as Patience, alias "Stacey," was born about 1766 at Eastchester, New York.[40] At some point during the Revolution her master sold her to Gabriel Fowler of Westchester County, and in August 1783 this seventeen-year-old "stout wench," named in Loyalist New York's "book of Negroes" as "Stach" and infant Joe arrived at Saint John harbour in Fowler's household.[41] Fowler sold Stacey to the Loyalist surgeon Joseph Clarke, and Clarke sold her to Phineas Lovitt, apparently a trader out of Annapolis Royal. While with Lovitt, Stacey entered into a marriage relationship, the formality of which is unclear, with Richard Hopefield Sr, a free Black from Virginia.[42] When pregnant with their second child, Stacey was "sent by ... Leavitt on board the Greyhound packet in order to be put on board a Brig lying off Partridge Island [Saint John] in which ... she was to be taken to the West Indies and sold." On learning that his wife was about to be carried off, Hopefield submitted his predicament to Governor Carleton. By his "order" Stacey was "sent for on shore and re-delivered to her ... Husband and told she was free and might go where she pleased within the King's dominions."[43] If Carleton had really done as Stacey understood, he had exceeded his authority. Nevertheless, she lived with her husband "quietly and undisturbed and in the enjoyment of her liberty" at Saint John for upwards of seven years. After Lovitt's difficulty in removing her from the province he apparently re-conveyed her to Dr Clarke, for it was Clarke who in 1792 advertised in the press for information about "Statia," a five-year-old son and infant daughter who had run off with a free Black servant named Dick/Richard Hopefield [Sr]. Then Clarke came to Saint John and "seized on her by violence and carried her to Magerville ... where he kept her upwards of two years and then (as she was informed) sold her to Mr Joseph Hewlett" of Hempstead, Queens County. Stacey's sad vicissitudes would have gone the way of other accounts of the slave experience but for the fact that the captive on whose behalf lawyer Street secured the 1805 habeas corpus was the child with whom she had been pregnant when threatened with abduction to the West Indies all those years earlier, Dick Hopefield Jr.

The irascible character to whom the writ was directed was Stair Agnew.[44] Agnew had been defendant in the second habeas corpus application of 1799 and then sponsored the attempt to have slavery recognized by the General Assembly, of which he remained a member. How Dick Hopefield was sold away from his mother (who in 1805 was still a slave of Joseph Hewlett) and came to be in Agnew's possession was never stated. Perhaps it did not occur until Hopefield was a teenager, for his dealings with Agnew were tense. In 1801 or 1802 (that is, when Hopefield was about eighteen) Agnew promised before a witness to free him at age twenty-one if he would agree to become an indented servant. But later that same day, when Agnew took him to the York County registrar of deeds to draw up the papers, Hopefield "declined being indented." Then on 7 May 1802 Agnew beat Hopefield three times, so severely that he was charged before the York County General Sessions of the Peace with "Cruel Treatment and abuse of two Negro Boys then his Servants." Agnew got the matter dropped by pledging in court to free them when they turned twenty-one.[45] One of these young men was Dick Hopefield. When Agnew broke that promise, Street applied for the habeas corpus on his behalf. His parentage became the subject of detailed enquiry because Street placed weight on the fact that the senior Hopefield was a free man. The defence countered by trying to show that Dick's parents had not married formally, so that he took the status of his slave mother rather than of his free father.[46]

The habeas corpus in *R. v. Agnew*, granted in February 1805, did not come to a hearing on the lawfulness of slavery until February 1806. Much of the delay was due to the side issue of whether Agnew had lied when deposing that *both* of Hopefield's parents were slaves.[47] Meanwhile, Hopefield commenced a lawsuit against Agnew for battery and false imprisonment arising from the beating incident of 1802. And, as noted below, Dick Hopefield's cause overlapped with legal manoeuvres centring on yet another member of the Hopefield family. Street acted for the slave in all proceedings, assisted on one occasion by Thomas Wetmore. Chipman, reversing his stance of five years earlier, defended the master.

Hopefield v. Agnew, the civil suit, may not have gone to trial, given that Hopefield's bid for freedom failed.[48] In *R. v. Agnew*, the habeas corpus application, argument on the broad question of slavery appears to have taken place on 7 February 1806. The result was that Chief Justice Ludlow and Judges Upham and Saunders dismissed Hopefield's claim for freedom.[49] At other points in the case's slow progress the Supreme Court minutes show a bench divided, but in this their ultimate ruling the three sitting judges were unanimous. Ludlow and Upham needed only to have adhered to their views from *R. v. Jones* in 1800, and by 1801 Saunders had come to agree with them. Judge Isaac Allen, the abolitionist, sat on some earlier stages of *R. v. Agnew* but at the final argument was not present. Surviving in the Court's case file is Chipman's lengthy brief defending the lawfulness of slavery in New Brunswick.[50]

Dick Hopefield's case was a legal triumph for slave-owning interests. Now, unlike in *R. v. Jones* six years earlier, they had received a clear decision upholding the lawfulness of slavery, something they could not have won from the General Assembly or from the court of any other British American province. Of four judges on the Supreme Court only one was an abolitionist. Faced with such a Court, it is not surprising that no later cases testing the lawfulness of slavery can be found. But while *R. v. Agnew* is the final case put in motion in the hope of striking down slavery outright, it was not the last case to consider an aspect of slave law. That final proceeding, at least as located thus far, introduces another member of the Hopefield family.

Late in 1805, while Dick Hopefield's status was still undetermined, an agitated clerk of the Supreme Court advised Ward Chipman that "Street has sued out another habeas corpus for *James* Hopefield (a

Brother I suppose of Dick) in the keeping of Dr Clarke – so that I suppose we shall e're long have half the negroes in the Province on Record."[51] This time the writ was directed to Joseph Clarke, a Connecticut surgeon settled at Maugerville in the central Saint John Valley.[52] It will be recalled that Dr Clarke had owned Stacey Hopefeld in the 1790s and presumably also her New Brunswick–born children. Although Clarke sold the mother to Joseph Hewlett, he must have kept James/Jim. On 1 November 1805 Jim Hopefield fled Dr Clarke's farm, crossed the Saint John River, and took refuge with a sympathetic family in Burton Parish. His kindly protector was none other than lawyer Samuel Street himself.

An angry Clarke sued Street, putting his claim on a legal theory ("trover") that, by harbouring the slave, Street was detaining Clarke's property away from him.[53] As this theory presupposed that Jim Hopefield was property, it invited Street to defend himself by arguing that in New Brunswick humans could not be property. But Street had tried that principled approach twice already and had failed. The tactic he adopted now was different: to resist the plaintiff's claim by raising a number of limited, somewhat technical issues, any one of which, if accepted, would allow the court to hold that Dr Clarke's suit against Street was defective without contradicting its recent holding that slavery was lawful. All that is known of the judicial handling of *Clarke v. Street* is the *Royal Gazette*'s report of civil trials held before Chief Justice Ludlow on Sunbury County circuit in mid-1806.[54] Ludlow accepted two of Street's objections to the validity of Clarke's suit: that the "uncontrolled and unlimited" right to property that is the foundation of a trover action was inapplicable to humans;[55] and that, even if the British Act of 1790 did contemplate slavery for enslaved Blacks newly imported into New Brunswick, it had no application to people born within the province, such as Jim. In the result, Ludlow dismissed Clarke's case against Street without putting it to the jury.

For Jim Hopefield personally, the result of *Clarke v. Street* implied quite strongly that he was not a slave, though just what became of him is not known. Whether other New Brunswick–born "slaves" and their masters found such an implication in the court's non-suiting of Dr Clarke is doubtful, as press references to local slavery continued occasionally after 1806. For lawyer Street, the result suggested that his earlier strategy of trying slavery cases on the bare question of principle had been asking New Brunswick's Supreme Court for too much. Better to have tried to "wear out the claim" in small legal graduations, as was occurring in Nova Scotia.[56] For Chief Justice Ludlow, who believed so strongly that the long existence of slavery in the American colonies and islands meant that it *must* be legal, *Clarke v. Street* was an opportunity to cloud the master's title to an individual slave without retreating from what he evidently saw as the law.

There is positive evidence that slavery in New Brunswick was understood as continuing as late as 1816. That was when Caleb Jones published an escape advertisement for Lidge, the very slave who, some thirty years earlier, had made an escape attempt in company with his mother Nancy (who herself was later the subject of *R. v. Jones*).[57] No doubt slaves were held for some time after 1816. But the underlying trend of converting slave status into service for a term of years, which Ward Chipman said was perceptible from the very beginning of the province, can only have continued and accelerated. Elderly and female slaves, even if freed, might have little economic option but to remain in service to the former owner.[58] Freedom might mean so little to the real relationship between master and servant/slave that some slaves may never have asked for freedom. Despite an 1822 report that there were already "no Slaves in the Province," it may be that, technically, some Blacks were freed only by the British abolition law in 1834.[59] But if ending slavery would not have embarrassed masters greatly, then why did judges Ludlow, Upham, and Saunders resist what they knew was the trend of events throughout the North Atlantic world? They did so not accidentally or incidentally but deliberately and explicitly, after elaborate argument. Why choose to confirm New Brunswick in a social hierarchy that had at its base a category of humans classed formally as chattels? What disposed them to value a master's claim to property more highly than a slave's claim to freedom?

A plausible, if speculative, case can be made linking the judges' comparative indifference to the claims of liberty to their peculiar experience as members of New Brunswick's governing elite. The colony was carved out of Nova Scotia in 1784 as an asylum for loyal exiles from the Revolution. The typical American Loyalist did not differ greatly in political principles from the typical Patriot, and at war's end most of them managed to make peace with the new order. But for those loyal Americans compelled by the fortune of war to make their loyalty conspicuous, a quiet submission was precluded, and exile seemed the only recourse. As one Canadian scholar put it succinctly, most exiled Loyalists "came because they could not stay."[60] That their intellectual baggage included political principles and techniques that, apart from republicanism, differed little from those of the Patriots is vividly clear in the tempestuous politics of early Saint John and in the province's constitutional crisis of the mid-1790s.[61] It is not likely, therefore, that the Supreme Court's response to the abolition question reflected an especially conservative consensus in New Brunswick society at large. As Ward Chipman asserted in 1800, the general provincial opinion was always against slavery's "admission or toleration."[62]

But the four Supreme Court judges were not typical Loyalists. All had occupied positions of wealth and standing in the old colonies. Because of their local prominence, they had been called on to articulate an opinion in America's controversy with Britain, and they had chosen empire over independence. All had served in positions of military command, ensuring that they would not be allowed to reconcile with the triumphant Patriots. In 1783 all were exiled from the old colonies, leaving behind property, heritage, almost their whole world. They faced ruin of their fortunes and careers and dramatic dislocation in the social hierarchy. A name such as Upham, Ludlow, or Saunders had commanded deference and access to the highest circles in Massachusetts, New York, or Virginia, but it would command nothing for an exile in Britain. Men born to play a large role on a small provincial stage faced the chilling prospect of insignificance. One senses the anguish with which Ward Chipman (himself a future judge) wrote from London that he "had rather move in a reputable and respectable line in that Country [New Brunswick] with a competent subsistence, than with the same income, support the mortification of seeing in obscurity millions insulting me with their wealth" in Britain.[63] For such men, their patronage appointment in the new colony of New Brunswick came as a godsend. More than salvation of careers and fortunes, it meant restoration of their former position in a colonial elite, and indeed improvement. In a revealing expression of such sentiment Edward Winslow (another future judge) exulted that immediately on arriving at Saint John harbour he had regained his proper place in the social hierarchy: "[I] have adopted a style that would astonish you. There's not a man from this quarter that presumes to solicit from head Quarters without my recommendation and I have effected some business for meritorious characters which has afforded me vast pleasure."[64] The most ambitious attempt to replicate former gentility was that of Judge John Saunders, who amassed a 12,000-acre New Brunswick estate aptly named "The Barony."[65]

Of all the Loyalists appointed to New Brunswick's governing oligarchy in the 1780s, the most fortunate were the judges. Theirs were among the few salaries borne by the British Treasury, and they occupied key positions in the executive as well as the judiciary. All were appointed to the lieutenant-governor's Council, in which capacity they could initiate bills or reject those sent up from the House of Assembly. As confidential councillors, they also advised the governor on exercise of the executive prerogative. The judges were thus at the very centre of the power structure, in the enviable position of interpreting the statutes that they, as legislators, had helped frame.

In addition to restoration of their economic and social status, the New Brunswick experiment afforded the Loyalist elite an opportunity to vindicate – to the world and to themselves – the wisdom of the imperial system for which they had been martyrs. Eschewing the institutional laxity and indulgence of dissent that had led to the downfall of the old American empire, they determined to make the constitution of their new colony, in the words of a future judge, "the most Gentlemanlike one on earth."[66] Administered on firm lines, New Brunswick would become the flourishing "envy" of the American states.[67] To this end they entrenched legal, educational, and religious establishments framed to reflect and reinforce a hierarchical social and political order.

If the concept of New Brunswick as political as well as personal vindication is one key to understanding the social attitudes of New Brunswick's governing elite, another is the threatened collapse of their dreams in the 1790s. Externally the attack was from the rise of democratic and atheistic discourse inspired by the French Revolution. Even in remote, obscure New Brunswick there was a Burkean outpouring of religious and civil jeremiads against the intellectual currents of the times.[68] According to one pillar of the governing elite, the principles of the French Revolution had "excited an alarm that was never known before."[69] This assault on the vitals of the established order was thought to have its local parallel in the growth of an opposition political faction, numerically a majority in the House of Assembly in the latter 1790s. With revealing hyperbole one member of the elite denounced the leader of the opposition alignment as a "most notoriously violent democrat and Jacobin" and as "one that would wish to overturn the *Church and State*."[70] Four years of political impasse between House of Assembly and the Council brought the legislative process nearly to a halt. Most of the opposition's grievances centred on the court system: the reception date for English statutes, the monetary jurisdiction of inferior courts, whether judges would go on legislated circuits, and the role of the judges in government. At the height of the controversy, the Supreme Court judges were denounced as being "much more dependent for their daily bread on the Minister of the Crown than any menial Servant in the Province is on his Master."[71]

By the early years of the nineteenth century, when the judges of New Brunswick were called on to retain or abolish slavery, the feeling was general that their larger social vision of a model colony in a new British Empire was gravely imperilled. The French revolutionary contagion threatened their world from without, and a powerful political faction, of which lawyer Samuel Street was a key member, made their life miserable within the colony. Equally alarming was the prospect, quite discernible by 1800, that the Loyalist settlers of New Brunswick would not attend the established church, vote for government candidates, tenant great estates, or reverence their betters. Against such a threatening background, the decision of three members of the colony's aging Supreme Court to affirm a society with Blacks at its legal as well as its social base was, in part, a statement in symbolic terms. It affirmed the old notion that God had appointed some to be great and some to be low. In a society in which the position of the great seemed increasingly precarious, it may have been with considerable satisfaction that three of the judges ensured that, as a matter of law, the province's Black slaves would continue to be very low indeed. Others might succumb to the seductive principles undermining the very pillars of North Atlantic civilization, but New Brunswick's judges would seize on the question of upholding or abolishing slavery to make a protest against the intellectual current of their time.

Slavery in Nova Scotia

As J.W. St.G. Walker has observed, "Though many Nova Scotians, most prominent among them Chief Justice Thomas A. Strange [1790–9] and Attorney-General S.S. Blowers [1785–97], sought to make perpetual bondage illegal, slavery remained a fact throughout the 1780s and 1790s." It will be argued here, as Blowers was to do, that Strange and Blowers, as consecutive chief justices, sought to debilitate slavery without declaring it illegal, at virtually the same time as unsuccessful attempts were being made to affirm it by legislation. Although Walker goes rather too far in describing Attorney-General Blowers as "a pioneer in the attempt to abolish slavery in the province," he was undoubtedly opposed to trafficking in slaves.[72] On at least one occasion during his tenure as attorney-general, moreover, Blowers had resolved to prosecute some unidentified slave-masters for sending a Black man "out of the province against his will, who had found means to get back again, but the master being willing to acknowledge his right to freedom nothing further was done."[73]

Blowers, who succeeded Strange as chief justice in 1797, was not only the first but also, until 1810, the only Loyalist judge on the bench of the Supreme Court of Nova Scotia. The judges of Loyalist Nova Scotia thus differed significantly from the New Brunswick bench, which did not have a non-Loyalist judge until 1834. Nor was the legality of slavery in Loyalist Nova Scotia merely a question of Loyalist legal attitudes, despite the preponderance of Loyalist attorneys at the bar after 1783. The issue not only divided the Loyalist lawyers among themselves, but also was one over which the abolitionist part thereof could make common cause with like-minded members of the pre-Loyalist bar, a rare, perhaps unique, instance of ideological convergence and professional cooperation between oldcomers and newcomers.

The legality of slavery, which tended to be reinforced indirectly on the infrequent occasions when it was challenged during the 1780s, began to be challenged successfully on the grounds of defect of title warranty in the 1790s. Yet this development took place only after two attempts at legislative regulation of Blacks in the late 1780s had failed. Why did the judges of Nova Scotia's Supreme Court during the Loyalist period consistently undermine the lawfulness of Black slavery when they might conveniently have abolished it? Why did the lawyers in Nova Scotia's legislature further undermine the lawfulness of slavery by declining to enact the regulatory bills, and yet fail to introduce an abolition bill until as late as 1808, when the virtual necessity of such a measure was conceded even by petitioning slave-masters?

On numerous occasions in the late 1790s and early 1800s, the mainly non-Loyalist judges of Nova Scotia's Supreme Court were confronted with the question of whether slavery was legal even though it was not legislatively recognized. Only among the advocates of its legalization, however, did the view prevail that slavery had been introduced by acts of Parliament extending either *proprio vigore* or at common law to the colonies. While it was no less entirely open to the Nova Scotia Supreme Court than to the New Brunswick Supreme Court to "mak[e] the law for the occasion,"[74] the judges of the former strove to prevent law being made, for fear that legislating by judicial decision might impute even the presumption of legality to institutional slavery. In choosing gradually to subvert slavery, the judges calculatedly rejected the option of declaring it illegal. The gradualist judicial policy developed and implemented by Chief Justices Strange and Blowers, the former an inexperienced English barrister, the latter an accomplished American Loyalist attorney from Massachusetts, may be judged to have succeeded, in that slavery eventually disappeared without having to be abolished through judicial fiat, much less legislative enactment. The rationale for this approach to the impasse was that slavery, though arguably a violation of human rights, was both customarily legal and seen to be so, and that prudent judges had therefore to proceed with extreme caution lest they find themselves in the invidious position of determining what the law should be rather than deciding what it was, and thus provoke the legislature into overruling their decisions. Despite there being neither judge-made nor statute law, both Strange and Blowers well knew that slavery existed in fact, if not in law.[75] It existed unchallengeably in default of either judicial decisions or legislative acts positively declaring it to be illegal.

If it was Nova Scotia's judges and its law officers who played a leading role in administering the coup de grâce to institutional slavery, legislators took the active part in trying to perpetuate it through express statutory regulation. The third (1787) session of Nova Scotia's Sixth Assembly, the first to which numbers of Loyalists belonged and in which the new Loyalist townships of Shelburne and Digby, having between them the bulk of the Black population, were represented, saw the first reading of *An Act for Regulating bound and free Negroes and Mulattoes, and for more effectually Punishing such Persons of that Description as shall in future be guilty of Offences*. Prominent among the five lawyer members of the House of Assembly (MHAs) were Attorney-General Blowers and Solicitor-General Richard John Uniacke. Blowers was Speaker, a position to which Uniacke would succeed scarcely more than a year later. Professional rivals as well as bitter personal enemies, whose enmity would endure a lifetime, Blowers and Uniacke were nevertheless united in their belief "that slavery in Nova Scotia had no basis in law."[76] A lifelong, committed ideological opponent of slavery, Uniacke had emigrated in early manhood from Ireland. If Blowers and Uniacke agreed on one thing only, it was that the perceived para- or quasi-legal status of slavery must not be enhanced by the passage of affirmatory Acts of any kind whatsoever.

The 1787 *Negro Bill*[77] passed through first and second reading, and had reached the committee stage, when Uniacke successfully moved that it be deferred until the next session. Recalling this event thirteen years later Blowers, wrote, "When the Law made in 1787 for the regulating of Servants was brought into the house of Assembly, there was a clause inserted for the government of Negro Slaves which was rejected by a great Majority on the ground that Slavery did not exist in the province and ought not to be mentioned."[78]

Nonetheless, the *Negro Bill* was substantially reintroduced in the House of Assembly at its next session in 1789. By that time Blowers had been promoted to the Council, and Uniacke had replaced him as Speaker of the House. The new *Negro Bill* was drafted and presented by Charles Hill, an Ulster Protestant immigrant who ran an auction house in Halifax while representing the country constituency of Amherst, and who was also a close friend and business associate of Uniacke's. *An Act for the Regulation & Relief of the free Negroes within the Province of Nova Scotia*[79] progressed through the Assembly (Uniacke seems not to have interfered) and was sent up to the Council, but was returned by the Council "not agreed to," presumably at the instigation of Blowers, who feared that language such as, "no person or persons whatsoever can by authority of Law enslave them [free Negroes) unless they are proved by Birth or otherwise to be bound to Servitude for Life" and "Negroes ... who are not Slaves by Birth or otherwise," implicated the existence of a statutory justification for slavery.

Despite the apprehensions of the senior law officer, the 1789 *Negro Bill* was conceived by its framers in the lower house partly as a vagrancy Act, a social-welfare-cum-civil-rights bill. Walker cites it as an honest attempt to address the worsening problem of the illegal seizure and export of free Blacks for sale in the United States or the West Indies.[80] This ad hoc compromise, however, born of expediency, was no more than an attempt to prevent the illegal re-enslavement of free Blacks; it did nothing to ameliorate the condition of slave Blacks, and indeed held out to indigent free Blacks the prospect of nothing better than involuntary indentured servitude. The bill's failure was nevertheless to provide both the inspiration and the occasion for later judicial attempts at debilitating slavery by converting perpetual bondage (or servitude) into indentured servitude.

It must have appeared to Blowers that socially dangerous "positive law," such as the proposed *Negro Bill*, would be far worse than no legislation at all. He remained an unflagging opponent of any species of statutory enactment "relating to Negroes." The legality or otherwise of slavery was far too serious and delicate a matter to be left to assemblymen, some of whom were slaveholders; it was a matter instead for the

Supreme Court, where, in Winks's memorable phrase, a "judicial war of attrition," would be waged upon slave-owners.[81]

Understandably of greater interest to Blowers, after he had become chief justice in 1797, was statutory interpretation. Given the failure of the 1789 regulatory bill, the only statute in which the words *Negro* and *slave* were conjoined was the 1762 *Innholders Act*, which prohibited retailing alcoholic beverages on credit to soldiers, sailors, servants, apprentices, indentured servants, and Negro slaves.[82] Replying in 1800 to an enquiry from Solicitor-General Ward Chipman of New Brunswick, "whether the question [of the legality of slavery] has ever been judicially determined, whether there was ever any act of Assembly in your province upon the subject, and upon what ground the right of the master is supported, if slavery is recognized at all among you," Blowers had stated, "We have no Act of the Province recognizing the slavery of negroes as a statute right."[83]

Chipman, however, in searching through the statutes, had discovered the *Innholders Act*; he supposed it would be construed by counsel for the master as securing their argument in defence of the legality of slavery: "Had the counsel for the master stumbled upon your [Nova Scotia's] Act passed in 1762 ... in the second section of which negro slaves are mentioned, the conclusiveness of their reasoning on their principles would have been considered as demonstrated."[84] Blowers, however, took the view that the "expression ... Negro Slaves in our province's *Law for regulating In[n]holders &c* has been considered here as merely a description of a Class of people existing in the province, and not as a recognition of the Law of Slavery."[85] The unpassed regulatory bills of 1787 and 1789 were another matter, however, for they would have legalized slavery by according it de jure statutory recognition.

Slavery adjudication in Loyalist Nova Scotia meanwhile began not in the Supreme Court, to which it was afterwards confined exclusively, but on the judicial side of the Court of General Sessions of the Peace. The judicial bench of the Court of Sessions, like the Inferior (civil) Court of Common Pleas, consisted of laymen, some of whom were themselves slave-masters and therefore interested personally in upholding the master's property right.[86] The judicial records of the Shelburne County Sessions, which survive almost complete from the late eighteenth century, contain numerous examples of freedmen attempting to escape re-enslavement at the hands of slavers or former masters, who were attempting to use due process of law not only as a means of reclaiming refugee slaves, but also as a cloak for trafficking or slave-market profiteering.[87] "If a master could prove a prior claim, of however long standing," writes Walker, "the black was liable to be returned to slavery."[88] Typical of those cases in which "the threat of being [re]claimed, in the courts and with the full sanction of the law, as a legal slave" was realized, was *R. v. Gray, ex parte Postell*,[89] in which the former master was tried and acquitted of a "misdemeanour" for having resold into slavery an emancipated slave.

In its concern for the property rights of slave-masters, the Court of Sessions, especially in early Loyalist Shelburne, resembled more closely the Supreme Court of New Brunswick, which consisted entirely of Loyalists, than the Supreme Court of Nova Scotia. During the same period (1785–1808) in which the Supreme Court of New Brunswick was presided over by George Duncan Ludlow, a chief justice who was partial to the legality of slavery, moreover, the Supreme Court of Nova Scotia was presided over by two consecutive chief justices who opposed slavery. While the Strange Court (1790–6) and the Blowers Court (1797–1833) were anti-slavery, however, they were emancipationist rather than abolitionist. Strange's policy, with which Blowers concurred and collaborated while attorney-general, and which he continued to implement after he had become chief justice, was to exploit to the full the resources of law and procedure in order to secure the emancipation of individual slaves rather than abolish slavery per se by judicial fiat. If habeas corpus did not succeed in favour of the slave as against the putative master, then the alternative was slow strangulation of the master's "property rights" through risky, prolonged, and expensive litigation.

Though it would be difficult to attempt to estimate the number of slave cases tried in the Supreme Court of Nova Scotia in the 1790s, most if not all of them were Crown proceedings for habeas corpus brought against masters on behalf of fugitive slaves, in order to determine whether slavery was a form of unjust and illegal detention. The criteria according to which such cases would have been decided were stated thus by Chief Justice Blowers: "The right to hold a negro by this tenure [i.e., slavery] is supposed by us to be maintainable, either by the Common Law of England, the Statute Law of England and the Colony, or upon adjudged cases."[90] As there was no provincial statute establishing, regulating, or even recognizing slavery, the principal point was adjudicable on the grounds of English law and colonial custom or usage having the force of law; Blowers rejected the latter as a mere pretext for adducing the false principle of "colonial" common law, as distinct from English.[91]

In lieu of even informal reports or a systematic survey of court records documenting slavery adjudication in the Supreme Court of Nova Scotia during the 1790s,[92] one has to rely almost entirely on Chief Justice Blowers's retrospective on the Strange Court, given a few years after Strange's resignation, in confidential correspondence with Solicitor-General Ward Chipman of New Brunswick. "The question respecting the slavery of negroes has often been agitated here in different ways," wrote Blowers in reply to Chipman's original request for information, "but has not received a direct decision":

My immediate predecessor [Strange] dexterously avoided an adjudication of the principal point, yet as he required the fullest proof of the master's claim in point of fact, it was found generally very easy to succeed in favour of the negro, by taking some exceptions collateral to the general question, and therefore that course was taken ... [A] summary decision of the question of slavery between master and negro here has always been resisted, and the party claiming the slave has been put to his action; and several trials have been had in which the jury has decided against the master, which has so discouraged them that a limited service by Indenture has been generally substituted by mutual consent. Mr Strange always aimed to effect this, and generally succeeded ... I had frequent conversations with Mr Strange upon the question, and always found that he wished to wear out the claim gradually, than to throw so much property as it is called into the air at once.[93]

The Blowers-Chipman correspondence also reveals that both men were aware of the 1778 Scottish leading case, *Knight v. Wedderburn*,[94] which had declared slavery unequivocally illegal in Scotland, and that Blowers at least considered it to stand "on Better reason" than *Somerset*. In 1800 he wrote to Chipman, "I doubt whether the determination in the Scotch Case would not be preferred by the Court of Kings Bench in England at this day."[95] For both men, *Knight v. Wedderburn* stood for the proposition that "the dominion assumed over the Negro under the law of Jamaica, being unjust, could not be supported in Scotland to any extent; that, therefore, the master had no right to the Negro's service for any space of time, nor to send him out of the country against his consent."[96]

It will become clear that the role of English habeas corpus in the judicial war of attrition against slavery in the province owed more to *Knight v. Wedderburn* than to *Somerset*. As in England, in Nova Scotia the key to liberating slaves without resorting to judicial abolition of slavery was habeas corpus, the remedial value of which both Strange and Blowers exploited to the full extent in the interest of fugitive or refugee slaves. Granting applications for habeas corpus was the preferred judicial tactic for setting slaves legally free, thereby asserting their basic civil right to personal liberty no less than any other of the King's subjects. The Nova Scotia cases would establish a neo-*Somerset* precedent, which demonstrated that proof of purchase and constructive possession did not amount to sufficiency on a return to habeas corpus in favour of Black slaves.

Blowers wrote to Chipman in January 1800, "Since I have been Chief Justice, a black woman was brought before me on *habeas corpus* from the gaol at Annapolis. The return was defective and she was discharged, but as she was claimed as a slave I intimated that an action should be brought to try the right, and one was brought against a person who had received and hired the wench. At the trial, the plaintiff proved a purchase of the negro in New York as a slave, but as he could not prove that the seller had a legal right so to dispose of her, I directed the jury to find for the Defendant which they did."[97] The action to which Blowers referred was probably *R. v. Ditmars, ex parte Van Embenow* [sic: *Emburgh*] *et al.*, concerning which the defendant's attorney, neophyte lawyer Thomas Ritchie,[98] boldly asserted that "the legality of Slavery in the Province ... will be determined on the return to the aforesaid writ of *Habeas Corpus*."[99]

A consortium of twenty-five Annapolis County slave-masters, headed by Loyalist MHA James Moody, and including Loyalist Councillor James DeLancey, executed a bond in favour of second-generation Loyalist Douwe Ditmars Jr of Clements Township, in which they undertook to share with him the burden of his legal costs. The efforts of the bondsmen, all but two or three of whom were Loyalists or their sons, however, failed to resolve the doubts that had arisen in the mind of the Loyalist chief justice on the legality of slavery. Proof of purchase availed nothing against the purchaser's failure or inability to prove the vendor's title to the property conveyed; as usual, the ground for instructing the jury to find against the defendant was breach of title warranty. This unsuccessful attempt by slave-masters to bring off a test case by trying their property right showed that allowing the prerogative writ of habeas corpus would not necessarily compel the court to declare whether the law of the colony recognized slavery. Yet every slave case potentially became a test case until the broad legal question was settled, either by judicial decision or by legislation.

In response to this uncertain situation, James DeLancey launched an action in the Supreme Court at Annapolis to recover the "fair market value" of a slave, Jack, who had run away to Halifax in May 1800, apparently to enlist in the Royal Nova Scotia Regiment, and who had eventually found gainful employment.[100] DeLancey's lawyer, Ritchie, wrote to Jack's employer, one William Woodin, alleging unlawful detainer and threatening legal action if the fugitive were not returned. Woodin's lawyer, Attorney-General Uniacke, denied the allegation on the grounds that Jack "as well as all other Negroes in this Province were Freemen; there not being any law here to make them otherwise."[101] DeLancey thereupon commenced an action for trover, which was tried at the Annapolis annual circuit court in September 1801. The trial judge was James Brenton, a New England Planter from Rhode Island, who was the first (and until 1807 the only) professionally trained lawyer to serve as a puisne judge of the Supreme Court of Nova Scotia.

DeLancey v. Woodin perfectly realizes D.B. Davis's characterization of "the earlier judicial cases concerning Negroes" as involving "civil disputes over the ownership of individual slaves, some of whom had obtained *de facto* freedom ... and had been employed for wages. In legal terms, the plaintiff commonly instituted an action of trespass or trover, the latter being a way of recovering the value of personal property wrongly converted by another for his own use. The specific issue raised by such actions was whether English laws protecting personal property could be extended to protect the owners of errant slaves."[102] The choice as to the form of the tort action, trover, rather than trespass *per quod servitium amisit*, was made on the advice of Joseph Aplin, who had been retained by DeLancey as watching counsel; Aplin was afterwards to describe Ritchie as a "younger Disciple of the Law," who had lost his "professional Maidenhead" in the case. A Rhode Island Loyalist and former solicitor-general and attorney-general of Prince Edward Island, "who for twenty years past, has been considered as one of the first special pleaders in America," Aplin was then living in indigent circumstances at Annapolis Royal, where he was the only other resident legal practitioner.[103]

Ritchie's original intention had been to commence the special action of trespass *per quod servitium amisit*, which, though well grounded in English adjudged cases, was tantamount to an admission that the plaintiff had no property in the alleged fugitive slave. From this cautious and reasonable course, however, Ritchie was dissuaded by Aplin, who considered the leading English case against trover for Black slaves not only not "to stand in the Way of [the] proposed Action," but also "as an Authority pointedly in their Favour."[104] The decision concerned was *Smith v. Gould*,[105] in which the judgment in the leading pre-*Habeas Corpus Act* case allowing trover for Black slaves had been overturned: "For *per totam Curiam* this action does not lie for a negro, no more than for any other man; for the common law takes no notice of negroes being different from other men. By the common law no man can have a property in another."[106] The precedent set by Lord Chief Justice Holt's anti-slavery decisions, however, had been overruled in 1749 by Lord Chancellor Hardwicke, who had "no doubt but trover will lie for a Negro slave; it is as much property as any other thing."[107] As *DeLancey v. Woodin* was to follow much the same course as *Smith v. Gould* a century before, there is sharp irony in Aplin's having persuaded young Ritchie that the judgment for the plaintiff in the latter, which exempted the Black from trover, favoured the plaintiff's case in the former.

The surviving sixteen pages of Ritchie's originally twenty-two-page "proslavery" brief[108] depends on English slave law, which is assumed to extend to the colonies, thereby providing the legal basis for American colonial slavery. Those first six pages of Ritchie's address that are no longer extant[109] shed light on the racist *mentalité* of Annapolis County's Loyalist plantocracy: "With us, why are they black and we white, there can be nothing more diametrically opposite to each other, than those two colours, which serves to evince their inferiority to us. It may be said that their colour is owing to the Climate in which they reside. If it was why are not those who live under the same parallels of Latitude, of the like cast? No doubt can remain but that they were designed to be subservient to others: therefore may be very justly termed slaves by Nature. I shall now endeavour to show that the right of Slavery exists in the Province of Nova Scotia; and that, that right, is constituted by acts of the Legislature of Great Britain."[110]

Despite his heavy emphasis on the statute law of England, Ritchie did not ignore the statute law of the colonies, which he considered to be purely regulatory of slaves rather than constitutive of the right of slavery. This important distinction prompted him to adduce the Nova Scotia *Innholders Act* of 1762, by which he supposed that "slavery is as much recognized as it is in those acts specially passed in regulation of slaves" – legislation, of course, that existed in the former thirteen colonies as well as in the West Indies but never in Nova Scotia.

Ritchie had the misfortune of finding himself opposed by the dean and head of the bar, not to mention its ablest advocate, Richard John

Uniacke, who was acting for the defendant Woodin. Then at the height of his rhetorical powers, Attorney-General Uniacke was afterwards to argue, rather circularly, "that it appearing in Evidence that the servant Jack was a Slave, and there being no Slaves in the Province, the Plaintiff could not recover the Loss of his Service."[111] In other words, if a fugitive slave could not legally enforce a claim for wages, then a putative master could not sue for the recovery of whatever wages may have been paid to the alleged slave.

But not even Uniacke's courtroom pyrotechnics could turn a sceptical Annapolis jury against an Annapolis plaintiff (who happened to be not only a former member of both the Council and the House of Assembly, but also the most prominent Loyalist in the county), in favour of a Halifax merchant defendant, against whom judgment was given for £70. Though it "was urged on the Trover Action against Woodin, that small Damages ought to be given, from the Consideration, that the Negro was a runaway Negro,"[112] the sum awarded seems to have been the amount sued for – the issue in trover, of course, being the value of the property wrongly converted.

Having lost at trial, Uniacke made a motion in arrest of judgment on the basis that trover did not lie for the recovery of a slave in the province. On the hearing of this motion he obtained a rule to show cause why the verdict should not be quashed on the grounds of excessive damages. The venue then changed to Halifax, where DeLancey retained the Loyalist Solicitor-General James Stewart to argue before Chief Justice Blowers in chambers against Uniacke's motion for a new trial. Stewart's failure led to DeLancey suing Woodin anew in trespass for £500 damages. The action was set down for the Circuit Court at Annapolis in September 1803 but seems never to have come to trial. Thomas Chandler Haliburton, who practised at Annapolis for eleven years preceding his own appointment to the bench in 1829, construed *DeLancey v Woodin* thus: "Some legal difficulties having arisen in the course of an action of trover, brought for the recovery of a runaway, an opinion prevailed that the Courts would not recognize a state of slavery as having a lawful existence in the country. Although this question never received a judicial decision the slaves were all emancipated."[113] Haliburton, whose *History* was published in 1829, denied that there were slaves in the province any longer, but allowed that slavery was still legal. The colony's other notable lawyer/author Beamish Murdoch, on the other hand, with a lack of candour, altogether ignored the leading case and denied both the historical existence and the legality of slavery.[114]

The failure of *DeLancey v. Woodin* produced a firestorm among the slave-masters of Annapolis County. Aplin had been concerned lest DeLancey attempt forcibly to repossess the slave, Jack, without a warrant; another of the Ditmars bondsmen, Loyalist Colonel Frederick Williams, found himself prosecuted and convicted for assault for that very reason.[115] Before his second lawsuit against Woodin could be settled, however, Colonel DeLancey died (in May 1804), poisoned, according to an unsubstantiated family tradition, "by a disgruntled female slave to whom he had promised freedom on his death."[116] The last slave sold at Annapolis was reportedly in October 1804,[117] but mention of slaves in the records of the Grand Jury continued to be quite frequent previous to the watershed year 1808, when the third and last *Negro Bill* failed to pass the House of Assembly.[118]

If, as argued above, the loyalist legal establishment in New Brunswick largely sympathized with slavery, then the non-Loyalist, essentially Anglo-Irish tradition of the Nova Scotia bar, exemplified by Uniacke, was generally hostile to it. Aplin himself commented that during the trial of *DeLancey* he had heard that the bar were generally against his opinion, namely that bringing an action of trover for Blacks necessarily meant imputing the character or quality of property to them, while Blowers observed to Chipman in 1800, "Though the question of slavery was much agitated at the Bar, I did not think it necessary to give any opinion upon it."[119] Ritchie himself might have formed more enlightened, humanitarian and progressive views, had he not trained under a Loyalist attorney who owned slaves and whose wife, another DeLancey, became notorious in oral tradition for her cruelty to them;[120] had he not fallen under the malignant influence of a much older, conservative New England émigré lawyer who was an advocate of the legality of slavery; had not his law practice numbered among its clients the most prominent Loyalist slave-masters of the county; had he not married into a family of slave-owning Georgia Loyalists; and had he not "made his name" as a young lawyer through a celebrated lawsuit, *DeLancey*, which achieved in Nova Scotia a mythic status comparable to *Somerset* in England. Within the profession generally, there was not even an implicit division for and against the legality of slavery along Loyalist and non-Loyalist lines. The Loyalist Chief Justice Blowers was opposed, as was the non-Loyalist Attorney-General Uniacke, while the Loyalist Solicitor-General James Stewart acted for slave-masters such as James DeLancey. Almost alone among his own, as well as the younger generation of Loyalist attorneys, Joseph Aplin adopted an aggressive, pro-legality stance towards slavery.

The next known slave case also involved an Annapolis military Loyalist, Colonel Frederick Williams, another of the Ditmars bondsmen, as plaintiff, and a partnership of Halifax merchants, John Stayner and John Allen, as co-defendants. The cause of action was identical to *DeLancey*: Jacob Francis, alias "Prince," was a fugitive slave whom Stayner and Allen had retained in their employ, despite having seen Williams's advertisement in a Halifax newspaper.[121] The case was set down for trial at Annapolis in September 1806, and though the outcome is not known, it seems probable, in light of the decision in *DeLancey*, that the plaintiff would have been non-suited.

Despite the notoriety of the slave-master lawsuits *DeLancey* and *Williams*, the case that verged most closely on the judicial abolition of slavery was *R. v. Ross, ex parte Edwards* (1806–7), a habeas corpus proceeding by the Crown that involved not an Annapolis but a Shelburne Loyalist. George Ross, a partner in the most successful mercantile firm in the town, daringly ignored a writ of habeas corpus directing him to bring up one Catherine Edwards and was afterwards prosecuted for contempt of court.[122] Another 1806 case, almost certainly the same one misremembered, was recorded in his brief memoirs by the nonagenarian former chief judge of the Cape Breton inferior courts, John George Marshall, who at the time of the case had been apprenticed to Lewis Morris Wilkins, MHA, the lawyer acting for the slave. Speaking of "individuals of the slave population," Marshall wrote,[123]

One of them abruptly left his [sic] master's service, in Shelburne, and came to Halifax. The master pursued him, and by some legal process, or other means, procured his arrest, and was about to convey him back to Shelburne. Application on his behalf was made to Mr Wilkins, who obtained a writ of *habeas corpus*, under which master and servant were brought before the Chief Justice, and the case, and the slave question were fully argued on each side, and the Judge legally and righteously decided, that this Province was not debased with that cruel and abominable slave system, which John Wesley appropriately characterized, as *"the sum of all villainies."* Thus the subject as to our free country, was settled for all time.

The *Edwards* case brought matters to a climax. The judicial war of attrition against slavery having nearly succeeded in extirpating it, the last offensive by the slave-masters was to be launched not in the courts but in the House of Assembly. Thomas Ritchie, who entered the legislature as MHA for Annapolis County in 1806, had at the top of his agenda to conciliate the slave-owning plantocrats of Annapolis County. All previous judicial attempts having failed to retrieve the situation, recourse was made to a legislative agenda. Ritchie also repaid his debt of gratitude to old and indigent Joseph Aplin, by arranging for him to be employed to draft bills.[124]

In December 1807, twenty-seven Loyalist slave-masters of Annapolis County, who among them owned some eighty-nine Black slaves – men, women and children – petitioned the House of Assembly for redress against the "firm judicial policy" of the Supreme Court that undermined their human property.[125] The material part of the petition reads, "But, unfortunately for your petitioners, owing to certain doubts now entertained by The King's Courts of Law in this Province, such property is rendered wholly untenable by your petitioners, whose Negro Servants are daily leaving their service and setting your petitioners at defiance. For, if it be no longer incumbent upon the Negro who claims his liberty within a Colony, to produce the Certificate of his emancipation; or to shew that he was born of free parents, or, at the least, to prove that at some former period of his life he exercised the rights of a free person, it is in vain that his possessor attempts to litigate with him."

The issue was where the burden of proof lay: the master to prove title, or the slave to prove that he was either born free or had been set free. Unlike the masters, the courts did not assume that a Black was a slave; the onus was on the master to establish his claim by offering "more than ordinarily clear" or quiet title to the so-called property.

Though the petitioners had not asked for a bill, they got one regardless. On the same day the slave-masters' petition was tabled (it appears to have been too controversial to proceed any farther), Thomas Ritchie introduced *A Bill for regulating Negro Servitude within and throughout this Province*, which addressed the grievances stated in the petition. These two initiatives had doubtless been pre-concerted, the former preceding the latter on the Assembly's order paper. After first reading, an unsuccessful attempt was made by Thomas Roach, MHA for Cumberland County, to give the *Negro Bill* the three-month hoist. The motion was lost by sixteen to ten; however, all the lawyers in the legislature voted against it. After second reading, the *Negro Bill* was committed for study by a Committee of the Whole House, which afterwards reported that they had deferred it for three months; this time the House agreed to the deferral.

At the next session Ritchie, not to be outdone, reintroduced the *Negro Bill*, having ameliorated the title from "Servitude" to "Servants";[126] it would be easier to regulate individuals than an institution that lacked *bona fide* existence. As on the previous occasion, the bill was read a first and a second time and committed, whereupon it was again given the three-month hoist. There is no evidence that the bill was ever presented again. Little useful purpose would have been served by resurrecting a twice-deferred bill in order to address the grievances of petitioners who professed themselves to be "far from pretending to advocate Slavery as a System" and who also conceded that "perhaps the true interests of Humanity, may require, in this Colony, the abolition of that particular species of property" that they claimed as their legal right.

Even if the 1808 bill had passed the House of Assembly, however, it would certainly have been rejected by the Council, just as its 1789 predecessor had been. Chief Justice Blowers, presiding ex officio, and Attorney-General Uniacke, a newly appointed member, remained implacable opponents of *Negro Bills*. It seems probable, moreover, that among the several lawyer MHAs, Ritchie was alone in advocating the legalization of Black slavery. He was merely playing to his audience of county constituents, on whom he made such a profound impression through his determined advocacy of their customary right to property in Black slaves, that he was returned by acclamation to the House of Assembly in four consecutive general elections.

It would appear that after 1808 there were neither any slave cases nor any further attempts tot enact a *Negro Bill*. The insecurity of title to their human "property," of which the petitioners had complained, was parenthetically noted in a Kings County deed of 1807, in which the administrators of Joseph Allison, late MHA for Horton Township, sold a young Black woman as part of the residue of his personal estate, "if a Negro can be considered personal property in Nova Scotia."[127] Four years later, moreover, the southern military Loyalist Captain Daniel McNeill attempted to retail in Nova Scotia "a considerable number" of slaves that he had accepted in North Carolina as settlement in kind of a debt. "However, Captain McNeill's slaves, on landing, were told by certain officious persons in Windsor that they were 'free niggers' [*sic*] when they touched British soil, and nearly all the male slaves ran away."[128]

Though Bell rejects the explanation that the difference of opinion between Chief Justices Blowers and Ludlow may have resulted from their respective legal training, there is no denying that the legal culture of slavery, no less than slave law itself, was far from monolithic, and that lawyers' attitudes towards the institution varied widely within the former thirteen colonies. Regional differences in slavery jurispru-dence and statute law among (and within) New England, the middle Atlantic colonies, and even the South might well account for ideologi-cal differences among lawyers and judges who had to grapple with the legality of slavery in a colonial backwater such as pre–American Revolution Nova Scotia, while at the same time acculturating them-selves to a small, insular indigenous bar that was generally hostile to and uncomprehending of the American view of any matter. It bears remarking that the only New York Loyalist lawyer practising in Nova Scotia was Thomas Barclay of Annapolis, with whom Thomas Ritchie articled; New Brunswick was perhaps the worse affected for having a New York Loyalist lawyer and judge as chief justice for the first twenty-odd years of its existence.

Perhaps the best formulation of the significance of the legal history of slavery in Nova Scotia is the sociological one offered by Joy Mannette, who argues that "a practice and its ideological forms cannot simply be overturned through a legal act [i.e., the failure to uphold slavery]. These practices merely become modified in terms of a new ideology."[129] The ideology is, of course, racism, and the rout of the slave-masters in the first decade of the nineteenth century fostered a heritage of re-sentment that has vitiated race relations in Annapolis-Digby until the present day. The judicial failure to deal equitably with the murder in 1985 of Graham Cromwell [Jarvis], himself the descendant of Annapo-lis County Loyalist slaves, shows indeed the truth of the adage *plus ça change plus c'est la meme chose*. Not even in late eighteenth-century Nova Scotia could a Black slave have been murdered by his white master with so high a degree of virtual impunity.[130]

Slavery in Prince Edward Island

In 1781 the legislature of Saint John's Island (Prince Edward Island) passed *An Act, declaring that Baptism of SLAVES shall not exempt them from BONDAGE* (emphasis in original). It stated that people of African descent "who now are on this Island, or may hereafter be imported or brought therein (being Slaves) shall continue such, unless freed by his, her, or their respective owners."[131] Ten years later, in an attempt to en-courage settlement, the local newspaper printed an Act of Parliament that promised the value of "forty shillings for every Negro brought by such white person."[132] The 1781 Act remained on the statute book as a dead letter until repealed in 1825.[133] But why did the Prince Edward

Island Assembly repeal the 1781 Act long after slavery had ceased to exist on the Island? And who promoted and introduced both Acts and why? These questions raise important issues about slavery, slave life, and slave emancipation on the Island. They also present historians with an interesting paradox: why did the Maritime colony with the smallest number of slaves and slaveholders pass the only statute relating to Black slavery? Ironically, while Prince Edward Island was the only jurisdiction in British North America that enacted a statute regulating slaves, the standard works about the history of Prince Edward Island do not examine slavery.[134] Indeed, in an otherwise excellent biographical entry about one of the Island's largest slaveholders, Colonel Joseph Robinson, J.M. Bumsted does not mention his slaveholding.[135] In many ways, the lack of attention to the Island's history of slavery says much about the general failure of Atlantic Canadian historians to examine the contours of slavery in the region. As Joanne Pope Melish has argued for New England, historians must rewrite the history of Atlantic Canada to include the experience of slaves.[136]

The enactment and repeal of formal slave law in Prince Edward Island also contributed to local understandings of race. The discrimination Black Islanders faced in judicial decisions and other ways after the decline and disappearance of slavery underlines the failure of emancipation to bring equality to local people of African descent. The formation of racial understanding on the Island had its roots in the attitudes and circumstances that gave rise to the 1781 slave law and the exploitation of Black slaves. In many ways, the making of slavery and race connected this peripheral island to broader notions of Black enslavement and inferiority that permeated the British Atlantic world in the late eighteenth and early nineteenth centuries.[137]

Slaves and people of African descent are absent from Prince Edward Island historiography for several reasons. There were an unknown number of Black people on the Island, and there is scant primary evidence about their experiences. It is problematic even to try to estimate the actual number of Black slaves on the Island without a significant number of advertisements for runaways, sales or estate inventories, manumissions or bequests, court records, or other primary sources. However, we have identified almost fifty slaves from primary and secondary sources. The omission of Black people and slavery from Island historiography is thus understandable because of small numbers. But this explanation goes only so far, and there is no doubt another, more subtle reason. Most histories of slavery are rife with stories of oppression of labouring, indentured, or enslaved groups. Prince Edward Island is no exception, but the focus on a landless class of workers has not included Blacks or Aboriginal people; instead, there has been an emphasis on whites who suffered under the absentee landlords. In writing about the Escheat movement and how the tenants resisted the landlords, the history of other oppressed peoples such as Blacks and Aboriginal people has been largely ignored.

Indeed, although slavery had ended by 1825, it became a symbol of the oppression of Islanders by the absentee proprietors and a useful tool in the arsenal of the Escheat movement. Those opposed to the system liked to characterize the landlords as slave-owners and the tenants as slaves. Tenant victims were fundamentally unfree because, like slaves, they were denied the right to hold property: the owned could not own. Rusty Bittermann has shown how slavery's legacy was appropriated and manipulated by the opponents of the landholding system.[138] Since the Escheat movement arose while slavery was still in full flower, it is unsurprising that tenant farmers should compare themselves – or be compared – with the slaves of their landlords (or landlords agents). Whether it was escheat of proprietors' land or emancipation of slaves, the fundamental issue was the same: infringing upon the rights of private property. The issue was negotiated differently, of course, depending on the context. In the land question, the government, after much uncertainty and hesitation, acted – and acted decisively. Emancipation of slaves was at first a matter of conscience by the individual slaveholder, and later this became generalized into a new, enlightened, social consensus in which the owning of human beings was seen as immoral and an undermining of the foundations of law and civil society. Public opinion came gradually to accept that owning Black people was sinful, which reflected poorly not on the victim but on the perpetrator.

While progressive imperial measures like the *Colonial Slavery Abolition Act* of 1833 may have encouraged the Escheat movement, the emancipation of slaves – which took place long before 1833 – caused not a ripple.[139] After all, it benefited no one other than Black people, who were conspicuous by their absence from the ranks of tenant farmers "enslaved" by the proprietors. The further slavery receded into the past, the more useful it became as an allegory of oppression for white persons who never were enslaved.

Thanks to the work of Hornby and some limited but enticing primary sources, we know something about the character of Island slave ownership, slave families, work patterns, and master–slave relations.[140]

On Prince Edward Island, masters came from the ranks of the elite. Generally, masters possessed one or two slaves with a few owning up to five.[141] The presence of Black slaves in the households of wealthy Prince Edward Island homes followed slaveholding patterns in colonial Boston, where, "for the most part, owners were people of wealth who lived opulently."[142] The use of slaves as symbols of wealth and status is underlined by the fact that the only "gentlemen" in eastern Prince County were those who "brought family slaves with them." Clearly, gentility among the Loyalists was inextricably linked to owning slaves. The two largest slaveholders, Loyalists Colonel Robinson and Lieutenant-Governor Fanning, both enjoyed wealth and high social status. Yet pre-Loyalists such as Chief Justice Peter Stewart and Governor Walter Patterson also owned slaves. Loyalist William Schurman owned a business, and his will indicates he enjoyed some degree of wealth. As Hornby points out, "The local elite – both Loyalists and others – was largely a slave-owning group."[143] In this sense, slaveholding differed greatly from Nova Scotia and New Brunswick, where it was common for the middling sort to possess slaves. For example, grocer Robert Wilkins of Shelburne owned at least one slave, while baker Richard Jenkins owned three.[144] Slave-owners on Prince Edward Island were wealthy and politically well connected; their human chattels, though, were usually isolated with only one or two per household.

Slaves were passed down through families and, in some cases, a new generation of slaves was born on the Island. For example, in 1802, Island slaveholder Thomas Haszard gave "to grand Daughter Hariot Clarissa Haszard and my grand Daughter [Louisa] Haszard one molatta girl about five years of age, named Catharine." Haszard also sold to William Haszard "a certain mollatta Boy of three years of age called Simon."[145] Given the relatively late date of this sale and the age of the child slaves, it is clear that the Haszard family intended to keep a new generation of slaves. Colonel Robinson also owned the children of his slave Amelia and, as he made clear in his ledger, an offer of freedom for Amelia and her husband did not extend to their children.[146] In Prince Edward Island, slavery lasted a few generations, and masters remained loath to give up the cheap labour that their slaves provided. They were, so to speak, a renewable resource.

Upper Canada's 1793 slavery abolition Act was, as Bruce Ziff states, "the first abolitionist statute in the Empire,"[147] but Prince Edward Island's 1781 Act was the only statute in the post-revolutionary, second British Empire to regulate slaves explicitly. Its enactment suggests a debate on the reception of law – whether or not settlers brought with them the laws of their place of origin and, if so, whether that law attached itself to slaves. In particular, would it have been thought that Scottish settlers brought Scots law with them into an English common-law colony where secure slave-hold tenure was customary? Paradoxically, a Scottish immigrant to Prince Edward Island might hold slaves though he could not do so in Scotland, where, as discussed above, the customary illegality of slavery was upheld by the supreme civil court in the famous case of *Knight v. Wedderburn* in 1778. The putative reception of the Scottish law of slavery plays no part in the legal history of Prince Edward Island. Nevertheless, the very existence of the 1781 Act prohibiting emancipatory baptism suggests that the Scottish law of slavery was implicitly "received" along with the Scottish immigrants arriving in numbers over the previous decade and deemed to be in force until barred by local legislation.[148]

From 1767 onward, most of the land in Prince Edward Island was owned by "proprietors" – absentee landlords in England and Scotland who operated through local agents. Among the more active proprietors was Sir James Montgomery, father of Scottish emigration to the Island, who in 1781 was lord advocate (attorney-general) of Scotland. It was Montgomery who tellingly referred to his tenants-servants-retainers shipped to PEI in 1770 as "white negroes."[149] The chief justice of the colony was another Scot, Peter Stewart – a protégé of Montgomery, brother of a proprietor, and known slave-owner. Stewart's biographer observes that "what legal training he had was in Scottish law rather than the English common law that Whitehall always expected to serve as the basis for a colonial judicial system."[150] But Stewart, as a slave-owner, was motivated to ensure that the Scottish law of slavery did not obtain in Prince Edward Island. The Island slave law was enacted in 1781, when Stewart, as ex officio president of the Council, was an active legislator. Stewart had come to Prince Edward Island in 1775, three years before the judges in Scotland declared the custom of the country to be that slavery was not and never had been legal. The reasoning was that Scotland was a Christian nation, and that Christian conversion and consequent baptism set a slave free from slavery as much as it did from sin. The Prince Edward Island Act did not discourage the baptism of slaves – that was accepted and it continued to be done – but neither could the Act be used to justify emancipation. Baptism made slaves Christians; it did not make them free.

Prince Edward Island's slave law drew little or no attention when

enacted. It came in the midst of a politically contentious time, which
J.M. Bumsted describes as "grabbing for land" – a kind of property different from slaves. At the same time, there was an interesting contrast.
When the governor and legislature were taking steps to confiscate and
sell absentee proprietors' lands on which quit-rent had not been paid,
they were also acting to uphold, in Bumsted's words, "one of the major watchwords of eighteenth-century Britain: the sacred right of property."[151] The slave law was a perfect example of what Bumsted, writing
about the legislature's 1780 session, saw as enactments "obviously looking forward to a conclusion of wartime hostilities, to the end of government largesse, and to a return to settlement and development."[152] In
anticipation of victory, peace, and a return to normality, government
wanted to ensure that slave-hold tenure was secured against potential
threats, such as legal birthright or "baggage" from Scotland.[153] That being said, there is no direct evidence of what triggered the slave law or
who promoted it. We do not know whether it was an initiative of the
Assembly or the Council. We do not even know who wrote it, though
Chief Justice Stewart seems a likely candidate. Another is Attorney-
General Phillips Callbeck, an Irish lawyer who was also a slave-holder,
as were Governor Patterson and Speaker of the House Walter Berry.
The same was probably also true of Thomas Desbrisay, lieutenant-governor and ex officio president of the Council in its legislative capacity.

What is known is that on 1 March 1781 Governor Patterson wrote
the secretary of state, "Though I had a meeting of our Assembly in July
last, yet I found it would be both for the interest of the Island to have an
other meeting this winter, and accordingly I call'd an Assembly on the
20th of last Month, when, after sitting 20 Days, they passed the following Laws to which I have given my assent."[154] Among the bills passed
was the slave Act, the appropriateness of which was such that the governor did not bother to provide an explanatory gloss.[155] Even the law
officer of the Board of Trade, Richard ("Omniscient") Jackson, KC, MP,
to whom colonial laws were referred for a legal opinion on their validity, pronounced it materially unobjectionable and "of public utility."[156]
How could any law for the greater protection of private property not
be?

Despite its title, preamble, and principal provision, the Act had three
separate and unrelated provisions that, taken together, amount to a
germinal slave code. If doubts had arisen "whether slaves, by becoming Christians, or being admitted to Baptism, should by virtue thereof,
be made free" (preamble), then the Scottish law of slavery was sus-

pected of being of full force and effect. The second provision secured the property right: enslaved Blacks or mulattoes already present and accounted for or imported remained slaves until manumitted by their owner. There was to be no emancipation otherwise. The third and last provision recited the Roman law from which Scottish law itself ultimately derived. Slavehood descended matrilineally: the children of an enslaved woman were themselves slaves, hence the reference to mulattoes (children whose fathers were white); slave paternity was not legally material.

Nothing more is known about this Act. Between 1781 and 1825, when it was repealed, slavery in Prince Edward Island was gradually extinguished. There was no further legislation. The first series of consolidated statutes (stating the law as of 1788) includes the Act without comment, so it must have remained good law until slavery ceased.[157] Lieutenant-Governor Fanning (a former lawyer and judge) set an example of public-spiritedness by manumitting both of his slaves. Some credit for the demise of slavery must also go to the Reverend James MacGregor (1759–1830), the Scottish Antiburgher Seceder missionary and radical abolitionist who in 1788 launched Canada's antislavery movement. In the 1790s MacGregor visited Prince Edward Island on more than one occasion and intervened with slave-owners on behalf of their slaves.[158] One of the few resident proprietors accused those on the other side of the land question of comparing the landlord-tenant system with slavery.[159]

In 1802 slave Sam ran away from his English owner Thomas Wright and got himself into the Supreme Court on habeas corpus so that the Court could investigate the lawfulness of his being owned. Wright was able to produce proof of purchase, the Court found no defect in title or on the face of the record, and Sam was reclaimed.[160] As we have seen, this approach to emancipation had been tested in Nova Scotia, where it worked, and in New Brunswick, where it had not. By the early nineteenth century, slavery had begun to decline, although while it is clear that slavery disappeared before 1825, it is unclear exactly when, why, or how it ended. Hornby is certainly right that "in practice [slavery] seems to have been eroded earlier [than 1825] by social and religious pressures."[161] Slaves were manumitted by will or otherwise, or simply absconded and were not pursued or reclaimed. The disappearance of slavery in Nova Scotia and later in New Brunswick probably also played a role. The famous Susannah ("Soak") Schurman was clearly no longer a slave in July 1819 when her former owner, Loyalist William

Schurman, made generous provision for her in his will. She was, he or-
dained, to be "provided for in the family with meat drink and clothing
as long as she lives but if it be her choice to leave the family my will is to
give her fifty pounds lawful money of this Island to be raised out of my
Estate.'[162] As there is no record of her manumission, it may be assumed
that slavery was untenable by that time.

The reasons for the repeal of the 1781 Act in 1825 are opaque. In October 1825, Ewen Cameron (1788–1831), high sheriff and member for
Queens, introduced in the Assembly a bill to repeal the law.[163] It passed
quickly and quietly, apparently without any debate at all. The likeliest
candidate for the drafter of the repeal Act is William Johnston, newly
reappointed attorney-general, who had been a senior solicitor in Scotland's Court of Session before emigrating in 1812.[164] By 1825 Johnston
was the recognized leader of the government in the Assembly. The repeal Act looks like a declaratory Act, which affirms that slavery was
and had always been illegal – no less in Prince Edward Island than in
Scotland – and that the 1781 slave law was therefore unconstitutional.
With this interpretation, slave law repeal was Scotland's revenge, as
it was a reinstatement of the Scottish law of slavery as it stood in 1781
when the slave law was enacted.

Attorney-General Johnston's involvement aside, why did an obsolete
Act regulating a class of personal property that no longer existed attract formal repeal? Clearly more was involved than the superficially
apparent purpose stated in its preamble, which declared, "Whereas by
the [1781] Act slavery is sanctioned and permitted within this Island,
... it is highly necessary that an Act so in variance with the laws of England and the Freedom of the Country should be forthwith repealed."
The preamble made false and unsustainable historical claims. The 1781
slave law did not "sanction" or "permit" slavery; it simply responded
to a perceived or anticipated socio-legal need by regulating slaves. Nor
was it "at variance with the laws of England" or the "freedom of the
country" at the time of its passage. It was, on the contrary, in full com-
pliance with them. Legal qualms and long memories dictated that the
slave law repeal Act passed with a suspending clause, which meant
it could not become law until confirmed by Whitehall. It was referred
to the committee of the Privy Council for Trade and Plantations and
by them to counsel, James Stephen, who reported favourably.[165] The
slave law repeal Act was subsequently confirmed by Order in Council
in November 1826.[166] The anti-slavery spirit of the age was in sync with
a minor colony's apology for once legislating an ad hoc slave code. In

theory, however, if no longer in fact, slavery still existed because it had not been abolished by an Act of Parliament.

Slave law repeal was cosmetic and its impact nugatory. It made the ruling class feel better about themselves and the society they governed. Getting rid of the slave law long after slavery had disappeared posed no legal or social risk whatsoever and did nothing to improve the lot of former slaves. By 1825 the British Atlantic world had changed. The old, defunct, and discredited slave law was the proverbial straw man – a relic of times past when the scope of property was significantly wider in one respect. Had slavery still existed in fact, repealing the slave law would have been much less straightforward. By 1825 the anti-slavery movement, which culminated in the *Colonial Slavery Abolition Act* (1833), was well underway. In 1823 the Society for the Mitigation and Gradual Abolition of Slavery was founded in England, and the government, in which George Canning was foreign secretary and House of Commons leader, passed resolutions in Parliament instructing colonial governors on measures to ameliorate slavery where it still existed.[167] By 1825, moreover, the Colonial Office had been expanded and reorganized "principally in response to the anti-Slavery campaign."[168] It therefore seems probable that Prince Edward Island's slave law repeal was a gesture of due diligence – complying, however symbolically, with the imperial initiative. Although it served no practical purpose, as propaganda it has flourished up to the present day and given rise to the myth that slavery in Prince Edward Island was abolished by local statute. Nothing could be further from the truth.

In 1825 no bill abolishing slavery in England – much less the colonies – had yet been enacted by Parliament, nor did any colonial legislature ever enact such legislation. Despite its rhetorical flourish, the preamble of the repeal Act says nothing more than that the slave law was effective in its time – a time when slavery was a legally and socially accepted form of personal property. Slave law repeal signified not the end of slavery but the beginning of the anti-slavery movement: the campaign to abolish slavery elsewhere while it still existed.

NOTES

1 D.G. Bell, "Slavery and the Judges of Loyalist New Brunswick," *University of New Brunswick Law Journal* 31 (1982): 9–42; J. Barry Cahill, "Slavery and the Judges of Loyalist Nova Scotia," *University of New Brunswick Law Jour-*

nal 43 (1994): 73–135; J. Barry Cahill and H. Amani Whitfield, "Slave Life and Slave Law in Colonial Prince Edward Island, 1769–1825," *Acadiensis* 38 (2009): 29–51.

2 John Johnston, "Research Note: Mathieu Da Costa along the Coasts of Nova Scotia: Some Possibilities," *Journal of the Royal Nova Scotia Historical Society* 4 (2001): 152–64.

3 Kenneth Donovan, "Slaves and Their Owners in Île Royale, 1713–1760," *Acadiensis* 25, no. 1 (Autumn 1995): 10–11.

4 Ibid., 3–32; Kenneth Donovan, "Slaves in Île Royale," *French Colonial History* 5 (2004): 25–42.

5 Margaret Conrad, ed., *Making Adjustments: Change and Continuity in Planter Nova Scotia, 1759–1800* (Fredericton, NB: Acadiensis, 1991); Margaret Conrad and Barry Moody, eds., *Planter Links: Community and Culture in Colonial Nova Scotia* (Fredericton, NB: Acadiensis, 2001); Allen Robertson, "Bondage and Freedom: Apprentices, Servants, and Slaves in Colonial Nova Scotia," *Collections of the Royal Nova Scotia Historical Society* 44 (1996): 57–69.

6 Jim Hornby, *Black Islanders: Prince Edward Island's Historical Black Community* (Charlottetown: Institute of Island Studies, 1991), 2.

7 The literature about free Blacks during and after the Revolutionary War is voluminous. For an overview of the historiography, see Harvey Amani Whitfield, "Black Loyalists and Black Slaves in Maritime Canada," *History Compass* 5 (2007): 1980–97. See also Mary Louise Clifford, *From Slavery to Freetown: Black Loyalists after the American Revolution* (Jefferson, NC: McFarland, 1999); Graham Russell Hodges, ed., *The Black Loyalist Directory: African Americans in Exile after the American Revolution* (New York: Garland, 1996); John W. Pulis, ed., *Moving On: Black Loyalists in the Afro-American World* (New York: Garland, 1999); Cassandra Pybus, *Epic Journeys of Freedom: Runaway Slaves of the American Revolution and Their Global Quest for Liberty* (Boston: Beacon, 2006); Simon Schama, *Rough Crossings: Britain, the Slaves and the American Revolution* (2005; repr., New York: Harper Collins, 2006); Carole Watterson Troxler, "Re-enslavement of Black Loyalists: Mary Postell in South Carolina, East Florida, and Nova Scotia," *Acadiensis* 37, no. 2 (Summer/Autumn 2008): 70–85; James W. St.G. Walker, *The Black Loyalists: The Search for a Promised Land in Nova Scotia and Sierra Leone, 1783–1870* (London: Longman and Dalhousie University Press, 1976); Ruth Holmes Whitehead and Carmelita A.M. Robertson, eds., *The Life of Boston King: Black Loyalist, Minister and Master Carpenter* (Halifax: Nova Scotia Museum and Nimbus, 2003); Ellen Gibson Wilson, *The Loyal Blacks* (New York: Capricorn Books, 1976); Barry Cahill, "The Black Loyalist Myth in Atlantic Canada," *Acadiensis* 29, no. 1 (Autumn 1999): 76–87; James W. St.G.

Walker, "Myth, History and Revisionism: The Black Loyalists Revisited," *Acadiensis* 29, no. 1 (Autumn 1999): 88–105 (Walker's response to Cahill); Robin Winks, *The Blacks in Canada* (Montreal: McGill-Queen's University Press, 1991).

8 The most reliable statistics are reproduced in E.C. Wright, *The Loyalists of New Brunswick* (Wolfville: printed by author, 1955), 247–9, but they are incomplete. The compilation – from which come the statistics reproduced in Walker, *Black Loyalists*, 33 – is unreliable.

9 It then consisted of all the territory between Kings to the east and Shelburne to the southwest.

10 In his review of *The Black Loyalists*, Winks candidly admitted that neither he "nor Dr Walker have provided sufficient information on the nature of the Black community in the Annapolis Valley, and what we do provide tends to be set against each other." Winks, "Review of *The Black Loyalists*," *Dalhousie Review* 57 (1977): 151.

11 Petition of Thomas Peters to secretary of state, 1791, qtd in Wilson, *Loyal Blacks*, 180–1.

12 It is claimed by eyewitnesses that the Ross-Thomson house in Shelburne, since 1791 a branch of the Nova Scotia Museum, formerly had manacles in the cellar. Needless to say, such artefacts of Shelburne's slave-owning heritage were not touristy and did not remain in situ. See W.A. Spray, *The Blacks in New Brunswick* (Fredericton: Brunswick, 1972), 21n11: "A number of slave-owners' homes had rooms in the basement equipped with chains, which were used to confine slaves who had attempted to run away." A 1949 pamphlet written by a former occupant of the house is quite candid about the material culture of slavery: D. Webster, *The Charlotte Lane House Which Is the Old Ross-Thomson House in Shelburne Nova Scotia* (Milton, MA: Turtle, 1949), 11.

13 (1772) Lofft I; 98 E.R. 499.

14 Reginald Coupland. *The British Anti-Slavery Movement* (London, 1933), 55.

15 *Somerset*, 510. In *The Problem of Slavery in the Age of Revolution* (Cornell: Ithaca, 1975), 476–7, David Davis argues that there is a significantly more accurate version of Mansfield's remarks; but, having been long ignored, it is irrelevant for the present purposes.

16 F.O. Shyllon, *Black Slaves in Britain* (London: Oxford University Press, 1974), 234.

17 Roger Anstey, *The Atlantic Slave Trade and British Abolition* (Atlantic Highlands, NJ: Humanities, 1975), 273, 321.

18 Winks, *Blacks in Canada*, 96–8.

19 Ibid., 100–2.

20 W. Chipman to S. Blowers (draft), 15 Dec. 1799, vol. 6, ser. 1, D 1, MG 23, Lawrence Collection, Library Archives Canada (hereafter LAC).

21 J. Hannay, *History of New Brunswick* (Saint John: John A. Bowes, 1909), 1:221–2; I.A. Jack, "The Loyalists and Slavery in New Brunswick," *Proceedings of the Royal Society of Canada*, ser. 2, vol. 4 (1898): 137–85; J.W. Lawrence, *Foot-Prints; or, Incidents in [the] Early History of New Brunswick* (Saint John: J. & A. McMillan, 1883), 57–8; Lawrence, *Judges of New Brunswick and Their Times* (Saint John: Acadiensis, 1907), 70–6; W.O. Raymond, "The Negro in New Brunswick," *Neith* 27, no. 1 (1903): 32–3; T.W. Smith, "The Slave in Canada," *Collections of the Nova Scotia Historical Society* no. 3 (1898): 98–105.

22 A. Gorman Condon, *Envy of the American States: The Loyalist Dream for New Brunswick* (Fredericton: New Ireland, 1984), 192; Gorman Condon, "1783–1800: Loyalist Arrival, Acadian Return, Imperial Reform," in *Atlantic Region to Confederation: A History*, ed. P.A. Buckner and J.G. Reid (Fredericton: Acadiensis, 1994), 200; Spray, *Blacks in New Brunswick*, 23–5; Winks, *Blacks in Canada*, 108–9.

23 Notoriously, s. 2 of Nova Scotia's *Innholders Act* (SNS 1762, cap 1) prohibited tavern-keepers from accepting pledges from various classes of persons including "negro slave[s]." When the first sitting of New Brunswick's legislature enacted s. 2 of its own *Inn-Holders Act* (SNB 1786, cap 36), which was based on Nova Scotia's law and was in nearly identical language, the reference to slaves was omitted. This was deliberate; and in transmitting the statute to London, the Executive observed that in New Brunswick "slavery has no Sanction from Law": vol. 1, CO 190, National Archives, UK (hereafter NA). Presumably this meant that, as there was no statute in New Brunswick establishing slavery, it would be improper to make any legislative allusion to its existence.

24 Ward Chipman anti-slavery brief [1800]: Archives and Special Collections, University of New Brunswick, Fredericton. View images of Chipman's eighty-one-page brief at http://www.lib.unb.ca/Texts/NBHistory/chipman/. Jack transcribed it in "Loyalists and Slavery," 155–85, and another transcription accompanies the images on the University of New Brunswick site. One early slave case about which little is known is a 1789 habeas corpus against Benjamin Davis for his slave Prince. The result was that "ye negro [was] ordered to be deliver'd to his Master as a servant for Life": Supreme Court Minutes (Crown Causes): vol. 2, RS 30B, RG 5, Provincial Archives of New Brunswick (hereafter PANB). (Note the reluctance of the clerk to use the term *slave*.) Concerning Davis and Prince, see also *Royal Gazette*, 17 June 1788.

25 W. Chipman to S. Blowers (draft), 15 Dec. 1799, vol. 6, ser. 1, D 1, MG 23, Lawrence Collection, LAC; Ward Chipman anti-slavery brief [1800], Archives and Special Collections, University of New Brunswick.

26 T.B. Vincent, "Samuel Denny Street," *Dictionary of Canadian Biography*, 1987, 6:739–41.

27 Four of the slaves dealt with in this chapter went by informal names – Nancy (for Ann) and Stacey, Dick, and Jim Hopefield (for Patience, Richard, and James). As it appears that formalization of the names was contrived for court proceedings, I use mostly the nicknames, as apparently more authentic.

28 Jones, a former captain in the Maryland Loyalists, advertised for five escaped slaves (including Nancy and her young son Lidge) in 1786, for another in 1787, and for Lidge again in 1816: *Royal Gazette*, 25 July 1786, 7 Mar 1787, 9 July 1816; W.A. Spray, "Caleb Jones," *Dictionary of Canadian Biography* (1983), 5:456. The not very extensive archival record of *R. v. Jones* is scattered across five repositories, a legacy of nineteenth-century souvenir hunting. Most documents are in the Supreme Court Records, RS 42 1800, RG 5, PANB. The writ and return for *R. v. Jones* are printed in Jack, "Loyalists and Slavery," 184–5, from contemporary copies that Chipman included at the end of his brief.

29 Two nearly simultaneous habeas corpus applications on behalf of two female slaves held by two ex-military Loyalists both living across the Saint John River from Fredericton was a coincidence so improbable that historians beginning with Jack and Lawrence (note 21) have generally conflated the two women into a single case concerning a "Nancy Morton," even to the extent of altering the name of the slave when reprinting documents.

30 W. Chipman to S. Blowers (draft), 15 Dec. 1799, vol. 6, D 1, MG 23, LAC; *Royal Gazette*, 18 Feb. 1800.

31 Bliss's thirty-one-page memorandum of authorities is F51, S 29B, Odell Family Collection, New Brunswick Museum, Saint John.

32 Allen is said to have freed his slaves as a result of the opinion he formed at the trial. Saunders is not known to have held slaves in New Brunswick but he had owned many in Virginia. As a result of the trial, Stair Agnew challenged Judge Allen to a duel, which the latter declined. It is sometimes said that words spoken at the slavery hearing led to a duel between Street and J.M. Bliss, a junior counsel for the master. A Street-Bliss duel (with Agnew as a second) did occur, but it was a few weeks prior to the slave hearing and had nothing to do with it: D.R. Jack, "An Affair of Honor," *Acadiensis* (1905): 176–7.

33 Chipman understood that Street would bring an action on Nancy's

behalf against Jones for false imprisonment but it seems not to have proceeded.

34 *Journal of the Votes and Proceedings of the House of Assembly* (Saint John: John Ryan, 1801), 641, 650–2; S14-B9.1, RG 2, House of Assembly Papers, PANB.

35 30 Geo. 3, c. 27 (UK).

36 Winks, *Blacks in Canada*, 106–7.

37 *Royal Gazette*, 28 July 1801. The paper had also reprinted the 1790 Act at the request of a "Constant Customer" on 14 January 1800, shortly before *R. v. Jones* had its hearing. John Ryan, editor of the *Gazette*, was a slave-owner himself and a steady supporter of the cause.

38 Saunders Papers, Miscellaneous, n.d. #7, UNB Archives.

39 Supreme Court Minutes (Crown Causes), vol. 2, RS 30B, RG 5, PANB.

40 As this little narrative progresses, one observes that the slave's name graduates from Stach to Statia to Stacey. Then, following an apparent convention of turning nicknames into formal names for court documents, the Stacey is converted to Patience – a name she likely never used.

41 Unlike his younger half-brothers Dick and Jim, Stacey's son Joe (known later as Joe/Joseph Hopefield, though his father is unknown) apparently does not figure in slave litigation. However, on 4 Feb. 1814 he apprenticed his seven-year-old son, Dick, to Joseph Clarke Jr of Maugerville: F1, S 34, Hubbard Family Papers, New Brunswick Museum. As noted in the text, Clarke's father had owned Joe's mother and half-siblings and so presumably Joe as well. This apprenticeship looks like part of one of those transitional arrangements mentioned by Ward Chipman whereby Joe's branch of the Hopefield family passed from slavery to freedom via conversion of service for life to service for a term of years.

42 To avoid confusion over the ultimately three Dick Hopefields in this family's story, I follow court documents in referring to the father as Richard Hopefield Sr.

43 G.R. Hodges, *Black Loyalist Directory: African Americans in Exile after the American Revolution* (New York: Garland Publishing, 1996), 78; *Saint John Gazette*, 29 June 1792; "Patience" Hopefield's deposition, 2 July 1805, and Richard Hopefield Sr's deposition, 5 July 1805: Supreme Court Records, 1805, RS 42, RG 5, PANB. At the time of her 1805 affidavit Stacey said that Dick Hopefield Jr was already upwards of twenty-two, which would put the attempted abduction and his subsequent birth at 1783 or early 1784. Her husband said that Dick was born shortly after Governor Carleton's arrival, which would put it in 1785 or the very end of 1784. Dick himself was under the impression that he had been born in New York.

44 M.C. New, *Maryland Loyalists in the American Revolution* (Centreville, MD:

Tidewater Publishing, 1996), 112; W.A. Spray, "Stair Agnew," *Dictionary of Canadian Biography* (1987), 6:6–7.

45 Statement of Garret Clopper, 9 Feb 1805, vol. 19, series 1, D 1, MG 23, Lawrence Collection, LAC; Affidavits of Cornelius Thompson and John Coombs, 10 Jan. 1805, RS 42 1805, RG 5, Supreme Court Records, PANB; W.G. MacFarlane, *Fredericton History: Two Centuries of Romance, War, Privation and Struggle* (Woodstock, NB: Non-Entity, 1981), 53 (puts the appearance before the York General Sessions at 1801). Given Hopefield's fraught relations with Agnew, it is more than curious that in February 1805 he put his mark to a deposition drawn up by Ward Chipman to the effect that Street had made the habeas corpus application without his knowledge or consent. With Hopefield still living with Agnew, it may have been politic to affirm this. It did not stop the habeas corpus application going forward or the Hopefield civil suit against Agnew that is noted below.

46 There was much evidence on this point. Hopefield Sr affirmed that he had "married" Stacey, and Joseph Clarke's 1792 slave advertisement for Stacey noted that Hopefield claimed her as his wife. Yet on other occasions in the past Hopefield had denied formal marriage. This denial was corroborated by Joseph Hewlett, who dismissed Hopefield and sent him away when he discovered that he and Stacey were unmarried. It was also corroborated somewhat by the Anglican rector of Gagetown (Clarke's brother), who recalled being approached by Hopefield to marry him to an unnamed ex-slave whose freedom Hopefield had purchased from William Peters. At that time Hopefield denied that he was already married to Stacey. Significantly, the cleric remained suspicious on this point and refused to marry them. Various affidavits, dated July 1805 (supporting Dick Hopefield Jr) and dated Jan. 1806 (supporting Agnew), are in RS 42 1802 (a large file of misplaced documents) and 1805, RG 5, Supreme Court Records, PANB; drafts in Ward Chipman's handwriting are at the Saint John Free Public Library.

47 Agnew's answer was that he had unthinkingly copied out what Caleb Jones had written as a return in *R. v. Jones*, without considering the possibility that Hopefield Sr might have been free. After much inquiry the Supreme Court accepted his error as a mistake rather than a lie.

48 RS 42 1805, RG 5, PANB. The final reference to the case in Supreme Court minutes is the defendant's successful motion for a special jury.

49 Supreme Court Minutes (Crown Causes), vol. 2, RS 30B, RG 5, PANB.

50 Chipman annotated his brief as if prepared for use in Trinity term 1805, corresponding to a hearing date of 4 July. Supreme Court minutes for that day show the court sidetracked on the question of whether Agnew had

made a false return to the writ and what should be done about it, with the court (Ludlow, Allen, Saunders) divided. However, if this were also the occasion of the principal argument on slavery itself, then the court's disagreement was presumably Ludlow and Saunders upholding it and Allen against.

51 W.F. Odell to [W. Chipman], 12 Nov. 1805, vol. 3, series 1, D 1, MG 23, Lawrence Collection, LAC.

52 On Clarke, see L. McNeill, *Cloud of Witnesses* (Fredericton: printed by author, 1995), 9–21. In 1785 Clarke had sued a fellow Loyalist for transporting a slave to Nova Scotia and in 1786 he advertised for an escaped slave.

53 *Clarke v. Street*, RS 42 1806, RG 5, PANB. Street was still a member of the House of Assembly. Clarke's statement of claim suggests that while Hopefield disappeared on 1 Nov. and Street made the habeas corpus application on his behalf within a couple of weeks, it was not until 15 Dec. that Clarke discovered that Hopefield was at Elysian Fields, Street's farm. Three days later, when Clarke's son showed up to reclaim Hopefield, one of Street's sons assaulted him, giving rise to yet another lawsuit.

54 *Royal Gazette*, 10 Sept. 1806. The report emphasized that the "general question of Slavery was not agitated."

55 Attempting to meet Street's argument against the applicability of trover, Clarke's lawyer (J.M. Bliss) quoted from a pamphlet of legal opinions prepared a few years earlier for use in a trover case in Nova Scotia, which Ludlow rejected as insufficiently authoritative: [J. Aplin?], *Opinions of Several Gentlemen of the Law, on the Subject of Negro Servitude, in the Province of Nova-Scotia* (Saint John: John Ryan, 1802); images of Ward Chipman's own copy of this rare pamphlet can be viewed at University of Victoria, http://spcoll.library.uvic.ca/Digit/slavery_opinion/facsimile/facsimile_cnt.htm. It was reprinted in its entirety in the *Royal Gazette* beginning 19 June 1805 in the obvious hope of influencing *Clarke v. Street*. For the pamphlet's Nova Scotia context, see Barry Cahill, "Mediating a Scottish Enlightenment Ideal: The Presbyterian Dissenter Attack on Slavery in Late Eighteenth-Century Nova Scotia," in *Myth, Migration and the Making of Memory: Scotia and Nova Scotia, c. 1700–1990*, ed. Marjory Harper and Michael E. Vance, 189–201 (Halifax: Fernwood, 1999)

56 S. Blowers to W. Chipman, 7 Jan. 1800, vol. 6, series 1, D 1, MG 23, Lawrence Collection, LAC.

57 *Royal Gazette*, 9 July 1816. There is an even later advertisement in the Saint John area for a runaway "Negro Boy," but it is not claimed expressly that he was a slave: *New Brunswick Courier*, 5 Sept. 1818.

58 Spray, *Blacks in New Brunswick*, 33–5; Walker, *Black Loyalists*, 57.

59 Blue Book return, 1822, vol. 5, CO 193, NA.

60 D.V.J. Bell, "The Loyalist Tradition in Canada," in *Canadian History before Confederation: Essays and Interpretations*, ed. J. Bumsted (Georgetown, ON: Irwin-Dorsey, 1972), 213–14; K. McRae, "The Structure of Canadian History," in *Founding of New Societies*, ed. L. Hartz (New York: Harcourt, Brace, 1964), 234–5; G. Rawlyk, "The Federalist-Loyalist Alliance in New Brunswick 1784–1815," *Humanities Association Review* 28 (1977): 142.

61 D.G. Bell, "The Reception Question and the Constitutional Crisis of the 1790s in New Brunswick," *University of New Brunswick Law Journal* 29 (1980): 157.

62 Jack, "Loyalists and Slavery," 180; W.S. MacNutt, *New Brunswick: A History, 1784–1867* (Toronto: Macmillan, 1973), 53–63, 94–117.

63 W. Chipman to J. Sewall, 9 July 1784, vol. 10, GII, MG 23, Sewall Papers, LAC. This aspect of the psychology of New Brunswick's governing elite is noted in Condon, *Envy of the American States*, 173: "The original Loyalist leaders … were intensely proud, self-conscious men. Although born in an apparently safe, secure world, where the path to distinction was illuminated by a series of well placed markers, their lives had in fact been characterized by flux, by a series of abrupt reversals and successes, over which they themselves had little control."

64 E. Winslow to W. Chipman, 7 July 1783, in *Winslow Papers, AD 1776–1826*, ed. W.O. Raymond (Saint John, NB: Sun Printing, 1901), 98.

65 W.A. Spray, "John Saunders," *Dictionary of Canadian Biography* (1987), 6:683–8.

66 E. Winslow to W. Chipman, 7 July 1783, *Winslow Papers*, 100.

67 E. Winslow to W. Chipman, 26 Apr. 1784, *Winslow Papers*, 193.

68 Some examples are given in S. Wise, "Sermon Literature and Canadian Intellectual History," in Bumsted, *Canadian History before Confederation*, 258–64.

69 J. Odell, "Reflexions on the Importance of Religion as a Support to the Civil Authority," 26 June 1795, pkg. 15, Odell Papers, New Brunswick Museum.

70 D. Lyman to J. King, 15 Apr. 1795, vol. 6, CO 188, NA.

71 *Royal Gazette*, 21 Aug. 1795.

72 Walker, *Black Loyalists*, 41, 121.

73 Blowers to Chipman, 7 Jan. 1800.

74 Chipman to Blowers, 27 Feb. 1800, vol. 6, D1, MG 23, Ward Chipman Papers, LAC.

75 Winks, *Blacks in Canada*, 102.

76 B.C. Cuthbertson, *The Old Attorney General: A Biography of Richard John Uniacke* (Halifax: Nimbus, 1980), 4 and n6.

77 The 1787 bill is not extant, but its text can be substantially reconstructed from the 1789 bill, the text of which is extant in two versions, draft and engrossed. The author and/or introducer of the original bill, however, are alike unknown.

78 Blowers to Chipman, 7 Jan. 1800, 141–143, vol. 4, D 1, MG 23, Ward Chipman Papers, LAC.

79 Vol. 1, series "U" [Unpassed Bills], RG 5, NSARM.

80 Walker, *Black Loyalists*, 51.

81 Ibid., 102.

82 Statutes of Nova Scotia, 1762, c. 1. This Act was still in force in 1804 ("Uniacke's Laws"), and remained "on the books" while Beamish Murdoch was composing his *Epitome of the Laws of Nova-Scotia*, 4 vols. (Halifax: Howe, 1832–3), 1:189. The Act was not repealed until 1851.

83 Chipman to Blowers, 15 Dec. 1799, and Blowers to Chipman, 7 Jan. 1800, transcribed in Jack, "Loyalists and Slavery," 148–9.

84 Ibid., 151, citing Chipman to Blowers, 27 Feb. 1800. Counsel's reasoning could hardly have been based on principles of statutory interpretation or reception at common law, however, as the Act concerned was not in force in the neighbouring province. New Brunswick's *Statute Law Declaration Act*, (1791), 31 Geo. 3, c. 2, provided "that no Law, passed in the General Assembly, of the Province of Nova Scotia, before the erection, of the Province of New Brunswick [1784], shall be of any force or validity whatever, in this Province; or so deemed, or taken, in any Court of Law, or Equity, within the same." Indisputably, therefore, the Nova Scotia Act of 1762 did not extend to New Brunswick in 1800, though it might have done ten years earlier, as the New Brunswick declaratory Act had "no retrospective force or operation."

85 Blowers to Chipman, Apr. 1800, 141–3, vol. 4, D 1, MG 23, Ward Chipman Papers, LAC.

86 New York Loyalist Isaac Wilkins, for example, the *custos rotulorum*, "is said to have brought a number of slaves" with him to Shelburne. T.W. Smith, "The Slave in Canada," *Collections of the Nova Scotia Historical Society* (Halifax: The Society, 1899), 10:24.

87 *R. v. McNeill, ex parte Reed et al.*, Court of Sessions of the Peace, 1786, RG 60 (SH), NSARM; M. Robertson, *King's Bounty: A History of Early Shelbourne Nova Scotia* (Halifax: Nova Scotia Museum, 1983), 94–6; Walker, *Black Loyalists*, 51. See also "Extracts from the Special Sessions of Shelburne, N.S." (typewritten transcript), 11, vol. 141, MG 4, NSARM. This case, which was

habeas corpus in everything but name, occurred when four free Blacks were spirited from Halifax to Shelburne, in irons, consigned to the Bahamian slave market for sale. The magistrates court divided five to two in favour of discharging the Blacks, Wilkins voting with the majority.

88 Walker, *Black Loyalists*, 51.

89 File 4 (1791), folder 49, RG 60 (SH), NSARM; file 40 (photocopy of case file), vol. 19, MG 15, NSARM; "Extracts from the General Sessions" (typewritten transcript), 47, vol. 141, MG 4. The defendant, one Jesse Gray, a southern Loyalist, brought four "servants" with him to Argyle township (now Yarmouth County) in 1786.

90 Jack, "Loyalists and Slavery," 149, citing Blowers to Chipman, 22 Dec. 1799 [*sic*: 7 Jan. 1800).

91 W.R. Riddell supposed it to have been admitted in *Somerset* that consuetudinary law made slavery legal in the American colonies: "The Slave in Canada," *Journal of Negro History* 5 (1920): 372n20. The reference is to Francis Hargrave, who opened the pleading on behalf of the Black ex-slave James Somerset: "The question ... is not whether slavery is lawful in the colonies, (where a concurrence of unhappy circumstances has caused it to be established as necessary)." (1772), 98 E.R 499.

92 An exception is *Douglass v. McNeill* (N.S.S.C. 1791), suit for damages "for falsely affirming a Negro Wench named Phebe to be a Slave & his property and selling her as such." (N.B. "Phebe" was probably the same Phebe Martin whom the defendant had brought from Halifax to Shelburne in irons in 1786, only to see her discharged by the magistrates.) Attorney-General Blowers represented the plaintiff in this case of actionable fraud ("breach of title warranty"): D.G. Bell and E.C. Rosevear, comps., *Guide to the Legal Manuscripts in the New Brunswick Museum* (Saint John: New Brunswick Museum, 1990), 17 – Blowers's private writ register (docket of causes); the original record is in file 62, box 62, series C (HX), RG 39, NSARM.

93 The correspondence, running from Dec. 1799 to Apr. 1800, was twice incompletely published: Jack, "Loyalists and Slavery," 148–51, and J.W. Lawrence, *The Judges of New Brunswick and Their Times* (1907; repr. Saint John: Acadiensis 1985), 71–5. The originals, Blowers's holographs and Chipman's letterbook copies, are in the Chipman family fonds at the LAC. Unless otherwise indicated, quotations are from the Jack edition, except where the text has been elided or mis-transcribed and I have therefore consulted the original directly. Chipman's holograph letters do not survive because Blowers destroyed his papers towards the end of his century-long life.

94 (1778) 33 Mor. Dict., Dec. 14, 545.

95 Blowers to Chipman, 7 Jan. 1800, 141–3, vol. 4, D1, MG 23, LAC.

96 Ibid., 172.

97 Ibid., cited in Jack, "Loyalists and Slavery," 150.

98 See A.C. Dunlop, "Thomas Ritchie," *Dictionary of Canadian Biography Online* (hereafter *DCB Online*). Having but recently been admitted to the bar, Thomas Ritchie inherited the extensive practice of Loyalist Thomas Henry Barclay, with whom he had articled.

99 Agreement with D. Ditmars to bear an equal proportion of the expense attending him about the slaves," n.d., doc. 86 (photocopy of Thomas Ritchie holograph at NA), vol. 20, MG 15, NSARM (hereafter Ditmars).

100 "But the Negro [Jack] never left his Master's Service, till after the Measure of enlisting Negro[e]s in this Quarter had been ado[p]ted: And about this Time it was universally believed among the Blacks, that whether they enlisted, or not, they would all be made free on coming to Halifax." J. Aplin to J. Stewart, 16 Nov. 1803, doc. 2, vol. 334, MG 1, Sir Brenton Haliburton fonds, NSARM. The measure was likely taken as a result of the ministerial decision to upgrade the provincial corps (1793–1802) from volunteer militia to fencible status.

101 Anon. [J. Odell, comp.,] *Opinions of Several Gentlemen of the Law, on the Subject of Negro Servitude, in the Province of Nova Scotia* (Saint John, 1802), 5 (hereafter *Negro Servitude*). There no longer remains a complete case report of *Delancey* extant. This pamphlet is the principal source of information available on the case. It may be inferred from the contents of the pamphlet that the compiler had access to the case file at the time it was compiled.

102 D.B. Davis, *The Problem of Slavery in the Age of Revolution, 1770–1823* (Ithaca, NY: Cornell University Press, 1975), 477 and n14. The *locus classicus* is *Butts v. Penny*, (1677), 12 E.R. 518 (K.B.), citing Co. Lit. 116: "There could be no property in the person of a man sufficient to maintain trover." The most concise and influential eighteenth-century exposition of trover as a tort remedy was given by Lord Mansfield, CJ in *Cooper v. Chitty* (1756), 97 E.R. 166 at 172 (K.B.). "This is an action of tort: and the whole tort consists in the wrongful conversion. Two things are necessary to be proved, to entitle the plaintiff to recover in this kind of action: 1st, property in the plaintiff; and 2ndly, a wrongful conversion by the defendant."

103 "Mr Taylor's Reply," in [J. Sterns and W. Taylor, comp.], *The Reply of Messrs Sterns & Taylor* (London, 1789), 42–3.

104 Original note 85.

105 Original note 86.

106 Original note 87.

107 *Pearne v. Lisle* (1749), 27 E.R. 47 at 48 (Ch), Hardwicke C.

108 Bell and Rosevear, *Guide*, 4. The legal opinion that Aplin intended to send may not have been his own, of course, but a copy of Ritchie's; doubtless he had received the original from Ritchie himself.

109 Author's pagination commences at 7. Though the fate of the missing holographs has not been determined, the New Brunswick Museum at least retains a photocopy of the remaining sixteen, courtesy of Professor Bell.

110 Ibid.

111 Aplin to Stewart, 16 Nov. 1803, no. 2, vol. 334, MG 1, Haliburton Papers, NSARM. "Surely," commented Aplin, "if there was ever a Bull born on Earth, this must be one; for I cannot possibly conceive, how this same Jack could be proved to be a Slave in a Province where no Slavery exists."

112 Ibid.

113 T.C. Haliburton, *Historical and Statistical Account of Nova Scotia*, 2 vols. (Halifax: Howe, 1829), 2:280.

114 Murdoch, *Epitome of the Laws of Nova-Scotia*, 1:43.

115 *R. v. Fennell et al.*, 243, vol. 2, RG 39 "J" [HX], NSARM. The incident is alluded to in Aplin's letter to Stewart, cited above.

116 B. Moody, "James DeLancey," *DCB Online*.

117 W.I. Morse, *Gravestones of Acadie and Other Essays on Local History, Genealogy and Parish Records of Annapolis County, Nova Scotia* (London, 1929), 70; the unacknowledged source is Smith, "The Slave in Canada," 64. The transaction was an unregistered private conveyance of an eight-year-old Black slave girl further to the settlement of an estate, not a public auction and sale; a typewritten transcript of the indenture is in the Miscellaneous Manuscripts Collection at NSARM: fol. 3(a), vol. 103, MG 100.

118 W.A. Calnek, *History of the County of Annapolis* (1897; repr., Belleville, ON: Mika Studio, 1972), 284.

119 Aplin to Blowers, n.d., Odell Family Fonds, New Brunswick Museum; and Blowers to Chipman, 7 Jan. 1800, 141–3, vol. 4, D 1, MG 23, Ward Chipman Papers, LAC.

120 "Mrs J.M. [Isabella A.] Owen, of Annapolis … has referred in the Halifax Herald to the tradition that Mrs Barclay, wife of Colonel [Thomas] Barclay, of Annapolis, was responsible for the death of a slave through a severe whipping she had ordered him." Smith, "Slave in Canada," 77. The psychology of guilt doubtless originated the folk tale that the restless spirit of Mrs Barclay haunts the scene of the crime, a seventeenth-century residence that still stands in Annapolis Royal: C.I. Perkins, *The Oldest Houses along St George Street Annapolis Royal, N.S.* (Saint John, 1925), 29,

31–2. Mrs Barclay (née Susan Delancey), 1754–1837, was a sister of James Delancey and a cousin of the Loyalist lawyer, provincial Lieutenant-Colonel Stephen Delancey; both families came from New York, where the conditions under which domestic slaves lived were harsher than in New England. Major Barclay himself, as he then was, arrived in Nova Scotia with seven slaves: Smith, "Slave in Canada," 24.

121 *Nova Scotia Royal Gazette*, 29 July 1802.

122 Vols 102, 208, and 232, RG 39 "J," Supreme Court Records, NSARM.

123 J.G. Marshall, *A Brief History of Public Proceedings and Events … in the Province of Nova Scotia during the Earliest Years of the Present Century* (Halifax, 1879), 9. It needs to be said that Judge Marshall was the son of a southern military Loyalist who owned slaves: Smith, "Slave in Canada," 26.

124 *Assembly Journals*, 7 Dec. 1807.

125 The subscribed original is at doc. 49, box 14, series A, RG 5, NSARM. A synopsis of the petition is given in *Assembly Journals*, 9 Jan. 1808, with some parts quoted verbatim. It is discussed in F.S. Boyd Jr, ed., *A Brief History of the Coloured Baptists of Nova Scotia [1895]* (Halifax: Afro-Nova Scotia Enterprises, 1976), xxi–xxii. Most, though not all, of the signatories were "proprietors of Negro Servants, brought from His Majesty's late Colonies now called the United States of America." A few, however, such as Dowset, Heloson [*sic*], and Winniett, were non-Loyalist old settlers.

126 *Assembly Journals*, 3 Dec. 1808.

127 The instrument is reproduced verbatim in Smith, "Slave in Canada," 65–6.

128 W.F. Parker, *Daniel McNeill Parker, M.D. … Daniel McNeill and His Descendants* (Toronto, 1915), 15–16.

129 J.A. Mannette, "Setting the Record Straight: The Experience of Black People in Nova Scotia, 1780–1900" (MA thesis, Carleton University, 1983), 24.

130 See J.A. Mannette, "Social Constructions of Black Nova Scotians: The Weymouth Falls Case, 1986" (paper prepared for the Atlantic Association of Sociologists and Anthropologists Annual Meeting, Acadia University, Wolfville, 13–16 Mar. 1986), 29; S. Kimber, "A Black Man's Death Puts White Man's Justice on Trial," *Atlantic Insight* 8, no. 4 (Apr. 1986): 32–4; and G.E. Clarke, "The Birmingham of Nova Scotia: The *Weymouth Falls Justice Committee vs. the Attorney General of Nova Scotia*," *New Maritimes* 5 (Jan. 1987): 4–7, repr. as I. McKay and S. Milsom, eds., *Towards a New Maritimes: A Selection from Ten Years of New Maritimes* (Charlottetown: Ragweed, 1992), 17–24.

131 *Statutes of Prince Edward Island*, 1781, c. 15.

132 *Charlottetown Royal Gazette and Miscellany*, 19 Nov. 1791.

133 AN ACT *to repeal an Act made and passed in the twenty-first year of his late Majesty's reign, intituled "An Act declaring that* BAPTISM *of* SLAVES *shall not exempt them from* BONDAGE," *Statutes of Prince Edward Island*, 1825 (2nd sess.), c. 7.

134 Francis W.P. Bolger, ed., *Canada's Smallest Province: A History of Prince Edward Island* (Charlottetown: PEI Centennial Commission, 1973); J.M. Bumsted, *Land, Settlement, and Politics on Eighteenth-Century Prince Edward Island* (Montreal and Kingston: McGill-Queen's University Press, 1987); W.S. MacNutt, "Fanning's Regime on Prince Edward Island," *Acadiensis* 1 (1971): 37–53. See also Rusty Bittermann, *Rural Protest on Prince Edward Island: From British Colonization to the Escheat Movement* (Toronto: University of Toronto Press, 2006); Andrew Hill Clark, *Three Centuries and the Island: A Historical Geography of Settlement and Agriculture in Prince Edward Island Canada* (Toronto: University of Toronto Press, 1959); D.C. Harvey, "Early Settlement and Social Conditions in Prince Edward Island," *Dalhousie Review* 11 (1932): 448–61; Matthew George Hatvany, "Tenant, Landlord and the New Middle Class: Settlement, Society and Economy in Early Prince Edward Island, 1798–1848" (PhD diss., University of Maine, 1996); Errol Sharpe, *A People's History of Prince Edward Island* (Toronto: Steel Rail, 1976). For a new synthesis and bibliography, see Cole Harris, *The Reluctant Land: Society, Space and Environment in Canada before Confederation* (Vancouver: University of British Columbia Press, 2008), 196–203, 226.

135 J.M. Bumsted, "Joseph Robinson," *DCB Online*.

136 Joanne Pope Melish, *Disowning Slavery: Gradual Emancipation and "Race" in New England, 1780–1860* (Ithaca, NY: Cornell University Press, 1998), xi–49.

137 David Armitage and Michael J. Braddick, eds., *The British Atlantic World, 1500–1800* (New York: Palgrave Macmillan, 2002).

138 Bittermann, *Rural Protest*, 370, index, s.v. "slavery."

139 On this subject generally, see Bittermann, *Rural Protest*, 153, 164, 169, 226, 272, 318–19n118.

140 Hornby, *Black Islanders*. Hornby's work may be read as a response and corrective to Harry Baglole, ed., *Exploring Island History: A Guide to the Historical Resources of Prince Edward Island* (Belfast, PE: Ragweed, 1977), which devotes chapters to First Nations people, Acadians, and "Island social history" but says not a word about the Island's historical Black community that emerged from slavery. See also H.T. Holman, "Peter Byers," *Dictionary of Canadian Biography Online*; Holman, "Slaves and Servants

on Prince Edward Island: The Case of Jupiter Wise," *Acadiensis* 41 (1982): 100–4; William Renwick Riddell, "The Baptism of Slaves in Prince Edward Island, *Journal of Negro History* 6 (July 1921): 307–9; Diane E. Whitcomb, "On Dembo's Trail: Black Ancestry on Prince Edward Island," *New England Historical and Genealogical Society NEXUS* 11 (Feb.–Mar. 1994): 18–21; Winks, *Blacks in Canada*, 44–5.

141 Bumsted, "Joseph Robinson"; Hornby, *Black Islanders*, 15, 3–11.

142 Peter Benes, "Slavery in Boston Households, 1647–1770," *Slavery/Antislavery in New England* (2005): 17.

143 Hornby, *Black Islanders*, 10.

144 Book of Negroes, doc. 10,427, Sir Guy Carleton Papers, UKNA; *Shelburne Nova Scotia Packet and General Advertiser*, 3 Aug. 1786.

145 "Declaration by Thomas Hazard re. selling mulatto children, November 1802," no. 878, ser. 22, Smith Alley Collection, acc. 2702, Public Archives and Records Office, Prince Edward Island (hereafter PARO-PEI).

146 *Charlottetown Examiner*, 11 Feb. 1881. As Hornby points out, Robinson probably wrote this document because two of his slaves were named Sack and Amelia.

147 Bruce Ziff, "Warm Reception in a Cold Climate: English Property Law and the Suppression of the Canadian Legal Identity," in *Despotic Dominion: Property Rights in British Settler Societies*, ed. John McLaren, John McLaren, A.R. Buck, and Nancy E. Wright (Vancouver: UBC Press, 2005), 106–8.

148 Two relevant recent essays on reception are J.M. Bumsted, "Politics and the Administration of Justice on Early Prince Edward Island, 1769–1805," in *Essays in the History of Canadian law*, vol. 9, *Two Islands, Newfoundland and Prince Edward Island*, ed. C. English, 48–78 (Toronto: Osgoode Society and University of Toronto Press, 2005); and Margaret McCallum, "Problems in Determining the Date of Reception in Prince Edward Island," *University of New Brunswick Law Journal* 55 (2006): 3–10. Interestingly, Bumsted observes, "Other aspects of the law, both in substance and in practice, might be adopted or adapted from other British jurisdictions, including Scotland" (51).

149 See J.M. Bumsted, "Sir James Montgomery and Prince Edward Island, 1767–1803," *Acadiensis* 7 (1978): 81.

150 J.M. Bumsted, "Peter Stewart," *DCB Online*.

151 Bumsted, *Land, Settlement, and Politics*, 83, 86.

152 Ibid., 82.

153 Thomas Garden Barnes, "'As Near as May Be Agreeable to the Laws of this Kingdom': Legal Birthright and Legal Baggage at Chebucto, 1749," in

Law in a Colonial Society: The Nova Scotia Experience, ed. Peter Waite, Sandra Oxner, and Thomas Barnes, 1–23 (Toronto: Carswell, 1984).

154 Walter Patterson to Lord George Germain, 1 Mar. 1781, 126, vol. 7, CO series 226, NA.

155 An excellent account, together with the full text of the Act, appears in Hornby, *Black Islanders*, 3–5. A modern paraphrase under the heading "Early Laws" appears in Douglas Baldwin, *Land of the Red Soil: A Popular History of Prince Edward Island*, 2nd ed. rev. (Charlottetown: Ragweed, 1998), 62. On slavery and conversion in the American colonies the *locus classicus* is John Codman Hurd, *The Law of Freedom and Bondage in the United States* (Boston: Little, Brown, 1858), 1:168. For a general account, see Marcus W. Jernegan, "Religious Instruction and Conversion of Negro Slaves" [1916], reprinted in Marcus W. Jernegan, *Laboring and Dependent Classes in Colonial America, 1607–1783* (New York: Ungar, 1931), 24–44. Jernegan points out that the English law officers in 1729 issued an advisory opinion that "baptism did not alter the status of the slave" (27). As far as the attorney general and solicitor general were concerned, such was the common law of England.

156 Jackson's report, dated 8 Mar. 1782, is in vol. 61, Colonial Office Series 226 (Prince Edward Island Original Correpondence), UKNA.

157 See Phillips Callbeck and Joseph Aplin, comps., *Acts of the General Assemblies of His Majesty's Island of Saint John …* (Charlottetown: James Robertson, 1789).

158 Hornby, *Black Islanders*, 29–31, 80. For historical context, see Cahill, "Mediating a Scottish Enlightenment Idea."

159 MacNutt, "Fanning's Regime on Prince Edward Island," 46.

160 Hornby, *Black Islanders*, 7.

161 Ibid., 8.

162 Will of William Schurman, 1819, fol. 130, lib. 1, ser. 1, RG 62, PARO-PEI.

163 *Statutes of PEI* 1825 (2nd), c. 7. Bittermann, *Rural Protest*, 132, describes Cameron as one of the "key members of the mercantile and professional communities"; clearly he was a social progressive who supported, among other good causes, Catholic Emancipation.

164 See generally M. Brook Taylor, "William Johnston," *DCB Online*.

165 James Stephen was an anti-slavery activist who went on to draft the *Colonial Slavery Abolition Act*. On his work as legal adviser to the Colonial Office, in which capacity he vetted all colonial legislation, see Paul Knaplund, *James Stephen and the British Colonial System, 1813–1847* (Madison: University of Wisconsin Press, 1952); and D.B. Swinfen, *Imperial Control of Colonial Legislation, 1813–1865: A Study of British Policy towards Colo-*

nial Legislative Powers (Oxford: Clarendon, 1970). For historical context, see Phillip Buckner, "The Colonial Office and British North America, 1801–1850," *DCB Online*. The authors would like to thank Buckner for determining that no report by Stephen on PEI's slave law repeal act exists among law officer reports in Colonial Office records.

166 Bathurst to Ready, 26 Feb. 1827, enclosing Order in Council, 20 Nov. 1826, 138, vol. 171, CO series 227, NA. On Bathurst's attitude towards colonial slavery, see N.D. McLachlan, "Bathurst at the Colonial Office, 1812–27: A Reconnaissance," *Historical Studies Australia and New Zealand* 13 (1969): 485–8.

167 Robin Blackburn, *The Overthrow of Colonial Slavery, 1776–1848* (New York: Verso, 1988).

168 Neville Thompson, "Bathurst, Henry, third Earl Bathurst (1762–1834)," *Oxford Dictionary of National Biography*, http://www.oxforddnb .comlview/article/1696. See also Neville Thompson, *Earl Bathurst and the British Empire* (Barnsley, UK: Leo Cooper, 1999), 170–82; see, for example, Thompson's comments that "the campaign for the abolition of slavery ... became the major reform issue of the 1820s" (170) and "nothing absorbed so much of Bathurst's time and effort in the years that he remained at the Colonial Office after 1823 as slavery" (182).

10

The Burden of History: Race, Culture, African-Canadian Subjectivity, and Canadian Law in *R. v. Hamilton*

DAVID SEALY

Introduction

There has recently emerged, in several Western liberal democracies, a series of controversies around the relationships among law, race, culture, penality, and justice. In the United States there are debates on the cultural defence, especially articulations of the Black rage defence. In Canada, the paradigmatic debate is about culturally articulated conceptions of justice that have emerged with the *Criminal Code*'s special sentencing provisions for Aboriginal offenders, as interpreted by the Supreme Court of Canada in *R. v. Gladue*.[1] Culture and criminal justice have also engaged Canadian courts in the African-Canadian context, most notably the controversy over what some have called racialized differential sentencing in *R. v. Hamilton*, where Justice Casey Hill drew on the Aboriginal provisions to the benefit of Black defendants.[2] Central to all these instances is the relationship between what philosopher Iris Marion Young has termed "the politics of difference" and mainstream conceptions of equality in the spheres of penality and justice.[3]

This chapter explores the interrelationship between the assumptions behind the Aboriginal provisions – that Aboriginal offenders have suffered numerous social and economic disadvantages that in turn create a special version of Aboriginal criminality – and those that underlie similar conceptions of Black criminality. It does so by comparing and contrasting the "principles of intelligibility" that create the dominant constitution of Aboriginal criminality as articulated in the *Gladue* decision, and those that influenced Justice Casey Hill's decision in the *Hamilton* case. The purpose is to highlight one approach to the problem of African-Canadian difference. By principles of intelligibility I mean what Fillon has called "the movement of thought (at a given time) that gathers around and structures itself around (or coalesces around) certain ways of making sense of privileged objects of concern." A principle of intelligibility, he argues, "describes the object, the goal, and the foundation of a particular exercise of reason or reasoning at a given time, arising out of specific conditions and responding to those conditions."[4] The claim here is that a certain set of principles of intelligibility underlie Mr Justice Hill's decision in *Hamilton* – principles that are in turn founded in racialized and gendered constitutions of the relationship between the figures of *homo economicus* (the rational actor guided by the principle of utility) and *homo criminalis* (the man who can legally be punished). In turn those understandings are informed by history – by the particular history of ideas about social and economic development and welfare subjectivity, out of which has emerged the discourse of "risky subjects." Such understandings are not static. As Stoler states in a different context, they are "subject to reformulation again and again."[5]

I will begin by briefly recounting the *Hamilton* case. I will then turn to an explication of the discourses of development that I see as grounding the principles of intelligibility that facilitate the analogy between Black and Aboriginal criminal subjectivity and therefore the deployment of s. 718(2)(e) of the *Criminal Code* in *Hamilton*. I shall then show how these principles are articulated in that decision. My point is not to argue either for or against that decision.[6] Rather, it is to show how the understandings that ground Hill J.'s association of low Black female socio-economic status with a Black culture of poverty and with s. 718(2)(e) of the *Code* are connected to a belief that what poor Black women living in neighbourhoods, referred to as ghettos, need are governmental technologies of economic and societal security and care aimed at protecting them and their children from themselves and from society. My argument is that these government programs are founded in a belief that poor Black females come from a sub-population that is highly at risk for both criminal involvement and criminal victimization. These women's children are also deemed to be similarly at risk. These women, like Aboriginal people, are less likely than others to have developed the habits, attitudes, and mores of the calculating economic actor that are deemed desirable by liberal economics. As McLeod says of similar female subjects in South Africa, such women are positioned in social scientific discourse as threatening economic security by "disrupting the production of the economic self."[7]

R. v. Hamilton

The *Hamilton* case involved two Black women – "welfare mothers" – who were arrested within six months of each other at the Pearson International Airport in Toronto, for the unlawful importation of cocaine from Jamaica. In sentencing them, Justice Hill of the Ontario Superior Court had to apply section 718.2 of the *Criminal Code*, which begins by stating that "a sentence should be increased or reduced to account for any relevant aggravating or mitigating circumstances relating to the offence or the offender." It then goes on to enumerate a non-exclusive list of criteria for the application of discretion, most of which comprise reasons for increasing sentences. Justice Hill found that sub-section (e) was relevant:[8] "All available sanctions other than imprisonment that are reasonable in the circumstances should be considered for all offenders, with particular attention to the circumstances of aboriginal offenders." In what turned out to be a highly controversial decision, in which he drew on material that he brought into consideration himself, and on his own stated experience as a judge in the Brampton courts, he concluded that "systemic and background factors, identified in this case … should logically be relevant to mitigate the penal consequences for cocaine importers conscripted as couriers."[9]

On appeal the Ontario Court of Appeal reversed this decision. For the court, Justice Doherty stated that the trial judge had "lost" the "narrow" focus that the provision mandated – a focus on only the circumstances of the individual offender. Rather, he "expanded the sentencing proceedings to include broad societal issues that were not raised by the parties. A proceeding that was intended to determine fit sentences for two specific offenders who committed two specific crimes became an inquiry by the trial judge into much broader and more complex issues. In conducting this inquiry, the trial judge stepped outside of the proper role of a judge on sentencing and ultimately imposed sentences that were inconsistent with the statutory principles of sentencing and binding authorities from this court."[10] To understand why Justice Hill apparently "stepped outside of the proper role of a judge" and conducted an inquiry into "much broader and more complex issues," I argue, we must take a broad diversion into ideas about social, moral, and economic development that have informed much of our modern world.

Development, Modernization, and Underdevelopment

The idea of developed and developing was inherent in the Enlightenment discourses of Kant, Hegel, et al., so that there emerged in the works of thinkers as different as Mill and Marx a distinctive hierarchy of place based on distinctions between developed and less-developed societies. After the Second World War, development studies emerged as a specific approach to societal development, with what the Colombian anthropologist Arturo Escobar calls "development as a discourse."[11] Development became a form of governmental discourse directed at poor countries, poor sections of developed countries, and poor populations. As April Biccum states, "Development was posited by the World Bank and other post war institutions as universal, inevitable, and inherently valuable and as something that naturally springs from the boon of the enlightenment."[12] Escobar puts it similarly: "The production of the Third World through the articulation of knowledge and power is essential to development discourse." There is a telos in human societies from undeveloped, or developing, to developed, and although the development of all human communities is somehow inevitable, it is also in the interests of both developed and developing societies to assist the latter. Development was not a political project to be undertaken by local regimes, as had been advocated by various anti-colonial nationalist movements in India, Africa, and Latin America, prior to and after the Second World War, but a socio-economic project to be undertaken by outside technical experts.

Important here, in the post-1945 period, is the epistemological relationship between development projects in the Third World and other poor nations, and welfare state projects in First World countries, such as the Africville relocation project in Halifax. Like the welfare state projects, development projects are, according to Escobar, bio-political strategies aimed at optimizing the life of the client population through intervention in the sphere of the social involving "education, health, hygiene, morality, and employment, and the instilling of good habits of association saving children and so on." Furthermore, he argues, as with welfare state projects, in the so-called First World, "development fostered a way of conceiving of social life as a technical problem, as a matter of rational decision to be undertaken by groups of people –

the development professionals – whose specialized knowledge alleg-edly qualified them for the task. Instead of seeing change as a process rooted in the interpretation of each society's history and cultural tradi-tion, these professionals sought to devise mechanisms and procedures to make society fit a pre-existing model that embodied the structures and functions of modernity."

The point, then, of locating the situation of two welfare mothers in the *Hamilton* case within the discourses of development is to, firstly, emphasize the "other place" aspect of the modern ghetto, as the site where these welfare mothers live. Like the so-called Third World, the ghetto is a site of social "underdevelopment." Secondly, this compari-son makes it clear that the discourses of welfare are grounded in the same evolutionary "will to improve" that subtends the discourses of development.

There is also a geography of development, what Edward Said called an "imaginative geography," that is able to define societies or commu-nities from developed to developing, from First World to Third World, and in our time from North to South.[13] This geography of development can also be articulated within the borders of a particular nation so that we have developed and developing areas of the nation. In this sense, it could be said that, in Canada, the Maritime provinces and Newfound-land and Labrador are not as developed as central Canada. The point is not only that these nations or parts of a nation are objectively poorer than other nations or more developed parts of a nation, but poverty and social deprivation is directly related to what could be called unde-veloped, or less-developed market relations, and therefore implicitly less-developed workforces. Important here is the way in which states with undeveloped or less-developed productive forces not only have less-developed market relations, but also have a less-developed labour force. Furthermore, development "provides a context in which poor countries (or, poor sectors of the population) are known, specified and intervened on."[14]

It was within the parameters of this discourse about the role of mar-ket forces in regulating subjectivity that there emerged the idea of a relationship between a highly developed society and a highly trained and disciplined workforce. There were therefore relationships between economic development, social development, the creation of a labour force, and the creation of *homo economicus* as a partner of exchange and production in the marketplace. Foucault has argued that the creation of the marketplace is not a natural process; he identifies two different instances of market development. On the one hand:[15] "The market, in the general sense of the word as it operated in the Middle Ages, and in the sixteenth and seventeenth century, was in a word essentially a site of justice … In the first place it was of course invested with extremely prolific and strict regulations: it was regulated with regard to the objects brought to market, their type of manufacture, the duty to be paid, and of course, the prices fixed. It was also a site of justice in the sense that the sale price fixed in the market was seen both by theorist and in practice as a just price."

On the other hand, by the mid-eighteenth century, the market "appears as something that obeyed and had to obey 'natural,' that is to say, spontaneous mechanisms." The argument here is that as the spontaneous mechanisms of the market appear natural, there emerged a standard of truth founded in this free market. And this standard of truth can be "a site of verification-falsification for governmental practices." As Foucault states, "The fundamental problem of liberalism" is "what is the utility value of government and all actions of government in a society where exchange determines the true value of things?"

From the eighteenth century, the free market emerged as the central site through which technologies of truth and freedom are articulated. And *homo economicus* emerged as a standard measure of free human subjectivity. This rational economic subject required "a whole range of legislation and governmental intervention in order to guarantee production of the freedom necessary to govern." As Foucault states in spelling out two different instances of liberal freedoms, "There must be free trade, of course, but how can we practice free trade, in fact if we do not control and limit a number of things and if we do not organize a series of preventive measures to avoid the effects of one country's hegemony over others which would be precisely the limitation and restriction of free trade. There must be free labour, but again there must be large enough numbers of sufficiently competent, qualified and sufficiently disarmed workers to prevent their exerting pressure on the labour market."

The discourses of development are based on a set of normative assumptions founded in the logic of market relations – assumptions about what constitutes a developed society in juxtaposition to a developing society or an undeveloped society and that allow for the articulation of how a developing society can become developed. Relatedly, this involves a moral geography of development, defining what constitutes a developed people as opposed to an undeveloped people, or even developed sectors of the population as opposed to undeveloped or developing sectors of the population. There is, of course, a marked difference between the internal frontiers of the nation state and its external borders. So, for example, Jamaica is constituted as very different from the Maritime provinces in Canada. However, it may be that Jamaicans, like Aboriginal peoples and Black peoples in Canada, can be constituted as developing peoples.[16] There is a supposed relationship between economic and social development and proper articulations of human freedom: mature, liberal, and self-governing. The freedom through which a particular subject position is articulated is in some sense related to its location in market processes. However, as Escobar claims, "Development assumes teleology to the extent that it proposes that the natives will sooner or later be reformed; at the same time, however, it reproduces endlessly the separation between reformers and those to be reformed by keeping alive the premise of the Third World as different, and inferior, as having limited humanity in relation to the accomplished European. Developmental theory thus relies on this perpetual recognition and disavowal of difference."[17]

It is within the parameters of this economically centred discourse about the role of *homo economicus* in the constitution of freedom that there emerged the idea that the prison could be a site for the disciplining of those incapable of disciplining themselves.[18] It was designed for those subjects who for some reason were thought incapable of translating themselves through the developmental disciplinary processes of modernization into *homo economicus*. Such people were "obdurately resistant to biopolitical revision," and thus became articulated as the criminal classes. What Marx called the lumpen proletariat, or others have called the underclass, are those likely to become *homo penalis*. As Foucault states, "At the end of the eighteenth century ... the mechanism of law was adopted as the economic principle of penal power, in both the widest and most exact sense of the word economic. *Homo penalis*, the man who can legally be punished, the man exposed to the law, is strictly speaking *homo economicus*. And it is precisely the law which enables this. When the reformative project failed, *homo penalis* became *homo criminalis*."[19]

It is not only that classical liberalism and neoliberalism share "the process of making economic activity a general matrix of social activity," but for governance through social welfarist developmental liberalism, economic activity is still an integral feature of the matrix of social activity. It is because we believe that humanity is best served by the development of *homo economicus* that the discourses of a culture of poverty, of the underclass, and of Aboriginal underdevelopment can be used to establish the analogy between Black female criminality and Aboriginal criminality. The analogy is in part located in what Mariana Valverde calls "common knowledges," or common-sense analogies made between the culture of poverty of Blacks and the cultural under-development of Aboriginals. As Valverde has demonstrated, it is these "common sense" analogies that often ground law's determination of "vice and virtue, and order and disorder."[20]

The *Hamilton* Decision, Development, and Modernization

I turn now to exploring how the ideas about the relationship between the culture of poverty and criminality, articulated in *Hamilton*, implicitly emerge from this developmental logic grounded in *homo economicus*. In implicitly extending the economically centred developmental logic articulated here to the two Black welfare mothers in *Hamilton*, the cycles of poverty and deprivation that constitute of the culture of poverty became crimogenic factors in the lives of these women. The women are highly "at risk" for both criminal victimization and criminal activity. Here we must return to s. 718(2)(e) of the *Code*.

As the Supreme Court stated in *Gladue*, "Section 718.2(e) is not simply a codification of existing jurisprudence. It is remedial in nature. Its purpose is to ameliorate the serious problem of over-representation of aboriginal people in prisons, and to encourage sentencing judges to have recourse to a restorative approach to sentencing."[21] The Court went on,[22]

Section 718.2(e) directs judges to undertake the sentencing of aboriginal offenders individually, but also differently, because the circumstances of aboriginal people are unique. In sentencing an aboriginal offender, the judge must consider: (a) the unique systemic or background factors which may have played a part in bringing the particular aboriginal offender before the courts; and (b) the types of sentencing procedures and sanctions which may be appropriate in the circumstances for the offender because of his or her particular aboriginal heritage or connection. In order to undertake these considerations the sentencing judge will require information pertaining to the accused. Judges may take judicial notice of the broad systemic and background factors affecting aboriginal people, and of the priority given in aboriginal cultures to a restorative approach to sentencing.

Furthermore, the Court also insisted that trial judges, in considering the systemic background factors that may have influenced the criminal conduct of the accused, consider the nature of the relationship between the offender and his or her community. Therefore, the Court ruled that the primary importance of s. 718.2(e) is that judges consider the way in which culturally specific factors might have played a part in the crime and may play a part in the sentencing.

In *Hamilton* Justice Hill concluded his decision by stating that "systemic and background factors, identified in this case ... should logically be relevant to mitigate the penal consequences for cocaine importers conscripted as couriers."[23] How did he get there? He began with this observation about the drug trade:[24] "The prosecution accepted that both offenders were couriers, 'mules' in the parlance of the drug trade, conscripted by overseers of illicit drug distribution networks to assume the exclusive risk of apprehension in transporting cocaine from Jamaica to Canada ... In this jurisdiction, the most common conscript is a courier living at the poverty level hired to transport cocaine to Canada for a few hundred dollars and an expenses-paid trip to Jamaica where she or he often has family to visit." Thus Justice Hill marked these women as belonging to a high-risk group for criminal behaviour. This involved locating them within the parameters of race, nation, and development, and therefore against the idealized version of *homo economicus* that, as stated earlier, has become crucial to dominant representation of the relationships between South and North (in this case, Canada and Jamaica), and to the representations of Aboriginal peoples' relationship to the nation state of Canada. This, however, was not a simplistic location of Black Jamaican female subjectivity as a site of atavistic moral otherness. Rather, it is a complex situating of their position within the parameters of a neocolonial relationship between Canada and Jamaica. As Hill J. stated, "Marsha Hamilton and Donna Mason risked their lives and their liberty by travelling to Canada after swallowing pellets of cocaine in Jamaica."[25] After going through some discussion of the effect of drugs on users and the extent of the drug trade, he resumed his characterization of the women:[26]

It is conceded that the offenders committed the importation crime for financial gain of a one-time payment but not participation in the equity or profit-sharing associated with trafficking distribution ... The offenders were "swallowers." The cocaine is ingested before leaving Jamaica in pellet form with the powder most often wrapped in condoms, the cut-off fingers of latex or rubber gloves, or other receptacle. The swallowing technique is a clandestine measure designed to defeat x-ray, canine or manual search interdiction efforts. There are risks to the courier's health from receptacle leakage and passage of an overdose of cocaine into the traveller's bloodstream. In the usual course, the receptacles are excreted in Canada and turned over to the domestic drug distribution network ... In the words of Canada Customs Superintendent Mark Hayes who testified in the sentencing hearing, drug couriers are "people normally in dire circumstance[s] that need money."

Judge Hill is here emphasizing that not only were these women desperate because of poverty, but they were desperate enough to risk their lives by ingesting condoms filled with cocaine, which could (and in the case of one of the accused, almost did) kill them. It is not only that these women were poor and desperate, and chronically peripheral to the processes of *homo economicus*, but also that they were at high risk for involvement in criminal activity and at risk of getting caught participating in crime. They did not even make very good cocaine importers.

This is not a characterization of the underclass welfare queen discussed in Dinesh D'Souza's conservative theories about "civilization gaps" and a "black civilizational crisis."[27] It is more redolent of the construction of a sociological culture of poverty and Black female subjectivity initially articulated by Daniel Moynihan,[28] that located the source of what could be called chronic Black poverty in social disorganization and cultural pathology. Both supposedly emerged with the break-up of the Black family structure and the emergence of female-dominated households during the period of Black slavery. In this characterization of Black life, crime is constituted as the product of a continuum of disorder located within Black communities, in which Black women emerge as incapable of parenting self-governing Black children. Pathological ways of life are passed down from generation to generation and inevitably lead to the creation of a Black underclass that exists permanently outside both the normative and opportunity structures of modern societies.

Hill J. then turned to the interdiction of cocaine importation, pointing out that in Canada fewer than 5 per cent of cocaine importers are caught. Thus these two women were likely caught as the result of some convergence of race profiling by customs officials and their own incompetence. He also noted that in his Brampton courtroom Black people, and increasingly Black women, were more and more often appearing before him on drug trafficking charges. He then returned to his characterization of the offenders: the convicted women's familial relationships to Jamaica inform the triple burden of race, gender, and poverty, while their lack of education, and what is called here "marketable skills," doom them to an existence on the periphery of legitimate *homo economicus*. The increasing prevalence of Black women in the drug trade was supported by official evidence about crime rates and gender. While there was "considerable overlap in the social characteristics of men and women in prison, particularly with respect to high levels of unemployment, low levels of education, and extensive family disruption," nonetheless some characteristics distinguished female offenders from male. "In addition to characteristics they shared with men, two-thirds of federally sentenced women are mothers, and 70% of these are single parents all or part of the time; 68% of federally sentenced women were physically abused ... 53% of federally sentenced women were sexually abused ... Fewer than one-third had any formal job qualifications beyond basic education prior to sentence, and two-thirds had never had steady employment ... [T]he female offender population is younger, and more likely to have primary child care responsibilities ... [M]en and women do not necessarily appear [before the court] in similar circumstances."[29]

To this Hill J. added an observation on the intersection of race and gender, noting that according to the Supreme Court of Canada, "African Canadians and Aboriginal people are over-represented in the criminal justice system," and that Black women account for a much larger proportion of those federally incarcerated than their population numbers warranted. Additionally, Black men and women have been "massively over-represented" among prison admissions – an over-representation "that has increased dramatically in recent years" with proportionally greater increases in the admission of Black women compared to white females. Women from minority ethnic groups who are federally incarcerated "are often very isolated" and "have no doubt also suffered the effects of racism."[30]

Hill J's point is to establish the relationships among women's gendered welfare status, their racial status, and risk factors not only for criminal activity, but for criminal interdiction. Hill J. then took judicial notice of the following facts derived from his experience of presiding in Brampton, Ontario:[31]

The face of importing that I see are black women charged with the crime of cocaine importing, beyond the percentage of black women that I see in a shopping centre or other public forum. Single women are disproportionate to the general population, single mothers are represented disproportionately in the prison population. And Justice Arbour made that point,[32] the studies from England make that point. Black women find themselves doubly disadvantaged frequently because of the effects of racial inequality ... And in any given year if one looks at cocaine trafficking or cocaine possession, women to their male counterparts usually are in the 16 to 18 percent ratio without exception. So that men are being charged at the rate of approximately 82 to 83 percent with those two cocaine offences. So there is something unique when it comes to women about cocaine importing, and I'm trying to figure out what it is, and I'm trying to figure out when I see black women before me, day in, day out, assignment court after assignment court, what it means in terms of the crime of cocaine importing, and what it should mean to me, if anything, as a sentencing judge obliged to apply equality principles, and constitutional principles in the exercise of a discretion, which sentencing is.

Judge Hill is here emphasising that not only are risk factors related to poverty and gender important in understanding the ways that these women are systematically victimized, but also that poverty and gender inform the ways that race and economics work with gender to constitute women like these as high-risk subjects. They are easy prey to drug dealers looking for "mules," but are also a danger to the rest of Canadian society. Like Aboriginal peoples, Black, single welfare mothers constitute a unique group for whom "the unique systemic or background factors which may have played a part in bringing the particular ... offender before the courts" must be taken into consideration by the judge when sentencing: "African Canadian women ... represent the single largest group of persons appearing before the court charged with cocaine importation." In part this is also the result of systemic racism against Black people in the criminal justice system, a point acknowledged by the prosecutor.[33]

Hill J. supported this point by the findings of the *Commission on Systemic Racism in the Ontario Criminal Justice System*, which found that the War on Drugs produces, or reproduces, racial inequality. It stated that "intensive policing of low-income areas in which black people live produces arrests of a large and disproportionate number of black male street dealers," and that the "intensive policing of airline travelers produces arrests of a smaller but still disproportionate number of black female couriers. Once the police have done this work, the practices and decision of crown prosecutors, justices of the peace and judges operate as a conveyor belt to prison ... It is clear from our findings that in

Ontario, as in many parts of the United States, one effect of the 'war on drugs,' intended or not, has been the increase in imprisonment of black people." This was especially true for some charges – trafficking in or importing of drugs, possession of illegal drugs, obstructing justice, and weapons possession – for which Black admission rates are more than nine time greater than white admission rates.[34]

Judge Hill's use of this evidence indicates that not only did he see a clear correlation between Black female deprivation and Black female criminality, but that when this correlation is coupled with the over-policing of Black communities, the result is a substantial increase in the incarceration rates for both Black men and Black women. Furthermore, in this case, he concluded, a term of incarceration could only re-victimize these already severely victimized women: "Poor, then exploited in their poverty, these women when captured and convicted have been subjected to severe sentences perpetuating their position of disadvantage while effectively orphaning their young children for a period of time." He stated in his concluding remarks, in refuting the prosecution's claim that a conditional sentence would change little in the life of the defendants, "The risk in surmising that a conditional sentence would change little in the life of [the defendants] is that we lose sight of those systemic and background factors relevant to the offenders' involvement in the importation crime."

The point about the inability of the justice system to address certain ills is very important. As Judge Hill had earlier stated, "While society often looks to the criminal justice system for solutions to its problems, the system cannot alone be expected to solve deeply rooted and profoundly complex social problems."[35] Thus these women are members of a group of people who are not only permanently at risk for criminal victimization but also beyond any kind of ameliorative reach of the criminal justice system.

Comparing Aboriginal Criminality to Black Female Criminality

How does this picture of Black female subjectivity structured by poverty and racism connect to the *cultural* constitution of Aboriginal subjectivity that informs the Supreme Court of Canada's interpretation of s. 718.2(e) in *Gladue*? Section 718.2(e) is about restraint in the use of imprisonment, especially, but not exclusively, for Aboriginal offenders. Restraint in sentencing is a feature of what Alan Cairns has called Aboriginal "citizen plus."[36] It recognizes the way in which the unique systemic risk factors, such as poverty, alcoholism, high rates of unemployment, and low levels of education in Aboriginal communities, rooted in Aboriginal cultural underdevelopment, has led to high incarceration rates among Aboriginal peoples. In other words, it is about the way that the effects of Aboriginal cultural underdevelopment mean that Aboriginal subjects are less likely than other Canadians to emerge as proper *homo economicus*. Restraint in sentencing and restorative justice, therefore, involves an attempt to address the effects of Aboriginal cultural underdevelopment.

Hill J. made a connection between Aboriginal and Black women. "Without minimizing the circumstances of aboriginal Canadians, many of the observations relating to systemic racism are equally applicable to African Canadians."[37] He cited with approval an extract from Rosenberg J.A.'s decision in *R. v. Borde*: "I accept that there are some similarities [between the plight of Aboriginal Canadians and African Canadians] and that the background and systemic factors facing African Canadians, where they are shown to have played a part in the offence, might be taken into account in imposing sentence."[38] Thus, to put the decision into the language of this chapter, some factors related to a culture of poverty for single, Black, poor women, which place them at the periphery of *homo economicus*, similarly locate Aboriginal peoples at the same periphery. Analogies drawn by the court between the situation of the two Black welfare mothers in *Hamilton* and the Aboriginal woman in *Gladue* require comparison between the effects of the cultural underdevelopment on Aboriginals and of a culture of poverty on the Black women in *Hamilton*. When this is done, section 718.2(e) can be extended to African-Canadian women. The process of doing so is facilitated by social science languages of social psychology, sociology, and economic statistics that hide within their very constitution common-sense normative judgments about vice and virtue, good and bad, civilized and uncivilized. Noteworthy here is the articulation of the relationships between *homo economicus* and *homo criminalis*, that wear the marks of colonial empire and are articulated through legal complexes and inscribed in racial knowledges. Those knowledges place certain people permanently at risk for criminal behaviour and criminal victimization.

NOTES

1 [1999] S.C.J. No. 19 [hereinafter *Gladue*]. The sentencing provision, discussed in more detail below, is s. 718(2)(e).

2 [2003] O.J. No. 532 (S.C.J.) [hereinafter *Hamilton*]. An appeal from Justice Hill's decision was allowed by the Ontario Court of Appeal: [2004] O.J. No. 3252 (C.A.).

3 Iris Marion Young, *Justice and the Politics of Difference* (Princeton: Princeton University Press, 1990).

4 Real Fillon, "Moving Beyond Biopower: Hardt and Negri's Post-Foucauldian Speculative Philosophy of History," *History and Theory* 44 (2005): 51.

5 Ann Stoler, *Along the Archival Grain: Epistemic Anxieties and Colonial Common Sense* (Princeton: Princeton University Press, 2009), 6.

6 See Sonia N. Lawrence and Toni Williams, "Swallowed Up: Drug Couriers at the Borders of Canadian Sentencing," *University of Toronto Law Journal* 56 (2006): 285–332, for an interesting critique of the deployment of what they call a social context analysis in the sentencing of poor racial minority women.

7 Catriona McLeod, "Economic Security and the Social Science Literature on Teenage Pregnancy in South Africa," *Gender and Society* 16 (2002): 649.

8 For a discussion, see Philip Stenning and Julian Roberts, "Empty Promises: Parliament, the Supreme Court, and the Sentencing of Aboriginal Offenders," *Saskatchewan Law Review* 64 (2001): 137–68.

9 *Hamilton*, para. 224.

10 [2004] O.J. No 3252 (C.A.), para. 3.

11 Arturo Escobar, *Encountering Development: The Making and Unmaking of the Third World* (Princeton: Princeton University Press, 1995); quotations below in this and the next paragraph are from 10, 23, and 75.

12 April Biccum, "Interrupting the Discourse of Development: On a Collision Course with Post-Colonial Theory," *Culture, Theory and Critique* 43 (2002): 39.

13 Edward Said, *Orientalism* (New York: Pantheon Books, 1978).

14 Escobar, *Encountering Development*, 45.

15 Michel Foucault, *Security, Territory, Population: Lectures at the College de France 1977–1978* (New York: Picador, 2007), 30. Quotations below in this paragraph and the next are from 30, 31, 46, 64, and 65.

16 The discourses of modernization and societal development are markedly different from the discourses of the undeveloped savage, as articulated in much enlightenment discourse. See John Stewart Mill's discussion in *On Liberty* of "rude nations and semi skilled and enslaved nations," discussed in P.A. Passavant, "A Moral Geography of Liberty: John Stewart Mill and American Free Speech Discourse," in *Law of the Postcolonial: An Insistent Introduction*, ed. Peter Fitzpatrick and Eve Darien Smith, 86–109 (Ann Arbor: University of Michigan Press, 1999).

17 Escobar, *Encountering Development*, 53.
18 Michel Foucault, *Discipline and Punish* (New York: Pantheon Books, 1979).
19 Foucault, *Security, Territory, Population*, 249–50.
20 Mariana Valverde, *Law's Dream of a Common Knowledge* (Princeton: Princeton University Press, 2003), 3, 4.
21 *Gladue*, para. 3.
22 Ibid., paras 97–8.
23 *Hamilton*, para. 224.
24 Ibid., para. 23.
25 Ibid., para. 1.
26 Ibid., paras 24–6.
27 Dinesh D'Souza, *The End of Racism: Principles for a Multiracial Society* (New York: Free Press, 1996).
28 Daniel Patrick Moynihan, *The Negro Family: The Case for National Action* (Washington: United States Department of Labor, 1965).
29 *Hamilton*, para. 79.
30 Ibid., paras 89, 90, and 97.
31 Ibid., para. 102.
32 The reference by Hill J. here is to then-justice Louise Arbour's *Report of the Commission of Inquiry into Certain Events at the Prison for Women in Kingston* (Ottawa: Public Works and Government Services Canada, 1996).
33 *Hamilton*, paras 10, 104–5.
34 *Commission*, cited in *Hamilton*, para. 106.
35 *Hamilton*, paras 150, 198, and 228.
36 Alan Cairns, *Citizens Plus: Aboriginals and the Canadian State* (Vancouver: UBC Press, 2000).
37 *Hamilton*, para. 187.
38 *R. v. Borde* (2003), 172 C.C.C. (3d) 225 (Ont. C.A.), cited in *Hamilton*, para. 189.

A Black Day in Court:
"Race" and Judging in *R. v. R.D.S.*

JAMES W. ST.G. WALKER

Introduction

This is a story about a boy on a bike, a Halifax policeman, a crusading lawyer and a courageous judge, and "race" and judging in Canada. In the 1997 case *R. v. R.D.S.* the Supreme Court of Canada broke with its tradition of silence and openly discussed racism in our society. The result was not without its hesitations and complications, but our top court did at last address this issue openly, and a majority confirmed the insidious existence of societal racism, and also confirmed the courts' role in confronting it. *R.D.S.* was the first case dealing explicitly with "race" to be argued before the Supreme Court under Section 15 of the *Charter of Rights and Freedoms*. It was the first case in Canada where a judge was accused of racial bias. It undoubtedly involved the largest number of African-Canadian lawyers in any single case at that level. And it became recognized as "the Supreme Court's leading judgment in the area of bias."[1]

Our story is important for what it reveals about policing in racialized communities as well as the treatment of "race" and racialization in the courts. As it unfolds, the narrative demonstrates the necessity of addressing racism directly in our legal system, and other areas of life, rather than hiding it behind a curtain of "colour blindness" in the supposed interest of "objectivity." The case thus has particular significance for critical race theory (CRT), as described in Barrington Walker's introduction to this volume. Racism in Canada, when not neglected completely, is frequently misrepresented. We often hear of "polite racism" in Canada, likened to a hair across the cheek: you can feel it but not see it. But for those who do feel it, it is much more than an obscure hair. It is also sometimes mistakenly characterized as an essentially individual phenomenon, a matter of personal ignorance or malice, something that could be eliminated if we just learn to "get along." The *R.D.S.* story combines and illuminates systemic racism and "street racism" in one poignant episode in the streets of North Halifax.

There is a substantial and respectable scholarly literature on *R.D.S.*, including several items written by lawyers and legal academics who were intimately engaged in developing and arguing the case. Their insights add immensely to any understanding of the complexities generated by this confrontation between a Black youth and a police officer.[2] Two scholarly journals, the *Dalhousie Law Journal* and the *Canadian Journal of Women and the Law*, have published forums where a variety of academic specialists offer their perspectives on the case.[3] All these contributions, with others found in academic journals, have informed the analysis offered in this chapter.[4] Together, these studies provide a thorough examination of the judgments associated with *R.D.S.* as it worked its way through the system, particularly of the Supreme Court of Canada decision and the reasoning of each justice in relation to trends and significance in Canadian jurisprudence.

The focus of this chapter differs somewhat from its learned predecessors. It proceeds through the incident itself, the trial in Halifax, the appeals in Nova Scotia and Ottawa, holding in centre place the defendant's counsel in the case, the street-fighter-turned-lawyer, the intellectual and activist B.A. "Rocky" Jones, who took an apparently insignificant case from Halifax Youth Court to the Supreme Court of Canada. April Burey, who represented one of the interveners at the Supreme Court, has observed, "The accused's lawyer, Burnley 'Rocky' Jones, is the unsung hero of this case. RDS is a testament to his courage, to his refusal to give up despite tremendous odds, and to his committed pursuit of a just result. His own life experience as an African Canadian, born and raised in the province where the events occurred, allowed him to see, understand and pursue the important issues of racial equality in this case."[5]

Jones was the propelling force underlying this entire episode, and his role will be recognized in the narrative that follows.[6]

A Day in the Street

It was a humid day on 17 October 1993 in Halifax, Nova Scotia, almost misty. An African-Canadian youth, identified in the courts only by his initials, "RDS," had spent the afternoon at his grandmother's house in the city's North End. Though he was fifteen years old at the time, RDS was small for his age, having the appearance perhaps of a slender twelve-year-old. Shortly before 4 p.m. he borrowed a mountain bike and started to ride it towards his own home, just a few streets away. En route he saw a crowd, mostly children under twelve, gathered around a police car. Driven by curiosity, he approached the scene on the borrowed bicycle. Someone in the crowd called to him, "They got N down." N, identified as "NR" in the documents, was RDS's cousin. He rode up to where the policeman had his cousin handcuffed and asked, "What's wrong with you N? What happened? What happened? I'll go tell your mother." Constable Donald Stienburg, who had NR under arrest, warned RDS, "Shut up, shut up or you'll be under arrest too." RDS persisted, asking his cousin, "What, what, do you want me to go tell your mother?" In the boy's version of the event, "boom," the officer suddenly grabbed him and put him in a chokehold. "I couldn't do nothing. I couldn't breathe and my face was like – I was almost knocked out. He had me right under the chin … I couldn't move. I was almost – I was dizzy … I was like flaking out." At the same time Constable Stienburg, twenty-nine years old, an eight-year veteran on the force, described as six feet tall, two hundred pounds, a "standard issue" police officer of the period, placed the handcuffed NR in a chokehold as well.

Seeing RDS's distress, a woman in the crowd yelled at the constable, "Let that kid go, let that kid go," and she said to RDS, "What's your phone number? What's your phone number?" RDS, still awkwardly straddling the bike, was unable to talk through his chokehold, but NR managed to cry out the grandmother's number. Constable Stienburg called his headquarters for back-up. Two more police officers arrived, and both boys were placed under arrest and taken to the station. NR, also fifteen years old, was arrested on suspicion of theft of an automobile. At the scene RDS was told that he was being charged with obstruction, but when the information was sworn at the station he found himself facing three charges: assaulting Constable Stienburg in the execution of his duty, assaulting him with intent to prevent the lawful arrest of NR, and unlawfully resisting arrest. The police ran a check and found that RDS had no previous record, so they telephoned his mother to come and take him home. A date was set for his trial in Youth Court.[7]

It had been a typical encounter in the streets of North End Halifax, between Black youths and white police officers. Nothing out of the ordinary. But precisely because 17 October was unremarkable, it deserves attention. Here is a real case with real people, revealing the daily experience of African Canadians when confronted by the law. No royal commission or scholarly study of "systemic racism" could be nearly so illustrative of how that abstract notion affects the lives of racialized Canadians. The incident that day also illustrates some characteristics of the Halifax Black community. RDS has been at his grandmother's. He enters the scene of the arrest to find out what's going on so he can inform NR's mother. The woman in the crowd intervenes so that she can contact RDS's family. This is a community operating, showing lines of support that come into play when the police become involved. *R. v. R.D.S.* offers observers a knot-hole through the fence that often blocks the view of what is called systemic racism, and it offers a knot-hole too, for outsiders, into the dynamics of Black community relationships.

Counsel for the Defence

History occasionally makes an appropriate call. When RDS and his mother went to the Dalhousie Legal Clinic to find a defence counsel for the impending trial, they were assigned a relatively junior lawyer named Burnley "Rocky" Jones, at that time the only Black lawyer on staff there. Though new to the legal profession, Jones was by no means an unknown quantity to the Halifax Black community. Born in Truro, Nova Scotia, he had drifted to Toronto following service in the Canadian army, and in 1965 became involved with Canadian support groups for the American civil rights movement. The Student Non-Violent Coordinating Committee (SNCC, pronounced "Snick") had a Toronto branch, Friends of SNCC, and Jones quickly became a leading public spokesperson for the group. Articulate, charismatic, and increasingly sophisticated in his analysis of the "race problem," Jones was sought out by the media, student groups, and others interested in hearing his interpretation of events in the American South. Inevitably, he drew upon his experience as an African Canadian in Nova Scotia, and this attention inspired one important group to take notice that racism and Black disadvantage were not unique to the United States. The Student Union for Peace Action (SUPA), which was establishing social movement projects in several Canadian regions, sponsored Rocky, his wife Joan, and several others to go to Halifax and found the Nova Scotia Project. In the summer of 1965, at the age of twenty-four, Jones returned to his home province and launched a grass-roots community development program aimed at involving African-Canadian youth in defining their needs and organizing for change. In its headquarters known as Kwacha ("Freedom") House, the project held sessions on historical and social analysis and strategies for community organization. Over the next several decades Jones was a leader in the Black community, representing a more radical and left-wing perspective than the traditional leadership offered by the African Baptist Church and the Nova Scotia Association for the Advancement of Coloured People. Most dramatically, he hosted the visit of Stokely Carmichael and other Black Panthers to Halifax in the late 1960s, and his name was thereafter associated with Black Power and an aggressive pursuit of equality for African Canadians.

Jones's conviction that you had to work outside the system to effect change became modified as he gradually discerned that the law was an area where decisions were being made that had a profound impact on the Black community. In the 1980s he undertook several legal-oriented projects for the Black United Front (BUF), an organization he had helped to found in 1968–9, and because of this experience and his general profile as a community leader he was selected by BUF to represent the Black community before the Marshall Inquiry. On the day of his presentation to the hearings chaired by Justice T. Alexander Hickman, Jones happened to sit at a table with Dalhousie law professors Richard Devlin, Wayne MacKay, and others.[8] Their discussion turned to the issue that there were not enough African-Canadian judges in the legal system, and to the necessity of training more Black lawyers before you can have Black judges. A committee was thereupon set up, including Devlin and Jones, to design a proposal to the Dalhousie Law School for a program to encourage African Canadians to study law. The committee received a boost from Justice Hickman's 1989 report, where it was recommended that more Black and other racialized minorities should be appointed to judicial and administrative positions, and that support should be given to Dalhousie's proposed program to recruit qualified minority students interested in a legal career. The result was the creation in 1989 of the Indigenous Blacks and Micmacs Program, designed to attract African-Canadian and First Nations students to the Law School and to facilitate their studies in an enriched curriculum leading to a bachelor of laws degree and membership in the bar.[9]

Jones's involvement in the IBM initiative was, to this point, void of self-interest. Now in his late forties, he intended to help get the program established, not to participate in it himself. But as the program began to take shape and Jones was actively recruiting applicants, he came under pressure from the community to "put his money where his mouth is," and send in his own application. Convinced that the law offered a route to progressive change, Jones succumbed to the pressure and in the fall of 1989 became part of the first IBM class at the Dalhousie Law School. He subsequently articled with his friend Jamie Armour in Windsor, Nova Scotia, working with Mi'kmaq at Shubenacadie and with the Black community in Windsor. Following his call to the bar he was offered a job by Dalhousie Legal Clinic, where he had served as a summer student. At that time the clinic had a three-pronged approach: academic pursuits for the students, the straight clinical practice of law, and law reform and community activism. Jones was given special responsibility for teaching the law students at the clinic, running a seminar every week on racism and other contemporary issues. He looked at legal problems as a reflection of societal problems and acted according to that perspective in working for community and legal reform from within the system. Besides community organizing, he took particular responsibility for defending young offenders.

The young RDS could hardly have found a better advocate. The scene was set for a case that, as it turned out, would provide an extension of Rocky Jones's career as a community and political activist and fulfil his ambition to utilize the legal system to confront racism in Canada.

The Day in Court

RDS and Rocky Jones appeared in Youth Court on 2 December 1994. There had already been four previous appearances dating back to 7 December 1993, all adjourned at the request of the Crown. This time the Crown seemed confident. It would be a snap case, totally routine. There were no witnesses and no experts, just two versions of a simple story: a Black kid charged with assault and interference with a police officer. The judge would make the right decision. But as they entered court it was apparent that this was not a standard situation. Present were Constable Donald Stienburg and Crown prosecutor Rick Miller, both white. The rest of the court was Black: the defendant, defendant's counsel, the court clerk, and, sitting at the bench, Judge Corrine (Connie) Sparks, the first and at that time the only African-Canadian judge in Nova Scotia. This was a complete reversal of the usual scene, where the defendant would be the only Black face in court. It was Constable Stienburg who was in the middle.[10]

The arresting officer was called and sworn. He testified that on 17 October 1993, while cruising in his patrol car, he had heard a call over the radio from another police unit that was chasing a stolen van. The van was abandoned, and "five non-white males, young kids" fled the scene. Stienburg and his partner Robin Atwell were approaching the same area at that moment and saw two Black teenagers running in a suspicious fashion. Stienburg went in chase of one of the youngsters, and his partner pursued the other in a different direction. Stienburg caught up to his suspect, NR, questioned him, and arrested him on suspicion of theft of a motor vehicle. A crowd of spectators assembled. The impression given by this testimony, whether deliberate or not, was that the crowd was intimidating. Into this tense situation came another boy on a mountain bike, driving right into his legs, Stienburg testified, and trying to push him away from the person under arrest, yelling at him and banging at his shoulders and arms. Crown counsel Miller interrupted to ask what NR was doing while this was going on. "He was standing beside me. I don't recall what exactly he would have been doing," Stienburg replied. This whole incident "lasted for approximately a couple of seconds, not very long." Again the Crown asked, "What physical contact over this period did you make with Mr S?," and the constable answered, "I was holding both of the accused at the time trying to control both of them, because there was two people there and I was by myself. I believe I had them in a neck restraint, both of them at that time."[11]

Jones, alert to the racial implications of the scenario, found an opening for his cross-examination. The only identification Stienburg and Atwell had of the suspects was that they were "non-white." Is this the usual description used by the police for people of African descent, he asked. "It has been, yes," said Stienburg. As the judge reported later, the constable grew tense and nervous under questioning by Jones; he was ruffled by Jones's attack on the use of a term that implied "white" was the standard against which all others were "non." They could have been Native kids, or East Indian, Jones suggested; "non-white" means nothing. "I am not 'non' anything," he has often asserted publicly; "I am *Black*." Jones also focused on the three charges, of assault, obstruction, and resisting arrest. "There's over-charging to say the least." When Miller challenged the relevance of Jones's lines of questioning, Jones claimed it was a matter of credibility. Doubts were raised by the non-specific and pejorative description of the suspects, and there was evidence to suppose that the officer had overreacted.[12]

RDS took the stand and gave his version of the encounter. He explained that when he saw the crowd, "I was like being nosey, I wanted to know what was going on." When he arrived, he recalled, NR was already handcuffed. He denied hitting the officer with his bike, or even speaking to him. "Did you tell the police officer, 'Let my cousin go?'" "No ... The police officer wasn't even in the conversation. I was talking to N." The crowd was made up mostly of little kids, seven or eight years old and, by implication, not a potential threat to a police officer. There was no rebuttal to the boy's version. The handcuffs, the chokeholds, RDS's attempt to speak with N and then being told to "Shut up or you'll be under arrest too": all this was left as uncontested evidence laid before Judge Sparks that morning.[13]

The judge began her oral judgment with a comment on RDS's credibility. He remembered the day quite clearly, she pointed out, even the weather, and he was candid in admitting that he was simply being nosey. The officer, on the other hand, had apparently forgotten or at least had not mentioned that N was handcuffed throughout the affair. "He gave the Court the distinct impression that he had a rather difficult job in trying to restrain NR. But I really query in my own mind if this young boy was handcuffed what was the big ordeal about." When RDS reported that his cousin was in handcuffs, "this has a ring of truth, and it certainly provides some detail with respect to the actual incident." RDS, in contrast to the officer,

presented in a very positive way ... He seemed to be a rather honest young boy. He said quite openly on cross-examination, he was being nosey. He wanted to go down to the street corner to see what was going on. He seemed to have been struck by the hostility which greeted him by the police officer ...

I don't say that I accept everything that Mr S has said in Court today, but certainly he has raised a doubt in my mind and, therefore, based upon the evidentiary burden, which is squarely placed upon the Crown, that they must prove all the elements of the offence beyond a reasonable doubt, and I have queries in my mind with respect to what actually transpired on the afternoon of October the 17th.

Crown counsel Miller interjected with a fateful question. Why would the officer say that events occurred in the way in which he has relayed them to the Court this morning? Judge Sparks had an answer.

I'm not saying that the constable misled the Court, although police officers have been known to do that in the past. And I'm not saying that the officer overreacted, but certainly police officers do overreact, particularly when they're dealing with non-white groups. That, to me, indicates a state of mind right there that is questionable.

I believe that probably the situation in this particular case is the case of a young police officer who overreacted. And I do accept the evidence of Mr S that he was told to shut up or he would be under arrest. That seems to be in keeping with the prevalent order of the day.

At any rate, based upon my comments and based upon all the evidence before the Court, I have no other choice but to acquit.[14]

It was perhaps not the most carefully crafted judgment, delivered orally that December morning in Halifax. However, Judge Sparks clearly and specifically said she was not accusing Constable Stienburg of lying, or of racially motivated overreaction. In response to the Crown's apparent presumption that police officers must be believed in any disputed testimony, she reminded Miller that sometimes police do mislead, and they sometimes overreact. But in this particular case it was only "probably" that the constable overreacted, a possibility sufficient to cast some doubt on his evidence. The evidence from the defendant rang true, because the judge was able to discern the pattern in the scene laid before her. That pattern, "the prevalent order of the day," represented the endemic and systemic racism in law enforcement in Halifax; Stienburg's behaviour toward the two boys revealed "a state of mind" with which Judge Sparks and the Halifax Black community were all too familiar. If Stienburg was not personally implicated by the evidence, certainly that evidence was redolent of daily experience in the streets of Halifax. In the circumstances, or as the judge put it, "At any rate," the boy's evidence was sufficiently plausible for her to find that the Crown had not proved its case beyond a reasonable doubt.

Drawing the Lines

If the incident with the bicycle offers a glimpse into the personal dimensions of systemic racism, the response of the Halifax establishment to Judge Sparks's decision gives a full-scale view of the "state of mind" of which she spoke. The judge found that RDS's story was consistent with life in the Black community, and when she said so, the "system" reacted with denial, recrimination, and silencing. What happened after the Youth Court hearing provides more than a knot-hole. The fence came down, from the inside.

Constable Stienburg, interpreting Judge Sparks's comment as a slur on his own integrity, complained formally to his chief and to his union, suggesting that the judge had acted with racial prejudice against a white police officer. The police chief publicly expressed his concern about the "racial bias" of the judge, and wrote similarly to the chief family court judge and the Judicial Council asking for action against Connie Sparks. A formal complaint was also made, but subsequently withdrawn, to the Nova Scotia Police Commission. Apparently someone inside the police force "anonymously" informed the *Halifax Chronicle-Herald*, which, supported by the CBC, sought access to a tape-recording that had been made of the trial in order to make this alleged transgression available to the wider public. Judge Sparks heard the newspaper's application on 7 December and issued a spirited but judiciously written decision denying access: although the hearing itself had been open to the press, in fact they had not attended; the transcript was now part of the "record," and under the *Young Offenders Act* a youth's record could not be released to the public. The young person had been tried and acquitted, she wrote, and release of the record could lead to his victimization all over again. Only those with a "valid interest in the administration of justice" deserve access, and journalists do not meet that criterion.

[A]ny disgruntled witness, even a police officer, could make an anonymous call to a reporter to, in effect, complain about a court ruling if that witness was not accepted by the court as presenting credible evidence. This would, in my view, open the floodgates, and not afford protection to young offenders as contemplated by Parliament. In the unique and troubling circumstances of this case if the concern is about the court commenting, in the course of an adjudication, about the treatment of an African-Canadian accused person; sadly this cannot be viewed as novel. There has been, and no doubt will continue to be, cases where the courts, rightfully in my view, examine and criticize when necessary the investigation of a police officer, and equally so, if not more so, when the investigation is of a person from a group which has historically endured discriminatory treatment in the justice system. There is no need to cite cases; however, suffice it to say this is one of the fundamental and necessary functions of the judicial branch of government and a cornerstone of judicial independence. For an exhaustive review of treatment of people of colour in the judicial system see: The Royal Commission on the Donald Marshall, Jr Prosecution.

And in closing, Judge Sparks almost seemed to throw down a challenge: "[I]f this court is to be scrutinized for the decision, then there is a procedure in place for such scrutinization. Consequently, the record of the youth court will be fully disclosed in due course, without any harm to the accused."[15]

The Crown immediately filed two notices of appeal on the last working day before Christmas, 22 December 1994. One was against the decision in *R. v. R.D.S.*, alleging that it manifested both actual and apprehended bias in favour of the accused and against the police officer on the basis of their "race." The second was against the refusal to grant the press access to the transcript. Both were set to be heard in April 1995.

With an appeal actually in the works, Sparks took a highly unusual step: on 13 January 1995 she issued written "supplementary reasons" to explain her original *R.D.S.* decision. They were an elaboration of the reasons she offered in her *Chronicle-Herald* ruling as well as of her oral judgment on 2 December and constituted a much more direct identification of the racialized nature of the case. She emphasized the obvious discomfort Constable Stienburg displayed in court, suggesting that "this may have been due to the racial configuration in the court which consisted of the accused, the defence counsel, the court reporter and the judge all being of African-Canadian ancestry." This visible discomfort became intense when defence counsel pressed him on the use of the term *non-white*. His demeanour, and especially the distinction in the clarity of memory between the officer and the accused, was sufficient evidence for her to express some doubt about the officer's testimony. Significantly, "the Crown did not call rebuttal evidence to contradict the evidence of the accused given the strikingly contradictory evidence … [I]t is not for the Court to reconcile such difference. The question is whether the Crown has proved all of the elements of the offence beyond a reasonable doubt." Furthermore, "the police officer is a full bodied man while the young person is slight and slender … The Court questioned the necessity of choke-holding a young person of such a slight and slender build. Also, in my mind, was the fact that, from other proceedings, it is not routine for a police officer to place a 15-year-old youngster in a chokehold. Certainly, in my experience as a trial judge, I cannot recall any young person having been subjected to such harsh physical restraint." In sum, she concluded, "The police officer, in my view, put his own credibility in issue when he did not state that the other young person was handcuffed, when he became tense when questioned about the use of 'non-white'; and further the Court asked, after the rigorous cross-examination, if racial dynamics came into play as the court was mindful of the Donald Marshall, Jr Prosecution, Province of Nova Scotia, December 1989 … in particular, which point to a prevalent view respecting the unequal application of the law to persons of colour."[16]

Besides the Marshall case, other recent events in the Halifax region pointed to difficult relations between Blacks and police that would have formed part of Judge Sparks's consciousness of the "prevalent order of the day." In July 1991, for example, a disturbance initiated by young Black men who had been consistently refused admission to downtown bars turned into an altercation between Blacks and the police. Allegations of excessive force and racial insult by members of the Halifax police department led to the establishment of an Incident Review Committee, though the committee split between police and community members in writing their reports. Even without a conclusive report, the Toronto *Globe and Mail* could comment in April 1992, just eighteen months before the RDS incident, "In Halifax, relations between the police and the city's black community have been strained in the wake of allegations that the police have used excessive force against blacks."[17] Such circumstances would have made it extremely unlikely, at least in the mind of any person in the Black community, that a scrawny fifteen-year-old would deliberately attempt to assault a "full bodied" police officer in October 1993.

The lines were drawn, with the police, the media, and soon the justice system itself aligned against Rocky Jones and Connie Sparks on behalf of the youth RDS.

The Appeals

Chief Justice Constance Glube of the Supreme Court of Nova Scotia heard the appeal on 18 April 1995, sitting as a summary conviction appeal judge. Counsel Adrian C. Reid, QC, for the Crown, argued that Judge Sparks's remarks made in the course of her decision "show clearly the Trial Judge's conclusions on credibility flow from a racially based bias against police, and not from the evidence. Further, the Crown submits that this creates an appearance of unfairness. The Crown goes further and alleges that the remarks exhibit real bias."[18] This charge of actual bias against a judge was highly unusual. Normally the allegation would be an "apprehension of bias," for it is very difficult to prove what was actually in a judge's mind when a decision was made. Jones, still only in his second year as a lawyer, sought the assistance of the staff and faculty at the Dalhousie Legal Clinic. They could not find a single Canadian case where a judge had been charged with racial bias against the police.

Despite the precedent-setting nature of the case before her, Chief Justice Glube chose not to take the time to craft a carefully worded written decision. Like that of Judge Sparks, it was issued orally. The chief justice began by rejecting Sparks's supplementary reasons from consideration. The release of those "gratuitous" reasons "caused me some concern," she admitted, for they contained information that was not in the original trial decision. In particular, the trial judge made new comments on "the demeanour of the police officer" and referred to "outside material," in citing the Marshall Inquiry, that had not been introduced at trial. Turning then to the actual judgment of 2 December, the chief justice commended the early part of the Sparks decision, up to the point where she declared her reasonable doubt raised by the conflicting evidence laid before her as to the facts of the case. "[H]ad it ended there," Glube said, "there would have been no basis for this appeal as the Crown has already conceded." However, statements made in the final two paragraphs of the Sparks decision, concerning the "prevalent attitude of the day" and "remarks made relating to the police," were not supported by evidence presented during the trial.[19]

The uncontested evidence that the two young suspects were handcuffed and placed in chokeholds, and the credible testimony that RDS had been threatened with arrest unless he "shut up," did not apparently convince Chief Justice Glube that they should be considered in court or form part of the trial judge's decision-making process. Or at least not *openly* considered, for the chief justice warned that a judge should "be extremely careful to avoid *expressing* views which do not form part of the evidence."

Chief Justice Glube then addressed the pertinent issue of whether bias could be discerned in the Sparks decision, for "an acquittal will only be set aside where the verdict is unreasonable or not supported by the evidence. In the case at bar, if there is to be found an apprehension of bias, then the verdict would not be supported by the evidence ... The test of apprehension of bias is an objective one, that is, whether a reasonable right-minded person with knowledge of all the facts would conclude that the judge's impartiality might reasonably be questioned. In my respectful opinion, in spite of the thorough review of the facts and the finding on credibility, the two paragraphs at the end of the decision lead to the conclusion that a reasonable apprehension of bias exists."

How or why Sparks's final paragraphs might violate the right-minded person's sense of impartiality was not elaborated in Glube's oral decision. Nor did she explain why she rejected the Crown's accusation of actual racial bias. She merely laid out the test for apprehension of bias and immediately concluded that the paragraphs support a finding that "a reasonable apprehension" exists. The "right-minded person" would seem to be the chief justice herself. She concluded by allowing the appeal and ordering a new trial "in front of a different trial judge."[20] On the surface, Chief Justice Glube's decision was racially neutral, for it simply and routinely ordered a new trial. But since Sparks was the only African-Canadian judge in Nova Scotia, this meant that RDS would appear before a white judge. The racialized aspect of the case was therefore enhanced by a decision that ostensibly ignored "race," demonstrating the liabilities of "colour-blind" justice that would be central to the subsequent deliberations.

Jones learned from his Dalhousie Law School mentors that only very rarely does the Crown claim an apprehension of judicial bias; usually it is the defence counsel in a criminal trial who would make such a claim. And most of the cases that do arise are dismissed, for there is a prevailing assumption in the judicial system that judges operate on good faith and with impartiality. There is therefore a high standard of proof that must be met by the party alleging that a particular judgment displayed a reasonable apprehension of bias.[21] Was it then mere coincidence that such a rare charge could be made, and upheld, against Nova Scotia's only Black judge? And was the high standard normally required applied in this case? The Black community had its doubts on both points. Connie Sparks was perceived as a victim of the very racism she had identified in her comments. The Glube decision seemed to confirm that no Black person, even a Black judge, could dare to confront the daily and systemic racism that every Black Nova Scotian recognized as a reality. Rocky Jones understood all these implications. Glube had to be appealed. Though initially concerned at the resources it would take, the Dalhousie Legal Clinic eventually agreed to back an appeal, and Jones was able to call on those resources and the pro bono engagement of Law School professors as the case proceeded.

With Richard Devlin, Dianne Pothier, Carol Aylward, and others from Dalhousie as his support team, Jones fashioned an argument to place before the Nova Scotia Court of Appeal. Jones contended that

Glube had inappropriately interfered with a finding of credibility by a trial court judge, that an incorrect standard had been applied for the reasonable apprehension of bias, and that a formal equality approach as implied in the Glube decision was unconstitutional. He described two potential approaches to the reasonable apprehension of bias as revealed in the jurisprudence. One was "the mere suspicion test," in which only a suggestion of bias needed to be found. The second was "the real danger test," where there was a genuine likelihood that a decision was biased. Jones claimed that Glube took the "mere suspicion" route, but the more appropriate test was the one for "real danger." No acceptable evidence of a "real danger" could be found in the Sparks judgment, and therefore it must be reinstated by the Court of Appeal. He also distinguished between two approaches to equality, which under the *Charter* should be considered in determining whether Judge Sparks's decision had exhibited an apprehension of bias. A formal approach would mean that the courts should be colour-blind and that all persons should be treated the same, regardless of age, gender, or colour. With such an approach, a court would abstain from any reference to "race" or acknowledgment of "race" as a factor in judgment. A substantive approach, on the other hand, recognizes the special needs of disadvantaged people. "Racism exists in Canadian society, and a recognition of that fact can help jurists remedy the effects of discrimination." Refusal to discuss "race" can have the effect of perpetuating racial inequality; only by confronting it directly can racism be dismantled. *Charter* Section 15, in particular, required the substantive definition of equality rights.[22]

The appeal was heard on 13 October 1995, before Justices Freeman, Pugsley, and Flinn. Their judgment, divided two to one, was delivered just twelve days later. For the majority, Justice Flinn dismissed the *Charter* argument on the simple ground that it had not been raised before Chief Justice Glube when she heard the appeal from the original Sparks decision. As Richard Devlin later commented, "While he is technically correct to suggest that the Charter analysis could have been raised in argument before Glube CJNS, the point is that it was her reasons for decision that generated the appellant's equality concerns."[23] The challenge on credibility was given equally short shrift. Glube's decision, Flinn wrote, "was not based upon a re-examination, and determination, of issues of credibility. Her decision was based solely on the issue of apprehension of bias." It was therefore to this ground of appeal that Justice Flinn paid most attention. He declined to recognize any distinction between various definitions of or approaches to "reasonable apprehension." "The appearance of bias, assessed objectively, and whether intended or not, is sufficient." The judge had based her decision to acquit at least in part on her general comments about the police. "Counsel for the appellant argues that these comments do not indicate that the Youth Court judge is biased against the police. He says they merely reflect an unfortunate social reality. That may very well be so; however, it does not address the real issue here." There was no evidence before Judge Sparks on the "prevalent attitude of the day," or that Constable Stienburg had overreacted. And if there were concerns in this regard, they were not canvassed in cross-examination and so the constable had no opportunity to address them. The reasonable person would therefore conclude that the judge had reached her decision "unfairly." Flinn, with Pugsley, denied the appeal.[24]

Justice Freeman saw matters quite differently. While he accepted the majority's interpretation of the applicable law, he did not agree with the way it was applied. "It was perfectly proper," he asserted, "for the trial judge, in weighing the evidence before her, to consider the racial perspective. I am not satisfied that in doing so she gave the appearance of being biased herself." Judge Sparks's reference to "the prevalent attitude of the day" may have been unclear, but Freeman accepted Rocky Jones's suggestion that she could have meant the attitudes exhibited *that* day, 17 October 1993. As Sparks recognized in her decision and her supplementary reasons, "race" was central in this case: "The case was racially charged, a classic confrontation between a white police officer representing the power of the state and a black youth charged with an offence ... It is unfortunately true and within the scope of general knowledge of any individual that police officers have been known to mislead the court and overreact in dealing with non-white groups."

The evidence placed before her in court was "enough to justify her in tipping the scales in an assessment of credibility." Trial judges have to incorporate their "wisdom and experience" to assess the credibility of witnesses, and appeal courts must defer to a trial judge in determining what evidence to believe. Judge Sparks's remarks were consistent with a fair inquiry, he ruled, and her original acquittal should be restored.[25]

Nevertheless the appeal was lost, and the new trial was scheduled for RDS. Jones turned again to his colleagues at the Legal Clinic, arguing for an appeal to the Supreme Court of Canada. Stretched for resources, the clinic again showed some reluctance to pursue this case further. Even some of his best friends doubted the wisdom of another appeal. But Justice Freeman's strong dissent gave Jones his arguments, and the clinic agreed to give it this final try. They were successful in gaining a Court Challenges grant, and Dalhousie promised the rest of the money required to carry the appeal to Ottawa.

Preparing for Ottawa

There is no automatic right to appeal to the Supreme Court of Canada (SCC). Appellants have to apply for leave to appeal, and from among the many applicants the Court will select cases that can demonstrate a degree of national importance. In designing their application, Jones and his Dalhousie team decided to ask the Court to establish the threshold of judicial bias, an issue that would affect every judge in Canada, and to determine by what right and under what circumstances judges can rely on their own experience in reaching their decisions. The grounds of appeal were carefully worded:

1. Did the Court of Appeal for Nova Scotia err in law in holding that the Chief Justice of the Supreme Court of Nova Scotia, sitting as a summary conviction appeal court judge, made no error in law with respect to the test for, or the application of the test for, or the finding of reasonable apprehension of bias on the part of the trial judge?
2. Did the Court of Appeal for Nova Scotia err in law in dismissing the ss. 7, 11(d) and 15 Charter requirement inherent in deciding the legal parameters of a reasonable apprehension of bias?[26]

Judge Sparks became the surrogate; it was *her* alleged racism that would be assessed.

Though the Crown submitted a memorandum denying that this was an issue of national importance requiring the intervention of the SCC, leave to appeal was granted on 6 May 1996.[27] It now became an issue of strategy for the appellants. Jones was invited to appear at the Law School one evening to submit his proposed arguments before an assembly of faculty and students, as if in a moot court. He began with the case he had presented before the Nova Scotia Court of Appeal, which had been substantially adopted by Justice Freeman in dissent. His mentors attacked him with "tough love," critiquing every statement and nuance and suggesting alternatives. One of their suggestions was to claim that Judge Sparks had in effect been taking judicial notice of societal racism when she made her disputed comments; they could then be legitimized under a standard judicial practice and not be considered as personal bias. Jones disagreed with this line of argument, seeing a huge downside risk if the SCC rejected it. Another suggestion from the Law School was to develop the *Charter* aspect more forcefully than at the Court of Appeal. Mindful of his own inexperience, Jones agreed to have Professor Dianne Pothier appear as co-counsel to make the *Charter* argument before the SCC. Dalhousie Law professors, including Devlin and Aylward, set to work with Jones and Pothier on writing a factum.

As soon as leave to appeal was granted, other groups began to offer themselves in support of Jones and Pothier. The Legal Education and Action Fund (LEAF) was first, engaging in strategy sessions by telephone and giving their advice. Together with the National Organization of Immigrant and Visible Minority Women of Canada (NOIVMWC), LEAF applied for intervener status; another joint application came from the African Canadian Legal Clinic, the Afro-Canadian Caucus of Nova Scotia, and the Congress of Black Women of Canada (the Coalition). Both were granted status and subsequently submitted factums.[28] Their assistance was appreciated, but there was a complication: the intervening teams wanted to categorize the Sparks comments as judicial notice, thus reinforcing the position taken by some members of the Law School. This was a strategy Jones had already rejected, fearing that judicial notice was too narrow and too specific to serve the broader purpose of this case. John Sopinka et al. offer a definition: "Judicial notice is the acceptance by a court or judicial tribunal, in a civil or criminal proceeding, without the requirement of proof, of the truth of a particular fact or state of affairs. Facts which are a) so notorious as not to be the subject of dispute among reasonable persons, or b) capable of immediate and accurate demonstration by resorting to readily accessible sources of indisputable accuracy, may be noticed by the court without proof of them by any party."[29]

Under these terms it seemed possible that Sparks's comments would not require "evidence" such as was demanded by the Nova Scotia courts. But Jones anticipated that the very existence of the Crown's argument would indicate that there was in fact a dispute over the racial dynamics represented by the RDS incident, and furthermore the Crown would have had to be advised of this interpretation at the time of the trial. The argument would quite probably fail, and this could be taken to imply a denial by the SCC of the existence of racism more generally. Jones preferred an alternative strategy. Sparks was correct in recognizing systemic racism because it was true, and she knew it from her own personal experience as a member of the Black community. She was authorized to do so by the doctrine of "contextualism," whereby a judge could take into consideration the social context of the case at trial. Not only Judge Sparks, therefore, but any judge should locate any case in the context in which it occurred and include that information in the process of adjudication.[30] It was Jones's case and therefore his call: judicial notice was omitted from the appellant's factum. Interveners are independent agents, however, offering their own expertise to the court, and therefore do not need the appellant's permission or approval of their arguments.

The first half of the appellant's brief of argument was written by Jones, in collaboration with his Law School colleagues. Arguing the first ground of appeal, Jones noted that Sparks had examined the evidence carefully, as Glube acknowledged, and had made her disputed comments only in response to the Crown's submission that there was no reason not to believe the constable's testimony. "The allegation of a reasonable apprehension of bias arose in this case because Judge Sparks, a Black female Youth Court judge, in adjudicating a trial of a Black accused, explicitly recognized that the case had racial overtones ... It is a mistake to assume that the identification of racial dynamics automatically gives rise to an apprehension of bias." The two approaches to the apprehension of bias were described, and Glube and the Court of Appeal were alleged to have applied the inappropriate "mere suspicion" approach. The "real danger" test was correct, because "[f]irst, any threshold test should reflect the presumption of judicial impartiality; those chosen for judicial office should be assumed to be persons of integrity, fully capable of exercising their duties with impartiality. Second ... before taking office, judges must take a Judicial Oath, in which they swear to carry out their duties honestly and with impartiality."

In applying the test, it should be acknowledged what "a fully informed *reasonable* person would know: that racism is pervasive in Canadian society and that practically and realistically police officers sometimes overreact, consciously or unconsciously, when dealing with Black youth." Sparks's remark about "the prevalent attitude of the day" referred to 17 October 1993; even if it was meant generally, "this is not a matter that requires evidence. Instead, it is a matter of *experience* of the trier of fact. In this case race was not a material fact that had to be proved, rather it was a matter of societal context. Accordingly it did not require evidence, nor did it require the taking of judicial notice."

Authorities were cited to support the widespread recognition of societal racism. "In *R. v. Parks* Justice Doherty (1992), speaking for a unanimous Ontario Court of appeal, wrote: Racism, and in particular anti-black racism, is a part of our community's psyche. A significant segment of our community holds overtly racist views. A much larger segment subconsciously operates on the basis of negative racial stereotypes. Furthermore, our institutions, including the criminal justice system, reflect and perpetuate these negative stereotypes."

This was echoed by "Judge Niedermayer (1992): The issue of racism existing in Nova Scotia has been well documented in the Marshall Inquiry Report. A person would have to be stupid, complacent or ignorant not to acknowledge its presence, not only individually, but also systemically and institutionally."

These judicial comments, together with the *Report of the Commission on Equality in Employment* (1985), the *Report of the Commission on Systemic Racism in the Ontario Criminal Justice System* (1995), and the *Royal Commission on the Donald Marshall, Jr Prosecution* (1989) meant that no reasonable person could dispute the existence of racism in Canada. Accordingly, Judge Sparks's comments "cannot properly be understood as giving rise to a reasonable apprehension of bias."[31]

Pothier was responsible for arguing the second ground. She began, "According to Glube CJSC, and the majority of the Court of Appeal, Judge Sparks would have demonstrated impartiality by never mentioning or noticing race in this case. It is that premise which, in the Appellant's submission, is inconsistent with the Charter. A judge cannot give rise to a reasonable apprehension of bias simply by letting it be known that the judge is alert to the *possibility* of racial bias, whether intentional or not, on the part of witnesses before the Court."

Charter sections 7 and 11(d) must be interpreted in light of section 15, for "[t]he relevance of equality to Charter analysis is not limited to s. 15; equality is a general value underlying other sections as well." Reinstating RDS into the case, Pothier argued that Section 7 should give the accused the benefit of Judge Sparks's reasonable doubt and not subject him to incarceration if convicted in a second trial; Section 11(d) guarantees an impartial tribunal, and to be impartial it must conform to the equality dictates of Section 15, which embraces a substantive notion of equality, recognizing that identical treatment does not always mean equal treatment. Contrary to Glube and the Court of Appeal, who had implicitly accepted that judges must be "colour-blind," Pothier insisted that a judge must be alert to the possibility of racial discrimination, as Judge Sparks had been; otherwise the courts could actually perpetuate racism. "To suggest that impartiality means factoring out race is to reflect the perspective of someone who has the luxury of never having suffered from racism ... For the justice system to take account of race in order to counteract racism is the antithesis of racial bias."[32]

The LEAF/NOIVMWC factum pushed further the idea that judges not only could but should articulate in their decisions any assumptions upon which they base their judgments. "This articulation would facilitate review by superior courts, guard against reliance on myths and prejudicial beliefs, and ensure that the inclusion in reasons for judgment of valid generalizations based upon well known social facts and observations is not construed as bias." They therefore argued that the SCC "should require judges to take judicial notice of the social context in which a case arises in order to give effect to the constitutional guarantee of equality enshrined in s. 15," and they urged the Court "to interpret the doctrines of judicial notice and judicial bias in a manner that is consistent with the Charter's guarantee of equality."[33] The second intervener's factum added a twist to the judicial notice theme: "Whether Judge Sparks took judicial notice of and/or used her common sense knowledge in taking race into account is not at issue in the Coalition's argument. The Coalition does, however, now invite this Honourable Court to take judicial notice of anti-black racism in Canada."[34]

The Crown had already contended that this was not a *Charter* case, and "if this court applies the Charter the Crown is at a distinct disadvantage because of the absence of opportunity to call s. 1 evidence." The essence of the respondent's argument was that Judge Sparks made comments that inferred that the actions of Constable Stienburg were racially motivated, and he was not given an opportunity to respond, and no literature was introduced to support the judge's generalizations. Therefore "[t]his case is about the fairness of the trial." In recent years, and especially since the Marshall Inquiry, the Halifax police had made serious efforts to improve their relationship with the Black community. Any judicial conclusions to the contrary should be supported by evidence and be subject to response by the Crown. The handcuffing of suspects was standard practice for the police, regardless of "race." "If the court is going to extrapolate and draw a negative inference from any particular action of an officer the opportunity must be provided to the officer to explain that action." The kinds of generalizations made by Judge Sparks constitute an impediment to the reduction of societal racism. When she "stepped outside the evidence before the court, imported unsubstantiated inferences or facts, and failed to consider possible explanations for the police action, the evaluation of the credibility became tainted by reason of apprehension of bias." The "appearance of justice" was violated by the judge reaching conclusions about "race" when "race" was not an issue at trial.[35]

The Hearing

Before leaving Halifax, Rocky Jones had half-heartedly conceded to pressure and added judicial notice to his notes for argument before the Court. The factum had already been submitted, but some of his Dalhousie collaborators and the interveners wanted this principle restored to his oral presentation. The night before the hearing, he told his sister, Lynn Jones, who accompanied him to Ottawa, that he was uncomfortable with this aspect of his presentation. Lynn encouraged him to rewrite it according to his own understanding of the issues, and he did, dictating to Lynn while she typed on a borrowed computer. Judicial notice would not be part of the appellant's case.[36]

The morning of 10 March 1997 dawned cold and drizzly. Jones, his wife Sharon, sister Lynn, Dalhousie students, the mother of RDS, and others who had come from Halifax arrived very early at the Supreme Court on Wellington Street in Ottawa. More Black people were coming from other Canadian cities, and from Ottawa itself, conscious of the significance of this case. They all formed a long line in front of the Court, while Jones went around to the back entrance reserved for lawyers pleading that day. Nobody else had yet appeared. Shortly before the public doors were to open, there arrived a busload or two of white law students, and they were admitted into the Court where they occupied all the seats available. An attendant explained to Lynn Jones and the Black people at the head of the line that these students had booked their seats in advance, an opportunity they had not been aware of. A fervent appeal was made to the students, and they gave up their seats and moved into an adjacent room to observe the proceedings on closed-circuit television. The Black people filed into the Court, and now they were the occupants of the full space available to the public. They formed an engaged and even a participatory audience, dressed in their finest, murmuring encouragement and disapproval and adding occasional laughter throughout the proceedings. It was a set-up that entirely suited the pleaders for the appellant and may have enhanced their performance.[37]

It was another Black day in court, in many ways. Surely there were never so many Black lawyers appearing before the SCC at a single time.

Arguing the case were Rocky Jones for the accused, Yola Grant for LEAF/NOIVMWC, and April Burey for the Coalition, all African Canadians. Even the respondent's counsel, Robert Lutes, QC, had brought a Black clerk with him.[38] Jones had his revised text all ready. At 9:46 a.m. he launched his presentation. He had spoken for scarcely four or five minutes when he began to be peppered with questions from the bench. His Dalhousie mentors had prepared him for this, and though he expressed some concerns about finishing his prepared remarks, he was given a full opportunity to make his points over the thirty-six minutes allowed to him. As with the factum, he argued the first ground of appeal.

"My Lords and my Ladies," he declared, "this case should have been about a young person, RDS, who was acquitted in 1994. The decision was based upon evidence and a determination of credibility which produced a reasonable doubt in the mind of Judge Sparks, the youth court judge ... The allegation of bias arose in this particular case because Judge Sparks, a black woman, was adjudicating the trial of a black accused and she explicitly recognized that the case had racial overtones."[39]

Justice Major asked about Sparks's alleged slur against the police. "Isn't that stereotyping that seems so out of favour these days? ... [I]f you substitute anything, any other group for police officers wouldn't it be condemned as being stereotyping?" And Chief Justice Lamer added, "Why single [the police] out in one given case ... We all know that everyone is capable of perjury, and we all know that policemen have perjured themselves in all kinds of circumstances, but here she has singled out the police officers in this particular case." Jones responded,

My Lord, the trial judge had to deal obviously with the evidence before her. The case dealt with police officers and this case dealt with the young accused. She, my Lord, was responding to a question and an assertion that was posed by the Crown Counsel at that time. The Crown had raised the issue as to why would a police officer mislead.

Lamer: Oh, I understand. It was the result of a question ... by the Crown and not something that she felt she had to factor in.

Jones: No, this wasn't something that came out of the blue.

Lamer: I see. I see. Well, it's been very helpful.[40]

Justice Sopinka wondered why Judge Sparks at first said the officer did not overreact, and later said that he did. Jones explained that she only said, "probably the police officer overreacted," a probability that raised a legitimate doubt in her mind. Justice Cory raised the issue of judicial notice, wondering why Jones had not included it at the Court of Appeal. Jones answered,

Yes, my Lord, it's the Appellant's position that in fact we do not address the issue of judicial notice because it was our position that the judge has a right, and a duty, to look at not only police actions, but what is happening in our society, to be aware of what is happening in society ...

What the Appellant is saying is that a reasonably aware, informed person in today's society should be aware of racism in our society, not that everyone's racist, I mean ...

At this point the Chief Justice interrupted:

But we don't know which ones are unless they do things to reveal it, and the smarter ones don't ... We have to decide whether this one was racist ... I accept the proposition with you, and it's an obvious proposition, that there is racism. To some people I'm a honky, to others I'm a frog. So we all are, unfortunately, in some form or fashion, subject to the intolerance and misunderstanding of others, but now we are talking about the credibility of a witness ... I'm wondering how far we're going? Why raise the issue of race at all?

This query from Chief Justice Lamer gave Jones the opportunity to make his major point extemporaneously:

I want the Court to address the issue if the Court will, that indeed the judge was right to acknowledge the existence of racism, or if not racism of racial overtones in a case, that in fact the same as we would now be aware of the imbalances in our society vis-à-vis women, we should be aware of the imbalances in our society because of race. And it's not asking something far out, it is a reality, and if we don't hide from the reality, if we address the reality, perhaps, and the Appellant submits that it is important for us as Canadians to address these issues and to work on them ...

My Lords and my Ladies, we cannot ignore the fact that for centuries people of colour have made claims about bias in the courts, and the courts have been deaf to those claims, but yet, as soon as one black judge even raises the issue of race, suddenly claims for an apprehension of bias in the judiciary seemed to be well grounded.

Jones then said that he was conscious of time passing, and he hadn't yet had an opportunity to go through his entire presentation. The chief justice said soothingly, "You may rest assured that we've prepared this case thoroughly and read all of your material and all of the evidence. So feel comfortable with that." These exchanges were generally good-natured. For example, when Justice LaForest made a helpful comment, Jones said, "Yes. Thank you very much, you're so much better than I am." Apart from the chief justice's assurance that he had thoroughly read all the appellant's materials, when in fact he seemed surprised to learn that Sparks's comments had been provoked by a question from the Crown, Jones's engagement with the Court was as effective as he could have wished.[41]

Pothier put the argument on the second ground. She too was interrupted from time to time, though she was able to make her case substantially as it was in the factum. Perhaps the most startling interruption came from the chief justice. From his experience as a practising lawyer, he claimed, he had learned that Chinese are "tremendous gamblers." If a Chinese individual were accused of illegal gambling, he asked hypothetically, should his community's "propensity for gambling" be factored into the evidence? And should a judge also factor in the possibility that the arresting officer, a non-Chinese, could be racially biased? "I am just trying to figure out how far down this slope we're going to go once we do this." The chief justice went on to raise rhetorical questions about "Gypsies" who pick pockets, and Black youths who steal cars, suggesting that judges should not rely on stereotypes when they are adjudicating a particular case. He was, as he later explained, raising hypothetical situations to show that "information" brought from outside could have a negative effect. "I'm afraid that it works both ways. While it might work for you today, it might work against you tomorrow."[42] Like Jones, Pothier tried to restore RDS to the discussion, indicating that his rights had been sacrificed and he had been "sort of lost in the shuffle … I think it is important that this Court not forget RDS in the process."

Yola Grant for LEAF suffered fewer interruptions, and April Burey for the Coalition, addressing the Court from her wheelchair, suffered none at all. Burey later wrote that she had been "close to tears at the end of my oral presentation. So too were many of those listening in the public galleries. And even all nine judges of the Supreme Court themselves seemed mesmerized."[43] Respondent's counsel Robert Lutes, on the other hand, experienced frequent questions and interjections from the bench. For example, when Lutes wanted to consider Sparks's supplementary reasons, which seemed to indicate that she was not talking just about the "prevailing attitude" on that particular day but was making a generalized comment, Justice McLachlin reminded him that the supplementary reasons were not an issue in this hearing, and that using his own argument about fairness, he could not bring this up at the end of the proceedings without the appellant having an opportunity to present opposing views.[44]

In a nine-minute reply for the appellant, Jones concluded the hearing by denying that Sparks had accused the officer of racism or that justice had not "seemed" to be done for Constable Stienburg. "That's not what this case is about ... [It] is that justice must in fact be done for this young person, RDS, and I submit to the Court that his acquittal should be upheld and he should not be faced, years later, as he is now, with going back for a new trial on what was only a summary offence in the first instance."[45]

The Decision

Rocky Jones was on a fishing trip in British Columbia when the SCC decision was issued on 26 September 1997. A Dalhousie student faxed a summary to Roger Jones in Vancouver, who passed it on to his brother Rocky a few days later. By a convincing margin of six to three, Canada's highest court had restored Connie Sparks's original judgment: RDS was acquitted; he would not have to face a new trial. That "bottom line" did not change, but when Jones had an opportunity to study the full decision, there were some complexities apparent. Four separate judgments were offered. The dissent was straightforward, written by Justice Major for himself and Lamer and Sopinka, denying the appeal. The six judges who participated in the majority decision to allow the appeal, however, wrote three different judgments: Justice Cory for himself and Iacobucci, Justice Gonthier, briefly, for himself and LaForest, and Justices L'Heureux-Dubé and McLachlin writing jointly. Of the nine individual judges, only four were unequivocal in their endorsement of Connie Sparks: L'Heureux-Dubé, McLachlin, Gonthier, and LaForest. Two were critical but nevertheless concurred in the acquittal: Cory and Iacobucci. And the three in dissent, Major, Lamer, and Sopinka, obviously rejected the Sparks judgment.[46]

As both Jones and Pothier had anticipated, RDS the person was "lost in the shuffle." No apparent significance was given to the fact that a fifteen-year-old boy, as he was in 1993, had been to court four times prior to the Sparks trial, and his case had been heard three more times since then. Eight appearances constitute a "water torture" of some kind, spread over four years, representing a substantial portion of his life by the time the SCC disposed of the charge hanging over him. But the "victim" described in the judgments is either Constable Stienburg or Judge Sparks, not RDS. He has no identity. The story is not his. To be sure, appeal courts are constrained by the grounds upon which a case is presented to them, but both the appellant's lawyers had made an urgent request, in their factum and in the oral pleadings, to put him back into the story.

On Systemic Racism

On the critical issue of systemic racism, the SCC acknowledged either directly or indirectly the appellant's assertion that racism pervaded Canadian society. The studies, commissions, and judgments cited in the Jones-Pothier factum were thoroughly quoted and sustained in the decision. Where the justices disagreed was whether the incident in October 1993 could be regarded as an example of that racism. The dissenting judges found that it could not and even denied that "race" was a concern in this case. Justice Major wrote, "This appeal should not be decided on questions of racism but instead on how courts should decide cases … Whether racism exists in our society is not the issue. The issue is whether there was evidence before the court upon which to base a finding that this particular police officer's actions were motivated by racism. There was no evidence of this presented at the trial." Justice Cory was prepared to accept that a judge might find racism to be the motive for the overreaction of a police officer "in some circumstances," but he found it "troubling" and "worrisome" that Judge Sparks had discerned racism in this incident. Regardless of the well-documented history of racism in Nova Scotia, "there was no evidence before Judge Sparks that would suggest that anti-black bias influenced this particular police officer's reactions." Only the L'Heureux-Dubé/McLachlin judgment, supported by Gonthier and LaForest, took advantage of the knot-hole supplied by the incident to find it representative of the kind of racism faced by Black people in Canada. They wrote that Judge Sparks had not in fact attributed the "probable overreaction" of Constable Stienburg to racism. She had, rather, tied her finding to the evidence that Stienburg had threatened to arrest RDS for speaking to his cousin. But, they wrote, there was "evidence capable of supporting a finding of racially motivated overreaction" in that NR was handcuffed throughout the encounter and both boys were placed in chokeholds.

"In the face of such evidence, we respectfully disagree with the views of our colleagues Cory and Major JJ. that there was no evidence on which Judge Sparks could have found 'racially motivated' overreaction by the police officer ... [I]f Judge Sparks had chosen to attribute the behaviour of Constable Stienburg to the racial dynamics of the situation, she would not necessarily have erred."[47] Even this minority declaration was nuanced ("she would not *necessarily* have erred"), and the SCC as a whole never seriously confronted the racial component; the constable's behaviour was in effect normalized by most justices on the SCC, as it was by the courts in Nova Scotia. More positively, and potentially much more revolutionary, the majority of the SCC (L'Heureux-Dubé, McLachlin, Gonthier, LaForest, Cory, and Iacobucci) offered a new definition of that legally significant fictional composite, "the reasonable person." The standard-bearer of Canadian fairness, the arbiter of judicial integrity, this "reasonable person," in the words of L'Heureux-Dubé and McLachlin, "supports the principles entrenched in the Constitution by the Canadian Charter of Rights and Freedoms ... includ[ing] the principles of equality set out in s. 15 ... [and in] human rights legislation. The reasonable person must be taken to be aware of the history of discrimination faced by disadvantaged groups in Canadian society ... The reasonable person is not only a member of the Canadian community, but also, more specifically, is a member of the local communities ... Such a person must be taken to possess knowledge of the local population and its racial dynamics."[48] This definition, adopted from the appellant's arguments, is perhaps a bit optimistic, but it is now enshrined in Canadian jurisprudence.

On Judging

The Supreme Court justices had much more to say about judging than they did about racism. Their *R.D.S.* report is virtually a seminar on judging in a multicultural society. As Justice Major put it, "The case is primarily about the conduct of the trial," and he and his colleagues proceeded to comment on how that best could be done. The judgments are schematically divided into discussions of the applicable theories relevant to *R.D.S.*, and then specific applications of those theories to the circumstances of the case. Thus they give both theoretical and practical advice on judicial impartiality, the apprehension of bias, the interpretation of the *Charter*, contextualism, judicial notice, the legitimate use of evidence and generalization, the assessment of credibility, and fairness in the courts. It was a seminar rather than a lecture, because the three main written judgments contain varying approaches to the issues under discussion. Difference and diversity, in fact, are held up as virtues, as fundamental features of Canadian society and of Canadian judging. "Canada is not an insular, homogeneous society," Justice Cory wrote. "It is enriched by the presence and contributions of citizens of many different races, nationalities and ethnic origins ... Section 27 provides that the Charter itself is to be interpreted in a manner that is consistent with the preservation and enhancement of the multicultural heritage of Canadians ... [O]ur judges must be particularly sensitive to the need not only to be fair but also to appear to all reasonable observers to be fair to all Canadians of every race, religion, nationality and ethnic origin. This is a far more difficult task in Canada than it would be in a homogeneous society." Justices L'Heureux-Dubé and McLachlin opened their judgment by endorsing Cory's comment on multiculturalism, adding, "[J]udges in a bilingual, multiracial and multicultural society will undoubtedly approach the task of judging from their varied perspectives."[49] What this might mean for the questions before the court would be revealed in the details.

On Judicial Bias

The appellants had argued that there was an inherent presumption of judicial integrity in Canada, which could be ignored only in the face of the strongest evidence of bias on the part of a judge. Their position was confirmed by Justice Cory: "A judge who happens to be black is no more likely to be biased in dealing with black litigants, than a white judge is likely to be biased in favour of white litigants. All judges of every race, colour, religion, or national background are entitled to the same presumption of judicial integrity and the same high threshold for a finding of bias."[50] Justices L'Heureux-Dubé and McLachlin took a different and more complex approach to this issue. "[I]t is necessary to distinguish between the impartiality which is required of all judges, and the concept of judicial neutrality." They cited Benjamin Cardozo to the effect that judicial neutrality is a fallacy and objectivity an impossibility because judges, like every other person, operate from their own perspectives.[51] "True impartiality does not require that the judge have no sympathies or opinions," they conclude; "it requires that the judge nevertheless be free to entertain and act upon different points of view with an open mind."[52] Taken together, these opinions, representing six of the nine justices, would set a very high threshold for a finding of bias against Connie Sparks. At the same time the entire Court accepted the test for an apprehension of bias articulated by Justice de Grandpré and summarized by Justice Cory as containing "a two-fold element: the person considering the alleged bias must be reasonable, and the apprehension of bias itself must be reasonable in the circumstances of the case."[53] Cory himself found that Judge Sparks's remarks "come very close to the line," but it must be understood that "she was rebutting the unfounded suggestion of the Crown that a police officer by virtue of his occupation should be more readily believed than the accused. Although her remarks were inappropriate they did not give rise to a reasonable apprehension of bias."[54] L'Heureux-Dubé and McLachlin "disagree[d] with Cory J's position that the comments of Judge Sparks were unfortunate, unnecessary, or close to the line. Rather, we find them to reflect an entirely appropriate recognition of the facts in evidence in this case and of the context within which this case arose – a context known to Judge Sparks and to any well-informed member of the community."[55] Justice Major in dissent accepted the same test for the apprehension of bias. "However I come to a different conclusion in the application of the test to the words of the trial judge in this case." She "was stereotyping all police officers as liars and racists, and applied this stereotype to the police officer in the present case ... I would uphold the disposition of [the Nova Scotia] Court of Appeal ... and dismiss the appeal."[56]

On Contextualism

The most dissension among the three substantial judgments, and the clearest distinction between the two majority judgments, was aroused by the appellant's contention that a judge may (or even must) apply personal experience and social context in adjudicating a case. Justice Major, consistent with his general approach, maintained, "A fair trial is one that is based on the law, the outcome of which is determined by the evidence." Judge Sparks concluded, in his view, that the constable's actions were motivated by racism, but "[t]here was no evidence of this presented at the trial." He did concede that the life experience of a judge "is an important ingredient in the ability to understand human behaviour, to weigh the evidence, and to determine credibility ... It is of no value, however, in reaching conclusions for which there is no evidence ... Life experience is not a substitute for evidence ... The trial judge presumably called upon her life experience to decide the issue. This she was not entitled to do."[57]

Evidence was also significant for Justice Cory, though he was more willing to admit personal experience into the process of adjudication. Neutrality and fairness, he stated, form "the cardinal rule of judicial conduct," but this "does not require judges to discount the very life experiences that may so well qualify them to preside over disputes." Whether such references are acceptable depends on the facts of the case. "On one hand, the judge is obviously permitted to use common sense and wisdom gained from personal experience in observing and judging the trustworthiness of a particular witness on the basis of factors such as testimony and demeanour. On the other hand, the judge must avoid judging the credibility of the witness on the basis of generalizations or upon matters that were not in evidence … If there is no evidence linking the generalization to the particular witness, these situations might leave the judge open to allegations of bias." This proposition, however, does not lead to the *automatic* assumption that the use of "generalizations" would result in an apprehension of bias. Having set out the theory, Justice Cory turned to the Sparks comments. Rather than justifying those comments on the basis that they accurately reflected the social context of racism in Halifax, as the doctrine of contextualism would normally suggest, he looked at the context in which the remarks had been made in the 1994 trial. Judge Sparks had already examined evidence to assess the credibility of the two witnesses and had found in favour of the accused. The subsequent remarks were intended as a rebuttal to the Crown's contention about the officer's credibility. In any case, Judge Sparks had not accused Constable Stienburg of misleading the court or overreacting on the basis of racism. It was not necessary for her to resolve the question of why the officer behaved as he did. "Judge Sparks' remarks could reasonably be taken as demonstrating her recognition that the Crown was required to prove its case, and that it was not entitled to use presumptions of credibility to satisfy its obligation."[58]

Both Major and Cory, speaking on behalf of five members of the Court, recognized a role for social context and personal experience in judging, but restricted them to certain circumstances. L'Heureux-Dubé and McLachlin, for the remaining four members, thoroughly embraced the doctrine of contextualism and based their decision upon it. "[J]udges must rely on their background knowledge in fulfilling their adjudicative function," they wrote. "There is more to a case than who did what to whom … Judges … must be aware of the context in which the alleged crime occurred." In fact "a conscious, contextual inquiry has become an accepted step towards judicial impartiality." They can gain their understanding of the context from expert witnesses, from academic studies, and "from the judge's personal understanding and experience of the society in which the judge lives and works. This process of enlargement is not only consistent with impartiality; it may also be seen as its essential pre-condition." Referring to the context within which a case occurred is not evidence of bias, they continued, "[O]n the contrary, such awareness is consistent with the highest tradition of judicial impartiality." Against this background, this judgment concluded, "Judge Sparks was under a duty to be sensitive to the nuances and implications, and to rely on her own common sense which is necessarily informed by her own experience and understanding." Nothing in the 1994 trial indicated that she had prejudged the case or exhibited bias. Connie Sparks, rather, should be regarded as a positive example of reasonable adjudication. "In alerting herself to the racial dynamic in the case, she was simply engaging in the process of contextualized judging which, in our view, was entirely proper and conducive to a fair and just resolution of the case before her."[59]

Implications

Thirteen judges reviewed Connie Sparks's original decision in *R.D.S.* Six of them rejected her judgment and decided that it displayed a reasonable apprehension of bias; seven supported her, denying the charge of bias and restoring the acquittal of RDS. Seven to six: it seems a narrow victory. But that number is misleading. Six of her seven supporters were, after all, from the highest court in the land. Though he had been largely ignored in the SCC's decision, the outcome was a resounding victory for RDS the person: four years after the incident, he at last was freed from the threat of another trial and potential punishment. His courage and that of his family in insisting that justice be done deserves recognition; the young man and especially his mother pushed for and cooperated with every stage in the appeal process.[60] It was undoubtedly a satisfying victory for Rocky Jones, extending his fight against racism in Canada into the highest reaches of our justice system. The victory was shared by Richard Devlin, Carol Aylward, and particularly Dianne Pothier, by their colleagues and students at the Dalhousie Law School, and by the interveners. And it had an enormous and stimulating impact on the Black communities of Halifax, of Nova Scotia, and even of Canada, who claimed the victory as their own and who gained a rare lesson that the Canadian legal structure could have positive relevance in their lives.

R.D.S. also represented a victory for contextualized judging. In some ways the case might be regarded as a contest between a kind of "scientific" method in judging and a more subjective and contextual method. Glube, Pugsley, Flinn, Major, Lamer, and Sopinka did indeed seem to adhere to a now-outdated assumption that judges simply apply existing rules and discover the applicable law, rather than interpret the situation before them in its context. Justice Anglin of the SCC epitomized this approach when he wrote in 1923, "Our common object is to make the administration of justice as nearly certain and scientific as it is possible that any human institution can become."[61] But the "scientific" judicial method was always more myth than science; judging was never autonomous and objective but imbued by social context and construed through the "legal sensibility" prevailing at the time.[62] Canadian courts, including the SCC, upheld a 1912 Saskatchewan law forbidding "Chinamen" from hiring white women, claiming that the discriminatory law was "in the moral interest." In a 1939 case, *Christie v. York*, the SCC denied that racial discrimination was "immoral," and the same language was used in the Ontario Court of Appeal in a 1949 decision confirming the validity of a racially restrictive property covenant. In criticizing the *Christie* judgment, then professor and future chief justice Bora Laskin charged that the Court was "reading social and economic doctrine into law."[63] Obviously our judges, even in an era ostensibly committed to objective and "scientific" adjudication, were applying moral values and their own "common sense" in deciding legal disputes. The problem was, "common sense" accepted the existence of discrete human "races," their genetically dictated attributes, and their natural inclination towards competition and even conflict. This common sense was upheld and reinforced by the courts in cases such as *Quong Wing*, *Christie*, and *Noble and Wolf*. Typically, the courts took the racial issue for granted, as too obvious to require consideration. *Quong Wing* was decided not on the ground of racial discrimination but the province's right to protect white women from Chinese, *Christie* became a case of freedom of commerce, and *Noble and Wolf* was a matter of the sanctity of contracts. "Race" pervaded each case but was never confronted directly. Common sense was elevated to scientific truth.[64]

Canadian judges, then, have historically allowed "context" to affect their decisions, but its practical application as judicial method depends on its being done openly, as an explanation for judgment and a measure for accountability. If the older "formalistic" approach to law was not entirely displaced by R.D.S., it did suffer a serious blow. In their 1997 decision, four judges expressly adopted contextualism, three were negative, and two were conditional. But again, numbers can be deceptive. Contextualism formed the essential foundation for the decision by the four justices, thus confirming its vitality and validity in judicial decision-making. Furthermore, the method received an elaborate articulation as written by Justices L'Heureux-Dubé and McLachlin, enabling it to be utilized and expanded in Canadian jurisprudence. Just three years later Antonio Lamer, who was part of the minority in R.D.S. that explicitly rejected contextualism, told the National Judicial Institute that we can produce "better judges ... by making them more aware of the broader social, economic, cultural and political context within which ... judges function in a society as diverse as Canada."[65] The movement towards the newer approach has not been without its obstacles, as Devlin and Sherrard have illustrated,[66] yet by 2006 McCormick could write that formalistic judging had been "replaced" by contextualism, and Sugunasiri claimed that this incremental trend was "clearly confirmed" by R.D.S.[67]

The implications of R.D.S. for racial equality in Canada are harder to monitor. It was, however, surely significant that the Supreme Court of Canada had abandoned its traditional reluctance to address "race." This time "race" and racism were directly confronted and, especially through the inclusion of social context and the revised definition of the "reasonable person," cognizance of racism was established as a standard practice in our courts. "Colour-blind" judging, the assumption that "race" is irrelevant, was left behind; acceptance of "race" as a factor in judgment was endorsed.[68] As the appellants had argued, racial disadvantage will be overcome only when it is brought into consideration, and so R.D.S. was a major step toward judicial participation in the fight against racism. The SCC majority accepted Rocky Jones's contention that "substantive equality" cannot be achieved by the old paradigm of "equal opportunity." Once more it was Beverley McLachlin (appointed chief justice in January 2000), who neatly articulated the direction in our jurisprudence. "This new paradigm of substantive equality," she has written, "requires us to recognize the context of historical, racial and ethnic inequality and the myths and stereotypes that this context has produced. It requires us to disabuse ourselves of these preconceived notions, acknowledged or unacknowledged, to understand the reality that disadvantaged groups face, and to examine the claim of unequal treatment afresh on the basis of this understanding."[69]

Chief Justice McLachlin pointed out that less than a year after *R.D.S.* the SCC held unanimously that an accused was entitled to challenge prospective jurors for racial bias, thus reinforcing the principle "that courts can and should take proactive steps to recognize racism and prevent it from compromising trials and thereby marring the justice system." The law, she claimed, has undergone an evolution and can now be seen "as a tool to combat inequality and enhance substantive equality."[70]

The *R.D.S.* saga as a whole can be regarded as a powerful illustration of the necessity of taking "race" into account in considering legal disputes whenever it is appropriate. This now has the sanction of the SCC. *R.D.S.* further demonstrates the value of narrative in legal proceedings. The accused RDS told a story of an incident that lasted only a few seconds. Judge Sparks accepted his story because it reflected the truth as she knew it for the Black community. His narrative was not only consistent with the Black experience with police in Halifax, it also offered clarity in the incident, a richness of uncontested evidentiary detail, that the officer was unequipped to match or deny. The youth's story, drawn out by questions from his own lawyer and from the Crown, conveyed an image so real that Judge Sparks could see the systemic pattern woven through it. She could connect those few seconds to a broader narrative, to a context.

At any rate, as Judge Sparks might put it, there are many profound implications from *R.D.S.* It has become common in academic discourse to describe "race" as a social construct. In Canada, as elsewhere, "race" was also a legal artefact, and this syndrome has been interrupted. SCC decisions are perpetuated through their use as precedents or interpretations in subsequent cases, they influence the way the law is to be administered by state authorities, and they set the standard that a law-abiding population uses to measure its behaviour. *R.D.S.* therefore has a shaping influence on the conditions that exist in society, becoming in effect a part of the "social context" within which future incidents and disputes will be defined. Reforms are not, of course, initiated by courts, or anywhere else on high; shifts in consciousness and in social structures, such as the achievement of racial equality would require, arise from alert citizens and especially from outspoken members of disadvantaged groups who articulate a new perspective of what is "right."[71] It depends on what *we* do. But if, as Clifford Geertz contends, law and judging reflect a prevailing legal sensibility, then *R.D.S.* and the developments it represented can be understood as a preliminary reflection of a new legal sensibility in Canada, one that is aware of the disadvantages created for many of our citizens by racism and determined to overcome them. The newly defined "reasonable person" can be nourished with the "enlargement of mind" identified in *R.D.S.*, contributing to the emergence of a new "common sense" about "race" and judging in our country. In the words of Chief Justice McLachlin, "While I cannot predict the future, I believe we are on the right road."[72]

NOTES

1 Shalin M. Sugunasiri, "Contextualism: The Supreme Court's New Standard of Judicial Analysis and Accountability," *Dalhousie Law Journal* 22 (1999): 159.

2 Carol A. Aylward, "'Take the Long Way Home': R.D.S. v. R. The Journey," *UNB Law Journal* 47 (1998): 249–310; April Burey, "No Dichotomies: Reflections on Equality for African Canadians in R. v. R.D.S.," *Dalhousie Law Journal* 21 (Spring 1998), 199–218; Richard F. Devlin, "We Can't Go On Together with Suspicious Minds: Judicial Bias and Racialized Perspective in R. v. R.D.S.," *Dalhousie Law Journal* 18 (1995): 408–46; and Richard F. Devlin and Dianne Pothier, "R.D.S.: Redressing the Imbalances," *Ottawa Law Review* 31, no. 1 (1999–2000): 2–37.

3 *Dalhousie Law Journal* 21 (Spring 1998), including articles by April Burey, cited above; Allen C. Hutchinson and Kathleen Strachan, "What's the Difference? Interpretation, Identity and R. v. R.D.S.," 219–35; Jennifer Smith, "R. v. R.D.S.: A Political Science Perspective," 236–48. *Canadian Journal of Women and the Law* 10 (1998), with an introduction by Christine Boyle, 160–3; Brenna Bhandar, "R. v. R.D.S.: A Summary," 163–70; Constance Backhouse, "Bias in Canadian Law: A Lopsided Precipice," 170–83; Marilyn MacCrimmon, "Generalizing about Racism," 184–99; Audrey Kobayashi, "Do Minority Women Judges Make a Difference," 199–212.

4 E.g., Bruce P. Archibald, "The Lessons of the Sphinx: Avoiding Apprehensions of Judicial Bias in a Multi-Racial, Multi-Cultural Society," *Criminal Reports* 10 (5th) (1997): 54–64; R.J. Delisle, "R. v. S. (R.D.)," *Criminal Reports* 10 (5th) (1997): 1–11; Shin Imai, "Problem Solving in Clinical Education: A Counter-Pedagogy for Social Justice; Core Skills for Community-Based Lawyering," *Clinical Law Review* 9 (2002): 195–222; Sherene Razack, "R.D.S. v. Her Majesty the Queen: A Case about Home," *Constitutional Forum* 9, no. 3 (1998): 59–65.

5 Burey, "No Dichotomies," 211.

6 In the interest of full disclosure, the reader should know that I have been a friend of Burnley A. "Rocky" Jones for over forty years, and I was close to him throughout the events described in this chapter. Furthermore Dr Jones and I, with Dr George Elliott Clarke, are collaborating on a book about the "Black Movement" in Nova Scotia and Dr Jones's pre-eminent role in it from the 1960s to the present. It is important to note, however, that the account of *R.D.S.* offered here is not intended to represent Dr Jones's perspective or to reveal his private thoughts. The chapter is my interpretation of the case, based on an analysis of the documentary record and, of course, my own lived experience, which includes my friendship with the defendant's counsel and my research into the legal construction of "race" in Canada. A full description of Dr Jones's involvement with the case will appear in our book. Jones was honoured with an LLD by the University of Guelph in 2004 and the Order of Nova Scotia in 2010, in recognition of his outstanding and lifelong contribution to the struggle for racial equality in Canada.

7 Details of the incident are taken from RDS's testimony, Case No. Y093-168, *Her Majesty the Queen v. R.D.S.*, Young Offender, 2 Dec. 1994, verbatim transcript, 43–53. RDS was charged under Criminal Code sections 270(1)(a), 270(1)(b), and 129(a). The charge of theft against NR was later dropped. Copies of the transcript are in Library and Archives Canada (LAC), RG 125, Vol. 5231. Interestingly LAC has the documentation on this case indexed under the full name of RDS. In this chapter, however, the juvenile's identity will be protected.

8 The Royal Commission on the Donald Marshall, Jr Prosecution was created to examine the wrongful conviction for murder of a young Mi'kmaq from Membertou (Sydney), Nova Scotia. Because the murder victim was a Black youth, and because racism in the justice system was a fundamental issue in the case, BUF sought and was granted status at the Inquiry. See below, note 16.

9 At the time, "Micmac" was the spelling generally used for the people now known as Mi'kmaq. The Dalhousie Law School website describes the program thus:

> The Indigenous Blacks & Mi'kmaq (IB&M) Initiative was established at Dalhousie Law School in 1989 with the purpose of reducing structural and systemic discrimination by increasing the representation of Indigenous Blacks and Mi'kmaq in the legal profession.
>
> The IB&M Initiative was the result of efforts by African Nova Scotian communities and Mi'kmaq First Nations to obtain access to legal education and the legal profession and to address racism in the justice system.

These efforts were the catalyst for Dalhousie University's study entitled
"'Breaking Barriers': Report of the Task Force on Access for Black and
Native People" and coincided with the work of the Royal Commission
on the Donald Marshall, Jr Prosecution, which recommended that the
then fledgling IB&M Initiative "receive the financial support of the Governments of Canada and Nova Scotia, and the Nova Scotia Bar."
   Through the hard work and persistence of the Advisory Board and
other community members, the directors, students, faculty, and staff,
the IB&M Initiative grew to become a model for access to legal education and the legal profession across Canada and the United States.

10 Verbatim Transcript, Youth Court Trial, *supra* note 7. Connie Sparks grew
   up in Loon Lake, NS, where she attended a segregated primary school.
   Her post-secondary education was at Mount Saint Vincent University
   (BA 1974) and Dalhousie University (LLB 1979 and later LLM 2001) in
   Halifax. She was appointed to the Nova Scotia Family Court in 1987, the
   first African Nova Scotian in the history of the province, and the first
   female African Canadian anywhere in Canada, to serve on the judiciary.
   (http://jamesrjohnstonchair.dal.ca/photo_gallery_and_biographies/
   Judge_Corrine_E._Spa.php). Since the RDS case, she has won many distinctions and awards, including the Canadian Bar Association's Touch-
   stone Award in 2008 "for her outstanding accomplishments in promoting
   equality in the Canadian legal profession." In 2007 the Dalhousie Black
   Law Students' Association created the Judge Corrine Sparks Award to
   recognize students who are "committed to using their legal education as
   a tool for change in their community," Canadian Bar Association, news
   release, 15 Aug. 2008.

11 Verbatim Transcript, Direct Examination of Donald Stienburg, 2–20.

12 Ibid., Cross-Examination, 22–41, and Redirect Examination, 41–2.

13 Ibid., 43–53.

14 Ibid., 54–60. Quotations at 59–60. Although the atmosphere in Youth Court
   is relatively informal, it is quite unusual to have a judicial decision interrupted in this way by the prosecution or the defence. Mr Miller may not
   have intended any disrespect towards Judge Sparks with his interjection,
   but it could be interpreted as such.

15 The Crown was not represented at the hearing, but Rocky Jones appeared
   on behalf of RDS. The associate chief justice of the Supreme Court of Nova
   Scotia, Ian H. Palmeter, would later allow the appeal and grant the *Halifax-
   Herald* access to the tapes. RG 125, Vol. 5231, Factum of the Appellant, Part
   I, Statement of Facts; Factum of the Respondent, Part I, Statement of Facts;
   Mail-Star, 9, 10, and 17 Dec. 1994; *Chronicle-Herald*, 13 Dec. The *Chronicle-*

Herald decision is indexed as *R. v. R.D.S.*, 1994 NSR (2d) Lexis 2010; 136 NSR (2d) 299; 388 APR 299. Quotations at paras 33 and 34.

16 Supplementary Reasons released by Judge Sparks, 13 Jan. 1995, RG 125, Vol. 5231, quotations at 2, 4, and 5. In 1971 Donald Marshall Jr, a seventeen-year old Mi'kmaq from the Membertou Reserve in Sydney, Nova Scotia, was convicted of murdering his friend Sandy Seale, also seventeen and an African Canadian. After serving eleven years of a life sentence Marshall was found to have been wrongfully convicted. An RCMP investigation discovered *inter alia* that a particular police officer, John MacIntyre, had thwarted the pursuit of justice through intimidation and perjured evidence. Nevertheless the Nova Scotia Supreme Court concluded, "Any miscarriage of justice is ... more apparent than real ... There can be no doubt that Donald Marshall's untruthfulness through this whole affair contributed in large measure to his conviction." This sparked a demand for a public inquiry, pressed in particular by the Mi'kmaq and Black communities, which was successful finally with the appointment in 1986 of Justice T. Alexander Hickman as chair of the Royal Commission on the Donald Marshall, Jr Prosecution. The Commission's seven-volume report, published in 1989, contained an exhaustive survey of injustice against African-Canadian and First Nations people throughout the justice system in Nova Scotia. Volume 4 was entitled *Discrimination against Blacks in Nova Scotia: The Criminal Justice System*, prepared for the Commission by Wilson Head and Don Clairmont. Useful accounts of the Marshall case can be found in Michael Harris, *Justice Denied: The Law Versus Donald Marshall*, 2nd ed. (Toronto: Harper-Collins, 1990), the essays in Joy Mannette and Alex Denny, eds., *Elusive Justice: Beyond the Marshall Inquiry* (Halifax: Fernwood, 1992), and Mary Ellen Turpel, "Further Travails of Canada's Human Rights Record: The Marshall Case," *International Journal of Canadian Studies* 3 (1991): 27–48.

17 *Globe and Mail*, 4 Apr. 1992, editorial, "Blacks and the police." For a discussion of this and similar incidents, see Aylward, "'Take the Long Way Home,'" 265–72.

18 Case Number 112401, In the Supreme Court of Nova Scotia, between Her Majesty the Queen, Appellant, and RDS, Respondent, 18 Apr. 1995, Oral Judgment by Chief Justice Constance Glube, RG 125, Vol. 5231.

19 Ibid., 9–10.

20 Ibid., 10.

21 The case law in Canada generally accepted the standard laid down by Justice de Grandpré in 1978: "[The] test is 'what would an informed person, viewing the matter realistically and practically – and having thought the

matter through – conclude'... The grounds for this apprehension must ... be substantial [and not simply] related to the 'very sensitive or scrupulous conscience.'" *Committee for Justice and Liberty et al. v. National Energy Board et al.*, [1978] 1 SCR 369 at 394, cited throughout the *R.D.S.* proceedings.

22 Application for Leave to Appeal (N.S.), RG 125, Vol. 5231. See also Devlin, "We Can't Go On Together with Suspicious Minds," 421, 423; Devlin and Pothier, "RDS: Redressing the Imbalances," 31; Aylward, "'Take the Long Way Home,'" 276, 280.

23 Devlin, "We Can't Go On Together with Suspicious Minds," 444.

24 *R.D.S. v. Her Majesty the Queen*, 1995 NSR (2d) Lexis 1865; 145 NSR (2d) 284; 418 APR 284. Quotations at paras 19, 31, 37, 38, 40, 41, 42, 44, 45, 47.

25 Ibid., quotations at paras 54, 59, 62, 63, 66, 68, 69.

26 Factum of the Appellant, Part II, Grounds of Appeal, RG 125, Vol. 5231.

27 Ibid., Part I, Statement of Facts; Memorandum of the Respondent, 30 Jan. 1996.

28 Another potential intervener, the Parent Student Association of Preston, Nova Scotia, applied too late to be accepted, RG 125, Vol. 5232.

29 John Sopinka et al., "Rules Dispensing with or Facilitating Proof," in *The Law of Evidence in Canada* (Toronto: Butterworths, 1992), 976, cited in LEAF/NOIVMWC factum, Part III, 4(a)(I), Interveners' Arguments with respect to the Issues, Judicial Notice, RG 125, Vol. 5232.

30 A useful examination of this doctrine can be found in Sugunasiri, "Contextualism: The Supreme Court's New Standard," 126–84. Sugunasiri explains that contextualism emerged as a distinct methodology in the SCC in the 1980s, and was most clearly articulated by Justice Wilson in *Edmonton Journal v. Alberta (Attorney General)*, [1989] 2 SCR 1326. At first applied only in *Charter* cases, by the mid-1990s it could be regarded as a standard approach in the SCC, thus encouraging judges to consider the broader social context in their application of legal regulations.

31 Factum of the Appellant, Part III, Brief of Argument, 9–30, *supra* note 26. The Doherty and Niedermayer citations can be found at *R. v. Parks* (1993) 84 CCC (3d) 353 at 369 (Ont. CA), leave to appeal denied [1994] 1 SCR x, and *NS (Minister of Community Services) v. SMS* (1992) 110 NSR (2d) 91 at 109 (Fam Ct), affirmed (1992) 112 NSR (2d) 258 (CA).

32 Ibid., 31–7.

33 Factum of LEAF and NOIVMWC, Part III, Argument, *supra* note 29.

34 Factum of the Coalition (African Canadian Legal Clinic, Afro-Canadian Caucus of Nova Scotia, and Congress of Black Women of Canada), Part III, Argument, RG 125, Vol. 5232.

35 Brief of the Respondent, Interventions and Charter, 17 Oct. 1996; Factum of the Respondent, Part III, Brief of Argument, RG 125, Vol. 5231.

36 Information received from Ms Lynn Jones in the course of many conversations.

37 Information from Lynn Jones; Aylward, "'Take the Long Way Home,'" 297–9; Burey, "No Dichotomies," 199.

38 Another African-Canadian lawyer, Carol Allen, participated on behalf of LEAF/NOIVMWC, but did not speak at the hearing.

39 Supreme Court of Canada, Case 25063, Transcription of Cassettes, Monday March 10, 1997, RG 125, Vol. 5232. Quotations at 1, 2 and 4.

40 Ibid., at 4–7.

41 Ibid., at 8–15.

42 Ibid., at 19–22 and 27. The Chinese Canadian National Council complained about these remarks to the Canadian Judicial Council. The complaint was rejected because Chief Justice Lamer was deemed to have been using a hypothetical example to make a serious point about stereotyping. *Toronto Star*, 4 and 5 Nov. 1997; Razak, "R.D.S. v. Her Majesty the Queen," 61; Devlin and Pothier, "RDS: Redressing the Imbalances," footnote 89.

43 Burey, "No Dichotomies," 218. Burey was confined to a wheelchair by multiple sclerosis.

44 Transcript, at 81.

45 Ibid., at 83, 86.

46 Indexed as *R. v. S (RD)*, Supreme Court of Canada, 1997 Can. Sup. Ct. Lexis 83. Justice Cory occupies fourteen pages in the printed decision, L'Heureux-Dubé and McLachlin five and a half, Major three, and Gonthier only six lines. See the items referenced in notes 2–4 for expert commentary, while noting that the commentators do not always agree and even the two authors in the jointly written article have differences in their analysis.

47 Major at paras 3 and 6; Cory at paras 123, 132, 149, 150, and 152; L'Heureux-Dubé and McLachlin at paras 55–7.

48 L'Heureux-Dubé and McLachlin at paras 46–7; Cory at para. 111.

49 Major at para. 3; Cory at para. 95; L'Heureux-Dubé and McLachlin at paras 28, 38.

50 At para. 116.

51 At para. 34. The quotation is from Benjamin N. Cardozo, *The Nature of the Judicial Process* (New Haven: Yale University Press, 1921), 12–13: "There is in each of us a stream or tendency, whether you choose to call it a philosophy or not, which gives coherence and direction to thought and action. Judges cannot escape that current any more than other mortals. All their lives, forces which they do not recognize and cannot name, have been tugging at them – inherited instincts, traditional beliefs, acquired convictions; and the resultant is an outlook on life, a conception of social needs ... In this mental background every problem finds its setting. We may try to see

things as objectively as we please. None the less, we can never see them with any eyes except our own." They add a quotation from the Canadian Judicial Council, *Commentaries on Judicial Conduct* (Cowansville, QC: Éditions Y. Blais, 1991), 12: "There is no human being who is not the product of every social experience, every process of education, and every human contact ... [T]he wisdom required of a judge is to recognize, consciously allow for, and perhaps to question, all the baggage of past attitudes and sympathies that fellow citizens are free to carry, untested, to the grave."

52 At para. 35.

53 See note 21, *supra*. Cory at paras 111 and 115; Major at para. 23; L'Heureux-Dubé and McLachlin at para. 31.

54 At paras 152–3.

55 At para. 30.

56 At paras 6, 23, 25.

57 At paras 3, 6, 13, 14.

58 At paras 118, 119, 121, 123, 128–30, 133, 134, 153–5, 158.

59 At paras 38–42, 44, 49, 59. At para. 42 they cite Jennifer Nedelsky, "Embodied Diversity and Challenges to Law," *McGill Law Journal* 42 (1997): 107, to support their notion of "enlargement": "What makes it possible for us to genuinely judge, to move beyond our private idiosyncrasies and preferences, is our capacity to achieve an 'enlargement of mind.' We do this by taking different perspectives into account. This is the path out of the blindness of our subjective conditions. The more views we are able to take into account the less likely we are to be locked into one perspective ... It is the capacity for 'enlargement of mind' that makes autonomous, impartial judgment possible."

60 Aylward, "'Take the Long Way Home,'" 287, suggests, "He was also perhaps in essence a Canadian Rosa Parks."

61 Qtd in Ian Bushnell, *The Captive Court: A Study of the Supreme Court of Canada* (Montreal and Kingston: McGill-Queen's University Press, 1992), 56. The same views were reflected in the United States Supreme Court at that time, where "the common law was recognized as the distinct subject matter of legal science," Paul W. Kahn, *Legitimacy and History* (New Haven: Yale University Press, 1992), 110.

62 The term "legal sensibility" comes from Clifford Geertz, who argues that legal systems are wound in culture, and that law and context are part of the same cultural process. Law and society cannot be separated, and its legal sensibility is an essential and active part of every society. *Local Knowledge: Further Essays in Interpretive Anthropology* (New York: Basic Books, 1983), 215, 218–19, 232.

63 Bora Laskin, "Tavern Refusing to Serve Negro – Discrimination," *Canadian Bar Review* 18 (1940): 314–16. The cases referred to are *Quong Wing v. the King*, (1914) 39 SCR 440, *Christie v. York Corporation*, [1940] SCR 139, *Re: Noble and Wolf*, [1949] 4 DLR 375, [1949] OR 503 (Court of Appeal). These cases are all discussed at length in my book *"Race," Rights and the Law in the Supreme Court of Canada: Historical Case Studies* (Toronto and Waterloo: Osgoode Society and Wilfrid Laurier University Press, 1997). For similar studies, see Constance Backhouse, *Colour-Coded: A Legal History of Racism in Canada, 1900–1950* (Toronto: Osgoode Society and University of Toronto Press, 1999). *Christie v. York* is described in chapter 7 in this volume.

64 As Pierre Bourdieu succinctly puts it, "Common sense speaks the clear and simple language of what is plain for all to see." *In Other Words: Essays towards a Reflexive Sociology* (Stanford: Stanford University Press, 1990), 52.

65 Qtd in Richard F. Devlin and Matthew Sherrard, "The Big Chill?: Contextual Judgment after R v. Hamilton and Mason," *Dalhousie Law Journal* 28 (2005): 409.

66 Ibid., in which the authors describe "perhaps the most important case since *R.D.S.* on the issues of social context and the appropriate judicial function." Though the trial judge followed *R.D.S.*, his decision was overturned by the Ontario Court of Appeal. *R. v. Hamilton* (2003) 172 CCC (3d), 114, and (2004) OR (3d), 1.

67 Peter McCormick, "The Serendipitous Solution to the Problem of Supreme Court Appointments," *Osgoode Hall Law Journal* 44 (2006): 539–45; Sugunasiri, "Contextualism: The Supreme Court's New Standard," 160–1. McCormick defines "formalism" as the doctrine that "there is always a single correct answer to any legal question, and judges are trained professionals who know the objective and logical processes that take them to that correct answer," 539.

68 It is disappointing that the term *race* is used throughout the SCC decision without any qualifications or explanation of what it is meant to convey. Since there is no generally accepted definition of the term, observers may read their own meaning into it. This could lead to very disturbing results.

69 Beverley McLachlin, "Racism and the Law: The Canadian Experience," *Journal of Law and Equality* 1 (2002): 20.

70 Ibid., 21–2. The case was *R. v. Williams*, [1998] 1 SCR 1128.

71 Historical case studies in support of this generalization are offered in *"Race," Rights and the Law*.

72 McLachlin, "Racism and the Law," 22.

Contributors

Eric M. Adams is an associate professor at the University of Alberta, Faculty of Law, where he researches and teaches constitutional law, legal history, and employment law. He has published a number of articles and chapters on Canadian constitutional history and is working on a book on that topic.

Constance Backhouse, CM, O. Ont., FRSC, is a professor in the Faculty of Law at the University of Ottawa. She has published a number of books on legal history, the most recent being *Carnal Crimes: Sexual Assault Law in Canada, 1900–1975* (Toronto: Irwin Law, 2008), which was awarded the Canadian Law and Society Association Book Prize and shortlisted for the Harold Adams Innis Prize. *Colour-Coded: A Legal History of Racism in Canada, 1900–1950* (Toronto: University of Toronto Press, 1999) was awarded the Joseph Brant Award. Her *Petticoats and Prejudice: Women and the Law in Nineteenth-Century Canada* (Toronto: Women's Press, 1991) was awarded the Willard Hurst Prize in American Legal History. She is the past president of the American Society for Legal History, was a Trudeau Fellow, received the Killam Prize in Social Sciences, and was awarded the Social Sciences and Humanities Research Council's Gold Medal.

D.G. Bell, professor of law at the University of New Brunswick's Fredericton campus, writes on the legal, religious, and intellectual history of the Maritime colonies. His book on Loyalist Saint John won the Canadian Historical Association's award of merit in regional history.

J. Barry Cahill, M. Litt., CAPP, is an independent scholar in Halifax. He is writing the official history of the Nova Scotia Barristers' Society.

Philip Girard is university research professor and professor of law, history, and Canadian Studies at Dalhousie University, where he is based at the Schulich School of Law. He has published widely on Canadian and comparative legal history. His biography *Bora Laskin: Bringing Law to Life* (2005) received the Chalmers Award for the best book published in Ontario history in that year, while his *Lawyers and Legal Culture in British North America: Beamish Murdoch of Halifax* received the Clio Atlantic award from the Canadian Historical Association in 2012. He is the associate editor of the Osgoode Society for Canadian Legal History.

Susan Lewthwaite holds a doctorate in Canadian legal history from the University of Toronto. She has taught at York University, Ryerson University, and the University of Toronto, and has also worked as a research archivist. She was co-editor of and contributor to *Essays in the History of Canadian Law*, vol. 5, *Crime and Criminal Justice*, and has published primarily in the field of Upper Canadian criminal justice history. She is an independent scholar living in Toronto, researching and writing about the lives and careers of prominent Ontario criminal lawyers in a socio-cultural historical context.

Susan McKelvey has a bachelor of science from Queen's University and a bachelor of arts from York University. She is pursuing a Juris Doctor degree at Queen's University.

David Sealy posthumously received his PhD in criminology from the University of Toronto in 2010. This is how he described his work shortly before his death in December 2009: "My work in areas pertinent to studies of law and society rotates around questions generated in two interconnected spheres directly related to the discourses of Black diasporic modernity. On the one hand, there are questions on the way that nineteenth-century colonial and imperial racial knowledges, articulated through, for example, discourses of the Negro question, are 'translated' into modern and late modern discourses of Black crime and criminality. On the other hand, there are the related and more fundamental questions about the social construction of racial and ethnic categories, and the multiple ways that racial and ethnic knowledges are deployed in the constitution of criminality and penalty and in the development of legal technologies to address the problems of minority populations. Here, it must be emphasized how racialization and ethnicization work through other categories such as gender, class, sexual orientation, and nation to constitute social identities or social identifications."

David Steeves is a member of the bars of Alberta, Nova Scotia, and Ontario, where he practises civil litigation in Toronto. He holds a BA (English) from Mount Allison University as well as LLB and LLM degrees from Dalhousie University, where research for the work in this volume was completed with the assistance of the Faculty of Graduate Studies and Dalhousie Law School.

Barrington Walker is associate professor of history at Queen's University. He is the author of *Race on Trial: Black Defendants in Ontario's Criminal Courts, 1858–1958* published in 2010. His most recent publications are "Jamaicans and the Making of Modern Canada" and "Following the North Star: Race and I.Q. Testing in the Work of H.A. Tanser."

James W. St.G. Walker is professor in the Department of History at the University of Waterloo, where he specializes in the history of human rights and race relations. His publications include *The Black Loyalists: The Search for a Promised Land in Nova Scotia and Sierra Leone* (2nd ed. 1992), and *"Race," Rights and the Law in the Supreme Court of Canada: Historical Case Studies* (1997). In 2003–4 he was the Bora Laskin National Fellow in Human Rights Research.

Harvey Amani Whitfield is an associate professor of history at the University of Vermont. In 2006, he published *Blacks on the Border: The Black Refugees in British North America, 1815–1860*. Whitfield has also written several articles about Black people in the Maritime colonies. His most recent essay is entitled "The Struggle over Slavery in the Maritime Colonies." He is working on a project about slavery and natural rights in Revolutionary Vermont.

2012   R. Blake Brown, *Arming and Disarming: A History of Gun Control in Canada*

Eric Tucker, James Muir, and Bruce Ziff, eds., *Property on Trial: Canadian Cases in Context*

Shelley Gavigan, *Hunger, Horses, and Government Men: Criminal Law on the Aboriginal Plains, 1870–1905*

Barrington Walker, ed., *The African Canadian Legal Odyssey: Historical Essays*

2011   Robert J. Sharpe, *The Lazier Murder: Prince Edward County, 1884*

Philip Girard, *Lawyers and Legal Culture in British North America: Beamish Murdoch of Halifax*

John McLaren, *Dewigged, Bothered, and Bewildered: British Colonial Judges on Trial, 1800–1900*

Lesley Erickson, *Westward Bound: Sex, Violence, the Law, and the Making of a Settler Society*

2010   Judy Fudge and Eric Tucker, eds., *Work on Trial: Canadian Labour Law Struggles*

Christopher Moore, *The British Columbia Court of Appeal: The First Hundred Years*

Frederick Vaughan, *Viscount Haldane: 'The Wicked Step-father of the Canadian Constitution'*

Barrington Walker, *Race on Trial: Black Defendants in Ontario's Criminal Courts, 1858–1958*

2009   William Kaplan, *Canadian Maverick: The Life and Times of Ivan C. Rand*

R. Blake Brown, *A Trying Question: The Jury in Nineteenth-Century Canada*

Barry Wright and Susan Binnie, eds., *Canadian State Trials, Volume III: Political Trials and Security Measures, 1840–1914*

Robert J. Sharpe, *The Last Day, the Last Hour: The Currie Libel Trial* (paperback edition with a new preface)

2008   Constance Backhouse, *Carnal Crimes: Sexual Assault Law in Canada, 1900–1975*

Jim Phillips, R. Roy McMurtry, and John T. Saywell, eds., *Essays in the History of Canadian Law, Volume X: A Tribute to Peter N. Oliver*

Greg Taylor, *The Law of the Land: The Advent of the Torrens System in Canada*

Hamar Foster, Benjamin Berger, and A.R. Buck, eds., *The Grand Experiment: Law and Legal Culture in British Settler Societies*

2007 Robert Sharpe and Patricia McMahon, *The Persons Case: The Origins and Legacy of the Fight for Legal Personhood*
Lori Chambers, *Misconceptions: Unmarried Motherhood and the Ontario Children of Unmarried Parents Act, 1921–1969*
Jonathan Swainger, ed., *A History of the Supreme Court of Alberta*
Martin Friedland, *My Life in Crime and Other Academic Adventures*

2006 Donald Fyson, *Magistrates, Police, and People: Everyday Criminal Justice in Quebec and Lower Canada, 1764–1837*
Dale Brawn, *The Court of Queen's Bench of Manitoba, 1870–1950: A Biographical History*
R.C.B. Risk, *A History of Canadian Legal Thought: Collected Essays*, edited and introduced by G. Blaine Baker and Jim Phillips

2005 Philip Girard, *Bora Laskin: Bringing Law to Life*
Christopher English, ed., *Essays in the History of Canadian Law: Volume IX – Two Islands: Newfoundland and Prince Edward Island*
Fred Kaufman, *Searching for Justice: An Autobiography*

2004 Philip Girard, Jim Phillips, and Barry Cahill, eds., *The Supreme Court of Nova Scotia, 1754–2004: From Imperial Bastion to Provincial Oracle*
Frederick Vaughan, *Aggressive in Pursuit: The Life of Justice Emmett Hall*
John D. Honsberger, *Osgoode Hall: An Illustrated History*
Constance Backhouse and Nancy Backhouse, *The Heiress versus the Establishment: Mrs Campbell's Campaign for Legal Justice*

2003 Robert Sharpe and Kent Roach, *Brian Dickson: A Judge's Journey*
Jerry Bannister, *The Rule of the Admirals: Law, Custom, and Naval Government in Newfoundland, 1699–1832*
George Finlayson, *John J. Robinette, Peerless Mentor: An Appreciation*
Peter Oliver, *The Conventional Man: The Diaries of Ontario Chief Justice Robert A. Harrison, 1856–1878*

2002 John T. Saywell, *The Lawmakers: Judicial Power and the Shaping of Canadian Federalism*
Patrick Brode, *Courted and Abandoned: Seduction in Canadian Law*
David Murray, *Colonial Justice: Justice, Morality, and Crime in the Niagara District, 1791–1849*
F. Murray Greenwood and Barry Wright, eds., *Canadian State Trials, Volume II: Rebellion and Invasion in the Canadas, 1837–1839*

2001 Ellen Anderson, *Judging Bertha Wilson: Law as Large as Life*
Judy Fudge and Eric Tucker, *Labour before the Law: The Regulation of Workers' Collective Action in Canada, 1900–1948*
Laurel Sefton MacDowell, *Renegade Lawyer: The Life of J.L. Cohen*

2000 Barry Cahill, *'The Thousandth Man': A Biography of James McGregor Stewart*

A.B. McKillop, *The Spinster and the Prophet: Florence Deeks, H.G. Wells, and the Mystery of the Purloined Past*

Beverley Boissery and F. Murray Greenwood, *Uncertain Justice: Canadian Women and Capital Punishment*

Bruce Ziff, *Unforeseen Legacies: Reuben Wells Leonard and the Leonard Foundation Trust*

1999 Constance Backhouse, *Colour-Coded: A Legal History of Racism in Canada, 1900–1950*

G. Blaine Baker and Jim Phillips, eds., *Essays in the History of Canadian Law: Volume VIII – In Honour of R.C.B. Risk*

Richard W. Pound, *Chief Justice W.R. Jackett: By the Law of the Land*

David Vanek, *Fulfilment: Memoirs of a Criminal Court Judge*

1998 Sidney Harring, *White Man's Law: Native People in Nineteenth-Century Canadian Jurisprudence*

Peter Oliver, *'Terror to Evil-Doers': Prisons and Punishments in Nineteenth-Century Ontario*

1997 James W. St.G. Walker, *'Race,' Rights and the Law in the Supreme Court of Canada: Historical Case Studies*

Lori Chambers, *Married Women and Property Law in Victorian Ontario*

Patrick Brode, *Casual Slaughters and Accidental Judgments: Canadian War Crimes and Prosecutions, 1944–1948*

Ian Bushnell, *The Federal Court of Canada: A History, 1875–1992*

1996 Carol Wilton, ed., *Essays in the History of Canadian Law: Volume VII – Inside the Law: Canadian Law Firms in Historical Perspective*

William Kaplan, *Bad Judgment: The Case of Mr Justice Leo A. Landreville*

Murray Greenwood and Barry Wright, eds., *Canadian State Trials: Volume I – Law, Politics, and Security Measures, 1608–1837*

1995 David Williams, *Just Lawyers: Seven Portraits*

Hamar Foster and John McLaren, eds., *Essays in the History of Canadian Law: Volume VI – British Columbia and the Yukon*

W.H. Morrow, ed., *Northern Justice: The Memoirs of Mr Justice William G. Morrow*

Beverley Boissery, *A Deep Sense of Wrong: The Treason, Trials, and Transportation to New South Wales of Lower Canadian Rebels after the 1838 Rebellion*

1994 Patrick Boyer, *A Passion for Justice: The Legacy of James Chalmers McRuer*

Charles Pullen, *The Life and Times of Arthur Maloney: The Last of the Tribunes*

Jim Phillips, Tina Loo, and Susan Lewthwaite, eds., *Essays in the History of Canadian Law: Volume V – Crime and Criminal Justice*

Brian Young, *The Politics of Codification: The Lower Canadian Civil Code of 1866*

1993 Greg Marquis, *Policing Canada's Century: A History of the Canadian Association of Chiefs of Police*

Murray Greenwood, *Legacies of Fear: Law and Politics in Quebec in the Era of the French Revolution*

1992 Brendan O'Brien, *Speedy Justice: The Tragic Last Voyage of His Majesty's Vessel Speedy*

Robert Fraser, ed., *Provincial Justice: Upper Canadian Legal Portraits from the Dictionary of Canadian Biography*

1991 Constance Backhouse, *Petticoats and Prejudice: Women and Law in Nineteenth-Century Canada*

1990 Philip Girard and Jim Phillips, eds., *Essays in the History of Canadian Law: Volume III – Nova Scotia*

Carol Wilton, ed., *Essays in the History of Canadian Law: Volume IV – Beyond the Law: Lawyers and Business in Canada, 1830–1930*

1989 Desmond Brown, *The Genesis of the Canadian Criminal Code of 1892*

Patrick Brode, *The Odyssey of John Anderson*

1988 Robert Sharpe, *The Last Day, the Last Hour: The Currie Libel Trial*

John D. Arnup, *Middleton: The Beloved Judge*

1987 C. Ian Kyer and Jerome Bickenbach, *The Fiercest Debate: Cecil A. Wright, the Benchers, and Legal Education in Ontario, 1923–1957*

1986 Paul Romney, *Mr Attorney: The Attorney General for Ontario in Court, Cabinet, and Legislature, 1791–1899*

Martin Friedland, *The Case of Valentine Shortis: A True Story of Crime and Politics in Canada*

1985 James Snell and Frederick Vaughan, *The Supreme Court of Canada: History of the Institution*

1984 Patrick Brode, *Sir John Beverley Robinson: Bone and Sinew of the Compact*

David Williams, *Duff: A Life in the Law*

1983 David H. Flaherty, ed., *Essays in the History of Canadian Law: Volume II*

1982 Marion MacRae and Anthony Adamson, *Cornerstones of Order: Courthouses and Town Halls of Ontario, 1784–1914*

1981 David H. Flaherty, ed., *Essays in the History of Canadian Law: Volume I*